P9-AOR-867

Chicago Public Library

REFERENCE

Form 178 rev. 11-00

Latino and
African American
Athletes Today

Latino and African American Athletes Today

A Biographical Dictionary

Edited by David L. Porter

GREENWOOD PRESS
Westport, Connecticut • London

Library of Congress Cataloging-in-Publication Data

Latino and African American athletes today : a biographical dictionary / edited by David
  L. Porter.
      p. cm.
    Includes bibliographical references and index.
    ISBN 0–313–32048–9 (alk. paper)
    1. Hispanic American athletes—Biography—Dictionaries. 2. African American
  athletes—Biography—Dictionaries. I. Porter, David L., 1941– .
  GV697.A1L345 2004
  796'.092'2—dc22   2003047241

British Library Cataloguing in Publication Data is available.

Library of Congress Catalog Card Number: 2003047241
ISBN: 0–313–32048–9

First published in 2004

Greenwood Press, 88 Post Road West, Westport, CT 06881
An imprint of Greenwood Publishing Group, Inc.
www.greenwood.com

Printed in the United States of America

The paper used in this book complies with the
Permanent Paper Standard issued by the National
Information Standards Organization (Z39.48–1984).

10 9 8 7 6 5 4 3 2 1

Contents _____

Introduction ————————————

African Americans and Latino Americans have figured prominently in the saga of American sports. African Americans have made major impacts on baseball, football, basketball, boxing, and track and field, whereas Latino Americans have left their greatest imprint on baseball and boxing. In *A Hard Road to Glory*, the late Arthur Ashe Jr. ably traced the historical struggles faced by African American athletes in boxing, baseball, football, track and field, basketball, and other sports.[1] Biographies and autobiographies have detailed the achievements and personal struggles of notable African American and Latino American athletes. During the last two decades, sports historians have compiled several collective biographies including notable African American and/ or Latino American athletes. Bill Mallon and Ian Buchanan's *Quest for Gold* (1984) contains brief biographies of numerous Olympic gold medal winners, including many African Americans and some Latino Americans.[2] This editor's multivolume *Biographical Dictionary of American Sports* series (1987–2000) profiles numerous notable African American and Latino American athletes.[3] James A. Riley's *The Biographical Encyclopedia of the Negro Baseball Leagues* (1994) covers over 4,000 Negro League baseball players.[4] This editor's *African-American Sports Greats* (1995) contains biographies of 166 African Americans representing 11 different sports.[5] Anne Janette Johnson's *Great Women in Sports* (1996) profiles notable women athletes, including several African Americans and Latino Americans.[6] David Pietrusza, Matthew Silverman, and the late Michael Gershman, in *Baseball—The Biographical Encyclopedia* (2000), cover numerous African American and Latino American major league and/or Negro League players.[7] Peter Bjarkman's *The Biographical History of Basketball* (2000) contains portraits of that sport's most significant personalities.[8]

Latino and African American Athletes Today: A Biographical Dictionary is the first comprehensive, multisport biographical resource that concentrates exclusively on notable African American and Latino American athletes of the last quarter century. This book profiles 174 important contemporary athletes, including 113 African Americans and 61 Latino Americans who have made a significant impact on sports in the United States since 1975. A majority of the athletes included made their biggest contributions to American sports after 1990. The sports represented include baseball (61), football (40), basketball (31), track and field (18), boxing (6), auto racing (3), bobsledding (2), speedskating (2), swimming (1), tennis (2), golf (1), horse racing (1), ice hockey (1), rodeo (1), soccer (1), softball (1), thoroughbred racing (1), and wrestling (1).

Seventeen of the athletes profiled—fourteen of them African Americans and four Latino Americans—are women representing seven different sports: track and field (7), basketball (5), tennis (2), bobsledding (1), softball (1), and speedskating (1).

Athletes achieving stardom in more than one sport are classified under the sport for which they won their greatest fame. Bo Jackson and Deion Sanders are listed under football, although both played professional baseball. Michael Jordan is listed under basketball, although he briefly played professional baseball. The profiles appear alphabetically and usually range from 700 to 1,200 words.

Selection of the biographical entries proved challenging. Before making final choices, the editor researched books, articles, and especially statistical guides on contemporary African American and Latino American athletes. The criteria used for selection were as follows. (1) The athletes were born in or spent their childhood years in either the United States or Latin American countries. (2) They compiled exceptional athletic records and profoundly affected the development of at least one major sport played in the United States, often overcoming formidable barriers. (3) Record-breaking sports achievements and major athletic honors and awards have filled their careers, such as starring in Olympic competition, winning gold, silver, or bronze medals. Most of the athletes profiled have been listed in sports statistical compilations and/or have won major races, tournaments, or championships. Although most have served as excellent role models for American youth, unfortunately a few have not demonstrated exemplary behavior outside of sports.

Twenty-five contributors, mostly members of the North American Society for Sport History (NASSH), the Society for American Baseball Research (SABR), and/or the Professional Football Researchers Association (PFRA), wrote biographical entries. Most contributors either teach or are employed in other capacities at colleges, universities, and public or private schools. Others are writers, librarians, editors, municipal government employees, or sports organization employees who share common interests in sports and biography. Contributors are listed after each entry and are cited alphabetically with their occupational affiliation following the index in About the Editor and Contributors.

The profiles contain information through the year 2002 and, in some instances, 2003. Each subject's personal, family, and educational backgrounds are delineated, often focusing on the enormous personal struggles and obstacles that many overcame to excel in their respective sports. Entries describe each subject's athletic career, including his or her entrance into sport, major accomplishments, records set, awards, and honors, and overall impact. The profiles of team sport participants identify positions played, team affiliations, All-Star Game appearances and selections, and postseason playoff performances. Each entry includes a brief bibliography that lists pertinent books, articles, and other sources. Cross-references between entries are indicated by an asterisk (*) following the athlete's name when mentioned elsewhere in the text.

Additional features include quotations by or about notable athletes, as well as alphabetical listings of all biographical entries listings by heritage and major sport, and entries about women by sport.

ACKNOWLEDGMENTS

The editor appreciates the enormous time, energy, and effort expended by the contributors in researching and preparing these profiles. In particular, I wish to thank John Evers, Frank Olmsted, Ron Briley, and Scott Crawford for contributing a large number of the entries. I also wish to thank Richard Gonsalves, Keith McClellan, and Terry Sloope for graciously agreeing to handle additional entries when last-minute cancellations occurred.

Wendi Schnaufer, Barbara Rader, and Anne Thompson of Greenwood Publishing Group and Lewis Parker of Westchester Book Services furnished guidance and valuable suggestions, facilitating the preparation of the volume. The staffs of the William Penn University Library and Computing Services also afforded valuable assistance. My wife, Marilyn, again demonstrated considerable patience, understanding, and support throughout the project.

NOTES

1. Arthur R. Ashe Jr., *A Hard Road to Glory: A History of the African-American Athlete, 3 vols.* (New York: Amistad Press, 1988).

2. Bill Mallon and Ian Buchanan, *Quest for Gold: The Encyclopedia of American Olympians* (New York: Leisure Press, 1984).

3. David L. Porter, ed., *Biographical Dictionary of American Sports, 9 vols.* (Westport, CT: Greenwood Press, 1987–2000).

4. James A. Riley, *The Biographical Encyclopedia of the Negro Baseball Leagues* (New York: Carroll & Graf, 1994).

5. David L. Porter, ed., *African-American Sports Greats: A Biographical Dictionary* (Westport, CT: Greenwood Press, 1995).

6. Anne Janette Johnson, *Great Women in Sports* (Detroit, MI: Invisible Ink, 1996).

7. David Pietrusza, Matthew Silverman, and Michael Gershman, *Baseball: The Biographical Encyclopedia* (Kingston, NY: Total Sports Publishing, 2000).

8. Peter C. Bjarkman, *The Biographical History of Basketball* (Chicago, IL: Masters Press, 2000).

Alphabetical List of Entries with Sport _____

Bobby Abreu—baseball

Edgardo Alfonzo—baseball

Marcus Allen—football

Ray Allen—basketball

Roberto Alomar—baseball

Moises Alou—baseball

Evelyn Ashford—track and field

Charles Austin—track and field

Harold Baines—baseball

Marcelo Balboa—soccer

Charles Barkley—basketball

Albert Belle—baseball

Armando Benitez—baseball

Jerome Bettis—football

Barry Bonds—baseball

Bobby Bonilla—baseball

Valerie Brisco-Hooks—track and field

Derrick Brooks—football

Tim Brown—football

Isaac Bruce—football

Kobe Bryant—basketball

Jose Canseco—baseball

Cris Carter—football

Vince Carter—basketball

Helio Castroneves—auto racing

Cesar Chavez—boxing

Bartolo Colon—baseball

Mike Conley—track and field

Cynthia Cooper—basketball

Chili Davis—baseball

Terrell Davis—football

Ron Dayne—football

Gil de Ferran—auto racing

Oscar De La Hoya—boxing

Carlos Delgado—baseball

Gail Devers—track and field

Eric Dickerson—football

Corey Dillon—football

Clyde Drexler—basketball

Tim Duncan—basketball

Anthony Ervin—swimming

Patrick Ewing—basketball

Marshall Faulk—football

Lisa Fernandez—softball

Tony Fernandez—baseball

Vonetta Flowers—bobsled

Andres Galarraga—baseball

Freddy Garcia—baseball

Jeff Garcia—football

Nomar Garciaparra—baseball

Kevin Garnett—basketball

Eddie George—football

Scott Gomez—ice hockey

Juan Gonzalez—baseball

Luis Gonzalez—baseball

Tony Gonzalez—football

Dwight Gooden—baseball

Maurice Greene—track and field

Alphabetical List of Entries with Sport by Heritage ———

AFRICAN AMERICAN

Marcus Allen—football

Ray Allen—basketball

Evelyn Ashford—track and field

Charles Austin—track and field

Harold Baines—baseball

Charles Barkley—basketball

Albert Belle—baseball

Jerome Bettis—football

Barry Bonds—baseball

Bobby Bonilla—baseball

Valerie Brisco-Hooks—track and field

Derrick Brooks—football

Tim Brown—football

Isaac Bruce—football

Kobe Bryant—basketball

Cris Carter—football

Vince Carter—basketball

Mike Conley—track and field

Cynthia Cooper—basketball

Terrell Davis—football

Ron Dayne—football

Gail Devers—track and field

Eric Dickerson—football

Corey Dillon—football

Clyde Drexler—basketball

Anthony Ervin—swimming

Marshall Faulk—football

Vonetta Flowers—bobsled

Kevin Garnett—basketball

Eddie George—football

Dwight Gooden—baseball

Maurice Greene—track and field

Ken Griffey Jr.—baseball

Florence Griffith Joyner—track and field

Tony Gwynn—baseball

Penny Hardaway—basketball

Tim Hardaway—basketball

Kenny Harrison—track and field

Marvin Harrison—football

Rickey Henderson—baseball

Grant Hill—basketball

Garrett Hines—bobsled

Chamique Holdsclaw—basketball

Evander Holyfield—boxing

Allen Iverson—basketball

Bo Jackson—baseball, football

Kevin Jackson—wrestling

Edgerrin James—football

Derek Jeter—baseball

Allen Johnson—track and field

Charles Johnson—baseball

Magic Johnson—basketball

Michael Johnson—track and field

Roy Jones Jr.—boxing

Michael Jordan—basketball

Jackie Joyner-Kersee—track and field

David Justice—baseball

Jason Kidd—basketball

Barry Larkin—baseball

Lisa Leslie—basketball

Carl Lewis—track and field

Ray Lewis—football

Kenny Lofton—baseball

Ronnie Lott—football

Tracy McGrady—basketball

Fred McGriff—baseball

Donovan McNabb—football

Steve McNair—football

Karl Malone—basketball

Cheryl Miller—basketball

Reggie Miller—basketball

Randy Moss—football

Alonzo Mourning—basketball

Dan O'Brien—track and field

Hakeem Olajuwon—basketball

Shaquille O'Neal—basketball

Terrell Owens—football

Gary Payton—basketball

Scottie Pippen—basketball

Michael Powell—track and field

Kirby Puckett—baseball

Tim Raines—baseball

Andre Reed—football

Butch Reynolds—track and field

Jerry Rice—football

David Robinson—basketball

Barry Sanders—football

Deion Sanders—baseball, football

Warren Sapp—football

Shannon Sharpe—football

Gary Sheffield—baseball

Bruce Smith—football

Emmitt Smith—football

Lee Smith—baseball

Darryl Strawberry—baseball

Sheryl Swoopes—basketball

Lawrence Taylor—football

Frank Thomas—baseball

Isiah Thomas—basketball

Thurman Thomas—football

Mike Tyson—boxing

Mo Vaughn—baseball

Michael Vick—football

Herschel Walker—football, track and field, bobsled

Chris Webber—basketball

Reggie White—football

Fred Whitfield—rodeo/calf roping

Ricky Williams—football

Serena Williams—tennis

Venus Williams—tennis

Tiger Woods—golf

Charles Woodson—football

Rod Woodson—football

LATINO AMERICAN

Bobby Abreu—baseball

Edgardo Alfonzo—baseball

Roberto Alomar—baseball

Moises Alou—baseball

Marcelo Balboa—soccer

Armando Benitez—baseball

Jose Canseco—baseball

Helio Castrovenes—auto racing

Cesar Chavez—boxing

Bartolo Colon—baseball

Chili Davis—baseball

Gil de Ferran—auto racing

Oscar De La Hoya—boxing

Carlos Delgado—baseball

Tim Duncan—basketball

Patrick Ewing—basketball

List of Entries by Major Sport

AUTO RACING

Helio Castroneves

Gil de Ferran

Juan Montoya

BASEBALL

Bobby Abreu

Edgardo Alfonzo

Roberto Alomar

Moises Alou

Harold Baines

Albert Belle

Armando Benitez

Barry Bonds

Bobby Bonilla

Jose Canseco

Bartolo Colon

Chili Davis

Carlos Delgado

Tony Fernandez

Andres Galarraga

Freddy Garcia

Nomar Garciaparra

Juan Gonzalez

Luis Gonzalez

Dwight Gooden

Ken Griffey Jr.

Vladimir Guerrero

Tony Gwynn

Rickey Henderson

Livan Hernandez

Orlando "El Duque" Hernandez

Roberto Hernandez

Bo Jackson

Derek Jeter

Charles Johnson

Andruw Jones

David Justice

Barry Larkin

Kenny Lofton

Javy Lopez

Fred McGriff

Edgar Martinez

Pedro Martinez

Magglio Ordonez

Russ Ortiz

Rafael Palmeiro

Jorge Posada

Kirby Puckett

Albert Pujols

Tim Raines

Manny Ramirez

Mariano Rivera

Alex Rodriguez

Ivan Rodriguez

Deion Sanders

Gary Sheffield

Lee Smith

Alfonso Soriano

Sammy Sosa

Darryl Strawberry
Miguel Tejada
Frank Thomas
Fernando Valenzuela
Mo Vaughn
Javier Vazquez
Jose Vidro
Omar Vizquel
Bernie Williams

BASKETBALL

Ray Allen
Charles Barkley
Kobe Bryant
Vince Carter
Cynthia Cooper
Clyde Drexler
Tim Duncan
Patrick Ewing
Kevin Garnett
Penny Hardaway
Tim Hardaway
Grant Hill
Chamique Holdsclaw
Allen Iverson
Magic Johnson
Marion Jones
Michael Jordan
Jason Kidd
Lisa Leslie
Tracy McGrady
Karl Malone
Cheryl Miller
Reggie Miller
Alonzo Mourning
Hakeem Olajuwon
Shaquille O'Neal
Gary Payton

Scottie Pippen
David Robinson
Sheryl Swoopes
Isiah Thomas
Chris Webber

BOBSLED

Vonetta Flowers
Garrett Hines
Herschel Walker

BOXING

Cesar Chavez
Oscar De La Hoya
Evander Holyfield
Roy Jones Jr.
Felix Trinidad
Mike Tyson

FOOTBALL

Marcus Allen
Jerome Bettis
Derrick Brooks
Tim Brown
Isaac Bruce
Cris Carter
Terrell Davis
Ron Dayne
Eric Dickerson
Corey Dillon
Marshall Faulk
Jeff Garcia
Eddie George
Tony Gonzalez
Marvin Harrison
Bo Jackson
Edgerrin James
Ray Lewis

Ronnie Lott
Donovan McNabb
Steve McNair
Randy Moss
Anthony Munoz
Terrell Owens
Andre Reed
Jerry Rice
Barry Sanders
Deion Sanders
Warren Sapp
Shannon Sharpe
Bruce Smith
Emmitt Smith
Lawrence Taylor
Thurman Thomas
Michael Vick
Herschel Walker
Reggie White
Ricky Williams
Charles Woodson
Rod Woodson

GOLF

Tiger Woods

ICE HOCKEY

Scott Gomez

RODEO/CALF ROPING

Fred Whitfield

SOCCER

Marcelo Balboa

SOFTBALL

Lisa Fernandez

SPEEDSKATING

Derek Parra
Jennifer Rodriguez

SWIMMING

Anthony Ervin

TENNIS

Serena Williams
Venus Williams

HORSE RACING

Laffit Pincay

TRACK AND FIELD

Evelyn Ashford
Charles Austin
Valerie Brisco-Hooks
Mike Conley
Gail Devers
Florence Griffith Joyner
Kenny Harrison
Allen Johnson
Michael Johnson
Marion Jones
Jackie Joyner-Kersee
Roger Kingdom
Carl Lewis
Dan O'Brien
Merlene Ottey
Michael Powell
Butch Reynolds
Alberto Salazar
Herschel Walker

WRESTLING

Kevin Jackson

List of Entries on Women with Sport

A

BOBBY ABREU
(March 11, 1974–   )

Baseball

Bobby Abreu, one of the Philadelphia Phillies' (National League) brightest young stars, is at once the product of one major league organization's cultivation of the rich vein of young talent in Latin America and for another organization that let him go, a poster boy for what might have been.

Bob Kelly Abreu, born on March 11, 1974 in Turnero, Venezuela, is the second of six siblings. All three of his brothers played professional baseball in the United States. Nelson, his late father, was a devoted baseball fan and tutored his sons on the finer points of the game. At age 14, Abreu was spotted by Houston Astros (NL) scouts and encouraged to attend the Astros' developmental school in Valencia, Venezuela. Two years later, at age 16, he signed with the Astros.

Abreu hit well as he progressed through the Astros' minor league system. After spending the 1995 and 1996 seasons playing Class AAA ball in Tucson, Arizona (Pacific Coast League), he was considered to be "the best pure hitter in the (Houston) system." Yet he still needed to improve his knowledge of the strike zone and to learn how to use his above-average speed on the base paths. At that time he was only an average outfielder with a strong arm.

The Houston Astros called Abreu up briefly at the end of the 1996 season. He went to spring training in 1997 and won the starting right-field job. He was so promising that his name often came up in preseason discussions of potential NL rookies of the year. But the 1997 season did not go as planned for Abreu. He suffered a fractured wrist in mid-May and went on the disabled list. He did not return to active duty until July 1, and was no longer a starter. After batting just six times between July 1 and July 16 and hitting only .240, Abreu was sent to Class AAA New Orleans, Louisiana (American Association). Unhappy with the demotion, he turned in a lackluster performance at New Orleans. After being recalled by the Astros, he raised his batting average to .250 by season's end.

Disappointed by Abreu's reaction to his demotion and blessed with fine outfielders (including Richard Hidalgo and Moises Alou), the Astros left Abreu unprotected during the 1997 expansion draft. The Tampa Bay Devil Rays (American League) selected him with their third pick and almost immediately traded him to the Philadelphia Phillies (NL) for shortstop Kevin Stocker.

The Phillies, having decided to launch a "youth movement," gambled on Abreu and hoped he would add some speed to the team. Abreu flourished in Philadelphia, batting over .300 from 1998 through 2000 and attaining a .335 average in 1999. After that season, the Phillies rewarded him with a three-year, $14.25 million contract. In 2000 Abreu was the only National Leaguer to reach double figures in doubles, triples, home runs, and stolen bases for the second consecutive season. His home run and stolen base totals increased each year from 1998 through 2001. Although his batting average dipped to .289 in 2001, he still became the first Phillie ever to record 30 home runs and 30 stolen bases during the same season. He also drove in over 100 runs (110) for the first time and scored 100 or more runs for the third consecutive year. In 2002 Abreu batted .308 with 20 home runs, 85 runs batted in (RBI), and 31 stolen bases and led the NL with 50 doubles in 2002. He hit .300 with 20 home runs and 101 RBIs and ranked fourth in the NL with 109 walks in 2003.

Two issues continue to hound Abreu. First, this 6-foot, 195-pound left-handed hitter struggles badly against southpaws both in batting average and in power production. He hit just .258 against lefties with a .365 slugging percentage in 2001, compared to .608 against right-handers. Through 2001, he clouted just four career major league home runs against left-handed pitching.

Second, Abreu is said to lack intensity and sufficient commitment to the game; this reputation has followed him from Houston to Philadelphia. Shortly after the Phillies acquired Abreu in 1997, Tim Wendel wrote in *USA Today Baseball Weekly* that "behind the scenes in Houston, there were rumblings about Abreu's desire and work habits." These problems resurfaced in Philadelphia when he was frequently late for team buses and games, resulting in a fine and brief benching by manager Terry Francona during the 2000 season. Abreu seems to be maturing, however. Larry Bowa, who took over as manager in 2001, has been pleased with Abreu's attitude and newfound maturity, noting that he has worked hard taking extra batting practice and studying films to pull himself out of slumps.

Abreu is single and has a daughter, Emily. During the off-season he lives in Aragua, Venezuela, and plays winter ball in the Venezuelan League. His career statistics through the 2003 season include a .306 batting average with 136 home runs, 569 RBIs, and 170 stolen bases.

BIBLIOGRAPHY

Chris Edwards, "The Book on . . . Bobby Abreu," *The Sporting News* 223, September 13, 1999, p. 51; Paul Hagen, "Abreu Jumps into 30-30 Club," *Philadelphia Daily News*, October 1, 2001; Chuck Johnson, "Abreu Everything Phillies Had Hoped For," *USA Today*, August 20, 1999 (Final Edition), p. 6C; Dana Pennett O'Neil, "A Horse with No Name: Bobby Abreu Might Be Baseball's Least Known Star," *Philadelphia Daily News*, September 11, 2001, p. 94C; Jeff Pearlman, "Thoroughbred Phillie," *Sports Illustrated* 93 (July 30, 2001), p. 40; "Philadelphia Phillies," *USA Today Base-*

ball Weekly 9, August 11, 1999, p. 17; Tim Wendel, "We Can Do More to Embrace Latin Beat," *USA Today Baseball Weekly* 7, March 11, 1998, p. 8; Lisa Winston, "Fan Favorite Abreu Still Is the Toast of Tucson," *USA Today Baseball Weekly* 6, April 3, 1996, p. 37.

Terry W. Sloope

EDGARDO ALFONZO   Baseball
(November 8, 1973–)

Affectionately known as "Fonzie" by New York fans, Edgardo Alfonzo was a fixture in the New York Mets (National League) infield from 1995 to 2002. He is noted for his slick fielding, clutch hitting, and dedication to the team. In an era of high-profile individualistic professional athletes, he emphasizes teamwork.

Edgardo Antonio Alfonzo was born on November 8, 1973 in Santa Teresa, Venezuela. His father, Edgar Alfonzo Sr., drove trucks and delivered medical supplies, while his mother, Mercedes Alfonzo, taught elementary school. Like many young baseball fans in his native land, he grew up admiring Dave Concepcion, Ozzie Guillen, and other Venezuelans who were successful major league players in the United States. Following graduation from Cecilio Acosto High School, Alfonzo was signed by the New York Mets in February 1991. His brothers, Roberto and Edgar, were also scouted by American major league baseball clubs and played in the minor leagues. Roberto now works as an international baseball scout, while Edgar managed in the farm system of the New York Mets. In 2000, Edgar managed the Kingsport, Tennessee, franchise (Appalachian League). When baseball returned to Brooklyn, New York, in the summer of 2001, Edgar Alfonzo piloted the Brooklyn Cyclones, the Mets' Class A affiliate (New York–Penn League).

Along with his brothers, Alfonzo faced many difficulties in making the transition to living and playing baseball in the United States. Perhaps his greatest challenge was learning to speak English. He studied English in school but had never used the language on a practical basis. He later recalled that the first phrase he learned in English was "let it go." This initial English lesson may reflect Alfonzo's personality; while competitive on the playing field, he offers a quiet confidence and leadership that reassures his teammates.

After four seasons in the minor leagues, the 5-foot 11-inch, 197-pound Alfonzo was promoted to the parent New York Mets and was installed as the team's third baseman. He enjoyed an outstanding rookie season with the Mets, batting .278 and appearing in over 100 games. In the 1996 and 1997 seasons, he played regularly at third base. After hitting over .300 in 1997, he increased his home run output to 17 in 1998.

In 1999, the Mets acquired Robin Ventura to play third base and asked Alfonzo to play second base. His popularity among Mets fans and teammates was assured when he graciously accepted this move to improve the team. In similar circumstances, most major league baseball players are not so accommodating. During the 1999 season, Alfonzo excelled defensively at second base and established career marks with a .304 batting average, 27 home runs, and 108 runs batted in (RBI).

Alfonzo, who bats and throws right-handed, led the Mets into the 2000 subway World Series with the New York Yankees. Continuing his assault upon NL pitching, he attained a .324 batting average, hit 25 home runs, drove in 94 runs, and earned selection to the All-Star team. His teammates quickly acknowledged their second baseman as the team's leader. Outfielder Darryl Hamilton told the *New York Times*, "When we get in a situation where we need a hit, where we need a guy to come through, everybody on this team wants Fonzie at the plate."

Alfonzo, however, was unable to carry the Mets to a World Series victory over the New York Yankees. During 2001, the Mets slumped and missed the playoffs. This decline occurred partly because Alfonzo missed numerous games with a bad back. His offensive statistics were impacted by his injury.

After the disappointing 2001 season in which his batting average fell to .243, Alfonzo was again asked to sacrifice for the team. Following the acquisition of second baseman Roberto Alomar* in a trade with the Cleveland Indians, the Mets requested that he return to third base when Ventura was not re-signed. Alfonzo was willing to accept a change in position as long as it would benefit the team. In 2002, he led the Mets with a .308 batting average, clouted 16 home runs, and recorded 56 RBIs. Through 2003, Alfonzo batted .288 with 133 home runs, and 619 RBIs. In December 2002, the San Francisco Giants (NL) signed him as a free agent. In 2003 he hit .259 with 13 home runs and 81 RBIs to help San Francisco win the NL West and .529 with four doubles and five RBIs in the NL Championship Series loss to the Florida Marlins.

Alfonzo's unselfish attitude inspires his teammates and his fans in New York City, where he and his wife, Delina, participate in many charity activities. He is a dedicated family man who tends to spurn New York's night life, and he has two young sons, ages 5 and 2.

The unassuming Alfonzo remains a hero in his native Venezuela where he continued to play winter baseball until 1999, when the Mets implored him to get more off-season rest. Only reluctantly did he comply with their wishes. As for his contributions, he states, "I just try to be a good role model for my kids and for the kids of the world, especially in the Latin countries." Alfonzo has certainly fit that bill.

BIBLIOGRAPHY
Joe Gergen, "Fonzie Back to the Future at Third," *Newsday*, March 21, 2002; Rafael Hermoso, "Alfonzo Grows on the Field and in the Dugout," *New York Times*, October 20, 2000, p. D1; Chris Jenkins, "Edgardo Alfonzo: Majors' Most Under-Rated Player," *Baseball Digest* 60 (March 2001), pp. 20–24; Tyler Kepnes, "When It Matters Most, Alfonzo Is the Mightiest Met," *New York Times*, October 14, 2000, pp. D1, D4.
Ron Briley

MARCUS ALLEN   **Football**
(March 26, 1960–)

Marcus Allen, one of professional football's all-time great running backs, played 16 National Football League (NFL) seasons from 1982 to 1997 with the Los Angeles Raiders and Kansas City Chiefs.

Marcus LeMarr Allen was born in San Diego, California, on March 26, 1960, one of six children of Harold "Red" Allen, a construction worker, and Gwen Allen, a licensed vocational nurse. His parents were his role models. "Of all the wonderful things that have happened to me, my parents are far and away the best," he recalled. "I grew up in a loving environment, watched over and encouraged by both my parents, learning their lessons of right and wrong. And, most of all, the value of family."

Allen compiled a remarkable record at Lincoln High School in San Diego, where he starred in basketball and football. As a senior, he quarterbacked his team to the county title with a 12–0–1 record in 1977. He completed 145 of 300 passes for 1,900 yards and 18 touchdowns and ran 97 times for 1,198 yards (12.4-yard average) and 12 more scores. As a defensive safety, Allen intercepted 11 passes, ran back four for touchdowns and made 311 tackles. In the championship game 34–6 win over Kearney High School, he scored all five touchdowns on runs of 85, 30, 20, and 10 yards and on a 60-yard interception return. He was named the San Diego Player of the Year and California Prep Athlete of the Year, being picked by three prep All-America teams. He was named to the San Diego Hall of Fame in 1998.

The highly recruited B+ student matriculated in 1978 at the University of Southern California (USC), the school of his boyhood idol, O. J. Simpson. Allen was moved from defensive back to tailback just before the start of his freshman season and gained 171 yards (5.5-yard average) as a backup for future Heisman Trophy winner Charles White. As a sophomore, Allen became the starting fullback and lead blocker for White, ran for 647 yards (5.7-yard average), scored eight touchdowns, and caught 22 passes (14.3-yard average). He returned to tailback in 1980 and rushed for 1,563 yards and 14 touchdowns, second nationally to Heisman Trophy winner George Rogers of South Carolina. Because of his receiving skills, Allen led the nation's running backs in total offensive yards with a 179.4 average per game. "With his all-around ability, he's a true Renaissance man as a football player," said USC coach John Robinson. "I've seen running backs who were a little faster and maybe even a little stronger . . . but none who had his combination of intelligence and competitiveness. Add balance and vision, ability to get into the holes quickly, explosion at the end of a run—and you've got the whole package."

As a senior in 1981, the 6-foot 2-inch, 210-pound Allen scored 23 touchdowns and set or tied 12 National Collegiate Athletic Association (NCAA) records, including most rushing yards (2,342) and most 200-yard games (8)

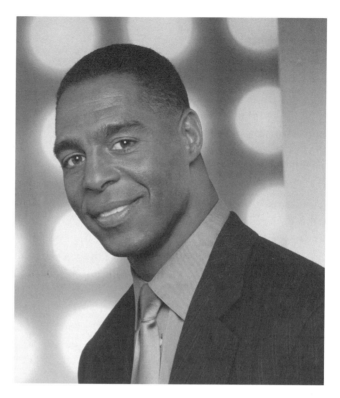

Marcus Allen ©Photofest

in a season. The consensus All-America averaged 212.9 yards per game and 5.81 yards per carry, was voted *The Sporting News*, *Football News*, Walter Camp, and United Press International (UPI) Player of the Year, and won the Maxwell Award and Heisman Trophy. Allen was inducted into the USC Athletic Hall of Fame in 1995 and the College Football Hall of Fame in 2001.

Several pro scouts questioned Allen's speed, durability, and toughness to excel in the professional game. In the NFL draft, he was passed over by nine teams before the Los Angeles Raiders finally selected him. "You've got to think positively to achieve the impossible, to be what you expect to be," he explained. "If you seek mediocrity, that's what you get out of life. I have a burning desire to be the best."

Allen quickly established himself with the Raiders as a superlative runner, blocker, receiver, and locker room presence with uncommon leadership skills. He finished the strike-shortened, nine-game 1982 season with 697 yards, an NFL-leading 11 touchdowns rushing, and 14 touchdowns overall. Named the Rookie of the Year, he also was selected All-Pro for the first of six times. In 1983 Allen rushed for 1,014 yards and led American Football Conference (AFC) backs with 68 receptions for 590 yards. He rushed for 121 yards and scored two touchdowns against the Pittsburgh Steelers in the playoffs and followed with a 154-yard effort in the AFC title game against the Seattle

Seahawks. He saved the best performance for Super Bowl XVIII, setting a Super Bowl record and winning Most Valuable Player (MVP) honors by rushing 191 yards against the Washington Redskins. His 74-yard burst for a touchdown on a broken play sealed a 38–9 victory for the Raiders. In 1984 Allen led the NFL with 18 touchdowns, rushing for 1,168 yards and 13 touchdowns and catching 64 passes for 758 yards and five touchdowns. His combined 1,926 yards (5.6 yards per play) won him a second All-Pro selection.

In 1985 Allen rushed over 100 yards in nine straight games to set an NFL record and gained 173 yards in the next game against the San Diego Chargers. He carried the ball for a league-leading 1,759 yards (4.6 yards per carry) and caught 67 passes for 555 yards. His 2,314 composite yards, a single-season record, and 14 touchdowns earned him the NFL, Associated Press (AP), and *Football News* MVP awards, selection as *The Sporting News* and UPI Player of the Year, and another spot on the All-Pro team.

Allen set a NFL record in 1986 for most consecutive games (11) with 100 or more yards and rushed for 759 yards. Knee injuries in 1989 and 1991, a personal feud with owner Al Davis over shared playing time with Bo Jackson* (1987–1990) and Eric Dickerson (1992), and a lingering salary dispute soured his remaining years with the Raiders. A new collective bargaining agreement allowed Allen to sign with the Kansas City Chiefs (NFL) in 1993. He ended his career with the Raiders as their all-time leader in carries (2,090), rushing yards (8,545), and touchdowns (98) and was voted their MVP ("Commitment to Excellence") award a record five times.

Allen experienced a remarkable turnaround with Kansas City in 1993. The 33-year-old back led the Chiefs in rushing with 764 yards and caught 34 passes for 238 yards. His 12 rushing touchdowns led the AFC, while his 15 total touchdowns ranked second in the NFL. Allen also won the Chiefs' MVP award and was selected All-Pro for the sixth time. In wins against his old teammates, the Raiders, he scored his 100th NFL career touchdown in the first game and averaged 5.0 rushing yards per carry in the second game. Kansas City coach Marty Schottenheimer reflected, "I don't think I have seen a better football player than Marcus Allen. . . . He is a guy who down after down, game after game, runs, blocks, catches, subordinates his own self-interest to that which is in the best interest of the team."

Slowed by an injury in 1994, Allen again paced the Chiefs in rushing. In 1995, he rebounded with 890 rushing yards and was again honored as Kansas City's MVP. He also became the first NFL player with more than 10,000 rushing yards and 5,000 receiving yards. In 1996, Allen broke Walter Payton's NFL career record for most rushing touchdowns with 112 and led the Chiefs in rushing for the fourth straight season.

Upon retiring after the 1997 season, Allen had appeared in more games (222), rushed for more touchdowns (123), and caught more passes (587) than any running back in NFL history. His lifetime 12,243 rushing yards and 17,648 total yards both currently rank the seventh all-time best. In 2003, he was elected to the Pro Football Hall of Fame.

Allen married Kathryn Eickstaedt on June 26, 1993 at the home of his friend O. J. Simpson in Brentwood, California. In 1994 rumors circulated of his alleged affair with Simpson's wife, Nicole. Allen denied the allegations, but rumors led to his divorce and loss of friendship with Simpson.

Allen joined CBS Sports in 1998 as a studio analyst and became a features/sideline reporter in 1999. He lives in Hollywood, California.

BIBLIOGRAPHY
Marcus Allen with Carlton Stowers, *The Autobiography of Marcus Allen* (New York, 1997); Marcus Allen file, College Football Hall of Fame Archives, South Bend, IN; Marcus Allen file, Pro Football Hall of Fame Library, Canton, OH; John T. Brady, *The Heisman: Symbol of Excellence* (New York, 1984); Jack C. Braun, telephone interview with Marcus Allen agent Mike Ornstein, August 30, 2001; *Current Biography Yearbook* (1986), pp. 3–6; David L. Porter, ed., *African-American Sports Greats: A Biographical Dictionary* (Westport, CT, 1995); David L. Porter, ed., *Biographical Dictionary of American Sports: Football* (Westport, CT, 1987); Ira Simmons, *Black Knight: Al Davis and His Raiders* (Rocklin, CA, 1990).

Jack C. Braun

RAY ALLEN   Basketball
(July 20, 1975–   )

Ray Allen starred with the Milwaukee Bucks (National Basketball Association) from 1996 to 2003. The 6-foot, 5-inch, 205-pound shooting guard has worked hard to improve his skills every season.

Walter Ray Allen was born on July 20, 1975 in Merced, California. His parents, Walter and Flora Allen, both played semiprofessional basketball. When Allen was age 10, his parents began teaching him basketball fundamentals. His father, a mechanic for the U.S. Air Force, moved his family from base to base, residing in Merced, California; Rosamond, California, Altus, Oklahoma; Ramstein, Germany; Suffolk, England; and Dalzell, South Carolina. Allen graduated from Hillcrest High School in Dalzell in 1993 and, as a senior, led his team to a State Basketball Championship with an average of 25 points and 10.5 rebounds per game. He was chosen All-State and the team's Most Valuable Player three straight years and was named Mr. Basketball in South Carolina following his senior season.

Allen attended the University of Connecticut between 1993–1994 and 1995–1996, where he earned a 3.6 grade point average as a communications science major. He led the Huskies to a 89–13 won-lost record and three National Collegiate Athletic Association (NCAA) Division I Tournament appearances. Connecticut advanced to the NCAA Regional Finals in 1995 before losing, with Allen averaging 24 points in four games. In 1995–1996, he was selected consensus All-America and was named United Press International's (UPI) College Player of the Year. He was chosen on the All–Big East Conference First Team, averaging 23.4 points, 6.5 rebounds, and 3.3 assists in 35 regular season games. Allen ranks third on the school's all-time scoring list with 1,922 points, establishing a single-season record with 115 three-point field goals. Allen, the first Husky to earn All-America recognition in consecutive seasons, was named as a junior to the Associated Press and the National Association of Basketball Coaches' Third Team in 1994–1995. In 2000, he was selected honorary captain of the 25-member University of Connecticut All-Century Basketball Team.

Following his junior season, Allen entered the 1996 NBA draft. The Minnesota Timberwolves (NBA) selected him in the first round as the fifth pick overall. In July 1996, Minnesota traded Allen, Andrew Lang, and a first-round draft choice in 1999 or 2000 to the Milwaukee Bucks (NBA) for the draft rights to Stephon Marbury. Allen started immediately for the Bucks and soon became one of the top NBA shooting guards. Everything he did on the floor seemed effortless. An explosive player, Allen demonstrated skills enabling him to shoot the runner, the finger roll, and the fadeaway jumper. He mastered the crossover dribble, letting him penetrate or shoot the long-range three-point field goal.

In his rookie season, Allen ranked third on the team in scoring at 13.4 points per game. The Bucks' three-point field goal threat, Allen led the team in free-throw percentage, participated in the Rookie Game and Slam Dunk contest at All-Star Weekend, and earned NBA All-Rookie Second Team honors. In his second season, he ranked second in scoring for Milwaukee at 19.5 points per game. In 1998–1999, Allen again finished second on the club in scoring at 17.1 points per game and led the Bucks in scoring in the first-round NBA playoff sweep by the Indiana Pacers. The following season, Allen was named to the NBA All-Star team and finished third in the American Telephone & Telegraph (AT&T) Long Distance Shootout. He averaged 22.1 points per game (17th in the NBA), made 88.7 percent of his free throws (5th), netted 42.3 percent of his three-point field goals (11th), and was ranked second in three-point field goals made. Indiana again eliminated Milwaukee in the first round of the postseason playoffs, as Allen averaged 22 points per game. In 2000–2001, he scored 1,806 points and averaged 22.1 points per game. He shot 88.8 percent at the free-throw line (7th in the NBA), 42.3 percent from three-point range (3rd), made 202 three-point field goals (1st), and was named to the All-NBA Third Team. Allen won the AT&T Long Distance Shooting Contest, making 33 of 50 attempts beyond the three-point arc. Allen recorded his first triple-double on February 7, 2001 against the Boston Celtics and posted a career-high 43 points against the Utah Jazz on April 12, 2001.

Allen helped lead Milwaukee to the 2001 NBA Playoffs, where the Bucks defeated the Orlando Magic in four games. Milwaukee triumphed over the Charlotte Hornets in a seven-game series but lost in seven games to the Philadelphia 76ers for the Eastern Conference Championship. In 18 playoff games, he led the Bucks in scoring with 452 points and averaged 25.1 points per game.

The Bucks finished a disappointing 41–41 in 2001–2002 and became the first franchise in NBA history to miss the NBA playoffs after leading its division as late as March 15. Allen averaged 21.8 points a game and led the Bucks with 1,503 points and 229 three pointers. Allen sometimes feuded with coach George Karl, who criticized his star for lack of intensity. In February 2003, the Seattle SuperSonics acquired Allen for Gary Payton.* Allen paced Seattle with 1,713 points and 201 three pointers and finished second in the NBA with a .916 free-throw percentage but the SuperSonics missed the play-offs. In seven NBA seasons from 1996–1997 through 2002–2003, Allen has compiled 10,391 career points and averaged 19.9 points in 523 regular season games. He has collected 2,423 rebounds, handed out 2,031 assists, and made 664 steals. He has made 1,129 of 2,809 three-point field goals for a career .405 shooting percentage. In 26 NBA playoff games, Allen has posted 629 points for an average of 24.2 points per game and made 76 of 164 three-point field goal attempts. He played in the 2000, 2001, and 2002 NBA All-Star games, scoring 44 points in the three games.

Allen resides outside Milwaukee in Mequon. He has a daughter, Tierra, born on September 25, 1992, who lives with her mother in Connecticut. In September 2000, he was engaged to long-time girlfriend and actress, Shannon Walker. Allen has one brother and three sisters, likes to play the piano, and enjoys bowling, claiming to have an average of 180. He also plays golf and has a ten handicap. He initiated the "Ray of Hope" Foundation in Connecticut to provide food and clothing for the needy. In 1997, he played the lead role of Jesus Shuttlesworth, the top high school basketball player in America, in Spike Lee's film *He Got Game*.

BIBLIOGRAPHY

"Ray Allen," Player Background, www.nba.com (2001); "Ray Allen," *Player Career Highlights*, www.nba.com (2001); "Ray Allen," *Player Career Statistics*, www.nba. com (2001); "Ray Allen," *Statistics*, www.cnnsi.com (2001); *NCAA Men's Basketball's Finest* (Overland Park, KS, 1998); *The Sporting News Official NBA Register*, 2002–2003; L. Jon Wertheim, "Acquired Taste," *Sports Illustrated* 9 (February 26, 2001), pp. 51–53.

John L. Evers

ROBERTO ALOMAR   Baseball
(February 5, 1968–   )

Roberto Alomar ranks among the greatest second basemen in major league baseball history.

Roberto Velasquez Alomar was born on February 5, 1968 in Ponce, Puerto Rico, the son of Santos "Sandy" Alomar Sr. and Maria Angelita (Velasquez) Alomar, and attended Luis Munoz Rivera High School in Salinza, Puerto Rico. His father played major league baseball with six different teams from 1964 to 1978, mostly as an infielder, and coached with the San Diego Padres,

Roberto Alomar ©Doug Benc/Getty Images

Chicago Cubs, and Colorado Rockies. His brother, Sandy Jr., caught for the Cleveland Indians and Chicago White Sox.

His father's dedication to baseball prepared Alomar (nicknamed "Robbie") for signing with the San Diego Padres (National League) organization in 1985 and making it to the parent club by 1988. Just 20 years of age, the 6-foot, 185-pound Alomar, who switch-hits and throws right-handed, had mastered second base. In his first major league season, the Padres led the NL in double plays for the first time in the club's history. Alomar possessed security and confidence, shown in his graceful movement as a fielder, and productive talents as a switch-hitter. Through teammate Tony Gwynn, who greatly assisted him in hitting, Alomar steadily improved. Manager Larry Bowa observed, "As far as fundamentals are concerned this kid is just as sound as Ryne Sandberg. . . . He doesn't give a damn who's out there pitching. He doesn't even know. He just plays."

In 1990, the San Diego Padres traded Alomar and outfielder Joe Carter to the Toronto Blue Jays (American League) for first baseman Fred McGriff* and shortstop Tony Fernandez.* With Toronto, Alomar played in the 1992 and 1993 World Series against the Atlanta Braves and Philadelphia Phillies, respectively. In the 1993 fall classic, he batted a stellar .480 with 12 hits in six games.

A free agent in 1995, Alomar signed with the Baltimore Orioles (AL) in December. His praiseworthy consistency and authority thrilled Orioles fans, who especially admired his exceptional range and fluid movement defensively between 1996 and 1998. In 1996, he hit .328 in 153 games.

A 1996 incident soiled his reputation considerably. In September following a called third strike, Alomar spat in the face of umpire John Hirschbeck and was suspended for the first five games of 1997. Some observers complained that the Orioles should also have withheld his salary during that week. "Really it's a five-day vacation" for Alomar, one reporter protested.

After three years with the Orioles, in December 1998, Alomar signed a $32 million, four-year contract with the Cleveland Indians (AL) rejoining brother Sandy Jr. for two seasons. Alomar attained a career high .336 batting average in 2001.

Alomar's achievements have been impressive. He has won the Gold Glove Award 10 times. Four games saw him clout homers from both sides of the plate. In 2001, he played in his twelfth consecutive All-Star Game. David L. Porter, in the *Biographical Dictionary of American Sports*, summarized: "He combines consistency and power at the plate with speed on the basepaths and exceptional range defensively."

In December 2001, Alomar was traded to the New York Mets (NL) in a big eight-player transaction. Atlanta Braves manager Bobby Cox, perhaps regretting Alomar's return to an opposing NL contender, observed: "He's probably one of the top ten players in the game today." Alomar slumped to a .266 batting average with 24 doubles and 53 runs batted in (RBI) in 2002. In July 2003, the Mets traded him to the Chicago White Sox. In 2003 he hit a composite .257 with just six home runs and 39 RBIs.

Through 2002, Alomar had batted .301 with 2,679 hits, 206 home runs, 1,110 RBIs, and 474 stolen bases. Despite one deplorable incident, his career has been devoted to achievement. He and his brother, Sandy Jr., have fulfilled their father's advice "to play the game hard."

BIBLIOGRAPHY
Joe Gergen, "How Long Will Family Ties Run in San Diego?," *The Sporting News*, March 20, 2001, p. 7; Dave Kindred, "Brat Ball Leads to Spitball," *The Sporting News*, October 14, 1996, p. 6; Bob Nightingale, "Thumbs Up on Ejections Is a Message from the Umps," *The Sporting News*, March 17, 1997, p. 32; David L. Porter, ed., *Biographical Dictionary of American Sports: Baseball—A–F* revised and expanded edition (Westport, CT, 2000); Roberto Alomar file, Research Center, *The Sporting News*, St. Louis, MO; *The Sporting News Baseball Register, 2003*.

William J. Miller

MOISES ALOU   Baseball
(July 3, 1966–)

Moises Alou, a five-tool baseball player, has starred in the field, on the bases, and at the plate. In major league seasons, he has compiled a .303 batting average with 217 home runs and 895 RBIs.

Moises Rojas Alou was born on July 3, 1966 in Atlanta, Georgia, into a famous baseball family. His father, Felipe, played 17 years in the major leagues and has managed for another decade. His uncles, Matty and Jesus, also played in the major leagues. Playing baseball on the family turf in the Dominican Republic proved difficult for the son of a former major league star. "It was tough," Alou said. "Dominican winter ball is one of the toughest leagues in the Caribbean. If I didn't do well, the fans would yell stuff at me. I was Felipe Alou's son. I was supposed to get a hit every at-bat." He has three sons and is concerned that the pressures of playing in the shadow of his famous family will be intensified for his own children. "I feel so bad for my kids now. They're Moises Alou's son and Felipe Alou's grandson."

Alou graduated from C.E.E. High School in Santo Domingo, Dominican Republic, in 1984 and attended Canada College in Redwood City, California. In 1986 he led the Coast Conference with a .447 batting average and hit nine home runs. He was selected by the Pittsburgh Pirates (National League) organization in the first round as the second pick overall of the free-agent draft.

Alou embarked on a four-year minor league career with seven different teams. He spent time on the disabled list with Macon, Georgia (South Atlantic League) in his second season. His major league career also was interrupted many times by stints on the disabled list. Injuries caused him the loss of the entire 1991 and 1999 seasons. "All the injuries I've had make me appreciate the game more," he said. "I think I enjoy the game more than anybody else in the league because it's been taken away from me a couple of times."

Alou made his major league debut with the Pittsburgh Pirates in 1990. After appearing in only two games, he was traded to the Montreal Expos (NL) and played 14 more games that year. During his six full seasons in Montreal, he went on the disabled list five times. (His father managed him for five years with that franchise.)

After his injury-plagued years in Montreal, Alou became a free agent and signed a $25 million, five-year contract with the Florida Marlins (NL). The Marlins assembled a club that became the first Wild Card team to win a World Championship. He contributed a .321 batting average and three home runs in the 1997 World Series triumph over the Cleveland Indians.

Despite their World Series victory, the Marlins dismantled their championship team and traded Alou to the Houston Astros (NL) in November 1997. "It's not what you prefer to do," explained Marlins' general manager Dave Dombrowski. "You don't want to trade a player like Moises Alou." Alou echoed those sentiments, "It was tough," he said of leaving the Marlins, "because we were like a family."

Houston's general manager Gerry Hunsicker welcomed the trade. "Moises Alou obviously is one of the premier players in the game today. Adding him to our lineup makes us a force to be reckoned with," Hunsicker said. Alou enjoyed his three best seasons with Houston in 1998, 2000, and 2001. During those three seasons, he batted .321 with 38 home runs; .355 with 30 home runs; and 331 with 27 home runs, helping the Astros make the playoffs in

1998 and 2001. Houston lost both NL Division Series. The second one especially disappointed Alou, who had considered the team's postseason chances "awesome."

Alou spent parts of the last three seasons with Houston on the disabled list. He became a free agent for the second time in his major league career after the 2001 season and signed with the Chicago Cubs (NL) in December 2001. In 2002, he batted .275 with 15 home runs and 61 runs batted in (RBI). Alou batted .280 with 22 home runs and 91 RBIs in 2003 to help the Cubs capture the NL Central Division. His sparkling .500 batting average, ten hits, and three RBIs helped Chicago defeat the Atlanta Braves in the NL Division Series. Alou hit .355 with two home runs and five RBIs in the NL Championship Series loss to the Florida Marlins, but protested when a fan deprived him of making a crucial catch along the left field stands in the eighth inning of Game Six.

Alou does not enjoy the spotlight, though he acknowledges that "It's nice to be recognized." Following the 1994 and 1998 seasons, *The Sporting News* named him as an outfielder on both the NL Silver Slugger and NL All-Star teams. He has appeared in four All-Star games (1994, 1997, 1998, 2001) with a composite .429 batting average. "Everybody who plays this game wants to go to the All-Star Game," he observed. "I think people are taking a lot more notice of what I'm doing."

Alou owns a stable of 35 race horses in the Dominican Republic. "I like race horses," he said. "It's my horses and my family."

BIBLIOGRAPHY
Seth Livingstone, "It's All about Bloodlines for Alou," *USA Today*, September 12, 2001; "Marlins Trade Alou to Astros, Miller Hired," *Athens News*, November 12, 1997; Brian McTaggart, "Alou, Berkman, Wagner to Be Named to NL Team," *Houston Chronicle*, July 4, 2001; *The Sporting News Baseball Register*, 2003; *Who's Who in Baseball 2002*; www.cubs.com.

James A. Riley

EVELYN ASHFORD   Track and Field
(April 15, 1957–)

Evelyn Ashford's sprint career as both amateur and professional ranks among the finest in track and field history.

The first of Samuel and Vietta Ashford's five children, Evelyn Ashford was born in Shreveport, Louisiana, on April 15, 1957. Since Samuel served as a U.S. Air Force noncommissioned officer, the family moved frequently. Ashford began running competitively at age 12. One of her earliest heroines was Olympic star Wilma Rudolph.

Ashford competed on the boys track team at Roseville, California High School near Sacramento and once ran the third leg of an otherwise all-boys relay team. In the fall of 1975, she entered UCLA. Her coach, three-time

Evelyn Ashford ©Tony Duffy/Getty Images

Olympian Pat Connolly, had placed fifth in the pentathlon at the 1968 Olympic Games in Mexico City.

As a 19-year-old, Ashford placed third in the 100 meters at the 1976 Trials to qualify for the U.S. Olympic team. At the Montreal, Canada, Olympic Games, she placed fifth, ahead of another teenager, East Germany's Marlies Oelsner, who as Marlies Goehr would become Ashford's greatest rival.

In 1977, Ashford won the 100- and 200-meter titles at both the collegiate and national championships. She broke the American record for the 200 meters in 22.62 seconds. She set seven more American outdoor records during her career. Ashford held the 200-meter record from 1977 to 1978 and from 1979 through 1984, and she owned the 100-meter record from 1979 through 1988. At that year's World Cup, she finished fifth and Goehr placed first in the 100 meters.

As a junior, Ashford repeated her sprint double victories at the 1978 collegiate and national meets. After that season, she left UCLA and married Ray Washington, a former California State University–Los Angeles basketball player. Washington eventually became her coach. In 1979, Ashford set an American record for the 100 meters in 11.07 seconds. She for the first time won sprint doubles at the national championships, the Pan American Games, and World Cup; *Track & Field News* ranked her best in the world in both sprints.

In 1980, the year of the U.S. Olympic boycott, Ashford did not rank in the sprint events for only the second time. She had not competed at the Olympic Trials because of an injury in 1978. Although she observed that the boycott "tore out my soul," it may have actually extended her career. "If I had gone to Russia and won my gold medals the way I expected to," she acknowledged, "I probably would have retired."

Ashford recovered from her injury in 1981, winning a third career sprint double at the nationals. She swept the sprint events at the World Cup, with *Track & Field News* naming her Female Athlete of the Year. She captured a fourth career national 100-meter title in 1982 at Knoxville, Tennessee, and completed a fourth sprint double at the 1983 U.S. Championships at Indianapolis, Indiana. Marlies Goehr defeated her at the USA–East Germany dual meet that same month, but on July 3 in Colorado Springs, Colorado, Ashford broke Goehr's world record for 100 meters with a 10.79-second clocking. Goehr got her revenge at the inaugural World Championships at Helsinki, Finland winning the 100 meters as Ashford fell to the track with an injury.

At the 1984 U.S. Olympic Trials in Los Angeles, California, Ashford qualified for her second Olympic team with a first-place finish in the 100 meters. She returned to the Los Angeles Coliseum for the Olympic Games that August, winning the 100 meters and anchoring the victorious U.S. sprint relay team. In Zurich, Switzerland, on August 22, she broke her own world record with a 10.76-second performance. Marlies Goehr, who did not compete in the Olympics due to a boycott, finished second. "That stands out more than anything else," observed Ashford. "She [Goehr] was my nemesis." Ashford was named Woman Athlete of the Year by *Track & Field News* for a second time.

Ashford gave birth to a daughter, Ashley Raina, on May 30, 1985. She and Pat Connolly split in 1986, a year in which she won all but two of her races and claimed top rankings in the United States for both sprints. A hamstring injury hindered Ashford throughout the 1987 season. In a world track federation poll that year, she was voted the all-time greatest female 100-meter performer. She finished ahead of both Rudolph and Goehr.

At the 1988 Olympic Trials, Ashford placed second to Florence Griffith Joyner,* whose stunning 10.49-second performance surpassed Ashford's world record. At the Seoul, South Korea, Olympic Games, Ashford competed in her fourth Olympics and finished second to Griffith Joyner in the 100 meters. At age 31, Ashford became the oldest sprint medalist in Olympic history. On the anchor leg of the 4×100 relay, she outran Goehr to give the United States a gold medal.

Four years later, the 35-year-old Ashford was considered a long shot to make the Olympic team. She ultimately edged out Carlette Guidry for third place in the 100 meters at the Olympic Trials to make the trip to Barcelona, Spain. Although she failed to make the 100-meter final, she ran the first leg of the 4×100 relay for the victorious U.S. squad.

Her last 100-meter U.S. race came on June 25, 1993 at the Indy Mazda Games in Indianapolis, Indiana. She finished fifth and ran a low-key 100-meter race in Sapporo, Japan, before retiring from competition. During her career, Ashford won 16 national titles (10 outdoor, 6 indoor), four gold medals and a silver medal in the Olympics, four World Cup titles, and two gold medals at the Pan American Games. She was ranked best in the world 14 times, 7 times in the 100 meters and 7 times in the 200 meters.

"When I started, I thought it basically was, 'One Olympics and you retire,' " admitted Ashford. "But the sport and its rules kept changing. The longer I stayed in it, the more open track became for athletes to make a living at it. So that helped me stay in a lot longer."

Ashford was elected to the National Track and Field Hall of Fame in 1997, an honor she considered icing on the cake. "Getting the victory isn't what it's all about," she claimed. "It's knowing what you went through to get there. That's what it's all about. The actual winning really is anticlimactic."

BIBLIOGRAPHY
Dave Carey, Scott Davis, and Don Potts, *The Progression of the American National Record* (Los Angeles, CA, 1999); Pete Cava, *Evelyn Ashford's Last Race*, USATF Media Notes, July 28, 1993; Scott Davis, Dave Johnson, and Howard Willman, *FAST United States Track and Field Annual 1994* (Los Angeles, CA, 1994); Jon Hendershott, "T&FN Interview: Evelyn Ashford," *Track and Field News* 45 (December 1992), pp. 44–46, 49; Bill Mallon and Jim Dunaway, "1993 TAC TAFWA Bio Data Sheet—Evelyn Ashford," *NBC Olympic Track & Field Research Manual*; USA Women's Biographies—Evelyn Ashford (New York, 1993); David Wallechinsky, *The Complete Book of the Summer Olympics* (Woodstock, NY, 2000).

Peter J. Cava

CHARLES AUSTIN   **Track and Field**
(December 19, 1967–)

Charles Austin took part in the high jump at three Olympic Games. He won the Olympic gold medal in 1996, the World Outdoor Championship in 1991, and the World Indoor Championship in 1997. He holds the American high jump record and captured six consecutive U.S. outdoor high jump championships, as well as the 1998 World Cup Championship.

Charles Austin was born in Bay City, Texas, on December 19, 1967 and graduated from Van Vleck High School in 1986. Remarkably, he never qualified for the Texas High School Championships and was not recruited for college track. Nonetheless, his high school coach asked coach Rock Light of Southwest Texas State University to look at Austin's jumping ability. When the 6-foot-tall Austin recorded a personal best jump of 6 feet 11 inches, coach Light gave him a scholarship at Southwest Texas State. At Southwest, Austin jumped 7 feet 1 inch in 1987 and 7 feet 2 inches in 1988. In 1989 he placed fourth in the National Collegiate Athletic Association (NCAA) Indoor Championships with a jump of 7 feet 3 inches and second in the NCAA Outdoor

Championships. He tied for fifth in the USA Track and Field Outdoor Championships. In 1989, he was ranked eighth in the United States by *Track & Field News*. As a college senior, Austin placed third in the NCAA Indoor Championships with a jump of 7 feet 6½ inches and won the NCAA Outdoor Championship with a jump of 7 feet 7¾ inches. In 1990 Austin again placed fifth at the USA Track and Field Championships. He was then ranked fourth in the United States by *Track & Field News*.

Austin experienced a breakthrough year in 1991. He set the American high jump record with a jump of 7 feet 10½ inches in Zurich, Switzerland. He also placed third in the USA indoor meet with a jump of 7 feet 6½ inches and tied for sixth at the World Indoor Championships at 7 feet 7 inches. During the outdoor season, Austin tied for second in the USA Outdoor Championships at 7 feet 6 inches, tied for tenth at the World University Games, and won the World Championships with a 7-foot 9¾-inch jump. He was ranked third in the world.

In 1992 Austin made the American Olympic team and placed eighth in the high jump at Barcelona, Spain, with a 7-foot 5¾-inch jump. His 1993 track and field season ended after the indoor season, when he placed second at the USA Track and Field Indoor Championship at 7 feet, 7 inches and ninth at the World Indoor Championships with a 7-foot 4¼-inch jump. At this point he suffered tendonitis in his knee and was told that he might never be able to jump again without surgery. In July 1993, he therefore agreed to undergo an operation. He bounced back to win the Olympic gold medal at the 1996 Atlanta, Georgia, games after a daring pass and two misses at 7 feet 9¼ inches. He cleared 7 feet 10 inches to set an Olympic record with his one remaining jump.

In 1997, Austin won the USA Indoor and Outdoor Championships and the World Indoor title with a 7-foot 8½-inch jump. In 1998, he triumphed in the USA Outdoor, World Cup, and Edwardsville Grand Prix. He finished second at the Goodwill Games and third at the Grand Prix finals. In 1999, Austin won the USA Outdoor Championship, tied for third in the USA Indoor, and placed third in the World Indoor meet. He again made the American Olympic team in 2000 but failed to reach the Olympic finals at the Sydney, Australia, games. In 2001, he won the Millrose Games Championship with a 7-foot 5¼-inch jump and placed second in the USA Outdoor Championships at 7 foot 6½ inches.

Austin, whose nickname is "Snake," is working toward a Master's degree in business administration. He married in 1989 and has two sons, Camron and Alex. He shares custody of the children.

BIBLIOGRAPHY

USA Track & Field Information Service; David Walechinsky, *The Complete Book of the Summer Olympics* (Woodstock, NY, 2000).

Keith McClellan

B

HAROLD BAINES   Baseball
March 15, 1959–)

Harold Baines ranked among the best designated hitters in major league baseball history. He played for five teams in his remarkable 22-year major league
career, becoming one of the finest hitters in baseball.

Harold Douglass Baines was born on March 15, 1959 in Easton, Maryland,
to Linwood Baines and Gloria Baines and has three brothers and one sister.
His father played sandlot baseball as a third baseman and worked construction
jobs. As a senior at St. Michael's High School, Baines batted .532 and made
high school All-America under coach Denver Leach.

Bill Veeck, legendary owner of the Chicago White Sox (American League),
witnessed Baines play in a 1971 Little League game. Six years later, Veeck
signed Baines as the number one pick of the draft ahead of Paul Molitor and
other players. When former Chicago White Sox general manager Paul Richards first saw Baines, he claimed that he "was on his way to the Hall of Fame.
He just stopped by Comiskey Park for 20 years or so."

Baines, a 6-foot 2-inch, 195-pound left-hander, became a regular with the
Chicago White Sox in 1980 and quickly earned a reputation as a good hitter,
especially when there were men on base. He hit 25 home runs in 1982 and
knocked in 105 runs while compiling a .271 batting average. He also clouted
three homers in a 1982 game against the Detroit Tigers and shared second in
the American League (AL) with seven triples. In 1983 Baines belted 20 home
runs, knocked in 99 runs, and batted .280 while helping the White Sox win
the AL Western Division Championship.

Baines thereafter posted good numbers for the White Sox, never hitting
below .271, hitting under 13 home runs, or knocking in fewer than 81 runs.
Unfortunately, Chicago never won an AL Championship Series while Baines
was with them. In 1986 he suffered a severe knee injury that required two
operations and forced him to be used almost solely as a designated hitter
thereafter.

Chicago dealt Baines to the Texas Rangers (AL) in July 1989 even though
he was batting .321 at the time. Soon after, in August 1990, he was traded
once again, this time to the Oakland Athletics (AL). He played in the post-

season for the first time since 1983 and batted .357 as the Oakland Athletics advanced to the World Series. The Cincinnati Reds won in four games. Although the Athletics slipped to fourth place in 1991, Baines hit .295, belted 20 homers, and knocked in 90 runs. In 1992 he experienced an off year, but Oakland reached the AL Championship Series. He hit .440, but the Athletics lost to the Toronto Blue Jays in six games.

In January 1993, Baines was traded to the Baltimore Orioles (AL). He continued to hit well, even though he was suffering constant knee problems. Between 1993 and 1995, he hit .313, .294, and .299. Baines returned to the Chicago White Sox in 1996, hitting 22 homers and batting .311. The Baltimore Orioles claimed him from the Chicago White Sox in January 1997. He helped the Orioles reach the AL Championship Series before losing to the Cleveland Indians in six games. The much-traveled Baines now joined the Cleveland Indians (AL) in August 1999 where he played in only 28 games before returning to the Baltimore Orioles that October. He started 2000 with Baltimore and rejoined the Chicago White Sox that August. He only played in 32 games for the White Sox in 2001, hitting just .131 with no homers and six runs batted in (RBI).

Career highlights for Baines included the first-ever RBI single by a designated hitter in an All-Star Game and a .306 lifetime average in postseason games. He shares the major league single-game record for most at-bats (12) on May 8, 1984 in a 25-inning marathon against the Milwaukee Brewers. In 1989 he was named the designated hitter on *The Sporting News* AL Silver Slugger team.

Baines retired following the 2001 season, with 2,866 hits, 384 home runs, 1,628 RBIs, and a career .289 batting average in 22 years. Baines married Marla Henry and has four children; they live in St. Michael's, Maryland.

BIBLIOGRAPHY
Baltimore Orioles Media Guide, 1994, 1999; *Chicago White Sox Media Guide*, 1982; *Oakland Athletics Media Guide*, 1991; Mike Shatzkin, ed., *The Ballplayers* (New York, 1990); John Thorn et al. eds., *Total Baseball*, 7th ed. (Kingston, NY, 2001).

Robert L. Cannon

MARCELO BALBOA Soccer
(August 8, 1967–   )

Marcelo Balboa ranks among the most determined, successful players in the history of U.S. major league soccer.

Marcelo Balboa was born on August 8, 1967 in Cerritos, California. His father, Luis Balboa, played professional soccer in Argentina and for the Chicago Mustangs (North American Soccer League) and coached him in the American Youth Soccer program in Southern California. Balboa, who speaks English and Spanish fluently, attended Cerritos Junior College in Cerritos,

California, and played soccer in 1988 and 1989 at San Diego State University, where he excelled as defender and made First Team All-America in 1988 and Second Team All-America in 1989. He led the San Diego State Aztecs to the National Collegiate Athletic Association (NCAA) tournament twice and was named among the top 10 soccer players in the United States by *Soccer America* in 1988.

Balboa captained the U.S. Under 20 team at the World Youth Championship Games in Chile in 1987. He performed on the U.S. World Cup Soccer team in Italy in 1990, in the United States in 1994, and in France in 1998. In the 1994 World Cup games, he played every minute of every game. Balboa, one of only three U.S. players to play in three different World Cup finals, won the U.S. Soccer's Chevrolet Male Athlete of the Year Award in 1992 and 1994. Only two players have captured the prize twice.

Balboa tore the anterior cruciate ligament in his right knee against Iceland on April 17, 1993, and spent seven months in rehabilitation. He bounced back quickly, winning the 1994 U.S. Soccer World Cup Most Valuable Player (MVP) Award and the 1994 Honda Player of the Year Award from the U.S. media.

Balboa became the first American player to appear in 100 international games when he scored a goal to help the United States defeat Nigeria, 3–2, on June 11, 1995. With over 125 appearances, he has played more games for the U.S. National team than any player in history and ranks among the top 10 in the world in career appearances.

Besides enjoying a phenomenal international and World Cup career, Balboa has ranked among the best, most consistent American professional players. He starred for the San Diego Nomads (American Professional Soccer League) from 1987 to 1989, the San Francisco Blackhawks (APSL) in 1990 and 1991, and the Colorado Foxes (APSL) in 1992, when he led his team to the APSL Championship. He signed with Leon, Mexico (Mexican First Division) in January 1995 and sparked his team to the playoffs in 1996.

Balboa joined the Colorado Rapids (Major League Soccer) just 72 hours before their 1996 home opener. He finished third on the Rapids in scoring despite missing 15 games. In 1997, he was honored as Colorado's Honda MVP and Bic Tough Defender of the Year and played central defense all season. Colorado owned the second worst record in the MLS in 1996. Balboa switched to defensive midfielder and led the Rapids to a second-place finish in the 1997 Major League Cup. He played 90 minutes in all four final playoff contests. He enjoyed a solid 1998 season for the Rapids, again contributing mostly from the defensive midfield position.

In 1999, Balboa moved to sweeper and led a Colorado defensive unit that surrendered only 39 goals over 32 games. On four occasions in 1999, he played all 90 minutes. During the 2000 season, he played at least 90 minutes nine times for the Rapids. Balboa's bicycle kick goal against Tampa Bay on April 15 earned him MasterCard Goal of the Year. He finished as the Rapids' second best scorer during 2001, contributing a career-high six assists. He and only one other Colorado player recorded 1,500 minutes of play without receiving a yellow card. On May 5, 2001, his assist of John Spencer's goal against San Jose made him the first defender in MLS's history to register a career 20 goals and 20 assists. Balboa observes that the secret to being a successful defender in soccer is keeping your eyes on the ball. "If someone is trying to dribble by you and he's coming right at you," he says, *"you've got to watch the ball*. No matter where the attacker's body moves—he can go to the right, he can go to the left—the ball always sits still." Second, he believes that it is always better to remain on your feet. "Any time you dive in there's a chance of you getting beat," he explains. "Only slide tackle if it's absolutely necessary."

Balboa entered 2003 with 24 goals and 23 assists, both MSL records for defenders, in 152 games. In 2002 he was traded to the New York/New Jersey MetroStars (MSL) for a third-round draft pick in the 2002 MLS Superdraft. He started five consecutive MLS All-Star games from 1997 to 2001 and was selected for the 1996 MLS All-Star Game, but was unable to participate due to injury.

Balboa, his wife, Cindy, and their son, Nicolas, reside in Superior, Colorado.

BIBLIOGRAPHY

Colorado Rapids, *Marcelo Balboa Player Biography* (Denver, CO, 2001); Major League Soccer, *Marcelo Balboa, Defender, MetroStars* (www.MLSnet.com, 2002); Marcelo Balboa, "Marcelo Balboa on Slide Tackling," *Soccer Skills* (www. Sweetspotsoccer.com, 1999); Soccer Times, *U.S. Teams* (www.Soccertimes.com, 2000).

Frank J. Olmsted

CHARLES BARKLEY   Basketball
(February 20, 1963–   )

Charles Barkley gained fame as a flamboyant college, professional, and Olympic basketball star. Charles Wade Barkley, nicknamed "Sir Charles," was born on February 20, 1963 in Leeds, Alabama, and grew up in a small, rural community outside of Birmingham, Alabama. The oldest of three sons of Frank Barkley and Charcey (Edwards) Barkley, Charles Barkley was still a baby when his parents were divorced. After Charcey's second husband, Clee Glenn, was killed in an automobile accident, he was brought up primarily by his mother and grandparents.

Barkley's first attempt at basketball failed; not only did he suffer anemia in early childhood, but he was also overweight and lacked the basic basketball skills. Undeterred, he began working on his game skills and conditioning his body. As a junior at Leeds High School in 1979–1980, he made the basketball team as a substitute. Prior to his senior year, Barkley grew 6 inches, developed his body, and improved his skills. He starred his final season, averaging 19.1

Charles Barkley ©Photofest

points and 17.9 rebounds per game while leading his school to the State Tournament. His scoring of 26 points in a semifinal game led Auburn University to recruit him.

At Auburn on a basketball scholarship, Barkley enjoyed immediate success. He led the Southeastern Conference (SEC) in rebounding for three years and in 1984 was named the SEC Player of the Year, averaging 15.1 points and 9.5 rebounds per game while pacing the Tigers to a 20–11 record and the school's first invitation to the National Collegiate Athletic Association (NCAA) Tournament. In three seasons at Auburn, the 6-foot 6-inch, 252-pound Barkley averaged 14.1 points and 9.6 rebounds per game. He failed to make the 1984 Olympic team and skipped his final college season to apply for the National Basketball Association (NBA) hardship draft.

Although concerned about Barkley's weight problems, work habits, and provocative attitude, the Philadelphia 76ers (NBA) selected the extremely talented power forward in the first round as fifth pick overall of the 1984 NBA draft. He joined veterans Julius Erving, Moses Malone, and Maurice Cheeks. Barkley exhibited a flamboyant personality throughout his basketball career, and fans reacted to his bruising play, taunts, and gestures. He constantly "badgered" his coaches, management, fans, officials, and opponents; he talked constantly. His aggressive behavior and reaction to crowd taunts caused numerous problems with management and the NBA office. Earvin "Magic" Johnson* said of Barkley, "He thrives on controversy."

Barkley spent eight years, from 1985 through 1992, with Philadelphia and registered 14.0 points and 8.6 rebounds per game in his first season when he was named to the NBA All-Rookie Team. He continually elevated his points and rebounds per game. After six NBA seasons, he began to gain star recognition. By 1990, he finished second to "Magic" Johnson in the Most Valuable Player (MVP) voting and was declared *The Sporting News* Player of the Year. Barkley ranked fourth in the 76ers' history in total points (14,184), third in scoring average (23.3 points), third in rebounds (7,079), eighth in assists (2,276), and second in field goal percentage. He led Philadelphia in rebounding and field goal percentage seven consecutive seasons and in scoring six straight years. The 76ers usually fared poorly in the NBA playoffs. When Philadelphia failed to qualify for postseason play in 1992, Barkley was traded that June to the Phoenix Suns (NBA) for Jeff Hornacek, Tim Perry, and Andrew Lang.

In his initial season, Barkley won the NBA's MVP Award while leading the Suns to the NBA's best record at 62–20 and a berth in the 1993 NBA Finals. He averaged 25.6 points and 12.2 rebounds per game and carried the Suns to the NBA Championship Series. Phoenix lost to the Chicago Bulls in six games, as he averaged 26.6 points and 13.6 rebounds per game. After achieving superstar status, in the next two seasons he suffered from injuries that hampered his performance. Even though Barkley improved considerably in 1995–1996, Phoenix traded him in August 1996 to the Houston Rockets (NBA) for Sam Cassell, Robert Horry, Chucky Brown, and Mark Bryant.

Barkley was given his last chance for an NBA title when he joined the 1994 and 1995 NBA Champion Houston Rockets with veteran campaigners Clyde Drexler* and Hakeem Olajuwon.* The Rockets, however, lost in the NBA playoffs in 1997 and 1998 to the Utah Jazz and in 1999 to the Los Angeles Lakers. He missed most of the 1999–2000 season because of injuries. Barkley announced his retirement in December but returned to play his final game in Houston in April 2000. He told the home crowd, "Basketball doesn't owe me anything. I owe everything in my life to basketball." He immediately joined the Turner Network as a television analyst for the NBA playoffs.

After 16 NBA seasons, Barkley ranked thirteenth with 23,757 points and fifteenth with 12,546 rebounds and finished with career averages of 22.1 points and 11.7 rebounds in 1,073 games. He joined Kareem Abdul-Jabbar, Wilt Chamberlain, and Karl Malone* as the only NBA players to compile more than 23,000 points, 12,000 rebounds, and 4,000 assists in his career. He led the gold-medal-winning U.S. Olympic basketball "Dream Team" in 1992 at Barcelona, Spain, and in 1996 at Atlanta, Georgia, in scoring. Barkley scored 2,873 points and collected 1,582 rebounds in 123 NBA playoff games, but his teams never won the NBA title. He made the All-NBA First Team in 1988–1991 and 1993, All-NBA Second Team in 1986, 1987, 1992, 1994, and 1995, and All-NBA Third Team in 1996. He was also selected to play in 11 NBA All-Star games, receiving more votes than any other player in 1994 and being named MVP in 1991. His most prestigious honor may have been his selection in 1996 as one of the 50 Greatest Players in NBA history. On March 30, 2001, Barkley became the seventh player to have his jersey number (34) retired by the Philadelphia 76ers, joining Julius Erving (6), Maurice Cheeks (10), Wilt Chamberlain (13), Hal Greer (15), Bobby Jones (24), and Billy Cunningham (32).

Barkley has written two books, *Outrageous* and *Wit and Wisdom of Charles Barkley.* Key to his mindset as a player was his belief that the "majority of the people in the world don't know what it takes to win. Everyone is looking for an easy road. I made up my mind a long time ago to be successful at whatever I did. If you want to be successful, can't nobody stop you!" He married Maureen L. Blumhardt on February 9, 1989 and has a daughter, Christiana.

BIBLIOGRAPHY
Charles Barkley and Roy N. Johnson, *Outrageous* (New York, 1993); Charles Barkley, www.nba.com; Charles Barkley, www.athletesdirect.com; James McMullan, "Michael and Me," *Sports Illustrated* 24 (December 2, 1999), pp. 64–69; *NCAA Men's Basketball's Finest*, 1998; Larry Platt, *Charles Barkley*, www.salon.com (May 30, 2000); David L. Porter, ed., *Biographical Dictionary of American Sports 1989–1992 Supplement* (Westport, CT, 1992); *The Sporting News Official NBA Register*, 2002–2003.

John L. Evers

ALBERT BELLE   Baseball
(August 25, 1966–   )

Outfielder Albert Belle led the American League (AL) three times in runs batted in (RBIs) and in 1995 became the first major leaguer to hit 50 doubles and 50 home runs in the same season.

Albert Jojuan Belle was born on August 25, 1966 in Shreveport, Louisiana, the son of teachers Albert Belle and Carrie Belle. Belle, nicknamed "Joey," has a twin brother, Terry, a financial analyst. Albert graduated near the top of his class from Huntington High School in Shreveport in 1984 and attended Louisiana State University from 1984 through 1987, twice making the All-Southeast Conference team.

The Cleveland Indians (AL) selected Belle in the second round of the June 1987 draft. He progressed rapidly through the minor leagues with Kinston, North Carolina (Carolina League) in 1987 and 1988, Waterloo, Iowa (Midwest League) in 1988, Canton-Akron, Ohio (Eastern League) in 1989 and 1990, and Colorado Springs, Colorado (Pacific Coast League) in 1991. The 6-foot 2-inch, 210-pounder, who batted and threw right-handed, split time between designated hitter and the outfield with the Cleveland Indians between 1989 and 1992 and became the Indians starting left fielder in 1993.

Belle, who remarked, "I play every game like it's the last game of my career," enjoyed several productive seasons between 1992 and 1996 with Cleveland. He led the AL in RBIs with 129 in 1993 and hit .357 with 35 doubles, 36 home runs, and 101 RBIs in just 106 games in 1994. In 1995 he helped the Indians win their first AL pennant since 1954, batting .317, pacing the league with 50 home runs and a .690 slugging percentage, and sharing the AL lead with 121 runs scored, 52 doubles, and 126 RBIs. No major league player had ever recorded at least 50 doubles and 50 home runs in the same season. *The Sporting News* named him major league Player of the Year, but the more popular Mo Vaughn,* who had a lower batting and slugging per-centage and fewer home runs, won the Most Valuable Player Award. In 1996 Belle led the AL with 148 RBIs and hit .311 with 398 doubles and 48 home runs, helping the Indians repeat as Central Division champions.

Belle appeared in the 1995 and 1996 postseasons. In 1995 he batted .273 with one double, one home run, and three RBIs as Cleveland swept the Boston Red Sox in the AL Division Series. The Indians defeated the Seattle Mariners in the AL Championship Series, but he hit only .222 with just one double, one home run, and one RBI. The triumphant Atlanta Braves limited Belle to a .235 batting average, two home runs, and four RBIs in the six-game World Series. In two World Series, he batted .231 with three home runs and nine RBIs in seven games. He also was named to the AL All-Star team between 1993 and 1996, with one hit and one RBI in the 1993 summer classic.

In November 1996, Belle signed a five-year $55 million contract with the

Chicago White Sox (AL) as a free agent and became the first major leaguer to earn over $10 million a year. He enjoyed another banner year in 1998, leading the AL in slugging percentage (.655) and total bases (399), finishing second in doubles (48), home runs (49), and RBIs (152), ranking third in batting average (.328), and placing fourth in hits (200).

In December 1998, the Baltimore Orioles (AL) signed Belle to a $65 million, five-year contract. He knocked in 117 runs in 1999 and 103 runs in 2000, sharing the AL lead for right fielders with 17 assists. Teammate Brady Anderson acknowledged, "When you have a guy who's as productive as he is and is willing to play every single inning of every game, you have to respect that." "As a teammate," he added, "he's the best you can have." Manager Mike Hargrove called Belle "one of the best right-handed right fielders in the game today."

Belle spent the entire 2001 season on the disabled list with an arthritic right hip and retired following that season with a .295 career batting average, 974 runs scored, 1,726 hits, 389 doubles, 381 home runs, and 1,239 RBIs in 12 major league seasons. He led all major leaguers in the 1990s with 1,099 RBIs. From 1990 through 2000, he ranked second among all major leaguers in RBIs, third in doubles and extra-base hits, fourth in total bases, fifth in home runs, and sixth in slugging percentage. Belle joined Babe Ruth, Lou Gehrig, and Jimmie Foxx as the only players to have eight consecutive seasons with 30 home runs and 100 RBIs. Belle made *The Sporting News* AL All-Star team and *The Sporting News* Silver Slugger team from 1993 through 1996 and again in 1998.

Defenders considered Belle a perfectionist, private, principled, focused, and intense, but critics called him angry, surly, bullying, and rude. He has done extensive charity work and given large donations to philanthropic organizations. Cleveland nominated him for the Roberto Clemente Award in 1993 and 1994 and the Branch Rickey Award in 1994. In 1997 he initiated a program that encourages first through eighth graders from low-income families in his hometown of Shreveport to read at least one hour a week.

Belle's quick temper led to numerous altercations with the fans and press during his playing days. On one occasion, in 1991, he threw a ball into the chest of a fan who taunted him. From 1990 to 1994, the AL suspended him once per season. He twice charged the mound after opposing pitchers, tore up a locker room with a bat, and spent 58 days in 1990 in the Cleveland Clinic being treated for alcohol addiction. Acting commissioner Bud Selig fined him a record $50,000 for his profanity-laced tirade against television reporter Hannah Storm during the 1995 World Series. In yet another incident Belle knocked down a Halloween vandal with his Ford Explorer pickup truck in 1995. Cleveland general manager John Hart said, "In a foxhole, I'll take Albert, but you're wasting your time if you're trying to figure him out."

BIBLIOGRAPHY
Albert Belle file, National Baseball Library, Cooperstown, NY; Michael Bamberger, "He Thrives on Anger," *Sports Illustrated* 74 (May 6, 1996), pp. 72–76ff; Cesar

Brioso, "Belle's Antics Could Hamper Hall of Fame Election Bid," *USA Today*, March 6, 2001, p. 3C; Chuck Johnson, "Oriole Ready to Answer the Call," *USA Today*, February 25, 2000, pp. 1C–2C; P. M. Johnson, "Albert Belle," *Sport* 87 (November 1996), pp. 22ff; David A. Kaplan, "Heavy Hitter," *Newsweek* 127 (March 25, 1996), pp. 62–63; B. Livingston, "Raging Belle," *Sport* 83 (February 1992), pp. 58–61; David L. Porter, ed., *Biographical Dictionary of American Sports: Baseball, A–F* revised and expanded edition (Westport, CT, 2000); *The Sporting News Baseball Register*, 2002.

David L. Porter

ARMANDO BENITEZ   Baseball
(November 2, 1972–   )

Armando Benitez has become one of the major leagues' premier relievers.

Armando German Benitez was born on November 2, 1972 at Ramon Santana, Dominican Republic, the son of Francisco Benitez, a rancher, and Constaza Benitez. His eventual 6-foot 4-inch, 229-pound frame anchored him in his successful pitching career. A nondraft selection in 1990 by the Baltimore Orioles (American League) at just age 17, Benitez reached the major leagues briefly in 1994 and 1996. In 1997, the Orioles finally retained him as a reliever.

His first major league appearance came against the Cleveland Indians in 1994, when Benitez fanned three hitters, including Albert Belle,* in just 2.2 innings. Benitez stirred much initial admiration. Orioles manager Johnny Oates observed; "He has command, and a good fastball, and a good slider. He was very impressive."

Benitez, a power-pitcher, possessed a fastball often clocked at 98 miles per hour. In 1993 he shared the Palmer Prize Award for being the best hurler in the Orioles farm system. As a closer, however, he too frequently surrendered home runs, and if left in too long, he often lost some speed. Sportswriter Peter Schmuck wrote, "Superior confidence is the closer's stock in trade. . . . At times that mentality is missing with Benitez." No doubt, he needed confidence. In 1995, he was discouraged and resentful and packed his bags, preparing to leave the club. The Orioles management persuaded him to stay. Benitez demanded the closer's job exclusively but sometimes could not preserve his team's precarious one-run lead in the last two innings or strike out batters at the right time. Most Orioles executives regarded Benitez as "one of the brightest relief products in baseball" and tried to "make sure he did not forget that," hoping to boost his confidence, as Schmuck expressed it. Benitez learned much from Randy Myers, veteran left-handed Orioles reliever who told the young pitcher how to deal with crisis situations.

Orioles manager Davey Johnson restricted Benitez to less stressful occasions until he could adapt to the bullpen and mature. Many expected him to eventually fulfill the same role for Baltimore as Mariano Rivera* did for the

New York Yankees, but Benitez surrendered too many critical hits in the 1997 and 1998 postseasons. The Orioles nonetheless signed him to a $900,000 contract for 1998. Baltimore coaches and executives told him "to grow in the closer's role," for they considered him the most overpowering hurler on the Orioles' staff.

The 1998 season marked Benitez's last with Baltimore. Benitez protested: "If you don't want me as a closer. . . . Then get me out of here." He was suspended during May 21–27, 1998 for throwing at the New York Yankees hitters and sparking mayhem involving both teams. It proved a troublesome year for Benitez. In December 1998, Baltimore traded Benitez to the New York Mets (National League) in a three-way deal also involving the Los Angeles Dodgers. The Orioles acquired catcher Charles Johnson.* This transaction teamed Benitez with relievers John Franco, Dennis Cook, and Turk Wendell, the NL's best bullpen at that time. He responded with a 4–3 record and 22 saves for 1999 and a 4–4 record with 41 saves in 2000, helping New York reach the World Series. Benitez had signed a four-year, $22 million contract the previous February. The postseason still troubled him as he converted only three of nine save situations. He was learning "how to face certain hitters, how to handle crises, overcome defeat, and deal with the New York pressures," as Schmuck wrote. Yet sportswriter Pete Caldera observed: "When Benitez is getting his high, 90 mph fastball over for strikes, his hard, downward-biting slider is unhittable. But when he's wild, he tends to groove pitches, and he still gives up too many homers."

The 2001 season, however, proved very productive for Benitez, as he recorded a career 43 saves, the best in Mets history and just one behind NL leader Robb Nen. Benitez fanned 93 batters in just 76.1 innings. He enjoyed a 6–4 record with a 3.77 earned run average (ERA). In 2002 he finished 1–0 with a 2.27 ERA, 33 saves, and 79 strikeouts in 67.1 innings. Through 2002, he had a 26–27 won-lost record, a 3.04 ERA, and 689 strikeouts in 511.1 innings. In July 2003, the Mets traded him to the crosstown New York Yankees (AL). Three weeks later, he was traded to the Seattle Mariners. In 2003 he compiled a composite 4–4 record, 2.96 ERA, and 75 strikeouts in 73 innings.

During his off-seasons, Benitez operates a 1,000-acre ranch in Quisesquea, Dominican Republic, reportedly with 100 cows and 50 horses. His hard work and dedication as a capable reliever paid dividends. Benitez has remained single.

BIBLIOGRAPHY
Armando Benitez file, Research Center, *The Sporting News*, St. Louis, MO; *New York Mets Information Guide*, 2002. *The Sporting News Baseball*, 2002 Annual; *The Sporting News Baseball Register*, 2003; *Who's Who in Baseball*, 2002; *Street & Smith's Baseball*, 2002.

William J. Miller

JEROME BETTIS
(February 16, 1972–   )

Football

"Go Bus Go!" For several seasons, Pittsburgh Steelers (National Football League) fans have used this cry to rally behind Jerome Bettis, "The Bus," the Steelers star running back. At 5 feet 11 inches and 255 pounds, the bull-like Bettis scatters potential tacklers like a runaway bus.

Jerome Abram Bettis, the son of Johnnie and Gladys Bettis, was born on February 16, 1972 in Detroit, Michigan. Bettis played football for McKenzie High School, and as a senior was named by the *Detroit Free Press* as Michigan's outstanding interscholastic football player. He starred at the University of Notre Dame, where he played running back and averaged 5.7 yards a carry. Nevertheless, he was not a natural running back and explained, "I had to teach myself how to run."

Bettis entered the NFL in 1993 as the first choice and tenth pick overall of the Los Angeles Rams. He gained 1,429 yards for an average of 4.9 yards per rush. He also recorded seven 100-yard games, tying him for the NFL lead, and scored seven touchdowns. In December, Bettis rushed for a career-high 212 yards against the New Orleans Saints. After the season, the Pro Football Writers Association, *The Sporting News*, Associated Press (AP), and *Pro Football Weekly* named him Rookie of the Year, and he was selected for the Pro Bowl.

The following season, Bettis again broke the 1,000-yard mark with 1,025 yards. He caught his first career touchdown pass and was named again to the Pro Bowl. After a 1995 contract dispute, his production declined markedly. During the off-season, the Rams traded him to the Pittsburgh Steelers for two draft picks.

In Pittsburgh, Bettis regained the skills that should propel him into the Pro Football Hall of Fame. In 1996, he ran for 1,431 yards for an average of 4.5 yards per rush and 11 touchdowns. He notched ten 100-yard games and was named American Football Conference (AFC) Offensive Player of the Month for November. Bettis was voted the Steelers Most Valuable Player (MVP) and made the *College & Pro Football Weekly* and *USA Today* All-Pro teams. He also returned to the Pro Bowl.

Statistically, 1997 marked Bettis's best year. He rushed for a career-high 1,665 yards on 375 carries, the second best mark in Steelers history. He ran for seven touchdowns and added two more on receptions. Bettis enjoyed ten 100-yard games and rushed for 105 yards in a losing effort against the Denver Broncos in the AFC Championship contest. He again was named Steelers MVP and made the Pro Bowl. The NFL also selected him AFC Offensive Player of the Month for October.

For the next two seasons, Bettis anchored a subpar Steelers team. Intelligent and dedicated, Bettis ran over 1,000 yards during both campaigns. In 2000, he posted a banner year. For the fifth consecutive year, he rushed for more than 1,000 yards with 1,341 yards. He scored eight touchdowns and enjoyed seven 100-yard games. His teammates again voted him the Steelers MVP.

After signing a six-year, $30 million contract, Bettis experienced an outstanding 2001 season until sidelined by a serious injury. His sixth consecutive 1,000-yard rushing season featured five 100-yard games, giving him then 51 for his career and an average of 4.8 yards per carry. In leading the Steelers to the AFC Central Championship, Bettis compiled single-game marks of 163, 153, and 143 yards rushing and returned to the Pro Bowl for the fifth time. Late in the season, however, he suffered a groin injury and did not play again until the AFC Championship game against the New England Patriots, where he performed ineffectively. Given his age and the physical pounding that he has taken over his career, some expressed concern over his ability to bounce back from this injury. Nevertheless, Steelers offensive coordinator Mike Mularkey has summed up his value to the team, "He is our ride, our rock, and we feed off his mind-set."

Bettis gained 666 yards for a 13.6-yard average and nine touchdowns in 2002, helping the Steelers win the AFC North with a 10–5–1 record. The Tennessee Titans limited him to six yards in their 34–31 AFC playoff victory over the Steelers. Through 2002, Bettis had rushed for 11,542 yards, which placed him second to Emmitt Smith* among active players and tenth on the all-time list. He ranks second behind Franco Harris as the Steelers' all-time rushing leader.

Bettis is single and divides his off-season between Detroit and Pittsburgh. An avid bowler who describes his 300 game in 1994 as his "greatest sports thrill of all time," the amiable, popular Bettis remains very active in charitable activities. In 2002 the NFL named him the Walter Payton NFL Man of the Year Award as the NFL player who best combines athletic ability on the field with off-the-field community service.

BIBLIOGRAPHY
Paul Attner, "Driving Force," *The Sporting News*, December 3, 2001, pp. 6–10; Ed Bouchette, "Jerome Bettis," *Sport* 87 (December 1996), p. 18; Darryl Howerton, "The Three Horsemen: Bettis, Brooks, and Watters Rush from Notre Dame to NFL Fame," *Sport* 85 (December 1994), p. 62; Peter King, "Busting Loose," *Sports Illustrated* 95 (October 29, 2001), pp. 74–76; *Pittsburgh Steelers Media Guide—2003*; Michael Silver, "Making a Statement," *Sports Illustrated* 85 (October 7, 1996), pp. 42–43; Michael Silver, "Smashing Success," *Sports Illustrated* 95 (December 10, 2001), pp. 50–54.

Frank W. Thackeray

BARRY BONDS   Baseball
(July 24, 1964–   )

Baseball scouts use five categories to judge a player's talent: hitting, hitting with power, running, fielding, and throwing. Barry Bonds has so excelled at each of these skills that some observers have concluded that he is the most complete player ever to take the field. His spectacular 2001 season, during which he broke the single-season major league record for home runs with 73 and became the first player in history to win four Most Valuable Player (MVP) awards, only serves to reinforce this judgment.

Barry Lamar Bonds was born on July 24, 1964 in Riverside, California, the son of former baseball star Bobby Bonds and Patricia (Howard) Bonds. His godfather is National Baseball Hall of Famer Willie Mays. Bonds attended Serra High School in San Mateo, California, where he played football, basketball, and baseball. The San Francisco Giants (National League) drafted Bonds in 1982, but he chose instead to attend Arizona State University. During his three-year collegiate career, he batted .347 with 45 home runs, 175 runs batted in (RBI), and 57 stolen bases. On three occasions, Bonds made the All-Pac-Ten Conference baseball team. In 1985, he made *The Sporting News* College Baseball All-America team. In June 1985, he signed with the Pittsburgh Pirates (National League) as their first-round selection in the free-agent draft and the sixth player taken overall.

Bonds played in only 115 minor league games before Pittsburgh called him up in May 1986. He hit .223 as a rookie, but his 16 home runs, 48 RBIs, 36 stolen bases, and 49 walks led all first-year players. Pirates manager Jim Leyland brought Bonds along slowly, dropping him from leadoff to the more productive five slot in the batting order only in 1990. Surrounded by good talent, including Bobby Bonilla,* Andy Van Slyke, and Doug Drabek, Bonds helped to lead Pittsburgh to three straight NL East Division titles from 1990 to 1992.

Standing 6 foot 2 inches tall and weighing 222 pounds, the fleet left-handed outfielder experienced a breakthrough season in 1990. He batted .301 with 104 runs scored, 33 home runs, 114 RBIs, and 52 stolen bases. He led the NL in slugging percentage (.565) and was named NL Player of the Month for July. Bonds was selected to the first of 11 All-Star teams and claimed his first of eight Rawlings Gold Gloves for his fine outfield play. He also won his first NL MVP Award, while *The Sporting News* tabbed him as its Major League Player of the Year.

Bonds's success in Pittsburgh continued through the 1991 and 1992 seasons. In 1991, he hit .292 with 95 runs scored, 25 home runs, 116 RBIs, and 43 stolen bases. He narrowly missed his second MVP Award, finishing a close second to Terry Pendleton. In 1992 he won his second NL MVP Award while batting .311 with 109 runs scored, 34 home runs, 103 RBIs, and 39 stolen bases. In 1991 and 1992, *The Sporting News* named Bonds its NL Player of the Year.

At the close of the 1992 season, Bonds became a free agent. The cash-starved, small-market Pirates did not make a realistic offer to their star player, causing Bonds to sign a six-year, $43.75 million contract with the San Francisco Giants (NL). The size of the contract stunned the sports world, but the egotistical Bonds replied, "I'm worth it."

In 1993 Bonds proved his worth. In yet another spectacular performance culminating in his third MVP Award, he led the Giants to 103 victories. His

Barry Bonds ©Photofest

46 home runs, 123 RBIs, and .667 slugging percentage topped the NL. He batted .336, with 181 hits and 129 runs scored. For the second year in a row, the Associated Press (AP) named him its Player of the Year.

Bonds's success continued through the rest of the decade. He hit more than 40 home runs on three occasions, drove in more than 100 runs five times, and hit more than .300 on four occasions. His performance in five postseason series before 2001 was disappointing, however, as he hit an anemic .196 with one home run and six RBIs. All this served as a prelude to his spectacular 2001 season. In winning his fourth MVP Award, he shattered Mark McGwire's single-season home run record with an astonishing 73 roundtrippers and hit .328 with a career-high 137 RBIs. His .863 slugging percentage broke Babe Ruth's major league record set in 1920. His 177 bases on balls also established a single-season major league record, while his homers every 6.52 times at-bat set a new standard. *The Sporting News* named Bonds its Major League Player of the Year and the AP tabbed him its Male Athlete of the Year.

At the end of the 2001 season, the Giants rewarded Bonds with a five-year

$90 million contract. In 2002 he won his first NL batting title with a .370 average, broke the major league record with 198 walks, and had a .799 slugging percentage, helping the Giants win the Wild Card and earning a fifth MVP Award. He enjoyed an exceptional postseason in 2002, batting .356 with eight home runs, 16 RBIs, 27 walks, a .581 on-base percentage, and a .978 slugging percentage. His .294 batting average, three home runs, four RBIs, and .824 slugging percentage helped San Francisco defeat the Atlanta Braves in the NL Division Series. In the NL Championship Series, he hit .273 with one triple, one home run, six RBIs, and 10 walks against the St. Louis Cardinals. Although the Giants lost the World Series, he feasted off Anaheim Angels pitching for a .471 batting average, four home runs, six RBIs, 13 walks, a .700 on base percentage, and a remarkable 1.294 slugging percentage.

Entering 2004, Bonds had belted 658 career home runs, placing him fourth on the all-time list. No other player in major league history has combined more than 600 home runs with 500 stolen bases. Through 2003, Bonds has batted .297 with 1,742 RBIs. He has 2,595 hits with six doubles, 2,070 walks, and 507 stolen bases. He stole his 500th career base in the 11th inning against the Los Angeles Dodgers in June 2003. Bonds enjoyed another sensational season in 2003, leading the NL with 148 walks, a .749 slugging percentage, and a .529 on-base percentage, ranking second with 45 home runs, and finishing third with a .341 batting average. He also scored 111 runs and drove in 90 runs, helping San Francisco capture the NL West. Bonds walked eight times, but batted only .222 with just two RBIs in the NL Division Series loss to the Florida Marlins. He won his record eleventh TSN Silver Slugger team award. In 2003, he became the first major league baseball player to win three consecutive MVP awards and six MVP awards total. Among the four major North American professional sports, only the National Hockey League's Wayne Gretzky has won more MVP awards with nine. Kareem Abdul-Jabar of the National Basketball Association also won six MVP awards.

Despite his accomplishments, this future Hall of Famer has experienced personal disappointment and controversy. His personality has not endeared him to many. Almost universally regarded as sullen, self-centered, and arrogant, he has often experienced strained relationships with both the press and his teammates. His unpopularity is perhaps best demonstrated by the anonymous remark of one of his former Pirate teammates who, upon learning of Bonds's departure for San Francisco, said, "I'd rather lose without Barry Bonds than win with him." Bonds's father, Bobby, replied, "Barry just wants to play baseball. He's not pushing ballots for popularity."

Bonds's personal life has also been troubled. His divorce from his first wife, Sun, resulted in a lengthy and vitriolic court battle that besmirched the reputations of both. He later married Liz Watson and now resides in Los Altos Hills, California. He is the father of a son, Nikolai, and two daughters, Shikari and Aisha Lynn. Bonds, a member of the Screen Actors Guild, has appeared in Hollywood films and on television.

BIBLIOGRAPHY
Barry Bonds file, National Baseball Library, Cooperstown, NY; Kevin Cook, "Playboy Interview: Barry Bonds," *Playboy* 40 (July 1993), pp. 59–72; Richard Hoffer, "The Importance of Being Bonds," *Sports Illustrated* 78 (May 24, 1993), pp. 13–21; Pam Lambert, "King of Swing," *People* 56 (July 9, 2001), pp. 63–64; Walter Leavy, "Barry Bonds: Baseball's $60 Million Man," *Ebony* 48 (September 1993), pp. 118–120; *Pittsburgh Pirates 1991 Record and Information Guide*, pp. 29–31; David Pletrusza et al., eds., *Baseball: The Biographical Encyclopedia* (Kingston, NY, 2000); David L. Porter, ed., *African-American Sports Greats* (Westport, CT, 1995); David L. Porter, ed., *Biographical Dictionary of American Sports: Baseball, A–F*, revised and expanded edition (Westport, CT, 2000); Steve Rushin, "Interest Bearing Bonds," *Sports Illustrated* 78 (April 26, 1993), pp. 18–23; *San Francisco Giants 2001 Record and Information Guide*; Tom Verducci, "The Producers," *Sports Illustrated* 94 (June 4, 2001), pp. 54–59.

Frank W. Thackeray

BOBBY BONILLA   Baseball
(February 23, 1963–   )

Bobby Bonilla ranks among the most powerful switch-hitters in major league history, setting the National League (NL) record for most home runs by a switch-hitter (247).

Roberto Martin Antonio Bonilla was born on February 23, 1963 to Roberto Bonilla, an electrician, and Regina Bonilla in New York City. After graduating from Lehman High School in the Bronx, New York, where he played baseball, he attended the New York Institute of Technology in Old Westbury, New York, for one semester. Bonilla was selected for a high school all-star team that played in Scandinavia in 1981. Syd Thrift, a Pittsburgh Pirates (NL) scout, saw Bonilla play and offered him a contract. He played two seasons with the Bradenton, Florida, Pirates (Gulf Coast League). In 1983 and 1984 at Alexandria, Virginia (Carolina League) and at Nashua, New Hampshire (Eastern League), he played first base and outfield and demonstrated some power potential. He broke his leg in a 1985 spring training collision with Bip Roberts and missed most of the season.

In December 1985, the 6-foot 3-inch, 240-pound Bonilla was selected by the Chicago White Sox (American League) from Pittsburgh in the Rule 5 Draft. After starting for the White Sox in 1986, he was returned to the Pirates in July for pitcher Jose DeLeon. For the next five seasons he sparked the Pirate attack, driving in 100 or more runs three times and clouting 103 home runs with 185 doubles. Bonilla moved from the outfield to third base in 1987 without complaint. "Bobby Bo," as teammates and fans called him, and Barry Bonds* provided a potent tandem that helped the Pirates win the NL Eastern Division crowns in 1990 and 1991, only to lose the NL Championship Series to the Cincinnati Reds and Atlanta Braves. Bonilla was runner-up to Barry Bonds in the NL Most Valuable Player voting in 1990.

Bonilla became a free agent and in December 1991 signed a $29 million, five-year contract with the New York Mets (NL). He quickly fell out of favor with New York fans and the media when he turned in his worst full-season performance. For the 1993 campaign, he lost some weight and coped better with an impatient, critical New York press. Bonilla belted a career-high 34 home runs and drove in 87 runs. He still was criticized for his fielding at third base and three times led NL third basemen in errors.

In 1995 Bonilla enjoyed his finest season. After hitting .325 with 18 home runs through late July, he was traded to the Baltimore Orioles (AL) for out-fielders Alex Ochoa and Damon Buford. As the Orioles' cleanup hitter, he batted .333 and clouted 10 more home runs. His 28 home runs, 107 runs scored, and 116 runs batted in (RBI) helped Baltimore grab the AL Wild Card in 1996. Bonilla's two home runs and five RBIs proved instrumental in the Orioles' defeat of the Cleveland Indians in the AL Division Series. New York Yankees hurlers, however, silenced his bat in the AL Championship Series, ending Baltimore's season.

A free agent, Bonilla was reunited in 1997 with Jim Leyland, his former manager in Pittsburgh and later pilot of the Florida Marlins (NL). Bonilla was signed to add veteran leadership to a young team and contributed 17 home runs, 97 RBIs, and a .297 batting average. The Marlins performed beyond expectations, winning 92 regular season games and the NL Wild Card. Florida captured the NL pennant and won the World Championship, defeating the Cleveland Indians (AL) in seven games. Bonilla scored five runs and had three RBIs in the Marlins' four wins and went hitless in their three losses.

When the Florida Marlins were sold after the 1997 season, the new owners dismantled the team to cut payroll and financial losses. In May 1998, Bonilla, outfielders Gary Sheffield* and Jim Eisenreich, and catcher Charles Johnson* were dispatched to the Los Angeles Dodgers (NL) for catcher Mike Piazza and third baseman Todd Zeile. In November 1998, Los Angeles traded Bonilla to the New York Mets (NL) for pitcher Mel Rojas. However, he spent most of the 1999 campaign disabled with patella tendinitis in the left knee and a contusion of the left knee.

Bonilla signed with the Atlanta Braves (NL) in January 2000 and played 114 games at third base, first base, outfield, and as a pinch hitter in 2000. He moved to St. Louis (NL) in January 2001, and played a similar role with the Cardinals, retiring after the 2001 campaign. In 16 major league seasons, he played 2,113 games, batted .279, got 2,010 hits, scored 1,084 runs, and hit 287 home runs, the fifth highest career total ever for a switch-hitter. Bonilla batted .385 in six All-Star games for the NL and is one of only six switch-hitters to drive in 100 runs in both leagues. Besides his World Championship, he played in seven League Championship Series with six different teams. Although often outspoken and argumentative earlier in his career, Bonilla became a positive clubhouse influence in his later years.

Bonilla sponsored celebrity bowling tournaments in New York to aid the Hispanic Scholarship Fund and received the Thurman Munson Award and Gary Carter Award for humanitarian service in the community.

Bobby and his wife, Migdalia, have a daughter, Danielle, and a son, Brandon. They reside in Greenwich, Connecticut, where they are part-owners of Performance Imaging, a home theater company.

BIBLIOGRAPHY
2000 Atlanta Braves Media Guide; Baseball Library, "Bobby Bonilla," www. BaseballLibrary.com (2002), pp. 1–5; Dan O'Neil, "The Bucs' Bobby Bonilla: His Best Is Yet to Come," *Baseball Digest* 49 (August 1990), pp. 25–27; David L. Porter, ed., *Biographical Dictionary of American Sports: Baseball, A–F* revised, and expanded edition (Westport, CT, 2000); *St. Louis Cardinals 2001 Media Guide*.

Frank J. Olmsted

VALERIE BRISCO-HOOKS Track and field
(July 6, 1960–)

Valerie Brisco-Hooks made history in the 1984 Los Angeles, California, Summer Olympic Games, when she won the gold medals in the 200- and 400-meter races, becoming the first runner to capture top honors in both events in an Olympics.

Valerie Ann Brisco was born on July 6, 1960 in Greenwood, Mississippi, the daughter of Arguster Brisco and Guitherea Brisco, and the sixth of 10 children. The Briscos moved to Los Angeles when she was 5 years old. Brisco attended Locke High School in the Watts area of Los Angeles, from which baseball greats Eddie Murray and Ozzie Smith had graduated. A track and field coach in a physical education class watched her outrun the fastest girl on the track and field team and insisted that she run track. Brisco drew strength and zeal for running from the memory of her brother, Robert, who was shot to death in 1974 while running on the track at Locke High School. As a senior in 1978, Brisco recorded national bests for high school girls by running a 100-yard dash in 10.5 seconds, a 100-meter sprint in 11.57 seconds, and a 200-meter run in 23.77 seconds. She also ran 400 meters in 53.7 seconds, the second-best time in the nation that year.

Brisco intended to enter the job market. Bob Kersee, the track and field coach at California State University at Northridge, convinced her that athletics could be her ticket through college and to a better life. She accepted a track and field scholarship and, under Kersee's tutelage, became an instant star, winning the 200 meters title in the 1979 Association of Intercollegiate Athletics for Women (AIAW) championship. Brisco finished second in the 200 meters in the Amateur Athletics Union (AAU) Championship and fourth in the Pan American Games that same year. She captured a gold medal, however, at the Pan American Games as a member of the 4×100 relay team.

Brisco's 1980 season was marred by injuries, but she narrowly edged Florence Griffith Joyner* for a place on the 1980 United States Olympic team. In 1980, however, the United States did not compete in the Olympics as a protest against the Soviet Union's invasion of Afghanistan. In 1981, she married Alvin Hooks, a track and field and football star at California State who played wide receiver for the Philadelphia Eagles (National Football League). She left

Valerie Brisco-Hooks ©Tony Duffy/Getty Images

track and field after competing for Long Beach City College in 1981 and moved to Philadelphia, Pennsylvania. In 1982, Brisco-Hooks gave birth to a son, Alvin Jr; she gained nearly 40 pounds during her pregnancy. The following year, her husband signed with the Los Angeles Express (United States Football League), and Brisco-Hooks found herself again craving the competitive arena. She therefore began a strict diet and training plan to lose weight and to regain running form. Her husband served as her manager when the Los Angeles Express released him. Her former coach, Bob Kersee, became a consultant who monitored her training and advised her on which competitions to tackle.

After a year of intense training, Brisco-Hooks entered the Track Athletic Congress (TAC) Championship and won the 400-meter race in 49.28 seconds, becoming the first American woman to break 50 seconds. She captured the 1984 U.S. national indoor 200-meter title and the outdoor 400-meter title. At the 1984 Olympic trials, she won the 200 meters and took second in the 400 meters. In the 1984 Los Angeles Olympics, boycotted by the Soviet Union probably in response to the U.S. boycott of the 1980 Moscow Olympics, Brisco-Hooks captured gold medals in the 200-meter, 400-meter, and 4×400-meter relay. She established new Olympic records with times of 21.81 seconds in the 200 meters and 48.83 seconds in the 400 meters. Her relay team set a record for the 4×400 meters in 3 minutes, 18.29 seconds. Not since Wilma

Rudolph in 1960 had a woman won three Olympic gold medals in track and field.

In 1985 Brisco-Hooks set the world indoor record for 400 meters in 52.99 seconds. She garnered the U.S. National Championship in the outdoor 400 meters in 1986. In 1987 she captured a gold medal with the U.S. 4×400 relay team in the Pan American Games in Indianapolis, Indiana. (Brisco-Hooks gave her medal to a deaf child who had watched the competition and asked to be photographed with her after the race.) She won her final Olympic medal in the 1988 Seoul, South Korea, Games when her 4×400 relay team captured the silver medal.

Brisco-Hooks, once Jackie Joyner's roommate, served as maid of honor when Jackie married Bob Kersee in January 1986. Valerie and Alvin Hooks Sr. were divorced in 1987.

BIBLIOGRAPHY

Athletic-heroes.net; *Valerie Brisco-Hooks* (www.sportingheroes.net, 2002), pp. 1–2; Michael D. Davis, *Black American Women in Olympic Track and Field: A Complete Illustrated Reference* (Jefferson, NC, 1992); Editors of Sports Illustrated, *Sports Illustrated 2001 Sports Almanac* (New York, 2001); Ralph Hickok, *Sports Biographies: Valerie Brisco-Hooks* (www.HickokSports.com, 2001); David L. Porter, *African-American Sports Greats* (Westport, CT, 1995).

Frank J. Olmsted

DERRICK BROOKS   Football
(April 18, 1973–)

Derrick Brooks has consistently led the Tampa Bay Buccaneers (National Football League) in tackles and anchored a defense that won Super Bowl XXXVII.

Derrick Dewan Brooks was born on April 18, 1973 in Pensacola, Florida, the son of Geraldine Brooks. Brooks was a class clown until fifth grade, when his stepfather, A. J. Mitchell, disciplined him before his classmates. Brooks recalled, "Thank God I had parents who cared." He graduated with a 3.94 average in 1991 from Booker T. Washington High School in Pensacola, lettering in football and basketball. As a senior, Brooks was named *USA Today* High School Defensive Player of the Year, first team *Parade* All-America, and first team all-state. Super Prep rated him the nation's best defensive safety.

Coach Bobby Bowden recruited Brooks to play football at Florida State University, where Brooks played safety in 1991, helping the 11–2 Seminoles finish fourth nationally and defeat the University of Texas, 10–2, in the Cotton Bowl. The 6-foot, 235-pounder switched to linebacker in 1992. Florida State ranked second nationally with an 11–1 mark, won the Atlantic Coast Conference (ACC), and triumphed over the University of Nebraska, 27–14, in the Orange Bowl. Brooks made All-America in 1993, recording two sacks and returning two interceptions 81 yards for touchdowns. Florida State won the

National Championship with a 12–1 mark, repeating as ACC champions and edging Nebraska, 18–16, in the Orange Bowl. He earned All-America again in 1994 with three sacks and three interceptions. Besides capturing a third consecutive ACC title, the 10–1–1 Seminoles finished fourth nationally and defeated the University of Florida, 23–17, in the Sugar Bowl.

Brooks graduated in December 1994 from Florida State with a Bachelor's degree in communications. For the Seminoles, he made 274 tackles, intercepted five passes for 133 yards and two touchdowns, recovered three fumbles, and recorded 8.5 sacks in 41 games. He was twice a finalist for the Vince Lombardi Award, symbolic of the nation's top lineman/linebacker. Brooks earned a Master's of Business Administration degree from Florida State in 1999 and attended the Craig James School of Broadcasting.

The Tampa Bay Buccaneers selected Brooks in the first round as the twenty-eighth overall pick in the 1995 NFL draft. He has started every game since 1996 and led the Buccaneers in tackles from 1997 through 2002. Brooks made the Pro Bowl from 1997 through 2000 and All-Pro in 1999, 2000, and 2002 helping revive the Tampa Bay franchise. "Just six, seven years ago, we were the laughingstock of the league," he recalled.

By 1999, the low-key, serious-minded, dedicated Brooks led a star-studded cast. He recorded two sacks, recovered two fumbles, and intercepted four passes for 61 yards, helping Tampa Bay win the NFC (National Football Conference) Central Division with an 11–5 record. The St. Louis Rams triumphed over the Buccaneers, 11–6, in the NFC Championship game. Tampa Bay finished second in the NFC Central Division with a 10–6 record the following year but was eliminated by the Philadelphia Eagles, 21–3, in the NFC Wild Card game. The Buccaneers slipped to 9–7 in 2001 and replaced head coach Tony Dungy with Jon Gruden of the Oakland Raiders.

Brooks combines skills as a bruising hitter, fast pursuer, and excellent open-field tackler with enough agility to cover wide receivers. An every-down linebacker, he epitomizes the old Dick Butkus–Ray Nitschke era. Coach Dungy observed, "Derrick's probably the best defensive player in football. If I had the first pick in a pickup game choosing any player in the league, he'd be my guy."

Brooks dominated the NFL in 2002 as Defensive Player of the Year. The Buccaneer defense allowed only 12.25 points and 252.2 yards per game, both NFL bests, and finished second in the NFL with 37 takeaways. Brooks led Tampa Bay with 93 solo tackles, paced linebackers in passes defensed, and made one sack. He intercepted five passes for 218 yards and three touchdowns, including a 97 yarder, and he returned a fumble for a touchdown. He scored more touchdowns than Tampa Bay's leading rusher Michael Pittman and NFL stars Troy Brown, Tim Brown,* Edgerrin James,* and Shannon Sharpe.* He recorded 15 tackles against the Green Bay Packers in November and 10 tackles by halftime against the Atlanta Falcons in December. "There's no way you can hide from him," teammate Warren Sapp* declared. "And you can't shake him down in the open field."

Tampa Bay finished first in the NFC Central Division with a 12–4 record and shared the best NFC record. Brooks vowed, "I want to stamp this defense as one of the greatest ever by winning a championship. We can't get into comparisons with the (Baltimore) Ravens of 2000 or the (Pittsburgh) Steelers of the '70s because they've got rings." Brooks helped Tampa Bay attain its first NFL title. The Buccaneers routed the San Francisco 49ers, 30–6, in the NFC playoffs, as he contributed five tackles and one-half sack, recovered one fumble, and intercepted one pass. Visiting Tampa Bay upset the Philadelphia Eagles, 27–10, in the NFC Championship game, as he made six tackles. The Buccaneer defense, utilizing coach Gruden's extensive knowledge of Oakland's offense, routed the Raiders, 38–20, in Super Bowl XXXVII. Besides making two tackles, Brooks returned a Rich Gannon pass 44 yards for a touchdown to give Tampa Bay a commanding lead. The Buccaneers defense held the Raiders to 19 rushing and 250 passing yards.

Through 2002, Brooks made 791 tackles, assisted on 255 tackles, intercepted 17 passes for 422 yards and four touchdowns, returned a fumble for a touchdown, and recorded 6.5 sacks in 128 games. Sapp reflected, "Derrick's been the best player since I've been here. I've been saying it for eight years now." Gruden added, "When you see . . . the seriousness with which he takes this game and the preparation, it's unbelievable."

Brooks and his wife, Lauren, have one daughter, Brianna and two sons, Derrick Jr. and Darius. Brooks participates in numerous community activities, including United Way, the March of Dimes, D.A.R.E, and the Audley Evans Center. In 1996 he started "Brooks Bunch"—a program for Boys and Girls Clubs in Tampa. He invites 20 youths to Buccaneer games and takes them on trips to Africa, the Grand Canyon, Washington, D.C., and college campuses. He owns Freedom Financial Mortgage Corporation and serves on the diversity committee of the NFL Players Association. His honors include being named to Florida State's Hall of Fame and second All-Time Team in 2000, sharing the Walter Payton Award for gridiron excellence and community service, and being selected the NFL Man of the Year in 2001. He was appointed a member of the Florida State University Board of Trustees in 2003.

BIBLIOGRAPHY
www.fsu.edu/FSUAlum/distinguished/BrooksDerrick.html; www.nfl.com/players/playerpage/3160/bios; sportsillustrated.cnn.com/football/nfl/players/3141; Jarrett Bell, "Brooks an All Star On, Off Field," *USA Today*, December 23, 2002, p. 3C; *ISN Pro Football Register*, 2002; Larry Weisman, "Bucs Ransack Raiders 48–21," *USA Today*, January 27, 2003, pp. 1C–2C.

David L. Porter

TIM BROWN   Football
(June 22, 1966–   )

Tim Brown starred as a receiver with the University of Notre Dame and the Oakland Raiders (National Football League).

Timothy Donnell Brown was born on June 22, 1966 in Dallas, Texas, the son of Eugene Brown, a cement finisher, and Josephine Brown. As a senior, Brown captained the football, basketball, and track and field teams at Woodrow Wilson High School in Dallas. He made Prep Football All-America, compiling over 4,000 career all-purpose yards. He returned six kickoffs and three punts for touchdowns and scored 16 others by rushing or receiving. In track and field, Brown leaped 24 feet, 3 inches in the long jump and also ran sprints and relays. The elusive Brown advised opponents on how to tackle him. "If I had to try and tackle me, I'd let me commit myself first. I'd let me go where I want to go and then tackle. Most guys commit before I even make a move."

Following high school graduation in 1984, Brown attended Notre Dame and majored in sociology. The 6-foot, 195-pound Brown, a speedy, talented, and deceptive athlete, played running back and receiver and returned punts and kickoffs for the Fighting Irish. At Notre Dame between 1984 and 1987, he carried the ball 48 times for 442 yards and four touchdowns and caught 137 passes for 2,493 yards and 12 touchdowns. Brown returned 36 punts and 105 kickoffs for 2,089 yards and six touchdowns. As a junior, he set the school record with 1,937 all-purpose yards. He broke school career records for receiving yards (2,493), kickoff return yards (1,613), and all-purpose yards (5,024). He played in the 1984 Aloha Bowl and the 1988 Cotton Bowl and lettered one year in track and field as a sprinter. Brown was named wide receiver on *The Sporting News* (TSN) College All-America First Team in 1986 and 1987 and United Press International and *TSN* College Football Player of the Year in 1987. His final year at Notre Dame culminated with winning the Walter Camp Trophy and Heisman Trophy, symbolic of the nation's outstanding college football player. Woodrow Wilson became the first high school to produce two Heisman trophy winners. (Davey O'Brien, quarterback at Texas Christian University, had won it in 1938.)

Brown was selected by the Los Angeles Raiders in the first round as the sixth pick overall of the 1988 NFL draft. He returned a kickoff 97 yards for a touchdown in his first NFL game and recorded 41 kickoff returns for 1,098 yards and 49 punt returns, all career highs, in his first season. He broke Gale Sayers' NFL record for most total yardage by a rookie (2,317) and was named kick returner on *TSN* NFL All-Pro Team. He played in the first of eight Pro Bowls, receiving this honor in 1988, 1991, 1993 through 1997, and 1999.

Brown played only one game during his second NFL season due to a serious knee injury. Then, he led the Los Angeles Raiders and ranked fourth in the American Football Conference (AFC) in punt returns in 1990, and the following season he recorded his first punt return for a touchdown with a 75-yard jaunt against the Cincinnati Bengals. He paced the Los Angeles Raiders in receptions, receiving yardage, and touchdowns in 1992, and the following year he led the AFC in reception yardage for the first of three consecutive years. Following the 1993 regular season, Brown caught a touchdown pass in the Wild Card game against the Denver Broncos and made an 86-yard touch-

Tim Brown ©Courtesy of the Oakland Raiders

down reception in the second round against the Buffalo Bills. He led the NFL with a career-high 487 punt return yards in 1994 and compiled six 100-yard reception games the following year, when the Raiders returned to Oakland. In 1996 he set the NFL mark for most career punt returns with 301, surpassing Vai Sikahoma's 292.

With a career-high 101 receptions for 1,408 yards during 1997, Brown surpassed Pro Football Hall of Famer Fred Biletnikoff as the Raiders' all-time leading receiver. Brown became the all-time total yardage recordholder with 13,022 yards and broke Art Powell's single-season total reception yardage record of 1,361 yards. His 14 pass receptions and three touchdown receptions in one 1997 game marked all-time highs for Brown, who was named to *TSN* NFL All-Pro Team as a wide receiver.

After compiling 1,012 receiving yards on 81 catches in 1998, Brown became the Raiders' all-time receiver with 9,600 yards. Against the New York Jets on October 24, 1999, he recorded 190 reception yards for a career single-game high. His eighth selection to the Pro Bowl in 1999 tied him with former Raiders Art Shell and Howie Long. Upon entering the 2000 season, Brown had caught at least one pass in 108 consecutive games. The string was broken when he failed to make a reception in the season opener against the San Diego Chargers. He recorded his thirty-seventh 100-yard reception game in 2000, a Raider record. In postseason play, Brown caught two passes in Oakland's Divisional playoff victory against the Miami Dolphins and five receptions in the Raiders' loss to the Baltimore Ravens in the 2000–2001 AFC Championship game. In 2001 Brown led the Raiders with 91 receptions for 1,165 yards and nine touchdowns. He caught three passes for 13 yards and a touchdown in the Raiders' Wild Card playoff triumph over the New York Jets and five passes for 42 yards in their second-round loss to the Super Bowl Champion New England Patriots. He caught 81 passes for 930 yards (11.5-yard average) and two touchdowns in 2002, helping the 11–5 Raiders win the AFC West and home field advantage in the playoffs. His three receptions for 52 yards helped Oakland defeat the New York Jets, 30–10, in the AFC playoffs. Brown caught nine passes for 73 yards, as the Raiders triumphed over the Tennessee Titans, 41–24, in the AFC Championship game. It took 15 seasons for him to make his first Super Bowl appearance. He remarked, "Now, I'm finally on my way. It's a great feeling." The Tampa Bay Buccaneers limited Brown to one reception for nine yards in Super Bowl XXXVII, outplaying Oakland 48–21.

After 15 NFL seasons from 1988 through 2002, Brown remains the Raiders' leader in receptions (1,018), receiving yards (14,257), touchdowns (102), and touchdown receptions (97). He trails only Jerry Rice* in career reception yards and ranks third in NFL career receptions and has been selected to the Pro Bowl 10 times.

He and his wife, Sherice, have one daughter, and twins, a son and daughter.

BIBLIOGRAPHY
Tim Brown file, Pro Football Hall of Fame, Canton, OH; Tim Brown file, Sports Information Office, University of Notre Dame, South Bend, IN; *Oakland Raiders Media Guide*, 2003; David L. Porter, ed., *Biographical Dictionary of American Sports 1989–1992 Supplement for Baseball, Football, Basketball, and Other Sports* (Westport, CT, 1992); *The Sporting News Pro Football Register*, 2003.

John L. Evers

ISAAC BRUCE   Football
(November 10, 1972–   )

Isaac Bruce ranks among the best wide receivers in the National Football League (NFL) with a graceful, fluid style, making him an excellent route runner.

Isaac Isidore Bruce was born on November 10, 1972 in Fort Lauderdale, Florida, one of 15 children of Jesse and Karetha Bruce. His parents created a close-knit, faith-filled family for their children. Bruce graduated from Dillard Village High School in Fort Lauderdale. After attending West Los Angeles Junior College and Santa Monica Junior College, he majored in physical education at Memphis State University in Memphis, Tennessee. His college football career included 113 receptions, 1,586 yards, and 15 touchdowns.

The Los Angeles Rams (NFL) drafted Bruce in 1994. He experienced a good rookie season with 21 receptions for 272 yards and three touchdowns. The 6-foot, 190-pound wide receiver moved with the Rams to St. Louis, Missouri, in 1995 and made 119 catches for 1,781 receiving yards, the second highest total in NFL history. Bruce earned Fox's Terry Award for best second-year pro, All-Pro recognition, and the Carroll Rosenbloom Memorial Rams' Most Valuable Player (MVP) Award. In 1996 he led the NFL with 1,338 receiving yards and topped Rams receivers with 84 receptions.

Although missing four games with a hamstring injury in 1997, Bruce paced St. Louis with five touchdown receptions and finished second with 56 receptions and 815 receiving yards. He reached a career-high 233 yards on 10 receptions against the Atlanta Falcons on November 22, 1997 and became the first receiver in Rams history to record three 200-receiving yard games. Another hamstring injury cost Bruce all but five games in the 1998 campaign, yet he managed 457 yards on 32 receptions for an average of 14.3 yards per carry.

A healthy Bruce proved instrumental in the Rams' dramatic reversal from a 4–12 record in 1998 to 13–3 National Football Conference (NFC) champions in 1999. He contributed 77 receptions, 1,165 receiving yards, and a team-leading 12 touchdowns and enjoyed four touchdown receptions against the San Francisco 49ers in Week Four. He led the Rams in receiving yards in the playoffs with 317. The biggest game of Bruce's career came in Super Bowl XXXIV on January 30, 2000 when he gained 162 receiving yards against the Tennessee Titans. With Tennessee defensive lineman Denard Walker only a foot away, Bruce grabbed a 73-yard pass from quarterback Kurt Warner, cut inside, and dashed past Anthony Dorsett for the winning touchdown in the 23–16 St. Louis victory, ending one of the most exciting games in Super Bowl history.

During 2000, Bruce made 1,471 receiving yards and nine touchdowns. On December 17, 2001, he caught passes from Kurt Warner for three touchdowns to defeat the New Orleans Saints, 34–21. That year, the head coach, Mike Martz, named him offensive team captain. Bruce recorded 1,106 receiving yards in 2001, setting a Rams team record for his fifth season of 1,000 receiving yards, despite playing with a broken finger, sprained foot, and a lower back injury. His efforts enabled the Rams to win the NFC Championship and a trip to Super Bowl XXXVI against the New England Patriots. Bruce caught five passes from Kurt Warner for 56 yards, but Ty Law intercepted a pass intended for him and returned it for a 47-yard touchdown to give New England a 7–3 lead. The Patriots upset the favored Rams, 20–17, in a final-seconds thriller. In 2002, he caught 79 passes for 1,075 yards (13.6-yard average) and led the 7–9 Rams with seven touchdown receptions. Bruce entered the 2003 season with 619 receptions for 9,480 yards (15.3-yard average), and 63 touchdowns in 125 games. He made receptions exceeding 40 yards on 28 occasions and was named to the NFC Pro Bowl team in 1996 and 1999.

In 1999 Bruce was driving on the interstate in St. Louis, Missouri, when a tire blew, flipping his car over. The vehicle was totaled, but Bruce walked away uninjured. He said a prayer when the tire burst and attributed the sparing of his life to the power of God. Kurt Warner testified, "Isaac is devout in everything he does." Bruce, who is single, contemplates becoming a Christian minister upon retiring from professional football.

BIBLIOGRAPHY

Acclaim Sports, "Chat with Isaac Bruce," *NFLPlayers.com* (www.Acclaimsports. com, 2002), pp. 1–4; Cliff Charpentier, *2001 Fantasy Football Digest* (Minneapolis, MN, 2001); David Lundy, "Warner Comes Up Big in Biggest Game of Year," *Sports Illustrated* (www.CNNSI.com, January 31, 2000), pp. 1–2; National Football League, "Isaac Bruce: Bio Info," *NFL Enterprises* (www.NFL.com, 2002), pp. 1–2; Nick Wishart, "Bruce Hits Several Milestones with Five Catches, 86 Yards, and Three TDs," *St. Louis Post-Dispatch*, December 18, 2001, p. D7.

Frank J. Olmsted

KOBE BRYANT **Basketball**
(August 23, 1978–   )

Kobe Bryant at age 18 became the youngest player ever selected in the National Basketball Association (NBA) draft. Following his senior year of high school in 1996, Bryant moved directly to the NBA rather than attend college. He was selected by the Charlotte Hornets (NBA) in the first round as the thirteenth pick overall of the 1996 NBA draft. The Charlotte Hornets traded his draft rights to the Los Angeles Lakers (NBA) for Vlade Divac in July 1996. Bryant reflected, "Playing in the NBA has been my dream since I was three." "I know I will have to work extra hard and I know this is a big step, but I can do it."

Kobe B. Bryant was born on August 23, 1978 in Philadelphia, Pennsylvania, the son of Joe "Jellybean" Bryant and Pamela Bryant. His father played

Kobe Bryant ©Stephen Dunn/Getty Images

basketball at LaSalle University and professionally with the Philadelphia 76ers
(NBA) from 1974–1975 through 1978–1979, the San Diego Clippers (NBA)
the following two seasons, and the Houston Rockets (NBA) in 1982–1983,
averaging 8.7 points in 606 NBA games. He moved his family to Rieti, Italy,
in the fall of 1984 to join the Italian Basketball League, playing for four
different teams in Italy and France. Kobe Bryant was constantly with his
father, learning basketball skills and fundamentals. He also studied tapes and
videos of the great American players, learning to use the moves of "Magic"
Johnson* and other stars. Bryant and his two older sisters, Shaya and Sharia,
attended school in Italy and became fluent in Italian. Upon returning to the
United States, Bryant completed eighth grade at Cynwyo Junior High School
in suburban Philadelphia.

In 1992–1993, Bryant entered Lower Merion High School in Philadelphia.
Under Coach Gregg Downer, he started in basketball as a freshman and led
the team in scoring. He led the Aces to a 77–13 won-lost record in his last
three seasons. Bryant averaged 30.8 points per game, 12 rebounds, 6.5 assists,

4.0 steals, and 3.8 blocked shots per game as a senior, helping Lower Merion capture the Class AAAA State Title. With a 31–3 won-lost record, the Aces ended the season with 27 straight triumphs. Bryant became the all-time leading scorer in southeastern Pennsylvania history with 2,883 points, breaking marks set by NBA great Wilt Chamberlain's 2,359 points and former St. Joseph's University standout Carlin Warley's 2,441 points. As a high school senior, he was selected by *USA Today* and *Parade Magazine* as the National High School Player of the Year, was named Naismith Player of the Year, Gatorade Circle of Champions Player of the Year, and McDonald's High School All-America, winning most valuable player (MVP) honors in their All-Star Classic.

The 6-foot 7-inch, 210-pound Bryant joined the Los Angeles Lakers (NBA) following the 1996 NBA draft and made his first start against the Dallas Mavericks on January 28, 1997. In his rookie season, Bryant averaged 7.6 points, 1.9 rebounds, and 1.3 assists per game in limited playing time and made the NBA All-Rookie Second Team. Bryant's highlight as a rookie came when he won the Nestle Crunch Slam Dunk Contest during the 1997 NBA All-Star weekend in Cleveland, Ohio. He also participated in the Schick rookie game, scoring 31 points to establish a rookie game record. In his second NBA season, the fans elevated Bryant to superstar status and voted him to start in the 1998 All-Star Classic. At age 19 he scored 18 points for the Western Conference (WC) All-Stars to become the youngest starter ever in an NBA All-Star game. ("Magic" Johnson was 20 years old when he played in the 1980 game.) During the 1997–1998 regular season, Bryant averaged 15.4 points per game as the Los Angeles Lakers' sixth man. Bryant registered 966 points in the shortened 1998–1999 season, averaging 19.9 points per game and made the All-NBA Third Team.

In 1999 the Los Angeles Lakers' management hired Phil Jackson as head coach. Jackson had coached the Chicago Bulls to six NBA Championships in eight years. During the 1999–2000 regular season, Bryant tallied 22.9 points per game while Shaquille O'Neal* averaged 29.7 points and 13.9 rebounds. The Lakers won the WC Pacific Division with a 67–15 won-lost record. In the NBA Finals, the Los Angeles Lakers captured the NBA Championship by defeating the Indiana Pacers in six games. Bryant, who averaged 21.1 points per playoff game, made the All-NBA Second Team and the All-NBA Defensive First Team. The Lakers won the Pacific Division in 2000–2001 but lost the top seed to the San Antonio Spurs. On April 18, 2001, just before the playoffs, Bryant married Vanessa Laine, a high school senior when they first met.

With Bryant averaging 28.5 points per game to complement O'Neal's 28.9-point average, the Los Angeles Lakers were ready for the playoffs. They had peaked for the championship drive, enjoying easy triumphs over the Portland Trail Blazers, Sacramento Kings, and San Antonio Spurs. In the NBA Finals, the Lakers defeated the Philadelphia 76ers in five games to capture their second straight NBA title under Phil Jackson. Los Angeles compiled a 15–1 won-lost playoff record, an all-time NBA standard. Bryant averaged 29.4 points in 16 playoff games and made the All-NBA Second Team and the All-NBA Defensive Second Team.

Bryant made the All-NBA First Team, started at guard for the WC All-Stars, and made the All-NBA Defensive Second Team in 2001–2002, finishing sixth in scoring with 2,019 points (25.2-point average. Bryant helped the Lakers finish 15–4 in the NBA playoffs and capture a third consecutive NBA title, averaging over 26 points per game. Los Angeles edged the Sacramento Kings, four games to three, in the WC finals and swept the New Jersey Nets in the NBA Finals. On January 7, 2003 he set an NBA record when he made 12 three-point shots, including nine consecutive, in a 119–98 victory over the visiting Seattle Supersonics in a 45-point performance. He again started at guard for the WC All-Stars in 2003 and scored 40 or more points in nine straight games. Bryant repeated on the All-NBA First Team and made the All-NBA Defensive First Team in 2002–2003, ranking second in the NBA in scoring with 2,461 points (30.0 average) and sixth in steals with 181 (2.2 average). The Lakers finished fifth in the WC and were eliminated by the San Antonio Spurs in the WC semifinals.

Bryant was arrested in July 2003 after a 19-year-old Colorado woman accused him of sexual assault in a Colorado hotel. He maintained his innocence, but Eagle County district attorney Mark Hulbert charged him with alleged sexual assault. The case is scheduled for a jury trial.

In six NBA seasons from 1996–1997 through 2002–2003, Bryant compiled 10,658 points in 496 games for a 21.5-point average. He snagged 2,458 rebounds (5.0 average), dished out 2,060 assists, and had 714 steals. He owns three NBA Championship rings and has played in five All-Star games. He won the Most Valuable Player Award at the 2002 All-Star Game, tallying 31 points in a 135–120 West win. In 97 playoff games, he has scored 2,155 points for a 22.2-point average. Bryant has posted 473 rebounds, 407 assists, and 119 steals.

Bryant has been described by coaches, players, writers, and fans as the "next Michael Jordan*" because he possesses many of the basketball skills that made Jordan an NBA legend. Bryant can run, shoot, pass, jump, and play solid defense. He has the ability to "change gears" and give the extra burst of speed to get by the defense. He has great "hang time," switching the ball from one hand to the other to create a better shot opportunity. Along with his brilliant ball handling, Bryant rebounds well and can play all positions.

He and his wife, Vanessa, have one daughter, Natalia.

BIBLIOGRAPHY
Allison Samuels, "Who Is the Real Kobe?" *Newsweek* 142 (July 28, 2003), pp. 48–49; Wayne Coffey, *The Kobe Bryant Story* (New York, 1999); Jonathan Hall, *Kobe Bryant* (New York, 1999); "Kobe Bryant," *Player Background*, www.nba.com (2001); "Kobe Bryant," *Player-Career Highlights*, www.nba.com (2001); "Kobe Bryant," *Player Statistics*, www.nba.com (2001); *The Sporting News Official NBA Register*, 2003–2004.

John L. Evers

C

JOSE CANSECO
(July 2, 1964–)

Baseball

Jose Canseco led the American League twice in home runs and once in runs batted in (RBI) and in 1988 he became the first major league player with at least 40 home runs and 40 stolen bases in the same season.

Jose Canseco Capas, Jr., was born on July 2, 1964 in Havana, Cuba, but lived nearly all his life in the United States. He is the son of Jose Sr., who taught English at a college in Cuba, and Barbara. Canseco has a sister, Teresa, and a twin brother, Ozzie, who also played in the major leagues.

When the Canseco boys were nine months old, the family left Cuba and settled in southern Florida. In their teens, Jose and Ozzie aspired to play major league baseball and starred for Coral Park High School. Scouts noticed Ozzie first, but by the time the twins were seniors in high school Jose Canseco outshone his brother.

Former major league pitcher Camilo Pascual urged the Oakland Athletics (AL) to draft Jose in 1982. Oakland selected him in the fifteenth round of the free-agent draft on June 7, 1982. Canseco became an Oakland Athletic, skipping college and joining the minor leagues. In 1983, while with Medford, Oregon (Northwest League), Canseco was named the "Best Hitting Prospect" and the "Hitter with the Best Power." The 6-foot 4-inch, 240-pound outfielder, who batted and threw right-handed, made the All-Star team as the designated hitter.

Canseco quickly moved through the ranks with the Huntsville, Alabama Stars (Class AA Southern League) and Tacoma, Washington, Rainiers (AAA Pacific Coast League) in 1985 and made Oakland by year's end. On September 2, Canseco debuted with the Athletics as a pinch hitter and struck out on three pitches. His first home run came on September 9, off Jeff Russell of the Texas Rangers. His second roundtripper off Joel Davis of the Chicago White Sox on September 21 marked only the fortieth time that a ball ever reached the roof at Old Comiskey Park.

In 1986, his first full year in the majors, Canseco earned a spot on the American League All-Star team. He collected 144 hits, 117 RBIs, 33 home runs, and 15 stolen bases to earn the Baseball Writers Association of America (BBWAA) and *The Sporting News' (TSN)* Rookie of the Year awards.

The following season Canseco became the first Oakland Athletic to post consecutive 100-RBI seasons. In 1987, he finished second on the club in home runs (31) behind Mark McGwire, and by July 21, he had homered at every AL ballpark.

The "Bash Brothers," McGwire and Canseco, led the Athletics to the 1988 AL title. Canseco created a completely new club that year, combining 42 home runs and 40 stolen bases to start the 40/40 Club. He reached his 100th career home run on August 1, and topped all players in All-Star votes. During the postseason, Canseco crushed three homers in the AL Championship Series against the Boston Red Sox and a grand slam to open the World Series against the Los Angeles Dodgers. The Athletics lost their first of three consecutive World Series.

During 17 seasons, Canseco earned six All-Star Game trips (1986, 1988–1990, 1992, and 1999); earned the AL MVP Award in 1988; led the AL in home runs twice; and ended his career with 462 roundtrippers. He stole 200 bases, batted .266, collected 1,877 hits, and had 1,407 RBIs, and earned the *TSN* Silver Slugger Award three times.

Injuries plagued Canseco, who moved around to eight different clubs. He performed for Oakland (1985–1992), Texas (AL, 1992–1994), Boston (AL, 1995–1996), Oakland (1997), Toronto (AL, 1998), Tampa Bay (AL, 1999–2000), New York (AL, 2000), and Chicago (AL, 2001).

On May 29, 1993, in a game against the Boston Red Sox, Canseco, an outfielder, strolled to the pitcher's mound. He walked three batters, gave up two hits, and surrendered three earned runs. He had blown out his right elbow and missed half the season. Over a period of 10 seasons, Canseco spent seven stints on the disabled list, losing close to two full seasons over his entire career.

When Canseco retired from baseball in 2002 after not making the Montreal Expos (National League) and Chicago White Sox, Tony La Russa, former manager of the Athletics, observed, "I thought he was the most complete athlete I've ever managed. This guy really could run and when he was concentrating, play defense. And, he loved to take the tough at-bat. Injuries just took the important part of his career from him."

Canseco showed great talent but fell short of 500 home runs and 2,000 hits. He left baseball, seeking to take care of his family life. He has been married and divorced twice with controversy surrounding each marriage. His second marriage to former Hooters waitress, Jessica, produced one child.

Prosecutors charged that he violated probation by taking steroids. Canseco denied any drug use while on probation. Prosecutors dropped the charges because conflicting testimony would not allow determining when Canseco allegedly took the drug.

In 2003, Canseco spent time in jail for violating his probation stemming from a brawl in which he and his twin brother fought with two men at a Miami Beach nightclub in October 2001. He wrote a tell-all book about the major leagues in which he described the use of steroids in the major leagues.

Not surprisingly, baseball insiders did not give the book an enthusiastic reception.

BIBLIOGRAPHY
Nathan Aaseng, *Baseball's 40-40 Man: Jose Canseco* (Minneapolis, MN, 1989); Lisa Arthur, "Canseco Is Jailed for Violating Probation," *The Miami Herald*, February 19, 2003; Jose Canseco file, National Baseball Library, Cooperstown, NY; Jose Canseco Statistics—Baseball Reference.com, www.baseball-reference.com/c/cansejo01.shtml; Jose Canseco, www.historicbaseball.com/players/canseco[su1]jose.html; Jose Canseco, www.sportingnews.com/baseball/players/3730/; *Tampa Bay Devil Rays Information Guide*, 2000; Pete Williams, "Past Tense, Present Calm: A Relaxed Jose Canseco Zeros in on 500 Homers," *USA Today Baseball Weekly*, February 10–16, 1999, pp. 8–10, 12.

Scot E. Mondore

CRIS CARTER   Football
(November 25, 1965–   )

Many football analysts ranked Cris Carter just behind Jerry Rice among the all-time great National Football League (NFL) receivers active in the 1990s. Yet Carter, who set the NFL record for most pass receptions in a season with 122 in 1994, was available four years earlier to any team willing to claim him off waivers for $100. At that time, although no one questioned his physical ability, he lacked the personal and moral discipline required to reach his potential.

Christopher D. Carter was born on November 25, 1965 in Troy, Ohio, to an athletic family. At nearby Middletown High School, he and older brother Butch excelled in football and basketball. Butch played seven seasons in the National Basketball Association and later coached the Toronto Raptors (NBA). Carter's first love was football, and he was named to the 1993 *Parade* High School All-American team after making 80 receptions for over 2,000 yards.

After being heavily recruited by National Collegiate Athletic Association (NCAA) colleges and universities, Carter matriculated at Ohio State University (OSU). By his junior year, he set Buckeye career records for receptions (168) and touchdown catches (27) and twice gained All–Big Ten Conference (BTC) honors. As a junior, his BTC-leading 68 catches and OSU single-season records for receiving yards (1,127) and touchdown receptions (11) gained him First Team All-American recognition. The 6-foot 3-inch, 200-pounder possessed widely admired speed, strength, and sure hands.

In April 1987, OSU suspended Carter for rules violations. Three months later, the Buckeyes ruled their star wide receiver ineligible for his senior season when he accepted money and signed a contract with sports agents Lloyd Bloom and Norby Wallers. The widespread scandal rocked the football world. A federal grand jury named Carter in criminal charges of mail fraud and obstruction of justice. His guilty plea led to a $15,000 fine and 600 hours of

Cris Carter ©Rick Kolodzie/Minnesota Vikings

community service. In a supplemental 1987 NFL draft targeting those involved, he was selected in the fourth round by the Philadelphia Eagles (NFL).

Carter's three years in Philadelphia featured occasional moments of brilliance. He averaged 19.5 yards per catch in 1988 and garnered 11 touchdown receptions in 1989. But coach Buddy Ryan was disgusted with his attitude and weak self-discipline. When the Eagles released him just before the 1990 season, only two NFL teams claimed him. In September 1990, he joined the Minnesota Vikings (NFL) and started a decade of play that increasingly showed him to be a "redeemed man" both athletically and spiritually.

"I had actually become a Christian in the spring after my rookie year in the NFL," Carter told *Sports Spectrum* in 1995. "My teammates Reggie White and Keith Byars were instrumental in leading me to Christ. But I was still holding onto the world. It took me a while to realize that giving your life to Christ and being fully committed to Him are two different things." In 1993, Carter enjoyed his breakthrough NFL season with 86 receptions for 1,071 yards. His life off the field was also transformed.

"I can't really point to an incident or moment that caused me to see that I needed to make a new commitment to the Lord," Carter has explained, "but I knew I needed to make my home life better." This new spiritual dynamic brought him recognition. In September 1994, he was given the NFL Extra Effort Award for his community service activities. The following year, he received the Athletes in Action Bart Starr Award for outstanding character and leadership. He also received the Midwest Sports Channel Citizen Athlete Award, and in 1996 he became an ordained minister.

Carter's on-field production soared. The acrobatic receiver caught 122 passes in both 1994 and 1995, reaching career bests of 1,371 yards and 17 touchdowns in 1995. During the next five years, he averaged 90 receptions and over 1,000 yards gained. His four-year, $11.5 million contract from 1995 through 1998 made him the highest paid player in Vikings history. His next contract almost doubled the amount. The Super Bowl ring, however, remained elusive. His farthest advance came in 1998, when the National Football Conference (NFC) Central Division champions finished 15–1 in the regular season and lost the NFC title game to the Atlanta Falcons in overtime.

Carter retired following the 2000 season, having set Viking team records for receptions (1,004), yards (12,383), and touchdown catches (110) and having made eight Pro Bowls from 1993 through 2000. He became an "Inside the NFL" analyst with Home Box Office (HBO) but was lured back on the field for five games by the injury-plagued Miami Dolphins (NFL) in 2002. In 16 NFL seasons, Carter has established Pro Football Hall of Fame credentials with 1,101 catches and 130 receiving touchdowns (both second to Rice) and gained 13,899 yards in 234 games.

Carter has shown maturity in many ways. His sensitive, plain-spoken mentoring helped talented, troubled Vikings receiver Randy Moss* garner the 1998 Rookie of the Year honors. "Cris is the main guy," Moss told *Sports Illustrated*. His Carter-White Charitable Foundation, founded with Kansas City's William White, has helped underprivileged children find success on the field and in the classroom. In 2000, brothers Cris and Butch Carter authored a unique, flip-format book, *Born to Believe*. Each contributed 25 concise chapters on addictive behavior and community service, the relationship with God and racism, and other topics. As on the football field, where every route had a purpose and sure hands reached for each opportunity, Carter plays the game of life with great passion. "God calls me to be truthful, to be frank and to step out in faith," he said. "I am responsible to use my influence and my resources for His glory."

Carter and his wife, Melanie, have two children, Duron and Monteray.

BIBLIOGRAPHY
Butch Carter and Cris Carter, *Born to Believe* (Full Wits Publishing, 2000); David Moriah, "Great Catch," *Sports Spectrum* 9 (October 1995), pp. 15–19; Troy Pearson, "Cris Carter," *Sports Spectrum* 13 (January–February 1999), pp. 26–27; Shirelle Phelps, ed., *Contemporary Black Biography* (Detroit, MI, 1999), pp. 34–36; *Sports Illustrated* (January 18, 1999); www.nfl.com/ Cris Carter, January 2003.

James D. Smith III

VINCE CARTER   Basketball
(January 26, 1977–   )

Vince Carter starred in basketball at the University of North Carolina and for the Toronto Raptors (National Basketball Association).

Vincent Lamar Carter, nicknamed "Showtime," was born on January 26, 1977 in Daytona Beach, Florida, and attended Mainland High School in Daytona Beach. He excelled in basketball, track and field, and volleyball and dunked a basketball as a 5-foot 8-inch fifth grader. Carter also played baritone, alto, and tenor saxophone in the band and wrote the school's homecoming anthem and songs for the marching band. His stepfather, Harry Robinson, whom he considers dad, directed the band. Carter was offered a music scholarship to Bethune-Cookman College as a drum major, not to play basketball. At the same time, the University of North Carolina offered him a basketball scholarship. When he decided to attend school in Chapel Hill, North Carolina, his mother, Michelle Carter Robinson, a teacher, made him sign a contract that he would complete the work on his Bachelor's degree if he left early for the NBA.

Following high school graduation in 1995, Carter entered North Carolina to play basketball and pursue a Bachelor's degree in communications. He did not dominate college basketball as some had predicted, but he improved steadily in his three years as a Tar Heel. He averaged 7.5 points as a freshman and 13.0 points as a sophomore. Carter starred as a junior, averaging 15.6 points and 5.1 rebounds and leading the Atlantic Coast Conference (ACC) with a .590 field goal percentage. He helped the Tar Heels make consecutive appearances in the Final Four. North Carolina lost to the University of Arizona, the eventual national champion, 66–58, in 1997 and 65–59 to the University of Utah, the runner-up in 1998. Carter made the NCAA All-East Regional Team in both years. Following the 1997–1998 season, he was named Second Team All-America, First Team All-ACC, and a finalist for both the Naismith and Wooden awards.

Coaches, teammates, fans, and friends describe the 6-foot 7-inch, 225-pound Carter as an impatient, restless, hyper individual, who appears to be a bundle of nerves and perpetual motion. He has a flair for the spectacular but is also a tremendously gifted athlete who can score, rebound, and block shots. Like Michael Jordan* he can "defy gravity." His "hang time" consists of taking off, cruising, and ending in an explosive slam dunk. Carter's favorite slam is the 360-degree dunk. In a charity game, he slammed one down with such force that the other players on the floor stopped to watch it on the replay screen. The highlight films showing his slams, orbital drives to the basket, and his 41-inch vertical jump have increased fan interest and television ratings everywhere.

Carter left North Carolina following his junior year to enter the NBA draft. The Golden State Warriors (NBA) selected him in the first round as the fifth overall pick of the 1998 NBA draft. His draft rights were traded with cash to the Toronto Raptors for the draft rights to college teammate Antwan Jamison* in June 1998.

In his first NBA season, Carter led all rookies in scoring (18.3-point average) and blocked shots (1.54), ranked third in assists (3.0) and double-doubles (6), fourth in rebounds (5.7), fifth in steals (1.10), sixth in field goal percentage (.450), and eighth in free-throw percentage (.761). No other rookie that year led his team in scoring. At the end of the 1998–1999 season, he received 113 of the 118 possible votes to win the NBA Rookie of the Year Award and was selected unanimously for the All-NBA Rookie First Team.

Carter played in 82 games in his second NBA season, scoring 2,107 points for a 25.7-point average. He collected 476 rebounds, averaging 5.8 boards per game. He led the Raptors in scoring and ranked fourth in the NBA. Carter received the most fan votes, nearly two million, for the 2000 NBA All-Star Game. During the All-Star weekend, he dazzled fans in winning the famed Slam Dunk Contest. He thrilled the crowd with his spectacular 360-degree slam and, in his final turn, captivated them with one of his best dunks, which included the catch and between the legs dunk. He was also named "Athlete of the Future" by *ESPN Magazine* and made the All-NBA Third Team.

In his third season with the Toronto Raptors, Carter ranked fifth in the NBA in scoring with 2,070 points for an average of 27.6 points and pulled down 5.5 rebounds per game. For the second straight year, fans voted him a starter for the East squad in the NBA All-Star Game. For the second consecutive season, he led Toronto to the NBA playoffs. The Raptors lost to the New York Knicks in the first round in 2000 but defeated them in 2001 and advanced to the semifinals. Carter and superstar Allen Iverson* of the Philadelphia 76ers squared off in a seven-game series. Carter and the Raptors fought valiantly. Iverson posted 54 points in Game Two, while Carter answered with 50 in Game Three. Iverson poured in 52 points in Game Five, but Carter tallied 39 points in Game Six to send the series back to Philadelphia. In the day off before the final game, he returned to North Carolina where he received his Bachelor's degree in communications. Upon returning to Philadelphia for the final game, he missed a jump shot as time expired. The 76ers escaped to the next round with an 88–87 triumph.

On August 1, 2001, Carter signed a six-year contract extension reported at $94 million with Toronto. He led Toronto in scoring in 2001–2002 with 1,484 points (24.7-point average), converted nearly 39 percent of his three-point shots, and snagged 313 rebounds in 60 games before having season-ending surgery on his left knee in March. Without Carter, the Raptors made a remarkable run to make the playoffs and lost to the Detroit Pistons in the first round. Carter started for the EC All-Stars in 2003. Injuries limited Carter to 42 games in 2002–2003, but he scored 884 points (20.6-point average) and made 188 rebounds for the struggling Raptors.

In five NBA seasons, Carter has compiled 7,458 points and averaged 24.1 points, 5.4 rebounds, 3.7 assists, 1.4 steals, and 1.1 blocked shots in 310 regular season games. In 15 NBA playoff games, he has registered 385 points for a 25.7-point average and snagged 6.4 rebounds per game.

Off the floor, Carter concentrates on the less fortunate and has given both his time and financial assistance for their cause. He donated $10,000 to Mainland High School to support their basketball programs and the marching band. In addition, he developed the Embassy of Hope Foundation, an organization that assists underprivileged children.

BIBLIOGRAPHY

"Vince Carter," *Biography*, http://www.AskMen.com (2001); "Vince Carter," *Players Background*, www.nba.com (2001); "Vince Carter," *Players Career Highlights*, www. nba.com (2001); "Vince Carter," *Players Statistics*, www.nba.com (2001); Michael Farber, "Raptor Rapture," *Sports Illustrated* 16 (April 19, 1999), pp. 54–55; *The Sporting News Official NBA Register*, 2003–2004; Jon Wertheim, "Rare Pair," *Sports Illustrated* 17 (November 1, 1999), pp. 72–74, 79–80.

John L. Evers

HELIO CASTRONEVES   Auto Racing
(May 10, 1975–   )

Helio Castroneves won consecutive Indianapolis 500 races in 2001 and 2002, the fifth driver to accomplish the feat.

Castroneves was born on May 10, 1975 in São Paulo, Brazil. He received his formal education in São Paulo schools and began his racing career in go-karts, competing in the São Paulo area as a 12 year old. His parents own a trucking company, and his father was himself once a race car driver. Both follow racing enthusiastically, and the father attends many of his son's racing events.

Castroneves's racing career progressed to Formula 3 racing, the Indy Racing League (IRL) Northern Light Series, and the Championship Auto Racing Teams (CART) FedEx Championship Series. He captured the 1989 Brazilian National Go-Kart Championship and participated in the 1991 World Cup Go-Kart Championship in Europe. He finished the 1992 season by placing second in the Brazilian Formula Vauxhall Championship and followed in 1993 with four victories and a second-place finish in the South American Formula 3 Championship. In 1994 Castroneves recorded four triumphs in the Brazilian Formula 3 championship series and the British Formula 3 Series. He ranked third in the 1995 British Formula 3 Championship driving for the Paul Stewart Racing Team.

Castroneves moved to the Indy Light Series (IRL) and drove for Tasman Motorsports in 1996 and 1997, capturing four victories. In 1997, he placed second behind Tony Kanaan for the driving title, losing by the closest margin in the series history. He drove for Bettenhausen Motorsports during 1998, scoring points in 8 of 19 starts. He came in second in Milwaukee, Wisconsin, the highest finish by a rookie. The following season, Castroneves won his first pole position in Milwaukee. For the Hogan Racing Team in the CART FedEx Championship Series, he finished in the top 10 six times.

In 2000, Castroneves captured three pole positions at Portland, Oregon, Toronto, Canada, and Laguna Seca and recorded three triumphs at Detroit, Michigan, Mid-Ohio, and Laguna Seca. He ranked seventh overall in points in the CART FedEx Championship Series. He received the first Greg Moore Legacy Award, which is presented annually to an excellent driver on the track and a charismatic personality within the racing world.

Castroneves finished fourth in the 2001 CART FedEx Championship Series, recording four triumphs at Long Beach, California, Detroit, Mid-Ohio, and the Indianapolis 500. The 2001 season marked his third year in the CART Series and the first with the Roger Penske Racing Team and racing partner Gil de Ferran.* Following his narrow victory in the Indianapolis 500 by 1.7373 seconds over de Ferran, Castroneves performed his crowd-pleasing climb of the safety fence at the Speedway to earn the nickname "Spiderman." The race marked a record 11 Indianapolis 500 triumphs for the Penske Racing Team. Castroneves captured three pole positions at Long Beach, Japan, and Detroit in 2001, leading the Long Beach and Detroit races from wire to wire. He led 411 laps, second on the CART Series list, and finished a career-best fourth in the CART point standings.

Castroneves and de Ferran competed exclusively in the IRL in 2002. With a controversial finish in the Indianapolis 500 and a season-ending race to determine the IRL driving championship, 2002 proved a dramatic season. After receiving the checkered flag as the Indianapolis 500 winner and repeating his "Spiderman" fence-climbing performance, Castroneves learned that the race results had been appealed. Car owner Barry Green and second-place driver Paul Tracy filed a protest, claiming Tracy had blown past Castroneves prior to the yellow caution light coming on due to a wreck in the second turn. This race, the fastest in Indianapolis 500 history, produced an average qualifying speed of 228.648 miles per hour. Racing officials rejected the protest, disallowing Tracy's pass. After finishing the three final miles of the race under the caution light, Castroneves became the first consecutive Indianapolis 500 winner since Al Unser in 1971 and the first driver to win the classic in his first two attempts. Castroneves led CART drivers in a sweep of the top five positions in the 2001 race. IRL drivers took five of the top six positions in the 2002 race, indicating that the balance of power may be shifting to the IRL.

Helio Castroneves ©Courtesy of Indianapolis Speedway

Castroneves captured one other IRL race in 2002. The IRL driving title for the 2002 season came down to the season-ending Chevy 500 at the Texas Motor Speedway. Sam Hornish Jr. and Castroneves battled for the driving championship. Hornish, the 2001 defending champion, led Castroneves by 12 points, after his .0024-second triumph over Al Unser Jr. in the closest IRL finish ever at the Chicagoland Speedway. Hornish and Castroneves had finished ahead of the other seven times during the season. In the finale at the Fort Worth, Texas, Motor Speedway, Hornish became the first driver to win two straight IRL season driving titles. After racing side by side for the last 25 laps and practically ignoring the other drivers, Hornish crossed the finish line .0096 second and only a few inches ahead of Castroneves to secure the championship in the second closest finish in IRL history. Hornish ended the IRL season with 531 points, 20 points ahead of Castroneves. Castroneves finished second at the Indianapolis 500 in 2003, trailing teammate Gil de Ferran by 0.0299 seconds. He finished third in the IRL driving standings in 2003, winning the Emerson Indy 250 in Madison, IL and the Firestone Indy 225 in Nazareth, PA in August.

Castroneves is single and divides his free time between Miami, Florida, and São Paulo, where he windsurfs, jet skis, and plays tennis.

BIBLIOGRAPHY

Mark Bechtel, "Indy-Structable," *Sports Illustrated* 23 (June 3, 2002), pp. 62–63; "Helio Castroneves," *Biography*, www.indyracing.com (2002); "Helio Castroneves," *Biography*, www.penskeracing.com (2001); "Helio Castroneves," *Career Event Results*, www.indyracing.com (2002); *The Evansville Courier and Press*, September 13, 2002, September 16, 2002.

John L. Evers

CESAR CHAVEZ   Boxing
(July 12, 1962–   )

Angelo Dundee, Muhammad Ali's manager and one of the greatest boxing trainers of all time, considers Cesar Chavez, "The Lion of Culiacan," or "JC" to his friends, "The toughest fighter I've ever seen, bar none." A national hero for most of his career in Mexico, Chavez causes massive traffic jams wherever he goes. One-time manager Emmanuel Steward notes, "When he appears he blocks streets." Chavez largely replaced World Boxing Council (WBC) featherweight champion Salvador Sanchez, who died in 1982 in an auto accident, in the Mexican imagination, even inspiring a raft of *corridos* (tales) about his life and career.

Julio Cesar Chavez was born on July 12, 1962, the son of Rodolfo Chavez, a railroad engineer, and Isabel Chavez, in Culiacan, Sinaloa, Mexico. The fourth of 10 children, he endured an impoverished childhood and soon honed such skills as selling newspapers, washing cars, and street fighting. He briefly studied civil engineering at the State University of Sinaloa but dropped out at age 16 to pursue boxing. In numerous informal fights in the countryside around Culiacan, Chavez received the Mexican equivalent of $5. The 5-foot 7-inch, 140-pounder turned professional in 1980 at age 18, knocking out Andres Feliz. By 1984, his won-lost record increased to 45–0 with a WBC Super Featherweight victory over Mario Martinez.

Thereafter, Chavez's rise proved meteoric. In November 1987, he overwhelmed World Boxing Association (WBA) lightweight champion Edwin Rosario in a fight stopped in the eleventh round. In October 1988, he unified the WBA/WBC lightweight titles in a victory over Jose Luis Ramirez. A savage body puncher, reminiscent of Pipino Cuevos in his prime, Chavez in May 1989 forced Roger Mayweather to retire after 10 rounds and forfeit his WBC welterweight crown. March 1990 found Chavez in his stiffest challenge yet,

Julio Cesar Chavez ©Photofest

as he almost lost to former Olympic gold medalist Meldrick Taylor for the WBC and International Boxing Federation (IBF) welterweight titles. Although his face was puffy from Chavez's onslaught, Taylor had outboxed Chavez and held a clear points advantage going into the final round. Chavez, however, caught Taylor with an overhand right in the closing seconds and knocked him down. The bewildered Taylor stood up at five but did not collect himself. Referee Richard Steele stopped the fight with two seconds remaining.

Two subsequent fights reestablished Chavez's shaken reputation. In September 1992, the bull-like Chavez pulverized game matador Hector Camacho over 12 rounds. In February 1993, he floored a condescending Greg Haugen in round five before a record 130,000 fans in Mexico City's Azteca Stadium. Haugen had enraged Chavez by referring to his early Mexican opponents as "stiffs . . . cab drivers from Tijuana." Afterward, Haugen ruefully admitted, "They must have been tough taxi drivers."

A further blot on Chavez's record occurred in September 1993, when he was awarded a majority draw against the smooth Pernell Whitaker to retain his WBC welterweight crown. An embittered Whitaker claimed that he had "put an old-fashioned project beating" on Chavez and had been a victim of a hometown decision. The fight took place in San Antonio, Texas, before a Mexican flag–waving crowd. Clouds loomed further in January 1994, when Chavez suffered his first career loss to Frankie Randall and was even knocked down once. Chavez defeated Randall four months later, but most boxing observers date Chavez's decline from the first Randall fight. The 31-year-old Chavez slowed steadily, losing on counts twice in June 1996 and 1998 to East Los Angeles, California, Golden Boy, Oscar De La Hoya.*

The second De La Hoya fight marked Chavez's last big showdown. Recent opponents have included Willy Wyse, Buck Smith, and Terry Thomas. With a glittering record of 103–6–2 and 83 knockouts, the pugnacious Chavez has trouble giving up a sport that has made him a multimillionaire. As noted Mexican psychiatrist Francisco Schnass observes, "Boxing has brought him self-esteem, self-determination, . . . well-being and security . . . being at home is immensely frustrating . . . few champion boxers have the courage to say enough is enough." His wife, Amalia, who filed for divorce in 1999, bluntly observed that Cesar is "in love with fighting . . . in love with winning." Chavez has three sons and lives in Culiacan.

BIBLIOGRAPHY

James Blears, "Sorry Farewell for Chavez," *BBC Sport*, http//news.bbc.com.co.uk; *Current Biography Yearbook* (1999), pp. 117–120; Clive Gammon, "Time to Hail Cesar; WBA Lightweight Champion Cesar Chavez of Mexico May Be the World's Best Fighter," *Sports Illustrated* 68 (February 22, 1988), p. 75; Richard Hoffer, "Head Case," *Sports Illustrated* 80 (May 16, 1994), p. 54; William Nack, "Beaten to the Draw," *Sports Illustrated* 79 (September 20, 1993), p. 14; William Nack, "The Brink: In the Final Seconds Meldrick Taylor Blew a Sure Win and Was KO'd by Julio Cesar Chavez," *Sports Illustrated* 72 (March 26, 1990), p. 16; Pat Putnam, "Down and Out in Mexico City," *Sports Illustrated* 78 (March 1, 1993), p. 28; Pat Putnam, "Friendly Fire," *Sports Illustrated* 77 (September 21, 1992), p. 28; Gary Smith, "Bearing the Burden," *Sports Illustrated* 78 (February 22, 1993), p. 50.

John H. Ziegler

BARTOLO COLON   Baseball
(May 24, 1973–   )

Bartolo Colon won 20 games in 2002, recording 10 victories each in the American League (AL) and National League (NL).

Colon was born on May 24, 1973 in Altamira, Dominican Republic, the son of Miguel Colon and Adriana Colon and has a brother and four sisters. His younger brother, José, saved 22 games for the Cleveland Indians (AL) Class A team at Columbus, Georgia (Southern League) in 2001. He grew up in a three-bedroom house without electricity, telephone, or plumbing. As a boy, he helped his father pick cocoa, coffee beans, and oranges, and he dropped out of school at 11 years of age. "When I was younger," Colon later explained, "the school was only 15 minutes away and I could walk. By the time I reached sixth grade, the school was an hour away and I had no way of getting there. Besides, I didn't like school much anyway." After learning to throw by knocking coconuts out of trees with stones, Colon began to play organized baseball at age 16. After starting as a catcher, he soon became a pitcher. Since his fastball soon was estimated at 75 to 80 miles per hour, other teams often refused to play against him.

Cleveland Indians (AL) scouts Virgilio Veras and Winston Llenas discovered the 6-foot, 230-pound right-hander, who began his minor league career in 1993 with Santiago (Dominican Summer League). Colon pitched for Winter Haven, Florida (Instructional League). He spoke no English at the time and had never eaten American food. He later admitted, "I was so homesick I didn't know what to do with myself." His adjustment was helped greatly by Puerto Rican–born Allen Davis, his interpreter, mentor, and director of community relations for the Indians.

Colon played rookie baseball in Burlington, North Carolina (Appalachian League) in 1994 and moved up to Class A, Kinston, North Carolina (Carolina League) the next year. Although faring 13–3 with a 1.96 earned run average (ERA) at Kinston, he suffered from elbow trouble the next two years at Canton-Akron, Ohio (Eastern League) in Class AA and Buffalo, New York (American Association) in Class AAA.

Colon broke into the major leagues in 1997, shuttling between Cleveland and Buffalo throughout the season. On June 20, 1997, he hurled a 4–0, no-hit victory over the New Orleans Zephyrs. In his rookie year with Cleveland, he won four games while losing seven with a 5.65 ERA. Colon did not appear in postseason play for the AL Champions, who lost to the Florida Marlins in the World Series. The next year he developed a two-seam fastball, which is slower than his 100-mile-an-hour four-seam fastball but sinks more. This led to great improvement in the following years, as he finished 14–9 in 1998 with an ERA of 3.71. That year he was the winning pitcher in the All-Star Game. Colon compiled a 1.59 ERA in his one AL Division Series start against the Boston Red Sox and won his only start against the New York Yankees in the AL Championship Series. He finished 18–5 with a 3.95 ERA in 1999 and 15–8 with a 3.88 ERA in 2000. His record slipped to 14–12 in 2001. Colon pitched well against the Seattle Mariners in the AL Division Series, splitting two decisions with a 1.84 ERA. After further developing his curve and slider, he rebounded in 2002 to 20–8 with a career-low 2.93 ERA.

In June 2002, the Indians traded Colon, then their ace pitcher, to the Montreal Expos (NL). Although he was very upset at leaving the Indians, the trade let him achieve a distinction. He finished 10–4 for each club, becoming only the second player to win 10 games in each league in the same season. (Hank Borowy had accomplished the feat in 1945.) In January 2003, the Chicago White Sox (AL) acquired him in a three-way trade. Through the 2003 season, Colon owned an 100–162 lifetime record, a .617 winning percentage, and a 3.86 ERA, fanning 1,120 batters in 1,388.2 innings. In 2003, Colon shared the NL lead with nine complete games, ranked second in innings pitched (242), and finished seventh in strikeouts (173). He compiled a 15–13 record with a 3.87 ERA.

Colon married Rosanna, his teenage sweetheart, in 1996 and has one son, Bartolo.

BIBLIOGRAPHY
Mary Kay Cabot, "Harnessing Colon's Fire," The Plain Dealer (Cleveland), June 26, 1998, pp. 1, 8; Paul Hoynes, "Tribe Has Colon's Number—28," *The Plain Dealer*

(Cleveland), February 23, 2002, p. D1; "Inside Baseball," *Sports Illustrated*, 96 (April 8, 2002), p. 90; *Who's Who in Baseball*, 2003.

Victor Rosenberg

MIKE CONLEY   **Track and Field**
(October 5, 1962–   )

Mike Conley specialized in the long jump and triple jump in track and field.

Michael Alex Conley was born on October 5, 1962 in Chicago, Illinois, and graduated in 1981 from Luther South High School in Chicago, where he made All-State in basketball. The 6-foot, 1-inch, 170-pound speedster also excelled in track and field, winning four events in the Class AA Illinois High School State track meet. Basketball meant a lot to him. He hoped to compete in both sports, but that did not happen. He won the Foot Locker Celebrity Slam Dunk Contest in 1988, 1989, and 1992.

Conley captured the USA Junior Triple Jump title and leaped 24 feet 5.75 inches and 51 feet 10 inches in the long and triple jumps before attending the University of Arkansas. Working with Razorback coach Dick Booth, Conley added 2 feet to his long jump and nearly 4 feet to his triple jump within a year. In his first World Championships in 1983, he won the bronze medal in the long jump and placed fourth in the triple jump.

Conley took nine NCAA (National Collegiate Athletic Association) horizontal jump (triple and long jump) titles while at Arkansas, and in 1985 he collected six All-America awards, including four at the NCAA Outdoor Meet. He earned 17 All-America certificates at Arkansas, more than any other Razorback athlete. With Conley as team captain his senior year, Arkansas won its first NCAA outdoor track title and became the second school to win the national triple crown. He swept the indoor and outdoor horizontal jump titles in 1984 and 1985, and placed second in the 200 meters in 1985.

Between 1981 and 1996, Conley concentrated on the triple jump and long jump at collegiate and international meets. During that span, he participated in nearly 100 major meets, including the NCAA Championships. He triumphed 31 times in the triple jump, recording first-place finishes at 12 USA Track and Field Championships, three Grand Prix Championships, one Pan American Games, one World Cup, and two World Championships. He finished first in the 1984 Olympic Trials and second in the 1992 Olympic Trials.

In the long jump, Conley captured three USA Track and Field Championships, one World Cup title, and one Grand Prix victory. Overall, he won his event in 35 of 86 major meets.

During 1984 and 1985, Conley enjoyed phenomenal success. He recorded six consecutive first-place finishes, placed second at the 1984 Los Angeles, California, Olympic Games, and followed with five more successive triumphs. By the end of the 1985 season, he had earned first-place honors in 15 of 18 major meets.

Conley captured a gold medal in the triple jump at the 1992 Summer Olympic Games in Barcelona, Spain. His leap of 59 feet 7.25 inches would have set a world record if not for a wind .01 above the legal limit. His jump was the only one aided by the wind during the competition. Conley also won a silver medal in the triple jump at the 1984 Olympic Summer Games in Los Angeles, California. First-place honors went to his U.S. teammate Al Joyner with a leap of 56 feet 7.5 inches, followed by Conley's jump of 56 feet 4.5 inches.

Conley recorded personal bests in the 100 meters of 10.36 seconds in 1986 and 20.21 seconds in the 200 meters in 1985. His best long jump came in 1996 with a leap of 27 feet 7.25 inches, and his best triple jump in 1987 with a leap of 58 feet 7 inches.

Conley worked as an assistant Razorback track and field coach when he completed his eligibility in 1985. A highly respected athlete nationally and abroad, he remained in this position for 14 years.

When asked if he thought he could make the 2000 Olympics team, the 38-year-old Conley replied, "I knew if I kept training, I'd make the team. But when I thought about what it would take to win a gold medal, I didn't want to train like that." University of Arkansas head track and field coach John McDonnell observed, "Conley is the best athlete we have ever had here, by-passing dozens other world-class stars. I think all you have to do is look at his record. Nobody won with the consistency he did and also ran at the high level he did."

In late 1998, Conley joined USA track and field as director of Elite Athlete Services. "It is my job to make sure our elite athletes are taken care of," he said. "I get them into meets in Europe before the Olympics and provide housing and travel arrangements for them."

Conley was inducted into the Arkansas Track and Field Hall of Fame in 1998. He trains police and attack dogs, serves as deputy sheriff for Washington County, Arkansas, and has earned a second-degree black belt in tae kwan do. He and his wife, Renee, have four children, Michael Alex II, Jordan, Sydney, and Jon.

BIBLIOGRAPHY

"Mike Conley," *Assistant Track Coach*, www.razorbacktrackandfield.com (1999); "Mike Conley," *Career Highlights*, www.sporting-heroes.net (1992); "Mike Conley," *Career Records*, www.usatf.com (1998); "Mike Conley," *Interviews*, www. fanaticzone.com (2000); "Mike Conley," *Track and Field Records*, www.ihsa.org (2002).

John L. Evers

CYNTHIA COOPER   Basketball
(April 14, 1963–   )

She Got Game, the title of Cynthia Cooper's autobiography, could be the anthem for Cynthia Cooper's life. Her staunch determination to overcome obstacles and to reach the heights of athletic success characterize her personal and professional story.

Cynthia Lynne Cooper was born on April 14, 1963. The youngest of eight children, she was brought up by a single parent, Mary Cobb, and never knew her father. Cooper grew up in the Watts area of south central Los Angeles, California. During her childhood, food was scarce. Their house burned down once, destroying all of their possessions. Sports provided the outlet for her energy and sparked her desire to be a leader. "As a kid I played detective with my friends," she said. "I was Sherlock Holmes because I wanted to be the leader."

At Locke High School, Cooper ran track and field and set a new city record in the 300-meter hurdles. She did not take up basketball until age 16 and only averaged 8 points as a junior. She worked hard on her game during the off-season and scored 31 points a game as a senior, leading her school to a championship. This gained Cooper an athletic scholarship to the University of Southern California. During her four years (1982–1984, 1986) there, the Women of Troy compiled an amazing 114–15 record and won the National Collegiate Athletic Association (NCAA) title in both 1983 and 1984. Southern California captured two West Coast Athletic Association and one Pac-West Conference titles and played in the 1986 national title game. Although winning many honors, Cooper frequently was overshadowed by Pamela McGee, Paula McGee, and Cheryl Miller* in the media. She usually ran the break, passed the ball, and defended the other team's best player. Coach Linda Sharp did not need another scorer. At Southern California, Cooper averaged 12.9 points, 4 rebounds, and 3.1 assists.

Europe provided the only professional basketball opportunity for Cooper after college. She played in Spain for two years and in Italy from 1987 to 1996, perfecting her game. "I wanted to be one of those players who took the clutch shots and carried teams on their shoulders," she told *Sports Illustrated*. Cooper led the European League in scoring eight times and finished runner-up the other two seasons. Nicknamed, "Coop," she played on several U.S. national teams, including the Olympic squads in 1988 and 1992, and Goodwill and World Championship teams. She presented her Olympic gold medal to her mother on Mother's Day in 1988.

When women's professional basketball came to the United States in 1997, Cooper was first drafted by the Houston Comets (Women's National Basketball Association). She led Houston to the championship in their first season. The Comets repeated in 1998, 1999, and 2000. Cooper, a four-time All-Star, was named league MVP twice, won the championship game MVP four times, and frequently paced in scoring. She won Excellence in Sports Performance for the Year (ESPY) awards for three consecutive years as the Outstanding Women's Professional Basketball Performer and became the first WNBA player to reach 300, 500, 1,000, 2,000, and 2,500 points in a career. In four WNBA seasons, she scored 2,537 points (21.1-point average), made 393 rebounds (3.3 average), and recorded 580 assists (4.8 average) in 120 games.

Cynthia Cooper ©Photofest

In 2001 Cooper became the head coach of the Phoenix Mercury (WNBA) and directed the team to a 19–23 record in one and a third seasons. She resigned 10 games into the 2002 season for personal and family reasons. Cooper came out of retirement and rejoined Houston in 2003.

Cooper was devoted to her mother and dropped out of college briefly to help her financially. Years later, she stayed with her mother during the last stages of her cancer. Cooper married Brian Dyke and has a large family of natural children, seven adopted nieces and nephews. Cooper has raised money for a foundation that aids children with cancer and for an inner-city after-school academic program, and has created the Mary Cobb "Building Dream" Foundation to collect funds for breast cancer research.

In 1999 Cooper wrote *She Got Game: My Personal Odyssey*, describing how she motivated herself to overcome obstacles and live a positive life. The book led to many speaking engagements, several videos inspiring young people, and work promoting reading for kids in Los Angeles. She endorses her own shoe, which NIKE called the Air C14, drawing an association to that other master of the game of basketball, Michael Jordan.*

BIBLIOGRAPHY
"Cynthia Cooper," Biography Resource Center, 2001; Cynthia Cooper, with Russ Pate, *She Got Game: My Personal Odyssey* (1999); Judith Graham, ed., *Current Biography Yearbook* (New York, 1998), p. 128; Richard Hoffer, "Family Ties," *Sports Illustrated for Women* (Summer 1999), p. 93; Gary Libman, "Alumni Profile: Cynthia Cooper," *USC Trojan Family Magazine* (Spring 1999); Kara O'Dell, *Cynthia Cooper website*, at www.angelfire.com; Jeff Savage, "Cynthia Cooper," *Top 10 Women's Basketball Stars*, 2001, pp. 6–9; Robert Schnakenberg, *Cynthia Cooper; Women Who Win*, October 2000.

Dennis S. Clark

D

CHILI DAVIS   Baseball
(January 17, 1960–   )

Chili Davis starred as a switch-hitter for several major league baseball clubs.

Charles Theodore Davis was born on January 17, 1960 in Kingston, Jamaica, the son of William Davis and Jenny (Baux) Davis. As a 6-foot 3-inch, 217-pound right-handed outfielder and switch-hitting designated hitter, Davis did not play baseball until his parents moved from Jamaica to Los Angeles, California, in 1970. In 1977, he graduated from Dorsey High School in Los Angeles. His nickname, originally "Chili Bowl," came following a haircut he received during his youth. He participated in the Los Angeles Inter-City baseball program.

The San Francisco Giants (National League) selected Davis in the eleventh round of the June 1977 free-agent draft and assigned him to Cedar Rapids, Iowa (Midwest League) in 1978. He spent 1979 in Fresno, California (California League) and 1980 in Shreveport, Louisiana (Texas League). He appeared in eight games for the San Francisco Giants in 1981 before being sent to Phoenix, Arizona (Pacific Coast League), where he compiled a .350 batting average, 19 home runs, 75 runs batted in (RBI), and 40 stolen bases in just 88 games. From 1982 through 1987, Davis played with San Francisco. On April 10, 1982, Davis hit his first major league home run off Mario Soto of the Cincinnati Reds. His best performances with San Francisco included career highs of 167 base hits in 1982 and 87 runs scored and six triples in 1984. Davis's best single season marks came in 1984, when he drove in 81 runs and batted .315, and in 1987, when he belted 24 home runs. In 1987, he slugged home runs from both sides of the plate twice, tying a major league record held by Mickey Mantle, Eddie Murray, and Kevin Bass. He also played in the 1987 NL Championship Series loss to the St. Louis Cardinals, batting .150.

After being granted free agency in November 1987, Davis signed with the California Angels (American League) in December 1987 and played three seasons there. He appeared in a career-high 158 games during 1988, shared the Owner's Trophy as Most Valuable Player (MVP) the following year, and moved from the outfield to designated hitter in 1988. He became a free agent in December 1990, joining the Minnesota Twins (AL) as their designated hitter for two seasons.

In 1991 Davis led AL designated hitters in home runs (29), RBIs (83), and total bases (269), contributing decisively to Minnesota's rise from a last place finish to a World Championship in seven games over the Atlanta Braves. In the AL Championship Series he batted .294 in the Twins' triumph over the Toronto Blue Jays. He hit .212 with two home runs to help Minnesota win the World Series.

In November 1992, Davis was granted free agency and rejoined the California Angels for four very productive campaigns. He hit his 200th career home run on May 17, 1993 and posted a career-high 112 RBIs that same season. Between 1993 and 1996, he recorded 101 home runs, 267 RBIs, and a career-high .318 batting average. On July 23, 1994, he became the 178th major league player and eighth switch-hitter to attain 1,000 career RBIs. Davis, who went hitless in the 1984, 1986, and 1994 All-Star games, was honored as the Angels MVP in 1994, and on June 24, 1996 he became the eighteenth switch-hitter in major league history to reach 2,000 career hits. In October 1996, the Kansas City Royals (AL) acquired him for starting pitcher Mark Gubicza. In 1997, he clouted his 300th career home run and belted a career-high 30 home runs while driving in 90 runs.

The New York Yankees (AL) signed Davis as a free agent in December 1997. In his final two seasons, he served as a designated hitter for the Bronx Bombers when they captured consecutive World Series crowns. After being injured most of the 1998 campaign, he finished 1999 with 19 home runs and 78 RBIs. The Yankees released him in December 1999, leaving Mickey Mantle and Eddie Murray as the only switch-hitters to top his 350 career round-trippers. New York Yankees general manager Brian Cashman said, " 'Chili' exemplifies character and class. . . . He was a veteran leader who, along with his offensive skills, brought professionalism and competitiveness to the ballpark every day."

Davis, who remains single, retired after 19 major league seasons. He scored 1,240 runs and made 2,380 hits in 2,436 games. He compiled a .274 batting average with 424 doubles, 30 triples, 350 home runs (including seven grand slams), 1,372 RBIs, 1,184 walks, 1,698 strikeouts, and 142 stolen bases.

BIBLIOGRAPHY
"Chili Davis," *ESPN Baseball*, www.espn.go.com (1999); "Chili Davis Retires After 19-Year Career," *Ballplayers*, www.totalsports.net (December 1, 1999); "Chili Davis," *The Baseball Online Library*, www.cbssportsline.com (February 16, 2001); David L. Porter, ed., *Biographical Dictionary of American Sports: Baseball, A–F* revised and expanded edition (Westport, CT, 2000); *The Sporting News Official Baseball Register*, 1999.

John L. Evers

TERRELL DAVIS   **Football**
(October 28, 1972–   )

Terrell Davis, the fourth National Football League (NFL) player to rush for over 2,000 yards in a season, helped the Denver Broncos (NFL) capture two Super Bowl titles.

Terrell Davis was born on October 28, 1972 in San Diego, California. He endured physical and verbal abuse from his father, Joe Davis, and grew up in a tough neighborhood. He attended Abraham Lincoln Prep School in San Diego, playing six different positions on the football team. As a senior, he was selected for the All-League first team and lettered in football and track and field.

Davis enrolled at Long Beach State University and played football for coach George Allen, gaining 262 yards from 55 carries while scoring two touchdowns. When the 49ers eliminated their football program following the 1991 season, Davis transferred to the University of Georgia. Georgia had produced outstanding tailbacks Herschel Walker,* Rodney Hampton, Garrison Hearst, and Tim Worley. He initially played behind Hearst, who finished third in the Heisman Trophy voting. During his three-year career at Georgia, Davis rushed for 1,657 yards on 317 attempts and 15 touchdowns. He appeared in the Florida Citrus Bowl in 1993, helping the Georgia Bulldogs defeat Ohio State University, 21 to 14.

The Denver Broncos selected Davis in the sixth round of the 1995 NFL draft as the 196th pick overall. In his first season with Denver, the 5-foot 11-inch, 210-pound Davis led the Broncos with 1,117 rushing yards with seven touchdowns.

The following year, Davis battled Detroit's Barry Sanders* for the NFL rushing title. Sanders won it by only 15 yards (1,553 yards to 1,538 yards), but Davis missed most of that season's finale because of an injury. His 345 carries for 1,538 yards and 15 touchdowns all set Broncos single-season records. He was selected to the Pro Bowl squad and won All-Pro honors.

Davis's 1997 production made him one of the most feared running backs in professional football. He rushed 369 times for 1,750 yards and 15 touchdowns to break his own team records. His three two-point conversions also tied the NFL mark. He again placed second to Sanders, who won the NFL's rushing title with 2,053 yards. In four playoff games that same year, Davis scored an NFL record eight touchdowns, all by rushing. Davis then capped that season by rushing for 150 yards on 30 carries with three touchdowns in Denver's 31 to 24 victory over the Green Bay Packers in Super Bowl XXXII, but missed the second quarter because of a migraine headache. His three touchdowns tied Super Bowl records for most points (18) and for most touchdowns, while his three rushing scores set a new Super Bowl standard. Davis was unanimously chosen the Super Bowl's Most Valuable Player and again won Pro Bowl and All-Pro honors.

Marty Schottenheimer, the San Diego Chargers head coach, acknowledged, "He is something. He brings a combination of speed and quickness and the ability to see the holes. He has the toughness of a fullback and the innate running ability of the great backs in the history of the game."

In 1998 Davis turned in a performance that ranked among the greatest-of-all-time running backs. He won his first NFL rushing title with 2,008 yards on 392 carries, becoming just the fourth player in NFL history to break the 2,000-yard barrier. By the seventh game of the season, he had 1,001 rushing yards to tie Jim Brown (1958) and O. J. Simpson (1973) as the fastest to reach 1,000 yards in a season. Davis also led the NFL in touchdowns (23), rushing touchdowns (21), first downs (112), and points scored by a running back (138). He became Denver's all-time career rushing leader with 6,413 yards, reaching this total in just 61 career games. This gave him the best per-game rushing average in NFL history of 105.1 yards. Davis also scored more rushing touchdowns per game (.918), recording 56 touchdowns. Davis virtually rewrote the Broncos' record book. He claimed his third Pro Bowl nomination and third All-Pro selection, earning the NFL's Most Valuable Player Award. Davis now joined a select group of nine players to win both NFL and Super Bowl MVP awards. He completed this brilliant season with 102 rushing yards on 25 carries in Denver's 34 to 19 win over the Atlanta Falcons in Super Bowl XXXIII.

"What I try to do is to remember the same things today that I did when I first came into the league," Davis reflected about his record-setting season. "I remember how hungry I was to play in my rookie year."

From 1999 to 2001, serious knee injuries slowed Davis down considerably. He finally announced his retirement from professional football prior to the 2002 season. In a brief six-year career, he rushed 7,160 yards on 1,559 carries and 65 touchdowns with three two-point conversions for 396 points. A life-long sufferer of migraine headaches, Davis established his own foundation for its treatment. Davis is single and resides in Aurora, Colorado.

BIBLIOGRAPHY
Jarrett Bell, "Davis Shows Value of Determination," *USA Today*, January 21, 1998, pp. 1c–2c; Terrell Davis and Adam Shefter, *TD: Dreams in Motion* (New York, 1998); *Denver Broncos Press Guide*, 2002; Sherelle Phelps, ed., *Contemporary Black Biography*, vol. 20 (Detroit, MI, 1999), pp. 52–54; *Pro Football Weekly*, August 3, 1997, November 29, 1998; *The Sporting News Pro Football Register*, 2002; Richard Weiner, "Davis: A Back at the Forefront," *USA Today*, November 16, 1998, pp. 1c-2c.

Richard Gonsalves

RON DAYNE   Football
(March 14, 1978–   )

Ron Dayne starred four years as a football tailback for the University of Wisconsin, winning the Heisman Trophy in 1999.

Ron Dayne Jr. was born on March 14, 1978 in Blacksburg, Virginia, the son of Ron Dayne Sr. and Brenda Dayne. After his parents divorced, his mother suffered from depression and used illegal drugs. He and his sister, Onya, were sent to live with separate relatives. Dayne moved as a teenager to Berlin, New Jersey, to live with his uncle, Rob Reid, a minister, and Debbie Reid, who became his legal guardians. He graduated from Overbrook High School, where he starred in football.

Bernie Wyatt, an assistant football coach at the University of Wisconsin, recruited the 5-foot, 10-inch, 253-pound Dayne, whom he called "a rare kind of athlete." Dayne entered Wisconsin in 1996 and starred in football four seasons under coach Barry Alvarez, exhibiting unusual power and breakaway speed. Archie Griffin, former Heisman Trophy winner, observed, "You've got a running back who's as big as a fullback. They're getting bigger and faster, and he's the leader of the pack."

Although not starting until his fifth game as a freshman, Dayne rushed for 1,863 yards and 18 touchdowns. Wisconsin fared 8–5 overall and seventh in the Big Ten Conference (BTC), defeating the University of Utah, 38–10, in the Copper Bowl. Dayne gained 1,421 yards and tallied 15 touchdowns as a sophomore in 1997, helping the Badgers finish 8–5 and fifth in the BTC. The University of Georgia defeated Wisconsin, 33–6, in the Outback Bowl.

Dayne rushed for 1,279 yards and 11 touchdowns as a junior in 1998, leading the Badgers to a 10–1 overall record, a share of the BTC crown, and a 38–31 victory over UCLA in the Rose Bowl. He contemplated entering the National Football League (NFL) draft but did not want to leave his one-year-old daughter, Jada. The mother was his girlfriend Alia Lester, a journalism major. "Being a father has changed my life," Dayne explained. "I can wait to make whatever money they say I might be able to make in the pros. Being around my daughter comes first."

As a senior in 1999, Dayne rushed for 1,834 yards and 19 touchdowns. He entered the season needing 1,717 yards to break Ricky Williams'* National Collegiate Athletic Association (NCAA) Division I-A career rushing mark of 6,279 yards. He ran for 231 yards against the University of Cincinnati but lost a fumble near the goal line in the Badger upset loss. Dayne sat out the second halves of routs against Murray State University, Ball State University, and Indiana University. His Heisman Trophy hopes dimmed when the University of Michigan defeated Wisconsin and held Dayne to no yards in eight carries in the second half. *Sports Illustrated* listed him among the season's ten biggest disappointments. "That really motivated me to go out and play harder," he said.

Dayne, meanwhile, passed Herschel Walker,* Charles White, and Tony Dorsett on the career rushing yardage list. After gaining 161 yards and scoring four touchdowns against Ohio State University, Dayne bulldozed for 234 yards against Michigan State University's top-ranked rushing defense. He finished three of his last four games with 200-yard-plus performances, rushing for 222 yards against Purdue University and scoring a 41-yard touchdown. Dayne set the NCAA career rushing record at Camp Randall Stadium in his last regular season game against the University of Iowa. He broke the record on a 31-yard run in the second quarter and gained 216 yards altogether. Coach Alvarez remarked, "I think it's going to take a while before it's broken." A consensus All-America, Dayne led Wisconsin to a 9–2 regular season record, an outright BTC title, a fourth-place national ranking, and a 17–9 victory over Stanford University in the Rose Bowl.

Dayne finished his career at Wisconsin with 1,115 carries for 6,397, yards—118 yards more than Williams. He played in 43 collegiate games, one fewer than Williams, and averaged 5.73 yards per carry, second all-time behind Williams' 6.21 yards per carry. He ranked second on the NCAA Division I-A list with 148.8 rushing yards per game, 30 100-yard games, and 63 touchdowns. Coach Alvarez acknowledged, "There's no one that's done any more for a program than what he's done for our program. His numbers speak for themselves."

Dayne won the 1999 Heisman Trophy by a landslide over quarterback Joe Hamilton of Georgia Tech University. Dayne became just the second Badger to win the trophy, joining Alan Ameche from 1954. He considered his Uncle Rob the real Heisman Trophy winner and recognized coach Alvarez for teaching him to be not just a football player, but also a father. His other major honors included winning the Associated Press Player of the Year, Walter Camp, Maxwell, and Doak Walker awards.

The New York Giants (NFL) selected the soft-spoken, reserved Dayne in the first round as the eleventh overall pick in the 2000 NFL draft. He helped New York win the Eastern Division of the National Football Conference (NFC) with a 12–4 record in 2000, rushing for 770 yards (3.4-yard average) and five touchdowns. He gained 53 yards to help the Giants defeat the Philadelphia Eagles, 20–10, in the divisional playoffs and 29 yards in a 41–0 romp over the Minnesota Vikings in the NFC Championship game. The Baltimore Ravens, however, vanquished New York, 34–7, in Super Bowl XXXV.

The Giants struggled with a 7–9 mark in 2001, sharing third place in the NFC. Dayne started seven games, rushing for 690 yards and gaining 3.8 yards per carry. He gained 428 yards (3.4-yard average) and three touchdowns in 2002 for the 10–6 Giants, who earned an NFC Wild Card berth. Through the 2002 season, he has rushed 533 times for 1,888 yards (3.5-yard average) and 15 touchdowns and caught 22 passes for 127 yards (5.8-yard average).

BIBLIOGRAPHY
Gary Mihoces, "Dayne's Great Run," *USA Today*, November 12, 1999, pp. 1C–2C; Tom Pedulia, "Runaway Dayne: With Warwick Woes, Heisman Won in Rout," *USA Today*, December 13, 1999, p. 17C; Randy Peterson, "Hawkeyes Bowled Over," *The Des Moines Sunday Register*, November 14, 1999, pp. 1D–6D; Richard Rosenblatt, "Dayne Runs Away with the Heisman," *The Des Moines Register*, December 13, 1999, p. 2C; *The Sporting News Pro Football Register*, 2003.

David L. Porter

GIL DE FERRAN
(November 11, 1967–   )

Auto Racing

Gil de Ferran ranks among only four CART drivers to win consecutive titles.

Gil de Ferran, nicknamed "Professor," was born on November 11, 1967 in Paris, France, to Brazilian parents. His family returned to Brazil when he was nine months old. As a 5-year-old in São Paolo, Brazil, de Ferran began driving go-karts under the supervision of his father. His parents continued to encourage him to drive. As a 13-year-old, he wanted to attend one of the best high schools in São Paolo. This school required a difficult admission test. His father promised, "Look, if you pass this test, we'll buy you a new go-kart and go racing." "I passed," de Ferran recalled, "they bought a new go-kart and we went racing."

For the next several years, de Ferran attended school and raced. Part of his education included visiting the United States as a foreign exchange student and living on a dairy farm in Mount Hope, Wisconsin. Following three years of go-kart racing between 1982 and 1985, he competed in the Brazilian Formula 3 1600 Championship Series for three seasons. In 1987 he captured the Brazilian Formula Ford Series with seven victories. At the same time, de Ferran studied at Maua Engineering College in São Paolo. He tried to balance education and racing until 1988, when he left school for the United Kingdom to concentrate on racing. By 1991, de Ferran advanced to British Formula 3 competition, winning the championship in his second season with seven victories. In 1993 and 1994, he earned third-and fourth-place finishes in the Federation Internationale de L'Automobile (FIA) International Formula 3000 Series.

Driving for the Hall Racing Team in 1995, de Ferran made his first start in the Championship Auto Racing Teams (CART) FedEx Championship Series and earned Rookie of the Year honors. He also recorded his first CART career win and pole position. As a second-year driver, he finished sixth in points and was one of only four CART drivers to win a race and a pole. In 1997 de Ferran recorded a career-best second-place finish in the Championship Series, posting seven top 3 finishes and two pole positions. The following year, he finished twelfth in the Championship Series. In his fifth year as a CART driver and his third with the Walker Racing Team, in 1999 he registered his third career triumph and his fifth and sixth career poles and placed sixth in driver points.

In his first season with the Marlboro Team Penske, de Ferran captured the 2000 FedEx Championship Series title with 168 points. He earned two victories and five pole positions and gave the Penske Racing Team its 100th Championship Car victory, joining Rick Mears, Al Unser, Danny Sullivan, and Al Unser Jr. on the Penske racing list of FedEx champions. In winning

Gil de Ferran ©Courtesy of Indianapolis Speedway

the pole position at California Speedway, he established a new world closed-course speed record of 241.428 miles per hour and broke the previous record of 240.942 miles per hour. Besides being selected as a member of the 2000 CART All-Star team, he led all drivers in season earnings with $1,677,000 and qualified among the top 5 drivers for 16 of 20 starts.

In 2001, de Ferran became only the fourth driver in the 23-year history of the CART FedEx Series to win consecutive titles. In his seventh full season, he joined Rick Mears (1981, 1982), Bobby Rahal (1986, 1987), and Alex Zanardi (1997, 1998) as the only consecutive series champions. Driving the Car No. 1 Marlboro Honda/Reynard, he posted two victories and five pole positions in 2001. Through 2001, de Ferran compiled seven career victories, 27 additional podiums, and 16 pole positions in 128 career starts, seventh best in CART FedEx Championship Series history. At the November 2001 CART FedEx Awards Banquet, he received the Vanderbilt Cup Driver's Championship and a $1 million bonus. The 33-year-old Brazilian, who now resides in Fort Lauderdale, Florida, vowed that "As long as I continue to improve, I'll continue to race. The day I feel that I'm not as good as I used to be, it will be time to reconsider." In 2002 he switched to the Indy Racing League (IRL). He posted one victory and finished third in the IRL standings behind Sam Hornish Jr. and Helio Castroneves.* De Ferran held off teammate Castroneves to capture his first Indianapolis 500 in 2003 by 0.0299 seconds. He had willed himself to come back from two broken vertebrae and a concussion incurred in a crash the previous march in Phoenix, Arizona. De Ferran ranked second in the IRL standings behind teammate Scott Dixon, winning the Firestone Indy 200 in Nashville, Tennessee in July and the Chevy 500 in Fort Worth, Texas, in October. He retired at the end of the 2003 season.

Gil de Ferran married Angela Buckland from the *Motoring News* publishing family in December 1993. They met while she was working for the Paul Stewart Racing Team in the United Kingdom. They have a daughter, Anna Elizabeth, and a son, Luke, and reside in Fort Lauderdale, Florida. In addition to a life-long study of English, de Ferran avidly reads works ranging from auto racing to mysteries and especially likes motor sports because of the thrill of competition. His racing heroes include Emerson Fittipaldi, Mario Andretti, and Rick Mears.

BIBLIOGRAPHY

Mark Bechtel, "Head of the Class," *Sports Illustrated* 2 (July 10, 2000), p. 68; "Gil de Ferran," *Background*, www.autocentral.com (2001); "Gil de Ferran," *Biography*, www.gildeferran.com (2001); "Gil de Ferran," *Career Highlights*, www.gildeferran. com (2001); "Gil de Ferran," *Clinches Title*, www.cart.com (2001); "Gil de Ferran," *Profile*, www.autosport.com (2001).

John L. Evers

OSCAR DE LA HOYA   Boxing
(February 12, 1973–   )

Oscar "Golden Boy" De La Hoya is a boxing anomaly. As Mark Kriegel notes, De La Hoya is "Mexican by his blood, American in his inclination." From East Los Angeles, California, De La Hoya has partly repudiated his heritage to move into the American mainstream. He remains a matador among Hispanic boxing *aficionados*, who prefer bulls like Genaro Hernandez, Julio Cesar Chavez,* and Rafael Ruelas. He angered many Latino fans by moving to affluent Anglo Whittier, California, and taking up golf at the tony Friendly Hills Country Club there. As boxing expert Richard Hoffer observes, "Oscar De La Hoya moves through life the same way he moves through a golf course—purposefully and to his own advantage."

De La Hoya was born in East Los Angeles on February 12, 1973, the second of three children, to Joel De La Hoya Sr., a shipping clerk, and Cecilia De La Hoya, a seamstress and professional singer. He grew up on a quiet street of small single-family homes, although gang violence was never far away. He was never involved in a street fight as a boy, preferring skateboarding and baseball. At age 6, De La Hoya was sent to a neighborhood gym to learn boxing for self-defense. The 5-foot 10-inch, 147-pounder enjoyed competing in the ring, compiling an astounding 223–5 amateur record with 163 knockouts. By 1988, De La Hoya won the Junior Olympic (119-pound class championship). The following year, he captured the National Golden Gloves (125-pound class) title. His other amateur honors included taking the Gold Medal at the 1990 Goodwill Games in Seattle, Washington, and becoming the only American boxing gold medal winner at the 1992 Barcelona, Spain, Olympics. De La Hoya's boxing success, however, was shadowed by personal tragedy. In October 1990, his mother died of breast cancer. She had skipped radiation treatment to watch her son perform in Seattle, Washington. De La Hoya often ran along a road next to the cemetery where she lies buried.

De La Hoya turned professional in November 1992, knocking out Lamar Williams in the first round of his debut. De La Hoya's ever-changing handlers moved him carefully through several preselected opponents. His most important early victory came in July 1994 with his two-round knockout of Jorge Paez for the World Boxing Organization (WBO) lightweight title. In 1995, he defeated such tough customers as John John Molina, Rafael Ruelas, Genaro Hernandez, and Jesse James Leija. The Molina fight forced the artful De La Hoya to grapple with the shorter, bull-like opponent who was not above an occasional head butt.

In June 1996, De La Hoya won his first of two victories over boxing legend Julio Cesar Chavez. In four rounds, he beat the Lion of Culiacan's face to pulp, stripping him of the World Boxing Council (WBC) super lightweight belt. In April 1997, he deprived the elusive Pernell Whitaker of the WBC

Oscar De La Hoya ©Photofest

welterweight title with aggressive strategy over 12 rounds. By late 1997, De La Hoya had reached his peak. After a September 1997 dominating victory over Hector Camacho, he defeated three highly regarded fighters, including Chavez again, Ike Quartey, and Oba Carr.

De La Hoya's career has taken a downward turn. In September 1999, he handed a gift-wrapped 12-round decision to a persistent Felix Trinidad* for the WBC welterweight title. After suffering his first loss in 32 fights to Trinidad, he lost a close, hotly contested bout with Sugar Shane Mosely in June 2000. De La Hoya pounded Arturo Gatti into submission in five rounds in March 2001 and easily decisioned Spaniard Javier Castillejo for the WBC junior middleweight title in June 2001. In September 2002, De La Hoya unified the junior middleweight titles and recaptured his place at the top of the boxing world with an eleventh-round knockout of Fernando Vargas, his Southern California rival. De La Hoya had not fought in 15 months because of surgery on his left hand and hoped to lure Trinidad out of retirement. De La

Hoya knocked out Yory Boy Campos in May 2003 at Las Vegas, Nevada and lost a decision to Shane Mosely in September 2003.

De La Hoya wants to leave the ring at the top of his game. With his good looks, smooth singing voice, and pleasant personality, he seems a show business natural. He has appeared frequently as a guest on the *Tonight Show* and was nominated for a Grammy for his rendition of *Ven a Mi* from his CD *Oscar*.

De La Hoya, who boasts a 36–3 record with 29 knockouts, has been an extremely generous champion. He bought and renovated the Resurrection Gym, where he trained as a boy. In addition, he funds the Oscar De La Hoya Foundation to assist underprivileged East Los Angeles children and contributes significantly to Garfield High School, which he attended as an amateur fighter.

De La Hoya loves to draw and wants to become an architect, having designed his two-story cabin at his training facility in Big Bear Lake, California. He is also an avid reader (his favorite work is *Hamlet*). He remains single.

BIBLIOGRAPHY
Lorraine Ali, "He's Singing in the Ring," *Newsweek* 136 (October 23, 2000), p. 78; *Current Biography Yearbook* (1997), pp. 136–139; "Heart and Soul of Boxing," *Sport* 90 (February 1999), p. 51; Richard Hoffer, "Looks Like a Star," *Sports Illustrated* 82 (February 27, 1995), p. 60; Richard Hoffer, "The Pugilist and the Professor," *Sports Illustrated* 84 (June 10, 1996), p. 80; Tim Kawakami, *Golden Boy: The Fame, Money, and Mystery of Oscar De La Hoya* (Kansas City, MO, 2000); Mark Kriegel, "The Great (Almost) White Hope," *Esquire* 126 (November 1996), p. 93; Richard O'Brien, "El Mejor," *Sports Illustrated* 75 (October 21, 1991), p. 66; Alex Tresniowski, "Moving on Up," *People Weekly* 47 (January 20, 1997), p. 93.

John H. Ziegler

CARLOS DELGADO   Baseball
(June 25, 1972–   )

Carlos Delgado, a 6-foot, 3-inch, 225-pound left-handed-hitting first baseman, epitomizes the Toronto Blue Jays' (American League) commitment to scouting Latin American talent.

Carlos Juan Delgado was born on June 25, 1972 in Aguadilla, Puerto Rico, and signed with Toronto for $90,000 in October 1988 at age 16. His father, Carlos Sr., a drug and alcohol counselor who passed along his love of baseball to Delgado, and his mother Carmen, a medical laboratory assistant, emphasized education. Delgado graduated from Jose de Diego High School in Aguadilla in June 1989.

Originally a catcher, Delgado was named Most Valuable Player (MVP) for three different minor league teams. He was selected *USA Today*'s Minor League Player of the Year for 1992, hitting .324, with 30 home runs and 100 runs batted in (RBI) for Class A Dunedin, Florida (Florida State League). After a fine 1993 season at Class AA Knoxville, Tennessee (Southern Association), he began 1994 as an outfielder with the Toronto Blue Jays. On opening day, Delgado launched a 428-foot home run that nearly hit the window of the Skydome's Hard Rock Cafe. Despite a torrid start with eight home runs in 13 games, he was demoted to Class AAA Syracuse, New York (International League) in June when his batting average dropped to .215. He spent the rest of 1994 and most of 1995 at Syracuse.

In 1996, his first full major league season, Delgado quickly began to pay dividends. He batted .270 with 25 home runs and 92 RBIs, primarily as the designated hitter. After another good season in 1997, he blossomed in 1998 and 1999. Delgado injured a shoulder in the Puerto Rican Winter League in early 1998. Although not scheduled to return to action until late May, he rejoined Toronto in mid-April and produced 21 RBIs in his first 35 games. He finished with a .292 batting average, 38 home runs, 115 RBIs, and a .592 slugging percentage.

Delgado's salary rose with his production. After making $2.4 million in 1998, he could not agree with the Blue Jays on a long-term contract. He eventually avoided arbitration, signing for $5 million in 1999. Delgado won his first *The Sporting News (TSN)* Silver Slugger Award, hitting .272 with 44 home runs, 134 RBIs, and a .571 slugging percentage. He signed a three-year, $36 million deal in November 1999. The contract also gave him the right to request a trade within 15 days after the 2000 World Series.

The 1998 and 1999 seasons marked just a prelude to a magnificent 2000 season. Delgado stayed in contention for the Triple Crown as AL leader in batting average, home runs, and RBIs until he hit a slump in September. He ended the 2000 season with 41 home runs, 137 RBIs, and a .664 slugging percentage. He batted .344, 70 points above his career average. Delgado finished fourth in the AL MVP voting, won another *TSN* Silver Slugger Award, the AL Hank Aaron Award as the best overall hitter in each league, and *TSN* Player of the Year Award. He also was named to the AL All-Star team for the first time. The Blue Jays rewarded his tremendous 2000 season with a record-setting four-year, $68 million contract.

Delgado took great pride when Toronto opened the 2001 season against the Texas Rangers in his native Puerto Rico. After receiving a prolonged standing ovation prior to the game, he contributed an RBI single to the Blue Jays' win. Although he recorded two three-homer games and another multi-homer game before April 21, the 2001 season disappointed Delgado and Toronto. He hit 39 home runs with 102 RBIs, but his batting average dropped to .279 and his slugging and on-base percentages declined significantly. The Blue Jays were never serious contenders that season, causing many people to blame Delgado. In 2002 he batted .277 with 33 home runs, 108 RBIs, 102 walks, and a .406 on-base percentage. Through the 2003 season, his career statistics include a .284 batting average, 304 home runs, 959 RBIs, and a .559 slugging percentage. In 2003, Delgado enjoyed a banner year with a .302 batting average, easily led the AL with 145 RBIs, finished second with 42 home runs, 109 walks, a .593 slugging percentage, and a .426 on-base percentage, and placed fourth with 117 runs. He finished second in the AL MVP Award balloting.

Delgado is friendly and well-respected by teammates and fans alike. Former teammate Darrin Fletcher praised him as "the most down-to-earth superstar there is . . . he never complains. If your son wanted a role model . . . Carlos is the guy." Delgado enjoys working with children. For one game of every home-stand, he buys a block of tickets for needy youngsters and treats them to dinner at the ballpark. For relaxation, he enjoys fine food, Cuban cigars, the theater, and going to the beach. He is single.

BIBLIOGRAPHY
Mel Antonen, "Delgado Fit for a Triple Crown; 'Pitchers Seem Slower to Me,' Says Blue Jays' Big Slugger," *USA Today*, September 8, 2000, p. 3C; Rod Beaton, "Delgado a Future Power Source," *USA Today*, September 30, 1992, p. 7C; Murray Chass, "Delgado Becomes Top-paid Player," *New York Times*, October 21, 2000, p. 14; "Delgado's Three Homers Power Blue Jays to Rout," *New York Times*, April 21, 2001, p. 7; Tom Maloney, "Delgado Is on the Rise Again," *The Sporting News*, July 20, 1998, p. 20; Tom Maloney, "Down the Stretch He Comes," *The Sporting News*, September 8, 2000, p. 60; Tom Maloney, "TSN's Baseball 2000 Awards: Carlos Delgado, Blue Jays," *The Sporting News*, October 30, 2000, p. 8; David Leon Moore, "Delgado's Homers Have Jays Seeing Greatness," *USA Today*, April 19, 1994, p. 4C; Phil Rogers, "Carlos Delgado: A Triple Crown Threat," *Baseball Digest* 59 (December 2000), p. 64; Rick Sorci, "Baseball Profiles; Carlos Delgado," *Baseball Digest* 60 (May 2001), p. 38; Tom Verducci and David Sabino, "Three Dimensional," *Sports Illustrated* 93 (August 28, 2000), p. 78.

Terry W. Sloope

GAIL DEVERS Track and Field
(November 19, 1966–   )

Gail Devers overcame illness to become the greatest female sprinter/hurdler in history. In 1993 she became the first woman in 45 years to win sprint and hurdles titles in Olympics/World Championship competition.

Born on November 19, 1966 in Seattle, Washington, Yolanda Gail Devers is the second of two children of Larry Devers, a Baptist minister, and Alabe Devers, a teacher's aide. She grew up in San Diego, California, and began running in neighborhood events organized by her brother, Parenthesis.

Devers attended Sweetwater High School in National City, California, starting out as a distance runner and switching to the shorter races after her sophomore year. In 1984 she won the bronze medal in the 100 meters at the Pan American Junior Championships and ran the third leg on the gold-medal-winning U.S. 4×100-meter relay team.

The first female athlete from Sweetwater High to earn an athletic scholarship, Devers attended UCLA and majored in sociology. She won Pacific-10 Conference titles, including two long-jump crowns. Under Bruins coach Bobby Kersee, she blossomed into a world-class sprinter and hurdler. As a junior in 1987, Devers placed first in the 100 meters at the Pan American Games. She twice lowered the American record for the 100-meter hurdles as a senior. She won the National Collegiate Athletic Association (NCAA) 100-meter title and qualified for the Olympics with a second-place finish in the 100-meter hurdles at the U.S. Trials.

Devers began suffering from migraine headaches prior to the 1988 Seoul, South Korea, Olympics and was eliminated in the Olympic semifinals. After two months off, she resumed training in December. Her practice times for the 100-meter hurdles slowed to the 13.50-second range and then to 14.30 seconds. Illness sidelined her for all of 1989 and 1990. In September 1990, doctors diagnosed the illness as Graves' disease, a thyroid disorder. Devers underwent radiation treatment, but her feet swelled and became infected. She soon began suffering from insomnia, dramatic weight fluctuation, fits of shaking, and temporary vision loss in one eye. "My face was constantly peeling," she said. "That's when I stopped looking in the mirror. I felt like a creature."

Devers' physician changed her therapy. "I was approaching the point where they would have to amputate my feet," she lamented. "Two more days and amputation would have been necessary." She even struggled to walk. Her brief marriage to former UCLA miler Ron Roberts ended in divorce.

Devers worked as an insurance underwriter and took courses in child-care management, planning to open a day-care center. But coach Kersee, she noted, "wouldn't let me quit. Bobby had a dream that I would be all right. We held onto that dream." Miraculously, in the spring of 1991, she returned to track. Devers claimed her first U.S. title that June, winning the 100-meter hurdles. She placed second at the World Championships. The following month, she lowered her American record to 12.48 seconds.

In 1992 Devers qualified for the Barcelona, Spain, Olympics by winning the 100-meter hurdles and taking second in the 100 meters at the U.S. Trials. After winning the sprint gold medal, she hoped to become the first Olympic sprint/hurdles double-winner since Fanny Blankers-Koen of the Netherlands in 1948. In the 100-meter hurdles final, she led coming off the final barrier, tripped, fell, and wound up fifth. "Afterwards, Bobby said that I had clipped the last hurdle with the heel of my lead leg," Devers explained. "I couldn't believe I failed three meters from the finish."

Devers in 1993 won the 60-meter U.S. indoor (6.99 seconds) and World indoor (6.95 seconds) titles in record U.S. times. Outdoors, she captured the 100 meters at the U.S. Championships. At the World meet, she matched Blankers-Koen's feat with 100-meter sprint and 100-meter hurdles triumphs. A hamstring injury kept Devers from hurdling in 1994, but she repeated as the U.S. 100 meters titlist. A year later, she finished first in the 100-meter hurdles at the U.S. Championships and retained the World Championship.

Between 1993 and 1996, Devers enjoyed win streaks in both her specialties. At the 1996 U.S. Olympic Trials, she qualified for the Atlanta, Georgia Olympics with a victory in the 100-meter hurdles and a second-place finish to Gwen Torrence in the 100 meters. She repeated as the Olympic 100-meter champion and ran the second leg of the triumphant U.S. sprint relay team but finished fourth in the 100-meter hurdles.

During the 1997 indoor season, Devers won both the U.S. and World 60-meter titles. Outdoors, she concentrated on sprinting and anchored the U.S. 4×100-meter relay team to first place at the World Championships in an American record time. She sat out the 1998 season and returned in 1999, triumphing in the 100-meter hurdles at the U.S. and World Championships. Her time of 12.37 seconds for the 100-meter hurdles established an American record.

Devers lowered the 100-meter hurdles record again to 12.33 seconds in 2000, claiming her sixth U.S. 100-meter hurdles title at the Olympic Trials. At the Sydney, Australia, Olympics, however, she pulled up in the semifinals with a hamstring injury. In 2001, Devers won the U.S. title in the 100-meter hurdles and finished second at the World Championships to American teammate Anjanette Kirkland. She dominated the 100-meter hurdles event in 2002, winning the USATF Outdoor Championships at Palo Alto, California in June and the IAAF Grand Prix Final at Paris, France in September and ranking second in the Grand Prix Season Standings. She ended Marion Jones'* five year domination of the female track and field athlete ESPY award in 2002. In 2003, she again prevailed in the 100-meter hurdles on the track circuit until she was eliminated in the semifinals at the World Championships at Saint-Denis, France in August.

The 5-foot 3-inch, 120-pound Devers has been ranked first in the world by *Track & Field News* twice in the 100 meters and eight times in the 100-meter hurdles. Her comeback from Graves' disease was portrayed in the 1996 film, *The Gail Devers Story*.

BIBLIOGRAPHY
Dave Johnson, "A Truly Amazing Comeback," *Track and Field News* 44 (December 1991), p. 11; Ruth Laney, "Devers Won Wrong Race," *Track and Field News* 45 (October 1992), p. 53; Sieg Lindstrom, "A Long Medical Chart," *Track and Field News* 44 (August 1991), p. 24; Kenny Moore, "Gail Force," *Sports Illustrated* 78 (May 10, 1993), pp. 41–43; *NBC Olympic Track & Field Research Manual*, USA Women's Biographies—Gail Devers (New York, 1996); Dick Patrick, "Devers Seeks Gold Medal after Clearing Huge Hurdles," *USA Today*, January 7, 1992, p. C5; Bert Rosenthal, "On the Road to Barcelona: Gail Devers," *American Athletics* (Winter 1991), pp. 34–36; *2001 USA Track & Field Media Guide and FAST Annual* (Indianapolis, IN, 2001); 2001 USA Track & Field Athlete Biography—Gail Devers; David Wallechinsky, *The Complete Book of the Summer Olympics* (Woodstock, NY, 2000).

Peter J. Cava

ERIC DICKERSON   Football
(September 2, 1960–   )

Wearing trademark goggles because of his poor eyesight and possessing a graceful loping running style, Eric Dickerson ranked among football's most successful collegiate and professional running backs during the 1980s.

Eric Demetric Dickerson was born on September 2, 1960 in Sealy, Texas, the son of Robert Johnson and Helen Johnson, and was legally adopted and brought up by his great uncle and great aunt, Kary Dickerson and Viola Dickerson. At age 14, Dickerson learned that Helen, whom he believed was an older sister, was his birth mother. But he still viewed Kary, who died when Dickerson was 17, and Viola as his real parents.

At Sealy High School, Dickerson starred in football, basketball, and track, winning the state 100-yard dash his junior year in 9.4 seconds. Nevertheless, football proved his best sport. During his senior year, he rushed for 2,653 yards and led Sealy to the Texas AAA state championship. *Parade* magazine selected him as the top high school running back of 1978.

Dickerson received numerous college football scholarship offers before finally honoring his mother Viola's advice to select Southern Methodist University (SMU) of the Southwest Conference (SWC). In his freshman year, he battled injuries and accumulated 477 yards on 115 carries. As a sophomore, he gained 928 yards on 188 rushes and made the All-SWC second team. Dickerson disliked sharing playing time with Craig James at tailback and considered transferring to the University of Oklahoma. When Viola expressed reservations regarding Oklahoma's coach Barry Switzer, the running back returned to SMU. Dickerson enjoyed outstanding junior and senior campaigns, amassing 1,428 and 1,617 yards, respectively. As a senior, he was named consensus All-American, finished third in the Heisman Trophy balloting, and led the Mustangs to a victory over the University of Pittsburgh in the 1983 Cotton Bowl. During his four years at SMU, Dickerson established a career SWC rushing mark with 4,450 yards on 790 carries. This record is even more amazing because Dickerson shared playing time with James, who amassed 3,742 career yards as a Mustang.

Dickerson, the second player selected in the 1983 National Football League (NFL) draft following John Elway, enjoyed an outstanding rookie season with the Los Angeles Rams (NFL), leading the NFL in rushing with 1,808 yards. The 6-foot 3-inch, 220-pounder was named Rookie of the Year by the Associated Press and National Football Conference (NFC) Player of the Year. His second season with the Rams proved even more productive. He established an NFL single-season rushing mark of 2,105 yards, surpassing the 2,003 yards set by his boyhood idol O. J. Simpson in 1973. He was selected as the NFL's Most Valuable Player and earned his second Pro Bowl berth.

Dickerson missed the first two games of the 1985 season in a contract dispute with the Rams but still rushed for 1,234 yards and 12 touchdowns. He led the Rams to the NFC title game, where the Chicago Bears prevailed. In 1986 he again led the NFL with 1,821 yards rushing. Although the Rams lost to the Washington Redskins in the playoffs, Dickerson was selected as NFC Offensive Player of the Year and again named to the Pro Bowl.

In the strike-shortened 1987 season, the Rams sent Dickerson to the Indianapolis Colts (NFL) in a three-team, 10-player transaction. In only nine games with the Colts, he amassed 1,011 yards. In 1988 he captured his fourth

NFL rushing title with 1,659 yards on 388 carries and 14 touchdowns, earning a fifth Pro Bowl selection. The following season, Dickerson gained 1,311 yards and became the only back in NFL history to achieve seven consecutive 1,000-yard rushing seasons. He missed an NFL first game because of a hamstring injury (November 1989 against the Miami Dolphins).

In 1990 Dickerson rushed for only 677 yards and missed five games because of injuries. The Colts management, thinking he could have played, accused him of exaggerating the extent of his ailments. The following year, he continued to feud with the Colts, who suspended him for "conduct detrimental to the team." After he finished the 1991 season with only 536 yards, the Colts traded him to the Los Angeles Raiders (NFL). When a subpar 1992 season netted him only 729 rushing yards, the Raiders released him. Dickerson then joined the Atlanta Falcons (NFL) for four games before being dealt to the Green Bay Packers (NFL). He failed a physical with the Packers when team doctors uncovered a spinal injury, and he retired in October 1993.

During his 11-year NFL career, Dickerson rushed for 13,259 yards on 2,996 carries with 90 touchdowns to rank fourth in total yardage behind Emmitt Smith,* Walter Payton, and Barry Sanders.* He also caught 281 passes for 2,137 yards and six touchdowns. Named to six Pro Bowls and five All-Pro teams, Dickerson was inducted into the Pro Football Hall of Fame in 1999.

The single Dickerson lives in Malibu, California, performing charity and youth work in the Los Angeles area. In response to the 1992 Los Angeles riots, he established a pioneering program "Dickerson's Raiders," providing social, cultural, and athletic activities for preteens. He cohosted *In the Huddle* for Fox Sports with former SMU teammate James, and in 2000–2001 he served as a sideline reporter for ABC's *Monday Night Football*.

Although his final NFL seasons were marred by accusations of malingering, his statistics reveal his excellence. Of the seven running backs to reach 10,000-yards career rushing, Dickerson achieved the mark the fastest in 91 games.

BIBLIOGRAPHY
Eric Dickerson with Steve Delsohn, *On the Run* (New York, 1986); Eric Dickerson with Richard Graham Walsh, *Eric Dickerson Secrets of Pro Power* (New York, 1993); Joe Horrigan and Bob Carroll, *Football Greats* (New York, 1998); William Nack, "He Put the Squeeze on the Juice," *Sports Illustrated* 61 (December 17, 1984), pp. 16–19; Nancy Neilson, *Eric Dickerson* (New York, 1988).

Ron Briley

COREY DILLON   Football
(October, 24, 1975–   )

Corey Dillon of the Cincinnati Bengals ranks among the most outstanding running backs in the National Football League (NFL).

Corey Dillon was born on October 24, 1975 in Seattle, Washington. Although he had contact with his father, Dillon was brought up by his mother, Jerline, in a single-parent household. During adolescence, Dillon encountered numerous brushes with law enforcement officials in Seattle and was convicted of conspiracy to sell cocaine to undercover police. This conviction occurred when he was only 15 years old, but he insists that he never sold drugs. Dillon enjoyed greater success on the athletic fields of Franklin High School in Seattle, where he starred as an All-State running back in football and center fielder in baseball. He was selected by the San Diego Padres (National League) late in the 1993 baseball draft but preferred football. His goal of playing Division I college football, however, was cut short by his failure to meet the National Collegiate Athletic Association's (NCAA)'s minimum academic requirements.

A disappointed Dillon enrolled in the fall of 1993 at Edmonds Community College in Lynwood, Washington, where he tried baseball. He quickly grew tired of the long 90-minute bus ride from home to campus and withdrew after six weeks. He lived with his mother and worked as a night janitor, a job he detested. In order to pursue his dream of playing college football, Dillon entered Garden City (Kansas) Community College in the fall of 1994. Although successful on the football field, he clashed with coach Jeff Leiker and was dismissed from the team. Leiker, however, recommended Dillon to coach Greg Croshaw at Dixie College in St. George, Utah. Dillon made the most of this opportunity at Dixie, rushing for almost 2,000 yards and earning junior college All-America honors.

The University of Washington offered Dillon a football scholarship. In 1996 he set Huskies' records for rushing yardage (1,555), carries (271), and touchdowns (23). Eschewing his senior year of eligibility, he opted for the 1997 NFL draft. His troubled past, however, made some teams wary. The Cincinnati Bengals (NFL) made him the forty-third pick of the draft. Although disappointed at not being drafted higher, he inked a three-year pact with the Bengals.

The 6-foot 1-inch, 225-pound Dillon did not start for the Bengals until 10 games into the 1997 season, but he completed the year with 1,129 rushing yards to establish a new rookie mark for the Cincinnati franchise. The Bengals struggled, but Dillon continued his top-flight rushing in 1998 and 1999 with 1,130 and 1,200 yards, respectively. After the 1999 season, however, he became a restricted free agent and missed three weeks of training camp before signing a one-year extension with the Bengals. During the negotiations, Dillon angered some Cincinnati fans by telling one radio station that he would rather flip burgers than play for the Bengals. Nevertheless, he made amends with the Cincinnati fans by rushing for over 1,400 yards during the 2000 season. He also established the NFL single-game rushing record of 278 yards on October 22, 2000 against the Denver Broncos, eclipsing the mark of 275 yards set by Walter Payton in 1977. Dillon followed up his successful 2000 campaign by signing a five-year multimillion dollar contract with the Bengals and rushing for over 1,300 yards in 2001. He surpassed 1,300 rushing yards for the third consecutive season in 2002 for the 2–14 Bengals. Dillon, who made the Pro Bowl in 1999 and 2000, has rushed for 7,520 yards (4.4-yard average per carry) and 43 touchdowns through 2002.

Off the field, Dillon finally has found some peace after yet more trouble with the law. In March 1998, he was arrested in Seattle for driving under the influence. He pleaded guilty to negligent driving and received two years' probation. After considerable soul searching, Dillon experienced a religious conversion in the spring of 1999. He lives with his wife, Desiree, and three-year-old daughter, Cameron, in their Seattle and Cincinnati homes.

BIBLIOGRAPHY
www.bengals.com/team/players (April 1, 2002); www.bengals.com/press/hobsononline.asp (April 1, 2002); http://espn.go.com/nfl/trainingcamp00.000723clayton/mainbar.html (April 1, 2002); Jeffri Chadiha, "Dillon for Dollars," *Sports Illustrated* 94 (March 5, 2001), pp. 42–45; Cincinnati Bengals, "Corey Dillon," 1999–2002; Cincinnati Bengals, "History Not Hype—Finally," October 25, 2000; John Clayton, "Bengals Convinced Dillon Not Carl Pickens," August 3, 2000.

Ron Briley

CLYDE DREXLER   Basketball
(June 22, 1962–)

Clyde Drexler ranked among the most dominant National Basketball Association (NBA) players as the sport's popularity spread.

Clyde Austin Drexler, nicknamed "The Glide," was born on June 22, 1962 in New Orleans, Louisiana, as one of five children and the son of James Drexler Sr. and Eunice Drexler, a supermarket cashier. His mother brought up the children and later married Manuel Scott, a butcher. Education was paramount in her philosophy and the top priority for her children. The family moved to Houston, Texas when Drexler was age 4. He did not play basketball until his junior year at Sterling High School in Houston. He played basketball two seasons, being named the team's Most Valuable Player (MVP) and making the All-Houston Independent School District first team as a senior.

Drexler attended the University of Houston, teaming with Hakeem Olajuwon* and Larry Micheaux in 1981–1982 to form a group referred to as "Phi Slama Jama." They popularized the "Slam Dunk" with their dramatic, spectacular, and acrobatic attack on the basket, leading the Cougars to two consecutive trips to the National Collegiate Athletic Association (NCAA) Final Four. In the 1983 NCAA Championship game, North Carolina State University upset Houston, 54–52. North Carolina State's Dereck Whittenberg fired up an errant shot that was caught near the basket by unguarded Lorenzo Charles, who "dunked" it in as time expired.

Drexler, who has a tremendous vertical jump, once dunked a ball on a goal that was mounted above 11 feet. In his three-year career at Houston, he scored 1,383 points in 96 games for a 14.4-point average and recorded 948 rebounds for 9.9 boards average. He was named Southwest Conference (SWC) Player of the Year in 1983 and saw his jersey number 22 retired by the University of Houston in February 1997.

Drexler entered the NBA draft following his junior year in 1983 and was selected by the Portland Trail Blazers (NBA) in the first round as the eleventh pick overall. In his rookie year, the 6-foot 7-inch, 222-pounder averaged 7.7 points in 82 games. He became known as "Clyde the Glide" because of his effortless takeoff, his gravity-defying "hang time," and his smooth move to the basket. In his second year, Drexler became a starter. He began 10 straight seasons as one of the NBA's top scorers, averaging between 17.2 and 27.2 points. On January 6, 1989, he scored a career-high 50 points against the Sacramento Kings. Drexler averaged a career-best 27.2 points during the 1988–1989 season. He twice led Portland to the NBA Finals, losing to the Detroit Pistons in 1990 and the Chicago Bulls in 1992. He made the All-NBA Second Team in 1988 and 1991 and the All-NBA Third Team in 1990 and 1995.

The 1991–1992 campaign marked Drexler's most enjoyable season as a Trail Blazer. He averaged 25.0 points (fourth in the NBA), became the second player in Portland history to make the All-NBA First Team, finished second to Michael Jordan* in the MVP voting, and took the Trail Blazers to the NBA Finals against the Chicago Bulls.

Drexler was selected for 10 NBA All-Star games but did not play in the 1997 Classic due to a strained hamstring. Besides averaging 10.7 points in the All-Star games, he also competed in four NBA Slam Dunk contests. A member of the gold-medal-winning 1992 U.S. Olympic basketball "Dream Team," he was selected in 1996 as one of the 50 Greatest Players in NBA History. "Winning the NBA title would be the highlight of my career," he acknowledged, "But right after that, it would be the Olympic gold medal."

Nagging injuries caused Drexler's point production to fall in 1993 and 1994. In February 1995, Portland traded him and Tracy Murray to the Houston Rockets (NBA) for Otis Thorpe, rights to Marcelo Nicola, and a 1995 first-round draft choice. Drexler returned to the city where he played high school and college basketball and reunited with his University of Houston teammate Hakeem Olajuwon.* Drexler left Portland as the Trail Blazers' all-time leader with 18,040 points, 5,339 rebounds, and 1,795 steals.

Although Drexler and Olajuwon adjusted to each other easily, the Rockets were seeded sixth when the 1995 Western Conference playoffs began and were not favored to win their second straight NBA crown. Houston excelled, and Drexler performed amazingly throughout the NBA playoffs. The Rockets upset the Utah Jazz, Phoenix Suns, and San Antonio Spurs, and humiliated the Orlando Magic in four games to capture their second consecutive NBA Championship. Drexler performed incredibly, averaging 20.5 points, 7.0 rebounds, 5.0 assists, and 1.5 steals.

Injuries limited Drexler's playing time over the next three seasons. In March 1998, he announced his retirement. In 15 NBA seasons from 1983–

1984 through 1997–1998, he scored 22,195 points (20.4-point average) and snagged 6,677 rebounds (6.1-boards average) in 1,086 regular season games. Drexler dished out 6,125 assists, made 2,207 steals, and blocked 119 shots. In 145 NBA playoff games, he averaged 20.4 points, 6.9 rebounds, 6.1 assists, and 1.92 steals.

Drexler served two seasons (1998–2000) as head basketball coach at the University of Houston with a 19–39 won-lost record. He moved to the Denver Nuggets (NBA) as special assistant to the general manager in September 2001 and as assistant coach in 2002. He married Gaynell Floyd, a lawyer, in December 1988. They have two sons, Austin and Adam, and two daughters, Elise and Enka.

BIBLIOGRAPHY

"Clyde Drexler," *Players Background*, www.nba.com (2001); "Clyde Drexler," *Players Career Highlights*, www.nba.com (2001); "Clyde Drexler," *Players Statistics*, www.nba.com (2001); J. Kelly, *Clyde Drexler* (Philadelphia, PA, 1998); David L. Porter, ed., *Biographical Dictionary of American Sports 1992–1995 Supplement* (Westport, CT, 1995); *The Sporting News Official NBA Register*, 2002–2003.

John L. Evers

TIM DUNCAN   Basketball
(April 25, 1976–   )

Tim Duncan starred in basketball at Wake Forest University and for the San Antonio Spurs (NBA).

Timothy Theodore Duncan was born on April 25, 1976 in St. Croix, Virgin Islands, the son of William Duncan, a mason and hotel employee, and Ione Duncan, a midwife. Duncan learned swimming from his older sister, Tricia, and by age 13 became one of the top swimmers in the 400-meter freestyle. His swimming career ended in 1989, when Hurricane Hugo destroyed his swimming complex training facility. Without a place to practice, Duncan began to concentrate on basketball.

Duncan attended St. Dunstan's Episcopal High School in St. Croix and began playing basketball as a 6-foot freshman. He grew 10 inches and became one of the Island's best players. "I remember thinking that after basketball season ended, I'd go back to swimming," he recalled, "but then basketball season never ended." As a high school senior, Duncan averaged 25.0 points, 12 rebounds, and 5 blocked shots. Wake Forest University offered him a basketball scholarship. In four seasons at Wake Forest from 1993–1994 through 1996–1997, he led the Demon Deacons to the Atlantic Coast Conference (ACC) Tournament Championship in 1995 and 1996 and to the National Collegiate Athletic Association (NCAA) Division I Tournament all four years. Wake Forest's highest advancement came in 1996, when the University of Kentucky defeated the Demon Deacons, 83–63, in the "Elite Eight" round

Tim Duncan ©Photofest

of the NCAA Tournament. Duncan averaged 16.5 points, 12.3 rebounds, 3.76 blocked shots, and a .577 shooting percentage in 128 games. His best scoring season came in 1996–1997, when he averaged 20.8 points and led the NCAA with 14.7 rebounds. He set the NCAA Division I record with 1,570 rebounds in a four-year career.

Duncan earned the National Player of the Year, Wooden, and Naismith awards and the NCAA Player of the Year in 1996–1997 and made First Team All-America and ACC Player of the Year in 1996 and 1997. He was named Defensive Player of the Year by the National Association of Basketball Coaches (NABC) in 1997 and was selected to the All-ACC First Team in 1995, 1996, and 1997. He led the ACC in blocked shots all four years and in rebounding his last three years. Besides ranking second in NCAA history in career blocked shots with 481, Duncan remains the all-time leader in ACC history in blocked shots and third in ACC history in career rebounds. Wake Forest University retired his jersey number 21 on February 25, 1997.

In June 1997, the 7-foot, 260-pound Duncan earned a Bachelor's degree in psychology. The National Basketball Association (NBA) draft on June 25, 1997 saw Duncan selected as the first pick overall by the San Antonio Spurs (NBA). The Spurs had just suffered through their worst season with a 20–62 won-lost record. He and David Robinson,* the formidable center of the Spurs, combined on an offense utilizing two premier centers to their advantage. When their two centers appeared together in the lineup, the Spurs began to dominate opponents. San Antonio in 1997–1998 compiled 56 victories, 36 more than in 1996–1997, but lost in the second round of the NBA playoffs. In his rookie season, Duncan averaged 21.1 points and 11.9 rebounds during the regular season and led the NBA in double-doubles for the first of four consecutive years with 57. He averaged 20.7 points, 9.0 rebounds, and 2.56 blocked shots in postseason play.

By the 1998–1999 season, the Duncan /Robinson "tandem" began to over-match opponents. Duncan led the Spurs to 37 victories in the strike-shortened 50-game season, tying the Utah Jazz for the best NBA record. He paced the Spurs in scoring with 21.1 points per game, in rebounds with 11.0 per game, and in blocked shots with 2.52 blocks per game. In the first round of the NBA Playoffs, San Antonio defeated the Minnesota Timberwolves, three games to one. The determined Spurs swept the Los Angeles Lakers and the Portland Trail Blazers and advanced to the NBA Championship Series against the New York Knicks. San Antonio dominated the Knicks in five games to capture the franchise's first NBA Championship. In four rounds of the playoffs, Duncan averaged 23.2 points and 11.5 rebounds. In the NBA Finals, he averaged 27.4 points and 14 rebounds. After just two years in the NBA, he had attained superstar status, was named MVP in the NBA Finals, and owned an NBA Championship ring.

The 1999–2000 season saw the Spurs compile a 53–29 won-lost record and Duncan average a career-high 23.2 points and 11.4 rebounds. With four games remaining in the regular season, however, he suffered a torn ligament in his knee and missed the NBA playoffs. He underwent successful surgery in May 2000. Without Duncan in the lineup, the Spurs lost in the first round of the NBA playoffs to the Phoenix Suns.

The following season, the Spurs earned the top seed with 53 victories. Duncan scored a career-high 1,820 points and collected 997 rebounds. San Antonio appeared headed for another NBA title when it easily eliminated the Minnesota Timberwolves and the Dallas Mavericks in the first two rounds of the NBA playoffs. In the Western Conference Finals, the Spurs were eliminated in four straight games by the Los Angeles Lakers. Duncan compiled 412 points for an average of 24.4 points in 13 2000–2001 playoff games, averaging 14.5 rebounds and 2.69 blocked shots. He averaged 23.0 points and 12.3 rebounds against the Lakers in the NBA Finals.

In 2001–2002, Duncan averaged career bests in points, rebounds, assists, and minutes played. He ranked second in the NBA in rebounds with 1,042 (12.7 average), fourth in blocked shots with 203 (2.48 average), and fifth in scoring with 2,089 points (25.5 average), helping San Antonio finish first in the Midwest Division with 58 wins. He averaged 27.6 points per game in the playoffs. The Spurs edged the Seattle SuperSonics in the first round but lost to the Los Angeles Lakers, four to one, in the Western Conference semifinals.

Duncan started at forward for the WC All-Stars in 2003 and led San Antonio to the best regular season record (60–22) in 2002–2003, finishing third in rebounding with 1,043 (12.9 average) and in blocked shots with 237 (2.9 average) and seventh in scoring with 1,884 points (23.3 average) and in field goal percentage (.513). The Spurs defeated the Phoenix Suns, Los Angeles Lakers, and Dallas Mavs en route to the WC crown, with Duncan averaging 24.9 points and 14.8 rebounds overall and 28 points, 11.8 rebounds, and 4.8 assists against the Lakers. Duncan dominated the NBA Finals, in which San Antonio took in six games against the New Jersey Nets. In a sterling Game 1, he totaled 32 points, 20 rebounds, six assists, and seven blocked shots. In the climactic Game 6, he delivered 21-points, 20 rebounds, 10 assists, and eight blocked shots—the closest anyone has come to a quadruple-double in the Finals. He won his second consecutive NBA MVP award and his second NBA Finals MVP award.

Duncan received multiple honors and awards in his six NBA seasons, including being NBA Rookie of the Year and making the NBA All-Rookie First Team in 1998. He made the All-NBA First Team each year, the NBA All-Defensive Second Team in 1998, and the All-Defensive First Team in the other five seasons. He was voted Most Valuable Player (MVP) in the 1999 and 2003 NBA Finals and was selected to play for the U.S. Olympic basketball team. Duncan appeared in the NBA All-Star Game each year except his rookie season and was named co-MVP with Shaquille O'Neal* in the 2000 Classic. Duncan won the ESPY award as NBA Player of the Year in 2002. He won NBA MVP honors in 2001–2002 and 2002–2003, emerging as a dominant force and team leader.

In six NBA seasons, Duncan has compiled 10,324 points and a 22.9-point average in 451 regular season games. He has collected 5,548 rebounds for 12.3 per game and has blocked 1,129 shots for 2.5 per game. In 72 NBA playoff games, he has recorded 1,739 points (24.2-point average), snagged 963 rebounds (13.4 average), and blocked 221 shots (3.1 average).

Duncan married Amy Sherrill, his college sweetheart, in mid-July 2001, in the Bahama Islands. They reside in San Antonio, Texas. He collects knives, watches movies, and plays video games. He helps the American Cancer Society.

BIBLIOGRAPHY
David Du Pree, "Duncan the Quiet Giant of the NBA," *USA Today*, January 29, 2003, pp. 1C–2C; *NCAA Official 1998 Men's College Basketball Record Book* (Overland Park, KS, 1998); *Spurs Game Time–Official Program of the San Antonio Spurs*, 2000–2001; *The Sporting News Official NBA Register*, 2003–2004; "Tim Duncan," *Players Background*, www.nba.com (2001); "Tim Duncan," *Players Career Highlights*, www.nba.com (2001); "Tim Duncan," *Players Career Statistics*, www.nba.com (2001).
John L. Evers

E
_____

ANTHONY ERVIN   Swimming
(May 26, 1981–)

In 2000 Anthony Ervin became the first African American to swim for the United States in the Olympics and win a gold medal in swimming.

Anthony Ervin, the son of Jack Ervin and Sherry Ervin, was born on May 26, 1981, in Burbank, California. Ervin attended William Hart High School in Newhall, California, and ranked as the top high school swim sprinter in the nation in the spring of 1999. He earned California Interscholastic Federation Southern Section Most Valuable Swimmer honors. Stanford University, Auburn University, and the University of South Carolina recruited him, but he finally accepted a swimming scholarship at the University of California in Berkeley.

As a freshman, Ervin placed second in the 50-meter freestyle and 100-meter freestyle in the PAC-10 Championships and participated on the Golden Bears' PAC-10 Champion 200 freestyle and 400 freestyle relays in 2000. He also won the National Collegiate Athletic Association (NCAA) 50-meter (21.21 seconds) and 100-meter (47.36 seconds) freestyle championships and led the Golden Bears' 400-meter freestyle relay team to a NCAA title.

The 2000 indoor swim season marked a breakthrough year of competition for Ervin. He made the U.S. Olympic swim team and trained with Gary Hall Jr. under the tutelage of coach Mike Bottom. Bottom called Ervin "the best racer I've ever seen," but the U.S. sprint team members "didn't like him at first" because he seemed overconfident and standoffish. During the training period before the Sydney, Australia, Olympic Games, Ervin and Hall became friends.

On September 16, 2000, at the Sydney Olympics, Ervin won a silver medal with the 4×100-meter relay team. The U.S. relay team broke the old world record, placing second to Australia. Eleven days later, Ervin and Hall tied for the gold medal in the 50-meter freestyle in 21.98 seconds before 17,000 screaming spectators. Only one other tie had occurred in Olympic swim history.

After his gold medal performance, Ervin recalled, "I started out just trying to make the team. A month ago that was in doubt. Now, I'm at the top of the mountain." When asked about his African American heritage, he responded,

"I want to be a role model, but I want to be a role model for all kids. People try to say I'm one thing or another. I don't think it's a big deal being from mixed heritage these days in America."

The 6-foot 2-inch, 165-pound Ervin returned to international competition the next year to win the 2001 World Championship in the 50-meter freestyle race in 22.09 seconds at Fukuoka, Japan. He placed second in the 100-meter freestyle at the Maine Messe in Fukuoka in July 2001 and broke the American record in the 100-meter freestyle in 48.33 seconds three days later.

BIBLIOGRAPHY
Keith McClellan, Telephone interviews with Mary Wagner, U.S. Swimming, 2001; Quinn Knapp, *San Francisco Chronicle*, 2001; and Scott Ball, swimming specialist, University of California Media Relations, 2001; Leigh Montville, "Double Take: The Surprisingly Strong American Swimmers Got the Biggest Surprise of All When Anthony Ervin and Gary Hall, Jr. Won in a Dead Heat," *Sports Illustrated* 93 (October 2, 2000), pp. 51ff; University of California, Media Services, Men's Swimming and Diving.

Keith McClellan

PATRICK EWING   Basketball
(August 5, 1962–   )

Patrick Ewing won acclaim as a tenacious player with Georgetown University and the New York Knicks of the National Basketball Association (NBA).

Patrick Aloysius Ewing was born on August 5, 1962 in Kingston, Jamaica, the son of Carl Ewing and Dorothy Ewing. As a youngster, Ewing played cricket and soccer. After moving to Cambridge, Massachusetts, in 1975, he began playing basketball. His first organized games took place at the Achievement School, where he worked on his language skills. A 1980 graduate of Cambridge Latin High School, Ewing, who already had reached his full height of 7 feet, led the Falcons as a center to three consecutive state championships and became the most-sought-after college recruit in the nation.

Ewing attended Georgetown University between 1981 and 1985, earning a Bachelor's degree in fine arts. He played basketball under legendary coach John Thompson, leading the Hoyas to a four-year 121–23 regular-season won-lost record and a 15–3 mark in National Collegiate Athletic Association (NCAA) Tournament games. He appeared in three NCAA Division I Championship games, helping Georgetown defeat the University of Houston 84–75 in 1984 to gain the national title. The Hoyas lost, 63–62, to the University of North Carolina in 1982, and 66–64, to Villanova University in 1985. Ewing was named Player of the Year by the Associated Press, *The Sporting News*, and the National Association of Basketball Coaches in 1985, Naismith Award winner in 1985, consensus All-America in 1983, and a unanimous All-America in 1984 and 1985. Ewing also played on the gold-medal-winning United States Olympic basketball teams in 1984 and 1992, was selected for

Patrick Ewing ©Photofest

the NCAA Tournament All-Decade Team of the 1980s, was chosen NCAA Tournament Most Valuable Player (MVP) in 1984, and made the NCAA All-Tournament Team in 1982 and 1985. Nicknamed the "Hoya Destroya" for his intimidation when playing defense around the basket, he remains George-town's all-time leader in rebounds (1,316) and blocked shots (493). His 2,184 career points rank him second, behind Eric "Sleepy" Floyd (2,304).

Ewing was selected by the New York Knicks (NBA) in the first round as the first pick overall of the 1985 National Basketball Association (NBA) draft. Ewing was known more for his defensive skills than for his scoring ability, but soon became an exceptional and deadly shooter in and around the basket. In 15 seasons with the Knicks, he became one of the NBA's top players. Ewing became an offensive threat during his first NBA season, averaging 20 points and being named Rookie of the Year. During the next two seasons, he continued averaging 20 points while collecting eight-plus rebounds a game. He established single-season records in points scored (2,347) and blocked shots (327) in 1989–1990, his best individual season. On March 4, 1990, Ewing scored a career-high 51 points and grabbed 18 rebounds against the Boston Celtics. In 1991 he became the fifth player in Knicks history to score 10,000 career points.

The Knicks hired Pat Riley as their coach in 1991, the sixth coach in Ewing's seven seasons. Ewing established a new one-game rebounding high, with 26 boards against the Miami Heat on December 19, 1992, but, for the third straight year, New York lost to the Chicago Bulls in the playoffs. In the 1993–1994 season, he led the Knicks to the NBA Finals, only to lose Game Seven and the NBA Championship to the Houston Rockets. On December 16, 1993, Ewing became the Knicks all-time leading scorer by eclipsing Walt Frazier's 15,581 points. He completed the season with 16,191 career points. After starting slowly in the 1994–1995 season due to knee surgery, Ewing returned to form the following season. On November 19, 1996, he became the twenty-third player in NBA history to reach 20,000 career points. He joined 21 other NBA players to be named an All-Star at least 10 times.

Ewing made the elite list of 50 Greatest NBA Players of All-Time. On March 30, 1999, he recorded his 10,000th career rebound to become only the tenth player in NBA history to combine 22,000 points with 10,000 rebounds. He was named to the All-NBA First Team in 1990, the All-NBA Second Team in 1988, 1989, 1991, 1992, 1993, 1997, and the All-NBA defensive Second Team in 1988, 1989, and 1992.

Following the 1996–1997 season, Ewing's point production and rebounds per game decreased sharply. On September 21, 2000, the New York Knicks acquired Luc Longley in a four-team deal that sent Ewing to the Seattle Supersonics (NBA). Ewing became the first player traded after 15 years with one team since Dolph Schayes of the Syracuse Nationals in 1963. After being elected president of the NBA Players Association in 1997, he represented the players during the lockout in 1998 and eventually worked out an agreement.

Ewing completed his 15-year career with New York as the NBA's thirteenth all-time leading scorer with 23,665 regular-season points. He paced the Knicks in games (1,039) and minutes played (37,586), career points, field goals made (9,260) and attempted (18,224), free throws made (5,126) and attempted (6,904), rebounds (10,759), blocked shots (2,758), and steals (1,061). He appeared in 135 NBA playoff games with New York, averaging 20.6 points, 10.5 rebounds, and 2.99 blocked shots.

With Seattle in 2000–2001, Ewing scored 760 points (9.6 average), posted 585 rebounds (7.4 average), and registered 92 assists, 53 steals, and 91 blocked shots in 79 regular-season games. The Orlando Magic (NBA) signed Ewing as a free agent in July 2001. He played a reserve role in 2001–2002, tallying 6.0 points a game. The Charlotte Hornets eliminated Orlando in the first round of the playoffs, as Ewing averaged 6.5 points per game.

Ewing retired following the 2001–2002 season. In 17 NBA campaigns, he scored 24,815 points (21.0 average), with 11,607 rebounds (9.8 average) and 2,894 blocked shots (2.5 average) in 1,183 regular-season games. He ranks fourth on the NBA career list in blocked shots, tenth in personal fouls (4,034), thirteenth in points, and nineteenth in rebounds. The Knicks retired Ewing's number 33 jersey in February 2003.

Ewing and his wife, Rita, have two daughters, Randi and Corey, and a son, Patrick Jr. He considers "graduating from Georgetown University with a Fine

Arts degree his finest moment as fulfillment of his late mother Dorothy's dream."

BIBLIOGRAPHY

NCAA Men's Basketball's Finest, 1998; "Patrick Ewing," *Player*, www.nba.com (2000); "Patrick Ewing," *Player Profile*, www.nba.com (2001); David L. Porter, ed., *Biographical Dictionary of American Sports—Basketball and Other Indoor Sports* (Westport, CT, 1989); *The Sporting News Official NBA Register*, 2002–2003.

John L. Evers

F

MARSHALL FAULK   Football
(February 26, 1973–   )

Marshall Faulk may be the best current National Football League (NFL) running back and ranks among the most determined and hardworking.

Marshall William Faulk was born on February 26, 1973 in New Orleans, Louisiana, the sixth son of Roosevelt Faulk, a truck driver, and Cecile Faulk, a department store clerk and housekeeper. Faulk grew up in the 1,800-unit Desire Housing Project in New Orleans, a complex known for broken plumbing and windows, violence, and drug abuse. He witnessed shootings, people overdosed on drugs, and youth gangs living on the streets. His parents divorced when he was 4 years old. He lived with his mother during the school year and spent summers with his father.

Faulk began playing football at age 7 and performed in the New Orleans Recreation Department League. In the eighth grade, he began practicing with the Carver High School varsity football team. The next year, Carver coach Wayne Reese played him at running back, quarterback, wide receiver, defensive back, punt returner, and punter. Reese taught him the fundamentals of the game and instilled in him a love for the game, personal discipline, and the motivation to attend college. Faulk exhibited diligence both in his studies and on the gridiron.

Faulk made the varsity football team as a freshman at San Diego State University and scored a touchdown against Long Beach State University in his first game. The following week, he established a National Collegiate Athletic Association (NCAA) record by rushing for 386 yards and scoring seven touchdowns on 37 carries against University of the Pacific. As a freshman, he amassed 1,429 yards, rushed for 21 touchdowns, caught two touchdown passes, and became the first freshman in history to lead the nation in rushing, averaging 159 yards and 15.6 points per game. Faulk broke or tied 13 NCAA records despite missing three games with a punctured lung and broken ribs. As a sophomore in 1992, he rushed for 1,630 yards and finished second in the Heisman Award voting. He rushed for 1,530 yards and 21 touchdowns in his junior year. When the San Diego State coaching staff was fired after that season, Faulk, a public administration major, skipped his senior year and entered the NFL draft.

The Indianapolis Colts (NFL) selected Faulk as the second player taken in the 1994 draft. In his first regular season game, he rushed for 143 yards and scored three touchdowns against the Houston Oilers. During 1994, he amassed 1,282 yards and 11 touchdowns to earn NFL Offensive Rookie of the Year. Named a starter for the American Football Conference (AFC), he was voted Pro Bowl Most Valuable Player (MVP). Faulk set a Pro Bowl rushing record with 180 yards and gained 27 yards on pass receptions. He established eight Colts' records and tied a ninth in 1994.

Between 1995 and 1998, Faulk rushed for more than 1,000 yards each season except 1996 when he missed three games due to injuries. In 1998, he rushed for 1,319 yards and caught 86 passes for 908 yards. Despite his great year, the Colts finished with a dismal 3–13 record. On April 15, 1999, Indianapolis traded him to the St. Louis Rams (NFL) for second- and fifth-round draft picks. Faulk supplied the ingredient needed to transform the 4–12 basement-dwelling Rams into 13–3 Super Bowl XXXIV champions. The 5-foot 10-inch, 210-pound running back performed with amazing consistency all season, recording seven 100-yard rushing games and one 200-yard receiving game. He finished with 1,381 rushing yards, caught 87 passes for 1,048 yards, and scored 12 touchdowns. His 2,429 total yards from scrimmage broke the single-season record of Barry Sanders.* He caught five passes for 90 yards but was limited to 17 yards rushing in the Rams' 23–16 triumph over the Tennessee Titans in Super Bowl XXXIV.

Although he missed two games with a knee injury in 2000, Faulk set an NFL record with 26 touchdowns. He enjoyed seven multiple touchdown games, collected 2,189 combined yards rushing and receiving, and earned NFL MVP and Offensive Player of the Year awards for the 10–6 Rams. The next season, he attained a career-high 1,382 rushing yards, exceeded 2,100 combined yards rushing and receiving for a fourth consecutive year, and scored 21 touchdowns on his way to a second NFL MVP award and a third Offensive Player of the Year accolade. Faulk returned home to New Orleans for Super Bowl XXXVI. The New England Patriots held him to 76 yards to upset the highly favored Rams, 20–17.

On July 26, 2002, head coach Mike Martz made Faulk the overall team captain. Three days later, Faulk signed a seven-year, $44 million contract that included a $9.3 million signing bonus. He agreed to restructure his contract to defer some of his salary so the team could stay under the salary cap and enable the Rams to keep other top players. He struggled with injuries in 2002, rushing for 953 yards (4.5-yard average) and making 80 receptions for 537 yards (6.7-yard average) and two touchdowns for the 7–9 Rams. Faulk made the Pro Bowl for the sixth time. He entered the 2003 season with 10,395 rushing yards, an average of 4.4 yards per carry, and 87 touchdowns in 135 games.

Faulk formed the Marshall Faulk Foundation to work for the improvement of community life for youth in St. Louis and New Orleans. His foundation includes the Rams 28 Club, the Lift for Life Gym, and the Right Step Shoe program. The Rams 28 Club encourages education and community service opportunities for youth, while Lift for Life Gym promotes physical conditioning and personal discipline for young people and the Right Step Shoe program supplies shoes for poor children. Faulk participates in charity auctions, golf tournaments, and football camps in St. Louis. "I help inner city youth because I am an inner city youth," he said. The "Marshall Plan" helping poor kids remains his passion as much as football.

BIBLIOGRAPHY
Cliff Charpentier, *2001 Fantasy Football Digest* (Minneapolis, MN, 2001); David Kindervater, "Marshall Faulk," *Pigskin Planet* (pigskinplanet.com, 2001), pp. 1–4; James Loving, "MARSHALL FAULK—Winner never quits," *National Radio Text Service* (February 1, 2002), pp. 1–3; Rob Rains, *Marshall Faulk: Rushing to Glory* (Champaign, IL, 1999); Jim Thomas, "Faulk Signs 7-Year Contract," *St. Louis Post-Dispatch*, July 30, 2002, pp. E1, E7; Jim Thomas, "Martz Names Captains, Calls Faulk Overall Leader," *St. Louis Post-Dispatch*, July 29, 2002, p. C7.
Frank J. Olmsted

LISA FERNANDEZ   Softball
(February 22, 1971–)

Lisa Fernandez ranks among the greatest softball players ever.

Lisa Fernandez was born in Lakewood, California, on February 22, 1971 to Antonio Fernandez and Emilia Fernandez. Both of her parents had an athletic background: Her father performed semiprofessional baseball in Cuba, and her mother, a Puerto Rican immigrant, avidly played stickball as a youngster in New York. They played slow-pitch softball together in Lakewood. Fernandez started playing slow-pitch softball at age 4 and fast-pitch softball by age 8. In her first game as a pitcher, she lost, 28–0, and at age 8 she walked 20 batters. She lost her first high school game and her initial college contest as well.

Fernandez developed as a pitcher, infielder, and hitter in high school. The 5-foot 6-inch right-hander hurled an incredible 69 shutouts in four years at St. Joseph High School in Long Beach, California. From 1990 to 1993 at UCLA, her pitching and batting statistics were almost mythical. She compiled a 93–7 won-lost record and a .930 career-winning percentage, establishing a National Collegiate Athletic Association (NCAA) record. In 1993 Fernandez led the nation with a .510 batting average and 0.23 ERA. She drove hits to all fields, compiling a career .382 batting average and establishing UCLA records for singles (225), runs scored (142), walks (65), hits (287), no-hitters (11), wins (93), and winning percentage (.930). She boasted a four-year 0.22 ERA before receiving a Bachelor of Arts degree in psychology in 1995.

Fernandez was selected All-America four times, Amateur Softball Association (ASA) Sportswoman of the Year in 1991 and 1992, Honda-Broderick Award winner three times, and Honda Cup winner in 1993. With Fernandez

Lisa Fernandez ©Donald Miralle/Getty Images

on the mound, the Bruins needed only a run or two to win. She usually had a role in producing those runs, too. No player equaled her in the college ranks.

Fernandez played on U.S. softball teams that won gold medals at the 1990 International Softball Federation (ISF) Women's World Championship, the 1991 Pan American Games, the 1992 Women's Challenger Cup in Beijing, China, the 1993 Intercontinental Cup in the Netherlands, the 1994 South Pacific Classic in Sydney, Australia, and the 1994 ISF World Championship in Canada. She led the United States to the gold medal in softball at the 1995 Pan American qualifying games in Guatemala, batting an incredible .511 and tossing a perfect game. She was named Women's Major Fast Pitch National Championship Most Valuable Player (MVP) in 1991 and 1992, and Women's Sports Foundation (WSF) Athlete of the Year in 1994.

Despite her spectacular accomplishments, Fernandez still had mountains to conquer. She made the U.S. Olympic softball team in 1996 in Atlanta, Georgia, hitting .348 and holding opposing teams with an incredible 0.33 ERA. She defeated China, 1–0, in the semifinals and picked up a save against China and a gold medal for Team USA in the championship game. When not on the mound, she played third base.

Fernandez continued to lead Team USA to victories in various world competitions from 1996 to 2000. She won all three starts without giving up an earned run in the 1999 Canada Cup competition, taking home the gold medal. She led the United States to more gold in the 1999 Pan American Games, triumphing in all three starts and hurling a no-hitter against Cuba.

Heading into the Sydney, Australia, Olympics in 2000, Team USA enjoyed a 112-game winning streak. Team USA, however, was stunned twice with extra-inning losses, but the horizon still looked bright with ace Fernandez on the mound against Australia. For 12 innings, she yielded just one hit while fanning 25 Aussie batters. In the bottom of the thirteenth frame, a runner was placed on second base as is done in every extra inning after the ninth. Fernandez retired the first two hitters but surrendered a home run and the game to Australia. The defeat marked the first time Team USA had ever lost three games in succession. The Americans needed to win five straight games to take the gold medal. Fernandez, however, put the United States into the medal round by shutting out Italy, 6–0, and clouting a two-run homer. She then defeated Australia with another stellar, 13-strikeout, 1–0 performance. In the championship game, Fernandez allowed Japan just three hits and helped Team USA snatch Olympic gold with a stunning 2–1 victory. She said it was a "tremendous lift for us to look up in the stands and see the USA baseball team and women's soccer team yelling, 'Lisa! Lisa! Lisa! Oi! Oi! Oi!'."

Fernandez has served as pitching and hitting coach for the UCLA women's softball team since 1996 and was named 1999 ASA USA Softball Female Athlete of the Year. She has been featured in over 30 magazines and newspapers and has designed and presented more than 50 softball and motivational camps and clinics across the United States. She accepts numerous speaking engagements for organizations like the WSF. Her strongest advice to women athletes is "to make certain they take advantage of the education available to them as a result of their athletic skills. My advice would be to keep your school work as a priority. Sports will get the coaches to look at you and even offer you a scholarship, but only grades will get you into the University."

BIBLIOGRAPHY
Jason King, "Olympic Pitcher Lisa Fernandez Inspires at Luncheon," *Kansas City Star* Sports on line (February 8, 2001), pp. 1–3; Greg Lewis, "Golden Arm," *Bruinwalk: Daily Bruin Online* (October 11, 2000), pp. 1–4; UCLA Athletic Department, "Lisa Fernandez Profile," *Softball* (2001); USA Softball, "2000 Olympic Games: USA Softball Player Bio: Lisa Fernandez," *Official Site of USA Softball* (Summer 2000), pp. 1–2; USA Today, "Softball: Olympic Team Biographies," *USA Today Online* (1996), pp. 2–3.

Frank J. Olmsted

TONY FERNANDEZ   Baseball
(June 30, 1962–   )

Tony Fernandez holds the all-time major league record for hits by a Dominican player.

Octavio Antonio Fernandez was born on June 30, 1962 in San Pedro, de

Macaris, Dominican Republic. His parents, Jose Fernandez and Andrea Fernandez, supported 11 children by sugar cane work. Fernandez attended Gaston Fernando de Ligne High School and was signed as an undrafted free agent at age 17 by the Toronto Blue Jays (American League). He played professional baseball for 22 seasons, and repaid the Blue Jays as an excellent fielder, good base runner, high-average hitter, and a winner. He played for Toronto 12 seasons and holds the all-time Blue Jay records for most hits (1,565), doubles (287), triples (72), and games played (1,402). His career included stints with seven major league teams and the Seibu Lions (Japanese Pacific League).

Fernandez began his career with Kinston, North Carolina (Carolina League) in 1980 at age 17. The next season, he played 75 games for Kinston and made the All-Star team at shortstop before being promoted to Syracuse, New York (International League). He suffered his first serious injury soon after and missed the rest of the 1981 season. Fernandez enjoyed a strong year for Syracuse in 1982, making the IL All-Star team and being named Syracuse's Most Valuable Player (MVP). The 1983 season marked another successful year for Fernandez at Syracuse and earned him his first promotion to the major leagues. He made his major league debut with Toronto on September 2, 1983.

A broken bone in his hand forced Fernandez to start the 1984 season at Syracuse, but the Toronto Blue Jays recalled him to the major leagues permanently. In 1985 he started 159 of 161 games at shortstop and batted .289. He hit .333 in the 1985 AL Championship Series, which Toronto lost to the Kansas City Royals. In 1986 Fernandez played in his first All-Star game. He led the AL in fielding (.983) and putouts (294), and won his first of four straight Gold Gloves. He also collected 213 hits, the most ever by a Blue Jay or any shortstop.

Fernandez spent four more seasons with Toronto, becoming one of the all-time best from that organization. He was traded in December 1990 in a blockbuster exchange of top stars with the San Diego Padres (National League). First basemen Fred McGriff* accompanied Fernandez to San Diego for second baseman Roberto Alomar* and outfielder Joe Carter. Fernandez played two years with the Padres, making the NL All-Star team in 1992. He was traded in October 1992 to the New York Mets (NL) but did not stay long with New York before returning to the Toronto Blue Jays in June 1993. This gave him the opportunity to play on the World Championship team that year. He batted .318 in the AL Championship Series against the Chicago White Sox and .333 in the World Series against the Atlanta Braves.

Fernandez became a free agent and signed with the Cincinnati Reds (NL) in March 1994. After one season with Cincinnati, he signed as a free agent with the New York Yankees (AL) in December 1994. He had a subpar season with the Yankees in 1995, batting only .245 and being sidelined with injuries twice. Fernandez missed the entire 1996 season because of a broken elbow. He showed his versatility by playing second base, third base, or shortstop.

In December 1996, Fernandez got his career back on track, signing as a free agent with the Cleveland Indians (AL). He batted .286 in 1997 and starred in the playoffs and the World Series, belting a home run against the Baltimore Orioles in Game Six of the AL Championship Series to break a scoreless tie in the eleventh inning and give the AL pennant to Cleveland. He hit .471 in the World Series against the Florida Marlins.

After two more solid seasons with the Blue Jays, Fernandez took his talents to Seibu, Japan (Japanese Pacific League) for the 2000 season. He compiled a .327 batting average, fourth best in the JPL and second best for a non-Japanese player. The 2001 season saw him play briefly with the Milwaukee Brewers (NL) before his release. Fernandez signed with the Toronto Blue Jays again and finished the 2001 season there. He retired following the 2001 campaign. In his playing days, Fernandez seldom let his teams down. During his 17 major league seasons, he batted .288 with 2,276 hits, 94 home runs, 844 runs batted in, and 246 stolen bases.

Fernandez resides in Boca Raton, Florida with his wife, Clara, and his three sons, Joel, Jonathan, and Abraham. He supported the baseball program in the Dominican Republic, where a Little League was named in his honor.

BIBLIOGRAPHY
San Diego Padres Media Guide, 1992; Tony Fernandez file, National Baseball Hall of Fame, Cooperstown, NY; *Toronto Blue Jays Media Guide*, 1999.

John E. Mosher

VONETTA FLOWERS   Bobsled
(October 29, 1973–)

In 2002 Vonetta Jeffery Flowers became the first African American to win a gold medal at the Winter Olympic Games, triumphing in the women's bobsled event.

Vonetta Jeffery Flowers was born on October 29, 1973 in Birmingham, Alabama, the daughter of Jimmie Jeffery and Barbara Jeffery, a domestic worker. When her parents divorced, she and her three brothers lived with their mother.

Flowers's interest in track and field was kindled at an early age. At age 9, she ran so fast her coach thought her sprint times belonged to a 13-year-old boy. A 1993 graduate of Jackson-Olin High School in Birmingham, she captured the Track Athletic Congress (TAC) National Championship in the 15–16 age group, made the All-State team in basketball, and ran for the Birmingham Striders Track Club.

Flowers attended the University of Alabama in Birmingham (UAB), earning a Bachelor of Science degree in physical education in 1997. She married Johnny Mack Flowers, a member of the Blazers football and track and field teams, in 1999.

At UAB, Flowers achieved enormous success in track and field. She competed in the long jump, triple jump, 100 meters, 200 meters, and relay teams.

She remains the school's recordholder in six individual events and two team events, and she retains three freshman marks. A four-year letter-winner, a seven-time National Collegiate Athletic Association (NCAA) All-America, and a six-time Great Midwest Conference (GMC) Most Valuable Player (MVP), she earned 35 GMC awards. She was named Newcomer of the Year in 1993 and Most Outstanding Athlete at the GMC Outdoor Championship, winning GMC blue ribbons in the 100 meters, 200 meters, the long jump, and the triple jump.

Flowers served as a graduate assistant at the University of Alabama between 1997 and 1999, coaching the field events and being head equipment manager. She returned to UAB in 1999, when she was named assistant coach to the cross country and track and field teams. Flowers, a three-time member of the U.S. Olympic Festival Team, earned a gold medal in the long jump in 1994 and the 4×100 meter relay in 1995. A nine-time USA Track and Field National Champion qualifier, a World University Game qualifier in 1995, and the 1996 Penn Relays long-jump champion, she has been ranked among the top 10 in the United States three times in the long jump.

Flowers had the talent to become a U.S. Olympic track and field team member as a sprinter and long jumper, but unfortunately injuries stymied her. She was unable to qualify in the 100 meters for the 1996 Summer Games in Atlanta, Georgia. Because of ankle surgery in the summer of 2000, she finished twelfth in the long jump and did not make the U.S. Olympic team for the Sydney, Australia games.

At this point, Flowers nearly quit participation in sports. When her husband told her about a USA Bobsled Team tryout, however, she decided to participate. She readily excelled in a six-event test that included sprinting, jumping, and putting a shot to earn a trial for the Olympic bobsled track team.

Bonnie Warner, a former Olympic luge athlete converted to bobsled driver, needed an athlete who could supply speed and power to get fast starts. In the fall of 2000, she and Flowers began racing as a team. In 2001 they ranked second in the United States and third in the world, while Flowers became the USA Push Champion and recordholder with a push time of 5.78 seconds. The team finished among the top 10 in all seven World Cup races in 2000–2001 and closed the season with four straight top three finishes, placing third in the overall World Cup standings. They also finished second at the national team selection in 2000 and eighth at the 2001 World Championship.

Flowers switched drivers for the 2001–2002 season, joining Jill Bakken as her push/brakeman. They took second place in the U.S. Olympic Trials and qualified for the 2002 U.S. Olympic team.

In the 2002 Winter Olympic Games at Salt Lake City, Utah, Flowers and Bakken were the tenth of 15 qualifying sleds. In their first run, they set a course record of 48.81 seconds. Their composite time following two runs stood at 1 minute 37 seconds, enough to capture the gold medal. No other African American had ever won a gold medal in the winter games. Flowers had pushed a 450-pound sled in an Olympic sport where American men had not won anything in 46 years. Debi Thomas, the only other African American to earn an Olympic medal in the Winter Games, won the bronze medal in figure skating in 1988. Flowers and Bakken were selected to carry the Olympic flag at the closing ceremonies, with Flowers being named the winner of the 2002 U.S. Olympic Team Spirit Award. The media praised Flowers as "a speed-suited Jackie Robinson, kicking the door in for future black Winter Olympians."

Flowers acknowledged that "This was a leap of faith. The way I see it, God put me in this sport for a reason." Johnny Flowers, her coach and husband, said, "God got us to this point. Vonetta is not strong enough to push that 450-pound sled and make it go that fast. I knew that it was prayer from many people that allowed the team to do what they did." They have twin sons, Jaden and Jorden.

BIBLIOGRAPHY
"Vonetta Flowers," *About Vonetta*, www.vonettaflowers.com (2001); "Vonetta Flowers," *Athlete Bios*, www.olympicgames.com (2002); "Vonetta Flowers," *Career Record*, www.usbsf.com (2002); "Vonetta Flowers," *Flowers' Story Is Wonderful, Wired*, www.freep.com (2002); "Vonetta Flowers," *Heart of Gold*, www. birminghamchristian.com (2002); "Vonetta Flowers," *Profile*, www.fansonly.com (2002); "Vonetta Flowers," *Realizing a Dream in the Coolest Way*, www.ajc.com (2002).

John L. Evers

G

ANDRES GALARRAGA   Baseball
(June 18, 1961–   )

Baseball is filled with wonderful stories involving sluggers promising a child they visited in a hospital to hit a home run at a game or other players battling some sort of adversity to reach the major leagues. Fans love to see the underdog prevail. Andres Galarraga, nicknamed the "Big Cat" because of his elegant defensive plays around first base for the San Francisco Giants (National League), is just one of these stories.

In February 1999, as spring training was getting under way for the Atlanta Braves (NL), Galarraga became the classic underdog. After completing 14 seasons in the major leagues, Galarraga suffered a nagging back pain and visited Atlanta's Piedmont Hospital to have it checked out. Doctors diagnosed his problem as lymphoma of the lumbar spine. His stellar career was put on hold so that he could deal with this critical situation. He, his wife Eneyda, and three daughters Andria, Katherine, and Andrianna, headed home to Caracas, Venezuela, so that the 37-year-old All-Star could receive the chemotherapy and radiation treatments.

Andres Jose Galarraga was born on June 18, 1961 in Caracas, Venezuela, the son of Francisco Galarraga, a house painter, and Juana Galarraga, a domestic maid. The 6-foot 3-inch, 235-pound first baseman, who bats and throws right-handed, attended Enrique Fermi High School in Caracas and signed with the Montreal Expos in January 1979 as a nondrafted free agent. The sure-handed first baseman spent six and a half years in the minor leagues before being brought up by Montreal in August 1986. The Big Cat made his first major league hit off Los Angeles Dodgers pitcher Rick Honeycutt on August 23 and hit his first major league home run against the St. Louis Cardinals close to one month later.

During 1987, Galarraga posted 90 runs batted in (RBI) and a .305 batting average. The following year, he knocked in 92 runs and hit .302, joining Rusty Staub (1970–1971) as the only Montreal players to collect consecutive 90 RBI seasons. The 1988 season marked the first of two *The Sporting News* Silver Slugger Awards (1988, 1996) for Galarraga. He led the NL in hits (184), doubles (42), and batting (.305), earning his first trip to the All-Star Game. He finished in the top 10 of 12 different offensive categories. After a knee injury sidelined him for part of the 1991 season, the Big Cat was traded to the St. Louis Cardinals (NL) for pitcher Ken Hill. He played for St. Louis in 1992 and was signed that November by the new expansion team, the Colorado Rockies (NL).

During 1993 with the Rockies, Galarraga did not let the fans down. He became the first player on an expansion team and the first Venezuelan to win a batting title. He batted .370 to equal Tony Gwynn's* 1987 season efforts, marking the NL's highest average since Stan Musial achieved a .376 mark in 1948. An All-Star for only the second time in nine seasons, he became the first Colorado player ever to represent his team at the midsummer Classic.

During 1995, Galarraga led the Rockies to their first ever postseason, broke the 100-RBI mark for the first time, and clouted 31 home runs for the second consecutive season. The Rockies lost to the Atlanta Braves in the NL Division Series, blowing a commanding 3-games-to-0 lead. The 1996 and 1997 seasons saw Galarraga extend his reputation as a premier NL power-hitter. He returned to the All-Star Game for the third time and led the NL in home runs (47) and RBIs (150) in 1996 and RBIs (140) in 1997.

The 1998 season brought a change of scenery for the Galarraga family. They moved to Atlanta, Georgia, where the Big Cat showcased his abilities for the Braves (NL). A reporter asked teammate Walt Weiss whether Galarraga could adjust. Weiss replied, "If you can hit, you can hit." Galarraga set Braves records for first basemen with 41 home runs and 121 RBIs. He reached the 300 career home run mark, enjoyed another .300 batting season, and a .595 slugging average. He made it back to the All-Star Game and the postseason. His postseason ended when the San Diego Padres ousted the Braves in the NL Championship Series and the Big Cat committed a record four errors at first base. After being treated for lymphoma in 1999, Galarraga faced incredible adversity in returning to the majors. His passion for oil painting while recovering from all the different therapies was not enough to tide him over. He wanted to play, make contact with the ball, and be around his teammates. After being out of baseball for 17 months, he was considered cured and returned to the team. John Schuerholz, the Braves general manager, called the Big Cat "their spiritual leader."

Everyone in baseball wanted Galarraga the Big Cat with the big smile to succeed. According to teammate Greg Maddux, "it's hard to put a number on the importance of chemistry, but that's where he's huge. You see it," Maddux added, "You feel it. That's what he brings." Galarraga played for the Texas Rangers (American League) and San Francisco Giants (NL) in 2001, returned to the Montreal Expos in 2002, and rejoined the San Francisco Giants in 2003. During 18 major league seasons, he has batted .288 with 398 home runs, 1,423 RBIs, and a .499 slugging percentage. Galarraga hit .301 in limited action in 2003 and went hitless in five at-bats in the NL Division Series against the Florida Marlins.

BIBLIOGRAPHY

Andres Galarraga Statistics—Baseball-Reference.com, www.baseball-reference.com/ g/galaran01.shtml., *Atlanta Braves Media Guide*, 2000; Ray Glier, "Galarraga's

Out of Coors, But Big Cat Still Has Bite," *USA Today Baseball Weekly*, May 13–19, 1998, p. 5; S.L. Price, "Cat & Mouth Game," *Sports Illustrated* 92 (March 13, 2000), pp. 40–45; Tracy Ringolsby, Galarraga Diagnosed with Cancerous Tumor, InsideDenver.com; *Rocky Mountain News*, http://insidedenver.com/rockies/0219and r1.shtml; National Baseball Library, Cooperstown, NY.

Scot E. Mondore

FREDDY GARCIA   Baseball
(October 6, 1976–   )

Freddy Garcia has developed into a star major league pitcher.

Freddy Antonio Garcia, a 6-foot 4-inch, 235-pound right-handed pitcher for the Seattle Mariners (American League), was born on October 6, 1976 in Caracas, Venezuela. The Houston Astros (National League) originally signed Garcia in October 1993 at age 17. He attended the Astros' baseball academy in Valencia, Venezuela, with future major leaguers Bobby Abreu* and Carlos Guillen.

Garcia began his professional baseball career in 1994 with the Dominican Astros (Dominican Summer League), finishing with 4 wins, 6 losses, and a 5.29 earned run average (ERA). With the Gulf Coast Florida Astros (Gulf Coast League) in 1995, he won 6 and lost 3 with a 4.47 ERA and exhibited excellent control, allowing 14 walks and 58 strikeouts in 58.1 innings. Garcia experienced some elbow problems in 1996 but still managed 5 wins, 4 losses, and a 3.12 ERA at Class A Quad City, Iowa (Midwest League). He struggled in early 1997 with Class A Kissimmee, Florida (Florida State League). After losing his first five decisions, he finished the season strong and led the FSL in complete games and shutouts. He ranked fifth in ERA (2.56) with a 10–8 won-lost record.

Garcia began the 1998 season with Class AA Jackson, Texas (Texas League). Poor run support led to a 6–7 won-lost record, but Garcia held opposing batters to a .215 batting average and led the TL in ERA (3.24). He was named to the TL All-Star team despite being promoted to Class AAA New Orleans, Louisiana (Pacific Coast League) in July. Garcia started two games for New Orleans with one triumph before being traded that July with infielder Carlos Guillen and pitcher John Halama to the Seattle Mariners (American League) for pitcher Randy Johnson. He finished the year with Seattle's Class AAA team at Tacoma, Washington (PCL), faring 3–1 with a 3.86 ERA in five games.

Garcia quickly exceeded Seattle's expectations. As spring training began in 1999, Mariners fans and the media believed Garcia would need another year of experience at Class AAA. He surprised everyone with an excellent spring training performance and won the Mariners' third starter role. Although sometimes lacking focus, Garcia finished 1999 with 17 wins, 8 losses, and a 4.07 ERA. He placed second in the AL Rookie of the Year voting behind Carlos

Beltran, leading all rookie pitchers in wins, ERA, games started (33), strike-outs (170), winning percentage (.680), and opponents' batting average (.263). He paced the Seattle staff in wins, strikeouts, and starts.

Garcia's 2000 season started badly. A fractured leg sidelined him from April 22 until July 7. Upon his return, he fared 1–0 with four no-decisions and a 2.51 ERA in July. In September, he responded when Mariners' ace Jamie Moyer struggled, winning four consecutive starts down the stretch. Garcia finished with 9 wins, 5 losses, and a 3.91 ERA. Two postseason wins against the New York Yankees in the AL Championship Series sweetened his year.

In 2001, Garcia pitched Opening Day against the Oakland Athletics. He compiled a 6–0 mark in his first 12 starts, not losing until June 9 against the San Diego Padres. He posted consecutive shutouts against the Anaheim Angels and the Los Angeles Dodgers in July and was named to the AL All-Star team with a 10–1 record. Before a home crowd at Safeco Field in Seattle, he pitched one scoreless inning and picked up the All-Star victory.

By September 2001, Garcia attained emerging star status. One advance scout observed that "Freddy Garcia is a Cy Young Award waiting to happen, and it might be this year." Garcia finished with 18 wins, 6 losses, and an AL-leading 3.05 ERA. His 18 victories tied former Mariner Eric Hanson for most triumphs by a right-hander in franchise history. He placed third in the AL Cy Young Award voting behind his idol Roger Clemens of the New York Yankees and Oakland pitcher Mark Mulder. In 2002 he won 16 of 26 decisions with a 4.29 ERA, and he struck out 181 batters in 223.2 innings. Garcia struggled with a 12–14 mark and 4.51 ERA in 2003, fanning 144 batters in 201.1 innings.

Through the 2003 season, Garcia boasted a career 72–43 record and a 3.97 ERA. His 72 victories exceed those of any active pitcher under age 27. He keeps his emotions in check and maintains excellent command of his fastball, curve, and change-up. According to one scout, "This guy throws three quality pitches . . . the most impressive thing is that he'll throw any of his pitches in any count." Garcia proves particularly effective when he utilizes his sinking fastball to get groundouts instead of trying to overpower hitters with his high fastball.

BIBLIOGRAPHY
Stephen Cannella, "Inside Baseball," *Sports Illustrated* 95 (July 30, 2001), p. 80; Stephen Cannella and Jeff Pearlman, "Inside Baseball: Armed and Ready in Seattle: Mariners' Pitching Picks Up," *Sports Illustrated* 91 (September 13, 1999), p. 102; Larry LaRue, "The Book on . . . Freddy Garcia," *The Sporting News* (August 23, 1999), p. 60; Bob Nightengale, "The Next Generation of Power Pitchers," *USA Today Baseball Weekly* 11 (May 23, 2001), p. 9; Ken Rosenthal, "It Ain't Broke, but M's Should Try to Fix It," *The Sporting News* (July 23, 2001), p. 13; "Seattle Mariners," *USA Today Baseball Weekly* 10 (September 13, 2000), p. 18.

Terry W. Sloope

JEFF GARCIA
Football
(February 24, 1970–)

Jeff Garcia has developed into one of the best quarterbacks in the National Football League (NFL).

Jeff Garcia was born on February 24, 1970 in Gilroy, California, and is the son of Bob Garcia, a football coach of Mexican heritage, and Linda (Elder) Garcia of Irish heritage. Linda's father, Maurice, starred as a halfback and defensive back at Kansas State University in the 1930s, while her two brothers coached football.

Garcia began playing youth football at age 8 and graduated in 1988 from Gilroy High School, where he started at quarterback two years. He played quarterback for his father at Gavilan Junior College, improving his footwork on the scout team in 1988. In 1989 his father made the Gavilan offense more wide-open to utilize Jeff's skills. Garcia passed for over 2,000 yards and 18 touchdowns and was named a Junior College All-America. He was later elected to the Junior College Hall of Fame.

At 6 foot 1 inch and 185 pounds, Garcia was considered too small to be an effective quarterback. Nevertheless, San Jose University offered him a full football scholarship. A three-year starting quarterback for the Spartans, he finished third nationally in passing efficiency as a sophomore and completed 61.9 percent of his passes for 1,519 yards and 12 touchdowns. As a junior, Garcia threw for 2,418 yards and 15 touchdowns, rushed for seven touchdowns, and earned United Press International All-America honors. He completed 196 of 356 aerials for 2,608 yards and 21 touchdowns in his final season, rushing for 559 yards and three touchdowns. He remains first on the Spartans' all-time list with 7,274 career yards of total offense and ranks third in passing with 6,545 yards, 504 completions, and a 129.4 passing rating, earning Most Valuable Player (MVP) honors at the 1994 East-West Shrine game.

Garcia graduated from San Jose State University in 1994 with a Bachelor's degree in business/marketing. NFL teams expressed little interest in him. He remarked, "I think when people doubted me, or when the doubts were out there, that added fuel to my desire to be the kind of player that I imagined I would be." Garcia signed with the Calgary Stampeders (Canadian Football League) and saw little action during his rookie season, backing up quarterback Doug Flutie. When Flutie was injured midway through the 1995 season, Garcia took advantage of his chance. He completed 230 of 364 passes (63.2 percent) for 3,358 yards and 25 touchdowns in 1995. In the semifinals on September 3, 1995, he threw for 546 yards and six touchdowns against Edmonton. Baltimore, however, defeated the Stampeders, 37–20, in the Grey Cup Championship game.

In 1996 Garcia finished third in the CFL with 4,225 passing yards and 25 touchdowns. The following year, he attained career highs in nearly all statistical categories. He completed 354 of 566 passes for 4,568 yards and 33 touchdowns and rushed for 739 yards and seven touchdowns. He was named West Division All-Star quarterback for the third consecutive time and finished second to Flutie as Canada's Most Outstanding Player. In 1998 Garcia led the Stampeders to the Grey Cup Championship, was chosen MVP of the Grey Cup game, and was selected All-Canadian and West Division All-Star quarterback. Calgary defeated Hamilton, 26–24, for the Grey Cup title, as Garcia completed 22 of 32 passes for 250 yards.

In five seasons with Calgary, Garcia converted 1,249 of 2,024 passes for 16,449 yards and 111 touchdowns and recorded a 61.7 completion percentage. He rushed for 2,370 yards and 24 touchdowns, averaging 6.2 yards per carry.

The San Francisco 49ers (NFL) signed Garcia on February 16, 1999 as a nondrafted free agent. He made his first NFL start against the Tennessee Titans on October 3, 1999, replacing the injured Steve Young. He started against the Cincinnati Bengals on December 5, 1999, throwing for a career-high 437 yards and completing 33 of a career-high 49 passes.

Garcia, who started all 16 games in 2000, threw for a team record and a career-high 4,278 yards and finished second in the NFL with 31 touchdown passes. Besides having a career-high 414 yards rushing, Garcia recorded the fifth 30-touchdown season in 49er quarterback history, joining John Brodie, Joe Montana, and Young. He threw a career-high four touchdown passes against the Dallas Cowboys on September 24, 2000, completing 36 passes and missing Montana's single-game team record by one. Garcia recorded six 300-yard passing games that season, one short of Young's club record. In 2000, Garcia also recorded a single-season-high 355 completions in 561 passing attempts for a 63.3 completion percentage.

In 2001 Garcia earned his second consecutive Pro Bowl honor and threw 32 touchdown passes to became the first 49er quarterback ever to toss at least 30 touchdown aerials in consecutive seasons. Garcia started all 16 games and led San Francisco to a 12–4 regular season record, but the 49ers lost to the Green Bay Packers in the National Football Conference (NFC) Wild Card game. In November 2001, he was named NFC Offensive Player of the Week and Offensive Player of the Month. Bill Walsh, former 49ers coach, commented, "He's the ultimate quarterback. He ranks right with Montana and Young in his performances."

Garcia led San Francisco to the NFC West crown with a 10–6 mark in 2002, completing 328 of 528 passes (62.1 percent) for 3,344 yards and 21 touchdowns. Garcia again made the Pro Bowl and engineered the second largest comeback in NFL history in the Wild Card game. The 49ers rallied from 24 points down in the third quarter to nip the visiting New York Giants, 39–38. He threw for three touchdowns and ran for another, as the 49ers scored the last 25 points of the game. Tampa Bay limited Garcia to 166 passing yards and no touchdowns, routing the 49ers, 31–6, in the next playoff round.

Between 1999 and 2002 with the 49ers, Garcia completed 1,224 of 1,968 passes for a 62.2 completion percentage while throwing for 13,704 yards and

95 touchdowns. He rushed 262 times for 1,252 yards and a 4.8-yard average and scored 14 touchdowns. The 49ers have compiled a 30–28 won-lost record with Garcia as starting quarterback.

During his professional career, Garcia has completed 2,119 of 3,421 passes for 25,573 yards and 173 touchdowns and has compiled a 61.9 completion percentage. Garcia, who is single, has rushed 571 times for 2,883 yards (5.64-yard average) and 31 touchdowns. He reflected, "People can't measure your heart. They wanted to look at my size, my arm strength or the physical aspects and knock me for that."

BIBLIOGRAPHY
Jeffri Chadii, "Panning Out," *Sports Illustrated* 23 (December 4, 2000), pp. 51–52, 56; "Jeff Garcia," *Career Stats*, www.nfl.com (2002); "Jeff Garcia," *Family, Youth, High School and Junior College*, www.jeffgarciafans.com (2002); "Jeff Garcia," *Player Profile*, www.yahoosports.com (2002); "Jeff Garcia," *Pro History and College Stats*, www.sf49ers.com (2002); *The Sporting News Football Register*, 2003; Larry Weisman, "Garcia Finally Finds Right Place, Right Time," *USA Today*, November 29, 2001, pp. 1C, 2C.

John L. Evers and David L. Porter

NOMAR GARCIAPARRA   Baseball
(July 23, 1973–)

Nomar Garciaparra, one of a new breed of hard-hitting shortstops, has won two American League (AL) batting titles.

Anthony Nomar Garciaparra was born in Whittier, California, on July 23, 1973 to Ramon Garciaparra and Sylvia Garciaparra. The name Nomar is his father's name spelled backwards. His father, one of his early baseball coaches, taught him to play every position in order to appreciate what each player had to accomplish. Garciaparra starred in soccer, baseball, and football at St. John Bosco High School in Bellflower, California. The Milwaukee Brewers (AL) drafted him in 1991, but he decided to attend Georgia Tech instead. Garciaparra studied business management, made the Dean's List, and played baseball with future Boston Red Sox teammates Jason Varitek and Darren Bragg. His three-year college career included 250 hits and a .372 batting average. He played for the 1992 U.S. Olympic baseball team at the Barcelona, Spain, Games.

Garciaparra, selected by the Boston Red Sox (AL) in the first round of the June 1994 free-agent draft, reported to Sarasota, Florida (Florida State League). He progressed rapidly through the Red Sox organization at shortstop for Trenton, New Jersey (Eastern League) in 1995 and Pawtucket, Rhode Island (International League) in 1996 before a late-season promotion to Boston. His first major league hit was a home run off John Wasdin of the Oakland Athletics on September 1, 1996. The next year, the 6-foot, 180-pound, right-handed Garciaparra enjoyed one of the greatest rookie seasons in major league baseball history. He led the AL in at-bats (684), hits (209), triples (11), and

Nomar Garciaparra ©Courtesy of the Boston Red Sox

putouts at shortstop (249). In addition, he set the major league mark for runs batted in (RBI) by a leadoff hitter (98) and home runs by a rookie shortstop (30) and established the AL record for longest hitting streak by a rookie (30 games). His 122 runs scored marked the fourth highest for a rookie in major league history, while his 365 total bases broke the Red Sox rookie record held by Ted Williams. Not surprisingly Garciaparra was selected 1997 AL Rookie of the Year, becoming only the fourteenth player chosen unanimously. The sophomore jinx eluded Garciaparra, as he collected 122 RBIs, raised his batting average to .323, and became only the fifth player to record 30 or more home runs in each of his first two full seasons. Although he spent time on the disabled list with an injured shoulder, he started the season in the leadoff spot, moved to third, and eventually filled the cleanup slot. Only twice all season did he go hitless two consecutive games.

In 1999 Garciaparra won the AL batting title with a .357 average, hit .417 with two home runs in the AL Division Series against the Cleveland Indians, and batted .400 with two home runs in the AL Championship Series against the New York Yankees. Garciaparra won a second AL batting title the next year with a lofty .372 and scored more than 100 runs for the fourth consecutive season. He played for the AL in All-Star games in 1997, 1999, 2000, 2002, and 2003. Garciaparra spent most of the 2001 campaign on the disabled list after undergoing wrist surgery, playing only 21 games. He led the Red Sox with 197 hits, 56 doubles, and 120 RBIs in 2002, batting .310 in 156 games. Through the 2003 season, Garciaparra had 1,231 hits, 685 runs, 272 doubles, 47 triples, 173 home runs, and 669 RBIs, with a .368 on-base percentage and an incredible .323 batting average in 928 games. Garciaparra batted .301 with 28 home runs and 105 RBIs in 2003, helping the Red Sox capture the AL Wild Card. He ranked second in triples (13) and runs scored (120), fourth in total bases (345), and fifth in hits (198). After hitting .300 in the AL Division Series against the Oakland A's, he struggled with a .241 batting average and eight strikeouts in the AL Championship Series against the New York Yankees.

Alex Rodriguez*, one of the premier AL shortstops, said, "I'm the youngest, Derek's (Jeter)* is the richest, but Nomar's the best." National Baseball Hall of Famer and Red Sox legend Ted Williams said of Garciaparra, "I'm looking at someone who is going to be as good as anyone who has ever played this game."

Garciaparra remains one of the nicest, most personable players in baseball. He signs autographs every day right after batting practice. Fans across the United States love him because he likes the fans and goes out of his way to accommodate them, especially the children. Garciaparra, humble about his own accomplishments, prefers to talk about his parents, two sisters, and his brother, Michael, a shortstop and the 2001 first-round draft pick of the Seattle Mariners (AL). Garciaparra is well-liked by his teammates because he plays every inning as if the World Championship rested on it. He earned $8.6 million with Boston in 2002, with the club holding options on his contract for $10.5 million in 2003 and $11.5 million in 2004.

BIBLIOGRAPHY
Boston Red Sox Media Guide, 2003; James Buckley Jr., *Super Shortstops: Jeter, Nomar, and A-Rod* (New York, 2001); Gordon Edes, "Nomar Garciaparra Lived Up to His Advance Billing in 1997," *Baseball Digest* 56 (December 1997); Jim Prime, "One-on-One with Nomar Garciaparra," *Baseball Digest* 59 (June 2000), pp. 22–29; I. J. Rosenberg, "Nomar Garciaparra: Defining Greatness at Shortstop," *Baseball Digest* 57 (December 1998), pp. 76–78; Alan Schwarz, "Rookie of the Year: Garciaparra Enjoys All-Star Campaign," *Baseball America's 1998 Almanac* (Durham, NC, 1997); Dan Shaughnessy, "There's No More Perfect Player Than Nomar," *Boston Globe* (August 10, 2000), p. D6.

Frank J. Olmsted

KEVIN GARNETT Basketball
(May 19, 1976–)

Kevin Garnett won acclaim as the first high school basketball player ever selected in the first round of the National Basketball Association (NBA) draft.

Kevin Maurice Garnett was born on May 19, 1976 in Greenville, South

Carolina, the son of O'Lewis McCullough and Shirley Garnett. His parents never married. Garnett's mother later married Ernest Irby and moved the family to Mauldin, South Carolina. During this time, Garnett developed a keen interest in basketball and practiced from daylight to dusk. His parents, however, believed that he should concentrate on education rather than basketball. Garnett attended Mauldin High School from 1991–1992 through 1993–1994, playing basketball for the Mavericks. His inner drive to excel in basketball and his rapid development as an excellent shooter, rebounder, and shot blocker led to his 1994 Mauldin Most Valuable Player (MVP) Award. At the end of his junior year, he also was selected Mr. Basketball in South Carolina.

Because of racial difficulties, Garnett's mother moved the family to Chicago, Illinois, and enrolled him in Farragut Academy. There he played under experienced, crafty coach William Nelson. As a senior, Garnett was named National High School Player of the Year by *USA Today* and was selected to the *Parade* magazine All-America First Team after leading Farragut to a 28–2 won-lost record and the quarterfinals of the Class AA Illinois State High School Basketball Tournament. Garnett averaged 25.2 points, 17.9 rebounds, 6.7 assists, and 6.5 blocked shots while shooting a .666 percentage, and he was named Mr. Basketball in Illinois. During his high school career, he compiled 2,533 points, 1,807 rebounds, and 739 blocked shots and was named the Most Outstanding Player at the McDonald's All-America Game.

Following his graduation from Farragut Academy, the 6-foot 11-inch, 220 pounder entered the 1995 NBA draft. The Minnesota Timberwolves (NBA) selected him in the first round as the fifth pick overall. Garnett, as noted earlier, became the first high school player ever chosen in the first round of the NBA draft. He successfully moved from high school to the NBA, improving and learning during his first year. At 19 years, 235 days, he was among the youngest players ever to start an NBA game. He established a franchise record with 131 blocked shots and was named to the NBA All-Rookie Second Team. The following season, he made the Eastern Conference All-Star team. Garnett blocked 163 shots to eclipse the record he set as a rookie. Besides being Minnesota's second leading scorer and rebounder, he helped lead the Timberwolves to their first ever appearance in the NBA playoffs. Minnesota lost to the Houston Rockets in three games in the first round. The 1996–1997 campaign marked the first of six consecutive seasons that Minnesota qualified for the playoffs.

During the 1997–1998 season, Garnett became the first All-Star Team starter in Timberwolves history. The following season, he led Minnesota in scoring, rebounds, blocked shots, and double-doubles. He ranked among the NBA's top 20 in scoring, rebounding, blocked shots, and steals and was named to the All-NBA Third Team. Garnett's most productive season came in 1999–2000, when he scored 1,857 points (22.9-points average) and collected 956 rebounds (11.8-boards average) and 5.0 assists per game, all career highs. He tallied a career-best 40 points against the Boston Celtics on March 22, 2000. He was named NBA Player of the Month in January 2000, averaging 25.8

Kevin Garnett ©Barry Gossage/Getty Images

points and 10.5 rebounds, and was selected to the All-NBA First Team and the All-NBA Defensive First Team. In 2000–2001, Garnett led the Timberwolves in scoring with 22.0 points per game and in rebounding with 11.4 boards per game. He ranked seventh in the NBA in rebounding and third in double-doubles with 54 and was selected to the All-NBA Second Team and the All-NBA Defensive First Team.

In 2001–2002 Garnett placed third in the NBA with 981 rebounds (12.1

average), repeating on the All-NBA Second Team and the All-NBA Defensive First Team. He tallied 1,714 points (21.2 average) and 126 blocked shots, helping Minnesota compile a 50–32 record. The Timberwolves were eliminated in the first round of the NBA playoffs for the sixth consecutive year. Garnett made the All-NBA First Team and All-NBA Defensive First Team, ranking second in rebounding with 1,102 (13.4 average) and ninth in scoring with 1,883 points (23.0 average) and blocking 129 shots. The Los Angeles Lakers ousted the Timberwolves in the first round of the NBA playoffs.

In eight NBA seasons from 1995–1996 through 2002–2003, Garnett compiled 11,877 points (19.4 average) and snagged 6,354 rebounds (10.4 average) in 611 regular season games. He dished out 2,250 assists, made 848 steals, blocked 1,053 shots, and played in six NBA All-Star games. In 29 NBA playoff games, he scored 611 points, pulled down 365 rebounds, and recorded 144 assists, 39 steals, and 47 blocked shots.

After seeing Garnett play, Michael Jordan* acknowledged, "He's come a long way, and you know what's scary about it? He's still got a long way to come. You are just seeing a touch of his skills."

Besides his mother and stepfather, Garnett has an older sister, Sonya, and a younger sister, Ashley. Tony Dorsett and Magic Johnson* were his sports heroes. Garnett portrayed Wilt Chamberlain in the movie *Rebound* (1998).

BIBLIOGRAPHY

Elizabeth A. Schick, ed., "Kevin Garnett," *Current Biography Yearbook* (New York, 1998); "Kevin Garnett," *Players Background*, www.nba.com (2001); "Kevin Garnett," *Players Career Highlights*, www.nba.com (2001); "Kevin Garnett," *Players Career Statistics*, www.nba.com (2001); *The Sporting News Official NBA Register*, 2003–2004.

John L. Evers

EDDIE GEORGE   Football
(September 24, 1973–)

Eddie George won the Heisman Trophy in 1995 and stars in the National Football League (NFL) as a running back with the Tennessee Titans (NFL).

Edward Nathan George was born on September 24, 1973 in Philadelphia, Pennsylvania, the son of Donna George. He attended Abington High School in Abington, Pennsylvania, near Philadelphia. Gravely concerned by his misbehavior and declining grades as a sophomore, his mother enrolled the 15-year-old at Fork Union Military Academy in rural Virginia, where he rushed for 2,572 yards with 32 touchdowns in football and won state titles in the high and low hurdles as a senior.

At Ohio State University, George gained 3,768 yards on 683 carries for 44 career rushing touchdowns in three seasons to rank second on the Buckeyes' All-Time rushing list in football. He played with losing teams at the 1993 and

1995 Florida Citrus Bowls. In 1995 he won the Heisman Trophy and the Doak Walker Award, given to the premier running back in the nation, and was unanimously chosen All-American.

The Houston Oilers (NFL) selected George in the first round of the 1996 NFL draft as the fourteenth pick overall. He became Houston's fourth Heisman Trophy winner, following Billy Cannon, Earl Campbell, and Mike Rozier. At 6 feet 3 inches and 240 pounds, he possessed an intriguing combination of size, power, vision, and ability to complete a run. George wanted his mother to attend his signing. His mother, a flight attendant with Trans World Airlines was supposed to fly that same day but changed her schedule so that she could be at the signing. Her originally scheduled plane, TWA flight 800, crashed soon after takeoff, killing all crew and passengers.

In his rookie year with Houston, George defied the Heisman jinx. In 1996, he finished sixth in the NFL rushing with 1,368 yards and eight touchdowns, and was unanimously selected to the NFL All-Rookie Team.

Jeff Fisher, Houston's head coach, admitted that George "was much more than what we thought he would be when we drafted him. He is a team player, a terrific guy in the locker room and on the field. He's got leadership qualities at a very young age."

The Houston franchise moved to Tennessee in 1997 and became the Titans. George opened the 1997 season by rushing for 216 yards against the Oakland Raiders to tie the 36-year-old team record set by Billy Cannon. George played in Super Bowl XXXIV against the St. Louis Rams in January 2000, carrying the ball 28 times for 95 yards. The Titans lost a 23–16 heartbreaker to the Rams when their pass receiver was stopped a yard short of a touchdown as time expired. George became the ninth Heisman Trophy winner to play in a Super Bowl, joining Cannon, Roger Staubach, Mike Garrett, Jim Plunkett, Tony Dorsett, Marcus Allen,* Desmond Howard, and Ron Dayne.*

George set career highs in 2000 for rushing yards (1,509), carries (403), rushing touchdowns (14), total touchdowns (16), receptions (50), total yards from scrimmage (1,962), and rushing touchdowns in a game (3). His 403 carries ranked fourth in NFL history, just seven shy of Jamal Anderson's 410 in 1998 with the Atlanta Falcons. George earned his fourth consecutive Pro Bowl berth and made All-Pro for the first time in his career. He posted the outstanding numbers while suffering from a turf toe injury. George became the first running back in NFL history to carry the ball at least 300 times in each of his first five seasons. He joined Pro Football Hall of Famer Eric Dickerson as the only backs to rush for 1,200 yards in each of their first five seasons.

George reflected, "I just try to go with the flow, I don't pay too much attention to people talking about me and what I have accomplished. There is still a lot of football to be played. . . . All I can do is focus on the game each week and try to do the best I can." During the off-season, surgeons repaired a torn tendon in his right toe. He rebounded in 2001 to run for 939 yards and five touchdowns. He helped Tennessee win the American Football Conference

(AFC) South with an 11–5 mark in 2002, rushing 1,165 yards (3.4-yard average) and scoring 12 touchdowns. George scored one touchdown, but fumbled twice in the 34–31 overtime victory over the Pittsburgh Steelers in the AFC playoffs. The Oakland Raiders limited him to 67 yards on 15 carries, defeating Tennessee, 41–24, in the AFC Championship Game.

During his seven-year NFL career, George has amassed 8,978 rushing yards on 2,421 carries for 59 rushing touchdowns. His 8,978 rushing yards since 1996 rank first in the NFL. George has started all 112 career games, topping active running backs in consecutive starts. Known for his durability, he was nicknamed "the Beast."

George returned to Ohio State during the off-seasons and earned his Bachelor's degree in landscape architecture in 2001. A "fitness freak," he has been featured in the *Sports Illustrated* swimsuit issue and *Muscle & Fitness* magazine. He has also appeared on several television shows. George, who is single, splits time between Nashville, Tennessee, and Columbus, Ohio, with his five-year-old son, Jaire.

BIBLIOGRAPHY

Pro Football Weekly, January 12, 1997, August 29, 1999; Jarrett Bell, "George Runs to the Front," *USA Today*, December 11, 1996, p. 3C; *The Sporting News Pro Football Register*, 2003; *Sports Illustrated* 95 (October 29, 2001), pp. 20–21; *Tennessee Titans Press Guide*, 2003; Tom Weir, "George Puts Stamina Talk to Rest," *USA Today*, January 18, 2000, p. 7C.

Richard Gonsalves

SCOTT GOMEZ
Ice Hockey

(December 23, 1979–   )

On June 2, 2001, the New Jersey Devils (National Hockey League) trailed the Colorado Avalanche two games to one in the Stanley Cup Finals and by a 2–1 score in the third period of Game Four. As the puck floated into the offensive end, goalie Patrick Roy mishandled a clearing attempt. The puck wound up on the stick of Jay Pandolfo, who then flipped it to Scott Gomez for a score. The Devils won that game 3–2. During New Jersey's 2000 and 2003 championship runs and their unsuccessful Stanley Cup defense in 2001, one of their primary cogs curiously was a Latino of Mexican and Colombian heritage. Gomez's energetic style and unusual heritage (for a hockey player) helped introduce the National Hockey League (NHL) to a new audience.

Scott Gomez was born in Anchorage, Alaska, on December 23, 1979 to Carlos Gomez and Dalia Gomez. Carlos Gomez's trek north began when his Mexican parents were deported, leaving him with an aunt in San Diego, California. During his teenage years, he developed a passion for hockey and particularly for Willie O'Ree. O'Ree, the first African American in the NHL, played for the San Diego Gulls. After moving to Alaska in 1972, Carlos met and married Scott Gomez's Colombian-born mother. When Gomez was only a toddler, Carlos began taking him to local rinks to watch hockey games.

Carlos wanted his son to pick up the game he loved but initially found it a tough sell. Gomez hated hockey because he had difficulty learning to skate and wanted to quit, but Carlos refused to let him. Carlos explained that "he had just bought me a brand-new pair of skates at the time and he didn't want them to go to waste." Gomez eventually grew to love the sport. Carlos and Dalia did everything possible to support him and even stood in doorways for target practice. The holes he knocked in the wall of the Gomez house eventually paid off.

Gomez led the Anchorage East High School Thunderbirds to the Alaska state title during his sophomore year. Later, he played for a team in the British Columbia Junior League and the Tri-Cities (Washington) Americans (Western Hockey League). The New Jersey Devils selected 18-year-old Scott as the twenty-seventh pick of the 1998 NHL Entry Draft. The selection of a Spanish-surnamed player surprised many. One Devils fan recalled that "When I heard he got drafted, a kid named Gomez from Alaska, I was like 'That's the best we can do? Can't we get someone from like, the University of Michigan?' " Still, New Jersey's management was impressed, as Gomez posted 12 goals and 37 assists in only 45 games with the Tri-Cities Americans in 1997–1998. Gomez came to the Devils' camp with hopes that he would stick with the NHL team, but management returned him to Tri-Cities for one more season. Gomez enjoyed another solid year, tallying 30 goals and 78 assists in 58 games. At his second Devils camp, he was quite confident, " 'I just had a feeling I was going to make the team.' " The Latino from Alaska made the opening day roster. Gomez called his parents and left an emphatic message on their answering machine, "You're talking to a 1999–2000 New Jersey Devil."

The 1999–2003 seasons have been a whirlwind for Gomez. He has become a fan favorite at the Continental Airlines Arena. His impressive totals for his first four NHL seasons included 56 goals and 180 assists in 314 games. In the NHL playoffs, he has scored 12 goals and added 24 assists. Gomez won the 2000 Calder Memorial Trophy as the NHL's Rookie of the Year, played in that year's NHL All-Star Game, and participated in the 2000 and 2001 Stanley Cup Finals. He fractured his left hand late in the 2001–2002 season and missed the NHL playoffs. He represented the United States in the junior (under 20) hockey World Championships during 1998 and 1999. On the 1999 USA squad, he fared second in scoring, with three goals and seven assists in six games.

Gomez enjoyed a very productive 2002–2003 season, scoring 13 goals and 42 assists, helping New Jersey to 46 wins and second place in the Eastern Conference. He recorded three goals and nine assists, as New Jersey eliminated the Boston Bruins, Tampa Bay Lightning, Ottawa Senators, and Anaheim Mighty Ducks en route to the Stanley Cup. New Jersey defeated Anaheim in seven games to win the Stanley Cup. What Jackie Robinson meant to African American children, pioneer Scott Gomez may be for Latinos in the twenty-first century. As one reporter stated, "Now that he is a first-round pick, Scott likely will be in an economic strata this his grandparents could not have envisioned." Latinos and other minorities have noticed Gomez's rise to stardom. Hockey's ethnic composition will likely become even more diverse.

BIBLIOGRAPHY
Kevin Allen, "Devils Rookie Gomez 'Torch Bearer' for Latinos," *USA Today*, October 19, 1999, C, p. 18; Keith Allen, "Gomez Primed to Break Barrier for Hispanics," *USA Today*, June 29, 1998, C, p. 6; Mike Brophy, "Go Go Gomez: Superb Rookie Sparks Veteran New Jersey Club," *The Hockey News*, February 4, 2000, pp. 11–12; Mark Everson, "Gomez Is One Hot Devil," *New York Post*, October 18, 1999, p. 65; "Scott Gomez," www.nhlpa.com, player profile at www.nhl.com, www.newjerseydevils.com, and www.scottygomez.com; Dan Shaughnessy, "El Diablo," *ESPN Magazine* (January 24, 2000), pp. 64–69; Doyle Woody, "Same as He Ever Was: Anchorage's Gomez Skates Through NHL Like a Kid at Play," *Anchorage Daily News*, December 5, 1999, p. A1.

Jorge Iber

JUAN GONZALEZ   Baseball
(October 13, 1969–   )

Following the 1998 baseball season, Texas Rangers (American League) outfielder Juan Gonzalez stood on top of the baseball world. Named the AL Most Valuable Player (MVP) for the second time, Gonzalez became the fifteenth player in major league history to win that award twice. His joy was doubled when close friend Sammy Sosa* was awarded the National League MVP title. For the first time in baseball history, Latino American players held both titles. "It's very special," Gonzalez told reporters, "Sammy is my friend, this is a special moment for all Latin America and all of baseball, too."

Gonzalez and Sosa began their professional careers as rookie outfielders with the Gulf Coast, Florida Rangers (Gulf Coast League) in 1986. Gonzalez hit no home runs during his first professional season at age 16. But in 1998, the 6-foot 3-inch, 220-pounder clouted 45 home runs and led the AL with 157 runs batted in (RBI), the most in the AL since 1949. His 101 RBIs at the All-Star break ranked second in history to Hank Greenberg's 103 RBIs in 1935. Gonzalez explained, "I concentrate more when I see men on base." Manager Lou Piniella observed, "It's hard to believe Juan has more than 100 RBIs already. One hundred used to be the barometer for a very successful *entire* season."

Juan Alberto Vazquez Gonzalez was born in Vega Baja, Puerto Rico, on October 16, 1969, the son of Juan Gonzalez and Lélé Gonzalez. Gonzalez began playing baseball at age 7. Because proper baseball equipment was scarce, he often played barefoot and used a broomstick for a bat and a bottle cap for a ball. Once, he even used "the head off one of my sister's dolls" for a ball.

At Vega Baja High School, where his father taught mathematics, Gonzalez played baseball on the school team. He was invited to play in an island-wide youth league, batting cleanup behind future New York Yankee outfielder Bernie Williams.*

Several major league teams wanted to sign Gonzalez. At age 16, he chose the Texas Rangers for a $75,000 signing bonus, the highest ever paid a Puerto Rican player. Ranger scout Luis Rose, who signed him, boasted, "Juan Gonzalez is the finest prospect to come out of Puerto Rico in years."

Gonzalez began his professional career in the GCL. In each of his five minor league seasons, he improved his skills. Although the youngest player in the American Association, in 1990 the 20-year-old led the AA with 29 home runs, 101 RBIs, and 252 total bases and was named AA MVP with the Oklahoma City 89ers.

As a starter for the Texas Rangers in 1991, Gonzalez clouted 27 home runs and 102 RBIs. The following season, he led the AL with 43 home runs, but his free-swinging style earned him a poor 143–35 strikeout to walk ratio. At age 22, he was the sixth youngest home run champion in major league history. Only five players, all National Baseball Hall of Fame members, had led the major leagues at a younger age. Puerto Rico had found a new national hero.

In 1993 Gonzalez achieved superstar stature, leading the AL with 46 home runs and producing 118 RBIs with a .310 batting average. His vigorous workout and bodybuilding regimen helped him become a mighty slugger but resulted in back problems and subpar 1994 and 1995 seasons. Other problems ensued. In 1994, his brother died, his marriage to Elaine Lopez ended in a month after a bitter feud between families, and the baseball season ended abruptly with the player's strike. Physical problems limited his 1995 playing time to 90 games.

Gonzalez confirmed his reputation as a great slugger with an AL MVP award-winning season in 1996, batting .314 with 47 home runs and 144 RBIs and leading the Rangers to an AL Division crown. The Rangers lost to the New York Yankees in the AL Division Series, but Gonzalez performed magnificently with a .436 batting average, five home runs, and nine RBIs in four games.

In his last three years with the Rangers from 1997 to 1999, Gonzalez averaged 42 home runs and 139 RBIs. When he finished fifth among AL outfielders in the 1999 All-Star balloting, he told the press that he would not go to the game, even though he was named to the team as a reserve player. "I respect the fans," he said, "but if they don't vote for me, I don't want to play." As a result, manager Joe Torre dropped him from the team. Fans began to boo Gonzalez at the plate. The All-Star incident came at a time when the exceptionally moody Gonzalez was distracted with marital problems. In December 1998, he had married Olga Tanan, a famous *merengue* singer in Puerto Rico.

The Detroit Tigers (AL) acquired Gonzalez in a nine-player trade in November 1999. The Tigers hoped to sign him to a long-term contract and reportedly offered to make him the richest player in baseball with a $143 million, eight-year deal. Gonzalez refused the offer and suffered through a miserable 2000 season in Detroit. Bothered by a bad back, distracted by persistent trade rumors, and disturbed by frequent fan and press criticism, he hit a subpar .289 with 22 home runs and 67 RBIs.

Gonzalez signed a one-year contract with the Cleveland Indians (AL) for the 2001 season and rewarded his new team with a spectacular year. He batted .325 with 35 home runs and 140 RBIs in 140 games, marking his eighth season with more than 100 RBIs. Indians manager Charlie Manuel noted: "Juan sniffs out RBI like a bloodhound." Both teammates and Indians fans embraced Gonzalez, whose behavior on and off the field was exemplary. In the five-game 2001 AL Division Series won by the Seattle Mariners, he batted .348 with two home runs and five RBIs. In January 2002, he signed a two-year $24 million contract with the Texas Rangers. Gonzalez batted .282 with only eight home runs and 35 RBIs in an injury-riddled 2002 season. Through 2003, he has batted .296 with 429 home runs and 1,387 RBIs. In limited action, he hit .294 with 24 home runs and 70 RBIs in 2003.

Like his hero, Roberto Clemente, Gonzalez never forgot his Puerto Rican roots. For his humanitarian work, Gonzalez was given the 1997 Texas Rangers True Value/Roberto Clemente Man of the Year Award. When Hurricane Georges left many Puerto Ricans without food and shelter, he helped coordinate relief efforts and donated $25,000 for supplies. For the youth of Southeast Dallas, Texas, he helped construct the Juan Gonzalez Youth Ballpark with a $50,000 gift.

BIBLIOGRAPHY
Daniel P. George, "Running Home," *Boys Life* 84 (May 1994), pp. 8–10; Evan Grant, *Juan Gonzalez: JUAN GONE!* (Champaign, IL, 1999); Paul M. Johnson, "Going Deep; Slugger Gonzalez Embarks on His Own Legacy with Clemente," *Sport* 88 (July 1997), pp. 62–65; Tom Verducci, "Puerto Rico's New Patron Saint," *Sports Illustrated* 78 (April 5, 1993), pp. 60–65.

Richard D. Miller

LUIS GONZALEZ   Baseball
(September 2, 1967–   )

Few baseball players have compiled three better consecutive seasons than Luis Gonzalez. From 1999 through 2001, he batted .324 with 114 home runs and 367 RBIs.

Luis Emilio Gonzalez was born on September 2, 1967 in Tampa, Florida, to Cuban parents. His father worked as a baker, while his mother was employed as a schoolteacher. Gonzalez graduated from Jefferson High School in Tampa Bay, Florida, in 1985 and was selected to the school's Hall of Fame. He played baseball at the University of South Alabama and was elected to their Hall of Fame in 1999. The Houston Astros (National League) selected him in the fourth round of the June 1988 free-agent draft. Signed as a third baseman, Gonzalez showed steady, undramatic progress in the minor leagues in 1988 and 1989. At Columbus, Georgia, in 1990, he led the Southern Association with 24 home runs and earned a September promotion to the Houston Astros. His first major league hit was a double off San Francisco Giants' relief pitcher Steve Bedrosian on September 8, 1990.

After moving to the Houston outfield in 1991, Gonzalez enjoyed a good rookie season with 13 home runs, 69 runs batted in (RBI) and a .254 batting average in 137 games. His first two major league home runs came off Chicago Cubs pitcher Greg Maddux on May 1 at Wrigley Field in Chicago. From 1991 to 1995, Gonzalez proved a dependable outfielder with an average arm but a quick release and a smart baserunner with average speed. The 6-foot 2-inch, 191-pounder, who bats left-handed but throws right-handed, displayed only modest power and hit above .270 only once in his tenure with Houston.

On June 28, 1995, Houston traded Gonzalez to the Chicago Cubs (NL) for catcher Rick Wilkins. After batting .271 for Chicago in 1996, Gonzalez returned to Houston via free agency in December 1996. The Astros released him after a 1997 campaign that saw his average drop to .258 with only 10 home runs. He signed with the Detroit Tigers (American League) in December 1997. For the Tigers, Gonzalez reached then career highs with 23 home runs, 35 doubles, and 84 runs scored. In December 1997, Detroit made one of the most lopsided trades ever recorded, sending Gonzalez to the Arizona Diamondbacks (NL) for light-hitting outfielder Karim Garcia.

Gonzalez, or "Gonzo" as his Arizona teammates call him, has become a franchise player for the Diamondbacks. His statistics from 1999 to 2001 frightened opposing pitchers. In 1999 he led the NL with 206 hits and batted a career best .336 with 112 runs scored and 111 RBIs. The following season, he hit .311, belted 31 home runs, scored 106 runs, produced 114 RBIs, and hit a career-high 47 doubles. Gonzalez reached a pinnacle in 2001 by clouting 57 home runs, scoring 128 runs, and producing 142 RBIs, all career bests, and batting .325. He batted .288 and led Arizona with 28 home runs and 103 RBIs in 2002. He was a key ingredient in the Diamondbacks' Western Division titles in 1999, 2001, and 2002. Gonzalez batted .200 in the 1999 NL Division Series, which the New York Mets won in four games. He hit .263 in the 2001 NL Division Series, helping the Diamondbacks defeat the St. Louis Cardinals in five games. He scored four times and drove in four runs in Arizona's 2001 NL Championship Series victory over the Atlanta Braves and tallied four runs and added five RBIs in the 2001 World Series against the New York Yankees. His bloop single off star reliever Mariano Rivera* in the bottom of the ninth inning of Game Seven gave the Diamondbacks a 3–2 victory and their first World Championship. Gonzalez played for the NL in the 1999, 2001, and 2002 All-Star games but missed the 2002 playoffs because of a separated shoulder. Through the 2003 season, he has appeared in 1,903 games with 1,959 hits, 430 doubles, 58 triples, 275 home runs, 1,060 runs, 1,124 RBIs, 115 stolen bases, and a .288 batting average. He also has been hit by pitches 79 times. In 2003, Gonzales hit .304 with 26 home runs, 104 RBIs, and 94 walks.

Gonzalez and his wife, Christine Lehman, had triplets, Megan, Jacob, and Allyssa on June 26, 1998. Luis says that becoming a father has made him a much better baseball player because he does not take bad games or poor performances home with him anymore. "When I come home after a game, I spend time with my wife and kids. I'm just dad there, not a ballplayer." They live in Scottsdale, Arizona. Gonzalez participates in numerous charitable causes, including the Boys and Girls Club, the Muscular Dystrophy Association, Make-a-Wish Foundation, the American Cancer Society, and Life Gift organ donors.

BIBLIOGRAPHY

Arizona Diamondbacks Media Guide, 2003; Baseball-reference.com, *Luis Gonzalez* (2002), pp. 1–4; Greg Boeck, "D'backs Work Their Own Magic in Game 7," *Baseball Weekly*.com (November 5, 2001), pp. 1–2; Paul Click, "Arizona's Luis Gonzalez Finds Late Success Rewarding," *Baseball Digest* 60 (September 2001), pp. 36–38; John Dewan, ed., *The Scouting Notebook 2002* (Morton Grove, IL, 2002); Bob Nightengale, "One Ring Is Not Enough," *USA Today Baseball Weekly* 12 (April 3–9, 2002), pp. 28–32.

Frank J. Olmsted

TONY GONZALEZ   Football
(February 27, 1976–   )

Tony Gonzalez spent part of June 2002 in Miami, Florida. This Kansas City Chiefs' (National Football League) star finalized an agreement with Pat Riley, coach of the Miami Heat (National Basketball Association), to participate in the team's summer league squad. Many Chief fans believed this was a ploy during contract negotiations, but Gonzalez countered, "I'm dead serious. I'm getting the experience, but at the same time you have goal in mind, too." He aspires to play in both the NFL and NBA. The logistics of this undertaking appears quite difficult, but this athlete has overcome many previous obstacles.

Anthony Gonzalez, the younger of two brothers, was born on February 27, 1976 in Torrance, California. His mother, Judith, worked at a hospital, where she eventually married an administrator, Michael Saltzman. When the clan moved to Huntington Beach, Gonzalez's "dark" complexion often drew attention. His paternal grandfather came from Cape Verde Islands. An error on immigration documents changed the family's name from Goncals to Gonzalez. He also has Jamaican, African American, and Native American ancestors. This unique background often led to anxious moments. "I get people who ask me questions in Spanish . . . (and) call me 'Big Mexican.' I've seen racism from whites, from blacks, from Hispanics. I've seen it from everywhere," he says.

In junior high school, Gonzalez faced ostracism because of his timid nature. His first attempt to overcome shyness involved sports but did not prove successful. "I was a big kid . . . But I didn't want to stick my nose in it. My attitude wasn't right," he acknowledged. Upon playing recreational league basketball, he developed the confidence to succeed. At Huntington Beach High School, he starred in two sports. As a senior in 1993, Gonzalez was named All County in football with 63 receptions as tight end and 131 tackles as a middle linebacker. He also earned All County in basketball, averaging 25.3 points and nine rebounds per game. His stellar ability in two sports drew national attention, but Gonzalez remained close to home and signed with the University of California—Berkeley.

Gonzalez showed much potential at California in 1994 and 1995 with 45 catches for 603 yards and three touchdowns. During his junior season in 1996, he caught 53 passes for 768 yards and five touchdowns and earned All-America status and selection to the All-Pac 10 Conference team. After the season, he declared for the NFL draft. Gonzalez also played basketball for the Golden Bears, who enjoyed a magical season in 1996–1997. During his first two years, Gonzalez averaged about six points and five rebounds for an improving team. Disaster then struck when leading scorer Ed Gray broke his foot just before the start of the National Collegiate Athletic Association (NCAA) Tournament. Gonzalez became a starter and scored in double figures in tournament wins against Princeton University and Villanova University. He took a tremendous risk during the drive to the Sweet 16 because an injury might have jeopardized millions of dollars. Still, he played for the love of the game, stating that "This is like when you were a little kid on the court going 'three, two one' and you beat Carolina at the buzzer."

The Kansas City Chiefs made Gonzalez the thirteenth pick in the 1997 draft. He has not disappointed them. Between 1997 and 2002, he has been acclaimed the prototypical modern tight end as a devastating blocker and downfield threat. Through the 2002 season, he ranked among the top 5 in team history in receptions (397) and yardage (4,731) and first in single-season catches (93 in 2000). His greatest game came on December 4, 2000, when he caught 11 passes for 147 yards against the New England Patriots. He appeared in the Pro Bowls following the 1999, 2000, and 2002 seasons.

In July 2002, Gonzalez' dream of playing in the NBA was postponed as he voluntarily left the Miami Heat's training camp. Although not yet achieving his dream of playing the two sports he loves professionally, he has clearly established himself as an elite athlete who takes his community responsibilities seriously. Success on the field and a social conscience combine to make him a very positive role model for all children regardless of ethnicity.

Gonzalez has exhibited a generous community spirit. He has worked with the Boys and Girls Club and Shadow Buddies Program, which provides smiling dolls to ill children and the elderly. He served as a United Way spokesman during 2000 and 2001 and supported both literacy programs and Race for the Cure. His charitable work earned him acceptance as part of Kansas City's

Ingram's "40 under 40" list, which honors the community's most influential individuals under 40 years of age.

BIBLIOGRAPHY
Jack Carey, "Cal's Two-Sport Gonzalez Realizes How Sweet It Is," *USA Today*, March 19, 1997, p. 6C; Jayda Evans, "Gonzalez Gets Word, Makes Adjustments," *Seattle Times*, December 23, 1999, p. D3; Leigh Montville, "Chief Weapon," *Sports Illustrated* 93 (December 27, 1999–January 3, 2000), pp. 44–46; C. W. Nevius, "Gonzalez Makes Presence Known," *San Francisco Chronicle*, December 1, 1997, p. C16; Keith Sugiura, "Chief's Tight End Rewrites Standards for His Position," *Atlanta Journal and Constitution*, December 24, 2000, p. 8E; *University of California 1996 Football Media Guide*, www.kcchiefs.com/rosters_stats/player.asp?ID=46, and www.tonygonzalezfoundation.shadowbuddies.com; Richard Weiner, "Gonzalez Makes Time for Others," *USA Today*, April 26, 2001, p. 3C.

Jorge Iber

DWIGHT GOODEN   Baseball
(November 16, 1964–   )

At the start of his professional baseball career, the 6-foot 3-inch, 190-pound fireball-throwing Gooden was untouchable. "He is in a group by himself," declared his former New York Mets (National League) and New York Yankees (American League) pitching coach, Mel Stottlemyre, at the time.

Dwight Eugene Gooden was born on November 16, 1964 in Tampa, Florida, the youngest of six children of Dan Gooden and Ella Mae Gooden. At age 6, Gooden went to the Hillsborough Park and learned the fundamentals of baseball from his father. The younger Gooden witnessed the smooth fluid pitching motion his father had learned as a semiprofessional on the sandlots of Americus, Georgia.

Dan Gooden had a long-range plan for his son. From the age of 4, Dwight watched the Atlanta Braves on television. The elder Gooden told his son, "Someday, you'll be out there with the pros." His father wanted him to concentrate on the game he loved and not worry about working, but his mother, Ella, a nurse, disagreed. She warned the two of them: "There's more to life than baseball."

Gooden was blessed with a loving family, but was brought up in a lower-income, safe neighborhood of Tampa, Florida, called Belmont Heights. Baseball provided an escape. His father planned for him to play baseball. Dwight did not have a real paying job or even need one until the New York Mets organization signed him up in 1982. After one minor league season, Gooden starred in 1983 with the Lynchburg, Virginia, Hillcats (Carolina League). He earned the Minor League Player of the Year Award, leading the league in wins (19), earned run average (ERA) (2.50), shutouts (6), and strikeouts (300).

Gooden's Hillcats performance earned him a job with the New York Mets the following year. The right-hander showed off his arm by establishing a

Dwight Gooden ©Photofest

record for strikeouts by a major league rookie and a teenager with 276. He posted 17 victories, becoming the NL Rookie of the Year and earning a trip to the All-Star Game. The next season saw him continue his pitching supremacy with 24 wins, the second of four trips to the All-Star Game (1984–1986, 1988), and a NL Cy Young Award. He is the youngest winner in the history of the award. During 1986, Gooden led the Mets to the postseason with a 17–6 record and first World Series Championship since 1969. He became the first pitcher in major league history to record 200 strikeouts in each of his first three seasons.

The hard-throwing Gooden won 33 games and struck out 323 batters over the next two seasons, and, in 1987, he visited the disabled list for the first time in his career. More importantly, he spent time in the Smithers Alcoholism and Treatment Center and tested positive for cocaine use, an event that started his downward spiral. After ineffective treatment at the center, Gooden pitched inconsistently for several years but still helped New York make it back to the NL postseason in 1988. After sustaining new injuries, he bounced back with the Mets in 1990 with 19 triumphs and 223 strikeouts in 232 innings.

In 1994, Gooden was injured again and once more tested positive for cocaine use, violating his aftercare program and baseball's drug policy. The punishment was quite severe for Gooden: he lost the entire 1995 season serving his suspension. The Mets released him, after which he signed with the New York Yankees in February 1996. Upon leaving the Mets, he ranked second in club wins and strikeouts behind National Baseball Hall of Fame pitcher Tom Seaver.

New York Yankees owner George Steinbrenner gave Gooden one piece of advice, "Don't embarrass me." On May 14, the 31-year-old completed one of baseball's grandest feats by pitching a no-hitter against the Seattle Mariners and ended the season with 11 wins, his first in double digits since 1993. He was not able to pitch during the postseason because of a tired arm, but he earned another World Series ring when the Yankees upset the Atlanta Braves.

Gooden spent 1998 and 1999 with the Cleveland Indians and 2000 with the Houston Astros, Tampa Bay Devil Rays, New York Yankees, and Toronto Blue Jays, retiring in 2001. He completed 16 major league seasons, winning 194 games, losing 112, striking out 2,293 batters, and compiling a 3.51 ERA.

BIBLIOGRAPHY
Dwight Gooden Statistics-Baseball-Reference.com, www.baseball-reference.com/g/goodenw01.shtml; *Houston Astros Media Guide*, 2000; George King, "The Doctor Is In: Gooden Begins New Career Behind Desk," *New York Post*, April 26, 2001, p. 74; George King, "Gooden: Mets Should Retire My Number," *New York Post*, February 17, 2003; George King, "Sad Doc: Lot of Fond Memories: Gooden Calls It a Career," *New York Post*, March 31, 2001; Bob Klapisch, *High and Tight: The Rise and Fall of Dwight Gooden and Darryl Strawberry* (New York, 1996); Dwight Gooden file National Baseball Hall of Fame Library, Cooperstown, NY.

Scot E. Mondore

MAURICE GREENE   Track and Field
(July 23, 1974–   )

Maurice Greene became known as the "World's Fastest Human" when he broke the world record in the 100 meters.

Maurice Greene was born on July 23, 1974 in Kansas City, Kansas, the youngest of four children of Ernest Greene and Jackie Greene. His brother, Ernest, influenced him to become a sprinter. Ernest himself had excelled as a sprinter, advancing to the semifinals of the 1992 Olympic Trials.

Greene began his track and field career at 8 years of age winning the 100 meters, 200 meters, and the shuttle relay at the All-City meet. He graduated in 1973 from F.L. Schlagle High School in Kansas City. As a senior, he was named an All-City tailback in football and captured his third straight Kansas High School State track and field titles in the 100 meters and 200 meters.

Greene attended Kansas City Community College and competed across the United States. Al Hobson, his high school coach, was enlisted that summer as his sprint coach. In 1995 Greene competed against top-ranked college sprinters in the Texas Relays. Former world recordholder and legendary Carl Lewis* was matched against Greene in the 100 meters. Greene captured his first major victory, defeating Lewis in the 100 meters sprint-off in a wind-aided time of 9.88 seconds.

Greene, however, faced numerous problems. He earned a spot on the 1995 U.S. World Championship team but did not reach the finals. Nagging injuries sidelined him in 1996 until the Olympic Trials. He failed to make the Olympic team and nearly gave up on sprinting.

Greene moved to California to begin training with sprint coach John Smith. Hobson agreed that Greene was making the right move. "I contacted Smith," Greene explained, "because he is simply the best coach around. You only have to look at what he has achieved to know how good he is. I wanted to be the best, and California was the place to make it happen."

Smith, a former 400-meter star, also trained Leo Drummond and Ato Boldon of Trinidad. Smith analyzed and restructured every step of Greene's 100-meter race and had him add 11 pounds to his upper body. For nine gruesome months, he drove Greene nearly to the breaking point with torturous workouts. Greene found the correct rhythm and developed Smith's precise mechanics.

Boldon, who competes against Greene daily, observed that "Maurice Greene is the most competitive human being I've ever known. Off the track, he's fun-loving, but on it, it's a hell of a contrast. He's tough. I've gotten tougher just being around him." Greene reads a verse daily and practices. "Every morning in Africa when a gazelle wakes up, it knows it must run faster than the faster lion or it will be killed. Every morning when a lion wakes up, it knows it must run faster than the slowest gazelle or it will starve to death. It doesn't matter if you are a lion or a gazelle, when the sun comes up, you better be running."

In the 1997 U.S. National Championship, Greene ran one heat of the 100 meters in a career-best 9.96 seconds. The next night he won his first National title in the 100 meters in 9.90 seconds, making him the third fastest American in history behind Leroy Burrell (9.85 seconds) and Lewis (9.86 seconds). On February 3, 1998, Greene set the indoor world record for 60 meters in 6.39 seconds. He won the sprint double in the Prefontaine Grand Prix and broke 10 seconds in the 100 meters 10 times that season.

The most productive year of Greene's career came in 1999, when he captured gold medals at the World Championships in the 100 meters, 200 meters, and on the 4×100-meter relay team. He became the first male to win the sprint double at the World Championships and only the fourth athlete in World Championship history to win three gold medals in a single meet. On June 16, 1999 in Athens, Greece, he set the world record in the 100 meters in 9.79 seconds. He also tied the 50 meters indoor world record in 5.56 seconds and was ranked best in the world in the 100 meters and 200 meters.

At Sydney, Australia, in the 2000 Olympic Games, Greene won the gold medal in the 100 meters in 9.87 seconds and ran a leg of the gold-medal-winning 4×100 relay team. His 2001 season was shortened due to a quadriceps injury, but Greene retained top ranking in the 100 meters and won his third World Championship. With his time of 9.82 seconds in winning the 2001 World 100-meter title, he owned the three fastest times in history. Greene won the 100 meters at the USA Track & Field Outdoor Championships in Palo Alto, California in June 2002. Tim Montgomery broke Greene's world record, being clocked in 9.78 seconds for the 100 meters at the 2002 IAAF Grand Prix Final, at Paris, France that September. Greene experienced his second consecutive disappointing season in 2003, pulling a thigh muscle in the semifinals of the WTAF Championships at St. Denis, France in August.

When referred to as the "World's Fastest Human," Greene replied, "I don't think of myself as the world's fastest human; if I did, I'd lose my edge. Being the fastest is only my job, it's not who I am."

Greene is single and has a daughter, Ryan Alexandria, from a past relationship. He lives in an upper-middle-class home in Granada Hills, north of Los Angeles.

BIBLIOGRAPHY

Frank Deford, "Time Bandits," *Sports Illustrated* 95 (August 6, 2001), pp. 53–63; "Maurice Greene," *Athlete Bio*, www.cnnsi.com (2000); "Maurice Greene," *Biography*, www.usatf.com (2000); "Maurice Greene," *Career Highlights*, www.usatf.com (2002); "Maurice Greene," *Early Years*, www.mogreene.com (1999); "Maurice Greene," *Later Years*, www.mogreene.com (2000); "Maurice Greene," *Profile*, www.unitedrunners.com (2002); "Maurice Greene," *SI Flashback*, www.cnnsi.com (1999); Tim Layden, "Gold Standard," *Sports Illustrated* 90 (June 28, 1999), pp. 55–63.

John L. Evers

KEN GRIFFEY JR.   Baseball
(November 21, 1969–)

The son of 19-year major league veteran Ken Griffey Sr., Ken Griffey Jr. debuted in the major leagues on April 3, 1989 with the Seattle Mariners (American League). He went to spring training as a nonroster player, hitting .359 with two home runs and 21 runs batted in (RBI) in just 26 exhibition games. Griffey Jr. earned a spot with the club as the youngest player in the major leagues that season. In his first game against the Oakland Athletics at Oakland, he doubled in his initial plate appearance off the All-Star pitcher

Dave Stewart. On April 10, at home against the Chicago White Sox, the 6-foot 3-inch, 205-pound outfielder blasted a home run off Eric King on the first pitch he ever saw at the Kingdome.

George Kenneth Griffey Jr. was born on November 21, 1969 in Donora, Pennsylvania, the son of George Kenneth Griffey Sr. and Alberta (Littleton) Griffey. Griffey Jr., who bats and throws left-handed, grew up as a natural athlete and graduated in 1987 from Cincinnati's Moeller High School, where he starred as a football player for three years and a baseball player for four seasons. In 1986 and 1987, he was named the league's Player of the Year. During the summer season as a child, he spent time with his father at the ballpark with the Cincinnati Reds (National League), the New York Yankees (AL), and the Atlanta Braves (NL). Griffey Jr. learned exactly what he needed to do to succeed in the big leagues. In 1987, without going to college, the 17-year-old began his professional career with the Everett, Washington, Aquasox (Northwest League). His first professional hit was a home run, and he soon led the club in batting average, home runs, and RBIs. In 1988, he played in the California League, was named to the All-Star team, and was selected the league's top prospect.

Griffey Jr. earned a spot with the Seattle Mariners in 1989, beginning his illustrious major league career. Over the next decade with the Mariners, he showed what he could do on the diamond. In 1990, the father and son were teammates and played together on August 31, marking the first time in major league history that a father/son tandem were teammates. On September 14 that year, the Griffeys clouted consecutive home runs in the first inning in a Seattle 7–5 loss to the California Angels. Pitcher Kirk McCaskill served up both home runs.

Griffey Jr. moved toward greatness. In 1990 he became the first Mariners player ever elected to the starting lineup of the All-Star Game. He returned 10 more times (1991–2000), winning the MVP Award in three games. Griffey Jr. unanimously was voted AL MVP in 1993 and became the first player to lead the AL in home runs for three consecutive seasons (1997–1999) since National Baseball Hall of Famer Harmon Killebrew accomplished it (1962–1964). He was the youngest player to reach 450 home runs and remains one of only four players to hit 40 home runs in five straight seasons, joining Babe Ruth, Hank Aaron, and Harmon Killebrew. He belted 56 home runs twice in his career (1997, 1998) and led the AL in home runs four times, ranking among the top 25 in career home runs. In 1999 fans voted Griffey Jr. to major league baseball's All-Century Team presented by MasterCard, while his peers voted him the Player of the Decade in the 1990s. Griffey Jr. has earned 10 Gold Glove Awards (1990–1999) and seven *The Sporting News* Silver Slugger Awards (1991, 1993–1994, 1996–1999).

Although his career has been filled with so much success, Griffey Jr. has also experienced disappointment. From his first major league season, injuries have slowed him down. In his first year, after leading all major league rookies in batting average (.287), home runs (13), and RBIs (45), he broke a bone in the little finger of his right hand. Since then, he has suffered lower back strains, sprained and broken wrists, tendon injuries, and knee and hamstring injuries.

In February 2000, Griffey Jr. was traded to the Cincinnati Reds (National League). He still owns Mariners records for all-time runs (1,063), hits (1,742), home runs (398), and RBIs (1,152). His new career with the Cincinnati Reds began well; he led his hometown team in home runs (40), RBIs (118), runs scored (100), total bases (289), and walks (94), despite a season-long hamstring injury. In the following two years, Griffey Jr. batted only 561 times, leading general manager James Bowden to state, "the trade (for Griffey Jr.) has been a bust." Bowden later retracted those remarks by saying, "He's one of the two or three best players in the game, with Barry Bonds* and Alex Rodriguez.*"

Griffey Jr. started his fifth season with the Reds in 2004, already having eclipsed the 2,000-hit and 400-home run plateaus, and being only the twenty-ninth player in baseball history to combine those marks. He was nearly traded to the San Diego Padres and may not end his career in Cincinnati. A torn tendon in his right ankle limited him to only 166 plate appearances in 2003. Through 2003, he has batted .294 with 481 home runs and 1,384 RBIs. He shares the major league record for most consecutive games with home runs (8), from July 20 to July 28, 1993. Griffey Jr. states, "I just want to come back, perform and let what I do on the field speak for itself. . . . Baseball is what I do, and it's what I love."

Griffey Jr. loves his family and his hometown. He and his wife, Melissa, have one son, Trey Kenneth, and one daughter, Taryn Kennedy.

BIBLIOGRAPHY
Cincinnati Reds Media Guide, 2003; Peter Gammons, http://espn.go.com/gammons/ s/2003/0122/1496934.html, January 22, 2003; Ken Griffey Jr. Statistics—Baseball-Reference.com, www.baseball-refernce.com/g/griffke02.shtml; Joe Kay, The Associated Press, *South Florida Sun-Sentinel*, June 6, 2002; Ken Griffey Jr. file, National Baseball Library, Cooperstown, NY; Josh Robbins, *The Orlando Sentinel*, The Miami Herald.com, posted March 12, 2003; The Sporting News: Baseball—Ken Griffey Jr., www.sportingnews.com/baseball/players/4305.

Scot E. Mondore

FLORENCE GRIFFITH JOYNER   Track and Field
(December 21, 1959–September 21, 1998)

The words beautiful, flamboyant, dazzling, nonconformist, and the fastest woman in the world describe Florence Griffith Joyner during her spectacular career in track and field.

Delorez Florence Griffith Joyner was born on December 21, 1959 in Los Angeles County, California, in the Mojave Desert to Robert Griffith, an electronics technician, and Florence Griffith, a seamstress, the seventh of 11 children. Her parents divorced when she was 4 years old. Her mother moved to a four-room housing project apartment in the poor Watts section of Los Angeles. With 11 children and a meager income, she sometimes skipped meals to make certain her children were fed and clothed. She maintained a tight discipline in the home and emphasized education as the top family priority. Recalling her childhood, Griffith Joyner said, "we didn't know how poor we were. We were always happy."

Griffith Joyner began participating in track and field at Ninety-second Street Elementary School and continued at Markham Junior High School. At David Jordan High School in Los Angeles, she set school records in the long jump and sprinting and competed against future track and field star Valerie Brisco.* In 1974 and 1975, she won track meets at the Jesse Owens National Youth Games.

Griffith Joyner attended California State University at Northridge in 1978–1979, but left because she could not afford the tuition. She worked as a bank teller until Bob Kersee, the sprint coach at California State, helped her find additional financial aid to return to college. When Kersee later took a track coaching position at UCLA, Griffith Joyner transferred there. Brisco narrowly edged her for a spot on the 1980 United States Olympic team. She made the 1981 United States World Cup relay team, which established the American record of 42.82 seconds, and she won the National Collegiate Athletic Association (NCAA) 200 meters in 1982 and the 400 meters in 1983.

Griffith Joyner earned a Bachelor of Arts degree in psychology from UCLA in 1983 and began training for the 1984 Olympics. To support herself, she worked as a hair stylist and began designing clothes. She captured the silver medal at the Los Angeles Olympics, finishing second to Brisco. Griffith Joyner irritated Olympic officials with her bright, colorful, shimmering bodysuits and extremely long red, white, and blue fingernails. She was removed from the U.S. Olympic relay team for refusing to cut her six-inch nails, which officials claimed would make passing the baton difficult and dangerous. Her flamboyance earned her the nicknames "Fluorescent Flo" and "FloJo."

Following her removal from the Olympic team, the bitter, depressed Griffith Joyner worked for Union Bank and scaled back her training. She quickly gained 15 pounds and added a full second to her 200-meter time. In 1986 she ended an engagement to Olympic hurdler Greg Foster. She realized she was at a crossroads if she was ever to be a premier runner and so she returned to former coach Kersee to train for the 1988 Olympics. Kersee gave Griffith Joyner a video of Olympian Ben Johnson winning the 100-meter race in Rome, Italy, and instructed her to study the way Johnson "exploded off the starting block, giving him an undeniable advantage." Griffith Joyner watched the tape daily and worked to imitate Johnson's start. On October 10, 1987, she married Al Joyner, 1984 Olympic triple jump gold medalist and brother of Olympic track and field star, Jackie Joyner-Kersee.*

At the 1988 Olympic trials in Indianapolis, Indiana, Griffith Joyner won the 100-meter sprint in 10.49 seconds. She trimmed .27 second off the world record and earned the press title, "Fastest Woman in the World." No woman had broken the record in the 100-meter event by more than 1/10th of a second.

Florence Griffith Joyner ©Photofest

She wore a white lacy running suit she designed and also frequently raced in eye-catching one-leg running suits. She was required to wear a standard running suit in the 1988 Olympics in Seoul, South Korea, but ran with her six-inch painted fingernails.

Griffith Joyner stole the limelight in Seoul and became the first American woman to win four medals in one Olympics, taking the gold medals in the 100-meter, 200-meter races, and the 400-meter relay and the silver medal in the 1,600-meter relay. Her 21.34 seconds 200-meter time set a world record. Her heroics earned her the 1988 Associated Press Female Athlete of the Year honors and the Sullivan Award as the best U.S. amateur athlete. Griffith Joyner retired from competition in February 1989. She and her husband had a daughter, Mary Ruth, in 1990.

Griffith Joyner came out of retirement in 1991 to train for the 1996 Olympics in Atlanta, Georgia, but Achilles tendon problems eventually ended the dream. She founded the Florence Griffith Joyner Youth Foundation and supported numerous charities to help children in poor neighborhoods. She continued to design clothes, accepted speaking engagements throughout the United States, and wrote several unpublished children's books. In 1996 she was hospitalized after suffering a cardiac seizure on a flight. On September 21, 1998, Griffith Joyner died at age 38 from suffocation caused by an epileptic seizure. Griffith Joyner, one of the world's greatest female athletes, reached heights in athletics that no woman had ever reached before, but she never forgot her humble beginnings or the people who enabled her to reach the top. At her funeral her husband, Al Joyner, eulogized, "One thing about Florence Griffith Joyner that not everybody saw was she gave unconditional love. She was my dream. I stayed focused on her for seven years until she looked my way. I'm going to miss you. I love you."

BIBLIOGRAPHY
Associated Press, *1,500 See FloJo Laid to Rest*, CNN Sports Illustrated Athletics, posted online September 26, 1998; Corine Naden and Rose Blue, *Heroes Don't Just Happen* (Maywood, NJ, 1996); Geri Speace, ed., *Newsmakers 1999 Cumulation* (Detroit, MI, 1999); Susan Wessling, "A Legacy of Caring," *Suite 101.com*: *Real People Helping Real People* (October 20, 1998), pp. 1–3.

Frank J. Olmsted

VLADIMIR GUERRERO Baseball
(February 9, 1976–)

Vladimir Guerrero, one of the most complete contemporary baseball players, combines great power, good speed, and the ability to hit for high batting average.

Vladimir Alvino Guerrero was born on February 9, 1976 in Nizao Bani, Dominican Republic, one of nine children. His older brother, Wilton, played infield for the Cincinnati Reds (National League) and Montreal Expos (NL), while younger brother, Julio, is an infielder in the Boston Red Sox (American League) farm system.

A high school dropout, Guerrero was discovered while playing sandlot baseball by Montreal Expos scouts. He came to his tryout with mismatched spikes that did not fit and signed for $2,000 as an amateur free agent on March 1, 1993, three weeks after his seventeenth birthday. He reported to the Expos Dominican Baseball Academy and batted .333 for the 1993 Expos entry in the Dominican Summer League (DSL). Guerrero batted .424 in the first 25 games of the 1994 DSL. The Expos promoted him to the Gulf Coast Expos (Gulf Coast League), where he hit .314. In 1995 he led the Florida State League with a .333 batting average for Albany, Georgia. Guerrero advanced in 1996 to Harrisburg, Pennsylvania, where he topped Eastern League (EL) batters with a lofty .360 batting mark. He won the EL MVP award and *The Sporting News* 1996 Minor League Player of the Year honors, earning him a September trial with the Montreal Expos. In 1997 the right-handed outfielder batted .302 for Montreal in 90 games and threw out four runners at the plate despite suffering a broken left foot and a broken hand.

Guerrero compiled staggering offensive numbers from 1998 to 2002, exceeding 30 home runs, 75 extra-base hits, 100 runs batted in (RBI), 100 runs scored, and a .300 batting average each season. He belted 42 home runs in 1999 and 44 roundtrippers in 2000. He reached a personal best 131 RBIs in 1999 and fashioned a 31-game hitting streak that included 12 doubles, 11 home runs, and 27 RBIs. Former Expos manager Felipe Alou limited Guerrero's base stealing, fearing injuries. Alou said, "At his age, he is the best talent I've ever seen. If he's pointed in the right direction, he's going to be one of the greatest players of all time." In 2001 manager Jeff Torborg encouraged Guerrero to utilize his excellent speed. Guerrero stole 37 bases, including nine swipes of third base.

Guerrero is a very aggressive hitter and often swings at the first pitch if it is anywhere near his liking. He ranks among the leaders in first-pitch home runs every year. Although he is not the most selective batter, his consistently high batting average demonstrates his ability to get base hits on pitches most hitters would take. The 6-foot 2 ½-inch, 204-pound right-handed right fielder, an excellent two-strike hitter, enjoys equal success against southpaws and right-handers. He hits to all fields and exhibits tremendous opposite field power. Guerrero led the Expos in home runs, RBIs, runs scored, stolen bases, total bases, and slugging percentage in 2001 and 2002, despite having little protection in the lineup. Atlanta Braves superstar Chipper Jones describes Guerrero as "a five tool guy: hit, run, throw, hit for power, and field. I've seen that throwing arm, and I've never seen a hitter like him." Guerrero may be baseball's best kept secret because he plays in Montreal before small crowds with no local radio or television coverage in English. He speaks very little English and remains comfortable playing in a French-speaking city, where most of his teammates also struggle with a language barrier.

Guerrero possesses one of the strongest and most accurate throwing arms in the NL. He shows the same aggressiveness in the right field that he demonstrates at the plate. He led NL flychasers in miscues from 1997 to 2000. Many of his errors resulted from charging or laying back on hard-hit bouncers and keeping his glove down.

Guerrero played on five NL All-Star teams from 1999 to 2003 and was named the Expos' team co-captain with Lee Stevens for the 2002 campaign. Guerrero seemed unruffled by the contraction and relocation adversity surrounding the Montreal franchise in 2002, producing 39 home runs, 111 RBIs, and a .336 batting average. Through the 2003 campaign, he played 1,004 games with 1,219 hits, 641 runs, 226 doubles, 34 triples, 234 home runs, 702 RBIs, and a .324 batting average. Injuries limited him to just 112 games in 2003, but he still hit .330 with 25 home runs and 79 RBIs. During the season, Guerrero lives in Montreal with Altagracia Alvino and their son, Vladimir Jr. In the off-season, Guerrero returns to the Dominican Republic. He enjoys spending free time with his family and listening to music.

BIBLIOGRAPHY
John Dewan, ed., *The Scouting Notebook 2002* (Morton Grove, IL, 2002); Dave George, "UnderEXPOSed: Montreal's Vladimir Guerrero Is a Superstar, What He Isn't Is Famous," www.Canadianbaseballnews.com (April 1, 2001), pp. 1–4; Chuck Johnson, "Vladimir the Great," *Baseball Digest* 60 (February 2001), pp. 38–40; Bob Kuenster, "Vladimir Guerrero: A Five Tool Phenom," *Baseball Digest* 58 (May 1999), pp. 22–25.

Frank J. Olmsted

TONY GWYNN
Baseball
(May 9, 1960–   )

Tony Gwynn's career refreshingly unfolded with one team. His remarkable 20-year career with the San Diego Padres (National League) ended with the 2001 season. Gwynn ranks among baseball's best pure hitters, and as such he is in a class with Ty Cobb, Honus Wagner, and Stan Musial.

Anthony Keith Gwynn was born on May 9, 1960 in Los Angeles, California, the son of Charles A. Gwynn and Vandella (Douglas) Gwynn. Gwynn and his brothers, Charles and Chris, excelled in sports. Charles starred in baseball for the California State University Los Angeles team, while Chris played on the 1984 U.S. Olympic team, made All-America in baseball at San Diego State University, and played with the Los Angeles Dodgers, Kansas City Royals, and San Diego Padres. Gwynn not only played baseball, but was also a highly recruited basketball point guard. In his freshman year, he concentrated on basketball. He was given a chance to play for the Aztecs in 1979, when the team's shortshop, Bobby Meacham, a future All-America and major leaguer, convinced Coach Jim Dietz to let Gwynn compete for a spot on the team.

Gwynn made the team as a left fielder and designated hitter. He became a two-time All-America and was selected as a first-team National Collegiate Athletic Association (NCAA) All-America. He also continued as point guard for the Aztecs, making the All-Western Athletic Conference team twice. Gwynn remains the only athlete in Western Athletic Conferences (WAC) history to be honored as an all-conference athlete in two sports.

On June 10, 1981, the San Diego Padres drafted Gwynn in the third round, and the San Diego Clippers (National Basketball Association) chose him in the tenth round. Gwynn quickly signed with the Padres and reported to Walla Walla, Washington (Rookie) Northwest League. He earned MVP honors that year, leading his team and the league in batting with a .331 batting average. He opened the 1982 season with Class AAA Hawaii (Pacific Coast League), hitting .328 in 93 games. Gwynn quickly was brought up to the San Diego Padres, debuting on July 19, 1982. In the game, he finished two for four with a double, a run scored, a sacrifice fly, and a run batted in (RBI) against the

Philadelphia Phillies. He broke his wrist on August 25 and missed the next three weeks before returning on September 13, compiling a .289 batting average with 55 hits in just 54 games.

That first season with the Padres marked the only campaign that Gwynn finished under .300. The 5-foot 11-inch, 225-pound Gwynn batted and threw left-handed, and won a NL record–tying eight batting championships (1984, 1987–1989, 1994–1997), tying Honus Wagner for second on the all-time list behind Ty Cobb. Many of Gwynn's 3,141 hits were singles. He never hit 20 home runs in a season (17 was his career high), and he drove in 100 runs only once. He became a baseball pioneer, studying videotapes of himself at bat. His strategy paid off. On August 6, 1999, he became only the twenty-second player in major league history to reach 3,000 hits. Gwynn acknowledged that he "never really concentrated on hitting; I'd play basketball, then switch over to baseball and start hitting . . . I started to realize I might be a pretty good hitter." Fellow 3,000-hit club member Wade Boggs said, "He's a truly amazing hitter. He rarely swings at bad pitches, he's very selective, he gets good pitches to hit and nine times out of 10, he hits it hard. . . . He's unbelievable, he really is."

Gwynn earned a spot on the NL All-Star team 15 times, being voted as a starter 11 times. His 11 All-Star starts equaled a major league record for outfielders, a record shared by National Baseball Hall of Fame member Reggie Jackson. Gwynn made *The Sporting News* Silver Slugger team seven times (1984, 1986–1987, 1989, 1994–1995, 1997). Although best known for his prowess in hitting, he earned five Gold Glove Awards, the Roberto Clemente Man of the Year Award, and the Lou Gehrig Memorial Award and was inducted into the World Sports Humanitarian Hall of Fame. He has always committed himself to community service, especially working with children throughout his career. He retired as a player at the end of the 2001 season.

During his major league career, Gwynn only struck out 434 times in 9,288 plate appearances and hit 534 doubles for seventeenth place on the all-time list. He attained a .338 career batting average with 3,141 hits and 1,138 RBIs, and he holds Padre records for career runs (1,383), hits, doubles, triples (85), RBIs, stolen bases (319), and highest batting average. He led his team to the postseason in 1984, 1996, and 1998, losing the 1984 and 1998 World Series.

Gwynn and his wife, Alicia, have two children, Anthony and Anisha Nicole. Gwynn coaches his alma mater's baseball team, the San Diego State Aztecs. His son, Anthony, played center field there and was drafted by the Milwaukee Brewers. When asked what it meant to be coaching his son, Gwynn said, "I'm proud as heck of him. He's got baseball smarts. He's a good player. As a coach, I lean on him a lot, to help me help these freshmen get to where they need to be."

Gwynn, who also is an analyst for ESPN, remains a caring, loyal husband, father, and humanitarian. Never a five-tool player or a World Series champion, he is nonetheless a superstar with a refreshing ability to teach his trade. During his "Goodbye" ceremonies in September 2001, the Padres presented him with a Harley-Davidson motorcycle. Bruce Bochy, the Padres manager, said, "It goes without saying the incredible career you've had and the impact you've had on the people of San Diego. . . . Plain and simple, you just make everyone better."

BIBLIOGRAPHY
Paul Attner, The Sporting News: Baseball—Tony Gwynn, www.sportingnews.com, September 18, 1999, National Baseball Library, Cooperstown, NY; Bob Baum, "Gwynn Makes Coaching Debut Vs. Sun Devils," The Associated Press, National Baseball Library, Cooperstown, NY; Nate Davis, USATODAY.com, What Is Tony Gwynn's Legacy? www.usatoday.com/sports/baseball/padres/2001-0627-gwynn; Ken Gurnick, MLB.com, "Gwynn Closes Out His Career," October 7, 2001, National Baseball Library, Cooperstown, NY; Montreal AP, "Gwynn Gets His 3000th Career Hit," *New York Post*, August 7, 1999, National Baseball Library, Cooperstown, NY; *San Diego Padres Media Guide*, 2001; Tony Gwynn Statistics—Baseball-Reference. com, www.baseball-reference.com/g/gwynnto.01.shtml.

Scot E. Mondore

H

PENNY HARDAWAY
(July 18, 1971–   )   **Basketball**

Penny Hardaway starred in high school, college, and professional basketball.

Anfernee Deon Hardaway was born on July 18, 1971 in Memphis, Tennessee, and grew up in a tough crime-infested area of Memphis. His father, Eddie Golden, taught him the fundamentals of basketball as a young boy. When his mother, Fae Hardaway Patterson, left for Las Vegas, Nevada, to become a singer, his grandmother, Louise Hardaway, took over his upbringing and kept him out of trouble. As a youngster, Hardaway constantly played basketball.

After learning basketball on the "hard nosed" playgrounds of Memphis, Hardaway attended Treadwell High School and became the leading basketball scorer. The 1990 graduate was named Mr. Basketball in Tennessee his senior year, and *Parade Magazine* selected him as National High School Player of the Year. He averaged 36.6 points, 10.1 rebounds, 6.2 assists, 3.3 steals, and 2.8 blocked shots. Later, Hardaway was inducted into the Memphis City School Alumni Hall of Fame.

Hardaway attended nearby Memphis State University (now the University of Memphis) but was declared academically ineligible to play basketball in 1990–1991. Later, however, he achieved a 3.4 grade point average there. As a sophomore in 1991–1992, he led the Tigers to the first of two straight appearances in the National Collegiate Athletic Association (NCAA) Division I Tournament. Memphis advanced to the Regional Finals in 1992. As a junior, he averaged 22.8 points, 8.5 rebounds, and 6.4 assists and established a school single-season record for points with 729. He was named Great Midwestern Conference Player of the Year twice, First Team All-America once, and a finalist for the Naismith and Wooden awards. Memphis State University retired his jersey number in January 1994.

The 6-foot 7-inch, 200-pound Hardaway skipped his senior year and entered the 1994 National Basketball Association (NBA) draft. The Golden State Warriors (NBA) selected him as the third pick and immediately traded him to the Orlando Magic (NBA) for Chris Webber* and three first-round draft choices. He became the starting point guard in midseason and led the Magic to their first NBA playoffs. Besides averaging 16 points, he was named to the 1994 NBA All-Rookie First Team, selected the Most Valuable Player (MVP) of the Schick All-Rookie Game, and finished second to Webber for Rookie of the Year.

The following two seasons, Hardaway became one of the top NBA point guards. He started in the NBA All-Star game and was named to the All-NBA First Team both years. In 1995, he helped the Magic achieve the best record in the Eastern Conference (EC). Orlando advanced to its first NBA Finals by defeating the Boston Celtics and Chicago Bulls and capturing the EC title in seven games over the Indiana Pacers. The Magic did not handle the power and strength of the Houston Rockets, losing in four games. In 1996 the Magic advanced in the playoffs until losing to the Chicago Bulls for the EC Championship. Hardaway played on the gold-medal-winning U.S. Olympic basketball team during the 1996 Summer Olympics in Atlanta, Georgia.

Although missing 23 games during the 1996–1997 season due to a knee injury, Hardaway led the Magic in scoring, was named to the All-NBA Third Team, and again started in the NBA All-Star Game. Hardaway was sidelined for all but 19 games of the 1997–1998 season because of torn cartilage in his left knee. He started all 50 games of the shortened 1998–1999 season, leading the Magic in scoring. In August 1999, he agreed to a sign-and-trade-deal with Orlando and was sent to the Phoenix Suns (NBA) for Danny Manning, Pat Garrity, and two future first-round picks. Hardaway played well with the Suns in 1999–2000, scoring over 1,000 points for the fifth time in his career. He missed nearly all the following season recovering from knee surgery but averaged 12 points in 80 games for Phoenix in 2001–2002 and 10.6 points in 58 games in 2002–2003.

In 10 NBA seasons from 1993–1994 through 2002–2003, Hardaway has compiled 9,646 points, averaged 16.9 points, handed out 3,232 assists, and made 1,006 steals in 571 regular-season games. He averaged 20.6 points and 6.2 assists in 60 playoff games and made four consecutive NBA All-Star Game appearances from 1995 to 1998, averaging 13.8 points.

During the summer of 1994, Hardaway co-starred with Shaquille O'Neal* in the motion picture *Blue Chips*. He is a national spokesman for UNICEF and has been involved with Special Olympics and other charities. His "Stay in School Campaign" promotes good grades and exemplary conduct.

BIBLIOGRAPHY

"Anfernee Hardaway," *Memphis City Schools Honor Hardaway*, www. pennyhardaway.net (2001); "Anfernee Hardaway," *Players Background*, www.nba. com (2001); "Anfernee Hardaway," *Players Career Highlights*, www.nba.com (2001); "Anfernee Hardaway," *Players Career Statistics*, www.nba.com (2001); "Anfernee Hardaway," *Sports Heroes*, www.myhero.com (1998); *The Evansville Courier and Press*, August 4, 2001, p. 12; *NCAA Men's Basketball's Best* (Overland Park, KS, 1998); *The Sporting News Official NBA Register*, 2003–2004.

John L. Evers

TIM HARDAWAY
Basketball
(September 1, 1966–   )

Tim Hardaway won acclaim in the National Basketball Association (NBA) for dishing out assists.

Timothy Duane Hardaway, nicknamed "Timbug," was born on September 1, 1966 in Chicago, Illinois, and grew up on the South Side of Chicago. His father, Donald Hardaway, drove a Coca-Cola truck and gained renown as a basketball player on Chicago-area playground courts. Although smaller than the average basketball player, Hardaway learned the fundamentals of basketball from his father and excelled as a point guard on Chicago playgrounds. His father's alcohol problem caused family tension and differences throughout young Hardaway's school days. His mother, Gwendalyn, a postal worker, divorced his father in 1979. Hardaway eventually informed his father that he wanted nothing more to do with him until he gave up drinking. After several years, his father overcame his drinking problem and the father/son relationship began to improve.

Hardaway starred in basketball at Carver High School in Chicago, and following his graduation in 1985, he attended the University of Texas at El Paso (UTEP), majoring in criminal justice. He played for veteran coach Don Haskins between 1985–1986 and 1988–1989, leading the Miners to 100 victories and four straight appearances in the National Collegiate Athletic Association (NCAA) Division I Tournament. The 5-foot 11-inch Hardaway was named the Western Athletic Conference (WAC) Player of the Year as a senior. He passed Nate Archibald in 1989 to become UTEP's all-time leading scorer with 1,586 points and won the Frances Pomeroy Naismith Award as the nation's best player under 6 feet tall. With the Miners, he perfected a move that the media dubbed the "UTEP TWO-STEP." Hardaway developed the maneuver after watching Pearl Washington of Syracuse University lose a defensive player with a crossover dribble. Hardaway acknowledged, "I added more to it in order to lose my man." "It is not a UTEP-TWO STEP. It's just a simple crossover move that I use." Many players have adopted this maneuver, but he perfected it.

The Golden State Warriors (NBA) selected Hardaway in the first round of the 1989 NBA draft as the fourteenth pick overall. A unanimous selection for the 1989–1990 NBA All-Rookie First Team, Hardaway averaged 14.7 points and led all rookies with 8.7 assists per game. The following three seasons, he became one of the top guards in the NBA thanks to his ability to produce points and assists. He averaged 22.6 points and 10.1 assists. Hardaway's crossover dribble became the best in the NBA in "freezing" the defense, leading to a drive to the basket for a score or a pass to an open teammate. Hardaway was named to the All-NBA Second Team in 1992 and the Third Team in 1993. He did not play during the 1993–1994 season owing to a knee injury.

Disagreements with the new coaching staff ultimately resulted in a trade. In February 1996, Golden State traded Hardaway and Chris Gatling to the Miami Heat (NBA) for Kevin Willis and Bimbo Coles. Hardaway returned to form as one of the top NBA point guards under coach Pat Riley. He enjoyed an outstanding season in 1996–1997, contributing possibly his best overall performance to date. Hardaway led the Heat in scoring, assists, steals, three-point field goals, and minutes played, helping Miami win its first division crown. He and Michael Jordan* were voted as guards on the All-NBA First Team.

Hardaway continued to use his crossover maneuver effectively, leading Miami to 61 victories in 1996–1997 and 55 triumphs the following season. The Heat, however, lost to the Chicago Bulls and the New York Knicks in the playoffs. An All-NBA Second Team selection in 1997–1998 and 1998–1999, Hardaway also played on the gold-medal-winning 1998 U.S. World Championship team. Over the next two seasons, knee and foot injuries limited his playing time. He became a step slower and saw his point production decline. In August 2001, Miami traded Hardaway to the Dallas Mavericks (NBA) for a future second-round draft choice. He was traded to the Denver Nuggets (NBA) in February 2002. In 2001–2002, he averaged 9.6 points in 68 contests.

Hardaway served as a basketball analyst on television for most of the 2002–2003 season, joining the Indiana Pacers (NBA) for the final 10 games. The savvy veteran averaged 4.9 points, providing Indiana with a stabilizing force at point guard late in games. The Pacers finished third in the Eastern Conference, but were upset by the Boston Celtics in the first round of the NBA playoffs. In 14 NBA seasons from 1989–1990 through 2002–2003, Hardaway compiled 15,373 points (17.7-point average), dished out 7,095 assists, and made 1,428 steals in 867 regular season games. He played in 56 NBA playoff games, scoring 943 points (16.8 point average), handing out 382 assists, and making 88 steals. He averaged 10.6 points, 4.6 assists, and one steal in five NBA All-Star games (1991–1993, 1997–1998).

Hardaway donates $20 per assist to the American Cancer Society and operates his own summer camp for youth in Chicago and El Paso. He co-founded "The Support Group," a Chicago nonprofit organization, in 1991. It has assisted over 15,000 youth to excel academically, athletically, and socially.

Hardaway and his wife, Yolanda, have a son, Timothy Jr., and a daughter, Nia.

BIBLIOGRAPHY
Darryl Howerton, "UTEP TWO STEP? Not Really," *Sport* 83 (February 1992), p. 19; *The Sporting News Official NBA Register*, 2003–2004; "Tim Hardaway," *Players Background*, www.nba.com (2001); "Tim Hardaway," *Players Career Highlights*, www.nba.com (2001); "Tim Hardaway," *Players Career Statistics*, www.nba.com (2001); "Tim Hardaway," *Profile*, www.WorldSportsmen.com (1998); "Tim Hardaway," *Profile and Statistics*, www.USABasketball.com (2000); Jeff Weinstock, "Steppin' Out," *Sport* 83 (May 1992), pp. 44–47.

John L. Evers

KENNY HARRISON   **Track and Field**
(February 13, 1965–   )

Kenny Harrison set an American record in the triple jump at the 1996 Atlanta, Georgia Olympic Games.

Kenny Harrison was born on February 13, 1965 in Milwaukee, Wisconsin, and graduated in 1983 from Central High School in Brookfield, Wisconsin. He set the Wisconsin State meet record for the triple jump with a leap of 48 feet 6.25 inches in 1983 and the all-time standard for a Wisconsin high school athlete at 52 feet 4.51 inches in 1983 at the Golden West meet. He was considered the second best prep in the triple jump in the nation.

Harrison graduated from Kansas State University in 1988 with a Bachelor's degree in journalism and public relations. The 5-foot 10-inch, 165-pounder performed equally well in the long jump, but dropped that event upon leaving Kansas State. He competed in the triple jump and long jump in both the indoor and outdoor National Collegiate Athletic Association (NCAA) Championships, recording three first-place finishes, two seconds, and one third.

In 1984, Harrison finished twenty-second in the Olympic Trials, won the USA Junior Championship, and placed second in the Pan Am Junior Games. In 1986 he was fourth in the USA Championships and ranked fourth in the United States in the triple jump and ninth in the long jump. The following year, he ended seventh in the USA Championships and second in the World University Games and was ranked seventh in the United States in the triple jump. In 1988 he was sixth in the Olympic Trials, ranked fourth in the United States in the triple jump, and ninth in the long jump. His best triple jump was 56 feet 3.25 inches, and his best long jump was 26 feet 3.75 inches.

Harrison trained for the 1992 Olympic Games, concentrating on the triple jump. Being small in stature, he found it very difficult competing against taller and physically stronger and faster athletes. He also suffered strains, sprains, fiber tears, torn cartilage, pulled muscles, and fractures.

The long journey to the Olympic gold medal began in 1989. That season Harrison finished only sixth in the USA Indoor Championships, with a best triple jump of 57 feet 3.75 inches. He was ranked fourth in the world and second in the United States. Harrison's performance the following two years made him the favorite for the 1992 Olympics at Barcelona, Spain. He prevailed in the USA Indoor Meet, captured first-place finishes twice in the USA Championships, and triumphed at the Goodwill Games and the World Championships. His best jump of 58 feet 10 inches helped him earn best ranking in the world. In 1992, a torn knee cartilage, which would later require surgery, blocked his way. Harrison, with a disappointing sixth-place finish in the Trials, did not qualify for the Olympics.

Following successful knee surgery and rehabilitation, Harrison began training for the 1996 Olympic Games at Atlanta, Georgia. For three years, he worked out daily and competed against others to reach the level that he had attained prior to his knee injury. He placed second in the USA Championships in 1993 and 1994, tenth in the World Championships in 1993, and first in the USA Indoor Meet. His best jump of 57 feet 2.25 inches helped him attain the second best ranking in both the United States and the world.

The year 1996 marked Harrison's finest, as he captured the Olympic Trials with a wind-aided leap of 59 feet 1.25 inches. In the Olympic Finals, he made a powerful jump of 59 feet 4.25 inches to establish an American record and capture the elusive gold medal. He was now ranked best in the United States and the world.

Battling age, Harrison began his journey to compete in the 2000 Olympic Games in Sydney, Australia. He captured first place in the USA Championships, dropped back to ninth place in the World Championships, and finished eighth in the Goodwill Games. In 1999 he did not get beyond the qualifying stages for the 2000 Olympic Games.

Prior to the 1996 Olympic Games, Harrison and Gail Devers* became romantically involved. They lived and trained together. Devers, an Olympic sprinter and hurdler, was a two-time 100-meter gold medalist and a member of the gold-medal-winning 4×100 relay team.

BIBLIOGRAPHY

Pete Cava, Executive Director, International Sports Associates, to John L. Evers, November 2002; "Kenny Harrison," *Athlete Bio*, www.usatf.com (1999); "Kenny Harrison," *Olympic Dreams Come True*, www.kstatecollegian.com (1996); "Kenny Harrison," *Wisconsin Track Athlete Bio*, www.wiaa.com (2001); *NCAA National Collegiate Championships*, 1986–1987.

John L. Evers and David L. Porter

MARVIN HARRISON Football
(August 25, 1972–)

Marvin Harrison, a wide receiver for the Indianapolis Colts (National Football League), has quietly developed into one of the best NFL pass receivers. Lacking the flair exhibited by his competitors, this hard worker and achiever often fails to attract the recognition he justly deserves.

Marvin Daniel Harrison Jr. was born on August 25, 1972 in Philadelphia, Pennsylvania. He was only 2 years old when his father, Marvin Sr., died of a genetic disease. He was brought up by his mother, Linda Harrison, who worked two jobs to support the family. A strict disciplinarian, Linda Harrison insured that her son focused on academics and stayed out of trouble. Harrison credits his outstanding work ethic as a professional athlete to the example set by his mother.

In 1991 Harrison graduated from Roman Catholic High School in Philadelphia, where he excelled in both football and basketball. The wide receiver

Marvin Harrison ©Rich Clarkson

and running back won three Maxwell awards, given each year to Philadelphia's top high school football player. Harrison's high school athletic achievements caught the attention of college recruiters. He accepted a football scholarship at Syracuse University and entered in the fall of 1991.

At Syracuse, the 6-foot, 187-pound Harrison earned four letters in football and established a school record for receiving yardage (2,718). He ranks second on the Orangemen's all-time records for touchdowns (20) and receptions (135). During his final college game, Syracuse defeated Clemson University, 41–0. He caught seven passes for 173 yards and two touchdowns.

Harrison was the nineteenth pick by the Indianapolis Colts in the 1996 NFL draft and signed a five-year, $5.8 million contract. During his rookie season, he led the Colts in pass receptions with 64 catches for 836 yards and eight touchdowns. The quiet, popular receiver had a high metabolism, which allowed him to consume vast quantities of junk food without putting on weight. During the football season, he reportedly consumed 30 Tastykakes—his favorite snack—a week.

Although the Colts' record remained abysmal, Harrison enjoyed successful campaigns in 1997 with 73 catches for 866 yards and six touchdowns and in 1998 with 59 receptions for 776 yards and seven touchdowns. A dislocated shoulder, however, sidelined him during the final six games of the 1998 season. He agreed to attend a 10-week 1999 spring training camp to work with the Colts' talented young quarterback Payton Manning. Harrison and Manning quickly established a personal and professional relationship, helping the Colts emerge as one of the top NFL teams with 13 wins and 3 losses. Indianapolis, however, lost in the playoffs to the Tennessee Titans. Although he was increasingly double-teamed by opposition secondaries, Harrison finished the 1999 season with 115 catches for an NFL best 1,663 yards and 12 touchdowns. He was named to the Pro Bowl and signed a four-year contract extension with the Colts worth approximately $25 million.

Indianapolis's fortunes declined in 2000 and 2001, but Harrison continued to establish excellent receiving marks. In 2000 he led Indianapolis with 102 catches and 14 touchdowns to tie a Colt record set by Raymond Berry in 1959. In 2001 he caught 109 passes for 1,514 yards and set a new Colts record with 15 touchdowns. After reaching the playoffs in 1999 and 2000, Indianapolis failed to qualify for postseason play in 2001. In a banner 2002 season, Harrison caught an NFL single-season record 143 passes for 1,722 yards (12.0-yard average) and 11 touchdowns to help the 10–6 Colts make the playoffs. Harrison, the first NFL receiver to have four consecutive 100-catch seasons, reached 600 career receptions in 102 games, the fastest in NFL history. He has caught more passes (528) in the last five years than any other NFL receiver, and he became the first NFL player to surpass 1,500 receiving yards in consecutive seasons, making the Pro Bowl. Through 2002, Harrison caught 665 passes for 8,790 yards and 73 touchdowns.

Harrison has finally gained the attention and respect he richly deserves. Colts team president Bill Polian admires Harrison's work ethic, "He does the most to get the maximum of an extremely talented body."

The low-key receiver remains single and resides in Philadelphia.

BIBLIOGRAPHY
Jeffri Chadiha, "Harrison Finally Getting His Due," *Sports Illustrated* 93 (November 6, 2000), pp. 101–102; P. G. Herman, "Marvin Harrison," *Current Biography* (New York, 2001); Pat King, "Hooked Up," *Sports Illustrated* 91 (October 4, 1999), pp. 106–109.

Ron Briley

RICKEY HENDERSON   Baseball
(December 25, 1958–   )

Rickey "Man of Steal" Henderson, professional baseball's acknowledged all-time greatest leadoff hitter, is the leader in baseball's career runs, walks, and stolen bases, and a member of its exclusive 3,000 hits club.

Rickey Henley Henderson was born on December 25, 1958, in Chicago, Illinois, the fourth of seven children of John Henley, a truck driver, and Bobbie (Earl) Henley, a registered nurse. His father left home when Henderson was an infant. His mother moved the children to live with her mother in Pine Bluff, Arkansas. When Henderson was 7 years old, she married Paul Henderson and moved to Oakland, California. Henderson credits his mother as being the "greatest influence in my life and my career."

Henderson, known for his blazing speed, excellent fielding, sharp batting eye, and ability to hit for power and batting average, initially won acclaim for his base stealing. Encouraged later to hit more for power, Henderson has clouted more leadoff home runs than any player in history (80). He also won a Gold Glove in his second full major league season. St. Louis Cardinals manager Tony La Russa called him "the most disruptive force in baseball."

The right-hand hitting, left-hand throwing Henderson became an outstanding athlete at Oakland Technical High School, participating in baseball, basketball, football, and track and field. He batted .716 as a junior and .465 as a senior, and was picked on the First Team All-Northern California. The Oakland Athletics (American League) selected Henderson in the fourth round of the June 1976 free-agent draft. A high school football All-America running back who rushed for 1,100 yards in his senior year, he also received two dozen football scholarship offers. Although football was his first love, his mother persuaded him to sign with the Athletics.

Switched to the outfield, Henderson spent over three years in the minor leagues and joined Oakland at midseason of 1979.

Henderson helped propel Oakland to second place in the Western Division in 1980. He broke Ty Cobb's single-season AL record with 100 steals and contributed a .303 batting average, 117 walks, 111 runs, and a .422 on-base-percentage. In the strike-shortened 1981 season, he batted .319, led the AL in stolen bases, hits, and runs, earned a Gold Glove, and finished second in the MVP balloting. Although the Athletics lost to the New York Yankees in the AL Championship Series (ALCS), Henderson batted .364. In 1982 he broke Lou Brock's single-season major league record with 130 stolen bases and led the AL with 116 walks. He stole 108 bases in 1983 to win his fourth straight title. The A's however, traded Henderson to the New York Yankees (AL) in December 1984.

Henderson batted .314 in 1985, belting 24 home runs, stealing 80 bases, leading the AL with 146 runs, and finishing third in the MVP voting. He became the first AL player to hit at least 20 home runs and steal 50 bases in a season. In 1986 Henderson accumulated a career-high 75 runs batted in (RBI), clouted 28 home runs, stole 87 bases to lead the AL for a seventh straight year, and scored 130 runs, an AL best for the second consecutive year. Baseball expert Bill James observed that Henderson's 1986 home run and stolen base totals represented the best single-season combination of power and speed in baseball history. He did not win universal acclaim, however. The Yankees critized Henderson for a lackadaisical attitude. In 1988, Henderson stole a league-leading 93 bases.

New York traded Henderson back to Oakland in June 1989. He batted .305, broke Bobby Bonds' career record for leadoff home runs with 35, and led the AL in stolen bases (77), walks (126), and runs (113), as Oakland won its second straight Western Division title. The 5-foot 10-inch, 195-pound left fielder was named the 1989 ALCS MVP, as the A's eliminated the Toronto Blue Jays in five games. He batted .400, clubbed two home runs, and compiled a .609 on-base percentage. Henderson also set a record for steals (8), and tied another mark with runs scored (8). "That was the best I've ever played," he declared. Henderson continued his stellar play in the World Series, hitting a home run and batting .474 to help Oakland sweep the San Francisco Giants. He also led in steals (3), total bases (17), and hits (9).

In 1990, Henderson led Oakland to its third straight Western Division title and was named AL MVP. He recorded career-high .325 batting and .577 slugging averages and a .441 on-base percentage, led the AL for the fifth time with 119 runs for a record tenth time with 65 steals, and shattered Ty Cobb's career AL stolen-base record of 892. His 28 home runs matched a career high. Oakland was swept by the NL champion Cincinnati Reds in the World Series, but Henderson excelled with eight hits, a .333 batting average, and three stolen bases. In 1991 he topped Lou Brock's career stolen-base mark of 938 and led the AL in thefts (58) an eleventh time, both major league records. Oakland traded Henderson to the Toronto Blue Jays (AL) in midseason 1993. He made a .435 on-base percentage as the Blue Jays captured their second straight AL and World Series Championships.

Henderson returned to Oakland in 1994 and two years later joined the San Diego Padres (NL). He led the Padres with a career-high 125 walks, a .410 on-base percentage, and 110 runs. He hit .333 in the NL Division Series against the St. Louis Cardinals. Henderson joined the Anaheim Angels (AL) in late 1997 and made a fourth visit to Oakland in 1998, pacing the AL at age 39 in walks (118) and stolen bases (66). In 1999, he batted .315 with the New York Mets (NL) and hit .400 with six stolen bases in the four-game NL Division Series victory over the Arizona Diamondbacks. He was named the 1999 NL Comeback Player of the Year by *The Sporting News*.

Henderson signed with the Seattle Mariners (AL) in 2000. In 2001, he rejoined San Diego and broke Babe Ruth's career walk record (2,062) and Ty Cobb's career runs record (2,246). In the season finale, he became the twenty-fifth major league player to achieve at least 3,000 career hits. He performed for the Boston Red Sox (AL) in 2002 and the Los Angeles Dodgers and in 2003.

Henderson, a 10-time All Star, batted .279 with 3,055 hits, including 510 doubles and 297 home runs, scoring 2,295 runs, and recorded 2,190 walks, 1,406 steals, and a .399 on-base percentage and a .979 fielding average through 2003.

Henderson resides with his high school sweetheart Pamela Palmer in Hillsborough, California. They have three children, Angela, Alexis, and Adriann.

BIBLIOGRAPHY

David Pietrusza et al., eds., *Baseball: The Biographical Encyclopedia* (Kingston, NY, 2000); David L. Porter, ed., *Biographical Dictionary of American Sports: Baseball*, revised and expanded edition (Westport, CT, 2000); "Rickey Henderson," *Current Biography Yearbook* (New York, 1990), pp. 293–297; Rickey Henderson file, National

Baseball Library, Cooperstown, NY; Rickey Henderson with John Shea, *Off Base*: (New York, 1992); *The Sporting News Baseball Register, 2003*; John Thorn et al., eds., *Total Baseball*, 7th ed. (Kingston, NY, 2001); Bernie Wilson, "Henderson Adds to Landmark Season," *USA Today Baseball Weekly*, October 10–16, 2001, p. 20.

Jack C. Braun

LIVAN HERNANDEZ   Baseball
(February 29, 1975–)

The day his Florida Marlins (National League) team won the 1997 World Series over the Cleveland Indians, in a 3–2, 11-inning victory, Livan Hernandez cried as he embraced his mother, Miriam Carreras, who had arrived from Cuba just hours before Game Seven. Hernandez had not seen her for over two years because of his daring defection from Cuba in September 1995. After the game, he beamed, "This is the happiest moment in my life. My mother's here and we are champions." In the postseason, Hernandez won two games over the Atlanta Braves in the NL Championship Series (NLCS) and defeated the Cleveland Indians in Game One and Game Five of the World Series. He was named most Valuable Player (MVP) for both the NLCS and World Series.

Hernandez's journey from Cuba to Mexico to Florida proved dangerous and difficult. Other baseball players had defected from Cuba and were declared "traitors" by the Fidel Castro government. Cuban officials kept close watch over the national team players. When in Monterrey, Mexico, with his older half-brother Orlando "El Duque" Hernandez* at the training camp of the Cuban national team, he left his motel secretly at midnight without any word even to his brother and met Joe Cubas, the noted recruiter of Cuban baseball players for U.S. major league teams. They drove to Mexico City, traveled to Venezuela, and ended in the Dominican Republic, where Cubas arranged interviews with American baseball teams. Hernandez signed with the Florida Marlins (NL) so that he could live in Miami. His contract entailed $6.5 million for four years with a $2.5 million signing bonus.

Livan Eisler Hernandez was born on February 20, 1974 in Villa Clara, Cuba, to Arnaldo Hernandez Montero and his second wife, Miriam Carreras. Arnaldo, an accomplished baseball player for Cuba's national team, played all positions. But his excellence as a pitcher won him the esteemed nickname, *El Duque*, "the duke." Arnaldo later managed Cuban baseball teams, including the Isle of Youth, an island 50 miles south of the mainland. Livan Hernandez grew up there with his mother, who worked as a typist in a government office after Arnaldo moved out of the house. They lived in a crowded fifth-floor apartment. As a teenager, he earned $5 a month as an electrician's assistant, a phantom job provided him as long as he played baseball.

Hernandez won acclaim across the island as the third superb pitcher from his family, following his father and brother. Trained in the best sport schools, he threw effortlessly with a three-quarters delivery. By his midteens, he mastered a curveball to complement a blazing fastball. He made Team Cuba before his twentieth birthday.

After signing as a nondrafted free agent with the Florida Marlins in January 1996, Hernandez struggled for a year. The Marlins sent him to Charlotte, North Carolina (International League), and Portland, Maine (Eastern League). He was separated from his family, had few American friends, and did not speak English, making communicating with his new coaches difficult. He gained 20 pounds and disagreed some with teammates. He also engaged in a bitter dispute with Cubas, leading to a split.

After compiling a 5–3 record with Charlotte in 1997, the 6-foot 2-inch, 222-pound Hernandez joined the Marlins in midseason and won his first nine decisions. He finished the year with a 9–3 mark, 3.18 earned run average (ERA), and two World Series wins. In 1998–1999, he made 53 appearances with the Marlins, a team greatly weakened by multiple budget-cutting trades after its World Series year. He fared 15–17 with a 4.74 ERA.

In July 1999, Hernandez's career was invigorated after his trade to the San Francisco Giants (NL) for two minor leaguers. He won three games in the regular season and capped his year with a 5–1 win over the New York Mets in Game One of the NL Division Series (NLDS), raising his lifetime postseason record to 5–0. His effectiveness continued in 2000 with a strong 17–11 record and 3.75 ERA.

On Opening Day of 2001, Hernandez threw 7.1 innings and drove in the Giants' first run in a 3–2 win over the San Diego Padres at PacificBell Park. Giants' manager Dusty Baker told reporters, "Livan was awesome. Not only did he pitch well, but he was an outstanding hitter, too." Hernandez's hot hitting continued through 2001. He made 12 hits in 13 at bats, including eight consecutive hits, at one stretch. He recorded four hits against the Chicago Cubs on August 11, becoming the first NL pitcher to accomplish the feat since 1997. In 34 starts in 2001, Hernandez won 13 games while losing 15 with a 5.24 ERA. He compiled a 12–16 record, three shutouts, and a 4.38 ERA in 2002, hurling 216 innings for the NL Wild Card winners. Hernandez won Game Four of the NL Division Series, fanning six in an 8–3 victory over the Atlanta Braves. Hernandez started Game Four of the NLCS against the St. Louis Cardinals, going 6.1 innings without a decision. He pitched poorly in the World Series, losing both Games Four and Seven with a 14.29 ERA and lasting a combined 5.2 innings in his two starts. In March 2003, the Montreal Expos (NL) acquired Hernandez. Through 2002, he had pitched 1,449.1 innings, with a 84–9 won-lost record and a 4.22 ERA. Hernandez led the NL in innings pitched (233.1) and complete games (8) in 2003, compiling a 15–10 record, 3.20 ERA, and 178 strikeouts.

BIBLIOGRAPHY

Milton H. Jamail, *Full Count: Inside Cuban Baseball* (Carbondale, IL, 2000); "Livan Hernandez," *People Weekly* 48 (December 2, 1997), p. 136; S.L. Price, "Delivering a Strong Pitch," *Sports Illustrated* 84 (March 25, 1996), pp. 72–75; "The Pride of Little Havana," *Marlins Magazine 6* (1998), pp. 61–63.

Richard D. Miller

ORLANDO "EL DUQUE" HERNANDEZ   Baseball
(October 11, 1965–)

As a rookie right-handed pitcher for the New York Yankees (American League) in 1998, Orlando Hernandez posted a 12–1 won-lost record with a 3.13 ERA and won two crucial postseason games en route to their World Series title over the San Diego Padres. "I dreamed of being a pitcher in the major leagues, but it never went through my mind that I would be a World Champion pitcher in less than a year," Hernandez acknowledged. Orlando had lived in Cuba, poor and forbidden to play baseball. Although a national hero as the pitching ace with the Cuban national team, he was banned from the sport in 1996 because his half-brother, Livan Hernandez,* who also played on the national team, had defected from Cuba to play baseball in the United States.

The day after Christmas in 1997, Hernandez and seven other Cubans secretly left the island on a small fishing boat and became shipwrecked on a deserted island. The United States Coast Guard picked them up and took them to Nassau, Bahamas. With the help of Joe Cubas, the player agent who aided Livan Hernandez in his defection, and Senator Robert Torricelli of New Jersey, Orlando was offered citizenship in Costa Rica. "In the short time I've been here I've been enjoying democracy and freedom. Here nobody can tell me what to say," he told reporters. In March 1998, he signed a four-year contract worth $6.6 million with the New York Yankees.

Orlando P. Hernandez was born on October 11, 1965 in Villa Clara, Cuba. His parents, Arnaldo Hernandez and Maria Julia Pedroso, separated. Orlando moved to Havana, Cuba, with his mother and older brother, Gerardo, to live in his grandparents' cramped two-room house. Stories are told that he slept on the floor until he was 16 years old. His mother's job as a typist for the Cuban government did not provide enough money for baseball bats and balls. Hernandez learned baseball on open lots with broomsticks as bats and large corks for balls. Despite all obstacles, he learned the game well. Like his father, he became a member of the Cuban national team.

His father, Arnaldo, was so skilled as a pitcher that Cuban fans nicknamed him "El Duque" or "the duke." Orlando Hernandez soon displayed his unique windup with his knee lifted against his ear and threw a blazing fastball as a pitcher for the strong Industriales team, the Yankees of Cuban baseball. Fans, who remembered his father, gave him the honored title, "El Duque" and chanted "El Duque" whenever he took the mound. During 10 years of competition, he became the most successful pitcher in Cuban amateur history with a 129–47 won-lost record. Cuba won two National Series titles and an Olympic gold medal.

As a celebrity on the national team, Hernandez left poverty behind. He was given a three-bedroom house in a nice neighborhood following his marriage to Norma Manzo and the birth of their two daughters, Yahumara and Steffi.

The good life ended abruptly, however, after his removal from the national team. Hernandez returned to poverty, and his marriage ended in divorce. He lived with dance teacher Noris Bosch, who accompanied him in his escape from Cuba. Life changed radically for him upon his arrival in the United States and acquisition by the New York Yankees.

After spring training in 1998, the New York Yankees sent Hernandez to their Triple A affiliate, the Columbus (Ohio) Clippers (International League). Hernandez dominated hitters, quickly posting a 6–0 record with a 3.83 earned run average (ERA). When Yankees starting pitcher David Cone suffered a sore arm, manager Joe Torre promoted Hernandez to fill the open spot in the rotation. Torre planned to pitch Hernandez one game and return him to Columbus. On June 3, the 6-foot 2-inch, 190-pounder pitched seven innings against the Tampa Bay Devil Rays. Hernandez displayed a wicked slider, a curveball, and a 90-mile-per-hour fastball, giving up five hits, striking out seven batters, gaining the 7–1 win, and never returning to Columbus. During his stunning rookie year, he posted a 12–4 record, 3.13 ERA, and a 9–3 World Series win over the San Diego Padres. His finest moment came when the U.S. State Department allowed his mother, ex-wife, and two daughters to visit New York, just 30 hours after the World Series win. That same day, he and his family stood on a float in the New York City ticker-tape parade for the World Champions. He raised his daughters above the crowd as his fans cheered, "Duque, Duque."

During 1999, Hernandez solidified his credentials with a 17–9 mark, 4.12 ERA, and three postseason victories to help the Yankees win their twenty-sixth World Championship. He also garnered the AL Championship (ALCS) Series Most Valuable Player (MVP) award. Hernandez enhanced his pitching ability with agile fielding. When a ball became stuck in his glove while fielding a ground ball, he tossed both ball and glove to first to record an out. He opened the AL Division Series (ALDS) with an 8–0 shutout over the Texas Rangers, clinched the AL pennant with a 6–1 win over the Boston Red Sox in the ALCS, and defeated the Atlanta Braves 4–1 in the opening World Series game, yielding only one hit in seven innings.

Although Hernandez was among the AL leaders in opposition batting average and runs allowed, his 2000 record fell to 12–13. Elbow discomfort and back spasms sidelined him in July. In the postseason, however, he again performed well, defeating the Oakland A's 4–2 in the ALDS and twice triumphing over the Seattle Mariners, 7–1 and 9–7, in the ALCS to bring his postseason record to 8–0. In Game 3 of the World Series against the New York Mets, he struck out 12 in his first postseason game loss, 4–2.

Injuries again plagued Hernandez in 2001, as he missed almost three months following toe surgery. He was sent to the minor leagues for rehabilitation and did not win his first game until September. He finished the year just 4–7 with a 4.85 ERA. Hernandez compiled an 8–5 record with a 3.64 ERA in 2002 and lost his only decision with a 2.84 ERA against the Anaheim Angels in the ALDS. In January 2003, the Montreal Expos (NL) acquired him in a three-way trade. Through 2003, he has pitched in 124 regular season games with a 53–38 won-lost record and a 4.04 ERA and was 9–3 in post-season play. Hernandez underwent shoulder surgery and missed the 2003 season.

Hernandez is married to Noris Bosch.

BIBLIOGRAPHY

Steve Fainaru and Ray Sanchez, *The Duke of Havana* (New York, 2001); Milton H. Jamail, *Full Count: Inside Cuban Baseball* (Carbondale, IL, 2000); Kenneth La-Freniere, *El Duque: The Story of Orlando Hernandez* (New York, 1999); Tom Ver-ducci, "El Duque," *Sports Illustrated* 89 (August 17, 1998), pp. 30–35.

Richard D. Miller

ROBERTO HERNANDEZ   Baseball
(November 11, 1964–)

Roberto Hernandez, a 6-foot 4-inch, 250-pound right-handed relief pitcher, still throws hard at age 40. He has added a split finger pitch to accompany his 90-plus-miles-per-hour fastball, making him an unwelcome sight to opposing batters as he enters from the bullpen to close out a game. He ranks fourth on the active list for saves and fifteenth overall with 320 career saves. His 60-plus appearances in seven straight seasons and his 81 percent save conversion ratio illustrate his durability and dependability.

Roberto Manuel Rodriguez Hernandez was born on November 11, 1964 in Santurce, Puerto Rico, but his family moved to New York City when he was a baby. Hernandez often played baseball in Central Park as a boy. He won a scholarship to New Hampton Prep School in New Hampshire, where he starred in football, basketball, and baseball. After graduating, he attended the University of South Carolina–Aiken and was honored in 1993 by having their refurbished stadium named after him. He caught until his sophomore year in college and believes that catching later helped him coordinate with his receivers when he became a pitcher.

The California Angels (American League) selected Hernandez in the first round of the 1986 draft. He was traded in August 1989 to the Chicago White Sox (AL) and reached the major leagues in September 1991 with the White Sox after five minor league seasons. His career almost ended before he ever reached the major leagues. During 1991 in Vancouver, Canada (Pacific Coast League), he developed blood clots in his right arm. This necessitated 11-hour, and 5-hour operations. His speedy recovery and September promotion to Chicago resulted in the only three starts of his major league career. The White Sox soon realized his potential as a relief pitcher. He served as the White Sox closer in 1993, saving 38 games.

The 1993 season marked Hernandez's first trip to postseason play, as he appeared in four games and recorded one save in the AL Championship Series (ALCS) loss to the Toronto Blue Jays. He enjoyed an outstanding year in 1996 with 38 saves, a career-high 84 innings pitched, a 1.91 earned run average (ERA), and his first All-Star appearance.

Hernandez experienced another strong campaign as the White Sox closer in 1997, but was traded that July with Wilson Alvarez and Danny Darwin to the San Francisco Giants (National League) for seven minor leaguers. Since the White Sox trailed first place by only 3½ games, this move caused owner Jerry Reinsdorf to receive much criticism in Chicago. The trade produced the desired result for the Giants. Hernandez pitched briefly in the NL Division Series (NLDS), in which the Giants were swept by the Florida Marlins.

Hernandez signed with the Tampa Bay Devil Rays (AL) on the day of the expansion draft in November 1997. He excelled as closer for the Devil Rays for three seasons, enjoying another All-Star appearance in 1999 with 43 saves. With Tampa Bay, he notched 101 saves in 111 opportunities from 1998 through 2000. The Kansas City Royals (AL), who had endured 59 blown saves in 1999 and 2000, were most interested in acquiring him. In January 2001, Hernandez was traded to Kansas City in a three-way transaction with the Oakland Athletics and the Tampa Bay Devil Rays.

Hernandez tried to stabilize the Royals bullpen. He described his approach as he became Kansas City's highest paid player at $6 million. "It's tough, as a closer. You get beat up physically and mentally. I prepare myself to pitch in 162 games. I think this is a day I might get into a game. I get mentally focused and involved in the game. It's your ego, you want to perform at the best of your ability every time." He gave the Royals quality relief work and leadership in 2001, pitching in 63 games and preserving 28 of 34 save opportunities, or 43 percent of the Royals' wins. In 2002 he preserved 26 of 33 save chances, or 42 percent of Kansas City's victories. The Atlanta Braves (National League) acquired him as a free agent in January 2003. In 2003, Hernandez appeared in 66 games as a spot reliever with a 5–3 record and 4.35 ERA in 60 innings and hurled one scoreless inning in the NL Division Series against the Chicago Cubs.

The Sporting News honored Hernandez as one of the 100 "Good Guys in Sports" with regard to civic responsibility and character. He donates $100,000 a year to the Puerto Rico All-Stars Fund, which provides youth-related educational and character-building programs. His 3.30 ERA, 320 saves in 760 games, and 53–54 won-lost record attest to his high standards in 14 major league seasons. He lives in Largo, Florida, near where he played for the Florida Marlins. He and his wife, Ivonne, have two sons and a daughter.

BIBLIOGRAPHY
Bob Dutton, "Royals Need Someone to Stop the Ugly Numbers," *Kansas City Star*, January 20, 2001; Dick Kaegel, "Hernandez Feels Fortunate His Career Didn't End Too Soon," *Kansas City Star*, January 20, 2001; *Kansas City Royals Media Guide*, 2002; Dick Kaegel, "Roberto Hernandez Is More Than a Stopper He's a . . . Strike Force," *Kansas City Star*, March 20, 2001; Roberto Hernandez Profile, Kansas City Royals Web Page player profiles, January 15, 2002; Roberto Hernandez Profile, 2001 Yahoo Inc., 2001 Stats Inc., 2001 MLBPA; "Roberto Hernandez Career Profile," 2001 CNN/*Sports Illustrated.*

John E. Mosher

GRANT HILL
(October 5, 1972–   )

Basketball

Grant Hill, the son of a famous professional football player, Calvin Hill, established his excellence in the collegiate and professional ranks among America's premier basketball players of the 1990s. Grant, also known for his intelligence, modesty, and character, saw his playing time and commercial endorsements diminished by injury during the 2000–2003 seasons.

Grant Henry Hill was born on October 5, 1972 in Dallas, Texas, the only child of Calvin Hill and Janet Hill. Calvin Hill had graduated from Yale University, starred as a running back in the early 1970s with the Dallas Cowboys (National Football League), and finished his career with the Washington Redskins (NFL) and Cleveland Browns (NFL). Janet Hill attended Wellesley College and shared a dormitory with Senator Hillary Rodham Clinton. She served as a special assistant to the secretary of the army and as a partner in the Capitol Hill consulting firm Alexander & Associates.

When Calvin was traded to the Redskins in 1976, the Hills moved to the affluent Washington suburb of Reston, Virginia. Hill's upbringing as the only child of successful parents was strict with high expectations. Homework always had to be completed before play. He reportedly never attended a dance until age 16. As an adult, he appreciated his parents, observing, "it was almost like being born into a royal family and being raised like a prince, being taught one day to become king. Not just how to be an athlete, but how to do things right."

Calvin refused to allow his son to play youth football. Upon entering ninth grade at South Lakes High School in Reston, Hill played basketball rather than football. During his junior and senior years at South Lakes, he led his team to two state championships. He averaged 25 and 29 points per game, respectively, and was selected as a high school All-American both years.

Widely recruited by major college basketball programs, Hill initially wanted to play for nearby Georgetown University. Disappointed with Georgetown's low academic expectations of athletes, he instead opted for coach Mike Krzyzewski and the Duke University Blue Devils. He joined a team with established stars Bobby Hurley and Christian Laettner, averaging 11.2 points with 79 assists and 51 steals and helping Duke defeat the University of Kansas for the 1991 National Collegiate Athletic Association (NCAA) Championship. The Duke small forward made the All-America freshman team. Duke was again national champion in 1992, with Hill averaging over 16 points and being named Second Team All-America.

Rejecting overtures to turn professional, Hill returned to Duke for his junior year in 1993. He led the Blue Devils in scoring with an 18-point average, but Duke was ousted in the NCAA tournament's second round. He also led Duke in steals (64) and won the Henry Iba Corinthian Award as the nation's best

Grant Hill ©Barry Gossage/Getty Images

college defensive player. Although Duke lost to the University of Arkansas in the 1994 NCAA Championship game, Hill's senior year was stellar. Hill led Duke in scoring (17.4 points per game), assists (176), and steals (64), while being named Atlantic Coast Conference Player of the Year and earning unanimous First Team All-America honors. During his four-year tenure at Duke, Hill compiled 1,924 points, 461 assists, 218 steals, and 133 blocks. The university retired Hill's number 33.

After earning a Bachelor's degree in history, Hill was selected by the Detroit Pistons (National Basketball Association) in the first round as the third overall pick of the 1994 NBA draft. He signed an eight-year, $45 million contract to play with the Pistons and garnered commercial endorsements from Sprite, General Motors, and Kellogg. He did not let financial success go to his head, however, and he earned a reputation for team play, leading the Pistons in steals (124) and points per game (19.9). In balloting for the 1994 All-Star Game, Hill emerged as the first rookie in NBA history to record the greatest number of fan votes. Fans were hungry for players who would display character and place team before ego. NBA officials hoped that he would replace Michael Jordan,* who was then attempting an ill-fated baseball career, as a gate attraction. Nevertheless, Hill downplayed such comparisons, observing, "No matter what I did, if I didn't score as many points as Michael, or win a title in as many years as him. I would still be a failure. Besides, I was never a scorer. Getting 30 points a night has never been what I'm about." Doug Collins, Hill's coach with the Pistons, concurred. "Grant doesn't have the killer instinct in scoring that Michael has. He can dominate a game more subtly, by getting the ball to open people, by rebounding and, with two dribbles, get his team into the open floor the way Magic Johnson* did as a rookie." He and the Dallas Mavericks' Jason Kidd* were selected the NBA's Co-Rookies of the Year for 1994–1995.

Hill continued his fine play with the Pistons during the 1995–1996 season, becoming only the fifteenth player in modern NBA history to lead his team in points (1,618), rebounds (783), and assists (548). The Pistons made it to the 1996 playoffs. Although Jordan had returned to the NBA, Hill led the NBA in All-Star votes. In the summer of 1996, Hill was chosen for the Olympic Dream Team III, which secured a gold medal for the United States in basketball.

For the next four seasons, Hill starred for the Pistons, averaging over 20 points. The Pistons, however, failed to make it past the first round of the playoffs. Hill started every All-Star Game from 1994 to 2000 but was increasingly frustrated with the lack of progress made by the Pistons organization. Young stars, including Kobe Bryant* of the Los Angeles Lakers, were being surrounded by other promising young players.

Hill suffered a broken ankle bone during a first-round playoff loss to the Miami Heat in 2000. Surgery involved the insertion of a pin in the ankle, but full recovery was expected for the 2000–2001 season. At this time, Hill, despairing of the Pistons' efforts to field a winning club, signed a seven-year, $92.96 million contract with the Orlando Magic (NBA). He wanted to win a championship in Orlando, proclaiming, "I can get into all the All-Star Games in the world, all the commercials and all the money, but it doesn't mean anything if you don't win." Hill's tenure with the Magic, however, brought disappointment. His ankle did not respond to the rigors of NBA competition and so required a second round of surgery in January 2001. Hill competed in only four regular season games in 2000–2001, in 14 games in 2001–2002, and 29 games in 2002–2003. Through 2003–2004, he had 300 blocked shots, 2,931 assists, 3,773 rebounds, 735 steals, and 10,104 points.

Hill plans to make a comeback for the 2003–2004 season. With a college degree in hand, as well as sound business investments, a home in Orlando, and his 1999 marriage to Grammy-nominated recording artist Tamie Washington, Hill is well poised for the future.

BIBLIOGRAPHY
Christopher John Farley, "Gentleman Slam Dunker," *Time* 145 (February 13, 1995), p. 78; Joshua Hill, "Grant Hill," *Current Biography* 63 (January 2002), pp. 52–57; Tom Junod, "The Savior," *Gentlemen's Quarterly* 65 (April 1995), pp. 170–175; Jackie MacMullan, "So He's Not Michael," *Sports Illustrated* 84 (January 22, 1996), pp. 53–59; Jackie MacMullan, "Grant's Tomb," *Sports Illustrated* 88 (February 9,

1998), pp. 64–66; Tom Singer, "One on One: Grant Hill," *Sport* 87 (April 1996), p. 17.

Ron Briley

GARRETT HINES
(July 3, 1969–)

Bobsled

Garrett Hines and teammate Randy Jones won silver medals as brakemen on the four-man bobsled at the 2002 Salt Lake City, Utah, Winter Olympic Games, becoming the first African American males to earn medals in Winter Olympic competition.

Garrett Hines was born on July 3, 1969 in Chicago, Illinois, the son of Edward Hines, a Korean War veteran, and Shirley Hines, and has three brothers and four sisters. He grew up in Memphis, Tennessee, and graduated in 1987 from Bartlett High School, where he participated in football his senior year and was named to Who's Who Among High School Students.

Hines attended Southern Illinois University at Carbondale, playing halfback on the football team and sprinting on the Saluki track and field squad. He competed in the 100-meter and 200-meter dashes. An exceptional scholar-athlete, he earned a Bachelor of Arts degree in biological science in 1992 and a Master's degree in education. Hines and his wife, Ileana, have three children, Kortnee, Nichole, and Kendall, and reside in Orlando, Florida. Hines works for Home Depot as part of the company's Olympic athletes program.

Because of his speed and strength, the 6-foot, 210-pound Hines was encouraged to enter bobsled competition. He attended a bobsled tryout camp in 1992 and has participated in the sport ever since. His commitment to the sport and his rigorous work habits landed him on the 1994 U.S. Olympic team as an alternate. A member of the United States Army Reserves, Hines holds the rank of first lieutenant and serves as an environmental engineer. He has received an army commendation for his meritorious service and was named the 1998 Armed Forces Athlete of the Year. He is the only athlete to score over 1,000 points in the national six-item test record event.

At the 1998 Winter Olympic Games at Nagano, Japan, Hines was the brakeman and the pusher for driver Brian Shimer aboard USA 1. They finished fifth in the four-man bobsled event, just missing the bronze medal by .02 second. The result marked the best finish for the United States in the four-man bobsled since a crew driven by Arthur Tyler won a bronze medal in 1956. Shimer and Hines came in tenth in the two-man bobsled competition at Nagano.

With his amazing strength, speed, and agility, Hines served as brakeman and pusher for the two-man and four-man bobsled teams preparing for the 2002 Winter Olympic Games at Salt Lake City, Utah. Between 1999 and 2001, the two-man bobsled team entered five races and won three times with Todd Hays as the driver. The four-man bobsled team consisted of Hays as driver, Pavle Jovanovic and Jones as crewmen with Bill Schuffenhauer as a replacement, and Hines as the brakeman and pusher. In 15 races, they recorded six first-place and three second-place finishes in World Cup races, World Championship Series, the Goodwill Games, and National Trials. Hays's team led the world tour in the four-man bobsled after five of seven events in 2001–2002. Hines won the Brakeman Push Championships in 1999, 2000, and 2001.

At the 2002 Salt Lake City, Winter Olympic Games, Hines placed fourth as the brakeman-pusher for Hays in the two-man bobsled, falling only .03 of a second short of medaling. "I don't know if there is any worse place in sports than fourth place in the Olympics," Hays acknowledged. Hines was very disappointed with his second near-miss for a medal. "I know what kind of pain he must be going through," Hays said of Hines, ". . . this is hard enough on me."

Hines captured the silver medal as brakeman-pusher on the USA 1 four-man bobsled team, trailing only Germany 2. Hays drove USA 1, while Jones and Schuffenhauer were crewmen. Hines and Jones became the first African American males to medal in the Winter Olympics. The USA 2 bobsled, driven by Shimer, won the bronze medal. No American team had medaled in the bobsled since the 1956 Winter Olympic Games at Cortina d'Ampezzo, Italy.

The twin medals lifted the spirits of the USA 1 team. Hays called the outcome "a storybook ending" and added, "This is a great way to end a drought." As Hays noted, "to come away with a medal is just absolutely amazing," and he beamed, "we are really happy with the silver." The victory held special meaning for African Americans Hines and Jones. "I think the doors are definitely open now," Jones explained. "It's something that we can do, and we can do well."

The dedicated Hines has represented the United States in four World Championships and two Winter Olympic Games. Since 1995, Hines has won two bronze, seven silver, and five gold medals in national and international competition. He wants to become the first African American athlete to drive a sled in World Cup competition, but he faces battles getting support.

In 2002, the Tennessee state legislature issued House Joint Resolutions 781 and 790 honoring Hines for his achievements. The legislature recognized "citizens who, through their determination, ability and endurance have distinguished themselves as champions in the realm of international competition."

BIBLIOGRAPHY
"Garrett Hines," *2002 Olympic Games-Bios*, www.sports.yahoo.com (2002); "Garrett Hines," *Career Record*, www.usabobsledandskeleton.org (2002); "Garrett Hines," *History-Years in Olympics*, www.usocpressbox.org (2002); "Garrett Hines," *USA Bobsled*, www.sportsline.com (2002); Greg Boeck, "U.S. Men Attempt to End Futility," *USA Today*, February 22, 2002, p. 4D; Greg Boeck, "U.S. Team Fourth in 2-Man Bobsled," *USA Today*, February 18, 2002, p. 4D; Charena Williams, "Bobsled Team End 46-Year Drought with 2 Medals," *Fort Worth Star-Telegram*, February 23, 2002, www.star-telegram.com.

John L. Evers and David L. Porter

CHAMIQUE HOLDSCLAW

Basketball

(August 9, 1977–)

Chamique Holdsclaw starred on three National Collegiate Athletic Association (NCAA) Championship basketball teams at the University of Tennessee.

Chamique Shawnta Holdsclaw, nicknamed "Mique," was born on August 9, 1977 in Flushing, New York, the daughter of Willie Johnson and Bonita Holdsclaw, a human resources worker. Holdsclaw's parents did not marry until the birth of her brother, Davon, in 1980. Her mother and father, constantly drank, cursed, fought and yelled until they finally separated. At age 10 she left home to live with her grandmother June Holdsclaw, who provided legal guardianship at the request of Children and Family Services.

Holdsclaw lived in a tough neighborhood and practiced basketball daily on the asphalt courts of New York, dominated by boys. She learned her basketball skills by competing with the older boys. She played better than most boys, earning their respect and concern for her safety.

June Holdsclaw insisted that her daughter go to a private high school and took on additional work to pay the tuition. Uncle Thurman assisted her in deciding what school she would attend. He knew that Christ the King Catholic High School in Queens, New York, fielded excellent athletic teams, and he was acquainted with their coach, Vinnie Cannizzaro, who could prepare her to advance to the next level. Cannizzaro also coached for Holdsclaw's AAU team in the summer and looked after her welfare. After seeing Holdsclaw at a pickup game, he observed: "I knew I had seen something special. I saw something I had not seen from a girl before, let alone one who was not yet in high school."

Holdsclaw attended Christ the King High School from 1991–1992 and through 1994–1995. She excelled in the classroom and on the court, leading her team to four straight state championships and only four losses in four years. Scholarship offers came from numerous schools, with Holdsclaw finally choosing the University of Tennessee at Knoxville.

Holdsclaw attended the University of Tennessee from 1995 to 1999, graduating in 1999 with a Bachelor's degree in political science. She also excelled on the basketball court, leading the Lady Vols to a 131–17 won-lost record. Pat Summitt, the highly successful Vols' coach, pushed Holdsclaw very hard to get the best out of her. There were times when Holdsclaw thought about leaving the program, but she stayed. Under coach Summitt, the 6-foot 2-inch, 172-pound forward helped Tennessee capture three consecutive NCAA Division I titles, two Southeastern Conference (SEC) regular season crowns, and three SEC Tournament Championships. Tennessee compiled a 21–1 won-lost record in four NCAA appearances and enjoyed a perfect 39–0 season in 1996–1997. In 1996 Holdsclaw was chosen the SEC Freshman of the Year, Rookie of the Year by the U.S. Basketball Writers Association (USBWA), and Third

Chamique Holdsclaw ©Andrew D. Bernstein/Getty Images

Team All-America, and was named to the All Final Four Team. Holdsclaw was selected as the NCAA Final Four Most Outstanding Player in 1997 and made the Kodak All-America First Team. She was named the SEC Female Athlete of the Year in 1998, ESPY'S Best Female Athlete, James E. Sullivan Memorial Sportsmanship Award winner, and the Honda-Broderick Cup recipient as the NCAA Athlete of the Year. In 1999 Holdsclaw was selected Kodak All-America and *USBWA* Player of the Year, and she finished her collegiate year as the SEC and the University of Tennessee all-time leading scorer with 3,025 points and the Lady Vols career-leading rebounder with 1,295 caroms. Holdsclaw set the all-time NCAA tournament record for scoring with 479 points and rebounding with 198 boards.

Holdsclaw was named to the SEC First Team in 1997, 1998, and 1999 and the All-America First Team the same three seasons. In 1998–1999, she was chosen SEC Player of the Year, Associated Press Player of the Year, and Naismith National Player of the Year.

Between her sophomore and junior seasons, Holdsclaw made the Women's USA Basketball World Championship team. In 1999 she was named USA Basketball Female Athlete of the Year and earned a silver medal in the World Championship qualifying tournament. She also earned gold medals in the 1998 World Championship, the 1999 Olympic Cup, and at the 2000 Olympic Games in Sydney, Australia.

The Washington Mystics (Women's National Basketball Association) selected Holdsclaw as the first overall pick in the May 1999 WNBA draft. In her first season as a professional, she averaged 18.9 points and 7.9 rebounds in 31 regular season games. Both marks ranked her among the top 10 in the WNBA. She was named Rookie of the Year and was chosen for the first of four consecutive times as a starting forward in the WNBA All-Star Game. Holdsclaw received the most votes among Eastern Conference players for the 2000 All-Star Game. During the regular 2000 season, she averaged 17.5 points and 7.5 rebounds in 32 games to rank seventh in the WNBA in both categories.

Holdsclaw finished the 2001 regular season fourth in the WNBA with 8.8 rebounds and fifth with 16.8 points per game, being named to the second All-WNBA team.

Although she missed 12 regular season games in 2002 due to injury, Holdsclaw led the WNBA with 17.6 points and 11.6 rebounds. She was ranked best in the WNBA in defensive rebounds, sixth in offensive rebounds, and second in double-doubles, making the All-WNBA team. She recorded a career-high 32 points against the Seattle Storm on July 27, 2002 and 21 rebounds against the Sacramento Monarchs on June 25, 2002.

Holdsclaw led the WNBA in rebounds with 294 (10.9 average) and finished second in scoring with 554 points (20.5 average) for last place Washington in 2003. She collided with Barb Ferris of the Detroit Shock in the season finale and suffered a sprained left knee. She also played for the East All-Stars. In five WNBA seasons, Holdsclaw scored 2,523 points (18.2-point average) and pulled down 1,268 rebounds (9.1-rebounds average) in 139 games. The Mystics lost in the first round of the WNBA playoffs in 2000, and the Eastern Conference title game to the New York Liberty in 2002. In seven playoff games, Holdsclaw averaged 17.7 points and 7.70 rebounds.

Holdsclaw, the "Female Michael Jordan," was selected as one of the Naismith College Basketball Players of the 20th Century. She has a street named after her in Tennessee, and she saw her number 23 jersey retired by the Lady Vols. She remains single and has published a book, *Chamique: On Family, Focus and Basketball.* She has released her own shoe style and has purchased a home in Virginia, where she practices between seasons and makes community appearances.

BIBLIOGRAPHY
"Chamique Holdsclaw," Background, www.wnba.com (2002); "Chamique Holdsclaw," Career Highlights and Personal, www.washingtonmystics.com (2002); "Chamique Holdsclaw," College and Pro Statistics, www.wnba.com (2001); Chamique Holdsclaw, *Chamique: On Family, Focus, and Basketball* (New York, 2000); "Chamique Holdsclaw," Hoop Dreams, www.tripod.com (2000); "Chamique Holdsclaw," Player Averages and Totals, www.washingtonmystics.com (2002); "Chamique Holdsclaw," Statistics and Averages, www.wnba.com (2002); "Chamique Holdsclaw," USA Basketball, www.usa.com (2001); *The Sporting News Official WNBA Guide and Register*, 2003.

John L. Evers and David L. Porter

EVANDER HOLYFIELD   Boxing
(October 19, 1962–   )

Boxer Evander Holyfield combines longevity and competitive zeal. On November 6, 1993, nearly one calendar year after losing the World Heavyweight Championship to Riddick Bowe, Holyfield regained the title from Bowe. Evander became only the third boxer in his weight class to regain his title by defeating the fighter who took away his title. In 1996 and 1997, he fought two epic, controversial, and scandalous fights with Mike Tyson.* Two years later, Holyfield fought Lennox Lewis of Great Britain and proved that he could still take and give punches. His reaction time and explosive power, however, had declined with age.

Evander Holyfield was born on October 19, 1962 in Atmore, Alabama, the youngest of eight children, and grew up with his mother, Annie Holyfield. Annie supported her four sons and four daughters by working 12 hours a day as a cook in an Atlanta, Georgia, hotel. She toiled until Holyfield was age 10. A serious heart attack then made her incapable of continuing this job.

Holyfield participated in the Warren Memorial Boys Club and was mentored by boxing coach Carter Morgan. He boxed for the first time as a 9-year-old. He continued boxing and graduated from Fulton High School. His breakthrough fight came in a victory over Ricky Womack for the National

Evander Holyfield ©Photofest

Sports Festival boxing title, making him a contender for a 1984 Olympic squad slot as a light-heavyweight. Despite an early loss to Womack, Holyfield defeated him in the final qualifying fight and was selected for the national team.

At the 1984 Los Angeles, California, Olympics, Holyfield suffered bad luck and almost ill-starred fortune. He knocked out Kevin Barry of New Zealand in the semifinal, but the referee disqualified him because Holyfield allegedly landed the knockout blow after the referee called for a break. Despite being the most muscular and athletic in his division, he settled for a bronze medal.

In November 1984, Holyfield turned professional after an amateur career of 160 wins, 75 knockouts, and 14 losses. Fight promoter Lou Duva signed him. In his early contests, Holyfield fought as a light-heavyweight at 175 pounds. He eventually gained the weight and muscle to compete effectively as a heavyweight. Tim Hallmark, a fitness consultant, devised a training program that made Holyfield among the best-conditioned boxers of his generation. According to *Current Biography*: "Hallmark's program put Holyfield in such superb condition that he twice reached the finals in television's Superstars competition, defeating the Olympic gold-medal sprinter Carl Lewis* in a half-mile running event in the process."

In his third professional heavyweight fight on March 11, 1989, Holyfield defeated Michael Dokes in the tenth round. *Ring* magazine rated the fight as the best heavyweight bout of the 1980s. Holyfield was poised to challenge Mike Tyson for the world title when Tyson was upset by James "Buster" Douglas. On October 25 1990, Holyfield easily defeated an out-of-condition Douglas and earned a challenger's purse of $8.5 million. In April 1991, Holyfield received $22 million in a decision over George Foreman, the "grand old man" of boxing.

In June 1992, Holyfield defended his title against Larry Holmes and received a $16 million purse. In an exciting, all-action brawl on November 13, 1992, Riddick Bowe won a 12-round decision over Holyfield and took the heavyweight crown. At this point Holyfield announced his retirement from boxing but changed his mind within two months. In the rematch with Bowe, he narrowly won a decision in a surreal Caesar's Palace in Las Vegas, Nevada, with a paraglider crashing into the ropes and holding up the contest during round seven.

In November 1996, the long-awaited Tyson–Holyfield fight took place. Tyson succumbed in the eleventh round. The July 5, 1997 rematch guaranteed Holyfield $35 million and earned him the highest amount from a single performance in the history of entertainment. The fight, arguably the most infamous in the history of pugilism, saw Tyson disqualified in round three for repeated "biting." Later in 1997, Holyfield defeated Mike Moorer to clear the road for an anticipated titanic tussle with Lennox Lewis. The March 1999 Lewis–Holyfield bout was ruled a draw by the referee and the two judges. The *Sports Illustrated* account of the bout, titled "Grand Larceny," referred to some highly questionable scoring. Richard Hoffer spoke of an "unconscionable draw."

In their November 1999 return fight, the 37-year-old Holyfield faced 34-year-old Lewis. Holyfield, 25 pounds lighter and two and a half inches shorter, lost the decision on points in a bout that disappointed spectators and commentators alike for its absence of fire and its dearth of either "dangerous" or "horrifying" action. Apart from the furious exchanges of round seven, the 12-round fight displayed curiously "cautious boxing." In August 2000, Holyfield defeated John Ruiz in a controversial unanimous decision in 12 rounds at Las Vegas, Nevada, for the vacant WBA title. Ruiz won a rematch in a 12-round unanimous decision at Las Vegas in March 2001. Ruiz retained the WBA title in a 12-round draw at Mashantucket, Connecticut, in December 2001. Holyfield won an eight-round technical knockout over Hasim Rahman at Las Vegas in June 2002 and lost to Chris Bird in December 2002. Holyfield has compiled a 38–7–2 record with 25 knockouts. James Toney soundly defeated him in nine rounds in October 2003.

Despite his well-known commitment to the teaching of Jesus Christ and biblical doctrines, Holyfield has lived a complex, convoluted life. He has six children—three with his former wife, Paulette, and three from relationships with three subsequent women.

The multimillionaire Holyfield owns several luxurious homes and sponsors the Warren Memorial Boys Club. Besides having sponsorship deals with Burger King and Coca-Cola, he has been featured in the *Fresh Prince of Bel Air* and has performed many other television vignettes.

BIBLIOGRAPHY
"Evander Holyfield," *Current Biography Yearbook* (New York, 1993), pp. 244–248; Richard Hoffer, "Floored by the Spirit," *Sports Illustrated* 87 (November 17, 1997), pp. 40–41; Richard Hoffer, "Grand Larceny," *Sports Illustrated* 90 (March 22, 1999), pp. 60–62; Richard Hoffer, "Lovestruck," *Sports Illustrated* 86 (June 30, 1997), pp. 22–30; Richard Hoffer, "Triumphant Timidity," *Sports Illustrated* 91 (November 22, 1999), pp. 60–63.

Scott A.G.M. Crawford

I

ALLEN IVERSON   Basketball
(June 7, 1975–   )

Allen Iverson ranks among the most prolific scorers in National Basketball Association (NBA) history.

Allen Ezail Iverson, nicknamed "Bubba Chuck," was born on June 7, 1975 in Hampton, Virginia, the son of Allen Broughton and Ann Iverson. Iverson's father lived apart from the family, had little contact with his son, and later received a prison term for stabbing his girlfriend. Shortly after Iverson's birth, Michael Freeman moved in with his mother. Ann was just 15 years old when Iverson was born and did "whatever she had to do" to make money to support the family. The family lived in poverty for some time. Ann, a former basketball player, and Freeman kindled Iverson's interest in basketball and taught him the fundamentals. Freeman became the only father he had and was concerned about the family welfare, but soon was imprisoned for possession of drugs with intent to distribute.

In 1990 Iverson enrolled in Bethel High School in Hampton, where he excelled in baseball as a pitcher, in basketball as a guard, and in football, his first love, as a quarterback. He enjoyed a fabulous sophomore year in 1991–1992, leading the football team to the State Championship. He passed for 1,423 yards, rushed for 781 yards, and scored 34 touchdowns. Iverson averaged 31.6 points, leading the basketball squad to the Virginia State Championship. As a sophomore, he scored a state record of 948 points in basketball and was named Virginia Player of the Year in both sports. During the summer, his Amateur Athletic Union (AAU) basketball team won the National Championship, and he was voted Most Valuable Player (MVP) in that tournament. As a junior in 1992–1993, he led the football team to their second straight State Championship and again was named Player of the Year. Iverson passed for 201 yards in the title game, returning a punt 60 yards for a touchdown and intercepting two passes. He began the basketball season with college recruiters and scouts watching his every move and put on an unbelievable performance. The 6-foot, 165-pound Iverson possessed a 40-inch vertical jump, dominated an opponent with his quickness, and shot accurately from anywhere on the floor. One scout remarked, "He has a level beyond quickness."

Iverson's basketball team was undefeated in 1993–1994. Iverson was en-

Allen Iverson ©Tom Pidgeon/Getty Images

joying a banner season until February 14, 1993, when a race-related brawl occurred in a Hampton bowling alley. He told the police he left when it started and played no part in the brawl. Nevertheless, he was charged and tried as an adult with maiming by mob gang-related incidents. Iverson was convicted and sent to the Newport News City Farm, a prison for young men. After serving four months in prison, he was given a conditional release by Governor Douglas Wilder. All charges were dropped by an appeals court because of insufficient evidence. Iverson worked with Sue Lambiotte, a tutor, both while in prison and after his release, toward completing the requirements for a high school diploma. After he passed his final test in September 1994, he accepted a basketball scholarship at Georgetown University.

At Georgetown, John Thompson became more than Iverson's basketball coach, sometimes serving as a substitute father. Iverson played basketball at Georgetown for two years. As a freshman in 1994–1995, he was named Big East Conference (BEC) Rookie of the Year after averaging a team leading 20.4 points and 4.5 assists. Iverson also was selected as the BEC Defensive Player of the Year in consecutive seasons. He led the Hoyas in consecutive trips to the National Collegiate Athletic Association (NCAA) Division I National Tournament. The Hoyas lost to the University of North Carolina in the 1995 regional semifinals and, the following year, came within one victory of reaching the Final Four before losing to the University of Massachusetts. As a sophomore, Iverson led Georgetown in scoring (25.0-point average), set a Hoya record with 129 steals in one season, and was selected on the All-BEC First Team and the All-America First Team. Prior to his sophomore season, he led the USA's gold-medal-winning basketball team to the Championship in the 1995 World University Games.

Iverson had a family of his own to support. In 1995 he and his girlfriend, Tawana Turner, began a family together, producing a daughter, Tiaura, and a son, "Deuce" (Allen Jr.). In 1999, they got married. Iverson left Georgetown to join the professional ranks and to meet his growing financial needs. The Philadelphia 76ers (NBA) selected him in the first round as the first pick overall.

In 1996–1997, Iverson proved he could play in the NBA. He was named to the NBA All-Rookie First Team, was selected Rookie of the Year, led the 76ers in scoring, and registered 40 or more points in five consecutive games to establish an NBA rookie record. Although averaging 22.0 points the following season, he experienced difficulty adjusting to his new coach, Larry Brown. When the pair made the necessary changes, the 76ers became a team with a plan. Iverson remarked, "I think God has sent me Larry Brown." In the shortened season of 1998–1999, Iverson averaged 26.8 points, captured the NBA scoring title, was named to the All-NBA First Team, and set an NBA playoff record with 10 steals in one game.

The following year, Iverson averaged 28.4 points and finished second in NBA scoring to Shaquille O'Neal.* Iverson was named to the All-NBA Second Team and led scorers in his first NBA All-Star Game. Named the 2000–

2001 NBA Most Valuable Player (MVP), he paced the NBA in scoring for the second time with an average of 31.1 points and 2.51 steals. The MVP in the All-Star Game, Iverson was selected All-NBA First Team. On January 6, 2001, he scored a career-high 54 points against the Cleveland Cavaliers. He led the 76ers to the NBA playoffs four straight years. The 76ers defeated the Orlando Magic in the first round in 1999 and triumphed over the Charlotte Hornets in 2000, losing both times to the Indiana Pacers in the second round. In the 2001 NBA playoffs, Philadelphia won the Eastern Conference Championship and lost in the Championship Series to the Los Angeles Lakers in five games. In the NBA Finals, Iverson averaged 35.6 points, 3.8 assists, 1.60 steals, and 5.60 rebounds.

Iverson led the NBA in scoring with 1,883 points (31.4-point average) and in steals with 168 (2.8 average) in 2001–2002 making the All-NBA Second Team and appearing in his third All-Star Game. The 76ers finished fourth in the Atlantic Division and were edged by the Boston Celtics in the first round of the Eastern Conference playoffs, as Iverson averaged 30 points per game. Iverson ranked third in scoring with a 27.6-point average and led the NBA with 225 steals (2.7 average) in 2002–2003, repeating on the All-NBA Second Team and playing in his fourth consecutive All-Star Game. Philadelphia placed fourth in the Eastern Conference. Iverson helped the 76ers defeat the New Orleans Hornets in the first round of the NBA playoffs, but the Detroit Pistons ousted Philadelphia in the second round.

Philadelphia police in July 2002 issued an arrest warrant for Iverson, who was accused of forcing his way into a West Philadelphia apartment with a gun displayed in his waistband and threatening two men while looking for his wife. Iverson thought that his wife had taken refuge there after a domestic dispute. He turned himself in a few days later and was arraigned on 14 counts, including four felonies, for his alleged actions. A Philadelphia judge reduced the charges to two misdemeanors.

In seven NBA seasons from 1996–1997 through 2002–2003, Iverson compiled 13,170 career points for an average of 27.0 points, 5.6 assists, and 2.4 steals in 487 regular season games. In 57 NBA playoff games, he has scored 1,743 points and has averaged 30.6 points, 5.8 assists, and 2.12 steals.

BIBLIOGRAPHY

"Allen Iverson," *Biography*, www.AskMe.com (2001); "Allen Iverson," *Players Background*, www.nba.com (2001); "Allen Iverson," *Players Career Highlights*, www. nba.com (2001); "Allen Iverson," *Players Career Statistics*, www.nba.com (2001); Rick Reilly, "Counter Point," *Sports Illustrated* 10 (March 9, 1998), pp. 82–90, 92; Charles F. Schmidt, *Allen Iverson* (Philadelphia, PA, 1998); Mark Stewart, *Allen Iverson: Motion and Emotion* (Brookfield, CT, 2001); *The Sporting News Official NBA Register*, 2003–2004.

John L. Evers

J

BO JACKSON
(November 30, 1962–)

Baseball, Football

By the time he became the Heisman Trophy winner in 1985 with the Auburn University Tigers, Bo Jackson had already overcome more than most people have in a lifetime to achieve success. Tragically, his career was cut short due to injury, begging the question what would have happened if he had remained healthy.

National Baseball Hall of Fame member and former teammate George Brett once observed, "With Bo, you never know when you're going to see something you've never seen before." With a decathlon win in high school, a 9–1 record as a high school pitcher, a monster home run clout in the major leagues, or a record-setting rushing Sunday afternoon in the National Football League (NFL). Jackson enjoyed an athletic career that has never been duplicated. His career parallels the earlier career of the great Jim Thorpe.

Vincent Edward Jackson was born on November 30, 1962 in Bessemer, Alabama, the son of A.D. Adams, a steelworker, and Florence Jackson Bund, a domestic. Jackson's childhood was not ideal. His mother, Florence, was left by his father to bring up 10 children. Jackson, who often went to school hungry, wrote in his book, *Bo Knows Bo*, "We never had enough food. But at least I could beat on other kids and steal their lunch money and buy myself something to eat. . . . But I couldn't steal a father's hug when I needed one. I couldn't steal a father's whipping when I needed one."

Jackson overcame adversity to star at Auburn University, lettering in three sports. He became an All-Star outfielder in the major leagues, an All-Pro NFL running back, created perhaps one of the most recognizable advertising campaigns in history with the athletic apparel company Nike, and has performed several movie and television roles since his athletic career ended. An entrepreneur, he owns his own motorcycle business and a restaurant with basketball superstar Charles Barkley,* and he serves as president and spokesperson for HealthSouth's Sports Medicine Council. He travels around the United States promoting education and nutritional programs for children. He and his wife, Linda Garrett, his college sweetheart, have three children, Garrett, Nicholas, and Morgan.

Jackson graduated in 1982 from McAdory High School where he excelled

Bo Jackson ©The Lovero Group

in every sport he tried, hitting a national high school record 20 home runs in 25 games during his senior season and posting a 9–1 record as a junior pitcher. After considering several offers from colleges around the nation, he stayed close to home so that his mother could see him play. Jackson finished his Bachelor's degree at Auburn, in honor of his mother. When the University of Alabama football recruiter told him he probably would not start in his first year, he quickly chose Auburn where he starred all four years.

At Auburn, Jackson lettered in baseball, football, and track and field. On the baseball team, he compiled a .335 batting average, 28 home runs, and 70 runs batted in (RBI) in just 89 collegiate games. He became the all-time leading rusher at Auburn (4,303 yards) and averaged 6.6 yards per carry during his collegiate career. In 38 games, he scored 43 touchdowns, which is still a record at Auburn. In 1985, Jackson enjoyed one of the best college football seasons ever, totaling four 200-yard games and averaging 162.4 yards per game. He compiled 1,786 rushing yards and a record 17 touchdowns in just

11 games, which remains an Auburn record. That year, he became the fifty-first Heisman Trophy winner. Jackson lettered in track and field as a freshman and sophomore, running the 60-yard dash and serving as a member of the 4×100-meter relay team. His career bests were 6.18 seconds in the 60-yard dash and 10.13 seconds in 100 meters.

Destined to be a superstar as a professional athlete, Jackson chose to play both professional baseball and football. Selected by the Kansas City Royals (American League) in the fourth round of the free-agent draft in 1986, he debuted with the double-A Memphis, Tennessee (Southern League) on June 30 against Columbus. He earned Player of the Week honors in July after going 11 for 26 (.423 batting average) with a double, three triples, two home runs, and eight RBIs. Jackson made his major league debut in right field on September 2, 1986 against the Chicago White Sox and singled in the second inning off future National Baseball Hall of Fame pitcher Steve Carlton for his first major league hit.

Jackson's amazing speed and ability to climb an outfield wall like Spider-man to track down a ball and make the catch were simply thrilling to watch. He displayed his talent on the big stage in 1989 as the starting left fielder for the AL All-Star team. He stole the show when he retrieved a long fly ball to end a first inning threat by the National League. Jackson led off the bottom of the first inning with a home run off pitcher Rick Reuschel and stole second base in the second frame, becoming the only All-Star besides Willie Mays to homer and steal a base in the same game. His lone All-Star appearance earned him Most Valuable Player (MVP) honors.

During an eight-year career marred by injury, Jackson batted .250 in 694 games with 86 doubles, 14 triples, 141 home runs, and 415 RBIs. He played for five years with the Kansas City Royals and in 1991 with the Chicago White Sox (AL). He sat out the entire 1992 season owing to reconstructive left hip surgery from a football injury, and, against all odds, he came back in 1993. In 1993 Jackson made it to his only postseason when the White Sox finished first in the Western Division with a 94–68 record. Chicago lost to the Toronto Blue Jays four games to two in the AL Championship Series. Jackson suffered a terrible postseason, going hitless with one run scored and six strikeouts. The next season, his last in the major leagues, saw him play 75 games for the California Angels (AL).

Jackson's NFL debut came on November 1, 1987 when the Los Angeles Raiders faced the New England Patriots. He rushed for 221 yards on 18 carries (a club record) and made a club-high and NFL season-high 91-yard run. He was named unanimously to the NFL All-Rookie Team.

During the next four years, Jackson carried the ball 515 times and compiled 2,782 yards at an impressive 5.4-yards-per-carry average. He scored 18 touchdowns and caught 40 passes for 352 yards. He set a Raiders' yardage record, dashing 91 yards for a touchdown against the Seattle Seahawks in a Monday night game in 1988. A devastating hip injury cost him a chance to be elected to the National Baseball Hall of Fame and Pro Football Hall of Fame. He was elected to the College Football Hall of Fame in 1999 and continues working with children.

BIBLIOGRAPHY
Auburn Tigers.com—The Official Website of Auburn Tigers Athletics, www.auburntigers.com/football/page.cfm?doc_id=643, 2003; Bo Jackson and Dick Schaap, *Bo Knows Bo: The Autobiography of a Ballplayer* (New York, 1990); Bo Jackson's Better, www.betterbar.com/bo.html, 2001–2002 Betterbar; "Bo Jackson Up Close," National Baseball Library, Cooperstown, NY; *California Angels Media Guide*, 1994; Ron Flatter, "Bo Knows Stardom and Disappointment," Special to ESPN.com, Vincent E. Jackson file, National Baseball Library, Cooperstown, NY; "NSCA—Interview with Bo Jackson," http://nsca-lift.org/interview/BoJackson.shtml, 2000, Vincent E. Jackson file, National Baseball Library, Cooperstown, NY; Jeanne Wolf, "Why Bo Hit the Books," *New York Daily News*, October 20, 1996, p. 8.

Scot E. Mondore

KEVIN JACKSON   Wrestling
(November 25, 1964–   )

Kevin Jackson, an Olympic gold medal and World Champion freestyle wrestler, coached USA Wrestling's national freestyle team.

Kevin Jackson, the fourth child of Leroy Jackson and Joyce Jackson, was born on November 25, 1964 in Highland Falls, New York. The Jacksons moved to Lansing, Michigan, where he graduated from Lansing Eastern High School. His older brother, Wayne, won a State Championship in wrestling and wrestled at Michigan State University.

Jackson was selected an All-State wrestler at 155 pounds in Michigan's Class A in 1981 and 1982. In 1982, 5-foot 9-inch Kevin pinned 29 opponents in 31 matches and finished undefeated. After Christmas, he pinned every foe. In 1982 Don Johnson, his high school principal and long-time wrestling coach, declared, "Kevin is the best wrestler at his weight in the country, and as good as any wrestler I can remember in Michigan. He doesn't even make wrestling a sport. It's just whooomp, pin. Last week at regionals, his three matches took 1:55. It disgusts me how good he is."

Jackson attended Louisiana State University (LSU) in the fall of 1982 and was named *Amateur Wrestling News* Freshman of the Year, when he won the Junior Nationals Greco-Roman Tournament. He earned All-America status all three years at LSU, placing third in 1983 and 1984 in the 158-pound division at the National Collegiate Athletic Association (NCAA) Championships and seventh in the 167-pound class as a junior.

In the summer of 1985 while attending a wrestling camp at the University of Northern Iowa, Jackson learned that LSU had eliminated its wrestling program. Several Iowa State University wrestlers at the camp persuaded him to transfer to their school that fall. Jackson redshirted for the 1985–1986 season, but enjoyed an outstanding year as an unattached wrestler. He finished with a perfect 13–0 record, winning both the Midwest Championship and the Northern Open.

In 1987 Jackson placed second at the NCAA Championships in the 167-pound division, losing to Royce Alger, two-time NCAA champion from the University of Iowa. Jackson's determination as a team leader helped the Cyclones break the University of Iowa stranglehold on college wrestling in the 1980s by winning the NCAA team championship in 1987.

After graduating from Iowa State in 1987, Jackson became an assistant coach there and one of the best freestyle wrestlers in the world. Although Alger blocked his path to a NCAA wrestling title, Jackson got his revenge by defeating him in the 180.5-pound weight class to become World Champion in 1991. He also triumphed over Alger to make the 1992 United States Olympic team and became an Olympic gold medalist at the Barcelona, Spain, games. The day after winning the gold medal, Jackson attended the track and field events and realized that "these are the ancient games that Jim Thorpe, Jessie Owens, and Muhammad Ali competed in, and now me, Kevin Jackson was a part of these historic games."

Jackson also won USA Senior Freestyle Championships and World Championships in 1991, 1993, and 1995, Pan American Games Championships in 1991 and 1995, the Yaser Dogu Tournament in Turkey in 1989, the Sunkist Open in 1989 and 1990, and the National Open Championships in 1990. In 1995 Jackson won the John Smith Award as Freestyle Wrestler of the Year. He later was selected to the Michigan Wrestling Hall of Fame. One of the best wrestlers in the world for nearly a decade, in 2000 Jackson was appointed USA Wrestling's national freestyle coach for the Olympic Training Center in Colorado Springs, Colorado. His understanding of technique and his preparation for world competition allowed him to coach with the same vigor and focus he brought to competitive wrestling.

In 2001, Jackson opposed the Federation Internationale de Lutters Amateur (FILA—the international governing body for world wrestling) decision to reduce the number of weight classes in international competition by three divisions (in comparison to 1996), even though women's freestyle wrestling was added as a sport for the 2004 Olympic Games.

Jackson and his wife, Robin, have two children, Robert Cole and Bailee Ann.

BIBLIOGRAPHY
"Cyclone Coach Jackson Earns Respect of His Peers," *Iowa State Daily*, June 24, 1991; "Former ISU Wrestler Ranks No. 1 in U.S., Eyes Olympics," *Ames Tribune*, June 24, 1991; Marc Hansen, "From Clumsy to Olympics," *Des Moines Register*, August 7, 1992, p. 1C; "A Host of Cyclone Heroes Bring the Trophy Home," *Iowa State Daily*, April 1987; *Iowa State Cyclones' Wrestling Media Guide, 1987*; "Jeers Won't Tarnish Jackson's Medal," *Cedar Rapids Gazette*, August 23, 1992, p. 1 ff; Keith Jackson file, National Wrestling Hall of Fame, Oklahoma State University, Stillwater, OK; Dan McCool, "Jackson Loses in Quest for 3rd Gold," *Des Moines*

Register, August 26, 1993, pp. 4C, 6C; Dan McCool, "Jackson Stops Alger for Spot on U.S. Team," *Des Moines Register*, June 5, 1994, p. 1C.

Keith McClellan

EDGERRIN JAMES   Football
(August 1, 1978–   )

Edgerrin James starred as a running back at the University of Miami and won consecutive National Football League (NFL) rushing titles with the Indianapolis Colts (NFL) in 1999 and 2000.

Edgerrin Tyree James was born on August 1, 1978 in Immokalee, Florida, and starred in football at Immokalee High School as a linebacker, kick returner, and placekicker, being named *Parade* All-America. At the University of Miami, James started two years as a running back. He was originally slated to be redshirted as a freshman but was forced into action for seven games because of injuries suffered by the Hurricanes' running corps. He established a school freshman rushing record with 446 yards on 71 carries and two touchdowns.

As a sophomore, James led Miami in rushing with 1,098 yards on 184 carries, with a 6.0-yard average and 13 touchdowns. Besides becoming just the third running back in Miami's history to gain more than 1,000 yards in a season, James also set a school record for most touchdowns in a season. As a junior, he established Hurricane season records for most yards with 1,416 on 242 carries and for most touchdowns with 17. His 17 rushing touchdowns also broke by three the 60-year-old Miami record set by running back Eddie Dunn in 1938. James scored 114 points to eclipse the old season standard of 107, set by placekicker Carlos Huerta in 1988. James became the only player in the school's history to post consecutive seasons with at least 1,000 yards rushing. During his career, he ranked second in Miami annals with 2,960 yards rushing on 497 carries. He was selected as a finalist for the Doak Walker Award, given annually to the nation's top running back.

James skipped his senior year to enter the 1999 NFL draft. Surprisingly, Indianapolis selected James in the first round as the fourth pick overall. Everyone associated with the sport expected the Colts to select Ricky Williams,* the Heisman Trophy winner who possessed outstanding size, strength, character, recognition, and countless NCAA rushing records.

Indianapolis president Bill Polian explained: "We felt with James' ability in the passing game to catch the ball and do something with it after he caught it, that he was the right fit with our quarterback Payton Manning. We were not necessarily looking for the player considered to be the best pure runner between tackles, but someone who can run outside as well as pound out yardage inside."

The 6-foot, 216-pound James with his trademark dreadlocks and five goldcapped teeth was an ideal replacement for Marshall Faulk,* who was traded to the St. Louis Rams. James produced one of the finest rookie seasons in

NFL history, gaining 1,553 yards on 369 carries and 13 rushing touchdowns. He became the thirteenth rookie to win the NFL rushing title and the youngest ever at 21 years, four months, and seven days. His 10 games rushing for at least 100 yards set an NFL rookie mark, while his 17 total touchdowns tied him for the third highest ever by a rookie. James caught 62 passes for 586 yards and four touchdowns, and he churned out 2,139 yards from scrimmage. James was selected the NFL's Offensive Rookie of the Year, named All-Pro, and voted to play in the Pro Bowl.

In 2000 James ran for 1,709 yards on 387 carries and 13 touchdowns to capture his second consecutive NFL rushing title. He became the eleventh player in NFL history to win consecutive rushing titles and just the fifth to accomplish it in each of his first two seasons. No NFL player had ever posted two consecutive 1,500-plus yard seasons. James set another team record by running for 219 yards against the Seattle Seahawks, the first time a Colt player ever gained over 200 yards in a game. James also caught 63 passes for 594 yards and five touchdowns, giving him 18 touchdowns for a career best 108 points. His 35 total touchdowns in his first two years established a new NFL record for that span of time mark. For the second straight year, he was nominated for the Pro Bowl.

James observed, "I am a lot smarter than I was in my first year: As a rookie, I made a lot of dumb moves and I was trying too hard . . . I have to stay focused, be patient, and wait for my openings. I now understand what the coaches want, which is important to being a good runner. If you understand exactly what the linemen are doing and what the coaches expect from you, the game becomes so much easier."

In 2001 James stood on the verge of becoming the only running back besides Jim Brown and Earl Campbell in NFL history to win the rushing title in each of his first three seasons. Midway through the season, however, James suffered a knee injury and missed the remainder of the year. His injury severely diminished the Colts' offense since he accounted for nearly 90 percent of the team's carries and rushing yards over his first two and a half seasons. James helped Indianapolis earn an American Football Conference (AFC) Wild Card berth with a 10–6 record in 2002, rushing 989 yards (3.6-yard average) and two touchdowns, and catching 61 passes for 354 yards (5.8-yard average) and one touchdown. Through 2002, James has rushed 1,184 times for 7,913 yards (4.1-yard average) and 31 touchdowns and caught 210 passes for 1,727 yards (8.2-yard average) and 10 touchdowns. James surpassed Lydell Mitchell as the Colts' all-time rushing leader in November 2003 with 5,540 career yards.

During the off-season, James participates in various charitable events in and around his Miami, Florida, hometown.

BIBLIOGRAPHY

Indianapolis Colts Press Guide, 2002; *Pro Football Weekly*, July 1999; Chris Jenkins, "Colts' James: Full Speed Ahead," *USA Today*, September 6, 2002, p. 3C; *The Sporting News Pro Football Register*, 2003.

Richard Gonsalves

DEREK JETER   **Baseball**
(June 26, 1974–   )

Perhaps no player is more synonymous with the New York Yankees' (American League) dynasty at the turn of the millennium than Derek Jeter. Jeter, among the game's best all-around shortstops and considered a clutch player in the postseason, has helped headline the nucleus of one of baseball's most successful teams in the postexpansion era.

Derek Sanderson Jeter was born on June 26, 1974 in Pequannock, New Jersey, the son of Charles Jeter, a drug and alcohol counselor, and Dorothy (Conners) Jeter, who worked in an accountancy firm. His family moved to Michigan when he was 5. A 1992 graduate of Kalamazoo Central High School, Jeter emerged among the nation's top prospects during his academic years. In his senior season, he batted .508 with four home runs, 21 walks, and just one strikeout in 23 games. His performance earned him High School Player of the Year honors from the American Baseball Coaches Association.

Impressed with his athleticism and production, the New York Yankees selected Jeter in the first round as the sixth overall pick of the June 1992 free-agent draft. The Yankees assigned him to the Gulf Coast Yankees (Gulf Coast League), but he struggled in his first professional season with Gulf Coast and Greensboro, North Carolina (Carolina League). His defensive play at shortstop raised particular concerns. He committed 21 errors in only 58 games.

Jeter batted .295 and stole 18 bases for Greensboro in 1993, being selected as the most outstanding prospect in the South Atlantic League. In 1994, he continued to improve in large increments. He started the season at Class A Tampa, Florida (Florida State League), moved up to AA Albany, New York (Eastern League), and finished the year at AAA Columbus, Ohio (International League), the Yankees' highest minor league affiliate. Despite switching leagues twice in midseason, he earned Minor League Player of the Year honors.

In 1995 New York gave Jeter the chance to win its starting shortstop position. He lost out to Tony Fernandez* and opened the season at AAA Columbus. When Fernandez was placed on the disabled list, the Yankees summoned Jeter to play shortstop. Jeter struggled at the plate in 13 starts and soon returned to the minor leagues, but impressed the Yankees with his soft hands, strong throwing arm, and calm maturity. He played well enough to make the International League's All-Star team.

Under new manager Joe Torre in 1996, Jeter became the Yankees' first Opening Day rookie shortstop since Tom Tresh in 1962. Jeter clouted a home run on the first day of the season. He contributed to the Yankees' AL East title by hitting .314 with 78 RBIs. Those numbers earned him the AL's Rookie of the Year Award. He batted .361 and scored 12 runs in the postseason, helping the Yankees win their first World Series since 1978.

After New York's disappointing finish in 1997, Jeter emerged as a full-throttle star in 1998. He batted .324 with 19 home runs and 84 RBIs and led the AL with 127 runs scored, numbers that looked even more impressive

Derek Jeter ©Photofest

coming from a shortstop. His All-Star performance coincided with Yankee supremacy, as New York steamrolled the competition for its second World Championship in three years. He batted .353 in a four-game World Series sweep of the San Diego Padres.

In 1999 Jeter experienced the finest season of his career. Establishing himself as one of the game's elite players, he led the AL with 219 hits and reached career highs in home runs (24), batting average (.349), walks (91), RBIs (102), and runs (134), while showing the durability to play 158 games at a demanding middle infield position. His level of play remained phenomenal in the Yankees' postseason run toward another championship. He hit safely in all 12 games, giving him hits in 17 consecutive postseason games to tie former Yankee Hank Bauer for the all-time record.

Jeter did not match his 1999 numbers over the next three seasons but remained a terrific baserunner and capable hitter while continuing his emergence as a team leader. In 2000, he became the first player in major league history to win All-Star Game and World Series MVP honors in the same season, as the Yankees defeated the New York Mets to stake claim to a third consecutive World Championship.

With his first five full seasons reading like a storybook, Jeter hoped for more glory in 2001. He found it in Game Three of the AL Division Series against the Oakland A's, making an incredible cutoff of an errant throw by Shane Spencer, and somehow snaring the ball near the first base foul line. He then made an off-balance, backhand flip of the ball to catcher Jorge Posada,* who applied the tag to Jeremy Giambi. "The Play" cemented Jeter's reputation as a winning player and preserved a 1–0 victory for the Yankees, who staved off elimination that night and came back to defeat the A's dramatically, three games to two. The Yankees once again advanced to the World Series, but Jeter's batting average declined for the second straight regular season. For the first time in his career, he slumped in both the ALCS and World Series partly because of nagging injuries. He also endured his first World Series loss, painfully watching the Arizona Diamondbacks celebrate their come-from-behind win in the ninth inning of Game Seven. Jeter batted .297 to help New York win the AL East in 2002, but the Anaheim Angels eliminated the Yankees in the AL Division Series. Through 2003, he batted .317 with 127 home runs and 615 RBIs. Jeter injured his shoulder in the first game of the 2003 season, but his .324 batting average helped the Yankees win the AL East again. After hitting .429 with a solo home run against the Minnesota Twins in the AL Division Series, he belted two doubles and a home run and sparkled defensively in the AL Championship Series against the Boston Red Sox. Jeter batted .346 with three doubles and two RBIs in the World Series loss to the Florida Marlins, but made his first World Series error.

Jeter's romantic and social life, often the subject of the New York City tabloids, has added to his unusually charismatic aura, but has drawn some criticism from Yankees owner George Steinbrenner. Jeter's star status, coupled with his good looks and friendliness with fans, have made the bachelor one of the most popular players in the history of the Yankees' franchise.

BIBLIOGRAPHY
Derek Jeter with Jack Curry, *The Life You Imagine: Life Lessons for Achieving Your Dreams* (New York, 2000); Tyler Kepner, "Jeter's Intangibles Hard to Quantify," *New York Times*, February 25, 2003; *New York Yankees Information and Record Guide*, 2003 New York Yankees Media Relations Department, 2003; Tom Verducci, "The Toast of the Town," *Sports Illustrated* 93 (November 6, 2000).

Bruce Markusen

ALLEN JOHNSON   **Track and Field**
(March 1, 1971–)

Allen Johnson won the gold medal in the 110-meter high hurdles at the Atlanta, Georgia, Olympic Games in 1996.

Allen Johnson was born on March 1, 1971 in Washington, D.C., the son of Ramon Judkins and Sandra Smith. Johnson graduated in 1989 from Lake Braddock High School in Burke, Virginia. He won the Virginia High School indoor state meet in the 55-meter hurdles in 14.21 seconds, the high jump with a leap of 6 feet 11 inches, and the long jump at 24 feet 5.25 inches, and he finished third in the 110-meter hurdles. During the outdoor season, Johnson high jumped 7 feet and triple jumped 49 feet.

Johnson was recruited out of high school because he performed well in numerous events and competed in the decathlon. The 5-foot 10-inch, 165-pound Johnson graduated from the University of North Carolina in 1993. Coach Dennis Craddock shifted Johnson from the decathlon to the hurdles and high jump because he was so injury prone, and Charles Foster, former great hurdler, taught Johnson much of his hurdling techniques. Johnson set the Tar Heel records in the 55-meter hurdles and the long jump. He won the National Collegiate Athletic Association (NCAA) Championship in the 55-meter hurdles in 1992, captured four Atlantic Coast Conference (ACC) titles in that event, and was named four-time All-America.

Johnson finished second at the NCAA Championships in both the 55-meter and the 110-meter hurdles and placed second in the 1994 World Cup in 13.25 seconds in the 110 meters. He enjoyed a highly productive season in 1995, winning the gold medal in the 110-meter hurdles at the World Outdoor Championships and the World and USA Indoor Championships. He became the fourth hurdler to break 13 seconds in the 110-meter hurdles, clocking 12.98 seconds in the Championships.

Johnson explained the key to winning the 110-meter hurdles: "I say the fifth hurdle is key because that's right in the middle of the race where I'm the fastest and I'm surging another two hurdles. So, if I'm ahead at the fifth, I feel by the seventh hurdle I'm going to be even further ahead of you, and after the seventh hurdle is when everybody in the race is going to start decelerating."

Johnson won the 1996 Olympic Trials in the 110-meter-high hurdles in 12.92 seconds, an American record. He shares the American record with Roger Kingdom* and is just 1/100th of a second off British hurdler Colin Jackson's world record of 12.91 seconds. He won the gold medal at the Atlanta, Georgia, Olympics in 12.95 seconds and ended the year ranked best in the world.

In 1997 Johnson won his second world title in the 110-meter hurdles and the USA Outdoor Championships. The following season, he ran 13.10 seconds or better five times and was ranked second in the USA and the world. He missed most of the 1999 season because of injuries but captured the 2000 Olympic Trials in the 110-meter hurdles in a world-best time of 12.97 seconds. Johnson recognized the pressure of being the defending Olympic champion. "That one competition (trials) is really nerve-racking. I just worry about making a mistake. I feel like if I do fairly well I should be in the top three, and that's the key about the Trials."

Johnson suffered a hamstring injury while competing in Japan just before the 2000 Olympic Games in Sydney, Australia. The injury hindered his performance, causing him to finish fourth at Sydney in 13.23 seconds. Injuries plagued him through most of 2000 and part of 2001, but he was still the top 110-meter hurdler. In 2001 Johnson finished first in the Goodwill Games and in the USA Outdoor Championships and recorded his third World Outdoor title. He captured both the USA Outdoor and Indoor Championships in 2002.

Johnson remains the only 110-meter hurdler in history to average 12.94 seconds for his five fastest times (12.92, 12.92, 12.93, 12.95, 12.97). Only four other hurdlers have ever run 12.94 or faster. Colin Jackson of Great Britain holds the world record at 12.91 seconds, while Roger Kingdom of the United States and Johnson share the American record at 12.92 seconds. Jack Pierce of the United States recorded 12.94 seconds, while Renaldo Nehemiah, also of the United States, became the first hurdler to break 13.00 seconds at 12.93.

The highlights of Johnson's career include being the 1996 Olympic gold medalist and three-time World Champion (1995, 1997, and 2001) in the 110-meter hurdles, the 1995 World Indoor Champion, and a five-time USA Outdoor Champion (1996, 1997, 2000, 2001, and 2002) in the 110-meter hurdles. He also was a two-time USA Indoor Champion in 1995 and 2002, a 1997 gold medalist as a member of the 4×400 relay team in the World Championships, and the 1992 NCAA Indoor 55-meter hurdle champion. He was named USA Track and Field (USATF) Jesse Owens Award winner and was the only double gold medal winner in the World Championships.

After a short stint as a volunteer assistant track and field coach at North Carolina, Johnson joined the University of South Carolina in 1995 as a volunteer track and field coach. He works with the hurdlers and belongs to Speed Elite. Former hurdle great Renaldo Nehemiah serves as his agent. In 1992, Allen's significant other, Marcia Williams, gave birth to his daughter, Tristine.

BIBLIOGRAPHY

"Allen Johnson," Athlete Bio, www.usatf.com (2002); "Allen Johnson," *High Hopes to Win 110 Hurdles*, www.modbee.com (2002); "Allen Johnson," *Hurdler Deserves Attention*, www.slam.com (2000); "Allen Johnson," *Olympic Update*, www.cnnsi.com (2001); "Allen Johnson," *Profile*, www.uscsports.com (2002); "Allen Johnson," *Telephone Conversation*, www.runnersworld.com (2000). *Pete Cava, Executive Director, International Sports Associates*, to John L. Evers, November 4, 2002.

John L. Evers and David L. Porter

CHARLES JOHNSON Baseball
(July 20, 1971–)

Charles Johnson rejoined the Florida Marlins (National League) on December 19, 2000, signing a five-year $35 million deal with his original team and returning to the area where he grew up.

Charles Edward Johnson Jr. was born in Fort Pierce, Florida, on July 20,

1971. His father, Charles Sr. teaches mathematics and coaches baseball at Westwood High School in Fort Pierce. Charles Jr. graduated from high school there. His mother, Gloria, works as an accountant for Fort Pierce. Charles Jr., three-time All State selection as a catcher at Westwood High, was named Gatorade Player of the Year for Florida in 1989.

Johnson attended the University of Miami and was named a three-time All America in baseball. He started at catcher on the United States Olympic team in the Barcelona, Spain, Olympic Games in 1992 and for the United States National Team in the Pan American Games in Havana, Cuba, in 1991. He played on the gold-medal-winning USA Junior National Team in 1988 in Australia.

Johnson attracted much interest from major league clubs. The Florida Marlins selected him in the June 1992 amateur draft, making him the first pick in their franchise history and the twenty-eighth selection overall. In May 1994, he became the first Marlin farm product to reach the major leagues as a power-hitting catcher with great defensive skills.

Johnson remained with Florida from May 1994 until May 1998. He set records and enjoyed some sterling moments with the Marlins. He holds the major league record for the most errorless games by a catcher (172), and he also tied a major league record with a 1,000 fielding percentage. His record streak of 1,295 consecutive chances without an error ended on Opening Day in 1998. Johnson played on the National League All-Star team in 1997 and 2001. He enjoyed a solid season in 1997 and won his third consecutive Gold Glove. The 1997 season produced his most satisfying achievements; that year he played on the World Championship Marlins team and starred in the World Series. He batted .357 with 10 hits in the World Series and clouted an upper deck home run in Game One off Orel Hershiser of the Cleveland Indians.

Johnson was traded to the Los Angeles Dodgers (NL) in May 1998 for financial reasons. Four other players accompanied him to Los Angeles for catcher Mike Piazza and infielder Todd Zeile. His time with Los Angeles started with a drought of 10 games, in which he went hitless in 35 official at-bats. Nevertheless, Johnson won his fourth consecutive Gold Glove, the longest string for a catcher since Johnny Bench. The Baltimore Orioles (American League) acquired Johnson in December 1998. Johnson enjoyed a solid year for the Orioles in 1999. The 2000 campaign marked his most productive season, as he batted .304 with 31 home runs and 91 runs batted in (RBI). In July 2000, he was traded to the Chicago White Sox (AL). He played in postseason for the White Sox in the AL Division Series and saw limited action against the Seattle Mariners.

Johnson, tired of moving around, accepted less money to return to the Florida Marlins. He declared, "For me to have a chance to come back here again is a thrill."

Johnson hit .264 with 18 home runs and 75 RBIs in 2001 and .217 with six home runs and 36 RBIs in 2002. He displayed his trademark strong game behind the plate and provided leadership for a young pitching staff. In November 2002, the Colorado Rockies (NL) acquired him. Through 2003, he batted .246 in 1,060 games with 154 home runs and 618 RBIs. Johnson struggled with a .230 batting average, 20 home runs, and 61 RBIs in 2003.

Johnson lives in Plantation, Florida, with his wife, Rhonda, and their two sons, Brandon and Beau. He has pledged a considerable amount to the Florida Marlins Community Foundation, which benefits Cornerstones for Kids, an organization that teaches children through education and baseball.

BIBLIOGRAPHY
Andrew Feirstein Florida Marlins Media Department, e-mail to John Mosher, November 6, 2001; "Charles Johnson returns Home," *Florida Marlins News*, January 9, 2001, pp. 1, 2; *Florida Marlins Media Guides*, 1994–1998, 2001–2002; John Mosher, conversations with Steve Gietschier and Jim Meier, *The Sporting News*, St. Louis, MO, September 5, 2001, September 11, 2001; John Mosher, telephone conversations with Maria Armella, Media Department, Florida Marlins, Miami, FL, September 20, 2001, October 9, 2001.

John E. Mosher

MAGIC JOHNSON   Basketball
(August 14, 1959–)

Magic Johnson ranks among the most popular ambassadors for professional basketball.

Earvin Johnson Jr. was born on August 14, 1959 in Lansing, Michigan, the sixth of 10 children of Earvin Johnson Sr. and Christina Johnson. To support his large family, Earvin Sr. worked night jobs after finishing his shift at a General Motors plant. In his spare time, he taught his son the basic fundamentals of basketball. Earvin Jr. attended Everett High School in Lansing between 1973 and 1977 and was selected to the Michigan All-State basketball teams each year. In his senior year, he led his team to the Class A State Championship. Named *UPI* Michigan Prep Player of the Year, Johnson averaged 28.8 points and 16.8 rebounds, and was credited with 208 assists and 99 steals. In his sophomore year, he was nicknamed "Magic" by a sportswriter after he had completely dominated an opponent in scoring, rebounding, and assists.

After graduating in 1977, Johnson attended Michigan State University and helped the Spartans win the 1977–1978 Big Ten Conference (BTC) Championship in his freshman year. The Spartans finished in a three-way tie for the BTC title the following year. An All-BTC team selection both years, Johnson helped Michigan State capture the National Collegiate Athletic Association (NCAA) Championship in 1979 with a 75–64 triumph over Larry Bird's Indiana State University. Bird was selected College Player of the Year, while Johnson was named Most Valuable Player (MVP) of the Final Four. Johnson, a First Team All-America in 1979, was named to the NCAA Final Four All-Time team and to the NCAA Tournament All-Decade team for the 1970s.

Magic Johnson ©Photofest

In 1979 Johnson entered the National Basketball Association (NBA) draft and was selected by the Los Angeles Lakers (NBA) as the first pick overall. The 6-foot 9-inch, 215-pounder played for Los Angeles from 1979–1980 through 1990–1991 and spent four seasons on the voluntary retired list. After being activated in January 1996, Johnson played in 32 games for the Lakers and retired permanently.

Johnson led the Lakers to five NBA Championships (1980, 1982, 1985, 1987, 1988). In 1980 he became the first rookie named MVP in the NBA Championship Finals. In the 1982 and 1987 NBA Finals, he again was selected the MVP. He also received regular season MVP honors in 1981, 1987, and 1990. His Lakers and Larry Bird's Boston Celtics dominated the NBA during the 1980s, renewing fan interest and attendance throughout the NBA.

In Johnson's rookie season, Los Angeles defeated the Philadelphia 76ers for the NBA Championship. He missed half the following season with a knee injury, as the Lakers lost to the Houston Rockets in the first round of the Western Conference (WC) playoffs. In 1981–1982, Los Angeles bounced back to defeat the Philadelphia 76ers for the NBA crown. Johnson won his second consecutive steals title during the 1981–1982 regular season and the first of four assists titles the following year, but the Lakers were swept in the NBA Finals by the Philadelphia 76ers. In 1983–1984, Johnson paced the NBA in assists and led Los Angeles to the NBA Finals, but the Lakers lost to Bird's Boston Celtics. Los Angeles rebounded the next season to defeat the Celtics in an NBA Finals rematch.

The Houston Rockets ousted the Lakers, four games to one, in the 1986 NBA WC Finals. In 1987 Johnson helped Los Angeles return to the NBA Finals against the Boston Celtics for the third time in four years. The Lakers won the NBA title four games to two. After Johnson recorded his career-high 23.9 points average in the 1987–1988 regular season, Los Angeles became the first team since the 1968–1969 Boston Celtics to win consecutive NBA Championships by defeating the Detroit Pistons in seven games. In a 1989 rematch, Johnson was injured in the first game and the Detroit Pistons swept the series. The Lakers boasted the best regular season record in their division in 1989–1990, but lost in the playoffs to the Phoenix Suns. Los Angeles returned to the NBA Finals in 1991 for the ninth time in 12 years, but Michael Jordan's* Chicago Bulls prevailed in five games.

On November 7, 1991, Johnson shocked the sports world when he disclosed that he had tested positive for HIV during a routine physical exam and was retiring from the NBA on the advice of his physician. He publicly acknowledged "that he had led a promiscuous and somewhat careless lifestyle, and urged others to learn from his example." Upon reflecting on his basketball career, he said, "As soon as I realized I had a God-given talent to play this game, I was determined to take it as far as I could. And I did. When the doctor gave me the test results, I knew that everything I had accomplished in my life was nothing compared to the battle I was about to begin."

Johnson was selected to play in his twelfth All-Star Game and received medical permission to play. Magic recorded 25 points, five rebounds, and nine assists, and was voted his second MVP Award, the other having been in 1990. Later that season, the Los Angeles Lakers retired his jersey number (32). In 1992, Johnson played on the United States Olympic basketball team. The "Dream Team" won the gold medal at the Barcelona, Spain, Olympics. Between 1992 and 1994, Johnson served as a broadcaster for NBC Sports. He also served as head coach of the Los Angeles Lakers for the final 16 games of the 1993–1994 season, compiling a 5–11 won-lost record. Since 1994–1995, Johnson has served as vice president of the Los Angeles Lakers.

In his illustrious career, Johnson compiled 17,707 points (19.5-point average), pulled down 6,559 rebounds, dished out 10,140 assists (second on the all-time NBA list), made 1,724 steals, and blocked 174 shots in 906 regular season games. He played in 190 playoff games, scoring 3,701 points (19.5-point average) and posting 1,465 rebounds, 2,346 assists, and 358 steals.

Johnson was named to the All-NBA First Team nine times (1983–1991), the All-NBA Second Team in 1982, and the NBA All-Rookie Team in 1990. He received the Walter Kennedy Citizenship Award in 1992 and the IBM Award for all-around contributions to the team's success in 1984. The Naismith Memorial Basketball Hall of Fame inducted him in 2002.

After announcing that he had tested positive for the virus that causes AIDS, Johnson became a national spokesman for AIDS awareness and prevention, promoted AIDS research, published a book, *What You Can Do to Avoid AIDS*, and served briefly on the President's Council on AIDS. He also co-authored the books, *My Life* (1992) and *"Magic"* (1983).

From his offices in Beverly Hills, California, Johnson directs and oversees numerous business interests under Magic Johnson Enterprises. These include Johnson Development Corporation, Magic Johnson Theatres, Magic Johnson All-Star Camps, Magic Johnson T's, and Magic Johnson Entertainment. He resides in California with his wife, Erletha "Cookie" Kelly, whom he married in September 1991, and their children, Earvin III, Andre (from a previous relationship), and Elisa (adopted).

BIBLIOGRAPHY
Big Ten Men's Record Book (Schaumburg, IL, 1987–1988); Earvin "Magic" Johnson and Robert Levin, *"Magic"* (New York, 1983); Earvin "Magic" Johnson and William Novak, *My Life* (New York, 1992); "Magic" Johnson, *Celebrities*, www.mrshowbiz. go.com; "Magic" Johnson, *Microsoft, Encarta, Online Encyclopedia* (Redmond, WA, 2001); *NCAA Men's Basketball's Finest* (Overland Park, KS, 1998); David L. Porter ed., *African American Sports Greats* (Westport, CT, 1995); *The Sporting News Official NBA Register*, 2003–2004.

John L. Evers

MICHAEL JOHNSON   Track and Field
(September 13, 1967–   )

For much of the twentieth century, Jesse Owens, the four gold medalist winner at the 1936 Olympics at Berlin, Germany, was considered the greatest sprinter of all time. No runner threatened Owens's feats until Michael Johnson. Johnson's 200 meters and 400 meters gold medal victories at the 1996 Olympics in Atlanta, Georgia, demonstrated extraordinary ability. Owens and Johnson were the greatest sprinters of all time.

Michael Duane Johnson's parents were Paul Johnson, a truck driver, and Ruby Johnson, a schoolteacher. Johnson, the youngest of five children, was born on September 13, 1967 in Dallas, Texas. His parents lived in Oak Cliff, a middle-class Dallas neighborhood and attached great importance to education. Although Johnson started running competitively at age 11, academics prevailed over athletics. Johnson, who wore black horn-rimmed glasses when he ran, resembled an "Oxford scholar" more than a Texas sprinter. He performed well at Skyline Senior High School and accepted a track and field scholarship at Baylor University, a school known for its academic standards. In 1986 he finished second in the State Championships in the 200 meters in a 21.30 seconds clocking.

Track and field coach Clyde Hart of Baylor University liked Johnson's relay potential. From 1987 to 1989, Johnson ran a blistering pace when healthy. At the 1988 Southwest Athletic Conference (SWC) championship, he ran 200 meters in 20.07 seconds.

The year 1990 proved a banner one for Johnson. He never lost a race in the 400 meters and was defeated only once in the 200 meters. His personal best times for the 200 meters and 400 meters were 19.85 seconds and 44.21 seconds, respectively. In the 1990 National Collegiate Athletic Association (NCAA) Championships, Johnson produced one of the great 4×400 relay legs of all time. Although recording a relay leg time of 43.5 seconds, he cruised home in a relaxed manner to conserve energy. Had Johnson sprinted all the way to the finish line, he would have completed the first-ever 400 meters in under 43 seconds. His running style was based on incredible power from arms and legs and a driving gait with very little knee lift.

In 1991 Johnson was ranked the world's top performer in the 200 meters and 400 meters. At the 1992 Olympics in Barcelona, Spain, he suffered food poisoning and was unsuccessful in both events. Nevertheless, he anchored the United States squad to a gold medal and world record in the 4×400-meter relay. The mind-boggling American time of 2 minutes 55.74 seconds translates into four consecutive runners, each covering 400 meters in under 44 seconds. His power and pace helped the U.S. squad defeat the Cuban team by the huge margin of nearly 4 seconds.

A year later, Johnson won the 400-meters race in 43.65 seconds at the World Championships in Stuttgart, Germany. He completed another sensational anchor leg in 42.94 seconds for the United States in the 1,600-meter relay and enabled the United States to lower its 1992 world record to 2 minutes 54.29 seconds.

In 1994 the United States Olympic Committee (USOC) and *Track and Field News* (TFN) made Johnson its Track and Field Athlete of the Year. During both 1994 and 1995, he toured extensively, ran frequently, won repeatedly,

Michael Johnson ©Mike Hewitt/Getty Images

and kept free of any nagging injuries. As the 1996 Atlanta, Georgia, Summer Olympics approached, he trained for a track and field feat never before accomplished. No Olympian had won both the 200 and 400 meters at the same games. According to Adam R. Hornbuckle, Johnson's goal in life was "being the best in the world at both" distances.

In 1996 *Newsweek* observed that Johnson possessed "a style so distinctive that it can be spotted on any track," "a torso as erect as a Beefeater's," "a gold chain bouncing against his weight lifter's chest," and legs that jut forward "swallowing his lane." Johnson's 6 foot 2 inches and 185-pound frame, along with his 325 pounds bench-pressing strength, made for a biped ideally contoured for the sustained sprint, one complete lap of the track. The 400-meter run remains one of the most physiologically and psychologically demanding events in track and field.

Johnson did not play down the importance of his winning a world championship. In 1995 he had won world championships over 200 meters and 400 meters. He stressed, however, that "nobody else in the world can say, 'I'm a double gold-medal winner in the 200 and 400.' I'm going to do it at the Olympics because no man has ever done it before."

With a physical frame possessing less than 3 percent fat, Johnson represents the quintessentially toned and sculpted superathlete. He works out less than a dozen hours a week spread over five or six days, featuring excellence and quality. His repetition sprints of five 400 meters or ten 300 meters are completed with brief intervals and take place at 80 percent or more of maximum speed. He follows a sane, simple life-style, eats whatever he wants to, gets lots of sleep, and enjoys computers, Formula 3 racing, television watching, and slalom moves on his "Jet Ski." Johnson enjoyed a Dream Olympics in 1996 at Atlanta, winning the 200 meters in a world record 19.32 seconds and the 400 meters in 43.49 seconds.

Before the 2000 Olympics in Sydney, Australia, Johnson seemed set to do the unthinkable with a double double! In a July 2000 U.S. Olympics Trials 200-meter race against arch rival Maurice Greene,* however, both pulled up lame. Nevertheless, the 400-meter world champion, who set the world record in 1999 with a 43.18 seconds clocking to break Butch Reynolds's* 11-year-old mark, performed majestically "Down Under." At Sydney, Michael won gold medals in both the 400-meter and the 1,600-meter relay. He explained, "I wanted to keep my record in track at my last games. I didn't want to get to the last one and mess up." All of his career Olympic medals were of the gold variety!

Roger Black, a leading European TV sports commentator, lauded Johnson as the "greatest athlete ever in track and field." Had Johnson indeed managed the double double with gold medals in the 200 meters and 400 meters at both Atlanta and Sydney, such an accolade would have been difficult to reject. Nevertheless, he proved a magisterial one-lap sprinter. He was unbeatable at his best and, even in the closing stages of a world record run, he seemingly could shift gears and run even faster.

In 2001 Johnson toured the world and enjoyed the celebrity existence of a much photographed star with several lucrative sponsorship deals. No other track and field athlete competes in gold-finished, one of a kind, shoes designed by Nike. He retired following the 2001 track and field season. Johnson has several long-term sponsorships, including "Samsung Digitall," and initiated his television career as a color commentator at the Sydney Olympics.

BIBLIOGRAPHY
Tom Lappin, "Sprinters Run Off at the Mouth," *Scotsman*, October 2, 2000, p. 4; Tim Layden, "How Are Michael Johnson and Maurice Greene Shaping Up After Their US Trials Debacle?," *Sports Illustrated* 93 (September 11, 2000), p. 94; David L. Porter,

ed., *African-American Sports Greats: A Biographical Dictionary* (Westport, CT, 1995); Mark Starr, "Good as Gold," *Newsweek* 128 (July 22, 1996), pp. 36–40.

Scott A.G.M. Crawford

ANDRUW JONES Baseball
(April 23, 1977–   )

Andruw Jones of the Atlanta Braves (National League) was only 19 years old when he set several World Series records. He has set even more records since then and has impressed baseball fans around the world with his natural talent and gifts. As Braves manager Bobby Cox says, "he can do it all. He has all the tools."

Andruw Rudolf Jones was born on April 23, 1977 in Willemstad, Curacao, Netherlands Antilles. At age 3, he received his first glove from his father, Henry, a former star catcher on Curacao's national baseball team with Road Runner–like speed. Jones grew up in Wellemstad, on a small island north of the coast of Venezuela, and was surrounded with people who loved baseball and admired his father. Baseball came naturally to Jones, who often outplayed kids his own age. His father recalls that, when Jones was age 5, he was "all alone (in his ability) . . . he was running too hard, throwing too hard and batting too hard, so they had to move him to the next level." At age 6, Jones loved watching games on television while his father listened on the radio.

Henry Jones fostered in his son a work ethic that, when combined with a natural love for the game, resulted in an unswerving devotion to being the best he could be. Jones fell off a roof at age 9 and broke his arm, but still played baseball the entire time he was wearing a cast. Henry Jones stressed the importance of having the right attitude and team spirit, noting that "all the guys on the field and ones on the bench, everyone on that bench are equal or better than the guys on the field—that's what makes a baseball team." Andruw Jones progressed through local leagues from 1991 to 1993, playing in senior and junior leagues. He was discovered at age 15 by Giovanni Viceisza, a Netherlands Antilles scout for the Atlanta Braves who spotted him in a baseball tournament in Puerto Rico.

In 1993, Jones turned age 16. Although the Toronto Blue Jays (American League) offered him more money, he signed with the Atlanta Braves for $46,000. He agreed with his father that the Braves organization was better equipped to develop him into a major leaguer. Jones began 1994 with the Gulf Coast Braves (Gulf Coast League) and finished with Danville, Virginia (Appalachian League), hitting .290 with 3 home runs and 26 runs batted in (RBI). Jones spent the 1995 season with Macon, Georgia (South Atlantic League). After hitting .277 with 25 home runs and 100 RBIs, he was named Minor League Player of the Year by *USA Today, Baseball Weekly*, and *Baseball America*.

In 1996 Jones completed his astonishing ascent to the major leagues. He rocketed through the minor leagues while clouting 34 homers, driving in 92 runs, and batting .339. He started the year in Durham, North Carolina (Carolina League) in Class A Ball. After 66 games, he was promoted to Class AA Greenville, South Carolina (Southern League) for 38 games, and then he joined Class AAA Richmond, Virginia (International League). Jones played only 12 games at Richmond when the Braves promoted him to the major leagues. One day later, he clouted his first major league home run. The Braves advanced to the World Series against the New York Yankees, enabling Jones to become the youngest player to perform in a fall classic since 1970 and to start in a World Series contest since 1935. In his first World Series at-bat in Yankee Stadium, he became only the twenty-fifth player in history to blast a home run. On his next at-bat he clouted another home run the next inning. Only six other players have accomplished that feat in consecutive innings. He also became the second player ever to hit homers in his first two World Series at-bats, the fifteenth player to drive in five runs in a game, and the youngest person ever to homer in the World Series.

Jones has continued to develop in the Atlanta Braves organization. After completing his first full season in the major leagues during 1997, he won a defensive Gold Glove in each of the next seven years. He has appeared in eight NL Division Series, five NL Championship Series, two World Series, and the 2000 and 2002 All-Star games. Jones has a career .269 batting average with 221 home runs and 675 RBIs. In 2002 the Braves signed him to a $75 million contract through the 2007 season.

Jones speaks fluent English, Spanish, Dutch, and Papamiento (an island dialect). He is building a home in the Atlanta, Georgia, area and plans to marry Nicole Derick. He has a young daughter, Madison, from a previous relationship.

BIBLIOGRAPHY
Atlanta Braves Media Guide, 2003; Mike Berardino, "Chipper Saw Andruw's Star Rise Early," *Augusta Chronicle*, October 22, 1996; S. J. Fletcher, "Father Figured in Andruw Jones' Rise: Live-in Role Model Molded Major-League Talent," *Richmond Times-Dispatch*, April 9, 1997; Carroll Rogers, "Andruw's Secure; Center Fielder Tapped Lessons from His Dad in Putting Place, Family Above Money," *Atlanta Journal-Constitution*, February 16, 2002; Alan Schwarz, "Impact Center of Attention," *Sport* 91 (April 2000), pp. 8–11; Jayson Stark, "The Legend of Andruw Jones," *Philadelphia Inquirer*, October 21, 1996; Mark Stewart, "Andruw Jones: Love That Glove," *Place*, 2001.

James A. Riley

MARION JONES   Track and Field, Basketball
(October 12, 1975–)

At the 2000 Summer Olympics in Sydney, Australia, America's Marion Jones made an unprecedented attempt to win five gold medals in track and field.

Marion Jones, the daughter of George Jones, a laundromat operator, and Marion Jones, a legal secretary, was born in Los Angeles, California, on October 12, 1975. Soon after her birth, her parents divorced. She remained estranged from her father until Thanksgiving 1995 when a brief reconciliation failed. Jones's mother married Ira Toler, who adopted her and her half-brother, Albert. Both children adored Ira, who died suddenly from a stroke only four years after the marriage. Albert recalled, "Ira was always there for my sister. He talked to her, answered her questions, helped her with homework, took her to tee-ball games."

In 1981 Jones was stretched out on the living room floor of her Los Angeles home watching television with her brother and mother. The 5-year-old enjoyed the British Royal wedding of Diana Spencer and Prince Charles. She remarked, "They have a red carpet to walk on, because they're special people. When will they roll out a red carpet for me?"

At the 1988 Olympics, in Seoul, Korea, Jones, then an eighth grader, admired Florence Griffith Joyner* and Jackie Joyner-Kersee* as they won gold medals in sprinting and long jumping. She confidently wrote, "I want to be an Olympic champion."

An early defeat sparked her will to win. At the Arcadia Invitational High School meet in Southern California in April 1990, Jones was defeated in both the 100 and the 200 meters by Inger Miller. This competition started a decade-long rivalry. A meet official told Miller, "It's a good thing you beat her now, because I don't think you'll ever beat her again."

In June 1991, Jones set a high school record in the 200 meters in 22.76 seconds. This performance amazingly took place in the finals of the U.S. senior event, in which she placed fourth. She was recognized as a prominent American and appeared on *Good Morning America.*

In 1991 Jones's mother moved the family from Camarillo, California, to Thousand Oaks, California, so that Jones could compete for Thousand Oaks High School in basketball. Her stellar sprinting, which included 22.67 seconds in the 200 meters and 11.14 seconds in the 100 meters, earned her the *Track and Field News* Female High School Athlete of the Year Award.

For the first time, Jones tried the long jump in 1992. Her first leap resulted in a promising 19 feet 10¾ inches. Later that season she soared to an impressive 23 feet, the second-longest-ever jump achieved by a high school female.

At the 1992 Olympic track and field trials, Jones finished fourth in the 200 meters and missed a spot on the national team by a minuscule seven-tenths of a second. The following year featured Jones as a high school star athlete in both basketball and track and field. Her 5-foot 11-inch height and her strength influenced her decision to accept a basketball scholarship with Sylvia Hatchell at the University of North Carolina. Jones played on their 1994 National Collegiate Athletic Association (NCAA) Championship team, winners of a 60–59 cliffhanger victory over Louisiana Tech. She also earned All-America honors in four events at the NCAA track and field championships.

Marion Jones ©Mike Powell/Getty Images

In 1996 she hoped to redshirt in basketball and compete in the Atlanta, Georgia, Summer Olympics, but twice broke a bone in her left foot.

Jones began dating Charles Hunter, seven years her senior and a track and field coach at North Carolina, in early 1996. Hunter, the divorced father of two, was a world-ranked shot putter. They married in the fall of 1996, but the marriage upset her mother. They later divorced.

Jones planned to concentrate on basketball in 1997 until she came under the tutelage of Jamaican Trevor Graham, a former Olympian 1,600-meter relay performer. Jones improved so much that she convinced herself that track and field, not basketball, was her avenue to fame, fortune, and success. She vowed, "I'm 22 years old; I'm going to get faster. Before my career is over, I will attempt to run faster than any woman has ever run and jump farther than any woman has ever jumped."

By the 2000 Olympics in Sydney, Australia, Jones and her mother had reconciled. She acknowledged, "My mother and I love each other very much. . . . If at the end of my life I can say that I was just a quarter of the woman she has been, I will be satisfied."

Jones's quest for five Olympic medals made her the center of attention. Her face and photograph became instantly recognizable, as she made six different American television advertisements. The October 2, 2000 issue of *Sports Illustrated* magnificently captured her striking muscularity and bunched levers (compact starting position) as she winds herself up in the starting blocks.

At Sydney, Jones came extremely close to grasping her "Holy Grail." She won the 100 meters (10.75 seconds) and 200 meters (21.84 seconds), and earned a gold medal in the 1,600-meter relay (3 minutes 22.62 seconds). Her 400-meter sprint in the relay was clocked at an impressive 49.57 seconds, an incredible achievement from an athlete who concentrated on explosive flat-out sprinting in the dash and long jump. Her dream of winning five gold medals, however, was torpedoed by her bronze medals in the 4×100-meter relay and the long jump (22 feet 8¼ inches). Nevertheless, she compiled a sterling string of competitive performances. Leigh Montville considered Jones one of a kind, being "the most celebrated of all the U.S. athletes as the Games began" and the supreme track diva as they concluded.

Jones considered retirement, but the lure of the 2004 Olympics and the rich rewards of massive sponsorship and professional track inspired her to continue her running and jumping career. She finished second in the 100 meters and first in the 200 meters at the IAAF World Championships at Calgary, Canada in August 2001, first in the 100 meters and 200 meters at the USA Outdoor Championships in Palo Alto, California in June 2002, and first in the 100 meters at the IAAF Grand Prix Final in Paris, France in September 2002. She missed the 2003 World Championships because of the birth of her first child. A 2001 *Vogue* magazine article, "Greater Than Gold—The New American Hero," featured Jones and the many opportunities that the hype and hoopla surrounding her Olympic saga opened for her.

Jones does not compete as a heptathlete, but her glorious attempt at the Sydney Olympics marks her as a mighty, yet mortal, superathlete. She wants to be spoken of in the same breath as a Muhammad Ali or a Michael Jordan.* If she returns to the Olympic arena in 2004 and succeeds, that just might happen.

Jones and sprinter Tim Montgomery, world record holder in the 100 meters, have one son, Tim Montgomery.

BIBLIOGRAPHY
CNN Sports Illustrated, http://sportsillustrated.cnn.com/olympics/features/2000/jones; Tim Layden, "The Fastest Lane," *Sports Illustrated* 93 (October 2, 2000), pp. 40–47; Leigh Montville, "Back to Earth," *Sports Illustrated* 93 (October 18, 2000), pp. 78–79; Julia Reed, "Hail Marion: Greater Than Gold—The New American Hero," *Vogue* (January 2001), pp. 146–154.

Scott A.G.M. Crawford

ROY JONES JR.   Boxing
(January 16, 1969–)

Roy Jones Jr. won boxing titles in the middleweight, super-middleweight, light-heavyweight, and heavyweight divisions between 1993 and 2003.

Roy Jones Jr. was born on January 16, 1969 in Pensacola, Florida, the son of Roy Jones Sr., a former electrician at the Pensacola Naval Air Station and bronze star Vietnam veteran, and Carol Jones. Jones grew up on a hog farm in nearby Barth and has a younger brother, Corey, and three younger sisters, Tiffany, Lakesha, and Catandrea.

His father, a middleweight boxer, kindled Jones's interest in boxing by play-sparring with him when he was 5 years old. Roy Sr. demanded much of his son, even to the point of physical abuse. He challenged Roy Jr. to go beyond what he thought he could do. When Roy Jr. did not live up to his father's expectations, Roy Sr. would hit him with anything available. Jones soon developed a tremendous fear of his father.

The hog farm was eventually sold and the family moved to Pensacola, where Jones graduated from Washington High School in 1988. His father managed a Boys Club boxing program for Santa Rosa County. Jones became a fierce, dominant fighter with an obsessive desire to win. He won the U.S. Junior Olympics in 1984 and the 1986 National Golden Gloves at 139 pounds and the 1987 National Golden Gloves at 156 pounds, two weight divisions higher. By age 19, Jones had compiled an amateur record of 106 victories and only four losses and was the youngest member of the 1988 U.S. Olympic Boxing team that competed in Seoul, South Korea. Jones was heavily favored to win the gold medal in the 156-pound weight class. He reached the championship bout with South Korean Si Hun Park. The ringside press scored the no-contest fight 86 to 32 in favor of Jones, but three of the five judges scored the match in favor of Park. Following the controversial decision, an investigation was conducted. Two of the three judges were accused of bribery. Since bribery could not be proved against the third judge, Jones was left with the silver medal. The International Boxing Association (IBA) awarded Jones the Val Barker Cup for being the outstanding boxer of the Olympic Games.

Roy Sr. now became his son's manager. Jones completed his amateur career with a 121–13 won-lost record and knocked out Ricky Randall in the second round of his first professional fight on May 6, 1989. Between June 1989 and

Roy Jones Jr. ©Photofest

August 1991, he faced relatively unknown opponents and won by knockouts in 14 contests. On January 10, 1992, he knocked out Jorge Vaca, former World Champion, in the first round, enabling Jones to challenge for the middleweight title. In August 1992, Jones, who had taken enough of his father's abuse, moved out of his parents' home. He employed Alton Merkerson, the assistant coach on the 1988 U.S. Olympic Boxing Team, as his trainer. His father seldom communicated with his son and refused to attend any of his fights. On August 18, 1992, Jones knocked out Glenn Thomas in the eighth round in his first match without his father. He won the vacant International Boxing Federation (IBF) middleweight crown on March 22, 1993 with a unanimous decision against Bernard Hopkins. One year later, he defeated Thomas Tate on a second-round knockout to retain his IBF middleweight title.

Jones captured the IBF super-middleweight crown with a unanimous decision over James Toney on November 18, 1994. Toney, the favored undefeated champion, was floored in the third round and was dominated by Jones during the entire contest. In 1995 and 1996, Jones retained his IBF super-middleweight title five times. He defeated Anthony Byrd, the top-ranked challenger, by a technical knockout (TKO) in the first round and Vinny Pazienza by a TKO in the sixth round. Against Tony Thornton, Jones threw 50 unanswered punches in the second round before the fight was stopped. In 1996 Jones signed to play point guard for the Jacksonville, Florida, Barracudas, a U.S. Basketball League (USBL) team. On June 15, 1996, he played in a USBL game during the day and knocked out Eric Lucas, a former Canadian champion, a few hours later to retain his super-middleweight crown. On October 4, 1996, he knocked out undefeated Bryant Brannon in the second round to retain his title.

Jones stepped up to the 175-pound light-heavyweight division on November 22, 1996 and captured the vacant World Boxing Council (WBC) championship belt with a 12-round decision against former three-time world champion Mike McCallum in Tampa, Florida. In the only loss of his career, Jones, who is 5 feet 11 inches tall and possesses a reach of 74 inches, was disqualified on March 21, 1997 for hitting Montell Griffin after knocking him down on one knee. In a rematch five months later, he knocked out Griffin in the first round. On July 18, 1998, Jones successfully unified the WBC light-heavyweight crown by dethroning Lou Del Valle, the World Boxing Association (WBA) champion. Although knocked down for the first time in his career, Jones won the fight easily. After capturing the IBF light-heavyweight title from Reggie Johnson in a 12-round decision on June 5, 1999, Jones was classified the undisputed champion in the IBF, WBC, and WBA. Between 1999 and 2002, Jones was challenged nine times and won seven by a knockout. Only Reggie Johnson, David Telesco, and Julio Gonzalez endured Jones's attack while losing 12-round decisions. Jones won a share of the heavyweight title with a seemingly effortless unanimous decision over the WBA champion John Ruiz in March 2003 despite giving away 33 pounds, at Las Vegas, Nevada. In November 2003, Jones, exhausted from shedding nearly 25 pounds, won a controversial 12-round decision over light heavyweight Antonio Tarver in Las Vegas.

Jones, recognized among the best fighters in the world, has won three division championships in 50 professional fights spanning 15 years. He has recorded 49 triumphs and only one loss with 38 knockouts.

Jones is not married and has two children. He owns an 81-acre homestead in Pensacola and spends much of his free time doing charity work there. Some of his boxing earnings have been used to build a boxing arena for children in the Pensacola area.

BIBLIOGRAPHY
"Roy Jones Jr.," *Boxing*, www.blackathlete.com (2000); "Roy Jones Jr.," *Career Record*, www.about.com (2002); "Roy Jones Jr.," *Current Biography Yearbook, 1999*

(New York, 1999); "Roy Jones Jr.," *Jones vs Ruiz*, www.secondsout.com (2002); "Roy Jones Jr.," *Personal Stats*, www.boxing'sfinest.com (2002); "Roy Jones Jr.," *Professional Record*, www.hbo.com (1998).

John L. Evers

MICHAEL JORDAN
(February 17, 1963–   )

Basketball

Michael Jordan may be the greatest professional basketball player in the history of the sport and among the most popular athletes of all time.

Michael Jeffery Jordan, nicknamed "Air Jordan," was born on February 17, 1963 in Brooklyn, New York, the son of James Jordan, an electrical engineer, and Deloris Jordan, a bank employee. Concerned about the drugs, violence, and crime in the streets where they lived, his parents moved the family of five children to Wilmington, North Carolina. Jordan first became interested in baseball rather than basketball, playing in the outfield and pitching. At age 15, he played basketball, football, and baseball at D. C. Virgo Junior High School. At Emsley A. Laney High School in Wilmington, he continued to compete in three sports and quarterbacked the football team. Before his senior year, he attended a basketball summer camp of high school all-stars and collected five trophies for outstanding performance. He was considered the best high school basketball player. Jordan later acknowledged, "It was the turning point in my life." As a senior, he averaged 28.1 points and 12 rebounds and was named the Buccaneers' Most Valuable Player (MVP). Following his high school graduation in June 1981, the not widely recruited athlete accepted a full basketball scholarship at the University of North Carolina.

As the Atlantic Coast Conference (ACC) Rookie of the Year, Jordan became a headline name as a 19-year-old freshman. In the 1982 National Collegiate Athletic Association (NCAA) Division I National Championship game, he made a 15-foot jump shot with 15 seconds remaining to give the Tar Heels a 63–62 victory over Georgetown University. He remarked, "I think that one shot really put me on the map." In Jordan's three years at North Carolina under coach Dean Smith, the Tar Heels compiled a 88–13 won-lost record and appeared in the NCAA Tournament all three seasons. In 101 collegiate games, he scored 1,754 points for a 17.4-point average. He played in 10 NCAA Tournament games, scoring 165 points. Jordan was selected the consensus College Player of the Year in 1984 and College Player of the Year by *The Sporting News* (*TSN*) in 1983 and 1984. He also won the Naismith Award and the Wooden Award and was selected unanimous First Team All-America in 1984. Jordan played on U.S. Olympic gold-medal-winning basketball teams in 1984 at the Los Angeles, California, games and on Dream Team I at the 1992 Barcelona, Spain, games. He was named to the NCAA Final Four All-Time Team, the All-Decade Team of the 1960s, and the 1982 NCAA All-Tournament Team.

Michael Jordan ©Photofest

After his junior year, the 6-foot 6-inch, 226-pound Jordan entered the 1984 National Basketball Association (NBA) draft and was selected by the Chicago Bulls (NBA) in the first round as the third pick overall behind Hakeem Olajuwon* and Sam Bowie.

Jordan finished ahead of Charles Barkley* and Olajuwon for NBA Rookie of the Year honors in 1985, ranking among the top NBA scorers with 2,313 points and averaging 28.2 points. Jordan suffered a broken foot in his second season, the only disabling injury in his career, and played in only 18 games. He soon became a superstar and perhaps the greatest player ever to play the game. The fierce competitor had tremendous quickness and defied gravity with his extended "hang time." He had the ability to do anything that could be done on a basketball court. Jordan owned six NBA Championship rings with the Chicago Bulls, including three straight from 1991 to 1993 and 1996 to 1998. Jordan was named the MVP in all six NBA Finals, averaging a record 41.0 points in the 1993 Finals. He started at guard in 12 NBA All-Star games in 1985, 1987 to 1993, and 1996 to 1998. In 1997, he became the first player ever to receive more than two million votes. He was chosen the Classic's MVP in 1988 after scoring 40 points, and repeated in 1996 and 1998.

Following the 1993 NBA Championship, Jordan's father was the victim of a senseless murder in North Carolina when he was robbed by two teenagers. As a result, Jordan lost the desire to play basketball and left the NBA to play professional baseball. In 1994 he signed a minor league contract with the Chicago White Sox (American League). Jordan batted .202 that summer with the Birmingham, Alabama, Barons (Southern League) and .252 later that year with the Scottsdale, Arizona, Scorpions (Arizona Fall League). He ended his retirement from basketball by rejoining the Chicago Bulls for the final 17 games of the 1994–1995 season. Now a world celebrity, he led Chicago to three straight NBA titles and paced the NBA in scoring each year. In 1995–1996 the Bulls became the first NBA team to win 70 games in one season, finishing with 72 victories. Jordan, selected as one of the 50 Greatest Players in NBA History, retired on January 13, 1999.

At the age of 38, Jordan trained to get his body in shape to return to the NBA as a player. Jordan philosophized, "Obstacles don't have to stop you. If you run into a wall, don't turn around and give up. Figure out how to climb it, go through it, or work around it."

On September 25, 2001, Jordan returned to the NBA as an active player for the Washington Wizards. Washington won 37 games in 2001–2002, 18 more than the year before he played. He led the Wizards with 1,375 points, averaging 22.9 points in 60 games before suffering a season-ending knee injury. In January 2003, he passed Wilt Chamberlain as the third leading scorer in NBA history. He was selected to his fourteenth All-Star Game in 15 seasons, the last appearance by a member of the United States' original Dream Team.

Jordan married Juanita Vanoy on September 2, 1989 in Las Vegas, Nevada. They reside in Highland Park, Illinois, and have three children, Jessica, Jasmine, and Marcus. Jordan retired after the 2002–2003 season, during which he averaged 20.0 points and led the Wizards with 123 steals. He was the only Wizard to play in all 82 games.

Jordan holds the NBA regular season career record for most seasons leading the NBA in scoring (10) and steals (3), and the most consecutive seasons leading the NBA in scoring (7). He was selected the NBA's MVP in 1988, 1991, 1992, 1996, and 1998 and Defensive Player of the Year in 1988; he won the IBM Award for all-around contribution to a team's success in 1985 and 1989; and he captured the NBA Slam Dunk Championship in 1987 and 1988. He dazzled fans in the 1988 competition with his "Superman Dunk."

In his final attempt, he took off from the free-throw line, extended his "hang time" by defying gravity, rose above the rim, and exploded his featured dunk for a perfect 50-point rating.

Jordan made the All-NBA First Team 10 times from 1987 to 1993 and from 1996 to 1998, All-NBA Second Team in 1985, All-Defensive First Team nine times between 1988 and 1993 and from 1996 to 1998, and the All-Rookie First Team in 1985.

In 15 NBA seasons, Jordan compiled 32,292 career points (third on the NBA All-Time list) and averaged an NBA-best 30.1 points in 1,072 regular season games. He collected 6,672 rebounds, dished out 5,633 assists, and recorded 2,514 steals (second best) and blocked 893 shots. He averaged 30 or more points eight seasons and scored 2,000 or more points in all but four seasons. His career-high 3,041 points came in 1986–1987. He scored a career-high 69 points against the Cleveland Cavaliers on March 28, 1990.

In 179 NBA playoff games, Jordan compiled 5,987 points and averaged 33.4 points per game, both postseason records. He posted 1,152 rebounds, 1,022 assists, 158 blocked shots, and a record 376 steals. He also holds the playoff record for most free throws made (1,463) and the single-game record for most points (63)—against the Boston Celtics on April 20, 1990.

Jordan tallied 262 points in 14 NBA All-Star games and holds career records for highest point average (18.7) and most steals (37). He recorded the only triple-double in All-Star Game history in 1997.

His basketball success led to numerous endorsements and commercials, and as a starring role in his first feature motion picture, *Space Jam.* Jordan become a household name throughout the United States and in most foreign countries as well. In 1994 the Chicago Bulls retired his jersey number (23) and erected a life-size statue of him in front of the United Center. From January 2000 to September 2001, he served as president of the Washington Wizards (NBA), handling the basketball operations.

BIBLIOGRAPHY
Frank Deford, "One of a Kind," *Sports Illustrated* 25 (June 22, 1992), pp. 48–50; *The Evansville Courier and Press*, August 17, 2001, p. D2; Bob Greene, *Hang Time* (New York, 1993); Bill Gutman, *Michael Jordan* (New York, 1991); "Michael Jordan," *Lycos Sports*, www.worldsportsman.com (1998); "Michael Jordan," *Pursuit of Excellence*, www.blink.org (2001); *NCAA Men's Basketball's Finest* (Overland Park, KS, 1998); David L. Porter, ed., *African-American Sports Greats: A Biographical Dictionary* (Westport, CT, 1995); *The Sporting News Official NBA Register*, 2003–2004.

John L. Evers

JACKIE JOYNER-KERSEE   Track and Field
(March 3, 1962–)

Jackie Joyner-Kersee was widely considered the greatest female athlete of the last half of the twentieth century.

Jacqueline Joyner was born on March 3, 1962 in East St. Louis, Illinois, to teenage parents, Alfred Joyner and Mary Joyner. She was the second of four children and was named for First Lady Jackie Kennedy. Alfred worked on the railroads and in construction, while Mary served as a nurse's aide. The Joyners struggled to break the cycle of poverty so common in East St. Louis. In the winter the pipes would freeze and the wind would whistle through the window frames in their little four-room house. Joyner's great-grandmother also shared the tiny dwelling.

Mary Joyner pushed her children to work harder and reach higher, desperately wanting a better life for them than she had known. As a child, Joyner studied modern dance at the Mary Brown Community Center in East St. Louis. When the Center started a track program, she switched to running. By age 12, Joyner competed in several track events with the East St. Louis Railers. Coach George Ward pushed her to excel in every event she tried. She and her brother, Al, also a runner, challenged each other. In 1975 Joyner watched a made-for-television movie, *Babe*, about athlete Babe Didrikson Zaharias. The movie inspired her to try multiple events in track and field. She won the first of four consecutive Junior Pentathlon Championships at age 14. She graduated from Lincoln High School in East St. Louis, the same school where her father played football and ran hurdles.

Joyner led Lincoln to the 1980 Illinois State Basketball Championship. Lincoln outscored its opponents by an average of 53 points. Joyner also played volleyball and was ranked second nationally in the Prep All-America long jump standings. Although offered a track and field scholarship at UCLA, the 5-foot 10-inch, 150-pound forward accepted a four-year full basketball scholarship instead. She started four years for the UCLA Bruins, earning All-America honors. UCLA track and field coach Bob Kersee encouraged her to train for multiple-event contests in track and field. Her UCLA teammate and future sister-in-law was Olympic gold medalist Florence Griffith Joyner.* Although a natural athlete, Joyner struggled with severe asthma and pollen allergies and was forced to use inhalers and wear masks during some competitions. Her mother died from spinal meningitis in 1982 before Jackie graduated with a Bachelor's degree in history.

In 1983 Joyner competed for the United States in Helsinki, Finland, in the World Championships. The following year, she broke the American record for the heptathlon with 6,579 points to win the Olympic Trials. The heptathlon included the high jump, shot put, 100-meter hurdles, 200-meter race, javelin, long jump, and 800-meter race. She took the silver medal at the 1984 Los Angeles, California, Olympic Games for the heptathlon, just five points behind Glynis Nunn of Australia, despite running the 800-meter race with a strained hamstring. The Olympic experience was made complete for Jackie when her brother, Al Joyner, made the Olympic team in the triple jump, and future sister-in-law Florence Griffith Joyner won four Olympic medals.

In 1986 Joyner collected the Sullivan Award for best amateur athlete, earned *Track and Field News* Athlete of the Year, and garnered the Jesse

Owens Award. On January 11, 1986, she married her track coach, Bob Kersee, in a Long Beach, California, Baptist church where he had once served as an assistant pastor. Her roommate, track and field star Valerie Brisco,* served as maid of honor.

From the fall of 1984 to the 1988 Summer Olympics, Joyner-Kersee was undefeated in the heptathlon. She held the world record in the heptathlon with 7,158 points. She broke that record by 57 points at the Olympic Trials in Indianapolis, Indiana, in 1988 and shattered it again with 7,291 points, taking the gold medal in the 1988 Seoul, South Korea, Olympics. Joyner-Kersee also won the gold medal in the long jump with an Olympic record 24 feet 3 ½ inches. In 1987 she received the Associated Press Female Athlete of the Year Award and became the first athlete to win the Jesse Owens Award twice. *The Sporting News* named her its 1988 Man of the Year, the first time it had ever given the award to a woman.

Joyner-Kersee won a third gold medal in the heptathlon at the 1992 Barcelona, Spain, Olympics and captured a bronze medal in the long jump. She garnered the *Track and Field News* Athlete of the Year a second time in 1994.

Despite injuries and asthma, Joyner-Kersee won a bronze medal in the long jump at the 1996 Atlanta, Georgia, Olympics. She played for the Richmond, Virginia, Rage (American Basketball League) in 1996. She closed her illustrious career with the 1998 Goodwill Games in New York. In one of the toughest competitions of her life, she edged past Dedee Nathan by 23 points to win her final heptathlon. She reflected, "I know I don't win by myself. God, my husband, and I are a team. I know my strength comes from God. That's why one of my favorite verses is, 'I can do all things through Him who strengthens me' " (Philippians 4:13, NASB).

The deeply religious Joyner-Kersee returned to the St. Louis area, becoming heavily involved in church, charitable, and civic activities. She established the Community Foundation, which provides scholarships, mentors for children, and leadership training. On March 1, 2000, she opened the Jackie Joyner-Kersee Boy's and Girl's Club in East St. Louis. She helped raise more than $12 million to build and operate the center, which provides learning resources and computer, music, dance, physical fitness, and martial arts classes for youth in her impoverished hometown. The club includes an Olympic-sized pool and a 13,000-square-foot gymnasium.

Joyner-Kersee's star was added to the St. Louis Walk of Fame on Delmar Boulevard on May 21, 2000. In 2001 the National Collegiate Athletic Association (NCAA) named her the Top Woman Collegiate Athlete of the past 25 years, and CNN/*Sports Illustrated* voted her the Greatest Female Athlete of the Century. From a life of poverty and sickness, she had achieved a happy marriage, a faith-filled life, commitment to serving others, and athletic success.

BIBLIOGRAPHY

Neil Cohen, *Jackie Joyner-Kersee* (New York, 1992); Brian Connor, "Jackie Joyner-Kersee: Walking with God," www.Christianity.com (2001); "Jackie Joyner-Kersee," *Current Biography Yearbook* (New York, 1987), pp. 293–296; Jackie Joyner-Kersee and Sonya Steptoe, *A Kind of Grace: The Autobiography of the World's Greatest Female Athlete*; Louise Mooney, ed., *Newsmakers* 93 (Detroit, MI, 1993); Rick Peterson, "Joyner-Kersee Faces New Challenges," *Topeka Capital Journal Online Sports* (August 7, 1998), pp. 1–2; David L. Porter, ed., *African-American Sports Greats* (Westport, CT, 1995); Ramona Cramer Tucker, "Jackie's Gold Medal Faith," *Today's Christian Woman* 20 (September/October 1998), pp. 46–50.

Frank J. Olmsted

DAVID JUSTICE Baseball
(April 24, 1966–)

David Justice appeared in the World Series with three different major league baseball teams.

David Christopher Justice was born on April 24, 1966 in Cincinnati, Ohio, and was brought up by his mother, Nettie Justice. His father, Robert Justice, a security guard, left the family when Justice was a small child. Justice attended Covington, Kentucky, Latin School, a private Roman Catholic institution, where he participated in baseball, soccer, basketball, and track and field. "Athletics always came second in my house," Justice has said. "Academics was always first." As a senior, he averaged 25.9 points and was named to the All-Catholic and All-America basketball teams. Following his graduation in 1982, Justice attended Thomas More College in Crestview Hills, Kentucky, on a basketball scholarship. As a sophomore, he dropped basketball to concentrate on baseball. In 1985 the Atlanta Braves (National League) selected him in the fourth round of the free-agent draft.

The 6-foot 3-inch, 200-pound Justice, who batted and threw left-handed, began his professional baseball career in 1985 as a first baseman with Pulaski, Virginia (Appalachian League). The following season, he spent with Sumter, South Carolina (South Atlantic League) and Durham, North Carolina (Carolina League). Although hampered by a broken wrist, he played in 1987 with Greenville, South Carolina (Southern League). Justice began 1988 with Richmond, Virginia (International League) but returned to Greenville to complete the season. In the following campaign, he played 16 games with the Atlanta Braves before returning to Richmond.

In 1990 Justice led all major league rookies with 28 home runs and 78 runs batted in (RBI) with Atlanta. The Braves returned him to his natural position in the outfield, as the Baseball Writers' Association of America and *The Sporting News* named him NL Rookie of the Year. Justice missed two months with a strained back in 1991 but led Atlanta with six RBIs, including five in one game, in their World Series loss to the Minnesota Twins. In the 1993 World Series, he batted only .158 as the Braves fell to the Toronto Blue Jays in six games.

In the following campaign, Justice placed third in the NL voting for Most Valuable Player (MVP) and finished the season ranked second in the senior circuit with 40 home runs and a career-best 120 RBIs. He batted .313 in the strike-shortened 1994 season and missed 40 games of the 1995 season due to a ligament tear in his right shoulder. He returned to the lineup in time to help the Atlanta Braves become the World Series Champion in six games over the Cleveland Indians. In the sixth game, Justice belted a spectacular sixth-inning home run to clinch the title, 1–0. A dislocated right shoulder and subsequent surgery limited him to 40 games during 1996.

In March 1997, Atlanta traded Justice and Marquis Grissom to the Cleveland Indians (American League) for Kenny Lofton* and Alan Embree. Justice remained with the Indians until June 2000 when he was traded to the New York Yankees (AL) for Ricky Ledee, Jake Westbrook, and Zach Day. In his first AL year, Justice enjoyed an outstanding season. He was named Comeback Player of the Year and batted .329 with 163 base hits, both career highs, to lead the Indians into the World Series. Justice batted only .185, as the Indians lost to the Florida Marlins in seven games. In 1998 he collected a career-high 34 doubles and 94 runs scored. He batted only .158 while the Indians lost the AL Championship Series (ALCS) to the New York Yankees in six games. Besides hitting .287 in his third year as an Indian, he slugged his fourth career grand slam home run. Justice split the 2000 season with the Indians and New York Yankees, hitting .286 and posting a career-high 41 home runs. In the ALCS against the Seattle Mariners, he drove in eight runs, registered six base hits, including two home runs, and earned Most Valuable Player (MVP) honors. He slumped offensively in the World Series, batting only .158 in the Yankees triumph over the New York Mets. Justice hit only .241 in 2001 for New York and batted .278 with four RBIs in the ALCS against the Oakland Athletics. He struggled again in the World Series, hitting only .167 in the Yankees' loss to the Arizona Diamondbacks. In December 2001, the Oakland Athletics (AL) acquired him in a trade. Justice helped the Athletics win the AL West in 2002 with a .266 batting average, 11 home runs, and 49 RBIs. The Minnesota Twins eliminated Oakland in the AL Division Series, as Justice hit .238 with four RBIs. He retired as a player following the 2002 season.

In his 14-year major league career from 1989 through 2002, Justice appeared in 1,610 games and compiled 1,571 base hits with a .279 batting average. He drove in 1,017 runs, belted 305 home runs, scored 929 runs, collected 280 doubles and 24 triples, coaxed 903 walks, and struck out 999 times. In postseason play, he appeared in 30 Division Series and 46 League Championship Series games with a combined .234 batting average. He batted 124 times in 36 World Series games, registering 25 base hits, 4 home runs, 21 RBIs, and a .202 batting average. In five times at bat, he managed one base hit in two All-Star games.

Justice was named to *The Sporting News (TSN)* Silver Slugger Team in 1993 and 1997 and as an outfielder on the *TSN* NL All-Star team in 1993 and the *TSN* AL All-Star team in 1997. He also was chosen to play in the 1993, 1994, and 1997 All-Star games.

Justice is single and lives in Cincinnati, Ohio, with his son, David Jr. He married actress Halle Berry on January 1, 1993, but they were divorced in 1997. He serves as an analyst for ESPN, enjoys swimming, golf, basketball, and billiards, and studies karate in the off-season.

BIBLIOGRAPHY
"David Justice," *David Justice Online*, www.geocities.com/indians (2000); "David Justice," *Players*, www.bravosweb.com/players/justice (1997); "David Justice," The *Yankees*, www.mlb.com (2001); David L. Porter, ed., *Biographical Dictionary of American Sports: Baseball*, revised and expanded edition (Westport, CT, 2000); *Sports Illustrated 2001 Sports Almanac* (Kingston, NY, 2000); *The Sporting News Baseball Register*, 2003.

John L. Evers

K

JASON KIDD
(March 23, 1973–)

Basketball

Jason Kidd has starred as a college and professional basketball player.

Jason Frederick Kidd was born on March 23, 1973 in San Francisco, California, the son of Steve Kidd, his black father, and Anne Kidd, his white mother, and has two sisters, Denise and Kim. His father served as a Trans World Airlines supervisor, while his mother worked as a bank bookkeeper. His father died suddenly of a heart attack at age 61 in May 1999, an event that profoundly affected Kidd. "My dad's death made me value things more," he noted, "Knowing that God can take things away from you, just like that."

Kidd grew up playing basketball on Oakland, California, playgrounds. He admired "Magic" Johnson,* who motivated him to perfect his passing abilities. His excellent passing, dribbling, and shooting skills, combined with his speed and quickness, made him a popular figure on the outdoor courts of the Bay Area.

Kidd attended St. Joseph's of Notre Dame High School in Alameda, California, where he played basketball under coach Frank LaPorte. During his high school career, Kidd led St. Joseph's to a 122–14 won-lost record. Between 1990 and 1992, the Pilots triumphed in 63 of 69 contests and captured two consecutive California Division I State Titles. At St. Joseph's, he scored 2,661 career points, collected 1,142 rebounds, made 719 steals, and became the all-time prep leader with 1,155 career assists. A high school All-America, Kidd was named a two-time California Player of the Year and *Street & Smith, Parade Magazine*, and *USA Today's* Player of the Year. He won the Naismith Award as the nation's top high school basketball player in 1991–1992.

In 1992 Kidd enrolled at the University of California at Berkeley on a basketball scholarship. He played two seasons with the Golden Bears and helped them compile a 43–17 won-lost record. In 1993 California made only its second appearance in the National Collegiate Athletic Association (NCAA) Division I Basketball Tournament. The Golden Bears lost in the Regional semifinals, but he became nationally known when California upset two-time defending champion Duke University. The Golden Bears returned to the

Jason Kidd ©Photofest

NCAA Tournament the following year but were eliminated in the first round by the University of Wisconsin–Green Bay. At California, Kidd averaged 14.9 points and 5.9 rebounds and recorded 499 assists and 204 steals. He led the nation in steals and paced all NCAA Tournament players in assists in 1993, when he was chosen unanimously for All-America honors, and led the nation in assists in 1994. The first sophomore ever named Pac-10 Conference Player of the Year and the first California All-America since 1968, he was named a finalist for both the Naismith and Wooden awards.

Following Kidd's sophomore season, the Dallas Mavericks (National Basketball Association) selected him in the first round as the second pick overall of the 1994 NBA draft. In his first season, the 6-foot 4-inch, 225-pounder guided Dallas to 23 more victories than the previous season, but the Mavericks still missed the playoffs. The first-year point guard was selected Co–Rookie of the Year with the Detroit Pistons' Grant Hill.* Later, differences arose between Kidd and some of his Maverick teammates, leading to a public dispute. Dallas began a rebuilding program and on December 2, 1996 traded Kidd, Tony Dumas, and Loren Meyer to the Phoenix Suns (NBA) for Sam Cassell, Michael Finley, A. C. Green, and a second-round draft choice. Kidd played over four seasons with the Suns before being sent with Chris Dudley to the New Jersey Nets (NBA) for Stephon Marbury, Johnny Newman, and Soumalia Samake in July 2001.

Kidd guided the Suns to a 56–26 won-lost record and the second of five consecutive NBA playoff appearances in 1997–1998. He became the first Sun ever to lead the NBA in assists with 10.8 per game and in triple-doubles with seven per contest in 1998–1999. He led the NBA in assists and triple-doubles for the second straight season. In 2000 Kidd was selected a tri-captain and starting point guard for the gold-medal-winning U.S. Men's National team at the Sydney, Australia, Olympic Games. In 2000–2001, Kidd became only the fourth player to pace the NBA in assists for at least three consecutive seasons, joining John Stockton, Oscar Robertson, and Bob Cousy. Kidd, who led the NBA in triple-doubles with seven, registered a career-high 43 points on March 28, 2001 against the Houston Rockets and a career-high 25 assists against the Utah Jazz on February 8, 1996. He directed New Jersey to the Atlantic Division crown in 2001–2002, ranking second in the NBA in assists with 808 (9.9 average) and third in steals with 175 (2.1 average). With Kidd's leadership, the Nets defeated the Indiana Pacers, Charlotte Hornets, and Boston Celtics before being swept by the Los Angeles Lakers in the NBA Finals. He averaged 19.6 points, 9.5 assists, and 6.9 rebounds in those 20 playoff games. Kidd again led the NBA in assists with 711 (8.9 average), and averaged 18.7 points in 80 games, helping New Jersey win the Atlantic Division with a 49–33 record in 2002–2003. He helped the Nets defeat the Milwaukee Bucks, Boston Celtics, and Detroit Pistons to win the Eastern Conference playoff, but lost to the San Antonio Spurs in the NBA Finals. He has played in seven All-Star games, starting in 1996, 2000, 2001, 2002, and 2003, and was the first Maverick to start an All-Star Game. He recorded 42 points, 48 assists, and 12 steals in six appearances. Kidd was named First Team All-NBA in 1998–1999, 1999–2000, 2000–2001, and 2001–2002, and Second Team All-NBA in 2002–2003, selected to the First Team All-Defensive Squad in 1998–1999, 2000–2001, and 2001–2002, and Second Team All-Defensive Squad in 1999–2000 and 2002–2003.

In nine NBA seasons between 1994–1995 and 2002–2003, Kidd has compiled 9,630 points for a 14.7 point average in 653 regular season games. He has dished out 9.4 assists and made 2.1 steals per game, ranking sixth on the all-time NBA list with 38 triple-doubles. In 62 NBA playoff games, he has scored 1,071 points and averaged 17.3 points, 9.5 assists, and 1.95 steals.

Kidd and his wife, Joumana, a correspondent for the entertainment show *Extra* and NBC TV, reside in Saddle River, New Jersey and have one son, Trey Jason (T.J.), and twin daughters, Miah and Jazelle. He has another son, Jason, who lives with his mother Alexandria Brown. They were never married.

BIBLIOGRAPHY
James Brant, *Jason Kidd* (Philadelphia, PA, 1997); "Jason Kidd," *Players Background*, www.nba.com (2001); "Jason Kidd," *Players Career Highlights*, www.nba.com (2001); "Jason Kidd," *Players Career Statistics*, www.nba.com (2001); *NCAA Men's Basketball's Finest* (Overland Park, KS, 1998); Phil Taylor, "Breath Taking," *Sports Illustrated* 23 (December 4, 2000), pp. 63–64, 66; *The Sporting News Official NBA Register*, 2003–2004.

                                                                                     John L. Evers

ROGER KINGDOM   Track and Field
(August 26, 1962–   )

Roger Kingdom earned nearly every track and field honor in the 110-meter high hurdles. He won an Olympic gold medal in 1984 and 1988; the Pan-American Championship in 1983 and 1995; the National Collegiate Athletic Association (NCAA) Outdoor Championship in 1983 and Indoor Championship in 1984; the Millrose Championship in 1988; the Track Athletic Congress (TAC) Championships in 1985 and 1988–1990; and the USA Track & Field Championship in 1995. He set the world record (12.92 seconds) in the 110-meter high hurdles in Zurich, Switzerland, on August 16, 1989.

The third child of Roy Kingdom and Christine Kingdom, Roger Kingdom was born on August 26, 1962 in Vienna, Georgia, near President Jimmy Carter's peanut farm. The son of a farmer and deliveryman, Kingdom grew up in rural southern Georgia near Unadilla. He attended Vienna High School, where his older brother and sister starred as athletes, and became a sensational athlete there. He won four letters each in football and track and field and was nicknamed "Super Rog" because "he could do almost anything." Kingdom rushed for more than 1,000 yards in 1980, averaging 7 yards per carry, and he set state records in the hurdles, discus, and high jump. He was named the Georgia High School Athlete of the Year in 1980 and 1981, nosing out Herschel Walker* in 1980. He also played in the school band and ushered at his church.

Over 30 colleges offered Kingdom scholarships. He initially accepted a football scholarship at the University of Tennessee, but finally entered the University of Pittsburgh in the fall of 1981 as a football player and track athlete because Tennessee would not allow him to participate in both sports until he was a junior.

During his freshman year at Pittsburgh, Kingdom played as a reserve running back in football. He switched to reserve defensive back as a sophomore. Discouraged about the slow pace of his athletic progress, Kingdom became a lazy track and field athlete during his first year. He would duck practice to watch television in the locker room. Nevertheless, he won his first collegiate 110-meter hurdles race at the twelfth Annual Pitt Invitational in May 1982. In the winter of 1982–1983, he became more focused on track and field.

Kingdom was named Most Valuable Performer at the Big East Conference (BEC) Indoor Track Championships, finishing second in both the high jump and the 55-meter hurdles. He opened the 1983 outdoor season by winning the hurdles at the Pitt Invitational despite losing his shoe midway in the race, and he ended that campaign by becoming the national NCAA high hurdles champion in June. He placed only seventh at the TAC Championships, but he won the high hurdles championship at the Pan-American Games in Caracas, Venezuela.

The titles he won at the NCAA and Pan-American Games changed Kingdom's life. Impatient for success, he saw himself as a potential Olympian. He redshirted in football to concentrate on training for the Los Angeles, California, Olympic Games. His speed and power enabled him to make the Olympic team, but his technical precision remained below average. In December 1983, he qualified for the NCAA finals with a 7.03 second race in the 55-meter hurdles at the George Mason Invitational. In January 1984, he was named the outstanding sprinter at the Joe Hilton Invitational at Chapel Hill, North Carolina. A few weeks later, Kingdom won the Eastman Kodak Invitational. In March, he collected his second NCAA title at the Indoor Championships in Syracuse, New York, with a 7.08 second clocking for the 55-meter highs. Kingdom redshirted for college track in the spring of 1984 and moved to Columbus, Ohio, where he prepared for the June Olympic Trials.

Kingdom's weakness in technique was exposed in late April at the 1984 Penn Relays, where he won the high hurdles only to be disqualified for "lack of effort" because he hit five hurdles. Knocking over hurdles troubled Kingdom. Yet, he solidified his status as an Olympic contender by placing second at the TAC Championships in early June. Before the Olympic Trials, he was ranked sixth in the world in the high hurdles. Despite a knee injury suffered when he banged a hurdle during a workout, Kingdom was encouraged by his mother and finished third to qualify for the Olympic team. Although projected to win the bronze medal, he surprised the pundits by winning the gold medal at the Los Angeles Olympic Games, despite knocking over six hurdles. After the race, he admitted, "winning the gold medal doesn't automatically make me the best hurdler in the world. If anything, it means I'm only number 2 or 3 right now."

Following the Olympic Games, Kingdom took a four-city tour of Europe and split four races with Greg Foster. Upon returning to Pittsburgh, Kingdom had a visible reward for his efforts: he was driving a new black Porsche. He earned his living endorsing athletic products and businesses and as a runner.

Kingdom was injured and inactive during much of 1986–1987, but completed the 1988 track and field season undefeated. He won a second Olympic gold medal at Seoul, South Korea, in 1988 and set a world record in 1989 without knocking down a single hurdle. In 1990, he won the Meadowlands Invitational and was named the Dapper Dan Club Pittsburgh Man of the Year. Kingdom was slowed by injuries in 1992 and did not make the Olympic team that year. He underwent reconstructive knee surgery in September 1992. He enjoyed an injury-free season in 1995, winning the Pan-American Games title and placing third in the World Championships in Sweden.

In 1996 he finished fifth in the U.S. Olympic Trials. He earned his Bachelor's degree from Pittsburgh in 2000. He and Joy Shepard have one daughter. A member of the Pittsburgh Marathon Board of Directors, Kingdom tried running the 10K in September 2001 and serves as a trainer.

BIBLIOGRAPHY
Valerie R. Gregg, "A Kingdom of Gold," *Pitt Magazine*, 1995; Jon Hendershott, "Kingdom Overcomes Favored Foster," *Track & Field News*, September 1984, pp. 24–25; Eddie Jefferies, "Kingdom's Best Is Yet to Come, Says Kennedy," *The Pittsburgh Courier*, August 25, 1984, p. B-5; Dave Johnson, "Kingdom Battling Himself," *Track & Field News*, February 1985, p. 44; "Kingdom 'Dapper Dan' Man of the Year 1989," *Pittsburgh Post-Gazette*, February 10, 1990, p. 1; Dave Kuehis, "Roger Kingdom," *Runner's World*, 2001; Gerald Lawson, *World Record Breakers in Track and Field Athletics* (Champaign, IL, 1997); Kenny Moore, "Track and Field," *Sports Illustrated* (October 3, 1988), p. 45; Charles O'Hara, "Fame Keeps Kingdom on the Run," *The Pittsburgh Press*, September 18, 1984, p. D20; Evan Pattak, "Blood, Sweat, and Tears," *Pittsburgh Magazine*, July 1984, pp. 34–40; University of Pittsburgh, Sports Information, Pittsburgh, PA; Linda Venzon, "Kingdom Dared to Dream," *Pitt Magazine*, September 1984, p. 6.

Keith McClellan

L

BARRY LARKIN
(April 28, 1964–)

Baseball

Barry Larkin has starred as a shortstop for the Cincinnati Reds (National League) since the late 1980s.

Barry Louis Larkin was born on April 28, 1964 in Cincinnati, Ohio, the son of Robert Larkin, a chemist for the federal government, and Shirley Larkin, a medical technician. Larkin has three brothers, Mike, who played football at the University of Notre Dame, Byron, who played basketball at Xavier University, and Stephen, who played outfield/first base in the Baltimore Orioles (American League) organization, and a sister. Larkin attended Cincinnati's Moeller High School, where he played baseball, football, and basketball.

Following his graduation from high school in 1982, Larkin matriculated at the University of Michigan. He played baseball there for three years and compiled a .361 career batting average. A two-time All-America and All–Big Ten Conference (BTC) member, he was selected BTC–Most Valuable Player (MVP) in 1984 and 1985 and became the first player to be named MVP twice. Larkin was chosen to the All-BTC Tournament team in 1983 as MVP and in 1984 and 1985. He batted .311 to help the 1984 United States Olympic Baseball team capture the silver medal.

Larkin was selected by the Cincinnati Reds (NL) in the second round of the June 1982 free-agent draft, but he did not sign. After he attended the University of Michigan for three years, the Reds chose him as the fourth pick overall in the June 1985 free-agent draft. The 6-foot, 185-pound shortstop, who throws and bats right-handed, began his professional baseball career by helping Vermont (Eastern League) capture the crown. The following season, he was assigned to Denver, Colorado (American Association) and won the AA Rookie of the Year and MVP honors. Larkin also made the AA All-Star team and was voted by the managers as the best AA defensive shortstop.

After being promoted to the Cincinnati Reds during the 1986 season, Larkin on August 15 recorded his first major league base hit off Dave Dravecky of the San Diego Padres. The sophomore jinx affected Larkin in 1987, as he batted only .207 in the first half of the season, but he recovered in the second half to hit a respectable .270. The following season, Larkin led all major league batters by striking out only 24 times in 588 appearances. An elbow injury sidelined him nearly half of the 1989 season. Nevertheless, he still played 97 games with a career-high .342 batting average. With 185 base hits in 614 plate appearances (both career highs), he led the 1990 Reds to a World Championship. He hit .300 in 10 postseason games, including .353 in the World Series sweep of the Oakland A's.

Larkin tied a major league record on June 27, 1991 with five home runs in two games. Upon batting .315 in 1993, he became the first shortstop in 40 years to hit at least .300 in five consecutive seasons. He reached 1,000 career base hits that same season and received the Roberto Clemente Award for his performance on and off the field. In the following campaign, Larkin won his first Rawlings Gold Glove Award and led NL shortstops in putouts. Cincinnati won the Central Division in 1995, when Larkin was honored by the Baseball Writers' Association of America with the MVP Award. He was rewarded not only for his offensive skills, but also for his excellent defensive play and leadership qualities. He recorded a career-high 51 stolen bases and continued his outstanding postseason play with a .387 batting average. Cincinnati swept the Los Angeles Dodgers in the NL Division Series but lost to the Atlanta Braves in the NL Championship Series (NLCS).

In 1996 Larkin became the first shortstop in major league history to post 30 home runs and 30 stolen bases in the same season. He established career bests with 117 runs scored, 33 home runs, 89 runs batted in (RBI), 96 walks, and a .567 slugging percentage. He played in only 77 games in 1997 due to surgery for an Achilles tendon injury. The following season, he batted .308 while slugging a career-best 10 triples and 34 doubles.

The 1999 season was a time of frustration and discontent for Larkin. Particularly damaging to Larkin's performance was Cincinnati Reds owner Marge Schott's repeated public references to her players with racial slurs, resulting in Larkin's subpar performance on the field and his request to be traded. The Cincinnati organization reacted slowly to his request. When Schott was reprimanded for her actions and Larkin was named team captain, however, the trade rumors diminished. He returned to form in 2000 with a .313 batting average, his ninth season of .300 or better. Larkin clouted the first grand slam home run of his career on April 29, 2001 off Al Leiter of the New York Mets. Larkin had led all active major leaguers in times at bat (6,734) without a grand slam homer. He batted just .256 in 95 games in 2001 and .245 in 145 games in 2002, but hit .282 in 70 games in 2003.

In his 18-year major league seasons from 1986 to 2003, Larkin scored 1,274 runs and made 2,240 base hits. In 1,879 games, he has had a career .295 batting average with 426 doubles, 73 triples, and 190 home runs, 916 RBIs, and 905 walks, 778 strikeouts, and 377 stolen bases. He has played in 17 postseason games, collecting 24 base hits for a .338 batting average.

Larkin was named shortstop on *The Sporting News (TSN)* National League All-Star Team 10 times (1988–1992, 1994–1996, 1998–1999) and *TSN* Silver Slugger Team nine times (1988–1992, 1995–1996, 1998–1999), and won the Gold Glove Award three times (1994–1996).

On January 6, 1990, he married Lisa Davis. They have three children, Brielle, DeShane, and Cymber.

BIBLIOGRAPHY

"Barry Larkin," *ESPN Baseball*, www.espnbaseball.com (2000); "Barry Larkin," *Major League Baseball*, www.mlb.com (2001); "Barry Larkin," *Official Web Site of the Cincinnati Reds*, www.cincinnatireds.com (2001); "Barry Larkin," *TSN Online*, www.tsn.com (2000); "Barry Larkin," *The Baseball Online Library*, www.cbssportsline.com (2001); *Big Ten Men's Record Book* (Schaumburg, IL, 1987–1988); David L. Porter, ed., *Biographical Dictionary of American Sports: Baseball, G–P*, revised and expanded edition (Westport, CT, 2000).

John L. Evers

LISA LESLIE   Basketball
(July 7, 1972–   )

Lisa Leslie has starred in both college and professional women's basketball.

Lisa De Shaun Leslie was born on July 7, 1972 in Compton, California. Her father Walter Leslie, a semiprofessional basketball player, left the family when she was 4, leaving her mother, Christine Leslie-Espinoza, to bring up Leslie and her sisters, Dionne and Tiffany. Leslie-Espinoza saved and borrowed to buy an 18-wheeler and became a semi-truck driver to support her family. She hired a live-in housekeeper to care for the girls during the school year while she traveled. Leslie enjoyed summers traveling cross country with her mother in the semi.

Leslie's height caused her embarrassment as a preteen. Disliked being asked if she was a basketball player, she initially hated basketball. However, when she joined the junior high school team upon her friend's urging, she learned to enjoy the game, and she quickly used her height and athletic ability to dominate opponents.

Leslie stood 6 foot 3 inches as a freshman at Morningside High School in Inglewood, California, and started every varsity game as a freshman. An A student, Leslie served as class president her sophomore, junior, and senior years and starred on the volleyball and track and field teams as well. By her senior year, every major college had recruited the 6-foot 5-inch, 168-pound basketball player. She averaged more than 27 points and 15 rebounds per game in high school, often sitting out the second half because the Lady Monarchs so dominated their opponents. Her greatest high school game came in the last contest of the 1989–1990 season against South Torrance High School. Leslie fired in 49 points in the first quarter and amassed an incredible 101 points by halftime, giving Morningside the lead, 102–24. The South Torrance players voted at halftime to forfeit the game rather than endure a second half of humiliation.

Leslie accepted a basketball scholarship to the University of Southern California (USC) and tallied 30 points and 20 rebounds in her first college game against the University of Texas. She led all U.S. freshmen women in scoring and rebounding and played center on the U.S. women's team at the World University Games in Great Britain. She dazzled fans with powerful slam dunks and led the United States to a gold medal over Spain. At USC, Leslie worked hard to improve her defense. As a sophomore, she compiled a .550 shooting percentage and earned Second Team All-America honors. As a junior, she broke the USC record for career blocked shots. She won All-America honors in 1992, 1993, and 1994 and was unanimously selected National Player of the Year in 1994. Under Leslie's leadership, USC made the National Collegiate Athletic Association (NCAA) Tournament four times and advanced to the Elite Eight in 1992 and 1994. Leslie ranks third in scoring, first in blocked shots, and fourth in rebounding in USC history. She played basketball for Sicilgesso, a professional team, in Alcamo, Italy, averaging 22.6 points during the 1994–1995 season.

In 1995 Leslie was selected for the U.S. Women's Basketball team for the 1996 Atlanta, Georgia, Olympic Games. Coach Tara VanDerveer took the squad on a year-long tour to play the best teams in the world. In 14 months, the U.S. team traveled 102,000 miles and captured 52 victories without a defeat. At the 1996 Olympics the U.S. Women's team cruised past Cuba, the Ukraine, Zaire, Australia, and South Korea. In the semifinals against Japan, Leslie set an American Women's Olympic record with 35 points. She tallied 29 points in the finals to help annihilate Brazil, 111–87, and she captured the gold medal. She shot an overall 65.3 percent in those games.

Leslie vowed that "If I could make a career out of this, that would be my dream." In 1997, she had her wish when she signed with the Los Angeles Sparks of the new eight-team Women's National Basketball Association (WNBA). In her debut against the New York Liberty on June 21, she scored 16 points and grabbed 14 rebounds. She averaged 15.9 points and 9.5 rebounds during her rookie season. In 1998 she averaged nearly 20 points and over 10 rebounds per contest. She was voted MVP in the 1999 WNBA All-Star Game, recording a 13-point, 5-rebound performance at center for the West All Stars. The Houston Comets' four-year reign as WNBA Champions came to an end on August 20, 2001, when Leslie scored 28 points and snatched 18 rebounds to lead Los Angeles to a decisive 70–58 victory and eliminated Houston from the playoffs. On September 1, 2001, the Sparks, led by Lisa's 24 points, 13 rebounds, and 7 blocked shots, pounded the Charlotte Sting, 82–54, to sweep the best-of-five series, 3–0, and win the 2001 WNBA title. She was named series MVP.

Leslie led Los Angeles to the Western Conference crown with a 25–7 record in 2002, ranking second in the WNBA in rebounding with 322 (10.4 average) and fifth in scoring with 523 (16.9 average). She finished second in the WNBA MVP voting and led Los Angeles to another WNBA title, besting New York in the WNBA Finals. USA Basketball named her Female Athlete of the Year for the third time in 2002.

Leslie helped Los Angeles repeat as Western Conference Champions with a 23–10 record, finishing third in the WNBA in rebounding with 232 (10.1 average) and fourth in scoring with 421 points (18.3 average). She led the West All-Stars to an 84–75 victory over the East All-Stars with 17 points.

In five WNBA seasons through 2003, Leslie has scored 3,614 points (17.6 average) and 1,957 rebounds (9.5 average) in 205 games. She made the All-WNBA First Team in 1997, 2000, 2001, and 2002 and the All-WNBA Second Team in 1998 and 1999. Leslie helped Los Angeles reach the WNBA Finals, but the Detroit Shock upset the Sparks in the three-game series.

Leslie has launched a second career for herself. She enjoys a successful modeling career with the Wilhelmina Modeling Agency of New York and has been featured in *Vogue, Newsweek*, and numerous sports publications. In October 1998, she dedicated the Lisa Leslie Sports Complex at Morningside High School. She received the 1999 Young Heroes Award for her work in the Los Angeles area with foster children through the Big Sisters Guild. In addition, she has been spokesperson for the WNBA Breast Health Awareness campaign.

BIBLIOGRAPHY

Oscar Dixon, "Goal Sparks Leslie's Mission," *USA Today*, August 21, 2001, p. 3C; "Leslie, Sparks End Houston's Four-Year Reign as Champions," *St. Louis Post-Dispatch*, August 21, 2001, p. E7; Robyn Norwood, "Sparks Win Another Title for LA in Series Sweep," *St. Louis Post-Dispatch*, September 2, 2001, p. D7; Mark Stewart, *Lisa Leslie: Queen of the Court* (New York, 1998); USA Basketball, *1998 USA Basketball Women's World Championship Media Guide* (1998); WNBA, *WNBA Player Directory, "Profiles: Lisa Leslie Player File"* (2001).

Frank J. Olmsted

CARL LEWIS
(July 1, 1961–   )

Track and Field

Carl Lewis ranked among the greatest track and field athletes in history. For the United States in the long jump, 100 meters, 200 meters, and the 400-meter relay, he won nine gold medals in four Olympiads in his phenomenal career.

Frederick Carlton Lewis was born on July 1, 1961 to William Lewis and Evelyn Lawlor Lewis in Birmingham, Alabama. His family moved several years later to Willingboro, New Jersey, where his parents served as high school track and field coaches. His two brothers and his sister excelled as athletes. Because of his small size, however, he was considered the family "runt."

Lewis explained that he "didn't mature until high school. There was talent there all the time, but it was only when I got older that I really blossomed." His younger sister, Carol, who later set a U.S. indoor long jump record for women even defeated him in races. "She was bigger than I was. Everybody was bigger than I was."

By his graduation from Willingboro High School in 1979, Lewis was the nation's top-ranked high school track and field athlete. Both Carl and Carol Lewis made the 1980 U.S. Olympic team, but that year the United States boycotted the Summer Olympic Games in Moscow in protest of the Soviet Union's invasion of Afghanistan.

Lewis attended the University of Houston, working with coach Tom Tellez on his mechanics. Tellez helped Lewis develop his unusual long jump style, the double-hitch kick. This maneuver involved a longer approach run than usual, a straight flight through the air rather than an arc, and a double pump of the legs in a bicycle motion while the arms spun backwards in flight.

In the early 1980s, Lewis began to excel at national collegiate track and field events. At the 1981 and 1982 National Championships, he won both the long jump and the 100-meter race. This feat had not been accomplished since Jesse Owens won both events in the 1930s. He trailed the field for the first half of the 100-meter race before accelerating. Lewis told a reporter after the race, "the reason I am so powerful in the last 40 or 50 meters is because I can relax very well, and when you relax you don't decelerate as much." Lewis won the Amateur Athletic Union's (AAU) Sullivan Award as the outstanding U.S. amateur athlete in 1981 and the Jesse Owens Award for outstanding track and field performance in 1982.

Because of academic difficulties at Houston, Lewis was disqualified from collegiate athletics for the 1981–1982 year. That year Lewis competed for the Santa Monica, California, Track Club under coach Joe Douglas. In 1983 he set several new records, including the indoor 60-yard dash, the 100-meter dash, and the outdoor high jump. He also won gold medals in the 100 meters, the long jump, and the 400-meter relay at the World Track and Field Championships in Helsinki, Finland.

At the 1984 U.S. Olympic Trials, Lewis qualified for the 100 meters, the 200 meters, the long jump, and the 400-meter relay. Winning four gold medals in track and field at a single Olympics posed a formidable challenge. Only Jesse Owens, at the 1936 Olympic Games in Berlin, Germany, had accomplished that feat. Lewis accepted the challenge, winning the 100 meters in 9.99 seconds, the long jump at 28 feet ¼ inch, and the 200 meters in 19.80 seconds, and anchoring the U.S. 400-meter relay team to a 37.83 seconds victory.

At the 1988 Olympics at Seoul, Korea, Lewis lost to Ben Johnson in the 100-meter race. Lewis was awarded the gold medal, however, when Johnson was disqualified for using performance-enhancing drugs. Lewis also won the long jump with a leap of 28 feet 7½ inches, but he was defeated at 200 meters by teammate Joe DeLoach.

Lewis struggled with unfavorable publicity throughout his career. He was criticized for waving the American flag during his victory lap following his 100-meter win at the 1984 Olympics. He was accused of passing up a chance to break the long jump record at those same Olympics after securing his victory, and he was also called aloof and arrogant. Coach Tellez countered that Lewis was "compassionate, friendly, and was unspoiled by celebrity."

At the 1992 Olympic Trials in New Orleans, Louisiana, Lewis experienced an off-day, finishing sixth in the 100 meters and fourth in the 200 meters, qualifying in the long jump and being selected as an alternate for the 4×100-

meter relay. He performed better at the Barcelona, Spain, Olympic Games, winning the long jump at 28 feet 5½ inches and anchoring the victorious U.S. relay team.

By 1996 when the Atlanta, Georgia, Olympic Games were held, Lewis was 35 years old and so competed only in the long jump. On July 29, he jumped 27 feet 10¾ inches to defeat the injured world recordholder, Mike Powell, to win his ninth and last Olympic gold medal. Lewis won eight gold medals at the World Track and Field Championships and broke world records in four events.

Lewis attempted to better his sport as an advocate of more stringent drug testing and of better working conditions, including pay for track athletes. He lives in Houston, Texas, and is involved in the sports apparel business.

BIBLIOGRAPHY

Great Athletes—The 20th Century, 10 (Englewood Cliffs, NJ, 1992); Carl Lewis, *Inside Track* (New York, 1992); "Carl Lewis," *Current Biography* (New York, 1983); *NBC Sports Research Manual* 8, pp. 474–478; *U.S. Olympic 1996 Team Media Guide*; David Wallechinsky, *The Complete Book of the Summer Olympics* (Woodstock, NY, 2000).

Robert L. Cannon

RAY LEWIS   Football
(May 15, 1975–   )

Linebacker Ray Lewis of the Baltimore Ravens (National Football League) ranks among the most outstanding defensive players in the NFL. At the same time, his off-the-field activities have made him one of professional football's most controversial athletes.

Ray Anthony Lewis Jr. was born on May 15, 1975 in Bartow, Florida. He had a distant relationship with his father, Raymond Lewis Sr., and was brought up primarily by his mother, Sunseria Keith. The oldest of five children, Lewis cleaned the house and cooked the meals while his mother worked two jobs to support the family.

Lewis excelled as an athlete at Kathleen High School in Lakeland. A linebacker, running back, and kick returner, he was named the football team's Most Valuable Player (MVP) in his junior and senior years. He won the State 4A Wrestling Championship in the 189-pound weight class.

Lewis's high school achievements led to a football scholarship to the University of Miami. With the Hurricanes, Lewis attained instant success and earned Freshman All-America honors from *The Gridiron Report*. He finished his junior year with a team-high 160 tackles, garnered consensus All-America honors, and placed runner-up for the Butkus Award. He opted for the NFL draft following his junior year.

Several brushes with the law at Miami from 1993 to 1995 marred Lewis's reputation. Coral Gables, Florida, police cited Lewis as a suspect in an August 1994 bar brawl on the Miami campus. A few weeks later, police investigated

Ray Lewis ©Photofest

an altercation between Lewis and his girlfriend, Tatyona McCall. No charges
were filed in that case. In September 1995, police investigated a fight between
McCall, the mother of Lewis's then three-month-old son, Ray III, and Kim-
berli Arnold, a former Lewis girlfriend. Lewis reportedly shook Arnold in a
threatening manner, but no charges were filed.

The Baltimore Ravens selected the Miami linebacker as their twenty-sixth
pick in the first round of the 1996 NFL draft. After signing a lucrative multi-
year contract, Lewis that year led the Ravens in tackles (142) and was named
to the *USA Today*'s All-Rookie team. In 1997, the Ravens linebacker paced
the NFL with 210 tackles. Although he missed three games because of an
injury, Lewis still led the Ravens with 154 tackles in 1998 and was named to
the Pro Bowl. In 1999 he again paced the NFL with 198 tackles. The 6-foot
1-inch, 245-pound Lewis signed a four-year, $26 million contract extension
with the Ravens in November 1998.

Off-the-field problems continued to plague Lewis in the 1990s. In 1997 McCall, who was expecting their second child, Rayshad, took Lewis to court to obtain child support. Then, in 1998, he was ordered to pay $2,700 in child support to a Maryland woman for a baby girl born in August 1997. But his major brush with the law occurred on January 31, 2000 in Atlanta, Georgia, following Super Bowl XXXIV. Lewis and several associates were seen fleeing an Atlanta nightclub in a 40-foot Lincoln Navigator Limo following the stabbing and murder of two young men. He and his friends Reginald Oakley and Joseph Sweeting were charged with murder and aggravated assault. He agreed to a misdemeanor charge of obstructing justice and cooperated with the prosecution. Oakley and Sweeting were acquitted, but NFL Commissioner Paul Tagliabue fined Lewis $250,000.

Ravens teammates and owner Art Modell backed Lewis, who returned to the football field for the 2000 season as a man on a mission. He recorded a team-high 184 tackles and was selected the NFL's Defensive Player of the Year, leading the Ravens to a Super Bowl XXXV victory over the New York Giants. Of his change in fortune, he remarked, "It's like a fairy tale, or a movie, where there's a bad start and a beautiful ending. But it's real life." Through 2002, Lewis has made 19.5 sacks and intercepted 14 passes. He continues to play an outstanding game at linebacker and remains active in Baltimore area charities, pledging $100 to the Police Athletic League for every 10 tackles. He also remains close to his mother, for whom he has purchased a home in the Baltimore, Maryland, suburbs.

BIBLIOGRAPHY

"Baltimore's Ray Lewis Tackles Murder Charges and Climbs Back to the Top a Year Later," *Jet* 99 (January 2001), pp. 49–50; Ray Didinger, "No Middle Ground with Ravens' Lewis," Superbowl.com, N.D., www.superbowl.com/XXXVI/ce/feature (April 1, 2002); Peter King, "Ravens Star Ray Lewis Sits in Jail on Murder Charges. Is He a Victim or a Killer?," *Sports Illustrated* 92 (February 14, 2000), pp. 58–61; Steve Rushin, "We Don't Know Jack: Ray Lewis Serves as a Reminder That What We Read Isn't Always the Whole Story," *Sports Illustrated* 92 (May 15, 2000), p. 26; Michael Silver, "Best of the Best," *Sports Illustrated* 94 (January 8, 2001), pp. 63–64.

Ron Briley

KENNY LOFTON   Baseball
(May 31, 1967–   )

Kenny Lofton starred in college basketball and concentrated on baseball after signing a professional contract. He quickly developed into one of the game's top center fielders, base runners, bunters, and leadoff hitters.

Kenneth Lofton was born on May 31, 1967 in East Chicago, Indiana, the son of Annie Person. He was brought up by his grandmother Rosie Person and played baseball and basketball at Washington High School there. A pitcher and outfielder, he started four years and batted .414 as a senior. "Baseball was my main sport from the beginning," he acknowledged. "But being from Indiana, if you didn't play basketball, people thought you were crazy."

In 1985 Lofton led Washington to the state basketball semifinals. Coach Lute Olson awarded Lofton a basketball scholarship at the University of Arizona. Arizona's sixth man as a sophomore in 1988, Lofton helped the Wildcats reach the National Collegiate Athletic Association (NCAA) Final Four. A year later, Arizona ranked first in the nation for much of the season. Lofton started at point guard and set Wildcat single-season and career records for steals. Arizona guard Steve Kerr, who later played in the National Basketball Association (NBA), called him "by far the best athlete on the team."

Lofton joined Arizona's baseball team in the spring of 1988. "I just wanted to play baseball again," he recalled. "I took a chance." Although Lofton played only five games and batted just twice, Houston Astros (National League) scout Clark Crist saw his potential. The Astros selected him in the seventeenth round of the June 1988 free-agent draft.

Lofton signed with Houston on condition that he could still play basketball at Arizona and complete his studies. He performed for Auburn, New York (NY-Penn League) in 1988, batting just .214. Two years later, he led the Florida State League in hits and batted .331 for Osceola, Florida. "After my second year I felt pretty comfortable," Lofton remembered. "I started to learn again."

Houston traded Lofton to the Cleveland Indians (American League) in December 1991. He batted .285 and finished second in AL Rookie of the Year voting to Milwaukee Brewers shortstop Pat Listach. He excelled with Cleveland, leading the AL in stolen bases every year from 1992 through 1996. His 66 stolen bases in 1992 set an AL record for rookies. He led the AL in assists three times (1994–1995, 1998) and hits (1994) and triples (1995) once each.

In a 1993 *Baseball America* poll of major league managers, Lofton was named the AL's "Most Exciting Player," "Best Bunter," and "Fastest Baserunner," and he ranked third in the "Best Defensive Outfielder" and "Best Baserunner" categories. Lofton attained a career-high .349 batting average in 1994. A 1996 scouting report described him as the "heart and soul of the Indians' offense."

As the Indians' center fielder and leadoff hitter, Lofton helped Cleveland win AL Central Division titles in 1995 and 1996. In the 1995 World Series against the Atlanta Braves, he tied a record by stealing two bases in one inning. In 1996 he became the Indians' all-time leading base stealer, surpassing Terry Turner's record of 254 set between 1904 and 1918. Turner set the record over 1,619 games, while Lofton broke it in just 531 contests.

Concerned about losing Lofton to free agency, Cleveland sent Lofton to the Atlanta Braves (NL) in March 1997 with pitcher Alan Embree for outfielders David Justice* and Marquis Grissom. Despite missing 40 games with injuries, Lofton batted .333 to help Atlanta win the NL East Division title. Lofton, who was not happy in the NL, returned to the Cleveland Indians in 1998. "In my heart, I'm an Indian," he declared. "I'll always be an Indian."

Lofton helped Cleveland capture AL Central Division titles in 1998, 1999, and 2001. Injuries in 1999 and 2000 limited his stolen base production, but he attained personal bests in home runs (15) and runs batted in RBI (73) in 2000. He became a free agent again after the 2001 season, signing with the Chicago White Sox (AL) in February 2002. Lofton batted .261 with 11 home runs, 51 RBIs, and 29 stolen bases in 2002, splitting the season between Chicago and San Francisco. After being traded to the Giants in July, Lofton proved a valuable leadoff hitter in their Wild Card quest. His .350 batting average with two RBIs helped San Francisco defeat the Atlanta Braves in the NL Division Series. Although hitting only .238 in the NL Championship Series, he homered in the 9–6 victory over the St. Louis Cardinals in Game One. In the World Series against the victorious Anaheim Angels, he batted .290 with a double, triple, two RBIs, and three stolen bases.

Lofton joined the Pittsburgh Pirates (NL) as a free agent before the 2003 season and was traded to the Chicago Cubs (NL) in July 2003. The 6-foot, 190-pound Lofton, who bats and throws left-handed, won AL Gold Glove awards from 1993 through 1996. He was selected to six All-Star teams from 1994 through 2000, batting .357 in five contests and sharing an All-Star Game record for most stolen bases (2) in a single contest. Through the 2003 season, Lofton's career statistics included a .298 batting average, 115 home runs, 1,245 runs scored, 648 RBIs, and 538 stolen bases. Lofton helped the Cubs win the NL Central in 2003, batting .296 with 97 runs scored, 32 doubles, 12 home runs, 46 RBIs, and 30 stolen bases as leadoff hitter. He hit .286 with three stolen bases in the NL Division Series triumph over the Atlanta Braves and .323 with ten singles and a double in the NL Championship Series loss to the Florida Marlins.

Lofton, who resides in Tucson, Arizona, earned a Bachelor's degree in radio and television. He co-chaired a summer reading program in Cleveland and was active in the Cleveland R.B.I. (Reviving Baseball in the Inner City) program. He hosted Kenny's Kids Press Conferences before each Saturday home game and donated 50 tickets for each Saturday game in Cleveland for organizations benefiting youngsters from the inner city.

Lofton has also been involved in charitable causes for disadvantaged children in East Chicago, Indiana, and was named East Chicagoan of the Year in 1995. The street where his grandmother lives was renamed Kenny Lofton Lane.

BIBLIOGRAPHY
Pete Cava, "Lofton 'Best Indiana-Born Player in Baseball,' " *Indianapolis Recorder*, October 21, 1995, pp. C6–C7; *Cleveland Indians Media Guide*, 1997; Bonnie DeSimone, "Indians' Kenny Lofton: He Was Born to Lead Off," *Baseball Digest* 56 (May 1997), pp. 34–36; "Indians Glad Lofton Went for Baseball," *Newark Star-Ledger*, August 3, 1993, p. 50; Sheldon Ocker, "Lofton Excels at Many Sports," *Indianapolis Star*, April 4, 1996, p. D10; Michael Silver, "Close to the Heart," *Sports Illustrated* 82 (May 1, 1995), pp. 96–101; *The Sporting News Baseball Register* 2003; Tim Wendel and Rob Rains, "Cluster of Rookies Rarin' to Shine," *USA Today Baseball Weekly*, March 11–17, 1992, p. 24.

Peter J. Cava

JAVY LOPEZ   **Baseball**
(November 5, 1970–   )

Javy Lopez of the Atlanta Braves (National League) made consecutive All-Star appearances in 1997 and 1998, clouting a home run in his first All-Star at-bat. His second All-Star season brought him then career highs of 34 home runs and 106 RBIs in 1998, and a Braves record for home runs by a catcher. That season, Lopez also batted .284 and led all major league catchers with a .995 fielding percentage.

Javier Torres Lopez was born on November 5, 1970 in Ponce, Puerto Rico, the son of Jacinto Lopez and Evelia Lopez. He attended Academia Cristo Rey High School in Ponce, where he played baseball and volleyball, and participated in track and field. His childhood baseball hero was Houston Astros star Jose Cruz Sr. "He was a big guy down in my hometown," Lopez said, "so I always admired him a lot."

Lopez performed as a pitcher, shortstop, and outfielder before becoming a catcher at age 13. "We usually played two games every weekend," he explained, "so one game I was catching, and the other game I was playing outfield." By age 16, he had mastered catching skills. The Atlanta Braves signed him as a nondrafted free agent one day after his seventeenth birthday.

After earning the Southern League Most Valuable Player (MVP) award with Class AA Greenville, South Carolina, Lopez made his major league debut at age 21 in September 1992 and appeared in one NL Championship Series (NLCS) game. The 6-foot 3-inch, 200-pound rugged receiver has caught regularly for the Atlanta Braves since then except 1999, when a partial tear of his right anterior cruciate ligament sidelined him for most of the season. During his stint, the Braves have won nine NL East Division titles, three NL pennants, and a World Series Championship in 1995 over the Cleveland Indians.

Lopez played an integral role in the Braves' success in the 1995 World Series, clouting a decisive two-run homer off Dennis Martinez in the second game. "I'm thinking he's going to try to surprise me with a fastball away or in. I was trying to be aggressive on that pitch," Lopez explained. "The next one was a fastball away and I took advantage of that." The baseball cleared the fence in dead center field over 400 feet away. "This is a great feeling," he said. "Everybody wants to a hero . . . I'm just glad that I am in the World Series."

After the final out of the 1995 World Series, Lopez celebrated by jumping into the arms of reliever Mark Wohlers. "Winning the World Series was one of the highlights of my career," Lopez reflected. "The other one was when I won the MVP in the NLCS. Those are the two unforgettable moments for me, and I'm really proud of them." As MVP of the 1996 NLCS against the St. Louis Cardinals, he hit .542 with two homers and six runs batted in (RBI). The Braves failed in their quest to repeat as World Champions, however, falling to the New York Yankees in the World Series. Lopez enjoyed his best major league season in 2003 with career-highs in batting average (.328), runs (89), hits (150), doubles (29), home runs (43), and RBIs (109), helping the Braves win another NL East title. Although hitting .333 with two doubles, he struck out six times in the NL Division Series loss to the Chicago Cubs.

Lopez's batting ability remains unquestioned. He constantly adjusts his swing to make better contact, hitting left-handers and right-handers equally well. Throughout his career, he has consistently hit for average and power except when hampered by nagging injuries. The two toughest pitchers for him remain Kevin Brown and Randy Johnson. "Those are the two that I'd really be happy not to face," he admitted.

Lopez has caught Greg Maddux, Tom Glavine, John Smoltz, and other premier major league hurlers. He considers catching these star pitchers "the best thing that happened in my life," but his ability to call a game should not be overlooked. He works hard and ranks among the best players at his position. His advice for aspiring young catchers is "just be positive all the time."

In his 12 major league seasons, Lopez has a career .287 batting average with 214 home runs and 694 RBIs. He likes playing with the Braves. "It's more than great—knowing that this team is going to the playoffs almost every year. I'm fortunate that I'm here playing with the Atlanta Braves."

Lopez lives in Duluth, Georgia, outside Atlanta with his wife, Analy, and their two young sons, Javier and Kelvin. He enjoys relaxing at his pool with his family, playing guitar, listening to rock music, and watching movies, especially the *Star Wars* films.

BIBLIOGRAPHY

"Javy Lopez Answers Your Questions," majorleaguebaseball.com, May 12, 2000; "Sports Focus: Javy Lopezbyline," *The Atlanta Journal—Constitution*, August 9, 2000; David Srinivansan, TSN.com, April 2002; *The Sporting News Baseball Register, 2003*; Thomas Stinson, "Braves v. Indians '95 World Series, Javy's Heroics: HR and Big Out," *The Atlanta Journal-Constitution*, October 23, 1995.

James A. Riley

RONNIE LOTT   **Football**
(May 8, 1959–   )

Ronnie Lott, one of the hardest-hitting defensive backs in football history, was enshrined in the Pro Football Hall of Fame in 2000.

Ronald Mandel Lott was born on May 8, 1959 in Albuquerque, New Mexico, the oldest child of Roy Lott and Mary Lott. He has a younger sister, Suzie, and a younger brother, Roy Jr. Roy Sr. served in the U.S. Air Force, requiring the Lott family to move frequently. The Lotts lived in Albuquerque, New Mexico, Washington, D.C., San Bernardino, California, and Rialto, California. Mary Lott claims the frequent moves made the family closer. "It was just the five of us. We made sure everybody shared, everybody gave. And we kept our focus humble."

Lott attended Eisenhower High School in Rialto and enrolled at the University of Southern California, where he played football and earned All-America honors at safety as a junior and senior. He graduated in four years with a Bachelor's degree in public administration. The San Francisco 49ers (National Football League) selected Lott eighth in the first round of the 1981 NFL draft.

When asked why he played defensive back, Lott replied, "I was put at defensive back because that was where my coaches felt I could succeed. The only choice I made was wanting to play, and that I wanted to do real bad." He says the hardest part about playing defensive back is "knowing you can beat on every play." Former Dallas Cowboys coach Tom Landry praised Lott, "He's like a middle linebacker playing safety. He's devastating. He may dominate the secondary better than anyone I've seen." Former San Francisco 49ers coach Bill Walsh praised Lott as the "best defensive back to ever play the game."

As a rookie with San Francisco, Lott started at the cornerback position and became only the second rookie in NFL history to return three interceptions for touchdowns. He finished second in the Rookie of the Year Award voting to linebacker Lawrence Taylor* of the New York Giants in 1981. One major highlight of Lott's rookie season was his team's victory over the Cincinnati Bengals in Super Bowl XVI. Lott played on four NFL championship teams during his nine-year career with the 49ers. He reflected on his experiences with the 49ers dynasty: "Everyone within that organization—from the secretary and equipment manager up to the players, coaches, and management—believes they are champions, and the only demand they make upon you is to be the best you can be. That attitude permeates the organization and rubs off on everyone, including the players."

Left unprotected by Plan B free agency, Lott signed a lucrative contract in 1991 with the nearby Oakland Raiders (NFL). He was determined to prove that he was still capable of playing at a high level and was motivated to show the 49ers that they were wrong to let him go. San Francisco fans were upset to see him go to the Raiders. A year later, he signed a $1.8 million contract with the New York Jets (NFL). The 49ers parted with Lott because he missed numerous games with injuries, including broken or sprained fingers, separated and dislocated right and left shoulders, a pinched nerve in his neck, torn cartilage in his right knee, and a cracked tibia in his right leg. Lott has been knocked unconscious making tackles. About his injuries he observed, "It's not important to be known as someone who hits hard. It's important to be thought of as a guy who gives his all. Sure, I'm taking a risk of getting injured or being burned. But one thing you don't do is sell out on your heart."

Lott holds several NFL records and numerous honors. He set the NFL record for the most interceptions (10) in a season (1986 and 1991) and the 49er record for the most career interceptions (51). Besides being named to the 1980's NFL All-Decade Team, he was selected to 10 All-Pro teams at three positions and earned four Super Bowl rings. Lott made the NFL's seventy-fifth anniversary all-time team and was enshrined into the Pro Football Hall of Fame in 2000 with his teammate, quarterback Joe Montana. Montana described Lott as "honest, upfront and genuine, and there's nothing phony about our relationship. What began as a competitive relationship founded on mutual respect blossomed into a friendship, and it'll last a lifetime." They collaborate in a high-tech investments firm, Champion Ventures.

Lott's other activities include serving as a Fox Sports Net analyst, co-owning a Toyota dealership, and forming All-Star Helping Kids, a group that raises money for underprivileged youth. He donates money to San Francisco churches to feed the homeless and visits sick patients. He has a genuine dedication to service: "I feel a responsibility to the community. It's easy to give to others, to give them some hope, some belief that they can make it. You've got to share yourself. You can't forget where you came from and that you should help people. The rewards you get from that are better than anything."

He and his wife, Karen, have two sons, Ryan and Isaiah, and two daughters, Hailey and Chloe.

BIBLIOGRAPHY

Glenn Dickey, "One on One," *Sport* 84 (August 1993), pp. 14–15; Peter King, "Letting Go: The 49ers Bid Roger Craig and Ronnie Lott Goodbye," *Sports Illustrated* 74 (April 15, 1991), pp. 15–16; Jill Leiber, "The Fab 5," *Sports Illustrated* 72 (January 23, 1990), pp. 68–78; Jill Lieber, "Hitter with Heart," *Sports Illustrated* 70 (January 23, 1989), pp. 44–48; Timothy Nolan, "A Lott to Cheer About," *Coach and Athletic Director* 66 (May-June 1997), pp. 68–75; "Ronnie Lott: Biography," www.pro footballhof.com/players/enshrinees/rlott.cfm; "Ronnie Lott's Enshrinement Speech," July 29, 2000, Canton, Ohio, www.profootballhof.com; Michael Silver, "Together Forever," *Sports Illustrated*, 93 (July 24, 2000), pp. 56–59.

Maureen M. Smith

M _____

TRACY McGRADY
(May 24, 1979–)

Basketball

Tracy McGrady of the Orlando Magic (National Basketball Association) jumped directly from high school to the NBA in 1997 and has emerged among the best-all-around NBA players.

Tracy Lamar McGrady Jr. was born on May 24, 1979 in Bartow, Florida, the son of Tracy McGrady Sr. and Melanise (Williford) McGrady and was brought up by his mother and maternal grandmother, Roberta Williford. Friends nicknamed him "Pumpkinhead" because the width of his skull was regrettably close to that of his shoulders. He attended Auburndale, Florida, High School, averaging 23.1 points and 12.2 rebounds in basketball as a junior in 1995. His name did not appear on any recruiting service lists of Division I prospects because he was never recruited to summer camps and Auburndale never appeared in high-profile tournaments. The undisciplined McGrady missed the district tournament after being suspended for talking back to a teacher.

In May 1996, Alvin Jones, basketball coach at neighboring Kathleen High School, told Joel Hopkins, basketball coach at Mount Zion Christian Academy in Durham, North Carolina, about McGrady. Jones observed, "The kid has never had much guidance or discipline in his home life, so he has always been a wanderer, and I felt he had reached a crossroads." Hopkins gave McGrady a basketball scholarship and much stricter discipline. McGrady averaged 28 points, 9 rebounds, and 8 assists in 1996, leading Mount Zion to a second-place national ranking in *USA Today* and making 36 points, 11 rebounds, 7 assists, 3 blocks, 4 steals, and 8 dunks in one game. Mount Zion assistant coach Cleo Hill explained, "There aren't many 6'9" guys who can score at will in the post and hit the three-pointer. When he turns it on, you can tell he simply doesn't belong here."

McGrady followed Kevin Garnett,* Kobe Bryant,* and Jermaine O'Neal in skipping college to play pro basketball. The Toronto Raptors (NBA) selected the 6-foot 9-inch, 210-pound shooting guard in the first round as the ninth pick overall of the 1997 NBA draft. McGrady signed a lucrative contract with NIKE shoes and donated $300,000 to Mount Zion. "If I was going to make all the money," he acknowledged, "I can't forget Mount Zion, they were a big part of this."

McGrady played a reserve role his first two seasons with Toronto, averaging 7 points in 1997–1998 and 9.3 points in 1998–1999. He started at guard in 1999–2000, averaging 15.4 points, 6.3 rebounds, and 3.3 assists. The Raptors finished third in the Central Division with a 45–37 record. He averaged 16.7 points, 7 rebounds, and 3 assists in the first round of the Eastern Conference playoffs, but the New York Knicks swept the three-game series.

Toronto traded McGrady to the Orlando Magic for a future first-round draft choice in August 2000. He enjoyed immediate success with the Magic. He was voted the NBA's Most Improved Player and made the All-NBA Second Team in 2000–2001, when he scored a career-high 2,065 points (26.8-point average), made 580 rebounds (7.5 average), and tallied 352 assists (4.6 average). The Magic finished in fourth place in the Atlantic Division with a 43–39 record and returned to the playoffs after a one-year absence. McGrady averaged 33.8 points, 6.5 rebounds, and 8.3 assists in the first round of the Eastern Conference playoffs, but the Milwaukee Bucks eliminated the Magic in four games.

McGrady enjoyed his second-best season in 2001–2002, making the All-NBA First Team. Besides scoring 1,948 points (25.6-point average), McGrady set career highs with 597 rebounds (7.9 average) and 400 assists (5.3 average). His 103 three-pointers nearly doubled his career high. He ranked eighth in the NBA with 555 free-throw attempts, far more than any other Orlando player. Although mostly playing the backcourt, McGrady led the Magic in rebounding and proved the team's best low-post player. McGrady and Kobe Bryant of the Los Angeles Lakers were the only two NBA players to average at least 25 points, 5 rebounds, and 5 assists.

McGrady demonstrated both versatility and flair. Although a good defender, with the absence of Grant Hill* he was forced to carry much of the load offensively and was often assigned to the opponent's best offensive player. He led the Magic to a 44–38 record and third-place finish in the Atlantic Division. McGrady and Mike Miller helped Orlando vault into the Eastern Conference playoffs, but the lack of an established inside presence and porous defense led to a first-round exit in four games to the Charlotte Hornets. McGrady averaged 30.8 points, 6.3 rebounds, and 5.5 assists in the playoffs.

McGrady took his game to an even higher level in November 2002, scoring over 40 points in consecutive games. He tallied 47 points in a 100–90 victory over the Milwaukee Bucks on November 2 and scored 41 points to help Orlando set a franchise point record in a 125–121 triumph over the Sacramento Kings three days later. McGrady led the NBA in scoring with 2,407 points (32.1 point average) in 2002–2003, making First Team All-NBA. He averaged 5.5 assists and 1.7 steals in 75 games, helping Orlando make the playoffs. The Detroit Pistons ousted the Magic in the first round of the playoffs.

Through the 2002–2003 season, McGrady tallied 8,542 points (20.3 average), 2,713 rebounds (6.5 average), and 1,637 assists (5.3 average) in 420 games. He has appeared in 18 NBA playoff games, averaging 29.4 points, 6.6 rebounds, and 5.4 assists per game. He played in the NBA All-Star Game in 2001, 2002, and 2003, scoring 29 points in 36 minutes in 2003.

BIBLIOGRAPHY

Tim Crothers, "Onward Christian Soldier," *Sports Illustrated* 86 (February 10, 1997), pp. 40–44; Tim Crothers, "A Tough Question," *Sports Illustrated* 87 (December 29, 1997–January 5, 1998), pp. 55–59; *Orlando Magic Media Guide*, 2002–2003; *The Sporting News Official NBA Register*, 2003–2004. L; Jon Wertheim, "Rare Pair," *Sports Illustrated* 91 (November 1, 1998), pp. 72–74.

David L. Porter

FRED McGRIFF
Baseball
(October 31, 1963–   )

Fred McGriff has clouted over 200 career home runs in both the American League (AL) and the National League (NL) and has homered in a record 42 major league ballparks.

Frederick Stanley McGriff was born in Tampa, Florida, on October 31, 1963 to Earl McGriff, who owned a television repair shop, and Eliza McGriff, an elementary schoolteacher. McGriff starred in baseball at Jefferson High School in Tampa before being drafted by the New York Yankees (AL) in June 1981. The 6-foot 3-inch, 210-pound first baseman spent the 1981 and 1982 seasons at Bradenton, Florida (Gulf Coast League). A five-player trade in December 1982 sent McGriff, outfielder Dave Collins, and pitcher Mike Morgan to the Toronto Blue Jays (AL). He progressed through the Toronto farm system from 1983 to 1986, demonstrating good home run power and struggling with his batting average.

McGriff was promoted to the Toronto Blue Jays in September 1986 and belted 20 home runs in 295 at-bats in 1987 while platooning at first base and designated hitter with Cecil Fielder. McGriff averaged better than 34 home runs from 1987 to 1994, pacing the AL with 36 for Toronto in 1989 and leading the NL with 35 in 1992 for the San Diego Padres (NL). No Padre player had ever led the NL in home runs. The left-handed McGriff hit right-handers for a slightly higher batting average than southpaws and clouted the vast majority of his home runs off right-handers. A low-ball hitter, McGriff drove the ball to all regions of the ballpark. His power came from fully extending his arms in his swing. He joined shortstop Tony Fernandez* in a blockbuster trade when Toronto sent them to the San Diego Padres for second baseman Roberto Alomar* and outfielder Joe Carter in December 1990. McGriff enjoyed his first 100 runs batted in (RBI) seasons with San Diego in 1991 and 1992 and averaged 100 walks due to lack of protection behind him.

The cash-poor San Diego Padres traded McGriff to the Atlanta Braves (NL) in July 1993 for three minor league players. He added a potent offensive threat to an anemic Braves attack. In 1994 he reached a career-high .318 batting average and became only the ninth major league player to swat 30 home runs in seven consecutive seasons. The other eight sluggers are in the National Baseball Hall of Fame. McGriff played in 322 consecutive games at first base in 1995 and 1996 and proved instrumental in Atlanta's Division Championships in 1993, 1995, 1996, and 1997. In 1995 he homered in his first World Series at-bat on the first pitch from Orel Hershiser in Game One and hit a second roundtripper in Game Three off Charles Nagy. The Braves won the World Series Championship over the Cleveland Indians in six games. McGriff also connected for two home runs in the Braves' six-game World Series loss to the New York Yankees in 1996.

In November 1997, Atlanta sold McGriff to the expansion Tampa Bay Devil Rays (AL). Nicknamed "the Crime Dog," McGriff provided leadership and proven RBI production for a young Tampa team from 1998 to midseason 2001. He drove in over 100 runs in 1999 and 2000 and belted 107 home runs with Tampa Bay. In August 2001, the Chicago Cubs (NL), who were contending for a Central Division Championship, acquired him from Tampa Bay to bat cleanup behind slugger Sammy Sosa.* McGriff delivered 12 home runs and 41 RBIs in 49 games, but the St. Louis Cardinals captured the Division crown. McGriff enjoyed playing in Wrigley Field and in 2002 clouted 30 home runs for the tenth time in his career. The Los Angeles Dodgers (NL) signed him in December 2002.

Defensively, McGriff possessed good hands and decent range. He led AL first basemen with a .997 fielding average in 1988 and in chances and double plays in 1989 and paced NL first basemen in chances in 1994, but more often ranked near the top of his league in errors.

McGriff played in four All-Star games for the NL and one for the AL. He was named the 1994 All-Star Game's Most Valuable Player for his two-run pinch-hit home run for the NL off Lee Smith to tie the game, 7–7, in the ninth inning, which the NL won 8–7 in the tenth inning. McGriff won *The Sporting News* Silver Slugger Award at first base for the AL in 1989 and the NL in 1992 and 1993. Through the 2003 season, he produced 2,477 hits, 1,342 runs scored, 438 doubles, 24 triples, 491 home runs, 1,543 RBIs, and a .285 batting average.

McGriff and his wife, Veronica, were married in October 1988, have two children, Erick and Ericka, and live in Tampa, Florida. His cousin, Terry McGriff, caught in the major leagues from 1987 through 1990 and 1993 through 1994, while his nephew, Charles Johnson,* catches for the Colorado Rockies (NL).

BIBLIOGRAPHY
John Dewan, ed., *The Scouting Report 1994* (New York, 1994); John Dewan, *The Scouting Notebook 2002* (Morton Grove, IL, 2002); Zander Hollander, *1992 Complete Handbook of Baseball*, 22nd ed. (New York, 1992); Zander Hollander, *1996 Complete Handbook of Baseball*, 26th ed. (New York, 1996); John Kuenster, "Unsung Fred

McGriff Earns His Keep with the Atlanta Braves," *Baseball Digest* 54 (June 1995), pp. 17–19; David L. Porter, ed., *Biographical Dictionary of American Sports: Baseball, G–P*, revised and expanded edition (Westport, CT, 2000).

Frank J. Olmsted

DONOVAN McNABB
(November 25, 1976–   )

Football

Donovan McNabb has starred as a quarterback at Syracuse University and for the Philadelphia Eagles (National Football League).

Donovan Jamal McNabb was born on November 25, 1976 in Chicago, Illinois, the son of Samuel McNabb, an electrical engineer, and Wilma McNabb, a registered nurse. McNabb began playing football in the seventh grade as a quarterback. He graduated in 1994 from Mt. Carmel High School, an all-male Roman Catholic institution on the southside of Chicago. He was selected an All-America and *Chicago Defender News* Player of the Year during his senior season. McNabb also played basketball at Mt. Carmel and was named a two-time all-area selection. He played football in high school with Tampa Bay Buccaneers (NFL) defensive end Simeon Rice and basketball with Dallas Mavericks (National Basketball Association) forward Antoine Walker.

Recruited heavily by numerous major universities, McNabb accepted a football scholarship from Syracuse University to play for coach Paul Pasgualoni. He was redshirted his first season in 1994 but started at quarterback for the Orangemen the next four seasons. He graduated as a fifth-year senior in December 1998 with a Bachelor's degree in speech communications. On the basketball court, McNabb served as a backup guard for coach Jim Boeheim's Orangemen for two seasons and played on the 1995–1996 squad that lost to the University of Kentucky, 76–67, in the National Collegiate Athletic Association (NCAA) Championship Game.

As a 6-foot 2-inch, 226-pound quarterback, McNabb started every game and recorded a 33–12 won-lost record. He led the Orangemen to four consecutive Bowl appearances. When Syracuse triumphed 41–0 over Clemson University in the 1996 Gator Bowl, he was selected the game's Most Valuable Player (MVP). The following season, the Orangemen conquered the University of Houston, 30–17, in the 1996 Liberty Bowl. Syracuse lost 35–18 to Kansas State University in the 1998 Fiesta Bowl and 31–10 to the University of Florida in the 1999 Orange Bowl.

McNabb was chosen the Big East Conference's (BEC) Player of the Decade for the 1990s, Offensive Player of the Year in 1996, 1997, and 1998, and First Team All-BEC quarterback for four seasons. He established Syracuse and BEC career records with 77 touchdown passes and 96 composite touchdowns, accumulating 8,389 passing yards, 9,950 total offensive yards, and

Donovan McNabb ©Photofest

1,403 total offensive plays. McNabb established the Orangemen's all-time records with 221.1 total yards per game, a 155.1 passing efficiency, and 9.1 yards per attempt. His 8,389 career yards passing, 548 completions, 938 attempts, and a 58.4 completion percentage rank him second in school history. As a freshman, McNabb was selected BEC Rookie of the Year and connected on a 96-yard touchdown pass against West Virginia University, the longest ever in Orangemen history. He tied a school record with four touchdown passes against the University of Cincinnati, and he set a school record in his junior season with 2,892 yards in total offense. As a senior, he completed 157 of 251 passes for 2,134 yards and a 62.5 completion percentage. His 22 touchdown passes matched the season record set by Don McPherson in 1987.

McNabb was selected by the Philadelphia Eagles in the first round as the second pick overall of the 1999 NFL draft. In his initial season he started six games, and he earned his first career victory against the Washington Redskins on November 14, 1999.

In 2000, his first full season as a starter, McNabb recorded career highs with 569 passing attempts, 330 completions, a 58.0 percent completion rate, and 3,365 passing yards. He led the Eagles to an 11–5–0 record and a playoff berth, defeating the Tampa Bay Buccaneers, 21–3, in a Wild Card game, before losing, 20–10, to the New York Giants in a National Football Conference (NFC) semifinal game. He led the NFL quarterbacks in rushing with 629 yards. His 569 passing attempts and 330 completions broke the Eagles' single-season standard, previously held by Randall Cunningham. McNabb's 55 pass attempts against the Pittsburgh Steelers on November 22, 2000 marked a career high, and he threw for a career-best 390 passing yards and four touchdowns against the Cleveland Browns on December 10, 2000. He finished second to Marshall Faulk* in the Associated Press voting for the NFL's MVP and was named the first alternate to the NFC Pro Bowl Team. When Kurt Warner was injured, he stepped in and led the NFC on a scoring drive in his first series. He also was selected 2000 NFL Player of the Year by CBS Radio, earned the Terry Bradshaw Award on Fox Sports, and was chosen to the All-Madden team.

Following the 2001 season, McNabb was named to the NFC Pro Bowl team for the second time. He combined for 3,715 yards of total offense and recorded a career-high 25 touchdown passes with an 84.3 quarterback rating in 2001. He was selected the Eagles offensive MVP in both 2000 and 2001. McNabb again led the Eagles to a 11–5–0 record and a berth in the playoffs in 2001. Philadelphia won the Wild Card game, 31–9, over Tampa Bay and the second-round divisional playoff game, 33–19, over the Chicago Bears, before losing, 29–24, to the St. Louis Rams in the NFC Championship Game. McNabb was chosen NFL Offensive Player of the Week after the playoff game in Chicago, completing 26 of 40 passes for 262 yards and two touchdowns and rushing for one touchdown. He became the fourth quarterback in Philadelphia history to pass for 3,000 yards in consecutive seasons, joining Sonny Jurgensen, Ron Jaworski, and Randall Cunningham.

Philadelphia finished with a 12–4 mark for the best NFC record and home advantage in the playoffs in 2002. McNabb completed 211 of 363 passes (58.4 percent) for 2,289 yards and 17 touchdowns with just six interceptions and rushed 63 times for 460 yards (7.3-yard average) and six touchdowns in 2002. He suffered a broken right ankle on the third play of the November 17 contest against the Phoenix Cardinals but played the rest of the game, completing 20 of 25 passes for 255 yards and four touchdowns.

Philadelphia defeated the Atlanta Falcons, 20-6, as McNabb converted on

20 of 30 aerials for 247 yards and one touchdown in the NFC playoffs. The Tampa Bay Buccaneers triumphed over the Eagles, 27–10, in the NFC Championship Game, limiting McNabb to 26 completions in 49 attempts for 243 yards and one interception.

In four NFL seasons, McNabb has started 48 games and completed 932 of 1,641 passes for 9,835 yards for a 56.7 completion percentage. He has connected on 71 touchdown passes, suffered 38 interceptions, and compiled a high quarterback rating. He has rushed 278 times for 1,884 yards and a 6.8-yard average, and scored 14 touchdowns.

During the off-seasons, McNabb, who married Raquel-Ann Nurse, a point guard on Syracuse's women's basketball team, in June 2003, spends two weeks of each month in Phoenix, Arizona working out at a training facility for professional and collegiate athletes. He participates in punishing exercises and intensive drills to condition his body for the next NFL season. He received the 2002 Wanamaker Award, given to the athlete or team that has done the most to reflect credit upon Philadelphia and their team or sport during the previous year.

BIBLIOGRAPHY
Gerry Callahan, "Head Games," *Sports Illustrated* 90 (May 17, 1999), pp. 38–41; "Donovan McNabb," *Career Highlights*, www.nfl.com (2002); "Donovan McNabb," *Career Stats*, www.nfl.com (2002); "Donovan McNabb," *College*, www. philadelphiaeagles.com (2002); "Donovan McNabb," *Personal*, www.philadelphia eagles.com (2002); Peter King, "Philly Flash," *Sports Illustrated* 96 (January 28, 2002), pp. 28–29; *The Sporting News Football Register*, 2003.

John L. Evers

STEVE McNAIR   Football
(February 14, 1973–)

Steve McNair starred at quarterback at Alcorn State University and guided the Tennessee Titans (National Football League) to a Super Bowl.

Steve La Treal McNair was born on February 14, 1973 in Mount Olive, Mississippi, the son of Selma McNair, an offshore oil rig worker, and Lucille McNary, a factory worker. McNair earned All-America and All-State honors as a quarterback and defensive back for Mount Olive High School. As a junior, he led his team to the State Championship on the final play of the game. He, together with Terrell Buckley, shared the state record for most career interceptions (30) and also excelled in basketball and baseball. The Seattle Mariners (American League) drafted him to play baseball, while Alcorn State recruited him as a defensive back in football.

As quarterback, McNair finished his career at Alcorn State with 938 completions in 1,673 attempts for 14,496 yards (55.5 percent average) and 119 touchdowns. He became only the third quarterback in Division 1-AA to throw for at least 100 career touchdowns. The 6-foot 2-inch, 225-pound quarterback

Steve McNair ©Photofest

also proved a threat as a runner, rushing 375 times for 2,327 career yards and 33 touchdowns. McNair broke nearly every Braves game, season, passing, and offensive record. He became the only player in collegiate history to gain over 16,000 career yards in total offense (16,823). He established two other collegiate records, averaging 400.5 yards in total offense and 8.18 yards per pass play. McNair finished his college career by setting Division 1-AA playoff records for completions (52) and passing attempts (82) while amassing 514 yards and three touchdowns against Youngstown State University. His outstanding performance made him a unanimous All-America choice. He also won the Walter Payton Award as the top Division 1-AA player and the Eddie

Robinson Trophy as the top player in an Afro-American college, finishing third in the Heisman Trophy race. Offensive Coordinator Rickey Taylor said, "Steve has the intelligence of a Montana, the release of a Marino, the scrambling ability of an Elway." He added, "I haven't seen anybody yet I can compare this kid with."

The Houston Oilers (NFL) selected McNair on the first round of the 1995 NFL draft as the third pick overall. He played behind starter Chris Chandler, seeing limited action. When Chandler was traded to the Atlanta Falcons in 1997, he became the starting quarterback. The team also moved to Tennessee and was renamed the Titans. That season, McNair completed 216 passes out of 415 attempts for 2,665 yards and 14 touchdowns and threw only 13 interceptions for a new team record. By rushing for 674 yards and eight touchdowns, he posed a double threat as a passer and explosive runner. His 674 yards marked the third highest rushing total by a quarterback in NFL history behind Randall Cunningham's 942 yards gained in 1990 and Bobby Douglas's 968 yards gained in 1972. Head coach Jeff Fisher said, "If you were going to put together a list of all the things you can't coach—poise, ability to lead, competitiveness, responsibility—he has them all."

McNair gained confidence as an NFL quarterback. In 1998, he developed a precise passing rhythm with a trio of second-year wide receivers, Joey Kent, Isaac Byrd, and Willie Davis. "I think I progressed pretty well," he claimed. "Now, I can play my game, go out confident that the offense is going to be wide open, half run, half pass. Things are going to get done and I feel great about that." Although beset by many injuries, McNair set career highs in passing attempts (492), completions (289), passing yards (3,228), and passing touchdowns (15). At age 25 he became the youngest quarterback in franchise history to pass for at least 3,000 yards. He again set a Titan record for fewest interceptions with 10, and he led all NFL quarterbacks in rushing with 559 yards.

McNair enjoyed his finest season in 1999 when he directed the Titans to a 13–3 record and their first-ever berth in a Super Bowl. With time running out in Super Bowl XXXIV, he completed a 16-yard pass to Keith Dyson. Only a game-saving tackle by Mike Jones of the St. Louis Rams at the one-yard line as time expired preserved a Rams 23 to 16 victory. McNair became the first Afro-American to lead an American Football Conference (AFC) team to a Super Bowl appearance.

McNair overcame a potentially career-ending shoulder problem in 2000 to direct the Titans to another 13–3 finish. In 2001, he passed for 3,350 yards and 21 touchdowns and set career highs in passer rating (90.2) and average yards gained per pass (7.77). He led the Titans to the AFC South crown with an 11–5 record in 2002, establishing career bests with 301 completions for 3,387 yards and 22 touchdowns. Tennessee defeated the Pittsburgh Steelers, 34–31, in overtime in the AFC playoffs, as McNair converted 27 of 44 aerial for 338 yards and two touchdowns. He scored two touchdowns, rushed 53 yards on five carries, and converted 21 of 36 passes for 194 yards in a 41–24 setback to the Oakland Raiders in the AFC Championship Game. His 44–20 record paced the NFL from 1999 through 2002. In nine NFL seasons, McNair completed 1,634 of 2,780 passes for 19,422 yards and 108 touchdowns.

McNair, his wife, Mechelle, and son, Tyler, split time in the off-season between Nashville, Tennessee, and Mount Olive, Mississippi. His brother, Fred, quarterbacked with the Toronto Argonauts (Canadian Football League), London Monarchs (World Football League), and Florida Bobcats (Arena Football League).

BIBLIOGRAPHY

Shirelle Phelps, ed., *Contemporary Black Biography*, Vol. 22 (Detroit, MI, 1999), pp. 145–148; *Pro Football Weekly*, August 16, 1998; *Pro Football Weekly*, January 8, 2000; *The Sporting News Pro Football Register*, 2003; *Tennessee Titans Press Guide*, 2003.

Richard Gonsalves

KARL MALONE   Basketball
(July 24, 1963–   )

Karl Malone ranks among the most prolific scorers in National Basketball Association (NBA) history.

Karl Anthony Malone, nicknamed "The Mailman" because he always delivers in the clutch, was born on July 24, 1963 in Summerfield, Louisiana, the son of J. P. Malone and Shirley Ann Jackson. When Malone was 3 years old, his father committed suicide. His mother married Ed Turner a few years later. To bring up nine children, she worked at two jobs. The family lived in a tin roof shack. As a teenager, Malone got his first job—cleaning out chicken coops. He excelled in basketball at Summerfield High School, graduating in 1981, leading the Rebels for three seasons in rebounding and scoring and averaging over 30 points.

Although heavily recruited, Malone was declared academically ineligible to play basketball in his first year of college. He attended nearby Louisiana Tech University, borrowing enough money to meet his expenses during his first year of attendance. He became eligible to play basketball for the 1982–1983 season and soon attained superstar status. He led the Bulldogs to a 74–19 won-lost record and to two appearances in the National Collegiate Athletic Association (NCAA) Division I National Tournament. He tallied 1,716 points and grabbed 859 rebounds in his three-year career at Louisiana Tech, and in 1985 he led all NCAA tournament players in rebounding average with 12.4 boards. Although selected to the All-Southland Conference First Team in 1983, 1984, and 1985, he considered "attaining a 3.6 Grade Point Average" his greatest accomplishment at Louisiana Tech.

After his junior year, Malone entered the 1985 NBA draft. The 6-foot 9-inch, 256-pound power forward was selected by the Utah Jazz (NBA) in the first round as the thirteenth pick overall. He made the NBA All-Rookie Team in 1986, becoming an excellent shooter inside and out, running the floor in the transition game, and playing very strong on defense against the opponent. His size, strength, quickness, and ability to make inside moves made him difficult to defend.

For the next 17 years with Utah, Malone averaged between 20.6 and 31.0 points per game. His Utah Jazz made the playoffs each year, but an NBA Championship eluded them. He and teammate John Stockton led the Jazz to the NBA Finals in the 1996–1997 and 1997–1998 seasons, but lost both times to the Chicago Bulls in six games. On December 5, 2000 against the Toronto Raptors, Malone registered his 31,420th career point to pass Wilt Chamberlain for the second position on the NBA's all-time scoring list. Malone trails only Kareem Abdul-Jabbar, who compiled 38,387 career points. On March 24, 2001 against the Washington Wizards, he broke the NBA career record for free throws made with 8,636, to surpass Moses Malone.

A consistently strong rebounder, Malone holds the Jazz career rebound standard with 14,601 caroms. For 13 consecutive years between 1986–1987 and 1998–1999, he snagged at least 800 rebounds. He has missed only eight games in his career. Malone led the Jazz with 53,479 career minutes played and has performed 3,000 or more minutes in 11 of his 18 seasons, with a season high of 3,329 in 1993–1994. Over a 17-year span, he and Stockton became the most compatible guard/forward combination in the NBA. Stockton owns the NBA record with 15,806 career assists. Malone became the fifth player in NBA history to compile 25,000 points and 10,000 rebounds, joining Chamberlain, Moses Malone, Elvin Hayes, and Abdul-Jabbar.

Malone made the NBA's 50th Anniversary All-Time Team in 1996 and participated on the gold-medal-winning U.S. Olympic basketball team in 1992 and 1996. He established NBA career records for most seasons with 2,000 or more points (12), most consecutive seasons with 2,000 or more points (11), most seasons leading the NBA in free throws made (8), and most consecutive seasons leading the NBA in free throws made (5). He was named to the All-NBA First Team 11 consecutive years (1989–1999), the All-NBA Second Team in 1988 and 2000, and the All-NBA Third Team in 2001. He was selected on the NBA All-Defensive First Team in 1997, 1998, and 1999, and the NBA All-Defensive Second Team in 1988.

In the 1996–1997 regular season, Malone gained recognition as the NBA's Most Valuable Player (MVP) after leading the Jazz to a franchise record 64 victories and their first berth in the NBA Finals. He was again named the NBA's MVP in 1998–1999, becoming only the ninth NBA player to win the Maurice Podoloff Trophy more than once. In July 2003, Malone signed a $1.5 million one-year contract with the Los Angeles Lakers (NBA).

In 18 NBA seasons from 1985–1986 through 2002–2003, Malone has compiled 36,374 points in 1,434 games for a 25.4-point average. Malone, the all-time Jazz leader in points, field goals made and attempted, free throws made and attempted, and rebounds, ranks second in steals and blocked shots and third in assists.

In 172 NBA playoff games, Malone has scored 4,519 points for a 26.3-

point average. He holds the single-game playoff record for most free throws made without a miss (18) and shares the record for most free throws made in one half (19).

Malone has played in 14 NBA All-Star games and posted 28 points and 9 rebounds in the 1989 game, being named the Classic's MVP. He led the Western Conference All Stars with 28 points and 10 rebounds in the 1993 game and was named Co-MVP with Stockton, who handed out 15 assists.

Malone married Kay Ann Kinsey, Miss Idaho USA, in 1990. They reside in Salt Lake City, Utah, and have three daughters, Kadee, Kylee, Karlee, and a son, Kai. Malone has become active in ventures outside of basketball. He owns a Toyota dealership in Albuquerque, New Mexico, and a cattle ranch in Arkansas. In addition, he and his wife have opened a bed-and-breakfast just outside Salt Lake City.

Malone has donated $100,000 to his university for a new weight room and has purchased uniforms and gym shoes for the boys' and girls' basketball programs at his high school. In 1997 he and his wife established the Karl Malone Foundation for kids who are abused, neglected, or abandoned and need help. He advises young African Americans, "I am a prime example of hard work and never letting people tell you, you can't do something. Because I'm a living witness that YOU CAN."

BIBLIOGRAPHY
"Karl Malone," *Broadband Sports*, www.athletesdirect.com (2000); "Karl Malone," *Player Background*, www.nba.com (2001); "Karl Malone," *Player-Career Highlights*, www.nba.com (2001); "Karl Malone," *Player-Career Statistics*, www.nba.com (2001); "Karl Malone Becomes NBA's 2nd Highest All-Time Scorer," *Jet* 3 (January 1, 2001), p. 49; *NCAA, Men's Basketball's Finest* (Overland Park, KS, 1998); David L. Porter, ed., *Biographical Dictionary of American Sports—1992–1995 Supplement* (Westport, CT, 1995); *The Sporting News Official NBA Register*, 2003–2004; *Sports Illustrated 2003 Sports Almanac* (Kingston, NY, 2002); "Transcript of Yahoo's chat with Karl Malone" (June 3, 1999), http://yahoosports.com/nba/malone_chat/html.

John L. Evers

EDGAR MARTINEZ   Baseball
(January 2, 1963–   )

Edgar Martinez ranks among the best pure hitters and the best designated hitter in major league baseball history.

Edgar Martinez was born on January 2, 1963 in New York City to Jose Martinez and Christina Salgado Martinez. The Martinez family returned to their native Puerto Rico when Martinez was 2 years old. He graduated from Jose S. Alegria High School in Dorado and attended American College in Puerto Rico before signing as a nondrafted free agent with the Seattle Mariners (American League) in December 1982.

Martinez began his professional baseball career inauspiciously at Bellingham, Washington (Northwest League), batting only .173 in 1983. At Wausau, Wisconsin (Midwest League), the following season, however, he hit .303 and showed patience at the plate by drawing 84 walks. He split the 1985 season between Chattanooga, Tennessee (Southern League) and Calgary, Canada (Pacific Coast League), and he spent the entire 1986 campaign at Chattanooga, leading SL third basemen with a .960 fielding average. Martinez played the 1987–1989 seasons at Calgary, with promotions each year to Seattle. In 1990, he batted .302 in 144 games for Seattle, demonstrating his great hitting prowess. He recorded more walks than strikeouts, a feat he duplicated nearly every year thereafter. He exhibited a strong arm at third base, but shoulder problems reduced his effectiveness.

Martinez batted above .300 every year from 1990 to 2001 except 1993 and 1994, when he was sidelined over 150 games with hamstring injuries. In 1992, he led the AL with 46 doubles and a .343 batting average and achieved a personal best 14 stolen bases. He was employed almost exclusively as a designated hitter from 1995 to 2000, producing batting averages above .320 and on-base percentages over .420. Martinez hit 52 doubles in 1995 and 1996, becoming the first player to record 50 doubles in consecutive seasons since Joe Medwick of the St. Louis Cardinals in 1936 and 1937. He led the AL with a career-high .356 batting average, .384 batting average with runners in scoring position, and .482 on-base percentage in 1995.

Martinez clouted three home runs against the Texas Rangers on July 6, 1996 and the Minnesota Twins on May 18, 1999. He exceeded 100 runs batted in (RBI) six times, peaking with an AL-leading 145 in 2000—the most ever by a player over 37 years old. For seven consecutive years from 1995 through 2001, he hit at least 23 home runs and 30 doubles. Martinez drew 90 or more walks each campaign, demonstrating an excellent batting eye and uncommon patience. The 5-foot 11-inch, 202-pound right-hander continued defying age in 2001 by driving in 116 runs, the most ever by a 38-year-old player. In 2003, he batted .294 with 24 home runs and 98 RBIs.

Martinez has suffered throughout his career from strabismus, a disorder that prevents his eyes from working in tandem. At times, his right eye drifts out so that he can use only his left eye. He sometimes sees the ball as the pitcher releases it, but then suddenly he loses sight of it. Eye specialist Dr. Nicholas Nikaitani has worked extensively with him to adjust for this difficulty. On April 11, 2002, Martinez ruptured a tendon behind his left knee and required surgery. He was on the disabled list until June 11 and finished 2002 batting .277 with 15 home runs in 97 games.

Martinez has played for the AL in six All-Star contests. He owns a .375 batting average with seven home runs and 20 RBIs in four AL Division Series, but has hit only .156, with one home run, in three AL Championship Series.

Through the 2003 season, Martinez recorded 2,119 hits, 1,174 runs scored, 1,198 RBIs, 491 doubles, 15 triples, 297 home runs, 1,225 walks, and a .315 batting average in 1,914 games. He has played all 17 major league seasons with the Mariners, which is a club record, and he has always worn uniform number 11. He remains one of only 17 players in major league history with a career .300 batting average, .400 on-base percentage, and .500 slugging percentage in at least 5,000 at-bats.

Martinez, a cousin of former major league first baseman Carmelo Martinez, lives in Kirkland, Washington, with his wife, Holli, and son, Alexander. He owns the Caribbean Embroidery Company in Redmond, Washington.

BIBLIOGRAPHY

John Dewan, ed., *The Scouting Notebook 2002* (Morton Grove, IL, 2002); ESPN, "MLB Player Index: Edgar Martinez," *ESPN.com* (April 20, 2002), pp. 1–2; Bob Kuenster, "Baseball's Most Productive Hitters with Men in Scoring Position," *Baseball Digest* 55 (May 1996), pp. 36–40; Ken Rosenthal, "Martinez Keeps the Hits Coming Despite Eye Disorder," *TSN*, TSN EXPERT on line (April 20, 2001), pp. 1–4; The Sporting News.com, *MLB Headquarters: Edgar Martinez* (February 20, 2002), pp. 1–2.

Frank J. Olmsted

PEDRO MARTINEZ   Baseball
(October 25, 1971–)

Pedro Martinez, star pitcher with the Boston Red Sox (American League), has won three Cy Young awards.

Pedro Jaime Martinez was born on October 25, 1971 in Manoguayabo, Dominican Republic. His parents, Paulino Martinez and Leopoldina Martinez, fought often when he was a small boy and divorced when he was 6. His family included three brothers, two sisters, and several foster children. His older brother, Ramon, pitched with the Los Angeles Dodgers (National League), while a younger brother, Jesus, played in the minor leagues.

The 5-foot 11-inch, 170-pound right-hander was signed by the Los Angeles Dodgers in June 1988 at age 16. After two seasons in the Dominican Summer League, Martinez pitched for Great Falls, Montana (Pioneer League) in 1990, recording eight wins, three losses. He began 1991 with Bakersfield, California (California League), going 8–0. At San Antonio, Texas (Texas League), Martinez won seven games and lost five. He finished the season with Albuquerque, New Mexico (Pacific Coast League) splitting six decisions. *The Sporting News* named him the 1991 Minor League Player of the Year.

Martinez spent most of 1992 at Albuquerque, winning seven games and losing six, with a 3.81 earned run average (ERA) and 124 strikeouts in 125.1 innings. He made his major league debut on September 24, 1992 in relief against the Cincinnati Reds.

Martinez led all NL relievers with 10 victories in 1993 and recorded 119 strikeouts in 107 innings. The Dodgers traded Martinez to the Montreal Expos (National League) in November 1993.

In 1994 Martinez flourished as a starter under manager Felipe Alou and pitching coach Joe Kerrigan. He had a 11–5 record in the strike-shortened 1994 season, with a 3.42 ERA and 142 strikeouts in 144.2 innings. In 1995 he won 14 games, lost 10, and posted a 3.51 ERA with 174 strikeouts in 194.2

Pedro Martinez ©Courtesy of the Boston Red Sox

innings. On June 3, Martinez took a perfect game into the tenth inning against the San Diego Padres, only to lose it on a leadoff double. In 1996 he was named to the All-Star team, finishing the season with a 13–10 record and a 3.70 ERA. He struck out 222 batters in 216.2 innings.

Martinez encountered difficulty controlling his fastball early in his career. In 1994 and 1995 he hit 22 batters, causing several brawls and a suspension. Kerrigan taught him a four-seam fastball that was easier to control. Martinez also mastered his curve ball and change-up, but his reputation as a "headhunter" lingers.

Martinez's persistence paid off in 1997 when he won 17 games against 8 losses with 305 strikeouts and led the NL in ERA (1.90) and complete games (13). He was selected an All-Star and won the NL Cy Young Award and *The Sporting News* NL Pitcher of the Year Award.

Montreal traded Martinez to the Boston Red Sox in November 1997. Boston quickly signed him to a six-year, $75 million contract. He finished 1998 with 19 wins, 7 losses, and a 2.89 ERA, leading Boston into the playoffs. He was selected an All-Star and finished second in the Cy Young voting.

The 1999 campaign saw Martinez dominate. He won his second Cy Young

Award, this time by a unanimous vote, and again he led the Red Sox into the playoffs. His 23 victories, 2.07 ERA, and 313 strikeouts paced the AL. He struck out a staggering 13.2 batters per nine innings, lost only four games, and walked just 37 batters. Martinez started the All-Star game at Fenway Park, fanning five of the six batters he faced and earning the All-Star MVP. He won Game Five of the AL Division Series against the Cleveland Indians with a gutsy, six-inning relief appearance despite a sore back. He won Boston's sole victory against the New York Yankees in the AL Championship Series. He finished second in the AL Most Valuable Player balloting and was voted the Associated Press Player of the Year and *Baseball Digest* Pitcher of the Year.

Martinez's success continued in 2000. He finished with 18 wins and 6 losses and compiled an AL-leading ERA (1.74), almost two runs per game better than his closest competitor. He led the AL in strikeouts (284) and shut-outs (4), was named to the AL All-Star team, and became the first AL pitcher to win successive Cy Young awards by unanimous vote.

Shoulder pain sidelined Martinez in 2001 from late June until early September. He was ineffective in several starts and finished 2001 with just seven victories, three losses, and a 2.39 ERA in 18 starts.

Martinez began an off-season training regimen that included weightlifting strengthening his shoulder and adding 10 pounds of muscle to his relatively small frame. He had a 20–4 record, with a 2.26 ERA, 239 strikeouts, and 40 walks in 199.1 innings pitched in 2002, finishing second in the AL Cy Young voting. Martinez led AL hurlers with a 2.22 ERA, ranked second with 206 strikeouts in just 186.2 innings, and won 14 of 18 decisions in 2003, helping the Red Sox capture the AL Wild Card and finishing third in the AL Cy Young Award balloting. He compiled a 1–0 record with a 3.86 ERA and nine strikeouts in the AL Division Series against the Oakland Athletics, but struggled with an 0–1 record and 5.65 ERA in the AL Championship Series against the New York Yankees. His beaning of Karim Garcia in Game 3 sparked altercations between the two clubs at Fenway Park. He surrendered a three run lead in the eighth inning of decisive Game 7 at Yankee Stadium.

Martinez has established himself as a team leader and keeps the team loose with his constant clubhouse and bench chattering. He has a large following among Hispanic fans, who come to Fenway Park with Dominican flags on days he is pitching.

In 11 major league seasons, Martinez has 166 wins and 67 losses, a 2.58 ERA, and 2,426 strikeouts. His dominance is attributed to masterful control of all three of his pitches and his willingness to throw any pitch on any count. Mark McGwire observed that "Martinez has such command of his pitches . . . you have no clue what he's going to do. That's not a good feeling."

Martinez is single. He enjoys gardening, loves young children, and quietly donates much of his time and money to charitable causes, particularly in the Dominican Republic.

BIBLIOGRAPHY
Tim Crothers, "The Inside Story," *Sports Illustrated* 86 (May 26, 1997), p. 82; Jack Etkin, "Pedro Martinez: A Little Guy Makes It Big Time," *Baseball Digest* 56 (No-

vember 1997), p. 34; Michael Farber, "The Case for Pedro Martinez," *Sports Illustrated* 87 (September 15, 1997), p. 84; Gary Graves, "All in Favor: Martinez Again Wins Cy Young," *USA Today* (November 14, 2000), p. C1; John Henderson, "Pitcher of the Year: Pedro Martinez Is King of the Hill," *Baseball Digest* 60 (January 2001), p. 24; Stephanie Myles, "Heating Up: At 27, Pedro Martinez Continues to Get Better," *Baseball Digest* 58 (September 1998), p. 24; Dan Shaughnessy, "Pitcher of the Year: Pedro Martinez," *Baseball Digest* 59 (January 2000), p. 24; Tom Verducci, "Martinez Mania," *Sports Illustrated* 83 (July 24, 1995), p. 26; Tom Verducci, "The Power of Pedro," *Sports Illustrated* 92 (March 27, 2000), p. 52.

Terry W. Sloope

CHERYL MILLER   Basketball
(January 3, 1964–   )

There have been many great women's basketball players, but none has been more decorated than Cheryl Miller.

Cheryl DeAnne Miller was born on January 3, 1964 in Riverside, California, the daughter of Saul Miller and Carrie Miller. Her father was selected an All-State high school basketball player in Tennessee and played forward at LeMoyne-Owen College, while her mother worked as a nurse. The Millers brought up five children, Saul Jr., Darrell, Tammy, Cheryl, and Reggie.* Miller's older brother, Darrell, played professional baseball with the California Angels (American League), while her younger brother, Reggie, starred in basketball with UCLA and the Indiana Pacers (National Basketball Association).

Miller enjoyed a supportive athletic-oriented childhood and starred at Riverside's Polytechnic High School from 1978 through 1982, lettering in basketball four straight years. She was the first four-time *Parade* All-America, male or female, to accomplish that feat. She was named *Street & Smith's* national High School Player of the Year in 1981 and 1982. In leading Polytechnic to an amazing 132–4 record, Miller averaged 32.8 points and 15.0 rebounds and captured national attention when she scored 105 points in a game against Notre Vista High School. She also played softball, maintained a 3.0 academic average, and finished runner-up for homecoming queen. Women's athletics began to emerge, following enactment of Title IX in 1972. She epitomized the grace, athletic potential, and promise of an approaching era.

Miller, recruited by 250 colleges, selected nearby University of Southern California (USC) and played basketball for coach Linda Sharp. The four-year, four-time All-American led her team to two National Collegiate Athletic Association (NCAA) national titles: over Louisiana Tech University 69–67 in 1983, and the University of Tennessee 72–61 in 1984. The Women Trojans compiled a cumulative 112–20 record. Miller set career records for points with 3,019 (23.6 average), rebounds with 1,534 (12.0 average), total field goals

Cheryl Miller ©Otto Greule, Jr./Getty Images

made, free throws made, steals with 700, and games played with 128. She won many conference honors, made the NCAA All-Tournament team three times, was voted NCAA Tournament Most Valuable Player (MVP) in 1983, was selected Naismith Player of the Year three times, won the Broderick Cup as the nation's best player in 1985 and 1986, and garnered the Wade Trophy her senior year. In 1986 she became the first female player nominated for the Sullivan Award. USC retired her number 31 jersey, making her the first Trojan athlete so honored.

The 6-foot 2-inch Miller represented the United States on many international basketball teams, including gold medal teams in the Pan American Games (1983), Los Angeles Olympic Games (1984), Goodwill Games (1986), and World Championships (1986). Leading the U.S. National team to its first Olympic gold medal ranked among Miller's biggest thrills in basketball, which she called "Cloud Nine." In 1984 she led the American team to the Women's Basketball Championship in Moscow, Russia. Miller served as commissioner for the 1985 Los Angeles Olympic Committee Summer Youth

Games and spokesperson for the Los Angeles Literacy Campaign, the American Lung, Diabetes, and Cancer associations, and the Muscular Dystrophy Association.

The fledgling National Women's Basketball Association drafted Miller on the first round in 1986 but folded the same year. During preparation for the Pan American Games, Miller sustained an injury that eventually ended her playing career.

Miller returned to USC as assistant basketball coach from 1986 through 1991 and then as head women's coach from 1993 to 1995. She directed the Trojans to a 44–14 record, collecting a Pac-10 conference title, making two NCAA tournament appearances, and reaching the Mideast Regional Final in 1994. Her first team finished 26–4 and held a high national ranking. "Coaching at USC was a great experience and I'll always have ties with the university," she remembered.

After earning a Bachelor's degree in sports journalism, Miller worked for ABC as a reporter on *Wide World of Sports* and as a commentator on college basketball telecasts. She joined Turner Sports in 1995 as a sideline reporter for TNT and TBS Superstation basketball games. In November 1996, she became the first female analyst to call a nationally televised NBA game. Miller also has been a commentator on ESPN.

Miller coached four seasons with the Phoenix Mercury (WNBA), compiling a 70–52 record from 1997 through 2000. Phoenix made the WNBA playoffs three of four seasons and reached the 1998 WNBA Finals, losing to the Houston Comets. Miller was the team's first coach/general manager and a big fan favorite. In her press release announcing her resignation, she stated, "I am the type of person who has to give 100 percent of myself, physically and emotionally, to each task I take on. And the grind of basically working 12 months a year for the last four seasons has taken a serious physical and emotional toll on me." Former college teammate, Cynthia Cooper,* replaced her as head basketball coach.

Besides being inducted into the International Women's Sports Hall of Fame in 1991, Miller was enshrined in the Naismith Basketball Hall of Fame in 1995 and in the inaugural class of the Women's Basketball Hall of Fame in 1999.

BIBLIOGRAPHY
Cheryl Miller file, Naismith Memorial Basketball Hall of Fame, Springfield, MA; David L. Porter, ed., *African-American Sports Greats* (Westport, CT, 1995); David L. Porter, ed., *Biographical Dictionary of American Sports: Basketball and Other Indoor Sports* (Westport, CT, 1989); Jeff Savage, "Cheryl Miller," *Top 10 Women's Basketball Stars*, 2001, pp. 34–37.

Dennis S. Clark

REGGIE MILLER
Basketball
(August 24, 1965–   )

Basketball writers describe Reggie Miller as a "pure shooter," "long-range bomber," or "shooting star."

Reginald Wayne Miller was born on August 24, 1965 in Riverside, California, the fourth of five children of Saul Miller and Carrie Miller. His father, a chief master sergeant in the United States Air Force, made All-State as a basketball player in Tennessee and played forward at LeMoyne-Owen College. His mother worked as a nurse. The Millers brought up five children, Saul Jr., Darrell, Tammy, Cheryl,* and Reggie. Reggie Miller's older brother, Darrell, played professional baseball with the California Angels, while his precocious older sister, Cheryl, starred in college and international basketball. "My family was almost perfect," he recalled. "I was very lucky."

Miller suffered from a congenital deformity of the hips and was required to wear leg braces until age 4. His father initially restricted him from outside play but encouraged him to play basketball. In backyard competitions, Miller was dominated by his tall sister, Cheryl. He consequently developed a high arching shot, which became his shooting signature. At Polytechnical High School in Riverside, Miller did not draw major college attention until his senior year in 1983. He averaged almost 30 points and 10 rebounds and led his school to the California Interscholastic Federation (CIF) 3A championship, averaging 36 points in the playoffs. He was named CIF 3A Player of the Year. "He reminds me of Walter Davis and tore up my league as much as anyone ever has," observed Greg Katz, director of the U.S. Olympic Basketball Development League.

The slender 6-foot 7-inch, 180-pound Miller made UCLA his college choice. Although a reserve in his freshman season, he excelled as the Bruins' best long-range shooter. In 1984–1985, he started at small forward and helped UCLA under coach Walt Hazzard win 12 of their last 13 games and a National Invitation Tournament (NIT) Championship. Miller was selected as the tournament's Most Valuable Player (MVP). UCLA struggled in his junior season, but he averaged 25.9 points, fourth in the nation. He also set a Bruin record with 202 free throws. His scoring average dropped to 22.3 points as a senior, but UCLA won the Pac 10 Conference Championship, made the National Collegiate Athletic Association (NCAA) tournament, and finished with a 25–7 record. He shot 54 percent from the field, made 83 percent of his free throws, averaged 5.4 rebounds, and recorded 71 assists and 64 steals. Upon leaving UCLA, Miller ranked second all-time in career scoring behind Kareem Abdul-Jabbar. Miller shot a remarkable 54 percent from the field and 43 percent from three-point range for his collegiate career. Magic Johnson* of the Los Angeles Lakers included Miller in pickup games with other professional players.

The Indiana Pacers (National Basketball Association) drafted Miller as the eleventh overall pick in the 1987 NBA draft. He has spent his entire 17-year career with Indiana, averaging around 20 points. The high-voltage off guard has made Indiana contenders in the Eastern Conference and holds many Pacer all-time game and career records. His best game came against the Charlotte Hornets in November 1992, when he scored 57 points, made 16 field goals, and converted 21 of 23 free-throw attempts. The NBA playoffs have brought out his best performances. In 1994 Miller scored 25 points in the fourth quarter against the New York Knicks. In the 2001 playoffs, he averaged 31.2 points. The Pacers, however, reached the NBA finals only once during his career and have never won a championship. Despite his NBA accomplishments Miller may be better known for his crowd-baiting and cocky attitude. One writer called him the king of "flash and trash" (talking). "I love being the villain," he replied.

Through the 2002–2003 season, Miller has scored 23,505 points, made 7,667 field goals and 2,330 three-point goals, and collected 3,838 rebounds, 3,746 assists, and 1,390 steals in 1,243 games. He remains the most prolific three-point scorer in NBA history. Besides being selected to the All-NBA Third Team three times in 1995, 1996, and 1998, he has appeared in five NBA All-Star games. Miller, a major contributor to Dream Team II, helped the United States win the gold medal in the 1996 Atlanta, Georgia, Olympic Games. USA Basketball named Miller Male Athlete of the Year in 2002.

The Southern California resident has made cameo appearances in two movies, *He Got Game* and *Forget Paris*. He has also appeared on television shows and provided sideline reporting on WNBA games for Lifetime in 2000. He established the Reggie Miller Foundation to aid fire victims, served as the national spokesperson for Reading Is Fundamental, and was honored by Make-A-Wish Foundation for his work with terminally ill children.

BIBLIOGRAPHY
Blue Ribbon College Basketball Yearbook, 1983–1984, 1984–1985, 1985–1986, 1986–1987, 1987–1988; Judith Graham, ed., *Current Biography Yearbook 1996* (New York, 1996), pp. 370–374; Player Profile, *Reggie Miller/31*, www.nba.com/ playerfile; "Reggie Miller," www.nba.com, playerfile/reggie_miller/printable_ playr_files.html; "Reggie Miller," *Yahoo!Sports*, www.sports.yahoo.com/nba/players/ 2/231.

Dennis J. Clark

JUAN MONTOYA   Auto Racing
(September 20, 1975–)

Juan Montoya captured the 1999 Championship Auto Racing Teams (CART) title and the 2000 Indianapolis 500.

Juan Pablo Montoya was born on September 20, 1975 in Bogotá, Colombia, the son of Pablo Montoya, an architect and former go-kart racer, and Libia

Montoya, and grew up in and attended school there. He has a brother, Frederico, and two sisters, Liliana and Katalina. Montoya began his racing career in go-karting at age 5 and in 1984 captured Colombia's Children's Division National Championship. He finished second in 1985 and registered Kart Championships in local and national competition the following two years. In 1990 and 1991 he won the Kart Junior World Championship racing in Italy and Spain.

Montoya began racing cars at age 17 after receiving a scholarship to the Skip Barber Driving School in the United States. He continued to race in Colombia but competed internationally. He registered four victories in the Copa Formula Renault in Colombia and won seven poles and seven races in the GTI National Championship.

In 1995 Montoya drove for the Paul Stewart Racing Team and finished third overall in the British Formula Vauxhall Championship. He moved to the more competitive British Formula 3 series, winning three races and one pole position in this Series in 1996. He also triumphed in the Bogotá Six Hours in his hometown. Montoya advanced to Formula 3000 in 1997 and drove with the RSM Marko Racing Team, which had taken a rookie to the title one year earlier. He won three races but lost the title by just 1.5 points to a strong team. He returned in 1998 for the second opportunity to win the Formula 3000 Championship and was supported this time by the Super Nova Team, the 1997 winner. Montoya won the pole in the season opener, but a lottery was used and his car was placed last. He found it difficult to make up the difference. He finished on the podium in seven of eight races. Montoya captured the Formula 3000 Championship by earning seven poles and four victories during the 12-race series. He became the test driver for the Winfield Williams Racing Team in Formula 1. When CART Champion Alex Zinardi joined the Williams Team for 1999 as an experienced Formula 1 driver, Montoya was bypassed. Nevertheless, he was named Colombia's 1998 Sportsman of the Year.

Upon joining the Chip Ganassi Racing Team in 1999, Montoya came to the United States to compete in the CART FedEx Series. He won his first race after just four attempts and built up a substantial point lead. After suffering a midseason slump, he fought off the challenges of drivers Dario Franchetti and Paul Tracy to win the championship. Although he tied Franchetti for total points, Montoya was crowned the CART Champion because of his seven victories to three for Franchetti. Montoya won the CART Championship in his first attempt. The Colombian was the youngest champion ever at age 24 and twice threatened the CART record of four straight victories. Racing on Chip Ganassi's new track in Chicago, Illinois, he won his sixth race of the series and broke the legendary Nigel Mansell's record for wins by a rookie.

Montoya returned to the CART Series in 2000 to defend his title, but the team changed its package to the unproven Lola-Toyota. Montoya won seven poles and recorded victories in the Miller Lite 225, the Michigan 500, and the Motorola 220, but soon fell out of contention for the title. After Montoya

Juan Montoya ©Courtesy of Indianapolis Speedway

won the CART Championship in 1999, the Indianapolis 500 remained the only triumph he had not accomplished in U.S. racing. For the first time, CART left an opening in its schedule over Memorial Day and allowed the teams to compete in the Indianapolis Classic. Only Ganassi's team crossed over. Montoya easily won the race at an average speed of 167.067 miles per hour in his first attempt. He dominated the race and was named the Indianapolis 500 Rookie of the Year. Otherwise, he did not have an outstanding racing year. He led more laps than any other driver but suffered numerous mechanical failures and wrecks and finished ninth in the CART standings.

Montoya returned to the Formula 1 circuit in 2001. He did not enjoy a successful year. He started 17 races in that year but won only the Italian Grand Prix and finished second in three other events. He ranked third in the Formula 1 Standings with 50 points in 2002, edging Rolf Schumacher and David Coulthard. Montoya placed fourth in the U.S. Grand Prix and Japan Grand Prix. Racing experts expect Montoya to be the next Michael Schumacher, the five-time world champion in Formula 1 racing. Montoya finished third behind Michael Schumacher and Kimi Raikkonen in the 2003 Formula 1 Standings, winning at Monte Carlo in June and at Hockenheim, Germany in August. Montoya has an aggressive driving style, but he must master the mental and technical aspects of the sport.

Montoya is single and enjoys playing golf and squash and listening to music.

BIBLIOGRAPHY

"Juan Montoya," *Career Highlights*, www.jpmontoya.com (2001); "Juan Montoya," *Driver Biography*, www.formula1.com (2001); "Juan Montoya," *Profile*, www. autosport.com (2001); "Juan Montoya," *Driver Racing Card*, www.target/ chipganassi.com (1999); "Juan Montoya," *Racing Record-2000*, www.ccnsi.com (2001); *Sports Illustrated Sports Almanac*, 2001; *USA Today*, June 12, 2001, p. 8C.
                                                                                                    John L. Evers

RANDY MOSS   Football
(February 13, 1977–   )

Randy Moss stands among the National Football League's (NFL) most exciting players at the wide receiver position.

Randy Moss was born in Rand, West Virginia, on February 13, 1977. His mother, Maxine Moss, a nurse's aide, brought up Randy, his brother, Eric, and his sister, Latisia. His father, Randy Pratt, had little contact with the family. Maxine Moss credits her dedication to Randy for much of his success. "I'm everything. A lot of people see Randy as an outstanding athlete, but when I see him, I see a young woman who's poured her life into him so he could have a life." At DuPont High School in Belle, West Virginia, Moss participated in baseball, basketball, football, and track and field. He was selected twice as West Virginia's Mr. Basketball. He lettered twice in baseball, attracting pro scouts as a center fielder, and in track and field, where he easily won conference and state titles. He lettered three times in basketball and track and field and was named West Virginia High School Player of the Year in football.

Moss was awarded a football scholarship at the University of Notre Dame but lost it when he pleaded guilty to two charges of battery for kicking a schoolmate during his senior year in high school. Florida State University offered Moss a scholarship. He redshirted his freshman year at Florida State, but in 1996 he tested positive for marijuana and was involved in a domestic dispute with his girlfriend. Moss was removed from the Florida State team and transferred to Marshall University in Huntington, West Virginia. During his freshman season, he caught 28 touchdown passes for 1,709 yards. His 28

Randy Moss ©Rick Kolodzie/Minnesota Vikings

touchdown catches marked the most by a freshman in National Collegiate Athletic Association (NCAA) history. Marshall enjoyed an undefeated season and won the Division I-AA football title against the University of Montana. Moss also competed in the Southern Conference Indoor Track and Field Championship, winning the 55-meter and 200-meter titles. The next football season, Marshall moved into the Mid American Conference at the Division I-AA level.

In his two seasons at Marshall, Moss made 174 receptions for 3,529 yards and 54 touchdowns. As a sophomore, he won the Biletnikoff Award as the best receiver in college football, finished fourth in Heisman Trophy voting, and was voted First Team All-America. He entered the 1998 National Football League (NFL) draft and was projected a top 5 pick. Because of his off-the-field troubles, however, many teams were hesitant to select him. He became the twenty-first overall pick by the Minnesota Vikings (NFL).

As a rookie, Moss led the NFL with 17 touchdown receptions. He caught 69 passes for 1,313 yards, averaging 19 yards per catch. He started in the 1999 Pro Bowl and was voted to *The Sporting News* (*TSN*) All-Pro and Associated Press (NP) All-Pro teams. Moss won numerous honors as a rookie, being named Offensive Rookie of the Year by *College & Pro Football Weekly* and *Football Digest*. He was selected Professional Football Writers of America National Football Conference (NFC) Rookie of the Year and won Rookie of the Year honors from *TSN, Sports Illustrated* and *The Football News and Weekly*. His brother, Eric, also played with the Vikings during Moss's rookie year. Former Vikings coach Denny Green praises Moss, "He is truly a great competitor. That is what I like best about him. He loves to compete, he loves to win."

The next season, Moss established a Vikings single-season receiving record with 1,413 yards, breaking the previous mark of 1,371 yards set by teammate Cris Carter.* Moss again made the Pro Bowl and was named MVP of the 2000 Pro Bowl with nine receptions for 212 yards. Seattle Seahawks coach Mike Holmgren proclaimed "Moss the scariest man in football and the best player, talentwise. You hold your breath every time they snap the ball. You just can't give him free access off the ball. He has such great focus and he plays the underthrown ball so well." *TSN* chose Moss as the best on its annual list of top 100 players and boasted that he made the "biggest single dramatic impact" in football.

Fans really like Moss, making his number 84 uniform the nation's hottest selling jersey. Vikings merchandise rose from twenty-fourth to fourteenth in the NFL. Vikings general manager Tim Connolly claimed, "Randy Moss is exactly what the NFL needs." In July 2001, Moss signed a $75 million contract extension, an eight-year deal with an $18 million bonus. In November 2001, he surprised his teammates and fans when he acknowledged, "I play when I want to play. Do I play up to my top performance, my ability, every time? Maybe not . . . case closed." His productivity decreased in 2001 with 82 catches for 1,233 yards and only 10 touchdowns. Moss was arrested in September 2002 for slowly pushing a police officer down a Minneapolis, Minnesota, street with his Lexus after she tried to prevent him from making an illegal turn. He was charged with two misdemeanors and released. He made the Pro Bowl again in 2002, making 106 receptions for 1,347 yards (12.7-yard average) and seven touchdowns. His career numbers remain impressive. He has made 414 receptions for 6,743 yards, averaging 16.3 yards per catch, and he has scored 60 touchdowns.

Moss works with the Twin Cities community through Randy's Purple Pioneers, a community service group he heads. He still enjoys playing basketball and played three games in the Southern California Summer Pro League, scoring 13 points and 6 rebounds. He has one daughter, Sydney, and one son, Thaddeus.

BIBLIOGRAPHY
Paul Attner, "As Great as He Wants to Be," *The Sporting News*, November 16, 1998, pp. 14–19; Paul Attner, "Ugly Solution to Moss Hysteria," *The Sporting News*, Jan-

uary 15, 2001, pp. 18–23; Peter King, "Cruise Control," *Sports Illustrated* 95 (December 17, 2001), pp. 128–130; Jack McCallum, "Moss Appeal," *Sports Illustrated* 90 (January 18, 1999), pp. 54–58; Dan Pompei and Steve Walentik, "Moss Appeal," *The Sporting News* 255, September 10, 2001, pp. 8–13; S.L. Price, "Cut Off from the Herd," *Sports Illustrated* 87 (August 25, 1997), pp. 130–140; Michael J. Watkins, "Randy Moss," in David A. Oblender, ed., *Contemporary Black Biography*, vol. 23 (Detroit, MI, 2000), pp. 141–143.

Maureen M. Smith

ALONZO MOURNING   Basketball
(February 8, 1970–   )

Alonzo Mourning ranks among the best defensive players in the National Basketball Association (NBA).

Alonzo Harding Mourning Jr., nicknamed "Zoo," was born on February 8, 1970 in Chesapeake, Virginia, and grew up as the only son of Alonzo Mourning Sr., a machinist in the shipyards, and Julia Mourning, a devout Jehovah's Witness. The tension between his parents led to their divorce. He left home at age 11 and lived in a group home for about a year. He became one of 49 children brought up by foster parent Fannie Threet until completing high school. "She taught me how to be a young man," Mourning recalled. He started playing basketball at age 13, practicing all of the time and in all weather conditions.

Bill Lassiter, his coach at Indian River High School in Chesapeake, became a guiding force in Mourning's life. He traveled as a consultant with Mourning's Amateur Athletic Union basketball team, Mourning became the only high school basketball player invited to the 1988 Olympic Trials. Indian River High School won 51 consecutive games and the 1987 Virginia Class AAA Championship, as Mourning received numerous recruiting offers.

Mourning played basketball at Georgetown University under coach John Thompson, another father figure. Mourning performed for the Hoyas between 1988–1989 and 1991–1992, leading the National Collegiate Athletic Association (NCAA) Division I with 4.97 blocked shots per game in 1989. A consensus First Team All-America in 1992 and a Second Team All-America in 1990, he led Georgetown to four straight NCAA Division I Tournament appearances. Georgetown advanced to the NCAA Regional Finals in 1989 before losing to Duke University, 85–77. Mourning finished his college career as the all-time Division I leader in blocked shots. As a senior, he averaged 21.3 points, 10.7 rebounds, and 5.0 blocked shots and became the first Big East Conference player to earn Player of the Year, Defensive Player of the Year, and Tournament MVP the same season. He received a Bachelor's degree in sociology in 1992.

The Charlotte Hornets (NBA) selected Mourning in the first round as the second pick overall of the 1992 NBA draft. Mourning played with the Hornets four seasons before being traded with LeRon Ellis and Pete Myers to the

Miami Heat (NBA) for Glen Rice, Khalid Reeves, Matt Geiger, and a 1996 first-round draft choice in November 1995. He made the NBA All-Rookie First Team, finishing runner-up to Shaquille O'Neal* for the NBA Rookie of the Year. In his first season with Charlotte, Mourning established a franchise record with 271 blocked shots. In 1993 he led the Hornets to their first ever playoff appearance, advancing to the Eastern Conference (EC) semifinals. Mourning was named to the NBA All-Star team five times from 1994 to 1997 and in 2000. The following summer, he played on the USA Basketball World Championship team and helped the United States win a gold medal. In 1995–1996, he led the Heat in scoring, rebounding, and blocked shots.

Mourning, one of the most hated NBA players, intimidated fans, players, writers, and officials. He was labeled arrogant, conceited, and ready to fight. He claims that his critics do not understand him and are misled by his actions: "I cannot control. I cannot change the way I play. My intensity is part of my game."

The 6-foot 10-inch, 261-pound Mourning led Miami in 1996–1997 to a club record 61 victories, advancing to the EC Finals. Besides leading the NBA in blocked shots and averaging a team-high 20.1 points and a career-high 11.0 rebounds, Mourning finished second behind Karl Malone* in the Most Valuable Player (MVP) voting. He was named Defensive Player of the Year in 1998–1999 and made the All-NBA First Team and All-Defensive First Team. In the 1999–2000 season, Mourning averaged 21.7 points, set a career high with 294 blocked shots, was named NBA Defensive Player of the Year, and made the NBA All-Defensive First Team and the All-NBA Second Team. The following year, Mourning was diagnosed with a kidney disease that sidelined him the entire season. Although not cured, he surprisingly returned to the Miami roster in March 2001 and appeared in 13 regular-season games and three playoff games. Mourning played in 75 regular season games in 2001–2002, scoring 1,178 points (15.7 point average) and blocking 186 shots for the struggling Miami Heat. His kidney disease leaves him susceptible to illnesses that can sometimes sideline him for weeks at a time and sidelined him for the 2002–2003 season. In July 2003, the New Jersey Nets (NBA) signed Mourning to a $20 million, four year contract. He played 12 games in 2003–2004 before the need for a kidney transplant forced him to retire from the NBA.

In 11 NBA seasons from 1992–1993 through 2003–2004, Mourning compiled 12,710 career points (20-point average), collected 6,137 rebounds (9.7 average), and blocked 1,889 shots (3.0 average) in 634 regular season games. Mourning tallied 15 points and seven rebounds as a starter in the 2000 NBA All-Star Game and 13 points in the 2002 NBA All-Star Game. In 55 NBA playoff games, he registered 1,095 points and 524 rebounds and averaged 19.9 points and 9.50 caroms.

Mourning and Tracy Wilson began dating as college freshmen and were married in 1997. They have a son, Alonzo III (Trey), and a daughter, Myka. His wife explains, "Yes, he can be testy, but his passion spills into everything he does, and his ups are more memorable than his downs."

BIBLIOGRAPHY
"Alonzo Mourning," *Players Background*, www.nba.com (2001); "Alonzo Mourning," *Players Career Highlights*, www.nba.com (2001); "Alonzo Mourning," *Players Career Statistics*, www.nba.com (2001); *NCAA Men's Basketball's Finest* (Overland Park, KS, 1998); S. L. Price, "The Man in the Iron Mask," *Sports Illustrated* 13 (March 30, 1998), pp. 72–78, 80–83; *The Sporting News Official NBA Register*, 2003–2004; Phil Taylor, "Say, Ain't It Zo?" *Sports Illustrated* 15 (April 9, 2001), pp. 54–55.

John L. Evers

ANTHONY MUNOZ   Football
(August 19, 1958–)

Anthony Munoz was anxious to start the 1979 football season. He hoped that his senior year at the University of Southern California (USC) would produce another National Championship and an Outland Trophy. He had appeared headed toward accomplishing these goals in 1978 when a knee injury sidelined him. The dream evaporated in the first game of the 1979 campaign when the 6-foot 6-inch, 280-pound tackle suffered another knee injury. But through diligence and faith, he played in the 1980 Rose Bowl against Ohio State University and cleared a path for the winning touchdown. This obstacle, however, was not the first this Mexican American had overcome.

Michael Anthony Munoz was born on August 19, 1958 in Ontario, California, the middle child of five siblings. His family struggled, as Esther Munoz brought up her children alone. Financially, these were difficult years, but Munoz recalled "We were provided for, but we didn't have any extras." He channeled his energies into the classroom and sports. His first love was baseball, but he also played basketball and football at Chaffey High School in Ontario. His bulk and skill eventually drew him to the gridiron. When he graduated in 1976, he signed with USC.

At USC, Munoz did not display all his abilities because of three knee injuries. The reduced playing time, however, did not diminish predictions of greatness. John Robinson, the head coach, declared, "Munoz is the best offensive tackle in America right now. He's one of the greatest football players I've ever been associated with at any position." Munoz lettered in football from 1976 to 1979, participated on a National Championship baseball team as a pitcher in 1978, earned Second Team United Press International All-America football honors in 1978, was named to the First Team All Pac-10 football squad in 1978, and graduated with a Bachelor's degree in public administration in 1980. Although he was huge, his legs were badly damaged. Ominously, he failed 14 physicals prior to the 1980 National Football League (NFL) draft.

The Cincinnati Bengals, a perennial also-ran from the American Football Conference (AFC) Central division, showed interest in Munoz. Paul Brown, the Bengals' legendary founder, liked what he saw at the 1980 Rose Bowl and so dispatched newly hired head coach Forrest Gregg to Los Angeles to look at this potential draft pick. During the scrimmage, Munoz knocked the coach on his rear. Gregg knew he had found his left tackle. The Bengals made him their first pick (third overall) in the first round of the 1980 NFL draft. The local media questioned drafting a player who had undergone several knee surgeries. In addition, Munoz held out briefly before reporting to camp.

The Bengals ironed out their differences with Munoz, starting one of the most impressive careers ever by an NFL lineman. Munoz became a starter in his first season and was named to the All-Rookie team. He was named All-Pro for 11 consecutive years from 1981 to 1991, anchoring an offensive line that took Cincinnati to the 1981 and 1989 Super Bowls. Munoz also caught four touchdown passes on tackle eligible plays. He was named to the All-NFL team of the 1980s and to the NFL's 75th Anniversary All-Time Team in 1994. A damaged shoulder and recurring knee problems prompted his retirement after the 1992 season. He was enshrined in the Pro Football Hall of Fame in 1998.

Munoz has distinguished himself by caring for the less fortunate. He has worked with youth groups, the Salvation Army, and the Cystic Fibrosis Foundation and has made missionary trips to Mexico on behalf of his church. He and his wife, DeDe, have two children, Michael and Michelle. The offspring continue the family's ties to sport, though at the University of Tennessee. Michael plays offensive tackle for the Volunteers, and Michelle committed herself to play basketball for Pat Summit's Lady Volunteers during her junior year in high school. Still, Anthony and DeDe Munoz are happiest with the moral aspects of their children's lives. "Athletics are nice," Munoz affirmed, "but character and integrity are the things we want from them the most." With a loving family, strong faith, enshrinement in the Pro Football Hall of Fame, and a potential future in broadcasting, Munoz achieved his life's goals on the field and off.

BIBLIOGRAPHY
Jim Bryant, "Anthony Munoz: The Living Legend of Ontario," *Ontario Daily Report*, pp. 9, 15; "Feature on Anthony Muñoz," www.profootballhof.com/players/enshrinees/amunoz.cfm; Nancy Mazmaniam, "Anthony Munoz: A Success in Any Uniform," *Touchdown Illustrated* (October 23, 1982), pp. 31–34; Michael Weinrob, "Heart, Soul & Knees: Ontario's Anthony Munoz Quelled Doubts about Physical Problems to Achieve Football Fame," *Ontario Press-Enterprise*, pp. C1, C9.

Jorge Iber

DAN O'BRIEN

Track and Field

(July 18, 1966–   )

Dan O'Brien has broken several decathlon records.

Daniel Dion O'Brien was born on July 18, 1966 in Portland, Oregon, of an African American father and half-Finnish mother, both college professors. His parents, Jim and Virginia O'Brien of Klamath Falls, Oregon, adopted him when he was two years old.

Upon entering Henley High School, O'Brien was a small, skinny youth with wide-ranging interests. He played trumpet in the school band, participated in the chess club, and tried out for school plays. His parents did not let him play football until his sophomore year, but he loved playing basketball and still enjoys playing a pickup game. He lettered in football, basketball, and track and field in high school.

O'Brien's dream of becoming an Olympic athlete was kindled in 1980, when he watched the underdog American ice hockey team win the gold medal against the Soviet Union team. O'Brien was not born a "great athlete," nor does he think most sport stars are really good without much hard work. "When an athlete achieves success," he said, "it is a small moment in time compared to what it took to get there. The hardest part is the journey."

O'Brien started lifting weights and conducting regular workouts in high school because he enjoyed it. He advises that "you have to be willing to do the work if you want success . . . I love the every day training. I keep working, sweating, and pushing the envelope because I enjoy it." But he warns, "don't let sports consume you"; there is more to life.

After graduating from Henley High School in 1984, O'Brien attended the University of Idaho and Spokane Community College. His prospects of becoming a champion, however, were seriously endangered when he began abusing alcohol. When he finally turned away from the party scene and dedicated himself to becoming the world's best decathlete, he surprised those who had given up on him.

For several years, O'Brien played second fiddle to Dave Johnson, another great American decathlete. In 1991 at age 25, O'Brien finally captured the USA Track and Field and World Decathlon Championships. He was favored to win the decathlon gold medal at the 1992 Barcelona, Spain, Olympics, but

Dan O'Brien ©Andy Lyons/Getty Images

had no height in his opening pole vault attempt and so failed to make the Olympic team. He was relegated to television commentary at the Barcelona Olympics.

On September 4–5, 1992 at Talance, France, O'Brien got his revenge when he set the world record for the decathlon with 8,891 points to become one of the best decathletes of all time. He won a gold medal in the 1996 Olympics at Atlanta, Georgia. He captured the U.S. Decathlon Championships from 1993 through 1996, the World Championships in 1993 and 1995, the Goodwill Games Championships in 1994 and 1998, and the International Amateur Athletic Federation (IAAF) Heptathlon Championship in 1993. He also set the world record in the men's heptathlon in 1993. Although he underwent knee surgery in 1999, O'Brien still competed in 2000. A dream and the spirit to overcome adversity and persist in day-to-day training made O'Brien a world champion.

BIBLIOGRAPHY

Gerald Lawson, *World Record Breakers in Track & Field Athletics* (Champaign, IL, 1997); Dick Patrick, "O'Brien Sets Course for 'Greatest' Tag," *USA Today*, August 4, 1992, pp. C1–C2; David L. Porter, ed., *African-American Sports Greats* (Westport, CT, 1995); Bob Schoner, ed., *The Olympic Dream and Spirit*, 1 (Grand Island, NE: 2000).

Keith McClellan

HAKEEM OLAJUWON   Basketball
(January 21, 1963–   )

Hakeem Olajuwon was the greatest African-born player in National Basketball Association (NBA) history.

Hakeem Abdul Olajuwon, nicknamed "The Dream," was born on January 21, 1963 in Lagos, Nigeria, one of five children of Salam Olajuwon and Abike Olajuwon, middle-class Muslims who operate a cement business in Lagos. Olajuwon at age 13 attended Muslim Teacher's College, where he excelled in soccer, team handball, field hockey, and track and field. He received an excellent education and learned to speak English, French, and four Nigerian dialects. He began playing basketball at age 15 when the handball team could not find competitors. Over the next two years, he learned the game from capable Nigerian coaches and improved enough to compete with the Lagos State team.

An American coached the Central African team and befriended Olajuwon. Christopher Pond recommended him to coach Guy V. Lewis at the University of Houston in Texas. In 1980 Olajuwon began attending Houston and played basketball for the Cougars. He was redshirted as a freshman and teamed with Clyde Drexler* and Larry Micheaux in 1981–1982 to form "Phi Slama Jama." They popularized the "Slam Dunk" with their dramatic, spectacular, and acrobatic attack on the basket. Olajuwon's tremendous strength and size was balanced by his unbelievable agility, individual moves around the basket, and shooting accuracy. During his three years at Houston, Olajuwon led the Cougars to a 88–16 won-lost record, two Southwest Conference Championships, and three consecutive trips to the National Collegiate Athletic Association (NCAA) Division I Final Four. In 1982 Houston lost 68–63 to the University of North Carolina. In 1983 the Cougars were upset on the final shot by the North Carolina State University's Wolfpack, 54–52, in the NCAA Championship Game. The following year, the Cougars lost to Georgetown University, 53–40, in the NCAA Championship Game.

At Houston, Olajuwon compiled 1,332 points (13.3-point average) and 1,067 rebounds (10.7 average). In 15 Division I Tournament games, he averaged 10.2 rebounds and 15.1 points. In 1984 Olajuwon, named the 1983 NCAA Tournament's Most Valuable Player (MVP), made consensus First Team All-America, was named to the NCAA All-Tournament Team, led the nation with a .675 field goal percentage, and averaged 13.5 rebounds and 5.6 blocked shots. He paced all NCAA Tournament players in rebounding in 1983 and 1984.

At the University of Houston, Olajuwon fell in love with Lita Spencer, a pre-law student at nearby Rice University. They later began living together. In July 1988, she gave birth to a daughter, Abisola. Because of their different religious beliefs, they never married and later separated. "I wanted her to become Muslim," Olajuwon explained. "But she is a Christian and felt she could not leave her religion." Lita agreed to have Abisola, who lives with her, brought up as a Muslim. Olajuwon married Dalia Asafi on August 8, 2000. They have two daughters, Rahmah and Aisha.

Olajuwon entered the 1984 NBA draft and was selected by the Houston Rockets (NBA) as the first pick overall. The 7-foot 255-pound center played 17 seasons with the Rockets and led Houston to the NBA playoffs 15 times in 17 seasons. In 1986 he teamed with 7-foot 4-inch Ralph Sampson to power the Rockets to the NBA Finals, only to lose to the Boston Celtics in six games. He and Sampson both averaged more than 20.0 points and 10.0 rebounds during that season, becoming the first duo to accomplish this feat since Wilt Chamberlain and Elgin Baylor of the Los Angeles Lakers in 1970.

In his first NBA season, Olajuwon was named to the All-Rookie First Team and finished runner-up to Michael Jordan* for Rookie of the Year honors. Olajuwon became the eighth NBA player to record 20,000 career points and 12,000 career rebounds. In 1993–1994, he became the only player in NBA history to win the regular season MVP Award, Defensive Player of the Year Award, and the NBA Finals MVP. Olajuwon was selected as the Defensive Player of the Year in 1992–1993 and NBA Finals MVP in 1995. He made the All-Defensive First Team in 1987, 1988, 1990, 1993, and 1994 and the All-Defensive Second Team in 1985, 1991, 1996, and 1997. He made the All-NBA Second Team in 1986, 1990, and 1996, the All-NBA First Team from 1987 to 1989, and in 1993, 1994, and 1997, and the All-NBA Third Team in 1991, 1995, and 1999.

Olajuwon led the Rockets to consecutive NBA Championships in 1994 and 1995. In 1994 Houston defeated the New York Knicks in seven games for the franchise's first NBA title and defended its title the next season with a four-game sweep of the Orlando Magic. Olajuwon averaged 28.9 points against the Knicks and 33.0 points against the Magic, earning him MVP honors in both battles.

Olajuwon played in 12 NBA All-Star games between 1985 and 1990 and between 1992 and 1997, starting eight times and averaging 9.8 points, 7.8 rebounds, and 1.92 blocked shots. In 1993 he received the IBM Award for all-around contributions to the team's success. Olajuwon, who had become an American citizen in 1993, was selected to the 1996 U.S. Dream Team III, which won a gold medal at the Atlanta, Georgia, Olympic Games. That same year, Olajuwon was named to the NBA's 50th Anniversary All-Time Team. The University of Houston retired his jersey number 34 on February 12, 1997. On January 27, 1999, he was inducted into the Texas Sports Hall of Fame. The Toronto Raptors (NBA) acquired him in August 2001. He retired following the 2001–2002 season.

In 18 NBA seasons, Olajuwon compiled 26,946 career points (seventh on the NBA All-Time list), averaged 21.8 points, collected 13,748 rebounds (11th), and averaged 11.1 boards in 1,238 regular season games. Olajuwon recorded 3,830 blocked shots (1st) for a 3.18 average, 3,058 assists, and 2,162 steals. He became the first NBA player to accumulate 2,000 blocked shots and 2,000 steals. He leads the Houston franchise in all-time scoring, rebounding, steals, and blocked shots.

In 145 NBA playoff games, Olajuwon compiled 3,755 points for seventh on the NBA's all-time list, ranks sixth with a 25.9-point average, and posted 1,621 rebounds and 472 blocked shots. After Houston's first NBA Championship, Olajuwon explained, "You must be enjoying what you are doing in life, not trying to do something to enjoy life. It's the journey, not the destination, that matters."

BIBLIOGRAPHY
Hakeem Olajuwon and Peter Knobler, *Living a Dream* (New York, 1996); "Hakeem Olajuwon," *Players Background*, www.nba.com (2001); "Hakeem Olajuwon," *Players Career Highlights*, www.nba.com (2001); "Hakeem Olajuwon," *Players Career Statistics*, www.nba.com (2001); *NCAA Men's Basketball's Finest* (Overland Park, KS, 1998); David L. Porter, ed., *African-American Sports Greats* (Westport, CT, 1995); *The Sporting News Official NBA Register*, 2002–2003.

John L. Evers

SHAQUILLE O'NEAL   Basketball
(March 6, 1972–   )

Shaquille O'Neal ranks among the most dominant players in National Basketball Association (NBA) history.

Shaquille Rashaun O'Neal, nicknamed "Shaq," was born on March 6, 1972 in Newark, New Jersey, one of four children of Phillip Harrison, a career Army drill sergeant, and Lucille O'Neal. Since his parents were not married at the time of his birth, his mother gave him her name. The children grew up on army bases in New Jersey, Georgia, Germany, and Texas. By age 13, O'Neal had grown to 6 feet 5 inches. When the family returned to the United States permanently, Harrison was stationed at Fort Sam Houston in San Antonio, Texas.

As a 15-year-old junior in 1987, O'Neal enrolled in the Robert G. Cole High School. He led the basketball team to a 32–1 won-lost record, suffering his only loss in the State Tournament. Cole won the State Tournament his senior year, finishing the season with a perfect 36–0 won-lost record. That year, O'Neal averaged 32.1 points, 22 rebounds, and 8 blocked shots. He was named to the *Parade* magazine All-America Team and was selected the Most Valuable Player (MVP) in the McDonald's All-Star Game and the Dapper Dan Classic.

After being offered a basketball scholarship by coach Dale Brown, O'Neal entered Louisiana State University in 1989. Brown described the 7-foot 1-inch, 295-pound center as an athlete with a tremendous work ethic and good attitude, who could run the court like a guard. O'Neal possessed the tenacity to pull down rims and played a hard intimidating game. In 1989, he led the Southeastern Conference (SEC) in rebounds and set a season record for most blocked shots. As a sophomore, O'Neal was selected to the All-America First

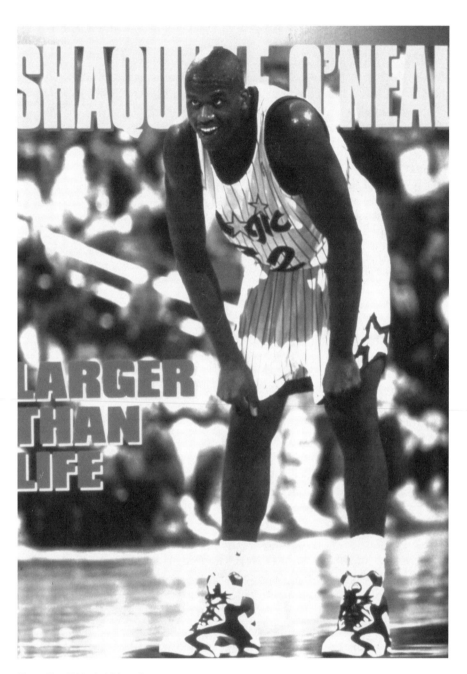

Shaquille O'Neal ©Photofest

Team and was named College Player of the Year by the Associated Press, United Press International, and *The Sporting News*. He was also chosen the SEC Player and Athlete of the Year, averaging 27.6 points, leading the nation in rebounds, setting a sophomore national record for blocked shots, and becoming the first player ever to lead the SEC in scoring, rebounding, field goal percentage, and blocked shots during the same season. As a junior, he paced the nation in blocked shots, ranked second nationally in rebounds, and made All-America and SEC Player of the Year for the second straight year. He was named National Player of the Year by L.A. Gear and finished runner-up for both the Naismith and Wooden awards.

O'Neal appeared in three National Collegiate Athletic Association (NCAA) Division I National Tournaments but lost in the first or second round each time. In five NCAA Tournament games, he averaged 24 points and 13.2 rebounds. In 80 regular season games, he averaged 21.6 points and 13.5 rebounds.

At the end of his junior year, O'Neal entered the 1992 NBA draft. The Orlando Magic (NBA) selected him in the first round as the first pick overall, and he signed a contract worth $39.9 million, the largest contract ever given to a rookie. He played four seasons with Orlando from 1992–1993 through 1995–1996. In his first year, O'Neal was named NBA Rookie of the Year, made the All-Rookie First Team, and appeared in the NBA All-Star Game. In his second year, the Magic advanced to the NBA Finals for the first time and were swept by the Houston Rockets. O'Neal made the All-Star Game for the second of ten times. An All-NBA Second Team selection in 1994–1995, O'Neal led the NBA in scoring with 2,315 points (29.3-point average) and played on the 1994 gold-medal-winning United States World Championship team. Following the 1995–1996 season, he accepted a $120 million offer from the Los Angeles Lakers (NBA). In 1996 he was named to the NBA 50th Anniversary All-Time Team and starred on the gold-medal-winning United States Olympic Basketball team in Atlanta, Georgia.

O'Neal has played seven seasons with the Lakers, from 1996–1997 through 2002–2003. An All-NBA Third Team member his first season, O'Neal missed 31 games because of a knee injury. An All-NBA First Team choice the following season, he missed 22 games with a fractured wrist. In the 1998–1999 "lockout" shortened season, he led the NBA in scoring with 1,289 points and made the All-NBA Second Team. When the Lakers hired former Chicago Bulls coach Phil Jackson as their head coach in 1999, O'Neal enjoyed his three most productive years. He led Los Angeles to three consecutive NBA Championships by defeating the Indiana Pacers in six games in 2000, the Philadelphia 76ers in five games in 2001, and the New Jersey Nets in four games in 2002. In 1999–2000, O'Neal led the NBA in scoring, averaged 29.7 points, and was chosen the regular season and NBA Finals MVP. That same season, he won the IBM Award, was selected to the All-NBA Defensive Second Team, and made the All-NBA First Team. In 2000–2001, he repeated as MVP of the NBA Finals and again made the All-NBA First Team. In his seventh NBA All-Star Game in 2000, he scored 22 points, snagged nine rebounds, and was honored as the Co-MVP with the San Antonio Spurs' Tim Duncan.*

O'Neal repeated as an All-NBA First Team member in 2001–2002, leading the NBA in field goal percentage (.579), free-throw attempts (717), and points per 48 minutes (27.2) and ranking second in scoring with 1,822 points. O'Neal dominated in the final two games of the Western Conference Finals against the Sacramento Kings and won his third NBA Finals trophy, setting an NBA mark with 195 points for a four-game series. He underwent toe surgery and missed the start of the 2002–2003 season. O'Neal averaged 27.6 points, 12.1 rebounds, and 2.37 steals in 67 games in 2002–2003 to help the Lakers finish second in the Pacific Division. Los Angeles defeated the Minnesota Timberwolves in the first round of the playoffs, but lost to the San Antonio Spurs in the WC semifinals.

In 11 NBA seasons from 1992–1993 through 2002–2003, O'Neal has compiled 20,475 career points and averaged 27.6 points, 12.1 rebounds, and 2.6 blocked shots in 742 regular season contests. He posted a career-high 61 points against the Los Angeles Clippers on March 6, 2000 and collected a career-best 28 rebounds and 15 blocked shots against the New Jersey Nets on November 20, 1993.

In 136 NBA playoff games, O'Neal has averaged 28.1 points, 12.9 rebounds, and 2.3 blocked shots. In the six-game 2000 NBA Championship Series against the Indiana Pacers, he tallied 38 points, 16.7 rebounds, and 2.7 blocked shots. He averaged 33 points, 15.8 rebounds, and 3.4 blocked shots in the five-game 2001 NBA Championship Series against the Philadelphia 76ers. O'Neal averaged 36 points, 12.25 rebounds, and 2.75 blocked shots in the four-game 2002 NBA Championship Series against the New Jersey Nets. Yao Ming of the Houston Rockets started ahead of O'Neal for the WC All-Stars in 2003.

O'Neal married Shaunie Nelson in December 2002, and they have three children. He has another child from a previous relationship. He starred in the movie *Kazaam* and appeared in *Freddy Got Fingered, Good Burger, Steel* and *Blue Chips*. O'Neal has released five rap albums, *Shaq Diesel, Shaq Fu: Da Return, You Can't Stop the Reign, Respect*, and a greatest hits album. As an entrepreneur, O'Neal owns a record label and clothing line named Twism. He co-authored *Shaq Attaq!* in 1993 and authored *Shaq Talks Back* in 2001. In December 2000, he graduated from Louisiana State University.

BIBLIOGRAPHY:
Bill Gutman, *Shaquille O'Neal* (New York, 1993); *NCAA Men's Basketball's Finest* (Overland Park, KS, 1998); "Shaquille O'Neal," *Biography*, www.Top Black.com (2001); "Shaquille O'Neal," *Players Background*, www.nba.com (2001); "Shaquille O'Neal," *Players Career Highlights*, www.nba.com (2001); "Shaquille O'Neal," *Players Career Statistics*, www.nba.com (2001); Shaquille O'Neal, *Shaq Talks Back* (New York, 2001); *The Sporting News Official NBA Register*, 2003–2004.

John L. Evers

MAGGLIO ORDONEZ   Baseball
(January 28, 1974–   )

Magglio Ordonez, the Chicago White Sox (American League) 6-foot, 210-pound right fielder, may be among the least known major league baseball stars largely because he does not talk extensively about himself with the American press. Ordonez, however, appreciates that he is a much-recognized hero in his native Venezuela: "Over there (Venezuela) you're a hero. Baseball players are the only positive thing they have. . . . You feel much better because you're doing something for your country and for your people."

Magglio Ordonez was born in Caracas, Venezuela, on January 28, 1974, the youngest of seven children. At age 16, he left home to attend the Houston Astros' (National League) baseball academy in Valencia, Venezuela. Originally a catcher, he suffered from subpar footwork and was released by the Astros after six months. Chicago White Sox scout Alberto Rondon signed him in May 1991 for a relatively small bonus.

Ordonez progressed steadily through Chicago's minor league system. His 1997 season for Nashville, Tennessee (American Association) marked a watershed for Ordonez. He won the AA's batting title with a .329 average and was voted the AA's Most Valuable Player and Rookie of the Year. Called up to the White Sox in August 1997, Ordonez hit .319 with four home runs in 69 at-bats. His first major league home run came off of Jose Lima against the Houston Astros on August 30.

Ordonez, who bats and throws right-handed, became the starting right fielder for Chicago in 1998. He was named to the *Baseball Digest* (1998) Rookie All-Star Team after hitting .282 with 14 home runs, 65 runs batted in (RBI) and 70 runs scored. In early 1999, he was moved into the cleanup spot in the lineup. Manager Jerry Manuel explained, "I want him to think RBI . . . He has evolved into one of the best young right-handed hitters in the game."

Ordonez quickly emerged as a rising young star. The lone White Sox representative to the All-Star Game in 1999, he hit .301 with 30 home runs, 117 RBIs, 100 runs scored, a .510 slugging percentage, and .349 on-base percentage. He became just one of three White Sox players to have recorded 30 home runs, 100 RBIs, and 100 runs scored in one season, joining Frank Thomas* and Albert Belle.* Ordonez's increased home run output pleasantly surprised Chicago. He never had hit more than 18 homers in one season in either the major or minor leagues.

Ordonez has continued to post impressive numbers since 1999. He made another All-Star appearance in 2000 and led the White Sox to the AL Central Division title, hitting .315 with 32 home runs, 126 RBIs, and a .546 slugging percentage. Ordonez, who made $425,000 in 2000, signed a one-year, $3.75 million contract for 2001, hitting .305 with 31 home runs, 113 RBIs, a .533 slugging percentage, and 25 stolen bases. Selected to his third straight All-

Star game, Ordonez joined three other American Leaguers with home runs in the midsummer Classic. Just after the All-Star Game, the White Sox signed him to a three-year, $29.5 million contract extension.

As a young hitter, Ordonez has exhibited patience at the plate. His on-base percentage has increased every year with Chicago, while his walk-to-strikeout ratio remains quite good. In 2001 he combined 70 walks with 70 strikeouts. Ordonez enjoyed his best season in 2002, ranking second in the AL in RBIs (135), third in total bases (352), fourth in doubles (47), fifth in batting average (.320) and slugging percentage (.597), and sixth in home runs (38) and runs (116). For his career, he has compiled a .307 batting average with 178 home runs, 666 RBIs, and a .527 slugging percentage. He kept the White Sox in contention in the NL Central race in 2003, ranking fourth in the AL in doubles (46) and fifth in batting average (.317), clouting 29 home runs, and knocking in 99 runs.

Ordonez and his wife, Dagly, have two children, Magglio Jr., and Maggliana. Ordonez enjoys playing pool, fishing, and going to the beach. His sports hero is Venezuelan first baseman Andres Galarraga.* He has supported numerous charitable activities, including fund-raising efforts for the American Red Cross to help the victims of the catastrophic flooding in Venezuela in December 1999.

BIBLIOGRAPHY:
Teddy Greenstein, "Movin' on Up: Magglio Ordonez: Hitting His Way to Big League Stardom," *Baseball Digest* 58 (November 1999), p. 24; Rick Sorci, "Baseball Profile: Magglio Ordonez," *Baseball Digest* 59 (June 2000), p. 65; Paul Sullivan, "Magglio Ordonez: A Major League Star on the Rise," *Baseball Digest* 59 (October 2000), p. 22; Paul Sullivan, "Chicago's Invisible Star: Magglio Ordonez Carries a Big Stick for White Sox," *Baseball Digest* 60 (June 2001), p. 70; Dave Van Dyck, "South Side Hit Men II: Young Hitters Come of Age for Chicago White Sox," *Baseball Digest* 59 (September 2000), p. 60; George Vass, "Baseball Digest's Rookie All-Stars of '98," *Baseball Digest* 57 (December 1998), p. 22.

Terry W. Sloope

RUSS ORTIZ   Baseball
(June 5, 1974–)

Native Californian Russ Ortiz has emerged as the pitching mainstay of the Atlanta Braves (National League).

Russ Reid Ortiz was born on June 5, 1974 in Encino, California. When Ortiz was a baby, his parents divorced. His mother worked multiple shifts as a dispatcher for the Los Angeles, California, Police Department. Ortiz and his older brother, Shad, now a financial adviser in the Los Angeles area, lived with their grandparents, Rocky and Natalie Magdaleno, in the San Fernando Valley. He credits his grandparents with fostering his interest in competitive athletics and respect for religion, marriage, family, and friendship.

After graduating in 1992 from Montclair Prep School in Van Nuys, California, Ortiz accepted a baseball scholarship at the University of Oklahoma. He roomed with his brother at Oklahoma. He pitched relief, helping the Oklahoma Sooners win the 1994 College World Series.

In June 1995, the 6-foot 1-inch, 210-pound right-handed Ortiz was selected in the fourth round of the free-agent draft by the San Francisco Giants (NL). Used primarily in relief, Ortiz recorded over 60 saves as he progressed through the Giants' farm system from San Jose, California (California League) to Shreveport, Louisiana (Texas League). In 1998 he split time between San Francisco and its Triple A farm team in Fresno, California (Pacific Coast League). Used mainly as a starter by the Giants, Ortiz compiled four wins and four losses with a 4.99 earned run average (ERA) during his rookie campaign. The 1999 season marked a breakout campaign for Ortiz, who won 18 games with a 3.81 ERA. He slumped during the first half of the 2000 season, winning only four games and struggling with his control. After regaining mastery of his fastball and hard overhand curve, he triumphed 10 times after the All-Star break and lowered his ERA from 6.92 to 5.01. In 2001 as Barry Bonds* established a new home run mark and the Giants struggled to reach the playoffs, Ortiz became the Giants' starting ace. He won 17 games, striking out 169 batters with a 3.26 ERA.

The religious, family-oriented Ortiz earned the praise of San Francisco manager, Dusty Baker, who described his new ace as "probably the calmest, most mature, emotionally stable young person I've seen in a long, long time." During the 2001 season, Ortiz and his wife, Stacy, welcomed their first child, Grace. Proud of his Latino heritage, Ortiz was invited in October 2001 by President George W. Bush to a White House event celebrating Hispanic Heritage Month. Later that same month, his beloved grandmother died from diabetes. In tribute, Ortiz remarked, "What I do with my family, when times get tough, whether in marriage or life in general, is to see how my grandmother felt for most of her life with diabetes and realize she was still very strong."

Ortiz helped San Francisco attain the Wild Card with a 14–10 record and 3.61 ERA in 2002, fanning 137 batters in 214.1 innings. He won both starts with a 2.19 ERA against the Atlanta Braves in the NL Division Series, striking out eight batters in 12.1 innings. He struggled against the St. Louis Cardinals in the NL Championship Series, lasting only 4.2 innings with a 7.71 ERA. Ortiz started two World Series games against the victorious Anaheim Angels, compiling a 10.13 ERA in eight innings. Ortiz led National League hurlers in wins (21) and suffered just 7 losses with a 3.81 ERA and 149 strikeouts in 212.1 innings, helping Atlanta capture another NL East title. He split two decisions with a 5.06 ERA in the NL Division Series loss to the Chicago Cubs.

In December 2002, the Atlanta Braves (NL) acquired Ortiz in a trade. Through 2003, Ortiz has compiled a 88–51 mark with a 3.97 ERA and has struck out 861 batters in 1,137 innings.

BIBLIOGRAPHY
John Hant, "The Pick of N. L. Pitchers: San Francisco Giants," *USA Today: Baseball Weekly,* February 3, 1999, p. 14; Alexander Kleinberg, "Batting Around with Russ

Ortiz," *San Francisco Giants News*, February 11, 2002, www.sfgate.com/cgi-bi . . . chronicle/archive/2002 (April 1, 2002). Henry Schulman, "Lessons from the Family Formed Ortiz," *San Francisco Giants News*, February 24, 2002.

Ron Briley

MERLENE OTTEY   Track and Field
(May 10, 1960–)

Merlene Ottey won more Olympic medals than any other female runner.

Merlene Ottey was born on May 10, 1960 in rural Pondside, Jamaica, the fourth of seven children of Hubert Ottey and Joan Ottey. She attended school at Rusea from 1976 to 1978 and Vere Technical School in 1978 and 1979. Both institutions were high schools with a strong vocational orientation. She was chosen for her first Jamaican track and field team as a 14-year-old, with her first officially recorded time for the 200 meters being 25.9 seconds in 1975. The successes of fellow Jamaican sprinter Don Quarrie at the 1976 Montreal, Canada, Olympics inspired her.

In August 1979, Ottey accepted a track and field scholarship to the University of Nebraska at Lincoln, Nebraska. As a star member of the Cornhuskers track and field team, she dominated U.S. intercollegiate track and field. Altogether, she garnered seven Indoor National Championships and 25 All-America honors and earned the Carreras Sportswoman of the Year Award in Jamaica in 1980. From 1982 through 1984, the truly versatile sprinter ran both short sprints and 400-meter dashes. In 1982 she held 9 of the 10 top times in the 300-yard sprint—in the world!

Ottey graduated from the University of Nebraska in 1984 with a Bachelor of Arts degree. Although track and field was her consuming passion, she began to acquire a great sense of style and fashion. On February 3, 1984, she married American hurdler/high jumper Nathaniel Page. At the 1980 Moscow, Olympics, she won a bronze medal in the 200 meters with a clocking of 22.20 seconds. At the 1984 Los Angeles, California, Olympics, she repeated her 1980 Olympics performance in the 200 meters with another bronze medal at 22.09 seconds and finished third in the 100 meters at 11.16 seconds.

At the 1988 Seoul, South Korea, Olympics, Ottey ran against the greatest female sprinter of all time, America's Florence Griffith Joyner.* Griffith Joyner proved unbeatable in 1988. Ottey took fourth place in the 200 meters at 21.99 seconds. In the World Championships from 1983 to 1999, Ottey was magisterial. At the 1983 World Championships in Helsinki, Finland, she garnered a silver medal in the 200 meters. At the 1991 World Championships in Tokyo, she earned two more bronze medals in the 100 and 200 meters. The Jamaican sprint relay team won the gold medal in 41.94 seconds by a significant .26 seconds. Two years later at Stuttgart, Germany, she won the 200 meters in 21.98 seconds and earned bronze medals in the 100 meters at 10.82

seconds and the sprint relay in 41.94 seconds. Upon receiving the gold medal on the Stuttgart podium, she was given a thunderous three-minute ovation from the crowd.

At the 1995 World Championships in Gothenburg, Sweden, Ottey won another 200-meter title. But it was a "hollow" victory achieved only because actual winner Gwen Torrence of the United States was disqualified for stepping on the curved line in the 200 meters. Ottey captured silver medals in the 100 meters and the sprint relay.

Ottey possessed both confidence and optimism before the 1996 Summer Olympics in Atlanta, Georgia. In the 100-meter final, Ottey and Gail Devers* of the United States finished in a dead heat in 10.94 seconds. The photo-finish showed Devers winning by a whisker! In the 200-meter final, the favored Ottey led with 40 meters to go and was eventually passed by Marie-Jose Perec of France. Along with her two silver medals, Ottey won a bronze medal with the Jamaican 4×100-meter relay. Her seventh Olympic medal meant that she equaled the Olympic record of Irena Szewinska of Poland.

In the 1997 World Championships at Athens Greece, Ottey won a bronze medal with a 22.40-second clocking in the 200 meters. When the 1999 World Championships opened in Seville, Spain, she was not allowed to compete because she tested positive for the drug nandrolone at an athletics meet earlier in 1999. An incredible amount of wrangling and legal maneuvering transpired, with Ottey claiming innocence on all charges. On June 15–16, 2000, at the International Amateur Federation (IAAF) headquarters in Monaco, the dope case against her was heard. The IAAF Arbitration Panel found Ottey not guilty of a doping offense and dismissed all charges against her. The 40-year-old Jamaican took part in her final Olympics in 2000 at Sydney, Australia. She ran the anchor leg for the Jamaican 4×100-meter sprint relay team and helped them earn the silver medal in 42.13 seconds. This achievement made Ottey the most decorated female Olympic runner of all time with eight medals (three silver and five bronze). The Olympic years saw her narrowly missing the gold medal she so desperately wanted.

Ottey recalled that "Nebraska taught me self-esteem, determination, honesty and the will to fight." After Jamaican authorities in late 1999 cleared her and found her not guilty of wrongdoing, she commented: "I am very relieved and happy about this ruling that confirms my innocence." Nevertheless, the controversy cast a black cloud over her credibility as a competitor.

Ottey lives alone in the tax haven of Monte Carlo, Monaco. Her web page proudly labels her "the greatest female sprinter in history," with her impressive longevity and double decade of Olympic endeavors. Her management firm *FKG* markets her with the slogan, "Running fast is my passion, fashion my challenge for the future."

BIBLIOGRAPHY:
D.K. Publishing, *Chronicle of the Olympics* (New York, 1996); Claire Forrester and Alvin Campbell, *Merlene Ottey: Unyielding Spirit* (Kingston, Jamaica, 1996); Jacob

M. Neilson, "The Greatest Female Sprinter in History," August 1999, Ottey tribute web page, www.merlene.subnet.dk.

Scott A.G.M. Crawford

TERRELL OWENS
(December 7, 1973–   )

Football

Terrell Owens, wide receiver of the San Francisco 49ers (National Football League), holds the NFL single-game record for most receptions with 20 against the Chicago Bears on December 18, 2000, breaking a mark that endured five decades. Tom Fears of the Los Angeles Rams had caught 18 passes against the Green Bay Packers on December 3, 1950.

Terrell Eldorado Owens was born on December 7, 1973 in Alexander City, Alabama, the son of Marilyn Heard, and grew up in Alexander City. He graduated in 1992 from Benjamin Russell High School, where he played football and basketball. He attended the University of Chattanooga, participating in football four years. He caught 38 passes for 724 yards (19.1-yard average) and eight touchdowns in 1993 and 57 passes for 836 yards (14.7-yard average) and six touchdowns in 1994. As a collegian, Owens made 144 receptions for 2,323 yards (16.1-yard average) and 16 touchdowns in 38 games. Owens also played as a reserve swing man for the Chattanooga basketball team in the National Collegiate Athletic Association (NCAA) Tournament.

The San Francisco 49ers selected the 6-foot 2-inch, 213-pound Owens in the third round as the eighty-ninth pick overall of the 1996 NFL draft. The draft produced several outstanding NFL receivers, including Keyshawn Johnson, Marvin Harrison,* and Terry Glenn. The 49ers utilized legendary Jerry Rice* as their primary receiver but increasingly drew Owens into their offense. After making 35 pass receptions for 520 yards and four touchdowns as a rookie in 1996, Owens caught 60 passes for 936 yards (15.6-yard average) and eight touchdowns in 1997. His 15-yard touchdown reception helped defeat the Minnesota Vikings in a National Football Conference (NFC) Wild Card game. He played in the NFC Championship Game, which was won by the Green Bay Packers.

After protracted, contentious negotiations, Owens signed a seven-year, $44 million contract in 1998. He caught 67 passes for 1,097 yards (career-high 16.4-yard average) and 14 touchdowns and rushed for one touchdown that year. In February 1999, the 49ers designated him as a franchise player. His production that year declined to 754 yards in pass receptions and four touchdowns. In 2000 San Francisco experienced its second consecutive losing campaign for the first time since 1979–1980 with a 4–12 record. Owens, however, set career highs with 97 pass receptions for 1,451 yards (15.0-yard average), scored 13 touchdowns, and enjoyed five 100-yard receiving games in 2000. The NFL suspended Owens one game for taunting the Dallas Cowboys on September 24.

Owens's best game came on December 17, 2000, when he took advantage of single coverage and caught an NFL record 20 passes from Jeff Garcia* for 283 yards to help defeat the Chicago Bears, 17–0. The 283 yards marked the eighth highest by an NFL receiver in a single game and included a 27-yard touchdown reception in the third quarter. Ironically his performance came in Rice's last home game with the 49ers and broke the 49ers' single-game franchise record of 16 receptions against the Los Angeles Rams in 1994. "Today is special, and I don't want to overshadow No. 80," Owens said. Rice replied: "He's been instrumental in my success. If you want to say the torch is being passed, then I hope to keep that tradition going." "Records are meant to be broken. I feel T.O. is going to carry on the tradition." Owens played in the Pro Bowl following the 2000 season, the first time a 49ers receiver other than Rice had been selected since John Taylor in 1989.

In 2001 Owens caught 93 passes for 1,412 yards (15.2-yard average) and scored a career-high 16 touchdowns. Propelled by an obsessive workout regimen, Owens led the NFL in scoring and recorded a career-best six 100-yard receiving games. On October 14 he made a career-high two touchdowns against the Atlanta Falcons and made consensus All-Pro as a wide receiver. The moody Owens, however, complained about being underused down the stretch and was branded the Barry Bonds* of the locker room. The Green Bay Packers defeated the 49ers, 25–15, in the opening round of the playoffs. Owens was upset because he made just four catches for 40 yards without a touchdown in that game.

Owens clashed often with head coach John Mariucci. Following the 2001 season, Owens said, "If there was a chance, I would have loved to (leave). I just needed a new start. I felt like I wasn't getting used to the best of my ability." He had an unfortunate war of words and asked the 49ers to put him on the expansion draft list of the Houston Texans, but general manager Terry Donahue sought to fix the strained relationship. The differences were largely resolved in an April 2002 meeting between Owens and Mariucci. Owens explained, "the best thing about it was both of us trying to get on the same page. And bringing our level of communication up for the upcoming season." He still trusts a few people in the 49ers facility and has few friends among the veteran players. "You don't know who to believe, who to trust," Owens observed. Owens believes the 49ers get too locked in on their scripted plays and do not get him the ball enough.

Owens helped the 49ers win the NFC West crown with a 10–6 record in 2002, catching 100 passes for 1,300 yards (13.0-yard average) and 13 touchdowns. He rested for the final two games of the regular season after battling nagging heel and groin injuries, but still made the Pro Bowl. He caught nine passes for 177 yards and two touchdowns, helping the 49ers rally from a 24-point third-quarter deficit to edge the New York Giants, 39–38, in the Wild Card game. The Tampa Bay Buccaneers limited him to just four receptions and 35 yards, routing the 49ers, 31–6, in the next round. Through 2002, Owens caught 512 passes for 7,470 yards (14.6-yard average) and 71 touchdowns.

Owens, who competes with Randy Moss* for recognition as the NFL's top wide receiver, has also rushed for two touchdowns and converted a two-point extra point, giving him 448 career points. A dominant young receiver, he gets off the line and goes for the ball like Jerry Rice and runs after the catch and blocks downfield like John Taylor.

Owens won the celebrity contest during the 2000 National Basketball Association (NBA) All-Star Game in Oakland, California.

BIBLIOGRAPHY

"Owens' 20 Receptions Lift 49ers Past Bears," *Des Moines Register*, December 18, 2000, p. C1; *San Francisco 49ers Media Guide*, 2003; *The Sporting News Pro Football Register*, 1996, 2003; Richard Weiner, "Calm Before the Storm?" *USA Today*, July 23, 2002, pp. 1C–2C.

David L. Porter

P

RAFAEL PALMEIRO
(September 24, 1964–   )   **Baseball**

After several mediocre seasons, the Texas Rangers (American League) entered 1989 with the hope that better times were near. One of the keys to this hope was a 25-year-old first baseman recently acquired from the Chicago Cubs (National League). Texas hoped that Rafael Palmeiro would provide both defensive and offensive spark. One of the first hints of this new dawn came on April 30. The Boston Red Sox were at Arlington, with Texas legend Roger Clemens on the mound. Clemens cruised into the eighth inning with a 1–0 lead when Palmeiro stepped up to the plate and promptly belted a fastball off the right-field pole. That clout gave the Rangers a 2–1 victory, serving notice that Palmeiro would challenge pitchers for years to come.

Rafael Corrales Palmeiro was born in Havana, Cuba, on September 24, 1964. His parents, José Palmeiro and María Palmeiro, struggled to provide their three sons with the basic necessities, given the austere and repressive conditions of the Fidel Castro regime. The Palmeiros fled Cuba in 1971 and settled in the Miami, Florida, area.

José, a construction worker, was a stern taskmaster. After coming home from work, he would take his sons to a nearby park "where he would make us hit and field until dark. He was tough, very critical." Palmeiro's swing became smooth and effective, as he starred for the American Legion and Miami Jackson High School. In his senior year in 1982, he led the Generals with a .442 batting average, hit seven home runs, and produced 36 runs batted in (RBI). He was named a Florida All-Star Game participant and a consensus choice for the all-county and all-city teams. The New York Mets (NL) selected him in the eighth round of that year's draft, but he instead decided to attend Mississippi State University.

During his three years at Mississippi State, Palmeiro generated imposing numbers. He clouted 67 home runs with 122 extra-base hits, 239 RBIs, and 530 total bases, and batted .372 in 183 games with the Bulldogs. The ever-floundering Chicago Cubs made him their first-round pick and twenty-second overall in 1985. In his first professional campaign, Palmeiro hit .294 for Peoria, Illinois (Midwest League). In 1986 he was promoted to Pittsfield,

Massachusetts (Eastern League), where he was named to the circuit's All-Star team.

With the Chicago Cubs well out of contention by September, Palmeiro was called up. He quickly showed his potential, hitting .247 with 12 RBIs in only 73 at-bats. His hitting improved during the next two seasons, climbing to .307, the second highest in the NL, in 1988. Defensively, he played 147 games in the outfield with a .983 fielding percentage. Palmeiro played in his first All-Star Game in 1988 and drew comparisons to first baseman Don Mattingly. The Cubs, however, shipped him to the Texas Rangers in December.

Palmeiro became a consistent, dangerous hitter for Texas. Between 1989 and 1993, he hit .296 with 107 home runs and 431 RBIs. The Rangers, however, brought in his Mississippi State University teammate Will Clark to replace him. Palmeiro next signed with the Baltimore Orioles (AL), where he continued his assault on AL pitchers by hitting .294 with 182 home runs and 553 RBIs between 1994 and 1998. Many of his peers recognized this quiet man as a true superstar. In 1997 Oriole teammate Roberto Alomar* complained: "he's never gotten the respect he deserves. But baseball people know what Raffy does for our team."

Lean times in Baltimore led Palmeiro to return to the Texas Rangers in 1999. He rewarded Texas with his best season, hitting .324 with 47 home runs and 148 RBIs. Despite such overwhelming numbers, he finished fifth in the voting for AL Most Valuable Player (MVP). He batted .288 with 39 home runs and 120 RBIs in 2000, .273 with 47 home runs and 123 RBIs in 2001, and .273 with 43 home runs and 105 RBIs in 2002. Through the 2003 season, he had punished major league pitching for a career .291 batting average, 528 home runs, and 1,687 RBIs. Going into the 2003 season, he ranked first in Ranger history in runs (958) and among the top three in home runs (321), hits (1,692), doubles (321), RBIs (1,039), extra-base hits (667), and total bases (2,585). He has appeared in four All-Star games. In 2003, Palmeiro belted his 500th career home run in May and hit .260 with 38 home runs and 112 RBIs.

Palmeiro and his wife, Lynn, were married in 1986 and have two sons, Patrick Ryne and Preston Connor. He supports various charitable causes in the Dallas–Fort Worth, Texas, area, including sponsoring the "Raffy's Readers" reading program in 1999, working with Coors Brewing Company to reduce underage drinking, and working with the Lena Pope Home to increase the number of foster families in north Texas. In 1992 he received the "21" Award, named in honor of Pittsburgh Pirate great Roberto Clemente. That same year, Palmeiro experienced another wonderful moment as he was reunited with his older brother, José, after 21 years of separation. Although he has not received the recognition he deserves, Palmeiro is a star both on and off the field. He is a shining example of the power of the American dream for people living in oppressed lands.

BIBLIOGRAPHY:

www.lenapopehome.org and www.rangers.mlb.com; Dave Anderson, "The Cubs' New Name," *New York Times*, June 2, 1988, p. B17; Athletic Media Relations, Mississippi State University, Starkville, MS; Rich Cimini, "Palmeiro, a Can't-Miss," *Newsday*, June 5, 1988, p. 3; Johnette Howard, "Star in the Shadows," *Sports Illustrated* 87 (September 8, 1997), pp. 42–44, 47; Susan Kucska, "Batting Tips from Dad Help Cubs' Palmeiro," *Los Angeles Times*, Part 3, June 19, 1988, p. 4; Phil Rogers, "Just Call Texas Trio the 3–4–5 Amigos," *The Sporting News*, July 31, 1989, p. 10; Mark D. Williams, "Power Rangers Unite!," *Sport* 90 (July 1999), pp. 38–41.

Jorge Iber

DEREK PARRA   Speedskating
(March 15, 1970–   )

Derek Parra won gold and silver medals in speedskating at the 2002 Salt Lake City, Utah, Winter Olympic Games.

Derek Dwayne Parra, of Mexican American heritage, was born on March 15, 1970 in San Bernardino, California. His parents were divorced when he was age 4. Parra, nicknamed "D. D.," was brought up by his father, Gilbert, who worked at a youth prison. He graduated from Eisenhower High School in 1988.

The diminutive 5-foot 4-inch, 140-pound Parra participated in football and wrestling as a youth but did not find his real interest until he was introduced to roller skating in 1984. He appeared to be in perpetual motion and proved a natural with wheels under his feet. "The disco, the lights, the music," he said, "It was like another world."

At age 17, Parra moved to the East Coast to improve his skating skills and enter more competitive races. Inline coach Virgil Dooley taught him how to train and skate. Parra enjoyed a phenomenal inline skating career and followed Dooley from California to Florida, Maryland, and then Delaware looking for the right place to train. Parra's strong work ethic and national and international racing enabled him by 1996 to become the most decorated athlete in speed roller skating history. A three-time National Champion, Parra won the overall World Championship twice and held world records in the 1,500-meter and 42-kilometer races. He captured 18 individual gold medals and earned the most medals at the 1995 Pan American Games, winning five golds, two silvers, and one bronze.

By 1995, Parra had won everything but an Olympic medal. Inline skating was not an Olympic sport, denying him the opportunity to win an Olympic medal. "I never would have given up inline and the salary I was making if I didn't think I could be a medal contender," Parra said. He was then earning up to $50,000 annually.

At age 25, in 1996 Parra switched from inline to speedskating. He found it difficult to go from the top of inline skating to the bottom of speedskating. Bart Schouten, the U.S. Allround coach who taught him speedskating, observed, "He's the smallest guy out there, and the crowd loves him." Parra had to eliminate certain characteristics natural to inline skating when he made the

Derek Parra ©Mike Hewitt/Getty Images

transition to ice. He had to learn to let the skates do the work for him and be more patient to get a long, powerful push. He also had to learn to control his upper body and arms to keep them from bouncing on the turns. Because of his short frame, he realized, he had to become technically better.

In 1998 Parra showed his determination to become a medalist by earning a place on the U.S Olympic team. After expecting to skate in the 5,000 meters at Nagano, Japan, however, he became frustrated and disappointed when told he would not be competing. The international officials had allowed Kazakstan to change its application form after the entry deadline had passed, and so a higher-ranked individual was put ahead of Parra. At this point Parra briefly contemplated retiring from skating but, determined, he set his sights on the next Olympics.

In preparation for the 2002 Winter Olympic Games at Salt Lake City, Utah, Parra trained and competed four years against the best skaters in the world. Among his many honors, he became North American Champion in 2001, U.S. National Champion from 1999 through 2001, and U.S. National Allround Champion in 2000. He medaled 12 times in the U.S. National Championships, making the U.S. National team five times and the U.S. World team four times. He won the silver medal at the 2001 World Single Distance Speedskating Championship in the 1,500 meters and finished fifth in the season World Cup standings in the 1,500 meters. He also was named the U.S. Olympic Committee Athlete of the Year in 1994. Parra, whose four-hour workouts consist of 30 repetitions of 32 different exercises, acknowledged, "I always come to the line knowing I have trained the hardest."

In the 2002 Winter Olympic Games at Salt Lake City, Parra won his leg of the 5,000-meter race and set a new world record in 6 minutes 17.98 seconds. It appeared that he might win his first Olympic gold medal in record time. He held the world record, however, for only about 20 minutes and settled for the silver medal. When the fifteenth pair faced off, Jochem Uytdehaage from the Netherlands knew what he had to do. He won his leg of the event to earn the gold medal, breaking Parra's world-record time in 6 minutes 14.66 seconds. Parra had another opportunity to defeat Uytdehaage in the 1,500-meter event and won the gold medal in world-record time of 1 minute 43.95 seconds, breaking the standard of 1 minute 44.57 seconds set earlier by Uytdehaage. Schouten noted, "Derek has it together when it counts. I think this is part of his personality and his mental preparation. His whole lifestyle is geared toward skating, and skating fast."

Parra plans to move to Orlando, Florida, to continue his education and bring up his family. He and his wife, Tiffany, have a daughter, Mia Elizabeth, born two months before the 2002 Winter Olympics. Parra, who works at Home Depot, enjoys Italian/Mexican food and always eats a package of Fig Newtons the night before a race. He reads the Bible, enjoys all kinds of music, movies, and books, and appeared on an album, "All I've Got," featuring Olympians.

BIBLIOGRAPHY
"Derek Parra," *Athlete Bios*, www.olympicusa.org (2002); "Derek Parra," Career Highlights, www.u.s.speedskating.org (2002); "Derek Parra," *Olympic Speedskater*, www.aca.com (2002); "Derek Parra," *Olympic Sports Figure*, www.nashspeaker.org (2002); "Derek Parra," *Speedskating*, www.olympicshiasys.com (2002); "Derek Parra," *Speedskating Bios*, www.usocpressbox.org (2002); Tom Weir, "Parra Doesn't Want to Come Up Short," *USA Today*, February 6, 2002, p. 7C.

John L. Evers and David L. Porter

GARY PAYTON   Basketball
(July 23, 1968–   )

Gary Payton of the Los Angeles Lakers (National Basketball Association) ranks among the most consistent All-Star performers.

Gary Dwayne Payton was born on July 23, 1968 in Oakland, California, and grew up in Oakland. He attributes his inner fortitude to his father, Al, who coached him in basketball and continues to give him advice. His favorite player as a youth was San Antonio guard George Gervin. Payton played basketball at Skyline High School in Oakland and Oregon State University, scoring 2,172 points in 120 games and averaging 18.1 points and 7.8 assists. In 1990 he was named *Sports Illustrated* College Player of the Year. His nickname is "the Glove" because "he covers opposing guards as snugly as one."

The Seattle Supersonics (NBA) drafted Payton as the second pick in the 1990 NBA draft. He excelled as a defensive player, an adept passer, and a cagey playmaker as a rookie, but only scored 7.2 points per game. He was named to the NBA All-Rookie Second Team. Since his rookie year, Payton has become one of the best all-around NBA point guards. Former Indiana Pacers coach Isiah Thomas* boasts, "He's the Deion Sanders* of the NBA. Defensively, he's so fast, he's there. The person he's guarding, you can just eliminate him from the offense."

Payton was named to the All-NBA First Team in 1998 and 2000; the All-NBA Second Team in 1995, 1996, 1997, 1999, and 2002; and the All-NBA Third Team in 2001. He was selected to the All-Star team from 1994 through 1998 and 2000 through 2003, starting the 1997 and 1998 games. He was named the NBA Defensive Player of the Year in 1996, becoming the first guard to win the award since Michael Jordan* in 1987–1988. Payton was selected to the NBA All-Defensive Team nine consecutive seasons. On March 19, 2001 against the Philadelphia 76ers, he became the eighth NBA player to tally 15,000 career points, 6,000 assists, and 1,000 steals. He was selected to America's Olympic Dream Team in 1996 and 2000, winning two gold medals. He has played in only one NBA Championship Finals, in which the Supersonics lost to the Chicago Bulls in 1996.

The durable Payton has missed only three games due to injuries in his NBA career. He held the longest consecutive streak of starts among active NBA players with 356. His streak ended when he was suspended for fighting in the locker room with coach Paul Westphal. During the 2000-2001 season, Payton was suspended twice. His off-the-court behavior concerned his coaches and Seattle fans. He arrived late to practice, bashed his teammates verbally to the media, and threw free weights at a teammate.

Payton remains highly competitive whether he is playing basketball or shooting pool. He engages in trash talking (talking gibberish), which is attributable to his younger years when learning the game on Oakland playgrounds.

Gary Payton ©Getty Images

He has worked tirelessly to improve his game. Former teammate Vin Baker says, "In the past Gary would let his competitiveness override his intelligence. He was always the best point guard physically; now he's become the best point guard mentally." Former coach George Karl adds, "What Gary has is excellent knowledge of the game. I think he has more of a mental edge than he gets credit for." Former coach Paul Westphal, explains, "The book on Gary used to be that he was talented but was so intense that you could rattle him and throw him off his game. He still has that edge, but he knows how to control it." Payton has matured during his career. In the 2001–2002 season, he averaged 9.0 assists and 22.1 points. Seattle traded Payton to the Milwaukee Bucks (NBA) for Ray Allen.* In 2002–2003, Payton averaged 20.4 points, 8.3 assists, and 1.7 steals to best his career averages of 18.3 points and 7.4 assists. He joined the Los Angeles Lakers (NBA) as a free agent in July 2003. In the 2002–2003 season, he scored 18,757 points and tallied 7,590 assists and 2,147 steals in 1,027 games. Payton leads the Supersonics in career points, assists, and steals (2,108). In 100 NBA playoff games, he has averaged 17.8 points, 6.2 assists, and 1.64 steals.

In 1996 Payton established the Gary Payton Foundation to help underprivileged children stay in safe recreational havens. He prefers charities that help children and the homeless and has authored a children's book, *Confidence Counts*. His favorite athletes are baseball player Barry Bonds* of the San Francisco Giants and former NFL quarterback Dan Marino of the Miami Dolphins. He lists John Stockton of the Utah Jazz as his most difficult NBA opponent.

Payton and his wife, Monique, have three children, Raquel, Gary II, and Julian.

BIBLIOGRAPHY

Phil Barber, "Gold Glove," *The Sporting News*, September 18, 2000, pp. 14–17; Dave D'Alessandro, "Payton Has Molded Sonics in His Bickering Image," *The Sporting News*, April 12, 2000, p. 58; Phil Taylor, "Still Dreaming," *Sports Illustrated* 93 (September 25, 2000), p. 58; Ian Thomsen, "Wild about Gary," *Sports Illustrated* 96 (February 11, 2002), pp. 68–69; L. Jon Wertheim, "The Hustler," *Sports Illustrated* 91 (December 20, 1999), pp. 92–97.

Maureen M. Smith

LAFFIT PINCAY
(December 29, 1946–   )

Horse Racing

Laffit Pincay may become the first jockey to record 10,000 victories. His family life revolved around horses, stables, the racetrack, and racing.

Laffit Alegando Pincay Jr. was born on December 29, 1946 in Panama City, Panama, the son of Laffit Pincay Sr., a jockey, and Rosario Pincay, who sold newspapers. His father soon left Laffit and Rosario to fend for themselves. The wild, undisciplined, deserted youth very nearly ran afoul of the law, but athletics saved him, giving his life substance, structure, and discipline.

Despite being just 5 feet 1 inch and 110 pounds, Pincay loved baseball. His skill and competitive fire made him aspire to become second baseman for the Panamanian national team. But his future lay elsewhere.

He began his jockey apprenticeship as a groom and "hot walker," helping a horse warm down after racing and exercising. He first raced in Panama in 1964 and quickly enjoyed consistent success, becoming the nation's premier jockey apprentice. In 1965 he became Panama's leading jockey. A year later, he followed fellow Central American riders Jorge Luis Velasquez and Braulio Baeza in migrating to the United States to race. Pincay signed a three-year contract with owner Fred Hooper in 1966. Two years later he married Linda Radkovich; they had two children.

Pincay has battled weight problems all his life, leading him to alternately try diet pills, diuretics, jogging, unusual diets, and protein and vitamin injections. He has also made extensive use of a sauna system at home and at racetracks. In 1978 he hired Joyce Richards, a food specialist who designed

Laffit Pincay ©Steve Grayson/Getty Images

a diet that kept him at 850 calories a day. Despite the alarmingly low caloric intake, the combination of grains, nuts, and fruits kept him healthy.

In 1975, at age 29, Pincay was elected to the National Museum of Racing Hall of Fame. He already had led jockeys in money earned from 1970 through 1974. He received the Eclipse Award as America's premier jockey on five occasions (1971, 1973, 1974, 1979, 1985) and won consecutive Belmont Stakes (one of the legs of the Triple Crown), aboard Conquistador Cielo (1982), Caveat (1983), and Swale (1984). On March 14, 1987 at the Santa Anita racetrack in Arcadia, California, Pincay became the first jockey to ride seven winners on a single program. His most special moment came in 1984 when he won the Kentucky Derby on Swale.

Pincay has set several mind-boggling records. In 1973 he became the first jockey to go over the $4 million mark in prize money. His defining moment in sports history came aboard Irish Nip in the sixth race at Hollywood Park in Inglewood, California, on December 10, 1999. The horse won by two lengths, giving Pincay his 8,834th career win and breaking Willie Shoemaker's seemingly invincible victory record. Shoemaker hugged the ebullient Pincay, who was given a white Porsche convertible. Pincay explained, "[I] love . . . the game, the love of riding horses."

Pincay has experienced, anguish, and adversity as well as triumph. In 1985 his wife of 17 years committed suicide. She had undergone unsuccessful surgeries and had been severely depressed. He remarried in 1992, and he and his wife, Jeanine, have one child.

Pincay won 170 races in 1999 and 202 races in 2000, and may well break the 10,000-win barrier. Richard Hoffer explains, "This is serious business, and to do it successfully at 54 suggests an almost pathological insatiability, the kind of hunger calories can't begin to satisfy. Poor Pincay, ever famished, coming down the stretch, all 116 pounds of him, 100% appetite." Through March 2003, Pincay had recorded 9,531 wins and ranks third in earnings with $225,612,657. He broke a bone in his neck when thrown from Trampus Too during a race at Santa Anita racetrack in March 2003.

Pincay's Hall of Fame induction plaque underscores his greatest asset as a jockey—a racing formula combining muscularity and command. The plaque reads: "He was a strong rider who could keep unruly colts to their task." No jockey has raced for as long and as well as Pincay. Hoffer notes that he "was always the man to beat down the stretch." With his big flickering hands controlling 1,100 pounds of horse flesh at speeds in excess of 40 miles per hour, he is "a gaunt picture of nobility."

BIBLIOGRAPHY
Andrew Beyers, "The Best in the Business Is Still Coming on Strong," *Washington Post*, December 11, 1999; Richard Hoffer, "It Takes a Hungry Man," *Sports Illustrated* 95 (September 3, 2001), pp. 66–69; George B. Kirsch, Othello Harris and Claire E. Nolte, eds., *Encyclopedia of Ethnicity and Sports in the United States* (Westport, CT: 2000); Arnold Markoe, ed., *Scribner Encyclopedia of American Lives: Sports Figures*, Vol. 2 (Detroit, MI, 2002); David L. Porter, ed., *Biographical Dictionary of American Sports: 1992–1995 Supplement* (Westport, CT, 1995).

Scott A.G.M. Crawford

SCOTTIE PIPPEN   Basketball
(September 25, 1965–   )

Scottie Pippen starred on six National Basketball Association (NBA) title teams.

Scottie Maurice Pippen, nicknamed "Pip," was born on September 25, 1965 in Hamburg, Arkansas, the youngest of 12 children born to Preston Pippen and Ethel Pippen. He developed slowly as a basketball player at Hamburg High School, not earning a starting berth until his senior year.

Following his high school graduation in 1983, Pippen attended the University of Central Arkansas in Conway, Arkansas. He served as a student manager during his first year. When several players quit the team, he begged the coaches to give him a chance and was given the chance to play. The 6-foot 7-inch, 228-pound Pippen played in 94 career games for the Bears, recording 749 rebounds, 253 assists, and 1,600 points for a 17.2-point average. As a senior, he averaged 10.0 rebounds and 23.6 points and was named the Bears' best player. Pippen's statistics made the NBA scouts take a look at this unknown quantity from a little-known school. At Central Arkansas, he

Scottie Pippen ©Otto Greule Jr./Getty Images

majored in Industrial Technology but did not graduate. According to his children's book, *Reach Higher*, he promised to return and get his degree.

Pippen's talent and ability were relatively unknown when he entered the 1987 NBA draft. The Chicago Bulls (NBA) probably made the most concentrated study on Pippen and were prepared to draft him, but the Seattle SuperSonics (NBA) selected him in the first round as the fifth pick overall. Chicago traded Olden Polynice and other draft considerations for Pippen. The versatile Pippen, who could play at a point guard position or a power forward, became one of the best NBA defensive players. He made the NBA All-Defensive First Team eight consecutive years from 1992 through 1999. Only Michael Jordan* and Bobby Jones matched this record. In his first season with the Chicago Bulls, Pippen was used primarily as a reserve; he did not earn a starting position until his second season. He, Jordan, Horace Grant, Bill Cartwright, and John Paxson led the Bulls to their first NBA Championship. When the exceptional talent, athleticism, and skills of especially Pippen and Jordan were blended together, Chicago captured six NBA titles from 1991 through 1993 and 1996 through 1998. The Bulls finished the 1995–1996 season with 72 victories, becoming the first NBA team to win at least 70 games in one season.

During the 1989–1990 season, Pippen increased his production in nearly every offensive category and was selected to play in his first NBA All-Star Game. In 1990–1991, Chicago won the organization's first NBA Championship. Pippen gained superstar status the following season when he helped the Bulls win their second consecutive NBA crown, was named to the All-NBA Second Team and the All-NBA Defensive First Team, and played on the U.S. Olympic gold-medal-winning basketball "Dream Team." Chicago captured its third straight NBA title in 1992–1993, but the mix changed the following year when Jordan retired to play professional baseball. Pippen carried the added load on his shoulders and compiled his finest statistical year since joining the Bulls, with 22 points, 8.7 rebounds, and 2.93 steals per game. With Jordan out of the lineup, the consecutive string of NBA titles was broken by the New York Knicks.

During the 1994–1995 season, Pippen continued to demonstrate his superstar status. Michael Jordan returned for 17 late-season games, but Chicago lost to the Orlando Magic in the Eastern Conference semifinals. Pippen easily adjusted to Jordan's return, leading the Bulls with 5.9 assists per game and a career-high 150 three-point field goals made. With assistance from Toni Kukoc, Dennis Rodman, Luc Longley, Ron Harper, and Steve Kerr, Chicago again captured three consecutive NBA titles. The Bulls defeated the Seattle SuperSonics in 1995–1996 and conquered the Utah Jazz the following two seasons.

When Jordan retired after the 1998–1999 season, the Chicago Bulls' dynasty was broken up. Pippen was traded to the Houston Rockets (NBA) in January 1999 for Roy Rogers and a second-round draft pick. Pippen played in 50 games with the Rockets before being traded to the Portland Trail Blazers

(NBA) in October 1999 for Kelvin Cato, Stacy Augmon, Walt Williams, Brian Shaw, Ed Gray, and Carlos Rogers. In Pippen's first season at Portland, the Trail Blazers advanced to the Western Conference Championship Series before losing to the Los Angeles Lakers in seven games. In 2000–2001 and 2001–2002, the Lakers swept Portland in the first round of the playoffs, leading Pippen to describe those seasons with the Trail Blazers as the most frustrating in his NBA career. In 2002–2003, Portland lost to the Dallas Mavericks in the first round of the NBA playoffs. Pippen rejoined the Chicago Bulls for the 2003–2004 season.

In 16 NBA seasons from 1987–1988 through 2002–2003, Pippen has compiled 18,804 points in 1,155 regular season games for a 16.3-point scoring average and ranks second in Bulls' franchise history in scoring with 14,987 points. Pippen has registered 7,426 rebounds, 2,286 steals, 6,085 assists, and 938 blocked shots. In 208 NBA playoff games, he has collected 3,642 points, 1,583 rebounds, 395 steals, 1,048 assists, 185 blocked shots, and six NBA Championship rings. In seven NBA All-Star games, he posted 85 points, 39 rebounds, 6 blocked shots, 17 steals, and 17 assists. Pippen was named Most Valuable Player (MVP) in 1994, recording 29 points, and snagged 11 rebounds.

Pippen made the All-NBA First Team in 1994, 1995, and 1996, All-NBA Second Team in 1992 and 1997, and All-NBA Third Team in 1993 and 1998. He was selected to the NBA All-Defensive First Team between 1992 and 1999 and was Second Team choice in 1991 and 2000. In 1996 he became a member of the NBA 50th Anniversary All-Time team.

Pippen has three children: Antron, born to his ex-wife, Karen McCullom; Sierra, born to his ex-fiancée, Yvette DeLeone; and Taylor, born to Sonya Ruby. He married Larsa Younan in July 1997.

BIBLIOGRAPHY
"Scottie Pippen," *Personal*, www.allstarsite.com (1997); "Scottie Pippen," *Player Background*, www.nba.com (2001); "Scottie Pippen," *Player Career Highlights*, www.nba.com (2001); "Scottie Pippen," *Player Career Statistics*, www.nba.com (2001); *The Sporting News Official NBA Register*, 2003–2004.

John L. Evers

JORGE POSADA   Baseball
(August 17, 1971–   )

As a young catcher playing under the publicity spotlight of baseball in New York City, Jorge Posada has guided a veteran New York Yankees (American League) pitching staff that dominated baseball for nearly a decade.

Jorge Rafael Posada Jr. was born on August 17, 1971 in Santurce, Puerto Rico, the son of Jorge Posada Sr. and Lamara Posada. The elder Posada possessed outstanding baseball talent in Cuba but defected in 1968 by stowing away on a Greek tobacco ship. Upon relocating to Puerto Rico, Jorge Sr. married and later pushed his young son to play baseball.

At Colegio Alejandro High School in Puerto Rico, Jorge Jr. played short-stop and competed in basketball, track and field, and volleyball. He even umpired girls' softball, where he met his future wife, Laura, a pitcher. After high school graduation, Posada was drafted by the New York Yankees. His father, however, wanted him to improve his skills and get an education before turning professional. A scholarship to a four-year college was not an option, however, for Posada failed to score well enough on the Scholastic Aptitude Test college entrance examination. Finally, Fred Frickie, the baseball coach at Calhoun Community College in Decatur, Alabama, offered Posada a base-ball scholarship. Although he was struggling with the English language and was homesick for Puerto Rico, Posada played well enough that the New York Yankees redrafted him as a twenty-fourth pick in 1990. After assuring the elder Posada that they would retain their draftee for at least three seasons, the Yankees signed Jorge Posada Jr.

The 6-foot 2-inch, 200-pound Posada performed in 1991 for Class A On-eonta, New York (New York-Penn League), where he hit only .235 and led the NYPL second basemen in turning double plays. The Yankee management believed that Posada, who switch hits and throws right-handed, lacked the speed to be a middle infielder and so converted him to a catcher. He learned his new position while progressing through the Yankees' farm system. In 1997, at age 26, Posada spent his first full year in the major leagues and appeared in only 60 games. In 1998 and 1999, he shared Yankee catching duties with Joe Girardi. After catching Roger Clemens in the final game of the 1999 World Series against the Atlanta Braves, Posada was ready to assume full-time Yankee catching duties. The Yankees allowed Girardi to depart via free agency.

Posada responded well to his new responsibilities in 2000, hitting 28 home runs and driving in 86 runs in 151 games and guiding the Yankee pitching staff to another World Championship over the New York Mets. Although the Yankees lost the 2001 World Series to the Arizona Diamondbacks in a dramatic Game Seven, Posada enjoyed another outstanding season with 22 home runs, 95 runs batted in (RBI), and a .277 batting average. The Yankees may not have made the World Series without Posada, whose home run accounted for the only run of the pivotal Game Three in the AL Division Series against the Oakland Athletics. In 2002 Jorge hit .268 with 20 home runs and 99 RBIs, helping the Yankees capture the AL East Division. Posada, who made the All-Star team in 2000, 2001, 2002, and 2003, has batted .270 with 135 home runs and 526 RBIs. He batted .260 in eight AL Division Series and appeared in five AL Championship Series and World Series. He hit .281 with 30 home runs and 101 RBIs to help the Yankees win another AL East title in 2003 and batted. 296 with 4 doubles, a home run, and 6 RBIs in the AL Championship Series against the Boston Red Sox. He struggled, however, in both the AL Division Series against the Minnesota Twins and the World Series against the victorious Florida Marlins. He finished third in the AL MVP Award balloting.

Posada, however, had more on his mind than baseball. He and his wife, Laura, spent August 29, 2001 at the hospital in New York with their son, Jorge

Posada IV, who suffered from cranosynostoris and required eight hours of surgery to properly align his facial bones. After a successful surgery, he remarked, "Baseball always was everything to me. Don't get me wrong, it's still very important. But now I look at it in a different way. You gain perspective." Both Jorge Posada IV and the Yankee pitchers appear to be in good hands.

BIBLIOGRAPHY

Chris Colston, "Posada Finds a Way to Triumph over the Pain," *USA Today*, October 23, 2001, www.USAtoday.com/sports/bbw/2001 (April 1, 2002); Jack Curry, "Posada's Father Basks as Teachings Pay Off," *New York Times*, July 11, 2000, p. D3; Tom Verducci, "The Posada Adventure," *Sports Illustrated* 94 (May 7, 2001), pp. 46–50.

Ron Briley

MICHAEL POWELL
(November 10, 1963–   )   **Track and Field**

The dramatic, historic, colorful front cover of the September 9, 1991 issue of *Sports Illustrated* has the airborne figure, cycling legs, and flailing arms of American long jumper Mike Powell and in bold yellow capitals the numbers 29' 4½". The cover spotlights Powell's amazing athletic feat of breaking what many consider the twentieth century's most extraordinary athletic accomplishment, Bob Beamon's gold medal leap of 29 feet, 2 inches at the 1968 Mexico City, Mexico, Summer Olympics. Upon improving the world record by 2½ inches, Powell flopped to the ground and exclaimed, "Tell me I'm not dreaming." He insightfully observed, "I stepped into a different realm."

Michael Anthony Powell was born on November 10, 1963 in Philadelphia, Pennsylvania, the third and last child of John Preston Powell and Carolyn (Eaddy) Powell. His father worked as a roofer, and his mother worked as an accountant. Powell was known in his neighborhood as a young boy with springs for legs and a penchant for bounding down flights of stairs with massive leaps.

After his parents divorced, Carolyn Powell relocated in 1974 to West Covina, California, near Los Angeles. Powell attended Edgewood High School in West Covina, where he loved basketball and showed incredible potential as a track and field athlete. With relatively little coaching and not much training, Powell high jumped 7 feet. Despite his athletic ability, considerable academic promise, a 3.2 grade point average, a 1,000 plus Scholastic Aptitude Test score, and an academic All-America status, Powell was not swamped with university scholarship offers. He finally accepted a track and field scholarship at nearby University of California at Irvine.

Powell gave up his first love, basketball, and settled for track and field. As a freshman, he considered the high jump his forte. But a soaring leap of 26 feet 5¼ inches as a sophomore convinced him of his real potential in the long jump. However, he lacked the consistency of archrival and nemesis Carl Lewis.*

At the 1984 U.S. Olympic Trials, Powell finished only sixth in the long

Michael Powell ©Michael Powell/Getty Images

jump. In 1985 he left California–Irvine and became a full-time athlete, enjoy-ing some success on the European circuit. In 1986 he went back to school and enrolled at UCLA, graduating with a Bachelor's degree in sociology. He now concentrated on becoming a world-class jumper.

Powell worked with the specialist coach Randy Huntington and was ranked sixth in the world in the long jump in 1987, winning the World University Games and passing 27 feet for the first time. He demonstrated enormous courage at the 1988 U.S. Olympic Trials when, only six weeks after undergoing an emergency appendectomy, he made the team. At the 1988 Seoul, South Korea, Olympics, Powell recorded a personal best of 27 feet, 10½ inches. The more consistent Carl Lewis won the gold medal, however, leaping 28 feet, 7½ inches. Lewis seemed repeatedly to defeat Powell when the stakes were highest. At the 1992 Barcelona, Spain, Summer Olympics, Lewis edged him for the gold medal by 28 feet 5¼ inches to 28 feet, 4 inches. At the 1996 Atlanta, Georgia, Summer Olympic Games, Lewis outlasted Powell. Powell's injuries kept him out of serious medal contention.

The greatest duel between Lewis and Powell may have occurred at the Tokyo World Track and Field Championships in 1991. Despite an air temperature of 81 degrees, 83 percent humidity, and a swirling wind, Powell defeated the Olympic Champion in the long jump. Lewis had won 65 consecutive competitions and had defeated Powell 15 times. Lewis performed magnificently in the event, but Powell took the event to a new level with a 29 foot 4½ inch leap, which most experts considered impossible at sea level. After winning, he hugged a "dumbfounded board judge" and his coach Huntington. Huntington replied gleefully, "We got it [the world record] and got him [Lewis]."

At his best, Powell proved an elegant jumper of incomparable technique. The *Encyclopedia of Sports Science* marveled at Powell's expertise, "late acceleration and a power take-off" and a "more propulsive last step" and rated the Lewis–Powell Olympic duel at Barcelona as "one of the greatest long-jumping contests of all time." *Current Biography Yearbook* reported that Powell's life "changed overnight" after breaking Beamon's record. Powell won the Sullivan Award and the Jesse Owens International Trophy and kept close with family members. His sister Linda Powell-Fitzgerald served as his manager.

Powell competed at a propitious time of financial rewards for track and field performers. His post–world record single-meet appearance fees approached $50,000. He signed endorsement contracts with Nike, Ray Ban, and Foot Locker and won television's Superstars competition in 1992.

BIBLIOGRAPHY:
"Mike Powell," *Current Biography Yearbook 1993* (New York, 1993); Kenny Moore, "Great Leap Forward," *Sports Illustrated* 75 (September 9, 1991), pp. 14–19; David L. Porter, ed., *African-American Sports Greats* (Westport, CT, 1995); John Sumerchik, ed., *Encyclopedia of Sports Science*, Vol. 1 (New York, 1997).

Scott A.G.M. Crawford

KIRBY PUCKETT   Baseball
(March 14, 1961–)

Kirby Puckett of the Minnesota Twins (American League) did not possess the prototypical athletic build of other superstars but nonetheless appeared headed toward 3,000 career hits when glaucoma abruptly ended his major league career.

Kirby Puckett was born on March 14, 1961 in Chicago, Illinois, the son of William Puckett, Negro League pitcher, and Catherine Puckett. Puckett, the youngest of nine children, grew up in the Robert Taylor House projects in southern Chicago and overcame his adverse environment. He wrote, "My mom was determined that the baby of the family would stay out of trouble. I was sheltered. I didn't hang out. I didn't even go to the movies. At night I was home."

Puckett played sandlot baseball between the project buildings. He graduated in 1979 from Calumet High School in Chicago, where he earned All-America recognition as a third baseman. He worked briefly at the local Ford plant until Bradley University baseball coach Dewey Kalmer spotted him at a Kansas City Royals (American League) tryout and gave him a baseball scholarship. Kalmer converted him to center fielder. After his father died in 1981, Puckett transferred to Triton Community College in River Grove, Illinois, to be closer to his mother. In 1982 he batted .472, clouted 16 home runs, stole 42 bases, and was selected the Region IV Junior College Player of the Year. The Triton Hall of Fame enshrined him in 1993.

The Minnesota Twins (American League) selected the 5-foot 8-inch, 178-pounder who batted and threw right-handed in the January 1982 free-agent draft as their first pick and third pick overall. Puckett progressed rapidly through the minor leagues. In 1982 he starred for Elizabethton, Tennessee (Appalachian League), leading the league in at-bats (275), batting (.382), runs (65), hits (105), total bases (135), and stolen bases (43) and making the All-Star team. *Baseball America* named him Appalachian League Player of the Year. In 1983 the Twins assigned him to Visalia, California (California League), where he paced the league in at-bats (548), finished second in doubles (29), fourth in triples (7), and sixth in batting average (.314), and made the All-Star team. He started the 1984 season with the Toledo, Ohio, Mudhens (International League).

Puckett became just the ninth player to make four hits in his major league debut, which came on May 8, 1984 against the California Angels. He batted .296 making the Topps' Major League All-Rookie team and placing third in the AL Rookie of the Year balloting.

Puckett was the mainstay of the Twins from 1985 to 1995. AL batting champion Tony Oliva improved Puckett's hitting and home run production. As part of his batting motion, Puckett started kicking his left leg, raising his batting average 40 points and hitting 31 home runs in 1986. In 1987 he paced the AL in hits and continued to hit with power to help Minnesota win the AL pennant. Puckett belted a three-run homer in the AL Championship Series against the Detroit Tigers, helping the Twins win in five games. He hit .357 and scored five runs against the St. Louis Cardinals in the World Series, as the Twins captured their first title in franchise history.

Puckett led the AL in hits in 1988 and 1989, joining the select company of Ty Cobb and Tony Oliva as the only AL players to accomplish that feat

Kirby Puckett ©Courtesy of the Minnesota Twins

for three consecutive seasons. Puckett's best offensive year came in 1988, when he batted .356 with 234 hits, 24 home runs, 109 runs scored, and 121 RBIs. He won his only AL batting title in 1989 with a .339 average, becoming the first AL right-hander to capture the crown over a full season since 1970.

Puckett batted .319 in 1991 and .429 with two home runs and six RBIs against the Toronto Blue Jays in the AL Championship Series to help the Twins win another AL pennant. In Game Six of the World Series against the Atlanta Braves, Puckett made a game-saving catch against Ron Gant and clouted a game-winning home run in the eleventh inning. The next night, the

Twins won their second World Series in five years. In 1992 Puckett led the AL with 210 hits.

In 1994 Puckett moved to right field to prolong his career. During that strike-shortened season, he paced the AL with 112 RBIs in just 108 games. He was batting .314 in 1995 when Dennis Martinez of the Cleveland Indians hit him on the left side of the face on September 28, breaking his jaw. He never played again in the major leagues. Doctors diagnosed him with glaucoma the following spring. The disease caused irreversible damage to his right eye and forced him to quit baseball. Puckett advised teammates, "Tomorrow is not promised to any of us, so enjoy yourself."

Puckett appeared in 10 consecutive All-Star games from 1986 to 1995, starting in 1986, 1989, 1992, 1993, and 1994. He batted .292 in All-Star competition and was named Most Valuable Player of the 1993 contest with a double, home run, and two RBIs. He won six Gold Glove (1986–1989, 1991–1992) and five *The Sporting News* Silver Slugger (1986–1989, 1992) awards, and he finished among the top 10 in MVP voting seven times.

During his 12-year major league career, Puckett batted .318 with 1,071 runs scored, 2,304 hits, 414 doubles, 207 home runs, and 1,085 RBIs in 1,783 games. The Twins retired his number 34 in 1997 and renamed the street outside the Hubert Humphrey Metrodome Kirby Puckett Place. He was elected to the National Baseball Hall of Fame in 2001.

The jovial, always smiling Puckett was very popular off the field and was involved in numerous charity activities. He received the Branch Rickey Award in 1994 for his extensive community service and donated $250,000 to the University of Minnesota for scholarships to minority students. His Puckett 8-Ball Billiards Invitational raised money for the Minneapolis-based Children's Heart Fund. He acknowledged, "All I want to do is thank God—He gave me the talent, the know-how. And there are a lot of people who helped me along the way."

Puckett served the Minnesota Twins as executive vice president of baseball operations and was on the board of directors from 1996 to 2003. The Minneapolis, Minnesota, resident was married to Tonya (Hudson) Puckett before their divorce in 2002 and has one daughter, Catherine, and one son, Kirby Jr. In September 2002 he was charged with sexually assaulting a woman in a Minneapolis-area restaurant-bar bathroom. Although a jury cleared him of all charges in March 2003, he no longer works for the Twins.

BIBLIOGRAPHY
Dave DeLand, "Helping Hands," *Beckett Baseball Monthly* 114 (September 1994), pp. 22–23; Henry Hecht, "Cal Can Bring 'em Up Right," *Sports Illustrated* 61 (July 23, 1984), pp. 56–57; *Minnesota Twins Media Guide*, 1996; Kirby Puckett and Mike Bryan, *I Love This Game: My Life and Baseball* (New York, 1993); *The Sporting News Baseball Register*, 1996; Rick Telander, "Minny's Mighty Mite," *Sports Illustrated* 66 (June 15, 1987), pp. 46–49.

David L. Porter

ALBERT PUJOLS   Baseball
(January 16, 1980–)

Albert Pujols recorded one of the best rookie seasons in major league baseball history in 2001 as a 21-year-old.

Jose Alberto Pujols was born on January 16, 1980 in Santo Domingo, Dominican Republic, and was brought up by his father, Bienvenido Pujols, and grandparents. His father played baseball in the Dominican Republic and worked many different jobs that often took him away from home for long periods. Albert Pujols started playing sandlot baseball at age 5 and, at age 16, moved with his father to New York City and then to Independence, Missouri.

At Fort Osage High School in Independence, Pujols twice won All-State honors in baseball. He batted .500 as a sophomore and .600 as a junior while leading Fort Osage to a Missouri Class 4A State Championship. Fort Osage baseball coach Dave Fry observed, "I felt like the baseball gods had smiled down on me." Pujols's frequent mammoth home runs caused opposing pitchers to walk him 55 of 88 plate appearances his junior year. He graduated from Fort Osage after the first semester of his senior year in 1999 and accepted a baseball scholarship to Maple Woods Community College in Kansas City, Missouri. After turning an unassisted triple play and clouting a grand slam home run in his first college game, he batted .461 for Maple Woods.

The St. Louis Cardinals (National League) selected Pujols in the thirteenth round of the June 1999 free-agent draft, and Pujols was signed by scout David Karaff. Pujols spent most of 2000 at Peoria, Illinois (Midwest League), being promoted to Potomac (Carolina League) in August and Memphis, Tennessee (Pacific Coast League) in September. He hit a combined .314 with 41 doubles, 19 home runs, and 96 runs batted in (RBI) while playing third base. In 2000 he was named ML Most Valuable Player (MVP) and PCL playoff MVP, hitting .367.

St. Louis assumed Pujols would start the 2001 season at Class AA New Haven, Connecticut (Eastern League) or Memphis. He was so poised at the plate, hit for both average and power, and played so well defensively that he remained on the Cardinals roster. Cardinals farm director Mike Jorgensen did not want to rush him to the major leagues but recognized his incredible talent and maturity. St. Louis skipper Tony La Russa observed, "He's really got a maturity about him you don't see very often in young players, and you really don't see it in older players either."

In 2001 the 6-foot 3-inch, 210-pound Pujols rewrote the record books for NL rookies with 360 total bases, 88 extra-base hits, and 130 RBIs. He finished one home run shy of the NL rookie record of 38 home runs. He became the first rookie in NL history to hit .300 with 30 home runs, 100 runs scored, and 100 RBIs, the first Cardinal to accomplish the feat since Stan Musial in 1952. The right-handed Pujols set the Cardinal rookie records for doubles, home runs, extra-base hits, runs, RBIs, and total bases while playing 161 games, including 55 at third base, 43 at first base for injured Mark McGwire, 39 in right field, and 39 in left field. Pujols batted over .300 every month except July and hit well to all fields. He was the first Cardinal rookie to play in the All-Star Game since third baseman Eddie Kazak in 1949, walking in his only plate appearance. Pujols homered off Randy Johnson in the 2001 NL Division Series, which the Arizona Diamondbacks won in five games. His postseason accolades included being the Baseball Writers' Association of America NL Rookie of the Year (only the ninth unanimous selection), *The Sporting News* (*TSN*), *Baseball Digest,* and *Baseball Weekly's* NL Rookie of the Year, Topps third baseman on the Rookie All Star team, and *TSN* NL Silver Slugger Award at third base.

In 2002 Pujols batted .314 with 40 doubles, 34 home runs, 127 RBIs, and a .561 slugging percentage to help the Cardinals repeat as NL Central Division Champions. He ranked second in the NL in runs (118) and RBIs, fourth in total bases (331) and hits (185, shared), seventh in batting, and tenth in home runs. He batted .300 with one triple, three RBIs, and three walks in the NL Division Series triumph over the Arizona Diamondbacks and .263 with one double, one home run, and two RBIs in the NL Championship Series loss to the San Francisco Giants. Pujols enjoyed a 30-game hitting streak in July and August 2003, tying Stan Musial for second longest in Cardinal history. A two-game suspension for punching San Diego Padres catcher Gary Bennett and a bout with the flu ultimately halted the streak. In August 2003 he clouted his 108th career home run, moving past Joe DiMaggio for third place for most home runs in a player's first three years. Through the 2003 season, Pujols batted .334 with 114 home runs and 381 RBIs in 475 games. His best season came in 2003, when he led the NL in batting average (.359), runs scored (137), hits (212), doubles (51), and total bases (394), and finished second in slugging percentage (.667), third in on-base percentage (.439), fourth in RBIs (124), and tied for fourth in home runs (43). He finished second to Barry Bonds* in the NL MVP balloting.

Pujols met his wife, Beidre, in a Latin dance club in Kansas City, when he was 18 years old and she was 21. They were married in November 1999. Beidre has a daughter, Isabella, with Down's syndrome from a previous relationship. Pujols said, "When I'm not home, I miss Isabella every day. I want to be there for her and do the best I can to be a dad. I don't think of it as a responsibility. God has blessed me." He and Beidre have one son, Albert "A.J.," and live in Roeland Park, Kansas.

BIBLIOGRAPHY

Steve DiMeglio, "Who's Afraid of Albert Pujols?" *USA Today* and *Baseball Weekly*, www.usatoday.com (April 15, 2001), pp. 1–3; John Dewan, ed., *The Scouting Notebook 2002* (Morton Grove, IL, 2002); Chuck Johnson, "Pujols Has Filled Cards' Power Void," *USA Today* and *Baseball Weekly*, www.usatoday.com/sports/baseball/front.com (May 21, 2001), pp. 1–5; MLB Advanced Media, *Albert Pujols* (MLB.com, 2002), pp. 1–3; *St. Louis Cardinals Media Guide*, 2004.

Frank J. Olmsted

R

TIM RAINES   Baseball
(September 16, 1959–)

Tim Raines ranks among the most prolific base stealers in major league baseball history.

Timothy Raines, the son of Ned Raines Sr. and Florence (Reynolds) Raines, was born on September 16, 1959 in Sanford, Florida. His brother, Ned Jr., played minor league outfield from 1978 to 1980. Raines attended Seminole High School in Sanford before being drafted by the Montreal Expos (National League) in June 1977. The 5-foot 8-inch, 185-pounder, who threw right-handed, was signed as a second baseman. After solid seasons with the Gulf Coast Expos (Gulf Coast League), West Palm Beach, Florida (Florida State League), and Memphis, Tennessee (Southern League) from 1977 through 1979, he was selected *The Sporting News* (*TSN*) Minor League Player of the Year in 1980 as a second baseman for the Denver, Colorado, Bears (American Association). He led the AA with 11 triples, 77 stolen bases, and a .354 batting average.

After September promotions to Montreal in 1979 and 1980, Raines batted .304 and stole a league-leading 71 bases for the Expos in 1981. He earned *TSN* Rookie Player of the Year honors and finished second to Fernando Valenzuela* for the NL Rookie of the Year Award. He continued as NL stolen base leader with 78 in 1982, 90 in 1983, and 75 in 1984. He paced the NL in runs scored with 133 in 1983 and 123 in 1987. Raines's outstanding speed and fearlessness on the basepaths enabled him to stretch singles into doubles and to take the extra base on singles by teammates.

The switch-hitting Raines batted for a higher average left-handed but exhibited good power from the right side. Primarily a leadoff batter, he hit hard line drives to all fields. A first-ball hitter, he demonstrated the patience and good batting eye to draw 80 or more walks in seven seasons. Raines played more often in the outfield than second base through 1984 and was employed exclusively thereafter in the outfield to capitalize on his great speed and ability to track down balls. He possessed an accurate, if only average, arm in left field. Raines played with the enthusiasm of a youngster on a sandlot diamond, making him popular with fans and teammates alike.

After leading the NL with a .334 batting average in 1986, Raines tested the free-agent market and missed the first month of the 1987 season. Nonetheless, he batted .330, reached career highs of 18 home runs and 68 RBIs, and hit for the cycle on August 16 against the Pittsburgh Pirates. He hammered switch-hit home runs against the Cincinnati Reds on July 16, 1988 and the Colorado Rockies on August 31, 1993.

From 1988 to 1990, Raines's offensive production dropped markedly, with fans and the media accusing him of lackluster play. In December 1990 Montreal traded him to the Chicago White Sox (American League) for outfielder Ivan Calderon and pitcher Barry Jones. Raines scored 102 runs for the White Sox in 1991 and 1992. Although slowed by a broken thumb in 1993, he batted .306 in 115 games and proved a key ingredient in Chicago's Western Division title. He set an AL Championship Series record with 12 hits while batting .444, but the Toronto Blue Jays prevailed in six games. He remained productive for Chicago through the 1995 campaign.

In December 1995, the White Sox traded Raines to the New York Yankees (AL). From 1996 to 1998, he platooned in left field and usually played against right-handed pitching. Despite serious hamstring injuries, he batted .284 in 1996, .321 in 1997, and .290 in 1998 for New York. After spending the 1999 campaign with the Oakland Athletics (AL), Raines temporarily retired in March 2000 after he was diagnosed with lupus. Montreal signed him in 2001. Raines batted .308 in 47 games as a pinch hitter and occasional outfielder despite suffering a torn biceps and labrum in his left shoulder.

Raines played in seven All-Star games for the NL and was on World Championship New York Yankees teams in 1996 and 1998. The greatest baseball thrills for Raines and his wife, Virginia, however, came in 2001. When the Expos faced the Baltimore Orioles in an exhibition game on March 6, he played against his son, Tim Jr., an outfielder. On rehabilitation assignment with Ottawa, Canada (International League), Raines again performed on August 21 against his son, then an outfielder for Rochester, New York. Both made one hit in three at-bats. In October, the Expos traded Raines to the Baltimore Orioles (AL) where he joined his son, who had been promoted there earlier that week. They joined Ken Griffey Sr. and Ken Griffey Jr.* as the only fathers and sons to play as teammates in the major leagues. Coincidentally, Raines had debuted in the major leagues on August 31, 1979, the day his son was born. Raines finished his major league career in 2002 with the Florida Marlins (NL). Used almost exclusively as a pinch hitter, the 42-year-old Raines batted .191 with a .351 on-base percentage.

In 23 major league seasons, Raines collected 2,605 hits, scored 1,571 runs, and produced 430 doubles, 113 triples, 170 home runs, 980 RBIs, 1,330 walks, and a .295 batting average in 2,502 major league games. His 808 stolen bases rank fifth highest in major league history.

BIBLIOGRAPHY
Associated Press, "Tim Raines, Sr. Joins His Son in Baltimore," http://cbs.sportsline. com (October 3, 2001), pp. 1–3; Steve Borelli, "A Final Push to Share the Raines," www.usatoday.com (July 13, 2001), pp. 1–5; John Dewan, ed., *The Scouting Notebook 2002* (Morton Grove, IL, 2002); John Dewan, ed., *The Scouting Report 1994* (New York, 1994); David L. Porter, ed., *Biographical Dictionary of American Sports: Base-*

ball, Q–Z, revised and expanded edition (Westport, CT, 2000); Marybeth Sullivan, *The Scouting Report 1986* (New York, 1986).

Frank J. Olmsted

MANNY RAMIREZ   Baseball
(May 20, 1972–)

Manny Ramirez has ranked among the most powerful American League (AL) sluggers in the last decade, having averaged over 30 home runs and 100 RBIs per season.

Manuel Aristides Ramirez was born on May 30, 1972 in Santo Domingo, Dominican Republic, the son of Aristides Ramirez, a factory worker, and Onelcida Ramirez, a seamstress. In 1985 the Ramirez family moved to a sixth-floor apartment in Washington Heights in upper Manhattan in New York City.

Baseball provided Ramirez a refuge from the drug culture of his neighborhood. He attended George Washington High School, joining the varsity baseball team as an eighth grader. He rose at 5 A.M. to run and practiced baseball from 6 A.M. until school started and from after school until dark. Coach Steve Mandl recalled, "He was a man among boys. It was dangerous. I always thought we should put a screen in front of the pitcher. He hit the ball that hard." Ramirez became the best high school baseball player in New York City, hitting .633 with 21 home runs in 1991.

The Cleveland Indians (AL) selected the 6-foot, 205-pound Ramirez, who bats and throws right-handed, in the first round as the thirteenth overall pick in the June 1991 free-agent draft. He progressed rapidly through the minor league system at Bristol, Tennessee (Appalachian League) in 1991, Kinston, North Carolina (Carolina League) in 1992, and Canton/Akron, Ohio (Eastern League) and Charlotte, North Carolina (International League) in 1993, leading the EL with a .340 batting average. He made his major league debut at age 21 with Cleveland against the Minnesota Twins in September 1993 and homered twice against the New York Yankees at Yankee Stadium.

Ramirez supplied enormous power for Cleveland, helping the Indians win the AL Central Division from 1995 through 1999. His .308 batting average, 31 home runs, and 107 runs batted in (RBI) helped Cleveland finish 100–48 in 1995. After going hitless against the Boston Red Sox in the AL Division Series, he batted .286 with two solo home runs against the Seattle Mariners in the AL Championship Series and .222 with one home run and two RBIs against the Atlanta Braves in the World Series. Ramirez, however, was picked off first base with his team trailing in Game Two to thwart a potential rally.

Ramirez hit .309 with 33 home runs, 112 RBIs, and a career-high 45 doubles in 1996. He excelled against the Baltimore Orioles in the AL Division Series, batting .375, doubling twice, and clouting two solo home runs. In 1997 he combined a then career-best 184 hits with a .328 batting average, 40 doubles, 26 home runs, and 88 RBIs. After struggling against the New York

Manny Ramirez ©Courtesy of the Boston Red Sox

Yankees in the AL Division Series, Ramirez hit .286, homered twice, and knocked in three runs against the Baltimore Orioles in the AL Championship Series. However he was picked off first base again in Game Three. Although batting just .154 and making an error in the World Series loss to the Florida Marlins, he clouted two home runs with six RBIs. During the off-season, he worked with team psychologist Charles Maher to improve his concentration.

Ramirez's offensive production soared during his final three seasons with Cleveland. He belted a career-high 45 home runs with 145 RBIs in 150 games in 1998. He homered three straight times against the visiting Toronto Blue Jays on September 15 and tied major league records for most consecutive home runs (4), most home runs in two straight games (5), and most home runs in three consecutive games (6). His home runs in the next two games came against the visiting Minnesota Twins. Ramirez enjoyed an outstanding postseason, batting .357 with two doubles, two home runs, and three RBIs against the Boston Red Sox in the AL Division Series and .333 with two home runs and four RBIs against the New York Yankees in the AL Championship Series.

Ramirez led the AL with a .663 slugging percentage and a career-high 165 RBIs in 1999, batting .333 with 44 home runs and breaking Hal Trosky's 63-year-old club RBI record. He clouted three home runs on August 25 against the Oakland Athletics at Oakland Coliseum. His defense in right field also showed marked improvement. Boston Red Sox pitchers limited him to only one hit in the AL Division Series. He enjoyed his best major league season in an injury-riddled 2000 campaign, leading the AL with a .697 slugging percentage and batting a career-high .351 with 34 doubles, 38 home runs, and 122 RBIs in just 118 games.

In December 2000 the Boston Red Sox (AL) signed Ramirez to a $160 million, eight-year contract, the third largest in major league baseball. He drove in a team-record 31 runs in April 2001, batted over .400 the first month, and paced the AL with 50 RBIs through mid-May. He hit .306 with 41 home runs and 125 RBIs in 2001. He broke his left index finger sliding into home plate against the Seattle Mariners in May 2002 and was sidelined for over a month, but still won the AL batting title, hitting .349 in 120 games. Ramirez helped the Red Sox win the AL Wild Card in 2003, leading the AL in on-base percentage (.427), ranking second in batting average (.325), fourth in slugging percentage (.587), tied for fourth in runs scored (117), fifth in walks (97), and seventh in home runs (37), and knocking in 104 runs. He batted .200 with one home run and 3 RBIs in AL Championship Series against the Oakland Athletics and hit .310 with one double, 2 home runs, and 4 RBIs in the AL Championship Series against the victorious New York Yankees. Boston placed the high-salaried Ramirez on irrevocable waivers following the 2003 season, but no team claimed him.

In 11 major league seasons through 2003, Ramirez has batted .317 with 959 runs scored, 1,585 hits, 347 home runs, and 1,140 RBIs. He was selected as an outfielder to *The Sporting News* All-Star team in 1995, 1999, and 2001 and to *The Sporting News* Silver Slugger team in 1995, 1999, 2000, and 2001. He made the AL All-Star team in 1995 and again from 1998 through 2002.

Cleveland shortstop Omar Vizquel* remarked, "He is a hitting machine. He can grab any bat at any time, and go out there and hit successfully." Ramirez possesses exceptional bat speed and demonstrates considerable power to the opposite field. Indian third baseman Travis Fryman observed, "He is a natural hitter, but one who works extremely hard at his craft." Fryman added, "He is the best opposite-field hitter with power I've ever seen." Minnesota Twins manager Tom Kelly noted, "Manny never seems fooled at the plate. He's fun to watch, but he's frightening when you're on the other side trying to get him out."

Ramirez married Juliana Monteiro of Brazil in October 2002 and resides in Boston, Massachusetts, and Weston, Florida. He has one son. The quick-witted, modest, and likable Ramirez, who enjoys hip-hop music and movies, is often moody and distant. His motto is "only the strong survive."

BIBLIOGRAPHY
Mel Antonen, "Right in the Swing of Things," *USA Today*, May 18, 2001, pp. 1C–2C; *Boston Red Sox Media Guide*, 2003; *Cleveland Indians Media Guide*, 2000; Mike Dodd, "An Invaluable Pair of Indians," *USA Today*, September 22, 1999, p. 3C; Manny Ramirez file, National Baseball Library, Cooperstown, NY; Russell Schneider, *The Cleveland Indians Encyclopedia*, 2nd ed. (Champaign, IL, 2001); *The Sporting News Baseball Register*, 2003.

David L. Porter

ANDRE REED   Football
(January 29, 1964–   )

An unknown from a small school in Pennsylvania, Andre Reed became one of the most prolific pass receivers in National Football League (NFL) history.

Andre Darnell Reed was born on January 29, 1964 in Allentown, Pennsylvania, the son of Calvin Reed and Joyce Reed. His father owned a concrete business and loved football, encouraging his sons to play the sport. When Reed was 8 years old, he played midget football for Allentown's Downtown Youth Center and was coached by Calvin.

Reed, a gifted track athlete, was most passionate about football and played quarterback at Louis E. Dieruff High School in Allentown, graduating in 1981. He attended nearby Kutztown University and converted to wide receiver. As a junior, he made 55 receptions for 791 yards and seven touchdowns, all school records. Reed set Kutztown career records with 142 receptions for 2,002 yards and 14 touchdowns. He was named to two collegiate All-Star teams after both his junior and senior seasons and drew the attention of NFL scouts.

Reed was selected in the fourth round of the 1985 NFL draft by the Buffalo Bills (NFL). After leading Buffalo in receiving during the preseason, he earned a starting job as a rookie. He played 16 NFL seasons, the first 15 from 1985 to 1999 with the Buffalo Bills and 2000 with the Washington Redskins. Reed ended his NFL career ranking third in receptions (951), fourth in yards (13,198), sixth in touchdown catches (87), and ninth in 100-yard receiving games (36). He was named to the Pro Bowl seven straight years from 1988 to 1994.

Reed consistently played well throughout his career, excelling during the 11 seasons he teamed with quarterback Jim Kelly from 1986 to 1996. Kelly observed, "He's been a great receiver all along. He just doesn't get the notoriety some of the other receivers get." Reed became Kelly's favorite receiver, enjoying four 1,000-yard seasons (1989, 1991, 1994, 1996) and five seasons with at least 70 pass receptions (1988–1991, 1994).

Reed set a single-game team record in 1994 with 15 receptions versus the Green Bay Packers, established a team season record with 90 catches in 1994 and 1,312 yards in 1989, and tied the team mark with 10 touchdown receptions in 1991. During his 15 seasons with Buffalo, Reed led the Bills in receiving yardage 9 times, receptions 10 times, and touchdowns 11 times. He also proved a dominant figure in playoff games. In Buffalo's 21 postseason games from the 1988 through 1999 seasons, he made 85 catches for 1,229 yards and nine touchdowns.

Although the most consistent receiver in the American Football Conference (AFC) during his career, Reed was often upstaged by Jerry Rice* of the San Francisco 49ers, the other great receiver in the 1985 NFL draft. Rice gained the fame and publicity that eluded Reed. Reed sometimes believed he was taken for granted, and he got tired of being overlooked, which also meant he was not paid as much as other wide receivers. The highly competitive Reed often complained to the Bills coaching staff about not being thrown to often enough.

Buffalo attained great success during most of Reed's career, reaching the AFC Championship Game in 1988 and making four straight trips to the Super Bowl from 1990 to 1993. The Bills lost them all. Several excellent draft choices brought Reed, Kelly, and running back Thurman Thomas* to the offense and lineman Bruce Smith* and linebacker Cornelius Bennett to the defense. The Bills' no-huddle offense proved almost unstoppable, with Reed playing a major role. Reed, the featured player in a multiple receiver formation, consistently made the key catch, usually over-the-middle, to keep drives alive. He masterfully ran exact pass routes and proved dangerous with the ball after the reception. Although mainly a possession receiver, Reed also served as a deep threat. Reed reflected, "I know every time I went on the field, I tried to do my best."

Reed's biggest challenge as a player came in 1995, when he suffered a torn hamstring and missed 10 games. His strong work ethic in off-season training helped him overcome the injury, as he returned that fall with his final 1,000-yard season.

Reed married his wife, Cyndi, in April 1993. They have two children, a daughter, Auburn, and a son, Andre Jr. Reed used his fame as an NFL star to help children, serving as a spokesman and contributor to the local chapter of the Big Brothers/Big Sisters program.

In September 2001, Reed returned to Buffalo and announced his retirement. He ended his NFL career as by far the greatest receiver in team history and one of the finest in NFL history. As Thurman Thomas said of Reed, "He always wanted to be the best receiver he could be."

BIBLIOGRAPHY
Mark Gaughan, "Home, But Not Alone; Andre Reed Returns to Buffalo to Make Sure He's Remembered with His Mates from Super Run," *Buffalo News*, September 9, 2001, Sect. C, p. 11; Hank Hersch, "Business as Usual," *Sports Illustrated* 81 (November 7, 1994), p. 170; Keith Joyner, "Andre Reed and the Hall of Fame: A Way of Evaluating Pass Receivers," *Coffin Corner* 19 (1997), pp. 17–21; Terry Larimer, "Andre Reed in Class by Himself in AFC," *Los Angeles Times*, October 22, 1989, Sect. C, p. 6; Salvatore Maiorana, *Relentless: The Hard-Hitting History of Buffalo Bills Football* (Lenexa, KS, 1994); Milt Northrop, "Catching up to the Greats; Superstar Reed Makes History, If not Headlines," *Buffalo News*, September 3, 1995, Sect. C, p. 7; Jerry Sullivan, "Durable and Dangerous; Reed Still Rolling in Longest-Running Show in Bills History," *Buffalo News*, December 19, 1998, Sect. C, p. 7.

Robert A. Dunkelberger

BUTCH REYNOLDS
(June 8, 1964–)

Track and Field

Butch Reynolds held the world 400-meter record for 11 years from 1988 to 1999.

Harry Lee Reynolds Jr., nicknamed "Butch," was born on June 8, 1964 in Akron, Ohio, the second of three children of Harry Reynolds Sr. and Catherine Reynolds. His father, a good high school athlete, worked in a factory and was later disabled. His mother worked for the Summit County Children's Home. His younger brother, Jeff, was a 400-meter sprinter at Kansas State University.

Reynolds tried out for track and field in ninth grade only because of the pretty girls on the Hoban Catholic High School team. Butch, soon considered one of the fastest runners in the state, won his first 400-meter race in 1980 at the Austintown-Fitch Class AA meet. He told his father, "That 400 isn't a race for human beings, that's what they have the Kentucky Derby for." Reynolds discovered that "if I did more sports, I could do less work [at home.]" He played football and basketball and ran the 400-meter dash in 48.1 seconds. He placed second in the 400-meter dash in the State High School Championships as a junior and was expected to win all the state sprint events as a senior until suffering a knee injury.

Sports infused Reynolds with inner strength, helping make him tough and self-reliant. His coaches also helped shape his character, while his participation in sports kept him out of trouble in a crime- and drug-infested neighborhood.

When Reynolds graduated from Hoban in 1983, his grades were below the 2.0 average required for a National Collegiate Athletic Association (NCAA) scholarship. He attended Butler Community College in El Dorado, Kansas. Coach John Frances taught him the value of hard work and distance running as a way of building running strength and avoiding injuries. In 1984 Reynolds won the National Junior College 400-meter championship.

Reynolds transferred to Ohio State University in 1986 and triumphed in the 400 meters at the NCAA Outdoor Championships the following spring. At Ohio State, he helped win the Big Ten Conference (BTC) Mile-Relay Indoor Championship and the 1,600-meter BTC Outdoor Relay Championship. He set Ohio State indoor records for the 400- and 500-meter dashes and the 440-yard and 600-yard dashes. Reynolds held the world record for the 500-meter dash (1 minute 86 seconds) and set the world record for the 600-yard run (1 minute 6.87 seconds). He established the world record for the 400-meter dash at sea level (44.09 seconds) and finished third in the 1987 World Championships.

Reynolds did not return to Ohio State in the fall of 1987 and made the 1988 Olympic team. In 1988 he set the world record in the 400-meter dash (43.29 seconds), a record that stood for 11 years. He won a silver medal in that event and helped win the 4×400 relay at the 1988 Seoul, South Korea,

Olympics. His relay team tied the world record (2 minutes 56.16 seconds) for 1,600 meters.

In November 1990, the International Amateur Athletic Federation (IAAF) suspended Reynolds for alleged use of the banned steroid Nandrolone. Despite evidence that cleared him, the IAAF refused to set aside his ban. Reynolds took the IAAF to court and won a judgment for just over $27 million. After an extended legal battle, the judgment was vacated because of jurisdictional problems.

The suspension cost Reynolds two of his best years of running and an opportunity to participate in the 1992 Olympics. Throughout the ordeal, he worked for charities and remained an excellent role model for young people. He completed his Bachelor's degree in education at Ohio State in January 1991 and advised youngsters, "It's cool to stay in school."

In 1993 Reynolds was elected captain by the U.S. World Championship team. After capturing the World Indoor 400-meter title that year, he won a silver medal in the 400-meter dash and helped the U.S. team set a world record in the 1,600-meter relay at the World's Outdoor Championship in Stuttgart, Germany. Reynolds was injured in the second round of the 1996 Olympic Trials after nearly defeating Michael Johnson* in the 400 meters, and so again he missed the Olympics.

Reynolds married Lillian Lumb on June 10, 1989, but the stress of the legal battle and the subsequent debts caused their separation in 1997. He retired from running in November 2000 after a 16-year career and now manages the Butch Cares for Kids Foundation in Akron, working closely with the city in youth development.

BIBLIOGRAPHY

Akron Beacon Journal (*Beacon Sunday Magazine*), August 1988–November 2000; *Cleveland Plain Dealer*, June 12, 1991, March 15, 1993; *Columbus Dispatch*, October 8, 1991, June 27, 1992, December 4, 1992, August 28, 1993; Keith McClellan, Interview with Harold "Butch" Reynolds Jr., December 6, 2001; *Ohio State Alumni Magazine*, July, August 1989, pp. 46–47; *Ohio State Lantern*, July, August 1987, p. 41, September 1987, p. 42, July 28, 1988, p. 4, October 1988, p. 38, July–August 1989, p. 46; *Runner's World*, June 1993, pp. 6–7.

Keith McClellan

JERRY RICE   Football
(October 13, 1962–   )

Jerry Rice set new standards for wide receivers, scoring more touchdowns and catching more passes than any other player in National Football League (NFL) history.

Jerry Lee Rice was born on October 13, 1962 in Starkville, Mississippi, the son of Joe Nathan Rice, a brick mason, and Eddie B. Rice. Rice, the sixth of eight children, has two sisters and five brothers. He grew up in Crawford, "a sleepy town of some 500 souls" 38 miles from Starkville. His childhood was "happy, idyllic," with his two passions being riding a neighbor's horse and cheering Dallas Cowboys wide receiver Drew Pearson. To attend B.L. Moor High School, he had to run five miles to and from Crawford. Rice observed, "That's what made [me] . . . running those dirt roads and country fields." As a senior in 1980, Rice starred in both football and basketball. He made 35 touchdown receptions in football and averaged 30 points a game in basketball.

Coach Archie Cooley of Mississippi Valley State University gave Rice a football scholarship. Rice developed wonderfully as a sophomore. By his junior year in 1983, he was named an All-America and set Division I-AA records with 102 catches and 1,450 season yards. A year later, he became one of the greatest college receivers of all time. Despite sometimes being triple teamed, he seemed unstoppable. His 1984 season saw him record 162 points, 103 receptions, 1,682 yards, and 27 touchdowns. Altogether, Rice set 18 Division I-AA career records, including most catches (301), receiving yards (4,693), and touchdowns (50). He surpassed 1,000 receiving yards three consecutive years, was selected the Most Valuable Player (MVP) in the Blue-Gray Game, played in the Freedom Bowl, and made SBN (Sports Block Network's) College Football All-Time team.

In 1985 Rice was selected as a first-round draft choice, sixteenth overall, by the San Francisco 49ers (NFL). His five-year contract was worth $2.1 million. His rookie year resembled a roller-coaster ride, but he was chosen National Football Conference (NFC) Rookie of the Year. He caught 49 passes for 927 yards, but was overwhelmed by the complexity of the 49er playbook and booed unmercifully by fans for dropping passes. Teammates bristled at Rice's seeming mix of arrogance and showmanship.

The following year proved a sensational one for Rice. He ranked among NFC leaders with 86 receptions and among NFL leaders with 1,570 receiving yards and 15 touchdown receptions. His flair and graceful athleticism netted him the *Sports Illustrated* NFL Player of the Year Award.

The NFL named Rice its MVP in 1987, as he made 1,078 receiving yards (16.6 average) and 65 receptions. His 22 receptions set an NFL record, statistically the acme of Rice's career. His next best season high of 17 touchdowns came in 1989. *Sports Illustrated, Pro Football Weekly, The Sporting News*, and *Football Digest* picked Rice as their NFL Player of the Year.

Rice dominated the NFL further in 1988, though tallying only nine touchdowns. He gained 1,306 receiving yards for an average of 20.4 yards. In Super Bowl XXIII, the 49ers defeated the Cincinnati Bengals, and Rice was designated MVP.

The 6-foot 2-inch, 196-pounder established a unique reputation in the NFL as a player who relished intense training and conditioning. His work ethic included being first into exercise drills and last back home after practice. Rice's absence of injuries revealed him to be a superbly conditioned athlete, who could absorb hits, bumps, and bruises.

Jerry Rice ©Courtesy of the Oakland Raiders

In 1990 Rice earned another Super Bowl ring in a win over the Denver Broncos and was unanimously selected to the Pro Football Hall of Fame NFL "Team of the 1980s." His achievements included winning a *Sports Illustrated*'s NFL Player of the Year Award and being the NFL leader in receptions (105) and yardage (1,502 yards).

From 1992 to 1996, Rice's career maintained its astonishing level. In 1992 he recorded his seventh consecutive 1,000-yard season. The following year, the Associated Press recognized him as the NFL Offensive Player of the Year, and he played in his seventh consecutive Pro Bowl. On September 5, 1994 against the Los Angeles Raiders, Rice broke the legendary Jim Brown's touchdown record with 127. In 1995, Rice widened his NFL touchdown record to 156 and became the NFL's receiving yardage recordholder with 14,040 yards. The 1996 season saw him record his 150th career touchdown reception against the Green Bay Packers.

In 1997 a torn anterior medial collateral ligament in his left knee caused Rice to miss 13 games. Until 1997, he had never missed a game at any level. When told that his injury might take six months to heal, he trained fanatically and returned within three months. Sadly, a great season-ending catch resulted in a fractured patella and two 1998 knee surgeries. Rice still started 16 games in 1998 and finished with 82 receptions for a team-high 1,157 yards and nine touchdowns. He became the first player in NFL history over age 35 to record a 1,000-yard season and the first player in NFL history to reach the 17,000-yard mark in rushing or receiving.

In June 2001, Rice left the San Francisco 49ers. He appeared at a news conference dressed in silver and black as an Oakland Raider (NFL). The Associated Press quoted him: "What I want to do is just come in here and do what I've been doing my entire career. That's basically just being a kid out there on the football field and doing something I love." In 2001 he caught 83 passes for 1,139 yards and nine touchdowns. Rice helped Oakland finish best in the AFC with an 11–5 record in 2002, making 92 receptions for 1,211 yards (13.2- yard average) and seven touchdowns. His 200th career touchdown came against the Denver Broncos on November 10, when he broke Walter Payton's record for all-purpose yardage.

Rice scored his twenty-first postseason touchdown on a nine-yard pass from Rich Gannon to tie Thurman Thomas* and Emmitt Smith* for most career playoff touchdowns and moved past Thomas for career playoff yards with 2,132 postseason yards in a 30–10 rout over the New York Jets in an AFC playoff game. Rice made five pass receptions for 79 yards, as the Raiders defeated Tennessee, 41–24, in the AFC Championship Game. The Tampa Bay Buccaneers limited Rice to five receptions for 77 yards and one touchdown in a 48–21 rout of Oakland in Super Bowl XXXVII.

Through the 2002 season, Rice's impressive career covered 270 games, 21,597 receiving yards, average reception of 14.8 yards, and 192 touchdowns. Rice has tallied 203 touchdowns altogether.

Rice is involved with the United Negro Fund and donates funds annually to the Bay Area Omega Boys Club through his 127 Foundation. He and his wife, Jackie Mitchell, have three children, Jacqui, Jerry Jr., and Jada, and live in Atherton, California.

BIBLIOGRAPHY
David L. Porter, ed., *African-American Sports Greats* (Westport, CT, 1995); Jerry Rice, http://sports.nfl.com/2000/playerhighlights; Jerry Rice, http://cbs.sportsline.com/u/football/nfl/players; Jerry Rice, http://encarta.msn.com/find; William Wagner, "Knowing When to Say When," *Football Digest* 30 (December 2000), www.findarticles.com/moOfcl/430/66760534/p1/article.jhtml.

Scott A.G.M. Crawford

MARIANO RIVERA
Baseball

(November 29, 1969–   )

Mariano Rivera has helped the New York Yankees (American League) win six AL pennants and three World Series titles, leading the AL twice in saves.

Mariano Rivera was born on November 29, 1969 in Panama City, Panama, the son of Mariano Rivera, a fisherman, and grew up in Puerto Caimito. Rivera has one sister, Delia, and two brothers, Alvaro and Giraldo. At age 7, he began playing baseball with a glove made of cardboard. He received his first real glove at age 10 and took it with him to school, church, and bed.

Despite their lack of equipment, the youngsters on those dusty streets of Panama really enjoyed playing baseball. When asked about the early introduction to the sport, Rivera replied, "It makes me smile and it makes me happy to think about that." Rivera spent hours playing on streets where the flow of the game was affected by the traffic. As for his role model, he responded, "You see most kids trying to be Nolan Ryan or Don Mattingly . . . I never thought about being a pro. I just got the ball, got my glove and enjoyed the game." His attitude may have come from his father, a fisherman. Captain Mariano told his son, "Don't even think about becoming a pro until after you sign a contract." Rivera, mindful of those years growing up without equipment, boxes up real gloves, balls, and bats and sends them off for children to use in Panama.

Rivera overcame his meager beginnings in baseball to become one of the premier major league closers. Minnesota Twins manager Tom Kelly observed, "Rivera should be pitching in a superior league." The New York Yankees signed him as a nondrafted free agent in February 1990. In his first season of professional baseball with the Gulf Coast Yankees in 1990, Rivera was so dominant that he was named the Gulf Coast League's "Star of Stars." He finished the season with a 5–1 record and allowed only one earned run in 52 innings. His earned run average (ERA) was a tiny 0.17, as he pitched a seven-inning no-hitter in his only start of the season. Rivera continued striking out batters in 1991 and 1992, but in 1992 he suffered through an injury-plagued season with the Class A Fort Lauderdale, Florida, Yankees (Florida State League). Despite the injury, *Baseball America* still rated him as the ninth best prospect in the Yankees system.

In 1994 Rivera was injured again and was placed on the disabled list twice with a strained right shoulder and a strained left hamstring. He pitched 22 games that season in three leagues, earning a 10–2 record. The following season, he split time between the majors and minor leagues. After starting with the Columbus, Ohio, Clippers (International League), he was brought up to the New York Yankees on May 16, 1995. Rivera made his first start on May 23, pitching 3.1 innings, giving up eight hits, five earned runs, three walks, and striking out five batters. He lost the decision, 10–0, becoming the first Yankee rookie to lose his debut start since Jeff Johnson in 1991.

Rivera's first win as a major leaguer came against the Oakland A's on May 28, when he gave up seven hits and one earned run and struck out one in 5.1 innings in the 4–1 victory. Rivera returned to Columbus but was recalled again on August 22 and appeared in the AL Division Series against the Seattle Mariners. He won his one start (in Game Two), but the Yankees lost the series.

Rivera was heralded as one of the most dominant pitchers in baseball in 1996, when he compiled an 8–3 record with a 2.09 ERA and five saves in 61 relief appearances. Ozzie Guillen of the Chicago White Sox called him "the finest pitcher in Baseball." Rivera set a record for Yankee relievers with 130 strikeouts in 107 innings, breaking Goose Gossage's record of 122 in 1978. He also notched another postseason victory, as the underdog Yankees won their first World Series in 18 seasons against the Atlanta Braves. When John Wetteland left the Yankees for the Texas Rangers, Rivera moved to the closer role with an untouchable 96-mile-per-hour fastball. Battery mate Joe Girardi called Rivera "sneaky," while Derek Jeter* said, "When Mo's pitching, you don't field nothing, he strikes out a lot of guys."

During the next three years (1998–2000), the Yankees won consecutive World Series with Rivera as the relief ace. In the 1999 postseason, he tossed 12.1 scoreless innings in eight games. In the World Series against the Atlanta Braves, he set a postseason career record with an 0.38 ERA in 47.1 innings. He pitched 4.2 scoreless innings with a win and two saves, earning the Series Most Valuable Player (MVP) honors.

The 2001 season ended with bitter disappointment for Rivera. The Yankees blew a 2–1 lead over the Arizona Diamondbacks, in the bottom of the ninth inning in Game Seven of the World Series. Rivera admits that it was his errant throw after fielding a Damian Miller bunt that "was the key to the inning." That game ended his 23-game postseason save streak, as he surrendered the winning hit to Luis Gonzalez.

The 6-foot 2-inch, 185-pound Rivera, who bats and throws right-handed, has earned a spot on six AL All-Star teams (1997, 1999–2003), won the 1999 and 2001 AL Rolaids Relief Award, and earned the 1999 World Series MVP and the 2003 AL Championship Series MVP. He finished third in voting for the AL Cy Young Award twice (1996, 1999) and led the AL in saves in 1999 (45) and 2001 (50). Through 2003, he has compiled a 43–29 mark and 2.49 ERA, converted 283 of 327 save opportunities, and struck out 582 batters in 649.2 innings. Rivera's 40 saves helped the Yankees win the AL pennant in 2003. He saved two games in the AL Division Series against the Minnesota Twins, finished 1–0 with two saves against the Boston Red Sox in the AL Championship Series, and saved one World Series game against the victorious Florida Marlins, giving him 9 World Series and 30 postseason career saves.

Rivera remains the Yankees' dominant closer. During the off-season, he and his wife, Clara, and their children, Mariano and Jafet, return to La-Chorrera, Panama, and live in a modest home near his parents.

BIBLIOGRAPHY
Michael Bamberger, "Strikeouts by the Boat Load," *Sports Illustrated* 86 (March 24, 1997), pp. 50–53; Jack Curray, "The Indispensable Yankee," *New York Times*, May 27, 1996, National Baseball Library, Cooperstown, NY; ESPN.com news services, "Rivera Still Wonders Why Yankees Didn't Turn Two," March 20, 2002; Kevin Kernan, "MVP Mariano: Killer Weapon," *New York Post*, October 28, 1999, National Baseball Library, Cooperstown, NY; Mariano Rivera Statistics—Baseball—Reference.com, www.baseball-reference.com/r/riverma01.shtm; *New York Yankees Media Guide*, 2003; Ben Walker, "Rivera No Longer Mr. Automatic," *Albany Times Union*, May 7, 2002, National Baseball Library, Cooperstown, NY.

Scot E. Mondore

DAVID ROBINSON   Basketball
(August 6, 1965–   )

David Robinson combined academic and athletic excellence, ranking among the most talented centers in National Basketball Association (NBA) history.

David Maurice Robinson, nicknamed "The Admiral," was born on August 6, 1965 in Key West, Florida, the son of Ambrose Robinson, a navy career man, and Frieda Robinson, a nurse. Robinson played basketball in high school at Virginia Beach, Virginia, but held varied interests. When his father was transferred in 1982, Robinson played basketball well enough his senior year at Osbourn Park High School in Manassas, Virginia, to attract the attention of U.S. Naval Academy coaches. His high test scores made it easy for him to be accepted, and he entered the Naval Academy in 1983. He already had reached 6 foot, 6 inches and grew an unbelievable seven additional inches while at the Academy.

As a Midshipman between 1984 and 1987, Robinson led the Naval Academy to a 106–25 won-lost record and three appearances in the National Collegiate Athletic Association (NCAA) Division I basketball tournament. The Midshipmen in 1986 advanced to the Regional Finals before losing to Duke University, 71–50. Robinson, in his first season, averaged just 7.6 points. He soon learned how to play the game, condition his body, and use his height and quickness to make the right moves near the basket. Over the next three seasons, his scoring average stood at 23.6, 22.7, and 28.2 points. Robinson registered 2,669 career points (21.0-point average) and 1,314 career rebounds (10.5-rebound average). He holds the NCAA Division I records for most blocked shots in a season (207) in 1986, the most blocked shots in one game (14), and the highest career average of blocked shots (5.9), and he became the first Division I player to complete his career with over 2,500 points and 1,300 rebounds, while shooting over 60 percent from the field. He was named 1987 Player of the Year by the Associated Press, United Press International, *The Sporting News (TSN)*, the U.S. Basketball Writers' Association, and the National Association of Basketball Coaches, Wooden Award and Naismith Award winner, and *TSN* First Team All-America in 1986 and 1987.

After graduation from the Naval Academy in 1987 with a Bachelor of Science degree in mathematics, the 7-foot 1-inch, 250-pound Robinson was selected as the number one draft pick by the San Antonio Spurs (NBA). He did not play until the 1989–1990 season because of his commitment to serve in the United States Navy. After leading the Spurs to a 56–26 won-lost record and a 35-win improvement, he averaged 24.3 points, 12.0 rebounds, and 3.89 blocked shots and was selected the NBA's Rookie of the Year. During his second season, Robinson was the only NBA player to rank among the top 10 in four categories: rebounding (1st), blocked shots (2nd), and scoring and field goal percentage (9th). He paced the NBA in scoring in 1991 and in blocked shots in 1991 and 1992. His other statistics virtually remained the same during the next three seasons. In the 1993–1994 season finale, Robinson scored 71 points against the Los Angeles Clippers. He led the NBA in scoring at 29.8 points per game that season and led the league for the first of three consecutive times in free throws made.

Robinson continued to score well over the next three seasons and again led the NBA in rebounding in 1995–1996. With the acquisition of 7-foot, 250-pound Tim Duncan* in the 1997 NBA draft, the Spurs contended for their first NBA Championship. Referred to as a "Twin Tower" with Robinson, Duncan soon developed into a premier scorer, rebounder, and shot blocker. Robinson adapted his game for the Spurs to use the two big men to their advantage. Sportswriters predicted, "Duncan and Robinson may prove to be the best two big men to ever play the game together." This cooperative effort produced the franchise's first NBA Championship in 1999 with a four games to one triumph over the New York Knicks.

With Duncan and Robinson at peak performance, San Antonio compiled the best overall won-lost NBA record in 1999–2000, and the Spurs were favored to win another title. The Spurs easily eliminated the Minnesota Timberwolves and Dallas Mavericks in the first two rounds but were humiliated by the Los Angeles Lakers in the Western Conference (WC) Finals. San Antonio barely captured the Midwest Division in 2001–2002 with a 58–24 record, but was again eliminated by the Los Angeles Lakers in five games in the Western Conference semifinals.

Robinson played his final NBA season in 2002–2003, averaging 8.5 points to help San Antonio compile the best record (60–22) in the NBA. The Spurs triumphed over the Phoenix Suns, Los Angeles Lakers, and Dallas Mavericks to win the Western Conference playoffs and defeated the New Jersey Nets in the NBA finals.

Robinson, the only male basketball player to appear on three different Olympic teams, was the leading scorer for the 1996 gold-medal-winning team and a member of the 1988 bronze medal and the 1992 gold medal teams. He holds the all-time scoring record of 270 points.

Robinson was named among the 50 Greatest Players in NBA History (1996), received the IBM Award for all-around contributions to team success (1990–1991, 1994–1996), was elected in 1999 to the San Antonio Sports Hall of Fame and the Texas Hall of Fame, and was selected the NBA All-Star Team 10 times. He made the All-NBA First Team in 1991, 1992, 1995, and 1996, the All-NBA Second Team in 1994 and 1998, and the All-NBA Third Team in 1990, 1993, 2000, and 2001. He also was named to the All-NBA Defensive First Team in 1991, 1992, 1995, and 1996 and All-NBA Defensive Second Team in 1990, 1993, 1994, and 1998.

In his 14 seasons with the Spurs from 1989–1990 through 2002–2003, Robinson compiled 20,790 points in 987 regular season games for a 21.1 point scoring average. He holds the Spurs' all-time record for points (20,790), rebounds (10,497), steals (1,388), and blocked shots (2,954). In 123 NBA playoff games, he registered 2,221 points, 1,301 rebounds, 312 blocked shots, and two NBA Championship rings. In 10 NBA All-Star games, he snagged 62 rebounds and scored 141 points.

Robinson proved an unselfish teammate, a tough defensive player, and a fierce competitor, rebounder, and shot blocker. A model husband, father, and philanthropist, he believes that his Christianity and his family are more important than basketball. Robinson married Valerie Hoggatt in January 1992 and has three sons, David Jr., Corey, and Justin. He serves as minister of Oak Hills Church in San Antonio.

Becoming a Christian and marrying gave Robinson's life a new meaning. He developed a basic belief that we are put on earth mostly to give back. "A lot of blacks find success and forget where they came from," he said. "I want to give other kids an opportunity." In 1992 Robinson and his wife developed the David Robinson Foundation (DRF), starting a scholarship and mentoring program, feeding the hungry, and assisting young mothers. In 1997 the DRF donated $5 million to establish the Carver Academy, which provided for a prep school, community center, and religious center in the African American part of San Antonio. Robinson won the NBA Sportsmanship Award in 2001.

BIBLIOGRAPHY:
Dave Branon, "David Robinson: It All Adds Up to Greatness," *Slam Dunk* (1994), pp. 217–224; Roland Lazenby, "Spurs: A Dynasty in the Making," *Spurs* (June 25, 1999), pp. 39–48; *NCAA Men's Basketball's Finest* (Overland Park, KS, 1998); David L. Porter, ed., *African-American Sports Greats* (Westport, CT, 1995); "David Robinson," *Player*, www.nba.com (2000); Lynn Rosellini, "Passing It Back," *Reader's Digest* (April 2001), pp. 94–101; *The Sporting News Official NBA Register*, 2003–2004; Phil Taylor, "Here's to You Mr. Robinson," Special Issue, *Sports Illustrated* 91 (July 7, 1999), pp. 20, 22–23, 25.

John L. Evers

ALEX RODRIGUEZ
(July 27, 1975–   )

Baseball

Alex Rodriguez ranks among the most prolific American League (AL) sluggers as a star shortstop with the Texas Rangers (AL).

Alexander Emmanuel Rodriguez was born on July 27, 1975 in New York

City, the son of Victor Rodriguez and Lourdes Navarro Rodriguez. Rodriguez was one of three children, who suffered a family tragedy when their father abandoned them. He was just 9 years old at the time. Lourdes often kept two jobs to support them. The situation left "deep scars" on their lives.

Rodriguez played baseball and basketball for Westminster Christian High School in Miami, Florida. The Seattle Mariners (AL) made the 17-year-old the very first selection in the 1993 free-agent draft. His father invited him to lunch after nine years, but he refused his invitation. "This was the man who walked away from my mom, who had spent her life working to give us all she could. . . . He walked away from my brother and sister, and from me."

The 6-foot, 195-pound Rodriguez, who bats and throws right-handed, reached the major leagues permanently with the Seattle Mariners at age 20 in 1995. He dominated the shortstop position from the outset. Teammate David Segui complimented his intensity and dedication: "He plays the game the way it's supposed to be played. He plays to win." In his first full season (1996), Rodriguez led the AL with a hefty .358 batting average, 141 runs scored, and 54 doubles, clouted 36 home runs, and produced 123 runs batted in (RBI). An admiring lady fan observed, "People fall in love with his image." Rodriguez, motivated by his own unfortunate family experience, worked frequently with young people. He supported the "Grand Slam for Kids" program in Seattle and authored *Hit a Grand Slam for Alex*, a book for youngsters in the project.

Rodriguez's remaining years with Seattle from 1997 through 2000 brought still more success, including a .316 batting average in his last year with the Mariners. Sportswriter Evan Grant praised Rodriguez as "the best player in the game today." He made the AL All-Star team every year from 1996 to 2002 except for 1999, when an injured knee shortened his season.

Advisors urged Rodriguez to leave Seattle for a larger city, where he could have more opportunities for commercials and off-field marketing. Another metropolis could enhance his media image to equal that of rival shortstops Derek Jeter* of the New York Yankees and Nomar Garciaparra* of the Boston Red Sox.

Rodriguez left Seattle at the December 2000 winter meetings with Scot Boras as his agent. After Rodriguez negotiated seriously with several clubs, Tom Hicks, owner of the Texas Rangers (AL), offered him an incredible $252 million, seven-year contract. Hicks, who liked Rodriguez personally and met with him frequently over several months, said, "The more I came into contact with the young man, the more I was impressed by him. The more I knew we had to sign him at whatever cost." Evan Grant termed it "the richest contract in sports history." An alarmed, frustrated Seattle general manager Pat Gillick warned, "What bothers me is not so much the money, but the amount of years. I thought we had gotten out of that sort of thing."

Despite predictions that with Rodriguez's signing, the Rangers would win the AL West Division title in 2001, Texas finished last in its division for the second straight season with a 73 win, 89 loss mark and a .451 winning percentage. Most blamed pitching woes for the disappointing finish, 44 games behind Rodriguez's former team. The Seattle Mariners tied the major league record with 116 wins and lost just 46 games for a .716 winning record.

Meanwhile, Rodriguez enjoyed a most productive 2001 season with a .318 batting average, 133 runs scored, 393 total bases, and 52 home runs. These last three figures significantly led the AL for a last-place team. Rodriguez compiled a Most Valuable Player–caliber season in 2002, batting .300, leading the AL in home runs (57), RBIs (142), and total bases (389), and finishing second in runs (125) and third in slugging percentage (.623) for another last-place team. In August 2003, he became the second player in major league history with six consecutive 40–home run seasons. In 2003, Rodriguez batted .298, led the AL in home runs (47), runs scored (124), and slugging percentage (.600), finished second in RBIs (118) and total bases (364), and won a second consecutive Gold Glove Award with the last place Rangers. Rodriguez won the AL MVP Award, becoming just the second player from a last place club to receive the award.

Rodriguez admired the dedication of baseball stars Cal Ripken Jr. and Dale Murphy. Through 2003, Rodriguez has batted .308, with 1,535 hits, 345 home runs, and 990 RBIs. Sportswriter Mike Shalin concluded: "Being the best at what he does is the most important thing in Alex's life."

BIBLIOGRAPHY:
Sean Deveney, "Getting from a Leverage Buyout," *The Sporting News*, December 25, 2000, pp. 54–55; Michael Knisley, "Cool Hand: In Face of Constant Playoff Pressure . . . ," *The Sporting News*, October 23, 2000, pp. 48–49; Bob McCullough, "A Squad for Now," *The Sporting News*, August 21, 2000, pp. 32–33; Alex Rodriguez file, Research Center, *The Sporting News*, St. Louis, MO; Mike Shalin, *Alex Rodriguez A + Shortstop* (Champaign, IL, 1999); *The Sporting News, Baseball*, 2003; *The Sporting News Baseball Register*, 2003.

William J. Miller

IVAN RODRIGUEZ
Baseball
(November 30, 1971–)

The call that all minor leaguers hope for came for Ivan Rodriguez on June 20, 1991. At the age of 19 years and 7 months, he moved up from the Class AA Tulsa, Oklahoma, Drillers (Texas League) and became the everyday catcher for the Texas Rangers (American League). Rodriguez started 88 of the team's final 102 games and provided management with a glimmer of his potential by hitting .264 and driving in 27 runs in 280 at-bats. Defensively, Rodriguez showed a powerful arm and threw out 48.6 percent of base stealers. Through hard work and raw talent, he overcame financial insecurity and a language barrier to emerge as one of the best catchers in baseball history.

Ivan Rodriguez was born on November 30, 1971 in Vega Baja, Puerto Rico, the second son of Jose Rodriguez and Eva Rodriguez. By the time he was 7 years old, Jose gave him hitting and defensive drills in the family's back-yard. Rodriguez played Little League baseball against boys from his *barrio*, including future slugger Juan Gonzalez.* Rodriguez began playing professionally upon graduating from Lino Padron Rivera High School in 1988. He signed with the Texas Rangers and joined their Charlotte, North Carolina (South Atlantic League) affiliate, being named an All Star in 1989. He drew rave reviews in the minor leagues, especially for his arm strength. At Tulsa, Oklahoma (Texas League), his throws from home plate to second base were timed at an astonishing 1.78 seconds. In 1991 the TL sportswriters voted him onto the circuit's postseason All-Star team. He also made the Major League Rookie All-Star team that season, capping an unusual double honor. A minor league coach nicknamed him "Pudge" for being small, cocky, and strong.

Rodriguez experienced a difficult transition to the major leagues and life away from his family, friends, and culture. He spoke little English and had difficulty adjusting. Although he earned more money than ever, he was unaccustomed to handling wealth and paying bills. Puerto Rican Luis Mayoral, the Rangers' liaison to the Hispanic community, helped straighten out his financial accounts. Rodriguez also focused on improving his English. He won Gold Gloves in both 1992 and 1993, made the AL All-Star team both seasons, and caught 38.5 percent of would-be base stealers.

Between 1994 and 2001, Rodriguez became a fixture at All-Star games and Gold Glove Award ceremonies. He has batted .305 and earned 10 Gold Gloves. His batting average increased steadily, topping out at .347 in 2000. His overall offensive production also improved, as he achieved career highs in home runs (35) and runs batted in (113) in 1999. He enjoyed a tremendous start in 2000, hitting 27 home runs and driving in 83 runs during the first 91 games. Then disaster struck when he broke his thumb against the Anaheim Angels in July.

His numbers behind the plate remain impressive. Through 2000, Rodriguez had thrown out 46.8 percent of attempted base stealers as the Rangers' backstop. In 1999 this figure peaked at 54.2 percent. His defensive prowess and his .990 fielding percentage led one teammate to observe that he "catches everything, and his arm—it impacts the whole game . . . they're not thinking . . . (of) running . . . they're just worried about not getting picked off."

Upon finishing his thirteenth major league season, Rodriguez has matured as a person and player. He played his career through 2002 with the Texas organization and helped the Rangers win three Western Division championships in 1996, 1998, and 1999. He battled injuries in 2000 and 2001 but still batted .308 and .314 in these seasons. He remains the Rangers' all-time leader in hits (1,723) and doubles (344) and ranks among the top three in games played (1,479), at-bats (5,656), runs (852), RBIs (829), extra-base hits (587), and total bases (2,768). In 2001 Rodriguez gave up the coveted third spot in the batting order when the Rangers signed superstar Alex Rodriguez.* Now wealthy and secure, he personally negotiated his $42 million contract through 2002 with general manager Tom Schieffer. In January 2003, the Florida Marlins (National League) signed him to a one-year, $10 million contract. Florida attained the NL Wild Card in 2003, as Rodriguez batted .297 with 36 doubles, 16 home runs, and 85 RBIs and caught a young Marlins pitching staff. He hit .353 with a double, home run, and 6 RBIs and blocked the plate to prevent J.P. Snow from scoring for the final out of decisive Game 4 of the NL Division Series against the San Francisco Giants. Rodriguez won NL Championship Series MVP honors, batting .521 with two doubles, 2 home runs, and 10 RBIs against the Chicago Cubs to make his first World Series. He hit .273 with 2 doubles and one RBI in the Florida's World Series triumph over the favored New York Yankees.

Rodriguez and Maribel, his wife of 11 years, have three children—Ivan, Amanda, and Ivanna. His Ivan Rodriguez Foundation, which the couple established in 1995, raises money to assist underprivileged children with cancer in Dallas, Texas, and Puerto Rico. He donated $500,000 from his contract to the Texas Rangers Baseball Foundation. The team used part of these funds to build a ballpark for inner-city youths in Fort Worth, Texas. Rodriguez's humanitarian work earned him the prestigious Roberto Clemente Man of the Year Award for 1998.

Rodriguez and his family have purchased their dream home in Miami, Florida. He plans a career in real estate and hopes to establish a baseball academy in Puerto Rico in order to pass along the love and skills of the game he loves so much to the next generation of *boriqua*—baseball hopefuls.

BIBLIOGRAPHY

Chris Colson, "The Heart of Texas: Ivan Rodriguez," *USA Today Baseball Weekly* (April 18–24, 2001), pp. 6, 8–9; Mat Edelson, "Catching Up," *Sport* 89 (September 1998), pp. 92–93; Mat Edelson, "Power Rangers Unite!," *Sport* 90 (July 1999), pp. 38–41; Johnette Howard, "Pudge Factor," *Sports Illustrated* 87 (August 11, 1997), pp. 42–44; Luis R. Mayoral, "Ivan Rodriguez Comes of Age as a Major League Star," *Baseball Digest* 26 (December 1994), pp. 55–57; www.pristinecards.com; www.pudge.org (official site of the Ivan Rodriguez Foundation); www.rangers.mlb.com.

Jorge Iber

JENNIFER RODRIGUEZ   Speedskating
(June 8, 1976–)

Jennifer Rodriguez captured two bronze medals in speedskating at the 2002 Salt Lake City, Utah, Winter Olympic Games.

Jennifer Rodriguez was born on June 8, 1976 in Miami, Florida, the daughter of Joe Rodriguez, a Cuban-American teacher of graphic arts at Miami-Dade Community College, and Barbara Rodriguez, an American who grew up in Boston, Massachusetts. She has a younger brother, Eric.

Rodriguez began roller skating at age 4 and started competing in both speed and figure skating the next year. She continued roller figure skating competition for 16 years, during which time roller speedskating gave way to inlines. She won medals in both roller speedskating and inlines. After graduating in 1994 from Palmetto High School in Miami, she attended Florida International University and Carroll College.

The 5-foot 4-inch, 128-pound Rodriguez became the only woman ever to medal in both roller figure and speedskating at the World Championships the same year. As a roller speed racer, she earned three gold and two silver medals as a two-time U.S. Olympic Festival participant, one silver and one bronze medal at the 1992 World Championship, five gold medals and one bronze medal at the 1992 Junior World Championship, and three gold and two silver medals at the 1993 World Championship.

Rodriguez was a five-time World team figure skating member and a four-time U.S. Olympic Festival participant, collecting one gold, two silver, and one bronze medals. In 1992, she captured one silver medal in the World Championships and was named U.S. Roller Skating Athlete of the Year. She added a bronze medal at the 1993 World Championships and a silver medal at the 1995 Pan American Games.

Rodriguez began dating roller skater KC Boutiette in early 1996. Boutiette converted to ice speed skating when convinced that roller skating would not be considered an Olympic sport. Boutiette became a three-time U.S. Olympic speedskater but found capturing a medal elusive. At the 1998 Nagano, Japan, Winter Olympic Games, he broke U.S. speedskating records in the 1,500, 5,000, and 10,000 meters without medaling.

Boutiette considered Rodriguez a natural for ice speedskating, so he tried to convince her to accompany him to Milwaukee, Wisconsin, which had the proper facilities and coaches to train her. She reluctantly agreed to go but lacked the confidence to speedskate on ice. After arriving in Milwaukee, Rodriguez had to be encouraged by everyone to try skating on ice. Progress initially was slow and the transition was not smooth. After several weeks, however, she began to improve and decided to stay.

Boutiette and the Olympic coaches helped Rodriguez improve enough to make the 1998 U.S. Winter Olympic team at Nagano. Rodriguez became the first Hispanic American and Florida-born athlete to make the Winter Olympic team. In less than 18 months, she incredibly went from never having ice skated to qualifying for the Winter Games. She became the only woman to compete at four different distances in the 1998 Winter Games. At Nagano, she finished fourth in the 3,000 meters, eighth in the 1,500 meters, tenth in the 5,000 meters, and thirteenth in the 1,000 meters. Her fourth-place finish surprised her coaches, who had projected her to finish about fifteenth. She began preparing diligently for the 2002 Winter Olympic Games at Salt Lake City, Utah.

During the four-year training period, Rodriguez established American records in the 500-, 1,500-, and 3,000-meter races. Rodriguez, a five-time U.S. World team and National team member, placed fifth overall in the 1998 World Allround Championships. After winning the U.S. Allround and North American Championships in 1999, she was the National Champion in the 500,

1,500, 3,000, and 5,000 meters, the U.S. Allround National Champion, and North American Champion the next two years, and captured the World Cup Silver Medal in 2000.

Rodriguez speedskated in World Cup competition in Europe between November 2001 and March 2002, capturing two gold, seven silver, and two bronze medals. She interrupted her European skating season long enough to take part in the Winter Olympic Games. At the trials, she became the first woman ever to earn a spot on the Olympic team in all five events and the only woman in the Olympics to compete at four different distances.

At the Olympic Oval in Kearns, Utah, in February 2002, Rodriguez finished seventh in the 3,000 meters in 4 minutes 4.99 seconds, bettering her previous best time by 1.5 seconds. She captured a bronze medal in the 1,000 meters in 1 minute 14.24 seconds, placing just behind Sabine Voelker of Germany. "I'm really happy with third," she acknowledged, "but I'm not happy with my race because of my mistakes. I know I can go faster." Rodriguez earned a second straight bronze medal in the 1,500 meters in 1 minute 55.32 seconds, trailing world recordholder Anni Friesinger of Germany. Rodriguez joined speedskater Derek Parra* as double medalists for the United States. The American team won eight medals to tie the 1980 team for the most successful in U.S. history. "I think it's special, because we've had so many different athletes on the podium," she said. "I don't think many of us expected to get as many medals as we have." She returned to Europe to complete the World Cup season.

Rodriguez and KC Boutiette were married on April 13, 2002 at a South Beach Hotel in Miami, Florida. They have four U.S. Allround titles, eight national records, and five Olympic berths between them.

BIBLIOGRAPHY:
Debbie Becker, "Rodriguez Finds a Quick Cure for the Jitters," *USA Today*, February 11, 2002, p. 6D; "Jennifer Rodriguez," *Hoping to Turn a Few Heads*, www.ccnsi. com (2000); "Jennifer Rodriguez," *Miami Native Takes Bronze*, www.sun_sentinel. com (2002); "Jennifer Rodriguez," *Rodriguez Shares Life*, ww.suntimes.com (2002); "Jennifer Rodriguez," *Speedskating—Athletes Bio*, www.usocpressbox.org (2002); "Jennifer Rodriguez," *Speedskating*, www.viagra.pl/olympics (2001); "Jennifer Rodriguez," *Speedskating: Women's 1,500*, www.houstonchronicle.com (2002); Tom Weir, "U.S. Speedskaters Tie '80 Medal Total," *USA Today*, February 21, 2002, p. 3D; Tom Weir, "Witty Steps Up in Olympics Again," *USA Today*, February 18, 2002, p. 4D.

John L. Evers and David L. Porter

S

ALBERTO SALAZAR
(August 7, 1958–)

Track and Field

Alberto Salazar set the world marathon record (2 hours 8 minutes 13 seconds) and the World five-mile mark (22 minutes 3 seconds) in 1981 and held six American records in distance running, including the 5-kilometer (5-K) and 10-kilometer (10-K) marks, during his running career. In 1982 Salazar set the Boston (2:08:51) and New York City (2:08:13) Marathon course records. He performed on the 1980 and 1984 United States Olympic teams.

The intense, gutsy Alberto Bauduy Salazar was born in Havana, Cuba, on August 7, 1958 to Jose Salazar, a civil engineer, and Marta Galbis (Rigol) Salazar, a portrait painter. He had two older brothers, Richard and Jose, an older sister, Maria Cristina, and a younger brother, Fernando. The Salazars had a keen sense of family status, genealogy, and individual potential. They came to the United States in the fall of 1960, after Jose, a classmate of Fidel Castro, former lieutenant in Castro's revolutionary army, and director of tourist construction in the Cuban government, fell out with Castro.

The Salazars lived in Manchester, Connecticut, for 10 years before moving to Wayland, Massachusetts, near Boston. Richard captained the U.S. Naval Academy cross-country team. Alberto Salazar emulated his brother by running in timed races at age 9 and later joining the Greater Boston Track Club. At Wayland High School, he finished second in the National Junior 5-K run, twice won the 5-K at the USSR–USA Junior Meet, and placed twenty-fourth in the National Amateur Athletic Union (AAU) Senior cross-country championships. In 1975 and 1976 he was named the top 5-K high school runner by *Track and Field News*.

In high school Salazar worked as a busboy and dishwasher at Mel's Restaurant in Wayland and graduated in the top 20 percent of his class. In 1976 he entered the University of Oregon because of its great running tradition. As a freshman, he failed to finish the National Collegiate Athletic Association (NCAA) cross-country race and placed a disappointing ninth in the NCAA outdoor 5-K. Salazar changed his technique, was encouraged to run fewer miles per week, and did less partying. As a sophomore he won the Junior NCAA 5-K and 10-K, and placed ninth in the NCAA cross-country championships. In 1978 he won the NCAA cross-country championships, placed second in the AAU cross-country championships, and captured the *Runner's World* Five-Mile Invitational in world-record time.

In 1979 Salazar placed second in the Pacific Coast Conference cross-country championship, finished third in the NCAA cross-country championship, and won the AAU cross-country championship. Crippled by tendonitis in his left knee, he trained for the Olympic Trials by swimming. He made the 1980 United States Olympic team, but the American boycott of the Olympic Games prevented him from participating in the Moscow, Russia, Games. On October 26 he won the New York City Marathon, his first race at the 26.2-mile distance.

On January 4, 1981, Salazar won his second *Runner's World* Five-Mile Invitational, breaking his own world record (22:04) at that distance. In his next race, he triumphed in a two-mile indoor event in Portland, Oregon, in 8:33.5. At Madison Square Garden on February 6 he set the American indoor mark in the 5-K (13:23.1). He won the NCAA 10-K in June, the Falmouth 7.1-mile Road Race in August, and placed third in the 10-K at the World Cup meet in Rome, Italy in September. He set the world record for the marathon (2:08.13), while he won his second New York City Marathon on October 25, 1981. Salazar finished the year by placing second in the 10-K at the Track Athletic Congress (TAC) cross-country championships, receiving the 1981 Nurmi Awards for best male road runner and best male distance runner. In 1981 he earned a Bachelor's degree in marketing from the University of Oregon, ran for Nike's Athletics West team, and married a distance runner, Molly Morton, in December. They have two sons, Antonio and Alejandro, and live in Eugene, Oregon.

The 6-foot, 144-pound Salazar peaked in 1982, when he won the U.S. Invitational 3-mile and the Boston Marathon in record-setting times. Salazar's duel with Dick Beardsley in the Boston Marathon, in which he surged in the last 100 yards of the race to win by 10 yards, is considered the most memorable finish in the meet's more-than-100-year history. During the summer of 1982, he set American records in the 5-K (13:11.03) and 10-K (27:25.61) at the Bislett Games in Norway. That October, he won his third consecutive New York City Marathon.

Salazar had a high tolerance for pain. He was able to maintain a high maximum volume of oxygen intake twice as long as most of his competitors but, after 1982, suffered from various physical ailments that hampered his running career.

In 1983 Salazar placed fifth in the Rotterdam, Netherlands, and Fukuoka, Japan, marathons. The following year, he finished second in the Olympic Trial marathon in Buffalo, New York, and fifteenth in that event at the Los Angeles Olympic Games. Injuries kept him out of the 1988 Olympic Trials. He failed to finish the marathon in the 1992 Olympic Trials but won the Comrades 53.8-mile Marathon in Durban, South Africa, in 1994.

BIBLIOGRAPHY
"Alberto Salazar," *Current Biography, 1983* (New York, 1983); Hal Higdon, *A Century of Running: Celebrating the 100th Anniversary of the Boston Athletic Association Marathon* (Emmaus, PA, 1995); *New York Times,* October 27, 1980, p. C-8, June 4, 1981, p. V-1, October 18, 1981, special section.

Keith McClellan

BARRY SANDERS   Football
(July 16, 1968–   )

Barry Sanders won the 1988 Heisman Trophy and four National Football League (NFL) rushing titles.

Barry David Sanders was born on July 16, 1968 in Wichita, Kansas, the son of William Sanders, a carpenter and roofer, and Shirley Sanders. William encouraged his son's interest in sports but also emphasized humility, Christian values, self-discipline, and Bible study. At North High School in Wichita, the coaching staff used the 5-foot 8-inch Sanders as a defensive back. Sanders started at running back the last five games as a senior in 1985, setting an All-City record with 1,417 yards. He performed as an outstanding running back for Oklahoma State University from 1986 to 1988, establishing 13 National Collegiate Athletic Association (NCAA) season records and playing in three Orange Bowl games. Sanders placed third among the Cowboys' all-time rushers with 3,797 yards. He won the 1988 Heisman Trophy and Maxwell Award in his junior and final year at Oklahoma State, leaving with one year of eligibility remaining.

The Detroit Lions (National Football League) selected Sanders in the first round of the 1989 NFL draft as the third pick overall. In his first NFL season, the 5-foot 8-inch, 203-pound elusive running back carried the ball 280 times for 1,470 yards and 14 touchdowns, both team records. The following year, he ran for 1,304 yards on 255 carries to win his first NFL rushing title. He became the first Detroit player to lead the NFL in rushing since Byron "Whizzer" White in 1940 and scored 16 touchdowns. In 1991 Sanders scored 17 touchdowns, the most ever by a Detroit Lion. When he reached the end zone, he never showboated or spiked the ball. "I just handed the ball to the referee," he explained. "That is what you are supposed to do."

During his sixth NFL season in 1994, Sanders began chasing the coveted 2,000-yard rushing mark right into the final week of that campaign. He finished with 1,883 rushing yards, the fourth highest single-season output in NFL history, and won his second NFL rushing crown. Thirteen of his 331 rushing attempts brought gains of at least 25 yards or more, with six being at least 60 yards.

Sanders had become a threat to go the distance anytime he took a handoff. With his small frame he ran with a low center of gravity, making it difficult to bring him down with the first contact. His quickness and stop-and-start ability allowed him to go from top speed to a dead stop. By making a lateral move either left or right, he could accelerate out of trouble and leave behind defenders grasping at air. Opposing defenses, too, had to adjust in their attempts to stop him and were left susceptible to Detroit's stretch-offense passing game. Head coach Wayne Fontes observed, "I've seen him make some three-yard runs that are better than any 50-yard runs. And I've seen him make 25-yard runs better than any 100-yard runs."

Sanders clinched his third NFL rushing title in 1996, running for 1,553 yards in 307 carries. He became the first offensive back in NFL history to gain at least 1,000 yards in each of his first eight seasons and the only running back ever to gain 1,000 yards or more in eight straight seasons.

In 1997 Sanders got off to the worst start in his nine-year NFL career when he managed just 53 yards rushing in the Lions' first two games. He quickly returned to his old form, reeling off an NFL record 14 consecutive games with at least 100 rushing yards. Against the Tampa Bay Buccaneers, he became the first player in NFL annals to record two touchdown runs of at least 80 yards in the same game. Sanders ended that season with 2,053 yards, making him only the third player in NFL history to surpass the 2,000-yard barrier in a year. The yardage, the second highest total in league annals, gave Sanders his fourth NFL rushing title.

Before the 1999 season, Sanders surprised everyone in professional football by announcing his retirement at age 31. He preferred to leave the game rather than face another losing season in Detroit. He compiled 15,269 career yards rushing, coming within 1,457 yards of eclipsing Walter Payton's then all-time record of 16,726 yards, and added 107 career touchdowns. "Truthfully, I got a lot of satisfaction out of doing well," Sanders reflected about his 10-year NFL career. "I think most people, if they do something they like doing and they are good at it, then I think that is gratification in itself. All other things will come after that."

Sanders set every Detroit Lions rushing record. His 10 seasons rushing for 1,000 yards or more tied Walter Payton's then NFL mark. His 10 consecutive seasons reaching this record also established an NFL milestone. Sanders was voted All-Pro eight times and was selected to play in nine Pro Bowls, being named the NFL's Most Valuable Player in 1997. Since retiring from professional football, he has resided in Michigan with his son, Barry Jr.

BIBLIOGRAPHY
"Barry Sanders," *Current Biography Yearbook 1993* (New York, 1993), pp. 504–507; *Detroit Lions Press Guide*, 1998; Michael La Blanc, ed., *Contemporary Black Biography*, vol. 1 (Detroit, MI, 1992), pp. 213–214; David L. Porter, ed., *African-American Sports Greats* (Westport, CT, 1995); *Pro Football Weekly*, January 14, 1990, February, 1991, December 8, 1996, January 4, 1998, August 22, 1999; *The Sporting News Pro Football Register*, 1999.

Richard Gonsalves

DEION SANDERS
(August 9, 1967–)

Baseball, Football

Deion Sanders was a gazelle on baseball's basepaths and a daring defensive back on the gridiron, mixed with a large dose of Hollywood flair and a larger measure of self-endorsement.

Deion Luwynn Sanders was born on August 9, 1967 in Fort Myers, Florida, to Fred Sanders and Connie Sanders. His parents divorced when he was a child. He lived with his mother, who married Willie Knight five years later. She directed Sanders toward sports, hoping to keep him from danger in their gang- and drug-infested neighborhood. He excelled in Little League baseball and Pop Warner League football, where, as a 10-year-old, he led his team to a 1979 national title as a running back, quarterback, and safety. He starred in football, basketball, and baseball at North Fort Myers High School, being named Florida High School Athlete of the Year in his senior year.

Sanders played football four seasons at cornerback for Florida State University from 1985 to 1988. He won the Jim Thorpe Award as the nation's best defensive back for the 1988 season. The Seminoles defeated the University of Nebraska, 31–28, in the 1988 Fiesta Bowl and Auburn University, 20–17, in the 1989 Sugar Bowl. Sanders, an excellent college runner in the 200- and 400-meter sprints and 4×100 relays in track and field, received accolades as a National Collegiate Athletic Association (NCAA) track and field All-America. He earned the nickname "Prime Time" for his showmanship on the basketball court. Sanders starred as a speedy, good-hitting outfielder for the Florida State baseball team and helped the Seminoles finish fifth in the 1987 College World Series. Sanders's mother thought he should focus on football; his stepfather encouraged him toward baseball.

The New York Yankees (American League) selected Sanders in the thirtieth round of the June 1988 free-agent draft. The handsome, 6-foot 1-inch, 190-pound outfielder played 14 games for New York in 1989. The Atlanta Falcons made Sanders the fifth overall selection in the 1989 National Football League (NFL) draft, beginning one of the most successful dual careers in professional sports. During his rookie NFL campaign, he averaged 10.4 yards per interception, 11 yards on punt returns, and 20.7 yards on kickoff returns. Sanders played five seasons for Atlanta from 1989 to 1993. In 1992 he paced the NFL with two touchdowns and 1,067 total yards on kickoff returns. He shared the NFL lead with seven interceptions in 1993.

In September 1994, Sanders signed with the San Francisco 49ers (NFL) and led the NFL that season with 303 yards and three touchdowns on interceptions at defensive back. He signed as a free agent with the Dallas Cowboys (NFL) in September 1995. He played for Dallas from 1995 through 1999 before moving to the Washington Redskins (NFL) in 2000. Sanders was named cornerback on *The Sporting News* (*TSN*) NFL All-Pro team seven times

Deion Sanders ©Photofest

from 1991 through 1997, was kick returner on *TSN* 1992 All-Pro team, and was selected National Football Conference (NFC) 1994 Defensive Player of the Year. Sanders played in the Pro Bowl in 1991, 1992, 1993, 1994, and 1997 but was unable to compete in the 1996 Pro Bowl because of injury. He participated in Super Bowl XXIX in 1995, when the 49ers defeated the San Diego Chargers, 49–26, and in Super Bowl XXX in 1996, when the Cowboys triumphed over the Pittsburgh Steelers, 27–17. Analyst John Madden observed: "Deion is the first NFL player to be able to dominate and direct a game from the defensive back position." His 12-year NFL career included 48 interceptions, 385 tackles, 89 assists on tackles, nearly 10 yards per carry average on punt returns, 23 yards per carry average on kickoff returns, and 18 touchdowns in 163 games. Sanders retired because "the Washington Redskins were a team in disarray."

Despite Sanders's enormous success in football, some believed he could have reached even greater heights in baseball. In January 1991, he signed with the Atlanta Braves (National League). When batting, Sanders was once described "looking like someone swinging an axe." He showed patience, however, and the ability to fight off tough pitches at the plate. His best season occurred with the Braves in 1992, when he batted .304 and stole 26 bases.

He led the NL in triples with 14, becoming the first player in history to pace the NL in triples while playing fewer than 100 games. He made history in the 1992 NL Championship Series when he performed in Game Five for the Atlanta Braves and then played for the Atlanta Falcons (NFL), becoming the first player to suit up for two professional sports on the same day. In the 1992 World Series, Sanders batted .533 with five stolen bases, but the Toronto Blue Jays defeated the Braves in five games. Sanders is the only athlete to play in both a Super Bowl and a World Series. Atlanta traded him to the Cincinnati Reds (NL) on May 29, 1994 for outfielder Roberto Kelly. He recorded 38 stolen bases that year. Sanders moved to the San Francisco Giants (NL) in an eight-player deal in July 1995 and skipped baseball in 1996. He returned in 1997 to have a productive season with Cincinnati, batting .273 in 115 games and stealing a career-high 56 bases. Sanders did not play baseball in 1998 or 1999 and signed with the Cincinnati organization in 2000, batting only .200 at Louisville, Kentucky (International League). In 2001 he hit .459 in 19 games at Louisville and was promoted to Cincinnati. The Reds released him in June 2001, however, after he batted just .173 in 32 games. The Toronto Blue Jays (AL) signed Sanders in June 2001 and sent him to Syracuse, New York (International League), releasing him a month later. Sanders's nine-year major league career included 558 hits, 308 runs scored, 72 doubles, 43 triples, 39 home runs, 168 RBIs, 186 stolen bases, and a .263 batting average in 641 games.

Sanders was a tremendous talent held back, many thought, by his own hype, temperamental personality, and contract disputes. All was well with "Neon Deion," when he was in the spotlight, but he tended to sulk when he was not. Sanders was a model for youngsters, however: he did not drink, use drugs, or curse. CBS hired him as a feature reporter and playoff contributor for NFL coverage. He and his wife, Carolyn (Chambers) Sanders, have one daughter, Deiondra, and one son, Deion Jr. Sanders enjoys spending leisure time with his family.

BIBLIOGRAPHY:
CNN/Sports Illustrated, *Pro Football: Deion Sanders* (cnnsi.com, 2002); John Dewan, ed., *The Scouting Report: 1994* (New York, 1994); Zander Hollander, ed., *Complete Handbook of Baseball*, 24th ed. (New York, 1994); David L. Porter, ed., *African-American Sports Greats* (Westport, CT, 1995).

Frank J. Olmsted

WARREN SAPP   Football
(December 19, 1972–   )

Warren Sapp won the 1994 Lombardi Award as an All-America defensive lineman at the University of Miami and has starred at defensive tackle for the Tampa Bay Buccaneers (National Football League).

Warren Carlos Sapp was born on December 19, 1972 in Orlando, Florida, the son of Annie Roberts. He graduated from Apopka High School in Plymouth, Florida, where he lettered in football, track and field, and baseball. He played three different positions for the football team: linebacker, tight end, and punter. As a punter, he compiled a 43.5-yard career average. In his senior year, Sapp was chosen All-State and *USA Today* Honorable Mention All-America. He entered the University of Miami in 1992 as a tight end but was switched to defensive tackle. In three years for the Hurricanes, he made 176 tackles, 19.5 sacks, and four fumble recoveries. He appeared with Miami in the Orange Bowl in 1992, the Sugar Bowl in 1993, and the Fiesta Bowl in 1994, making 13 tackles and 3 sacks. After his junior year, he was named to the All-America team. He won the Lombardi Award, symbolic of the nation's top lineman, and was a finalist for the Outland Trophy, given to the most outstanding interior lineman.

Sapp skipped his senior year to enter the 1995 NFL draft. The Tampa Bay Buccaneers selected the 6-foot 2-inch, 303-pound defensive lineman in the first round as the twelfth pick overall. He impressed his coaches so much with his speed and moves that he won the starting right defensive tackle job. He finished the 1995 season with 27 tackles, three sacks, one interception, and one forced fumble. His lone interception came against the Atlanta Falcons, when he picked off a shovel pass and returned it five yards for a touchdown, a lineman's dream come true. Being so agile at his size, Sapp was used as a blocking back on goal line plays in four games, and he led the Buccaneer offense to three touchdowns. His outstanding first-year NFL performance made him a consensus First-Team All-Rookie choice. Sapp's sacks increased to nine in 1996 and 10.5 in 1997. He made 51 tackles in 1996 and 68 tackles in 1997 and was selected to play in his first Pro Bowl following the 1997 season.

By 1998, Sapp became one of the most dominant NFL defensive linemen. In an effort to shut him down, opponents constantly double and triple teamed him. His pass-rushing skills and run-stopping abilities helped place Tampa Bay's defense among the NFL's top three. Sapp's sack production dropped to seven in 1998 because he was overweight and slow, but he made his second Pro Bowl. No Buccaneer player had made consecutive trips to the postseason Pro Bowl since Lee Roy Selmon from 1979 through 1984.

"I kind of set the goal for myself after 1998 when I finished watching all the tapes of that season and me being out of shape and not helping my team very much," vowed Sapp, leader of the NFL's third-ranked defense. "It was just a matter of me taking off the weight, getting myself into top physical condition so I can get in and hunt down those quarterbacks."

Sapp reported to training camp 40 pounds lighter in 1999. One teammate joked that he had shed a person. Sapp made just 50 tackles, but his sack total increased to 12.5. He fell just a half sack shy of the Buccaneers' season club record, set by Lee Roy Selmon in 1977. Sapp made the 1999 Pro Bowl, his third straight appearance. For the first time in his five-year NFL career, Sapp

Warren Sapp ©Photofest

was voted All-Pro and was named the NFL's Most Valuable Defensive Player. He played in his first National Football Conference Championship Game against the St. Louis Rams that season. St. Louis prevailed, 11 to 6, in this tight battle.

Sapp was even more formidable as a pass-rusher in 2000. He registered 16.5 sacks to set a new team record and made 76 tackles, both career highs. He also blocked a field goal against the Minnesota Vikings before a national television audience on Monday Night Football. Teammate Donnie Abrams recovered the ball and returned it 53 yards for a touchdown. Sapp made his fourth consecutive Pro Bowl appearance and repeated as an All-Pro. His output dropped in 2001, when he recorded just 3 sacks and 20 tackles. Sapp remained a dominant force on defense, being chosen for the fifth consecutive year to play in the Pro Bowl and being voted All-Pro for the third straight time. He recorded 7.5 sacks and two interceptions in 2002, anchoring a defense helping Tampa Bay win the NFC South with a 12–4 record. Tampa Bay defeated the San Francisco 49ers, 31–6, in the NFC playoffs, as Sapp combined with Derrick Brooks* on one sack. He made one tackle in the 27–10 triumph over the Philadelphia Eagles in the NFC Championship Game, and two tackles and one sack in the 48–20 rout over the Oakland Raiders in Super Bowl XXXVII. During his eight-year NFL career, he has recorded 327 tackles, 13 forced fumbles, 7 fumble recoveries, and 68.5 sacks. Although in a very physical position, the durable Sapp has missed only three games in his eight-year career.

Sapp and his wife, Jamiko, whom he married during the 1998 Pro Bowl festivities in Honolulu, Hawaii, reside in Tampa, Florida, with their daughter, Mercedes.

BIBLIOGRAPHY

Pro Football Weekly, January 23, 2000; *The Sporting News Pro Football Register*, 2003; *Tampa Bay Buccaneers Press Guide*, 2003.

Richard Gonsalves

SHANNON SHARPE   Football
(June 26, 1968–   )

Shannon Sharpe of the Denver Broncos (National Football League) ranks among the finest tight ends who have ever played football. He helped the Denver Broncos win the 1997 and 1998 Super Bowls and the Baltimore Ravens (NFL) win the 2000 Super Bowl. At 6 feet 2 inches and 240 pounds, Sharpe possessed the size needed to be a top NFL tight end and exhibited good speed. He also leads the NFL in career receptions and receiving yards by a tight end.

Shannon Sharpe was born in Glennville, Georgia, on June 26, 1968. "I grew up," Shannon recalled, "in a house with ten people, no running water, no cable TV." During a rainstorm, the impoverished family got wet when they lay in their beds at night because they could not afford to fix the leaky roof. His grandmother, Mary Porter, helped bring up Sharpe, his brother, Sterling, who also became a pro football star, and their sister.

At Glennville High School, Sharpe made All-County, All-Region, and All-Area in football. He attended Savannah State College, being named a three-time football All-America and All-Southern Intercollegiate Athletic Conference. During his college career, he caught 192 passes for 3,744 yards and 40 touchdowns.

Shannon Sharpe ©Rich Clarkson

The Denver Broncos selected Sharpe as a wide receiver in the seventh round of the 1990 draft but developed him slowly. During his first year, he caught seven passes for 99 yards and one touchdown. In 1991 he caught 22 passes for 322 yards and one touchdown. He led all Denver receivers in 1992 with 53 pass receptions for 640 yards and two touchdowns. The same year, he and his brother, Sterling, of the Green Bay Packers became the only siblings to pace their teams in receiving in the same season.

Sharpe made the Pro Bowl team in 1993 for the second consecutive season. That year, he grabbed 81 passes, third in the American Football Conference (AFC), and caught nine touchdown passes, tied for second best in the AFC.

He continually improved. In 1994 he caught 87 passes, fourth in the NFC, and was chosen Second Team All-Pro at tight end in 1995 by the Associated Press, despite missing the final three games due to an eye injury.

Sharpe also developed a reputation for talkativeness both on and off the field. His interviews with sports writers were often very colorful. As he observed, "I think he [Denver coach Mike Shanahan] has finally realized now that I am a guy who has to talk. That's who Shannon Sharpe is, and to ask him to be quiet and not talk is really taking him out of his element."

In 1996 Sharpe was selected to his fifth consecutive Pro Bowl and was named All-Pro. He led all NFL tight ends in receptions (80), receiving yards (1,062), and receiving touchdowns (10). The following year, he was selected to his sixth straight Pro Bowl and repeated as All-NFL. In Denver's 31–24 victory over the Green Bay Packers in Super Bowl XXII that season, Sharpe paced the Broncos with five pass receptions for 38 yards. He enjoyed another excellent year in 1998, making the Pro Bowl again and making All-NFL for the fourth time. He led all NFL tight ends in receiving yards (768) and recorded his seventh straight 50-reception season, a first for a tight end.

Sharpe's 1999 season was cut short in the fifth week when a fractured left clavicle sidelined him for the rest of the year. In July 2000, he left the Broncos to sign with the Baltimore Ravens (NFL). Baltimore won the Super Bowl, 34–7, over the New York Giants that year. He led the Ravens with 67 catches for 810 yards and five touchdowns and was voted a Pro Bowl alternate.

In 2001 Sharpe surpassed Ozzie Newsome as the all-time leader among NFL tight ends with 663 pass receptions. He shared the lead among NFL tight ends with 73 catches for 811 yards and two touchdowns. He was also named to the AFC Pro Bowl team and rejoined the Broncos as a free agent in April 2002. He caught 61 passes for 686 yards (11.2-yard average) and three touchdowns. Sharpe set the NFL record for most touchdown receptions by a tight end with 61, surpassing Jerry Smith of the Washington Redskins in November 2003.

Sharpe, considered one of the best tight ends to ever play professional football, overcame a poverty-filled childhood and developed into a top-notch pro football player. He holds the NFL career records for passes caught (753) and yards gained (9,290) by a tight end for 54 touchdowns, and remains a very productive player. He is single, continues to reside in Glennville, Georgia, and has three children.

BIBLIOGRAPHY

Baltimore Ravens 2001 Fan and Media Guide; www.NFL.com/players/playerpage/1329/bios; www.denverbroncos.com/lockerroom/bios/sharpe/shannon.php3; *Great Athletes—The 20th Century*, vol. 7 (Pasadena, CA, 2002); Clay Latimer, "I Am the Guy Who Has to Talk," *Football Digest* 29 (September 1999), pp. 17–22; Rick Reilly, "Lip Shtick," *Sports Illustrated* 90 (February 1, 1999), pp. 41–43.

Robert L. Cannon

GARY SHEFFIELD
(November 18, 1968–)

Baseball

Gary Sheffield is one of the most naturally gifted, yet controversial, players in major league baseball.

Born to Betty Jones in Tampa, Florida, on November 18, 1968, Gary Antonian Sheffield is a nephew of former National League Cy Young Award winner Dwight Gooden.* His stepfather, Harold Jones, worked in the shipyards. Sheffield played in the Little League World Series and graduated in 1986 from Hillsborough High School in Tampa, Florida. The Milwaukee Brewers (American League) made him the sixth overall pick in the June 1986 free-agent draft. A shortstop, he drove in 71 runs and batted .365 at Helena, Montana (Pioneer League) in 1986. The next season at Stockton, California (California League), he led the CL with 103 RBIs but proved a liability defensively at shortstop. Sheffield captured *The Sporting News* (*TSN*) 1988 Minor League Player of the Year Award for clouting 28 home runs and collecting 119 runs batted in (RBI), splitting the campaign between El Paso, Texas (Texas League) and Denver, Colorado (American Association).

After batting .247 and platooning at shortstop with Bill Spiers in 1989, Sheffield was moved to third base by the Milwaukee Brewers. He batted .294 in 1990 but struggled defensively. Two lengthy stays on the disabled list and a 100 percentage point drop in batting average caused the Brewers to trade him to the San Diego Padres (National League) in March 1992. The 5-foot 11-inch, 205-pound, right-handed Sheffield responded with a career-best and NL-leading .330 batting average. He clouted 33 home runs, recorded 100 RBIs, and grew more adept at third base, collecting *TSN* Comeback Player of the Year, Major League Player of the Year, and Silver Slugger awards for 1992.

In June 1993, the San Diego Padres trimmed their payroll by trading Sheffield to the Florida Marlins (NL) for relief pitcher Trevor Hoffman. In the strike-shortened 1994 campaign, the Marlins moved Sheffield to the outfield, where he seemed more at home. He crushed 27 home runs in just 87 games despite a bruised rotator cuff muscle. Torn thumb ligaments limited him to 63 games in 1995 for Florida. The following season, Sheffield made career bests with 118 runs and 120 RBIs for the Marlins. Many claimed Sheffield possessed the best bat speed in baseball. He hit change-ups, breaking balls, and fastballs alike.

The 1997 campaign marked one of the statistically least productive of Sheffield's career but brought him the greatest satisfaction. He batted only .250 and declined in most offensive categories, but led a young Marlin team that shocked the baseball world by winning the NL Wild Card. Florida defeated the Cleveland Indians in seven games for the World Series Championship as Sheffield contributed a home run, five RBIs, and a .292 batting average.

Marlins owner Wayne Huizenga, citing $34 million in losses for 1997, slashed operating costs in a fire sale by sending Sheffield, Bobby Bonilla,* and Charles Johnson* to the Los Angeles Dodgers (NL) in May 1998. Sheffield comprised the most productive offensive threat in the Dodger lineup from 1999 to 2001, scoring 306 runs with 113 home runs, 310 RBIs, and a .312 batting average. Sheffield was dispatched to the Atlanta Braves (NL) for outfielder Brian Jordan and pitcher Odalis Perez in January 2002. He helped Atlanta win the NL East in 2002, batting .307 with 25 home runs and 84 RBIs. Sheffield homered for his only hit in the NL Division Series against the San Francisco Giants. Through 2003, he has played 1,882 games with 2,009 hits, 1,190 runs, 356 doubles, 23 triples, 379 home runs, 1,232 RBIs, 200 stolen bases, and a .299 batting average. He performed for the NL in six All-Star games. Sheffield helped the Braves win another AL East title in 2003, ranking second in the NL in RBIs (132), third in total bases (348), and fourth in runs scored (126). He tied for fourth in batting average (.330), fifth in slugging percentage (.604) and on-base percentage (.419), and seventh in hits (190). Chicago Cubs pitchers, however, held him to a .143 batting average with just one RBI in the NL Championship Series.

Sheffield has encountered numerous problems on and off the baseball diamond. He fought with owner Bud Selig in Milwaukee over his contract in 1992. In 1995 he claimed a former girlfriend tried to frame him by reporting he carried illegal drugs on a flight; no charges were filed. Sheffield hired bodyguards because he thought he was being stalked. He filed charges against another girlfriend for writing bad checks, only to have her countersue for false imprisonment. Another female acquaintance was accused in a plot to murder his mother; she was later cleared. Sheffield was shot in the left shoulder while driving to a Tampa barbershop in an apparent carjacking attempt in October 1995. His feud with Marlins' general manager Dave Dombrowski further damaged his persona to the point that he engaged a public relations firm to reshape his public image. He wore out his welcome in Los Angeles after frequent criticism of the Dodgers' general managers Kevin Malone and Dan Evans in 2001. Some called him the talented wild child of baseball. Yet Jim Leyland, his manager at Florida, spoke nothing but praise for Sheffield. "I love the guy. He played hard everyday. He doesn't say much, but he's intense." Former Dodger manager Davey Johnson also praised Sheffield's talent and ability to inspire other players.

Sheffield affirmed that the power of God in his life and the love of his wife, DeLeon, a gospel singer who released a 1996 CD, *My Life*, have enabled him to mature and become a positive role model. Teammate Terry Pendleton strongly influenced his religious conversion. Sheffield has three children, Gary Jr., Ebony, and Carissa, from three earlier nonmarital relationships, and takes an active role in their lives. Sheffield grew up in the Belmont Heights projects, considered the worst in Tampa, Florida, and gave something back to disadvantaged children by strong support for the Boys and Girls Clubs and Returning Baseball to the Inner City (RBI) program. He founded the Gary Sheffield Foundation to assist underprivileged children in spiritual and personal growth.

BIBLIOGRAPHY
Rod Beaton, "Gary Sheffield: Growing into Major League Stardom," *Baseball Digest* 60 (March 2001), pp. 56–58; John Dewan, ed., *The Scouting Notebook 2002* (Morton Grove, IL, 2002); David L. Porter, ed., *Biographical Dictionary of American Sports, Baseball—Q–Z*, revised and expanded edition (Westport, CT, 2000); Gary Sheffield file, National Baseball Library, Cooperstown, NY; Tom Stinson, "Gary Sheffield: He Wants It All in Atlanta," *Baseball Digest* 61 (July 2002), pp. 56–61.

Frank J. Olmsted

BRUCE SMITH   Football
(June 18, 1963–)

Although he struggled with weight issues throughout his adolescence, Bruce Smith overcame his poor eating habits and emerged among the outstanding National Football League defensive linemen during the 1990s. He anchored the defense for the Buffalo Bills (NFL), who appeared in an unprecedented four consecutive Super Bowls during the early 1990s.

Bruce Bernard Smith was born on June 18, 1963 in Norfolk, Virginia, the youngest of five children of George Smith and Annie Smith. His father, who had boxed as an amateur, worked as a shipping clerk and truck driver. Smith remained close to his father and enjoyed fishing trips, even though the elder Smith often worked 10- and 12-hour days. His mother, who played high school basketball, labored at various minimum-wage jobs. Smith especially enjoyed her Southern-style cooking, so that by his sophomore year at Booker T. Washington High School in Norfolk he weighed over 270 pounds. He was teased and bullied by his classmates for being overweight.

With the encouragement of his parents, however, Smith turned to high school sports as a way to enhance his self-esteem. At Washington High School, he developed into an outstanding athlete. He achieved All-America honors as a football lineman and led his school to a State Basketball Championship. College recruiters, however, remained wary of Smith's weight and questioned his quickness. He enrolled at Virginia Tech University and enjoyed an outstanding collegiate athletic career there. During his four-year tenure at Virginia Tech, he made 180 tackles and achieved consensus All-America status. In 1984 he was awarded the Outland Trophy as the best interior lineman in college football.

The Buffalo Bills made Smith the first overall pick in the 1985 NFL draft. Buffalo was disappointed, however, when its recruit reported to training camp weighing over 300 pounds. Nevertheless Smith continued to display an amazing quickness for someone of his size, leading the Bills in quarterback sacks and earning recognition as the American Football Conference's (AFC) Defensive Rookie of the Year. The Bills continued to struggle during 1986, but Smith established a team record with 15 sacks. Although he missed three games during the 1987 players' strike, he led all AFC defensive linemen with 12 sacks. He was selected for the Pro Bowl, earning Most Valuable Player (MVP) honors.

Smith's promising career suffered a setback in 1988 when the NFL suspended him for the first four games of the season after he tested positive for illegal drugs. When he returned to Buffalo, he helped the Bills make the playoffs with a record of 12 wins and four losses. He was again selected for the Pro Bowl and was named by United Press International (UPI) as AFC Co-Defensive Player of the Year.

The Denver Broncos (NFL) attempted to lure Smith from Buffalo, but the Bills retained his services when they matched Denver's offer of a five-year $7.5 million contract. Although the Bills stumbled to a mark of nine wins and seven defeats in 1989, Smith made 13 sacks and earned selection to the Pro Bowl for the third consecutive year.

Smith approached the 1990 season with a new sense of dedication. He gave up his favorite fast foods in favor of a fish and pasta diet and reduced his playing weight to 265 pounds. Utilizing his speed, he became a defensive leader on a Bills squad that appeared in four consecutive Super Bowls between 1991 and 1994. Smith was named Defensive Player of the Year in 1990, but Buffalo lost an exciting Super Bowl to the New York Giants, 20–19. In 1991, he missed 11 regular season games because of arthroscopic surgery on his left knee. Yet, the Bills returned to the Super Bowl and lost to the Washington Redskins.

Smith was once again a defensive stalwart during the 1992 season. He made the Pro Bowl for the fifth time and registered 14 sacks for a Buffalo team, which was routed by the Dallas Cowboys in the Super Bowl. The Bills re-negotiated his contract and awarded him a $13.5 million deal. The defensive end responded with one of his finest seasons in 1994, recording a career-high 108 tackles. Despite Smith's efforts, the Bills again lost the Super Bowl to the Dallas Cowboys.

Slowed for much of the 1995 season by a bruised tendon, Smith registered only 10 sacks and the Bills failed to make the playoffs. The fortunes of the Buffalo franchise declined for the remainder of the decade. Smith, nevertheless, remained a fixture at defensive end for the Bills, recording from 10 to 14 quarterback sacks a year from 1995 to 1998. After his 1999 output fell to only seven sacks, Smith signed as a free agent with the Washington Redskins (NFL). He has averaged eight sacks from 2000 through 2002 with Washington. Through the 2002 season, he appeared in 263 NFL games and was credited with 195 sacks. Smith tied the NFL career sacks record with 198 in November 2003.

Although teased as a child for being overweight, Smith achieved NFL success and eventually will take his place in the Pro Football Hall of Fame. He lives in Norfolk, Virginia, with his wife, Carmen, and son.

BIBLIOGRAPHY
"Bruce Smith," *Current Biography Yearbook, 1995* (New York, 1995), pp. 540–543; "Forget Taylor, Smith Says He's the Best," *Washington Post*, December 22, 1990, p. F1; Thomas George, "A Force Grows in Buffalo," *New York Times*, December 9, 1990, p. 8; *The Sporting News Pro Football Register*, 2003; Rick Telander, "Lean, Mean Sack Machine," *Sports Illustrated* 75 (September 2, 1991), pp. 28–33.

Ron Briley

EMMITT SMITH   **Football**
(May 15, 1969–   )

Emmitt Smith has devoted much of his life to achieving excellence on the football field, becoming professional football's all-time rushing leader, and returning the Dallas Cowboys to prominence in the National Football League (NFL).

Emmitt James Smith III was born on May 15, 1969 in Pensacola, Florida, to Emmitt Smith Jr. and Mary Smith and was the oldest male child in a family of four boys and two girls. The close-knit family emphasized hard work, self-discipline, and religion. His father, who was an outstanding high school athlete and played semiprofessional football, drove a bus for Pensacola, while his mother worked as a documents clerk in a local bank. Although insisting that his father never pressured him to play football, Smith participated at age 7 in the minimite football division of the Salvation Army–Optimists League.

Smith began to gain national attention as a star running back for Escambia High School in Pensacola. Before he arrived in the fall of 1983, Escambia had not compiled a winning football season in 21 years. Coach Dwight Thomas, who came the same season as his promising running back, quickly turned things around. Thomas described his simple game plan, "Hand the ball to Emmitt, pitch the ball to Emmitt, throw the ball to Emmitt. It was no secret. Everyone knew we were going to get the ball to him. It was just a question of how." Escambia won Florida State Football Championships during Smith's sophomore and junior seasons. Escambia compiled 42 victories against seven losses, as Smith rushed for 8,804 yards and 101 touchdowns from 1983 through 1986. He finished his career at Escambia ranked as the second leading all-time high school rusher behind Ken Hall of Sugarland, Texas.

Smith's high school exploits attracted the attention of numerous college recruiters. Wanting to remain near his family, Smith opted for the University of Florida, where he earned All-America honors and finished among the top 10 candidates for the Heisman Trophy his freshman year. After three seasons at Florida, he held 58 school records and a career rushing mark of 3,298 yards. As a college junior, however, he declared himself eligible for the 1990 NFL draft. His decision to leave the university early was influenced by a National Collegiate Athletic Association (NCAA) recruiting investigation of the football program at Florida. The allegations of NCAA violations, however, did not involve the recruiting of Smith.

Some NFL scouts doubted Smith's potential as a professional running back, citing his lack of speed (4.7 seconds in the 40-yard dash) and relatively small size (5 foot 9 inches and 209 pounds). The Dallas Cowboys (NFL) traded with the Pittsburgh Steelers (NFL) to obtain the seventeenth pick of the draft. Coach Jimmy Johnson was delighted that Smith was still available. After Dallas owner Jerry Jones asserted that Smith was the fourth best player in the draft, the running back insisted that Jones pay him like a top pick. Smith held out for the entire preseason before agreeing to a three-year contract worth $2.75 million.

Smith joined a Dallas team that had lost 16 games in 1989. With the new talented running back, however, the Cowboys' fortunes rapidly improved. In 1990 Smith led the Cowboys to seven wins and nine losses, while rushing for 937 yards, scoring 11 touchdowns, and earning Offensive Rookie of the Year honors.

In 1991 Smith and the young Cowboys posted 11 wins against five defeats. Smith led the NFL in rushing with 1,563 yards on 365 carries. The Dallas franchise, built around Smith, quarterback Troy Aikman, and wide receiver Michael Irvin, made significant strides toward gaining its status among the dominant NFL franchises. In 1992 Smith repeated as NFL rushing leader with 1,713 yards on 373 carries, as the Cowboys thrashed the Buffalo Bills, 52–17, in the Super Bowl.

Smith believed that he deserved to be the highest paid NFL running back. Jones, however, refused to meet his demands, as the running back began a protracted holdout. After the Cowboys lost the first two games of the 1993 season, Jones signed Smith to a four-year contract worth $13.6 million. Smith, who always remained in good physical condition, immediately returned to the Cowboys and helped Dallas repeat as Super Bowl champions. He finished the 1993 season with 1,486 yards and became only the fourth player in NFL history to win three consecutive rushing crowns. He also was the first Cowboys player selected for the NFL's Most Valuable Player (MVP) Award and was chosen as the MVP in the Dallas rematch Super Bowl victory over the Buffalo Bills, 30–13.

In 1995 Smith established a single-season team record of 1,773 yards rushing and broke the NFL mark for rushing touchdowns with 25. He scored six more touchdowns during the postseason. In January 1996, the Cowboys won their third consecutive Super Bowl, defeating the Pittsburgh Steelers, 27–17.

During the late 1990s, however, the Dallas dynasty began to crumble. Although Aikman and Irvin retired, Smith remained the team's primary running threat. In 1999 Smith passed place kicker Rafael Septien as the all-time leading scorer for the Cowboys. During 2001, he established an NFL record with his eleventh consecutive season of rushing for at least 1,000 yards. Although Dallas struggled to a mark of 5 wins and 11 losses, Smith completed the season with 16,187 career yards. He surpassed the Chicago Bears' Walter Payton as the leading ground gainer in NFL history on October 27, 2002, against the Seattle Seahawks. He gained 975 yards for the 5–11 Cowboys in 2002, falling under 1,000 rushing yards for the first time since his rookie season. Through 2002, he rushed for 17,162 yards (4.2-yard average) and 153 touchdowns and scored 11 additional touchdowns via pass receptions. Smith joined the Phoenix Cardinals (NFL) as a free agent in 2003.

Smith's dedication to excellence has paid off on the football field. Off the field, he has remained true to traditional family values. Fulfilling a promise made to his mother, he returned to the University of Florida and secured a B.A. degree in recreation in May 1996. He married Southall Lawrence in April 2000, and they have two daughters. A devout Christian, Smith participates in many religious and charitable activities.

BIBLIOGRAPHY

Steve Delsohn, *The Emmitt Zone* (New York, 1994); Barry Horn, "Family, Not Football, Ranks Highest with Emmitt Smith," *Dallas Morning News*, January 15, 1993, p. H14; Jimmy Johnson with Ed Hinton, *Turning Things Around: My Life in Football* (New York, 1993); Peter King, "Dare to Be Great," *Sports Illustrated* 80 (January 31, 1994), pp. 22–23; David L. Porter, ed., *African-American Sports Greats* (Westport, CT, 1995); "Emmitt Smith," *Current Biography Yearbook, 1994* (New York, 1994), pp. 552–555; *The Sporting News Pro Football Register*, 2003.

Ron Briley

LEE SMITH   Baseball
(December 4, 1957–)

Lee Smith holds the major league baseball record for most career saves.

Lee Arthur Smith Jr. was born on December 4, 1957 in Jamestown, Louisiana, the son of Lee Smith Sr. Smith graduated from Caster High School in Caster, Louisiana, where he lettered in baseball, basketball, and track and field and received many awards, including outstanding state athlete. The 6-foot 5-inch, 220-pound right-hander attended Northwestern State University at Natchitoches, Louisiana, and married Diane Sanders. After being selected in the second round of the June 1975 draft by the Chicago Cubs (National League), he spent six years in their farm system as a starter but without significant success. His switch to relief pitching in 1978 proved decisive. At this stage in his career, he had seriously considered pursuing basketball with the New Orleans Jazz (National Basketball Association). Billy Williams, Cubs' star outfielder from 1959 to 1974, persuaded Smith to stay with baseball. "If I hadn't been a high draft choice, I probably would have gone before Billy got here," Smith admitted. He explained: "I always thought I had a better fastball than a jump shot." Upon joining the Chicago Cubs in 1980, Smith became an especially effective closer. *The Sporting News* reporter Joe Goddard observed that the Cubs had "found relief in relief."

Between 1984 and 1987, Smith recorded 30 saves for four consecutive seasons for an unsuccessful club. The Cubs finished 40 games behind in 1986, but Smith held opponents scoreless in 73 percent of his appearances. He led the NL in saves in 1983 for Chicago, in 1991 and 1992 for the St. Louis Cardinals (NL), and in 1994 for the Baltimore Orioles (American League). His peak season came in 1991 with 47 saves, a NL record. "I like to pitch," Smith affirmed. The power-pitcher relied on the "high, hard one." His ability to get that first strikeout with runners on base and preventing their advance often proved decisive. Billy Connors, Cubs pitching coach, used Smith's more effective slider to set up his fastball. Connors also suggested that Smith push off the mound with the ball of his foot rather than his heel. Connors observed, "He has a good, sound delivery, and he knows the hitters." From 1980 to 1987, Smith compiled 180 saves in 230 games with 644 strikeouts in 682 innings for the Cubs.

Since Smith was eligible for free agency in 1988, the Cubs traded him to the Boston Red Sox (AL) for pitchers Al Nipper and Calvin Schiraldi. Smith did not find Fenway Park or the AL congenial, although manager John Mc-Namara called him "one of the top relievers in all of baseball." After being traded to St. Louis for outfielder Tom Brunansky in May 1990, Smith achieved the pinnacle of his career.

St. Louis fans became increasingly aware how venerable number 47 dominated as he entered a game in the late innings to face an intimidated hitter. Smith took charge when the game was on the line, as his well-developed, muscular figure gave him a commanding presence. He proved the ideal reliever to preserve a one-run lead in the final inning. Always projecting confidence, he amassed 160 saves and 246 strikeouts with the Cardinals. His fastball consistently surpassed 90 miles per hour.

Between 1994 and 1997, Smith performed with the New York Yankees (AL), Baltimore Orioles (AL), California Angels (AL), Cincinnati Reds (NL), and Montreal Expos (NL). During 18 seasons, he compiled 71 wins and 92 losses with a 3.03 earned run average (ERA) and 1,251 strikeouts in 1,290 innings. His impressive statistics included a major league record 478 saves and NL record 347 saves, surpassing Rollie Fingers's 341 saves.

Smith, an eight-time All-Star, was named *The Sporting News* Co-Fireman for 1983 and 1992, NL Fireman for 1991, and AL Fireman for 1994. Chicago Cubs manager Jim Frey aptly called Smith "The top of the class."

BIBLIOGRAPHY
Bob Broeg and Jerry Vickery, eds., *St. Louis Cardinals Encyclopedia* (Chicago, IL, 1998); Dave Van Dyck, "A Mature Battler Bolsters Cubs' Pen," *The Sporting News*, April 7, 1986; Joe Goddard, "The Fast Ball was Better Than the Jump Shot," *The Sporting News*, June 22, 1987; Joe Giuliotti, "Giant Step with Smith," *The Sporting News*, December 21, 1987; Lee Smith file, Research Center, *The Sporting News*, St. Louis, MO; David L. Porter, ed., *Biographical Dictionary of American Sports: Baseball, Q–Z*, revised and expanded edition (Westport CT, 2000); *The Sporting News Baseball Register*, 1997; *Who's Who in Baseball*, 82nd ed. (New York, 1997).

William J. Miller

ALFONSO SORIANO Baseball
(January 7, 1978–   )

In 2002, Alfonso Soriano of the New York Yankees (American League) became the first second baseman to hit 30 home runs and steal 30 bases in the same season, and he fell just one home run short of becoming the fourth major league player to have 40 roundtrippers and 40 stolen bases in the same campaign.

Alfonso Soriano was born on January 7, 1978 in San Pedro de Macoris, Dominican Republic, the son of Andrea Soriano, and as a child dreamed of playing shortstop in professional baseball. His older brothers, Julio and Frederico, and an uncle, Hilario Soriano, played minor league baseball. Today Hilario serves as scouting supervisor for the Toronto Blue Jays (AL). Soriano attended Eugenio Maria de Osto High School in the Dominican Republic.

At age 16, Soriano attended a baseball camp sponsored by the Hiroshima Toyo Carp (Japan Central League). The Toyo Carp signed Soriano in November 1994. He played in their minor league system for two years, batting .366 with 55 runs batted-in (RBI) in 63 games for Hiroshima in the summer league (DSL) in 1995. Soriano played outfield the next two seasons with Hiroshima (Japan Western League) but batted only .118 in nine games for the Toyo Carp in 1997. At this point he retired from the Japan Central League and spent 1998 out of organized baseball.

The New York Yankees signed the 6-foot 1-inch, 160-pound Soriano, who bats and throws right-handed, to a four-year, $31 million contract as a nondrafted free agent in September 1998. Lin Garrett, New York director of scouting, told Brian Cashman, Yankees general manager, "You better not screw this up. You can't lose this guy." Cashman recalled, "Our blood was pumping." After playing in the Arizona Fall League in 1998, Soriano batted .305 for Norwich, Connecticut (Eastern League) in 1999 and .290 for Columbus, Ohio (International League) in 2000. The Yankees gave Soriano brief trials in 1999 and 2000, but he struggled in 31 games.

Soriano came to spring training in 2001 with an opportunity to make the Yankees. Several major league teams tried to acquire him. The Chicago Cubs (National League) reportedly offered outfielder Sammy Sosa* in a trade. New York projected Soriano as its left fielder in 2001, but second baseman Chuck Knoblauch's continuing throwing problems convinced manager Joe Torre otherwise. Torre moved Knoblauch to left field and put Soriano at second base.

As a rookie in 2001, Soriano learned a new position and batted ninth in New York's batting order. He hit .268 with 34 doubles, 18 home runs, 73 RBIs, and 43 stolen bases to help the Yankees win their sixth consecutive AL East Division crown. He started all 17 postseason games, hitting .222, with three doubles and three RBIs against the Oakland Athletics in the AL Division Series and .400 against the Seattle Mariners in the AL Championship Series. In the ninth inning of Game Four of the AL Championship Series, Soriano clouted a two-run, game-winning walk-off home run. He struggled against the Arizona Diamondbacks in the World Series, batting only .240 with one home run, two RBIs, and three defensive errors. His twelfth-inning single won Game Five at Yankee Stadium. Coach Willie Randolph, a former Yankee second baseman, said, "When young players get big hits like that, it does wonders for their confidence. Alfonso is going to build on that."

Alfonso Soriano ©Rich Clarkson

Soriano hit leadoff in 2002, becoming the first second baseman to hit 30 home runs and steal 30 bases in the same season. He sparked New York's most powerful offense since the franchise returned to baseball dominance in 1996, changing the expectations of his position in an era of big-time offense. Besides batting .300 with 102 RBIs, he led the AL with 128 runs scored, 209 hits, and 41 steals, finished third with 51 doubles, and ranked fifth with 39 home runs. He hit only two fewer home runs than slugger Jason Giambi and fell just 19 total bases short of 400, a milestone only Babe Ruth, Lou Gehrig, and Joe DiMaggio among Yankees have exceeded. Soriano also led AL second basemen with 23 errors, including eight in April. His defensive mistakes usually resulted from inexperience at second base. "When he can go behind second base and throw a strike to first while he's running toward left field," manager Joe Torre observed, "you know he's capable of making all the plays. It's a matter of polishing." Soriano struggled against the Anaheim Angels in the AL Division Series, batting only .118 with one double, one homer, two RBIs, and the lone Yankee stolen base. Soriano helped the Yankees win the AL East in 2003, ranking third in the AL in total bases (358), fourth in stolen bases (35), sixth in runs scored (114) and home runs (38), and seventh in hits (198). After hitting .368 with one double and 4 RBIs in the AL Division Series against the Minnesota Twins, he batted only .133 with one double and 3 RBIs in the AL Championship Series against the Boston Red Sox and .227 with one home run and 2 RBIs in the World Series against the victorious Florida Marlins. Through 2003, he has hit .284 with 98 home runs, 270 RBIs, and 121 stolen bases.

Soriano, who is single and a leadoff hitter like Rickey Henderson,* possesses strong, quick wrists, flexible hips, and a strong arm. He has long legs and a fluid motion, uses a 34.5-ounce bat, and drills pitches into the gaps with his uppercut swing. "He's Ted Williams-strong," Giambi observed. "He might not be big in stature, but he's lean and strong. The biggest thing is his bat speed is unbelievable." Although lacking patience and striking out too often at the plate, Soriano is a constant threat to steal bases. Torre observed, "You don't find many players this young with this kind of ability." Giambi summed up, "He can do it all, run, hit for power, hit for average."

BIBLIOGRAPHY
Mel Antonen, "Seconding an MVP: Soriano," *USA Today*, September 25, 2002, p. 3C; *New York Yankees Media Guide*, 2003; Alfonso Soriano file, National Baseball Library, Cooperstown, NY; *The Sporting News Baseball Register*, 2003.

David L. Porter

SAMMY SOSA   Baseball
(November 12, 1968–   )

Sammy Sosa, one of the most prolific home run hitters in major league history, remains the only player to hit 60 or more home runs three times.

Samuel Sosa Peralta was born on November 12, 1968 in San Pedro de Marcoris, Dominican Republic, to Bautista Sosa, a farmer, and Lucretia Peralta Sosa, a homemaker. Juan died when Sosa was 7, leaving Lucretia to bring up five boys and two girls in a two-room house. As a boy, Sosa sold oranges, shined shoes, and served as a janitor in a shoe factory to help support the family. He played stick ball with tightly rolled up socks for balls and a milk carton for a glove.

The Philadelphia Phillies (National League) signed Sosa in 1984, but the contract was voided because he was only 15 years old. In July 1985, the Texas Rangers (American League) signed Sosa for $3,000 after watching him at a tryout. He led the Sarasota, Florida, Gulf Coast Rangers (Gulf Coast League) with 19 doubles in 1986, his first professional season. In the Rangers minor league system, Sosa demonstrated great base-stealing ability, limited power, and a free-swinging approach. He reached the major leagues in June 1989 with the Texas Rangers. After only 25 games, he was traded in July 1989 to the Chicago White Sox (AL) in a five-player transaction. He started in right field for the White Sox in 1990 and 1991 and constantly threatened on the base paths, but batted only .233 and .203 while striking out often.

In March 1992, the White Sox sent Sosa to the crosstown Chicago Cubs (NL) for outfielder George Bell. Sosa's power surge began in 1993, when he clouted 33 home runs and drove in 93 runs for the Cubs. In the following campaign, Sosa recorded his first .300 batting average. In 1995 the hard-hitting right fielder amassed his first 100 runs batted in (RBI) season. From 1995 to 1997, he hit 36, 40, and 36 home runs, respectively, and continued to pilfer bases with his third 30-plus season in 1995.

In 1998 Sosa constructed one of the greatest offensive seasons in history, battling St. Louis Cardinal slugger Mark McGwire virtually all season. McGwire once led Sosa 24 home runs to nine, but Sosa eventually surged past McGwire, 57 to 46. He finished with 66 home runs, but McGwire batted five roundtrippers in the final three games to amass 70 home runs. The good-natured, humble sluggers made it a friendly rivalry and packed people into the ballparks. Sosa hit 20 home runs in June, a major league record for roundtrippers in one month. In the last two months of the season, baseball fans across the United States went to their televisions and radios when Sosa or McGwire came to bat. Sosa compiled a NL-leading 134 runs scored and 158 RBIs while posting a .308 batting average. The Baseball Writers' Association of America (BWAA) selected him NL Most Valuable Player in 1998. He earned the Roberto Clemente Man of the Year Award, *The Sporting News* Sportsman of the Year and Player of the Year awards, and *Baseball Digest* Player of the Year. He led the Cubs to the NL Wild Card, but the Atlanta Braves swept Chicago in the NL Division Series.

Sosa produced another sensational season for the Cubs in 1999, recording 63 home runs, 114 runs scored, and 141 RBIs. The following season, he clouted 50 roundtrippers, drove in 138 tallies, and posted a .320 batting average. Yet 2001 statistically marked his greatest season. Sosa drove 64 baseballs beyond the outfield fences and led the NL with 146 runs scored and 160

Sammy Sosa ©Stephen Green/Chicago Cubs

RBIs, 94 more than any teammate that season. He batted a career-best .328 but finished second to Barry Bonds* of the San Francisco Giants in the NL MVP balloting. Sosa's home run and RBI feats proved even more incredible because he enjoyed almost no protection in Chicago's lineup from 1998 to 2001. The 6-foot, 220-pound right-handed Sosa learned to hit to all fields and to stop lunging for pitches in the dirt and unreachable sliders. Ironically, he finished second each time he hit over 60 home runs, twice to McGwire and once to Bonds. With Fred McGriff* batting behind him for the entire 2002 campaign, Sosa came within one home run of being the first player to hit 50 or more home runs in five consecutive seasons. He surpassed 100 RBIs for the eighth straight year but could not lift a weak Chicago team. Sosa became the eleventh major leaguer to attain 500 career home runs, connecting off Scott Sullivan of the Cincinnati Reds in a 10–9 loss at the new Great American Ball Park on April 4, 2003. He was ejected in the first inning of an early June game with Tampa Bay at Chicago when home plate umpire Tim McClelland discovered cork in his broken bat when he grounded to second base. Major League Baseball suspended him for seven games. His 332 home runs from 1998 to 2003 remain the greatest six-year total in baseball history. He played on the NL All-Star team in 1995 and 1999–2002, and was selected in 1998, but was replaced due to injury. His career through 2003 included 2,099 hits, 319 doubles, 43 triples, 539 home runs, 1,450 RBIs, 233 stolen bases, and a .278 batting average in 2,012 games. Sosa batted .279 with 103 RBIs and ranked sixth in the NL with 40 home runs in 2003, helping the Chicago Cubs win the NL Central. Atlanta Braves hurlers limited him to a .188 batting average and only one RBI in the NL Division Series, but he batted .308 with one double, 2 home runs, and 6 RBIs in the NL Championship Series against the victorious Florida Marlins.

Sosa and his wife, Sonia, have two daughters, Keysha and Kenia, and two sons, Samuel Jr. and Michael. They reside on Lake Shore Drive in Chicago during the baseball season but return to Santo Domingo, Dominican Republic, for the winter months. His brother, Jose, played in the Cubs farm system. In 1997, Sosa formed the Sosa Foundation to aid the poor of the Dominican Republic. He built a multimillion dollar retail and office complex in his old neighborhood. Sosa purchased 60,000 pounds of rice and 20,000 pounds of bottled water for his countrymen when Hurricane Georges ravished the Dominican Republic in September 1998. In 1999 the Sosa Foundation opened the Sammy Sosa Medical Center for Preventive Medicine in San Pedro de Macoris. Sosa donates hundreds of Cubs tickets to Chicago's disadvantaged children each year. President George W. Bush, once part-owner of the Texas Rangers, acknowledged the worst move he ever made was allowing the Rangers to trade Sammy Sosa. The Rangers surely must agree.

BIBLIOGRAPHY
John Dewan, ed., *The Scouting Notebook 2003* (Morton Grove, IL, 2003); Louise Hightower and Terrie M. Rooney, eds., *Newsmakers 99 Cumulation* (Detroit, MI, 1999); Bernie Miklasz et al., *Celebrating 70: Mark McGwire's Historic Season* (St. Louis, MO, 1998); Chuck Wasserstrom, *Chicago Cubs 2003 Information Guide* (Chicago, IL, 2003).

Frank J. Olmsted

DARRYL STRAWBERRY   **Baseball**
(March 12, 1962–)

Darryl Strawberry gained the limelight for his home runs and off-the-field problems.

Darryl Eugene Strawberry was born on March 12, 1962 in Los Angeles, California, one of four children of Henry Strawberry and Ruby Strawberry. His brother, Michael, played outfield in the minor leagues. Strawberry spoke devotedly of Ruby. "She cared about her kids and wanted them to grow up happy. . . . She taught us to realize that life is what you make it." Strawberry graduated in 1980 from Crenshaw High School, where he played football, basketball, and baseball. He has noted that "he couldn't remember a time when I didn't love the game of baseball." His coach called the 6-foot 6-inch, left-handed-hitting outfielder "the black Ted Williams." Strawberry idolized both Williams and Pete Rose, but was more graceful than both of them, representing true poetry in motion.

Word of Strawberry's remarkable talents spread nationally when the New York Mets (National League) made him their first selection of the June 1980 draft. *The Sporting News* (*TSN*) speculated that "since he moved with effortless grace so smooth and so talented, that quite soon right field at Shea Stadium would become known as 'the Strawberry patch.' The mark of promise weighs heavily on Strawberry. . . . the next Willie Mays." Strawberry joined the New York Mets in 1983, hitting .257 with 26 home runs and a .512 slugging percentage in just 122 games. The Baseball Writers Association of America named him NL Rookie of the Year. After Strawberry clouted 27 homers and 97 runs batted in (RBI) in his second year, *TSN* called him "the Super Sophomore" and predicted he would become "the apple of New York's eye." He played in his first World Series in 1986, helping the Mets edge the Boston Red Sox, four games to three.

Strawberry belted at least 26 homers every year for his first nine major league seasons. *TSN* named him to its Silver Slugger Team for 1988 and 1990. Personal difficulties, however, surfaced with teammate Keith Hernandez and Manager Davey Johnson, who fined him several times for being late to workouts. Strawberry and Mets' pitcher Dwight Gooden* became close friends when both were having substance abuse problems. Gooden described their friendship: "He was a person I came to rely on as a friend. Darryl stood up for me in my difficult periods." Strawberry enjoyed his best year in 1987, hitting .284 with 39 home runs and 104 RBIs. Biographer Bob Klapisch observed that "Darryl could always make the world his own once he got to the plate." Klapisch added, "Certainly, Darryl and Dwight were not the only Mets into drugs—they just happened to fall the farthest." A 1989 divorce from his wife, Lisa, followed, leaving two children, Darryl Jr. and Diamond. She accused him of striking her in the face and breaking her nose. The Mets sent Strawberry to a treatment center in 1990. Strawberry told critics: "I'm not a bad person. I'm a sick person getting well. Thank God for that."

Strawberry signed with the Los Angeles Dodgers (NL) in November 1990, but a painful herniated disc limited his production. Stints with the San Francisco Giants (NL) and the New York Yankees (American League) between 1994 and 1999 proved disappointing. He underwent surgery for colon cancer in October 1998. Strawberry failed a drug test in January 2000, was suspended for one year, and retired as a player. In 17 major league seasons, he batted

.259, with 335 home runs, 990 RBIs, 1,401 hits, and 221 stolen bases. He set major league records for most pinch grand slams in a season (2) and most strikeouts in a major league game (5). His 1985 home run off St. Louis Cardinals left-hander Ken Daley hit the scoreboard and jammed the clock at Shea Stadium in New York.

Strawberry found baseball his life's fulfillment: "Baseball gave me goals to achieve, to strive for. It provided a purpose for my life."

BIBLIOGRAPHY
Barry Jacobs, "Huge Pressure on Rookie Strawberry," *The Sporting News*, August 15, 1981; Bob Klapisch, *High and Tight: The Rise and Fall of Dwight Gooden and Darryl Strawberry* (New York, 1996); David L. Porter, ed., *Biographical Dictionary of American Sports: Baseball, Q–Z*, revised and expanded edition (Westport, CT, 2000); *The Sporting News Baseball Register*, 2000; Darryl Strawberry file, Research Center, *The Sporting News*, St. Louis, MO; *Who's Who in Baseball*, 85th ed. (New York, 2000).

William J. Miller

SHERYL SWOOPES   Basketball
(March 25, 1971–   )

The incredible athletic prowess and shooting ability of Sheryl Swoopes led many to call her the female Michael Jordan.*

Sheryl Denise Swoopes was born in Brownfield, Texas, on March 25, 1971 to Louise Swoopes. Her parents divorced when she was young, leaving her mother to bring up Sheryl and her three brothers. Swoopes learned a very physical, aggressive style of basketball by playing with her brothers in neighborhood games. She made All-State and All-America in basketball for Brownfield High School.

Many major colleges recruited Swoopes, but she wished to remain near home. She enrolled at South Plains Junior College in Levelland, Texas, where she was selected a Junior College All-America and Player of the Year. Swoopes averaged better than 21 points and nearly 12 rebounds in her second year at South Plains. She transferred to Texas Tech University in August 1991. In her two seasons at Texas Tech, the women's basketball team won 58 of 66 contests and its first ever national championship. She averaged over 28 points and almost 10 rebounds in her senior year. In the National Collegiate Athletic Association (NCAA) women's title game in 1993, she led the Lady Red Raiders to a 84–82 victory over Ohio State University with 47 points, an NCAA record for a championship game. Swoopes's 1,645 points rank fourth highest total in school history. She was named women's basketball Player of the Year by nine different organizations, including the Associated Press. Texas Tech retired her jersey number 22.

In the fall of 1993, Swoopes played in 10 games for the Bari team (Italian Women's League) before returning to Texas Tech to complete her Bachelor's degree in sports science. The following year, she won a bronze medal for the

Sheryl Swoopes ©Allen Einstein/Getty Images

USA team at the World Championships in Sydney, Australia, and a gold medal at the Goodwill Games in St. Petersburg, Russia. She earned gold medals on the USA 1996 and 2000 Olympic teams, averaging 13 points and four rebounds.

Swoopes married Eric Jackson in June 1995. Two years later she signed with the Houston Comets of the newly formed Women's National Basketball Association (WNBA) but did not start the inaugural campaign in 1997 because she was pregnant. Six weeks after giving birth to Jordan Eric on June 25, 1997, the 6-foot, 144-pound forward returned to the hardwood with the Comets. Her husband Eric, an Arena League football player, became a stay-at-home father so that Swoopes could play professional basketball.

Swoopes joined Lisa Leslie* and Rebecca Lobo as the marquee WNBA players. Swoopes led the Houston Comets to four straight WNBA titles from 1997 through 2000, averaging 14.4 points and 5.7 rebounds. She was named to the All-WNBA First Team from 1998 through 2000 and was selected the WNBA Most Valuable Player (MVP) and Defensive Player of the Year in 2000. She played in the 1999 and 2000 WNBA All-Star games, scoring 14 points and making 14 rebounds.

Swoopes missed the entire 2001 campaign with a torn anterior cruciate ligament and lateral meniscus in her left knee but played for the USA National team and the USA Basketball World Championship team in 2002. She started every game for Houston during the 2002 WNBA season and led the Comets to their sixth straight playoffs, averaging 18.5 points for third best in the league, pacing the WNBA with 221 field goals, and placing second with 88 steals. She again was named WNBA MVP, edging 2001 MVP Lisa Leslie,* and Defensive Player of the Year. She finished as the top vote getter for the 2002 WNBA All-Star Game. Swoopes helped Houston finish second in the Western Conference with a 20–13 record in 2003, ranking ninth in scoring with 484 points (15.6 average) and tenth in assists with 121 (3.9 average) in 31 games. She also made the West All-Stars.

Through the 2003 season, Swoopes recorded 862 rebounds, 407 steals, 543 assists, 1,065 total field goals with 154 from three-point range, and 537 free throws in 164 regular season games. She remains the only player in WNBA history to record over 2,000 points, 400 assists, 700 rebounds, and 300 steals. She became the first woman to have a shoe named for her when Nike introduced the Air Swoopes women's shoe. She sponsored a basketball camp for women at Houston Baptist University, Houston, Texas, in July 2002.

BIBLIOGRAPHY
Elisa Ast All, "Bouncing Back from Baby," *Pregnancy Today* (Pregnancytoday.com, 2002), pp. 1–3; Michael A. Lutz, "Sports: Sheryl Swoopes' Surgery Successful," *Nando Media* (nandotimes.com, May 1, 2002), pp. 1–3; Terrie M. Rooney, ed., *Newsmakers 98 Cumulation* (Detroit, MI, 1999); USA Basketball, "Sheryl Swoopes" (usabasketball.com, 2002), pp. 1–4; WNBA, "Swoopes Named WNBA MVP Presented by Buick," *WNBA News* (WNBA.com, October 2002); *WNBA Official WNBA Guide and Register, 2003.*

Frank J. Olmsted

T

LAWRENCE TAYLOR   Football
(February 4, 1959–   )

Lawrence Taylor ranked among the most skilled defensive players in National Football League (NFL) history. He helped the New York Giants (NFL) win two Super Bowls, but also became a self-proclaimed "renegade," suspended from play for using hard drugs.

Lawrence Taylor was born on February 4, 1959 in Williamsburg, Virginia. His father, Clarence, worked in the shipyards in Newport News, while his mother, Iris, taught school. Taylor was the middle child of the three boys in the family but played baseball rather than football until he was 15 years old because he was short. His Lafayette High School's assistant coach advised him that "if you were black and came from a small town in the South and you wanted to go to college . . . , you had better think about things like football."

Taylor began playing football for the local Jaycees and then tried out for his Lafayette High School football team, but he did not blossom until his senior year. He grew to 6 feet, 3 inches, and 240 pounds. One of Taylor's senior teammates recalled, "Taylor was almost saying, 'I'm going to be great'. . . . When he was on the field, he'd just go wacko on people."

Taylor did not receive many college football scholarship offers but was finally recruited by the University of North Carolina (Atlantic Coast Conference). In his senior year in 1980, he made 69 solo tackles and made consensus All-America while helping the Tar Heels win the Bluebonnet Bowl against the University of Texas.

Taylor became the first draft pick of the New York Giants (NFL) and the second selection overall in 1989. The Giants had not won a championship since 1956. During his rookie year in 1981, the Giants made the NFL playoffs for the first time since 1963. Taylor was named both NFL Rookie of the Year and NFL Defensive Player of the Year.

Taylor's play was characterized by a ferocious rush in attacking the opposing quarterback or runners. He used his strength and speed to pursue relentlessly and to harry opposing players. He took particular pride in tackling the opposing passer behind the line of scrimmage, often "sacking" the quarterback. His success at trapping the enemy quarterback led the NFL to start keeping official count of sacks in 1982.

After that first year, Taylor continually improved. In his first nine years, he made the Pro Bowl each year. In 1986 he was chosen All-NFL, NFL Player of the Year, and NFL Defensive Player of the Year.

The Giants' road to the Super Bowl, however, met detours. In 1982 New York posted four wins and five losses in a season shortened by a player strike. At the end of that year, Bill Parcells took over as coach. The Giants fared worse in 1983, winning four and losing 12 games. Fortunately for Taylor, who hated to lose and was becoming frustrated by the way opponents now assigned two and sometimes three linemen to block him, the Giants improved. In 1984 New York finished nine and seven, making the playoffs. Taylor started in the Pro Bowl that year because of his 88 solo tackles and 11.5 sacks.

The Giants won 10 and lost 6 in 1985 before being eliminated in the playoffs by the Chicago Bears, the eventual Super Bowl champions. That season Coach Parcells noticed that Taylor did not seem his usual aggressive self and suspected that he was involved with drugs. In March 1986, Taylor entered a rehabilitation clinic because of his addiction to cocaine. He did not stay long in the clinic, however, and embarked on a cross-country trip, claiming that playing golf helped him kick his drug habit.

The 1986 season brought a Super Bowl victory to Taylor and the Giants. Taylor was unanimously selected as the NFL Most Valuable Player. In Super Bowl XXI, the Giants defeated the Denver Broncos, 39–20.

In 1987 Taylor crossed the picket line set up by the striking players and missed some games because of an injury. He again tested positive for drugs in August 1988 and was suspended for four games. He encountered no more public drug problems for the rest of his NFL career but he was continually regarded as boastful and was criticized for refusing to abide by the rules.

Taylor led the Giants to their second Super Bowl win in 1990, edging the Buffalo Bills, 20–19, in Super Bowl XXV. He was not selected to the Pro Bowl team after the 1991 season and missed much of the 1992 season because of an injury. In 1993 he helped the Giants earn a spot in the playoffs. He retired before the 1994 season, finishing his career in second place all-time in the NFL with 132.5 sacks.

Taylor ranked as the top defensive player of the 1980s, was named to the Pro Bowl team 10 times, and redefined the role of the outside linebacker in pro football. Other teams started to develop players who could attack and harass the passers from the outside linebacker spot.

Taylor married Linda Cooley in 1981; they have three children and live in New Jersey.

BIBLIOGRAPHY
Bob Carroll et al., *Total Football* (New York, 1997); *Great Athletes—The 20th Century*, vol. 17 (Englewood Cliffs, NJ, 1992), pp. 2478–2480; "Lawrence Taylor," *Current Biography, 1990* (New York, 1990); *The Lincoln Library of Sports Champions,*

vol. 18 (Columbus, OH, 1991); David L. Porter, ed., *African-American Sports Greats* (Westport, CT, 1995).

Robert L. Cannon

MIGUEL TEJADA Baseball
(May 25, 1976–   )

Miguel Tejada represents an exciting new breed of major league shortstop, combining excellent fielding ability with powerful hitting and a high batting average.

Miguel Odalis Tejada was born on May 25, 1976 in Bani, Dominican Republic. He grew up on the edge of starvation in a Dominican *barrio* with no plumbing and seldom any electricity. When Tejada was only three years old, his family lost their home in Hurricane David. For five years, the Tejadas moved from one homeless shelter to another until settling in a shantytown outside Bani. Tejada left school at age 11 to work full time in a garment factory. When his mother died two years later, his father moved north to seek work elsewhere. For four years, Tejada and his older brother led a subsistence existence.

Knowing baseball was his only possible ticket out of poverty, the teenaged Tejada connected with a talent scout. The scout helped him develop the discipline and baseball skills that major league scouts seek. Barely 17 years old, Tejada was signed in July 1993 by National Baseball Hall of Fame pitcher Juan Marichal for $2,000 and sent to the Oakland Athletics (American League) Dominican Baseball Academy. He played second base for the Dominican Athletics (Dominican Summer League) in 1993 and 1994, hitting a home run in his first at bat and showing good power at the plate and excellent speed on the bases. He moved to shortstop and advanced a level each season in the Oakland farm system, topping his minor league career with 22 home runs and 97 runs batted in (RBI) at Huntsville, Alabama (Southern League) in 1997.

After spending the first two months of the 1998 season on the disabled list, Tejada batted a modest .233 with 11 home runs in 105 games for Oakland. The 1999 campaign, however, produced a clearer picture of the potential the 5-foot 9-inch, 185-pound right-handed shortstop possessed. He unleashed 21 home runs, collected 84 RBIs, and scored 93 runs in 159 games. He showed good range, great hands, quick reflexes, and a rifle arm, leading AL shortstops with 292 putouts. Tejada has a compact, very quick throwing style and turns double plays well. In 2000 he hit 30 home runs, scored 105 times, and drove in 115 runs while leading AL shortstops with 501 assists. The following season, he played in all 162 games for Oakland, hit 31 home runs, scored 107 times, and recorded 113 RBIs. Although directing most of his home runs to left field, Tejada hits the ball to all fields. He demonstrates a willingness to learn and has improved his game each year, but he still needs greater selectivity at the plate and more patience to take walks.

On September 29, 2001, Tejada became the first player to hit for the cycle (single, double, triple, home run) at Safeco Park in Seattle to help the Athletics defeat the Seattle Mariners, 8–4. He was the fifth AL player ever to include a grand slam home run in the cycle, joining Jimmie Foxx, Nap Lajoie, Tony Lazzeri, and Jay Buhner. His three grand slam home runs in 2001 marked only the ninth time a player had accomplished the feat. Tejada's 31 round-trippers set the season record for an Athletics shortstop. Third baseman Eric Chavez belted his thirtieth home run, joining Tejada as the first third baseman-shortstop combination in major league history to each connect for that figure in the same season. Tejada established the Athletics' franchise career mark for home runs by a shortstop (117) in July 2002. He became one of only five major league shortstops to hit 30 home runs in a season more than once, joining Alex Rodriguez,* Ernie Banks, Nomar Garciaparra,* and Vern Stephens. The only Oakland shortstop to drive in 100 runs in a season, he has accomplished the feat in four consecutive campaigns. Tejada batted .278 with 42 doubles, 27 home runs, and 106 RBIs in 2003, hitting several clutch round-trippers in August and September to help the Athletics win the AL West. Boston Red Sox pitchers, however, limited him to just two hits and two RBIs in the AL Division Series.

The Baseball Writers' Association of America voted Tejada the 2002 AL Most Valuable Player, as he reached career bests with a .308 batting average, 108 runs scored, 34 home runs, and 131 RBIs while leading Oakland to the AL Western Division Championship. Through the 2003 campaign, Tejada batted .270, with 968 hits, 191 doubles, 11 triples, 156 home runs, 574 runs scored, and 604 RBIs in 936 games. He hit a composite .212 in AL Division Series appearances in 2000, 2001, 2002, and 2003. His aggressive style of play and determination to play every game, which includes 624 consecutive games through the 2003 season, make him a favorite of fans and his teammates. Tejada has joined Rodriguez, Garciaparra, and Derek Jeter* among the elite ranks of slick fielding, great hitting shortstops. Only time will tell how far he ascends. During the off-season, Tejada lives in Los Barranconez, Dominican Republic. He and his wife, Alesandra, have one daughter, Alexa, and one son, Miguel.

BIBLIOGRAPHY

Associated Press, "Historic Evening: Ichiro Sets Rookie Record; Tejada Hits for Cycle," *CNN Sports Illustrated* (cnnsi.com, September 30, 2001), pp. 1–4; Marcus Breton, *Away Games: The Life and Times of a Latin Baseball Player* (New York, 1999); Marcus Breton, "Fields of Broken Dreams: Latinos and Baseball," *ColorLines Magazine*, Archive Issue (Spring 2000), pp. 1–7; John Dewan, ed., *The Scouting Notebook 2002* (Morton Grove, IL, 2002); Gwen Knapp, "A-Rod, Jeter, Nomar, Omar, . . . and Miguel Tejada Are the Best All-around Shortstops in the Majors," *Baseball Digest 61* (November 2002), pp. 62–64; MLB Advanced Media, http://MLB.com: Miguel Tejada (http://mlb.com, 2002), pp. 1–3; Stats, Inc., "Miguel Tejada," www.ESPN.com (ESPN Internet Ventures, 2002), pp. 1–2.

Frank J. Olmsted

FRANK THOMAS   Baseball
(May 27, 1968–   )

Frank Thomas, one of the most feared hitters of the 1990s, consistently lived up to his nickname, "The Big Hurt," for the relentless punishment he inflicted on opposing pitchers.

Frank Edward Thomas Jr. was born on May 27, 1968 in Columbus, Georgia, the youngest of five children of Frank Thomas Sr., a textile worker and bail bondsman, and Charlie Mae Thomas. Thomas excelled in baseball, football, and basketball at Columbus High School, clouting 400-foot home runs. He credited his high school coach Bobby Howard for giving him the confidence to play baseball. Above all, Thomas hoped to play baseball in college or professionally. Yet, despite his Herculean homers in high school, few colleges expressed interest in him. Auburn University, however, offered him a football scholarship to play tight end. He played football his freshman year but also made the baseball team in the spring of 1987 and belted 21 home runs. After batting .385 in 1988, he had one of the finest college seasons ever in 1989, batting .403 with 83 runs batted in (RBI) and earning *The Sporting News* (*TSN*) All-American College Team honors. His 49 career home runs established the Auburn school record. Despite his spectacular record, he was left off the 1988 U.S. Olympic team in favor of future major league first basemen Tino Martinez and Ed Sprague.

The Chicago White Sox (American League) scouted Thomas for three years and made him their first pick (seventh pick overall) in the June 1989 draft. After batting .323 and drawing 112 walks in 109 games at Birmingham, Alabama (Southern League) and being named *Baseball America's* Minor League Player of the Year in 1990, he joined the Chicago White Sox that August. His ninth-inning RBI defeated the Milwaukee Brewers in his first major league game. The next night, his seventh-inning two-run triple defeated the Brewers. He finished with a .330 batting average in 60 games. Thomas underwent shoulder surgery after the 1991 campaign but recovered fully.

From 1991 to 1998, he collected more than 100 runs, walks, and RBIs every season. He clouted 40 or more home runs in 1993, 1995, 1996, 2000, and 2003. Between 1990 and 2000, he failed to hit .300 only once. In 1997 his .347 batting average led the AL. He attained a personal high .353 batting average in 1994, with his .729 slugging percentage topping the AL.

Besides his excellent batting eye and his patience to lay off pitches outside the strike zone, Thomas had a knack for fouling off two-strike pitches until finding one he could drive. National Baseball Hall of Fame pitcher Nolan Ryan observed, "Thomas hits fastballs and breaking balls. He doesn't mind going deep into the count and he doesn't mind walking. That's unusual for a power hitter." Sportswriter Phil Rogers advised that the best strategy to contain Thomas was to "throw him four balls and try your luck with the next guy." Thomas's home runs often exceeded 425 feet. The 6-foot 5-inch, 268-pound right-handed first baseman provided his infielders with a huge target and adeptly scooped throws from the dirt, but he lacked range at first base and sometimes made suspect throws. He became the White Sox's primary designated hitter in 1997 and preferred that role to defensive play.

Thomas was selected *TSN* 1993 Player of the Year. In 1994, he received all 28 first-place Most Valuable Player (MVP) votes and became the first player since Roger Maris of the New York Yankees (1960–1961) to win consecutive AL MVP awards. He finished second to Jason Giambi in AL MVP voting in 2000. He won AL Comeback Player of the Year in 2000, when he reached career highs with 115 runs, 191 hits, 43 home runs, and 143 RBIs. He is the only major league player in history to bat over .300, score 100 runs, drive in 100 runs, receive 100 walks, and hit more than 20 home runs a season seven consecutive years, accomplishing the feat from 1991 through 1997.

Thomas left the 2001 White Sox's spring training camp for six days in a contract dispute. Failing to get his swing or timing down well in spring training, he tore a tendon in his right arm in April while diving for a ball at first base. A more devastating blow came a few days later when his father died. The torn tendon required surgery, causing Thomas to miss the rest of the season. A healthy Thomas in 2002 anchored a great hitting lineup that included Kenny Lofton,* Magglio Ordoñez,* Paul Konerko, and Ray Durham, batting .252 with 28 home runs and 92 RBIs. He entered the 2004 season with 1,851 games played, 2,048 hits, 1,255 runs, 428 doubles, 11 triples, 418 home runs, 1,390 RBIs, 1,386 walks, and a .310 batting average. Thomas holds the White Sox career record for home runs. He played for the AL in the 1993, 1994, and 1995 All-Star games, making four hits in five at-bats. He hit .353 and drew a record 10 walks in the 1993 AL Championship Series against the victorious Toronto Blue Jays. Thomas batted .267 with 105 RBIs in 2003, sharing second in the AL with 42 home runs and ranking fourth with 100 walks.

Thomas married Elise Silver, whom he met during 1991 spring training. Now divorced, they have a son, Sterling Edward, and two daughters, Sloan Alexandra and Sydney Blake. Thomas remains very close to his mother and extended family. He participates in numerous charities, having established the Frank Thomas Charitable Foundation in 1993. He contributes $50,000 per year to the Leukemia and Lymphoma Society of America in remembrance of his younger sister, who died from the disease at age 3. Thomas has marketed the Big Hurt necktie and Big Hurt candy bar, with all proceeds going directly to charities. He founded Big Hurt Enterprises to oversee his sponsorships, endorsements, and charitable grants. He is often described as a well-spoken, personable, optimistic, and thoughtful man who never forgets his friends or his roots. This image has been tarnished somewhat as a result of his 2001 walkout, contract dispute, firing of his agents, on-field shouting match with White Sox manager Jerry Manuel in 2002, and twice failing to slide at home, resulting in outs.

BIBLIOGRAPHY
John Dewan, ed., *The Scouting Notebook 2002* (Morton Grove, IL, 2002); "Frank Thomas," *Current Biography Yearbook 1994* (New York, 1994), pp. 593–596; Frank

E. Thomas file, National Baseball Library, Cooperstown, NY; Zander Hollander, ed., *The Complete Handbook of Baseball, 1994*, 24th ed. (New York, 1994); Paul Ladewski, "Big Hurt Puts Up Big Numbers," *Baseball Digest* 59 (December 2000), pp. 56–58; Skip Myslenski, "Perfectly Frank," *Chicago Tribune*, August 7, 1994, sec. 3, pp. 1, 8–9; Michael Pagel, ed., *Beckett Great Sports Heroes: Frank Thomas* (New York, 1996); David L. Porter, ed., *African-American Sports Greats* (Westport, CT, 1995).

Frank J. Olmsted

ISIAH THOMAS   Basketball
(April 30, 1961–)

Isiah "Zeke" Thomas, one of professional basketball's all-time great point guards, played 13 National Basketball Association (NBA) seasons from 1981 to 1994 with the Detroit Pistons and was elected to the Naismith Memorial Basketball Hall of Fame in 2000. He was renowned for his outside shooting touch, flashy ball-handling skills, ability to penetrate the line in a drive, and running the length of the court on both offense and defense.

Isiah Lord Thomas III was born on April 30, 1961 in Chicago, Illinois, the youngest of nine children of Isiah Lord Thomas II, an International Harvester plant supervisor, and Mary Thomas. When Thomas was an infant, his father lost his job and could not find comparable work elsewhere. Embittered and frustrated, he left home when Thomas was 3. Mary brought up the children in one of the toughest, most poverty-stricken neighborhoods of Chicago. She worked as a cook at a local church and housekeeper and later as a counselor with Chicago's Department of Human Services to put her children through Catholic schools. "Without a doubt, my greatest role model and the most important figure in my life is my mother," stressed Thomas. "There's not anything I can do or say that could repay my mother for the years she gave me and my family."

The recipient of a sports scholarship to attend St. Joseph High School in suburban Westchester, Illinois, Thomas became an honor student. As a junior, Thomas led the school to a 31–2 record and a second-place finish in the State Championship Tournament and was selected to the All-State team. "He is a natural born leader," said coach Gene Pingatore. "Isiah has intelligence, mental toughness, the determination to win, plus charisma." After leading St. Joseph's to a 26–3 record his senior year, Thomas selected a scholarship offered by coach Bobby Knight to play basketball at Indiana University. In the summer following graduation, Thomas helped the Knight-coached United States team win a gold medal in the 1979 Pan American Games. He led the team in assists, averaged 9.2 points, and scored 21 points in a 113–94 title game victory over Puerto Rico. He also was selected to the U.S. Olympic Basketball team in 1980.

As a freshman and sophomore at Indiana, Thomas made All–Big Ten Conference (BTC) and led the Hoosiers in assists (5.7 average), steals, and scoring

Isiah Thomas ©Tim Defrisco/Getty Images

(15.4 point average) to help his team compile 21–8 and 26–9 records and capture two BTC titles. As captain in 1981, Thomas became a consensus All-American and was named the Most Valuable Player (MVP) in the National Collegiate Athletic Association (NCAA) tourney after scoring 91 points and making 43 assists in five games. His five assists and game-high 23 points led the Hoosiers to a 63–50 title game victory over the University of North Carolina. In 1999 he was cited as one of the 50 Greatest Players to have played in Indiana.

In April 1981, Thomas applied for the NBA draft citing family considerations. He was selected second in the opening round by the Detroit Pistons

(NBA), which had won only 37 out of 164 games the previous two seasons. He signed a four-year, $1.6 million contract and immediately purchased a home for his mother in Clarendon Hills, Illinois. Later, in 1987, Thomas earned a B.A. degree in criminal justice from Indiana.

The 6-foot-1-inch, 182-pound rookie guard made an immediate impact. He quickly established himself as the Pistons' leader in 1981–1982, helping Detroit improve to a 39–43 record. Thomas averaged 17 points, led his team in assists (565) and steals (150), was picked for the All-Star team, and was named *The Sporting News* 1982 NBA Rookie of the Year. In his second season, he averaged 22.9 points and 7.8 assists and again made the All-Star team.

Thomas consistently outplayed his teammates. The first NBA player voted to the All-Star team in his first five seasons, he was named the game's MVP in 1984 and 1986. His honors included 12 consecutive All-Star game selections. He was selected to the All-NBA First Team from 1984 through 1986 and to the All-NBA Second Team in 1983 and 1987. Under new coach Chuck Daly, Thomas in 1983–1984 guided Detroit to its first winning record (49–33) in seven seasons. He scored 16 points in the final 94 seconds of regulation to force overtime in a 1984 playoff game against the New York Knicks. In 1984–1985 he set a season NBA record of 1,123 assists (13.9 average).

In 1986–1987, the Pistons challenged for the NBA crown. Thomas averaged 20.6 points and 10 assists and led Detroit to a five-game victory over the Atlanta Hawks in round two of the playoffs. The Pistons pushed the Boston Celtics to the limit before losing in the seventh game of the Eastern Conference Finals, 117–114.

Thomas averaged 19.5 points and 8.4 assists in 1987–1988, when Detroit won its first Central Division title and overcame the Boston Celtics in six games in the playoffs for the Eastern Conference Championship. The Pistons lost to the Los Angeles Lakers in seven games in the NBA Finals, but Thomas made a gutsy performance in the sixth game. Although playing on a severely sprained ankle, he finished the game with 43 points, eight assists, and six steals, and set an NBA playoff record for points in a quarter with 25.

Team captain Thomas led Detroit to NBA Championships in 1989 and 1990. In 1988–1989 the "Bad Boys," as the Pistons were called because of their surly demeanor and rough tactics, compiled a 63–19 record and triumphed in the six-game Eastern Conference Finals against the Chicago Bulls and in a four-game sweep of the Los Angeles Lakers in the NBA Finals. The Pistons followed with a 59–23 record in 1989–1990 and defeated the Portland Trail Blazers in the five-game NBA Finals for their second straight NBA title. Thomas was named the 1990 NBA Finals MVP, averaging 27.6 points, seven assists, and 5.2 rebounds. "He's a big game guy," said coach Daly. "He plays best when the challenge is there."

In 1991 the Pistons were defeated by the Chicago Bulls in the Eastern Conference Finals. In 1991–1992 the Pistons finished third in their division and lost in the first round of the playoffs. Retirements, questionable trades, injuries, and age all contributed further to Detroit's misfortunes in Thomas's two remaining years with the club. His statistics declined as the Pistons won only 60 games and failed to make the playoffs in 1993 and 1994.

After suffering a torn Achilles tendon, Thomas retired after the 1994 season as the greatest player in Pistons franchise history. "I have no regrets," he reflected. "As a basketball player, you give everything to your sport, give everything to the organization and to the team you play for." He remains the career club leader in points (18,822; 19.2 average), assists (9,061; 9.3 average), steals (1,861; 1.9 average), and games played (979). He ranks among only four players in NBA history to reach 9,000 assists. In 111 playoff games, Thomas leads the franchise with 2,261 points (20.4 average), 987 assists (8.9 average), and 234 steals. The Pistons retired Thomas's number 11 jersey on February 17, 1996. In 1996 he was also named one of the 50 Greatest Players in NBA history. From 1988 to 1994, Thomas served as president of the NBA Players Association. He helped increase player salaries, form the NBA player salary cap, and create one of professional sports' first antidrug policies.

In May 1994, Thomas became part-owner, executive vice president of basketball operations, and general manager of the Toronto Raptors, Canada's first NBA expansion franchise. The Raptors won 51 games in their first two seasons (1995–1997) to tie a modern-era expansion record. After his bid to buy the entire team was rejected in 1997, Thomas became a sportscaster with NBC Sports in New York City from 1997 to 2000. He purchased the foundering nine-team Continental Basketball Association (CBA) in July 1999 but lost $10 million when it folded a year later. In July 2000, Thomas became the head coach for the Indiana Pacers (NBA). He compiled a 41–41 record and lost a four-game playoff series to the Philadelphia 76ers in 2000–2001. In 2001–2002, he posted a 42–40 record, but lost a five-game playoff series to the New Jersey Nets. Under Thomas, the Pacers finished third in the Eastern Conference with a 48–34 mark in 2002–2003, but were upset in a six-game playoff series with the Boston Celtics. He was released as head coach in August 2003, having compiled a 131–115 regular season record and a 5–10 playoff mark.

Thomas founded the Isiah Thomas Foundation, an organization that promotes and creates educational and recreational opportunities for inner-city youth in the Detroit area. He also participates in anticrime and antipoverty programs. He was the recipient of the 1985 Michiganian of the Year Award, the NBA Walter Kennedy Award, and the University of Detroit Mercy President's Cabinet Medallion Award in 1992.

Thomas married Lynn Kendall, a teacher, in 1985. They have two children, Joshua Isiah and Lauren, and reside in Indianapolis, Indiana.

BIBLIOGRAPHY
Barbara Bigelow, ed., *Contemporary Black Biography*, vol. 7 (Detroit, MI, 1994), pp. 257–261; Peter C. Bjarkman, *The Encyclopedia of Pro Basketball Team Histories* (New York, 1994); Paul C. Challen, *The Book of Isiah: The Rise of a Basketball Legend* (Toronto, Canada, 1996); "Isiah Thomas," *Current Biography Yearbook 1989*

(New York, 1989), pp. 571–576; Jan Hubbard, ed., *The Official NBA Encyclopedia* (New York, 2000); David L. Porter, ed., *African-American Sports Greats* (Westport, CT, 1995); Isiah Thomas, *The Fundamentals: 8 Plays for Winning the Games of Business and Life* (New York, 2001); Isiah Thomas with Matt Dobek, *Bad Boys! An Inside Look at the Detroit Pistons 1988–89 Championship Season* (Indianapolis, IN, 1989); Isiah Thomas file, Naismith Memorial Basketball Hall of Fame Library and Archives, Springfield, MA.

Jack C. Braun

THURMAN THOMAS
(May 16, 1966–   )

Football

Thurman Thomas starred as a running back for Oklahoma State University and the Buffalo Bills (National Football League).

Thurman Lee Thomas was born on May 16, 1966 in Houston, Texas, the son of Gilbert Cockrells. He was heavily recruited by college football scouts during a stellar gridiron career at Willowridge High School in Missouri City, Texas. Thomas made All-State and was selected Offensive Player of the Year by the Houston Touchdown Club and a *Parade* and *USA Today* All-America.

Thomas accepted a football scholarship at Oklahoma State University (OSU). He enjoyed a sensational sophomore year, was hobbled by injuries his junior year, and enjoyed extraordinary success his senior year.

Thomas established himself among the nation's top running backs and as the most prolific rusher in OSU football history. He became the all-time leading rusher in OSU history with 4,847 yards. In the regular season finale against Iowa State University (1987), he carried the ball for 293 yards for the best single-game performance in OSU history. He was named consensus All–Big Eight Conference (BEC). Both wire services recognized him as BEC Offensive Player of the Year, with the Associated Press (AP) naming him a First Team All-America. During the 1987 regular season, Thomas ranked as the nation's third-leading rusher and second in the National Collegiate Athletic Association (NCAA) in all-purpose yards.

Thomas's OSU career included 21 100-yard performances and six 200-yard performances. When he rushed for 100 or more yards, the Cowboys compiled 19 wins and only 2 losses. When Thomas gained at least 200 yards, OSU prevailed all six times. He scored 43 touchdowns and compiled nearly 600 career receiving yards. As a Cowboy, Thomas even threw for four touchdown passes. He was voted BEC Player of the Week seven times, including his last three games. His other honors included being named Most Valuable Player of the 1984 Gator Bowl, placing tenth in the 1985 Heisman balloting, and being consensus All-BEC three straight years.

Thomas was selected by the Buffalo Bills in the second round as the fortieth pick overall of the 1988 NFL draft. As a rookie, he led the Bills in rushing with 881 yards and ranked as the third leading rookie rusher in the NFL. He enjoyed his first career 100-yard rushing game against the Green Bay Packers on October 30, gaining 116 yards.

In 1989 Thomas was selected to the Pro Bowl, the United Press International All-AFC squad, *Pro Football Weekly* and All-American Football Conference (AFC) team, AP Second Team All-Pro, and *Sports Illustrated* All-Pro Team. He rushed for 1,244 yards and six touchdowns and caught 60 passes for 669 yards and six scores.

In 1990 Thomas rushed for 1,297 yards and a career-high 11 touchdowns and caught 49 passes for 532 yards and two scores. With star quarterback Jim Kelly injured, he carried the Bills singlehandedly against the Miami Dolphins on December 23, amassing 154 yards rushing with one touchdown on 30 carries.

Thomas rushed for 1,407 yards and seven touchdowns in 1991, 1,487 yards with nine touchdowns in 1992, 1,315 yards and six touchdowns in 1993, and 1,093 yards and seven touchdowns in 1994. In 1991 he became only the eleventh player in NFL history to gain over 2,000 combined yards from scrimmage in a season. His sixth consecutive 1,000-yard season moved him past football icon O. J. Simpson for the most in Buffalo history.

In 1995 Thomas became the third player in NFL history to rush for over 1,000 yards in seven consecutive seasons, joining Eric Dickerson* and Barry Sanders.* The following year, he recorded another 1,000-plus-yard season (1,033 yards and eight touchdowns) to join Barry Sanders as the only NFL players to compile eight or more consecutive 1,000-yard rushing seasons. In 1997 Thomas did not reach the 1,000-yard target. In the season opener against the Minnesota Vikings in August, Thomas made an 80-yard catch to become just the third NFL player to combine 10,000 rushing yards with 400 receptions. The other players are Walter Payton and Marcus Allen.*

In March 2000, Thomas signed with the Miami Dolphins but suffered a knee injury after playing 9 games. He was signed by the Buffalo Bills on February 27, 2001 and retired that same day.

Thomas, a rushing genius, ranks ninth among NFL rushing leaders. During 13 NFL seasons, he gained 12,074 yards (4.2-yard average), scored 65 rushing touchdowns, and caught 472 passes for 4,458 yards (9.4-yard average) and 23 touchdowns. His two fumbles in the 1994 Super Bowl against the Dallas Cowboys hurt Buffalo, and the Bills' repeated inability to win the Lombardi Trophy in four consecutive tries has cast a shadow over Thomas's legacy. A November 4, 2002 *Sports Illustrated* essay by Paul Zimmerman does not include Thomas among the 12 greatest running backs of all time.

Stan W. Carlson, in *African-American Sports Greats* (1995), called Thomas an "excellent role model" with his contributions to health services, educational facilities, religious charities, and youth sports programs. Thomas has contributed to Oklahoma State Athletics and the Buffalo Bills Foundation. He has also raised funds for the American Heart Association, Arthritis Foundation, Camp Good Days, Cystic Fibrosis, Diabetes Foundation, Easter Seals, Sickle Cell Anemia, and Variety Club Telethon.

BIBLIOGRAPHY
David L. Porter, ed., *African-American Sports Greats* (Westport, CT, 1995); Sports Information Release, Oklahoma State University, Stillwater, OK, November 6, 2002; Thurman Thomas file, Pro Football Hall of Fame, Canton, OH; Paul Zimmerman, "Dynamic Dozen," *Sports Illustrated* 97 (November 4, 2002), p. 56.

Scott A.G.M. Crawford

FELIX TRINIDAD   Boxing
(January 10, 1973–   )

Felix "Tito" Trinidad Jr. combines sound boxing skills with surprising power, claiming the mythical title of best contemporary pound-for-pound fighter. Trainer Emmanuel Steward believes that Trinidad would "have given trouble to any of the great welterweights I've seen, including Tommy Hearns and Sugar Ray Leonard." Boxing writer William Nack puts Trinidad in similar company: "among great Puerto Rican fighters, he has already been named an heir to tradition built by the likes of Wilfredo Gomez and Wilfred Benitez." Eric Raskin, boxing analyst for *Ring* magazine, proffers the best compliment: "(Harry) Greb, (Sugar Ray) Robinson, and (Marvin) Hagler . . . Trinidad. The name doesn't sound out of place."

Felix Trinidad Jr. was born on January 10, 1973 in Cupey Alto, Puerto Rico to Felix Trinidad Sr. and Irma Dores. His imperious father, known as Don Felix, held the Puerto Rican Featherweight Championship in the mid-1970s and manages his son's career. His father labeled the quiet, serious Felix Trinidad Jr. "an old man as a kid." Trinidad began boxing at age 8 in a former tire repair shop refashioned as a gym. Before turning professional in 1990, won five amateur Puerto Rican championships and boasted a 51–6 record with 12 knockouts. Due to his father's anger when he failed to make the 1988 Puerto Rican Olympic boxing team, Trinidad turned professional in 1990, knocking out 9 of his first 10 opponents. The 5-foot 10-inch, 159-pound Trinidad changed from boxer to puncher. "I started planting myself, with my feet more firmly on the ground, and the punches got stronger."

Trinidad showed heart against tough Jake Rodriguez in December 1991. Though injuring both hands midway through the bout, Trinidad kept up the pressure and won a 10-round decision. He tended to get knocked down early, get up, and finish his opponent. Trinidad first showed this pattern against well-regarded Alberto Cortes in October 1992, when he was knocked down in the second round. Trinidad regained his feet and knocked Cortes senseless, prompting the referee to stop the fight in the third round.

Trinidad won the International Boxing Federation (IBF) welterweight title in June 1993, knocking out two-time world champion Maurice Blocker. In subsequent title defenses, he outdueled luminaries Hector Camacho, Oba Carr, Freddie Pendleton, Pernell Whitaker, and Oscar De La Hoya.* Trinidad's 12-round decision over Camacho in January 1994 established his reputation,

Felix Trinidad ©Al Bellow/Getty Images

although Camacho had passed his prime. His most convincing victory may
have been his dismantling of Yory Boy Campos in four rounds in September
1994.

Trinidad's most recent fights have combined the bizarre with the rigorous.
He fought De La Hoya in September 1999 when De La Hoya jabbed and
back-pedaled. The judges ceded the 12-round decision and World Boxing
Council (WBC) welterweight title to the persistent Puerto Rican. In March
2000, Trinidad added the World Boxing Association (WBA) junior middleweight title to his collection with a brutal mugging of David Reid, although
he was dumped in the third round. December 2000 saw Trinidad survive a
fourth-round knockdown to knock out Fernando "El Feroz" Vargas in the
twelfth round, sending Vargas to a Las Vegas, Nevada, hospital for observa-
tion. After dethroning William Joppy for the WBA middleweight crown in
May 2001, Trinidad suffered his first loss that September to 36-year-old Ber-

nard "The Executioner" Hopkins at Madison Square Garden in New York. The cagey Hopkins eluded Trinidad's fearsome left hook while peppering him with left jabs and overhand rights to win the undisputed Middleweight Championship. When a tired Trinidad was knocked down in the twelfth round, Don Felix jumped into the ring to spare his son further punishment.

Trinidad retired with a 40–1 record and 33 knockouts. He lives in Cupey Alto, Puerto Rico, with his wife, Sharon, and two daughters, Ashley and Leysha. His hobbies include collecting classic cars, raising horses, playing basketball, and cockfighting (legal in Puerto Rico). He serves on the boards of the Children AIDS Foundation.

BIBLIOGRAPHY:

"Felix Trinidad," *Current Biography Yearbook, 2000* (New York, 2000), pp. 564–567; Richard Hoffer, "The Upper Hand," *Sports Illustrated* 92 (March 13, 2000), pp. 52ff; Richard Hoffer "Worth the Wait," *Sports Illustrated* 95 (October 8, 2001), pp. 54ff; William Nack, "Star Power," *Sports Illustrated* 84 (February 19, 1996), p. 30; Eric Raskin, "Felix Trinidad Prepares to Conquer Another Division," *The Ring* 80 (April 2001), pp. 34–38; "Spurred to Greatness," *Sports Illustrated* 94 (May 14, 2001), pp. 54ff.

John H. Ziegler

MIKE TYSON   Boxing
(June 30, 1966–   )

Mike Tyson was the youngest boxer to hold a World Championship belt. At his most destructive, he was both awesome and terrifying and seemed headed toward establishing a legacy of invincibility.

Michael Gerald Tyson, the youngest child of John Kilpatrick Tyson and Lorna Tyson, was born on June 30, 1966 in Brooklyn, New York. He grew up in the Bedford Stuyvesant area of Brooklyn, a neighborhood where it was literally the survival of the fittest and gang acceptance or exclusion meant safety or danger. "I was very shy, almost effeminately shy," remembered Tyson. "I don't know what possessed me to fight, but when I started hitting, I was loving it. I let so much frustration out."

Bullying tempered Tyson's psyche and transformed him into a successful pugilist, with steely resolve and animal anger. At age 13, he was placed in an upstate New York reform institution, the Tryon School for Boys. Legendary trainer Cus D'Amato, one of America's grand old men of boxing, took an interest in Tyson. D'Amato became much more than Tyson's coach, assuming the unofficial role of foster father and mentoring and counseling him with a rare balance of iron discipline and paternal affection.

Unlike the celebrated Muhammad Ali, Tyson was neither an Olympian nor a gold medalist. He won the national Golden Gloves Heavyweight Championship in 1984 and became the World Boxing Council (WBC) heavyweight champion at age 20 on November 22, 1986. He later gained both the World

Boxing Association (WBA) and International Boxing Federation (IBF) titles. In June 1988, he knocked down Michael Spinks in less than two minutes and became undisputed heavyweight champion of the world.

Scandal, controversy, and public debacles, however, have plagued Tyson ever since. The deaths of D'Amato and co-manager Jim Jacobs deprived Tyson of wise and sober advisors. Without them, he seemingly became an ill-fated raft tossed to and fro on the cruel sea of professional boxing. His divorce from actress Robin Givens generated much negative publicity. Her bleak accounts of life with Tyson, in an ABC television interview, left Tyson exposed as a fearsome fighter possessed of a suspect, unstable temperament.

In February 1990, James "Buster" Douglas sprang a massive surprise with a tenth-round knockout of Tyson. When Tyson seemed heading back to redemption, social acceptance, and a chance to regain the world crown in 1992, an Indianapolis, Indiana, jury found him guilty of raping African American beauty queen contestant, Desiree Washington. Following his release from prison in March 1995, Tyson joined the Don King "road show." A mega-dollar deal was set up with the MGM Grand Gorden Arena in Las Vegas, Nevada, and Showtime to make King and Tyson fabulously rich. King's promotion of Tyson's comeback fight in August 1995 with Evander Holyfield* generated over $90 million worldwide and set a U.S. pay-per-view record. In a slugfest, a superbly conditioned Holyfield triumphed over Tyson. Promoter King's gate revenues topped $14 million.

The July 1997 rematch took place with 16,331 in attendance at the same site. A colossal American and world pay-per view audience expected a "fight of the century." What actually took place was incredibly bizarre. Tyson, incensed and frustrated with Holyfield's tactics, bit the champion twice! He was disqualified by referee Mills Lane. The Nevada State Athletic Commission fined him $3 million and suspended him for one year. British boxing writer Hugh McIlvanney labeled Tyson a "marketable psychotic" who "flounders in the dark turbulence of his mind." McIlvanney saw this event as "the most grotesque episode" in the history of boxing.

Tyson remains a confrontational character whose behaviors polarize society. Jeffrey Sammons, African American sports historian, called the black male support for Tyson over the rape of Washington predictable, "lamentable," "shocking and deplorable." John Sugden, in *Boxing and Society*, summarized Tyson "had destroyed everything put before him in the ring. Unfortunately, he also destroyed everything he touched outside boxing." Tyson's fragile personality shaped a fragmented existence, in which he seemed increasingly unstable and isolated.

Since 1997, Tyson has engaged in several fights. Until American underdog Hasim Rahman defeated world heavyweight champion Lennox Lewis in April 2001, it seemed that Lewis and Tyson would battle for the heavyweight title in a financial bonanza. The fight was delayed until June 2002.

In April 2001, Tyson was featured on a CBS television *48 Hours* special. He seemed to be working hard at reinventing his image, discussing a "rocky road" and his image as "an out of control bad guy." He lamented that his four children were being taunted at their schools because they had a father who "seemingly is a monster." The Las Vegas, Nevada, resident began to meditate and to take medication to control his mood swings.

Tyson knocked out Brian Nielson in seven rounds at Copenhagen, Denmark, in October 2001 but was knocked out by Lennox Lewis in the eighth round in June 2002 at Memphis, Tennessee. In February 2003, he knocked out Clifford Etienne in the second round at Memphis. His lifetime record is still a remarkable 50-41-1 with 44 knockouts.

In his prime, Tyson was a frightening pugilist. Joyce Carol Oates described a younger Tyson as a man with an "unsettling air," "unwavering stare," and "impassive death's head face." "The single-mindedness of his ring style suggests that his grievance has the force of a natural catastrophe. That old trope, 'the wrath of God', comes to mind."

Tyson and his second wife, Monica Turner, were divorced in January 2003. They had two children, Rayna and Amir. Tyson filed for bankruptcy August 1, 2003 despite earning an estimated $300 million in his career.

BIBLIOGRAPHY
Jeffrey T. Sammons, "Rebel with a Cause," in Elliot J. Gorn, ed., *Muhammad Ali: The People's Champ* (Urbana, IL, 1995); Hugh McIlvanney, *McIlvanney on Boxing* (Edinburgh, Scotland, 1997); David L. Porter, ed., *African-American Sports Greats* (Westport, CT, 1995); Joyce Carol Oates, *On Boxing* (Hopewell, NJ, 1994); John Sugden, *Boxing and Society* (Manchester, England, 1996).

Scott A.G.M. Crawford

V

FERNANDO VALENZUELA
(November 1, 1960–)

Baseball

Fernando Valenzuela created a public relations sensation as a major league baseball pitcher in the 1980s.

Fernando Anguamea Valenzuela was born on November 1, 1960 in Navajoa, Mexico, the youngest of nine children of Avelino Valenzuela and Hemeregilda (Anguamea) Valenzuela. His parents farmed in Etchohuaquila, Mexico. As a teenager, Valenzuela played baseball with his seven brothers on an organized local team. He began his professional career in the Mexican League (ML) and was spotted by Los Angeles Dodgers (National League) scout Mike Brito in 1978.

After Valenzuela won 10 of 22 decisions and compiled a 2.49 earned run average (ERA) in 26 starts for Yucatán, Mexico (ML), in 1978, the Los Angeles Dodgers (NL) purchased Valenzuela's contract in July 1979. His 13 victories, four shutouts, and 162 strikeouts with San Antonio, Texas (Texas League) earned him a September 1980 promotion to the Los Angeles Dodgers. Valenzuela won two, saved one, and allowed no earned runs in 10 relief appearances. The pudgy, 5-foot 10-inch, 202-pound southpaw joined a Dodger rotation that boasted Jerry Reuss, Burt Hooton, and Bob Welsh in the strike-shortened 1981 season. Valenzuela won his first eight decisions, compiled a 13–7 record, posted a 2.48 ERA, and led the NL with 25 starts, 11 complete games, 192 innings, 180 strikeouts, and eight shutouts. His 1981 accolades included garnering NL Rookie of the Year honors, the NL Cy Young Award, and *The Sporting News* Silver Slugger, NL Pitcher of the Year, and NL Rookie Pitcher of the Year awards.

Valenzuela anchored the Dodger rotation throughout the 1980s with a fastball, curve, and slider. His primary pitch, however, was a screwball, on which he would change speeds from the low 60s to the low 80s miles per hour. He rarely threw his screwball in the strike zone but induced hitters to swing at it. He fielded his position extremely well, getting off the mound very quickly. Valenzuela possessed a fine pickoff move and fired the ball to any base. He hit well for a pitcher, showing occasional home run power, and ran the bases aggressively.

With Los Angeles from 1981 to 1990, Valenzuela won 10 games or more every year except 1988 when he was sidelined two months with shoulder problems. He won 19 games, completed 18 contests, and registered a 2.87 ERA in 1982. He played left field and right field in a 21-inning, 2–1 victory over the Chicago Cubs on August 17–18, 1982, when manager Tommy Lasorda used all 25 players. Valenzuela began the 1985 season by pitching 33 consecutive innings without allowing an earned run but split four decisions due to poor defense and lack of offense. He led the NL with a career-best 21 victories and 20 complete games in 1986 and pitched more than 250 innings every year from 1982 to 1987. He hurled a 6–0 no-hitter against the St. Louis Cardinals on June 29, 1990, a feat he predicted to teammates before the game. Valenzuela appeared in five All-Star games, hurling 7.2 scoreless innings. In the 1986 contest, he struck out Don Mattingly, Cal Ripken Jr., Jesse Barfield, Lou Whitaker, and Teddy Higuera in succession.

The Dodgers released Valenzuela in March 1991. He pitched ineffectively for the California Angels (American League) in 1991 before returning to the ML for the 1992 season. The Baltimore Orioles (AL) signed him in February 1993. He won 8 and lost 10 decisions before rejoining Jalisco (ML) for the 1994 campaign. Valenzuela returned to the major leagues for eight games with the Philadelphia Phillies (NL) in June 1994. After signing with the San Diego Padres (NL) in April 1995 and now relying on a curve and slider, he resurrected his career with 8 victories in 11 decisions that year and 13 wins against 8 losses in 1996. His fine major league career ended the next season when he lost 12 of 14 decisions for the Padres and St. Louis Cardinals (NL). He pitched for the Hermosillo Orange Growers (Mexican Pacific Coast League) from 1998 to 2001 and broadcasts Los Angeles Dodgers games in Spanish for a radio station.

Valenzuela played on the World Championship Los Angeles Dodgers in 1981 and 1988. In his lone 1981 World Series appearance, he defeated the New York Yankees, 5–4, in a complete game performance. He missed the 1988 World Series against the Oakland Athletics with a shoulder injury. In 17 major league seasons, he won 173 and lost 153 decisions, hurled 31 shutouts, struck out 2,074 batters in 2,930 innings, and recorded a 3.54 ERA in 453 games.

Valenzuela was always a fan favorite, whose portly appearance belied an athlete in good physical condition. His round face, wide, engaging smile, exuberant personality, and pitching feats inspired a decade of "Fernandomania" in Los Angeles and around the NL.

Valenzuela married Linda (Burgos) Valenzuela on December 28, 1981. They have four children, Ricardo, Fernando Jr., Linda, and Maria, and reside in Los Angeles during the summer months. Fernando Jr. played first base for the University of Nevada at Las Vegas and was drafted in June 2003 by the San Diego Padres organization.

BIBLIOGRAPHY

Paul Click, "20 Years Ago Fernando Valenzuela Was King of the Hill," *Baseball Digest* 60 (July 2001), pp. 62–65; John Dewan, ed., *The Scouting Report: 1997* (Skokie, IL, 1997); David L. Porter, ed. *Biographical Dictionary of American Sports: Baseball—Q–Z*, revised and expanded edition (Westport, CT, 2000); John Thorn and John Holway, *The Pitcher* (London, United Kingdom, 1987).

Frank J. Olmsted

MO VAUGHN   Baseball
(December 15, 1967–)

Mo Vaughn starred as a first baseman with the Boston Red Sox (American League).

Maurice Samuel Vaughn, a 6-foot 1-inch, 230-pound left-handed slugger, was born on December 15, 1967 in Norwalk, Connecticut. He was adopted at birth by educators. His father, Leroy Vaughn, served as a school principal, while his mother, Shirley Vaughn, taught grammar school. Vaughn captained three sports teams by his junior year at Trinity-Pawling High School in Pawling, New York, graduating in 1986. At Seton Hall University, he hit .417 with 57 home runs (a school record) and 218 runs batted in (RBI) over three seasons. He was named the 1980s Player of the Decade in the Big East Conference.

The Boston Red Sox selected Vaughn in the first round of the 1989 amateur draft. Vaughn debuted in the major leagues in 1991 and batted .260 with four home runs and 32 RBIs in 219 at-bats. He began 1992 as Boston's first baseman but spent 39 games with Pawtucket, Rhode Island (International League). After rejoining the Red Sox, he finished 1992 with a .234 batting average, 13 home runs, and 57 RBIs.

Vaughn's true ability emerged in 1993, as he batted .297 with 29 home runs and 101 RBIs. He raised his batting average to .310 during the strike-shortened 1994 season, hitting 26 home runs with 82 RBIs over 111 games. He made the 1995 AL All-Star team, clouting 39 home runs with an AL-leading 126 RBIs to earn the Most Valuable Player Award and help Boston capture the AL East title.

Vaughn also became a clubhouse leader, quickly earning his teammates' respect. Infielder Tim Naehring noted: "It's more than the RBIs, it's more than the homers, it's more than anything you can see on the field. . . . It's his presence. He brings a confidence and an attitude to this team that is hard to explain." Red Sox fans also took Vaughn to their hearts, a notable achievement for an African American player in Boston.

In 1996 Vaughn batted .326 with 44 home runs and 143 RBIs, becoming the fourteenth major leaguer with 40 home runs and 200 hits in the same season. He also made the AL All-Star team and won the Bart Giamatti Award for Community Service. His production suffered slightly in 1997 when a knee injury sidelined him for 20 games. He hit .315 with 35 home runs and 96 RBIs.

Vaughn was eligible for free agency after the 1998 season but wanted to stay in Boston. He rejected a five-year, $62.5 million contract offer, believing it was well below his market value. His relationship deteriorated with general manager Dan Duquette, who made several unpopular personnel decisions after coming to Boston in 1994.

Off-the-field events created more problems for Vaughn. In January 1998, he crashed his truck while driving home from a strip club late one night and was charged with drunk driving. He was found "not guilty," but stories surfaced about his bachelor lifestyle, active nightlife, fondness for strip clubs, and the events surrounding a 1995 brawl with a gang member in a Boston nightclub. Boston management publicly questioned Vaughn's physical conditioning, including his expanded waistline, and asked him to submit to an evaluation for alcoholism. He refused Boston's request.

Vaughn finished 1998 with a .337 batting average, 40 homers, and 115 RBIs. Vaughn and the Boston front office spent most of the summer sniping at each other in the press. Vaughn claimed that Boston had hired a private detective to follow him. He rejected a four-year, $37 million offer at the All-Star break, and became a free agent at the end of that season.

In November 1998, Vaughn signed a six-year, $80 million contract with the Anaheim Angels (AL). The Angels expected him to provide veteran leadership on a team made up mostly of young players. In the first inning of the first game in 1999, however, Vaughn injured an ankle tumbling down the dugout steps while chasing a foul ball. He spent two weeks on the disabled list and finished 1999 with 33 home runs and 108 RBIs. His batting average dipped to .281, the first time it had dropped below .300 since 1993. In 2000, he knocked in 117 runs, hit 36 homers, and saw his batting average fall further to .272.

Vaughn later discovered he had played the last month of the season with a torn bicep muscle. Corrective surgery sidelined him for the entire 2001 season. The Angels traded Vaughn to the New York Mets (National League) in December 2001 for Kevin Appier. In 2002, Vaughn batted .259 with 26 home runs and 72 RBIs. An arthritic right knee limited Vaughn to just 79 at-bats and a .190 batting average in 2003. Through 2003, he has hit .293 with 328 home runs and 1,064 RBIs. His Mo Vaughn Youth Development Center provides after-school tutoring and life-skills education to high school students in the Dorchester section of Boston.

BIBLIOGRAPHY
Michael Arace, "Family Feud," *The Sporting News*, August 3, 1998, p. 24; Gerry Callahan, "Sox Appeal," *Sports Illustrated* 83 (October 2, 1995), p. 42; Matt Christopher, *At the Plate with . . . Mo Vaughn* (Boston, MA, 1997); Tim Crothers, "Vaughn's Trying Times," *Sports Illustrated* 88 (March 16, 1998), p. 126; Rick Folstad, "Mo Vaughn Sets Sights on Career Consistency," *Baseball Digest* 57 (September 1998), p. 56; Tim Kurkjian, "Seeing Is Believing," *Sports Illustrated* 84 (June 24, 1996), p. 64; Walter Leavy, "Baseball's Two of a Kind," *Ebony* 51 (July 1996), p. 100; Michael Shalin, *Mo Vaughn: Angel on a Mission* (Champaign, IL, 1999); Rick Sorci, "Baseball Profile: Mo Vaughn," *Baseball Digest* 56 (January 1997), p. 43; Mo Vaughn, *Follow Your Dreams* (Dallas, TX, 1996).

Terry W. Sloope

JAVIER VAZQUEZ
(July 25, 1976–)

Baseball

Although the future of major league baseball in Montreal, Canada, is problematic, Montreal Expos (National League) pitcher Javier Vazquez seems to have a tremendous career ahead of him.

Javier Carlos Vazquez was born on July 25, 1976 in Ponce, Puerto Rico, and graduated in 1994 from Colegio de Ponce High School where he starred in both basketball and baseball. The Montreal Expos selected Vazquez in the fifth round of the 1994 free-agent draft. Desperate for pitching help, Montreal rushed Vazquez to the major leagues. The Puerto Rican native joined the Expos' starting rotation at age 21 in 1998 but was hit hard by NL batters. He won 5 games against 15 losses, allowed 31 home runs, and posted a 6.06 earned run average (ERA).

Vazquez retained his confidence, however, and kept his perspective: "I never lost focus on what I was trying to accomplish. I knew everything would work out if I kept working hard." The hard work gradually paid off.

Although assigned briefly to Class AAA Ottawa, Canada in 1999, Vazquez returned to the major leagues permanently around mid-July. David Cone of the New York Yankees pitched a perfect game against the Montreal Expos in Vazquez's first start after returning from the minor leagues. Despite his initial hard luck, Vazquez enjoyed a strong 1999 campaign with nine victories against eight defeats, 113 strikeouts, and a 5.00 ERA. The hard-throwing right-hander also batted .286 in 1999.

Vazquez matured further during 2000. Although initially Montreal's number three starter, he became the staff ace by season's end. He completed the 2000 campaign with 11 wins against nine losses on a team that finished only 67–95 overall. Besides registering a then career-high in victories, Vazquez set then personal bests in innings pitched (217), strikeouts (196), and ERA (4.05). He attributed his success to growing confidence, experience, and good health. He pitched late into the game in most of his starts and demonstrated good control of his fastball, slider, curve, change-up, and cutter.

By 2001, Vazquez ranked among the best young NL pitchers. He earned the NL's Pitcher of the Month Award for August, recording five wins against one loss with a 0.55 ERA. He seemed destined for a 20-win season with the lowly Expos when he was hit in the forehead by a pitch thrown by Ryan Dempster of the Florida Marlins on September 17. Vazquez suffered multiple hairline fractures above his right eye and in his right sinus cavity and did not pitch for the remainder of the season. His injury received little media attention because the game was played on the night when baseball resumed action after the terrorist attacks of September 11. The baseball world was instead focused on New York's response to a national tragedy.

Vazquez refused to blame Dempster. The strongly religious Vazquez commented, "God is with me, that's the way I feel. Even though I'm not finishing my season, he may have a purpose for me. I leave everything in his hands." His abbreviated season concluded with 16 victories against 11 defeats, 208 strikeouts, and a 3.42 ERA.

In 2002 Vazquez struggled with only 10 victories in 23 decisions and a 3.91 ERA, striking out 179 batters in 230.1 innings. Through the 2003 season, he appeared in 192 games with 64 wins against 68 defeats, 1,076 strikeouts, and a 4.16 ERA. He compiled a 13–12 record with a 3.24 ERA, ranking second in the NL in innings pitched (230.2) and third in strikeouts (241) in 2003.

At age 27 Vazquez appears to be on the edge of baseball stardom, although whether he will continue to wear the uniform of the Montreal Expos remains uncertain. Contraction or relocation of the Montreal franchise remains a possibility, but the poised young Vazquez seems ready to cash in on either eventuality. Mature beyond his years, he continues to work hard and to put his faith in God and family.

Vazquez married Kamille Rodriguez on November 14, 1998 and prefers to spend his free time "chilling out" with his wife. With his exceptional talents, the Vazquez family should live comfortably for many years to come.

BIBLIOGRAPHY
Mark Bowman, "It's Coming Together for Vazquez," *Montreal Expos News*, July 30, 2001, http://mlb.mlb.com/NASApp/mlb/mon/news/mon_news_story.jsp?article_id—on_200_108 (May 1, 2002); *The Sporting News Baseball Register*, 2003; "Javier Vazquez: An Exclusive Interview," *Montreal Expos News*, January 26, 2001, http://mlb.mlb.com / NASApp.mlb/mon/news/mon_news_story.jsp?article_id—on_200_101 (May 1, 2002); Pierre Moussette, "Vazquez Sidelined for the Remainder of the Season," *Montreal Expos News*, September 18, 2001, http://mlb.mlb.com/NASApp/mlb/mon/news/mon_news_story.jsp?article_id—on_2001_09 (May 1, 2002); Rick Reilly, "Underexposed," *Sports Illustrated* 95 (October 8, 2001), p. 112; J.S. Trzcienski, "Vazquez Shines in Comeback Game," *Montreal Expos News*, March 3, 2002, http://mlb.mlb.com/NASApp/mlb/mon/news/mon_news_story.jsp?article_id—on_200_203 (May 1, 2002).

Ron Briley

MICHAEL VICK   Football
(June 28, 1980–)

Michael Vick starred at quarterback for Virginia Tech University (Big East Conference) and was selected by the Atlanta Falcons (National Football League) in the 2001 NFL draft, becoming the first African American quarterback ever chosen first overall. He has emerged as the leading NFL rushing quarterback.

Michael Dwayne Vick was born on June 28, 1980 in Newport News, Virginia, the son of Michael Boddie, a shipyard painter, and Brenda (Vick) Boddie and second cousin of New Orleans Saints (NFL) quarterback Aaron

Brooks. Vick grew up in adverse circumstances in Newport News and graduated in 1998 from Warrick High School, where he starred in football. He inherited speed from his father, a premier scholastic sprinter in Virginia.

Warrick football coach Tommy Reamon groomed Vick to be quarterback, taking him to summer football camps. He sold Vick on weight training and academics and inspired him to practice speaking before a mirror to develop his interviewing skills. Reamon also insisted that schools interested in Vick allow him to redshirt during his first school year so he could get acclimated to college life. Vick considered Reamon "a father figure" and recalled that "he took me under his wings and molded me."

Virginia Tech head football coach Frank Beamer recruited the 6-foot, 214-pound Vick and redshirted him in 1998. Vick made several All-America First Teams and was named *The Sporting News* College Freshman of the Year in 1999, when he led the Hokies to an 11–0 regular season record and the BEC title with a 7–0 record. Virginia Tech outscored opponents, 455–116, and finished second nationally. The Hokies led the nation in scoring offense, scoring defense, and total offense, averaging 509 yards. Virginia Tech overwhelmed Rutgers University, 58–20, Syracuse University, 62–0, Temple University, 62–6, and the University of Miami, 43–10.

Vick led the nation in passing efficiency, completing 90 of 152 passes (59.2 percent) for 1,840 yards and 12 touchdowns and throwing just five interceptions. He rushed for 585 yards (5.4-yard average) and eight touchdowns, finishing third in the Heisman Trophy balloting. Florida State University defeated Virginia Tech, 46–29, in the Sugar Bowl National Championship game. Vick completed 15 of 29 passes for 225 yards and one touchdown and led the Hokies in rushing with 97 yards, including a 43-yard scamper and one touchdown.

As a sophomore, Vick paced Virginia Tech to a 10–1 regular season record and a sixth-place national ranking. The Hokies outscored opponents, 484–269, and finished second to Miami in the BEC with a 6–1 record. Vick completed 87 of 161 passes (54 percent average) for eight touchdowns and threw just six interceptions. He also rushed 617 yards (5.9-yard average) for eight touchdowns, helping Virginia Tech defeat Clemson University, 41–20, in the Gator Bowl.

At Virginia Tech, Vick completed 177 of 313 passes (56.5 percent) for 3,074 yards and 20 touchdowns and threw just 11 interceptions. He rushed 212 times for 1,202 yards (5.7-yard average) and 16 touchdowns.

The Atlanta Falcons selected Vick the first overall in the 2001 NFL draft. He possessed a left arm that could launch a football 70 yards, legs that could speed him through a 40-yard dash in 4.3 seconds, fluid moves that could leave defenders grasping and gasping, and uncanny instincts and mental toughness. Vick, drafted two months shy of his twenty-first birthday, replied, "It freaks me out, because it's like a 1-in-2 million shot to be the first pick in the draft."

Vick spent his rookie year as a backup for quarterback Don Chandler, learning to adjust to NFL offenses. Vick had followed instructions in college that often dictated that he run rather than search for secondary receivers. Virginia Tech's unsophisticated passing game rarely had used spread formations and included limited receiving options. He started two games as a rookie, completing 50 of 113 passes (44.2 percent) for 785 yards and two touchdowns and rushing 31 times for 289 yards (9.3-yard average) and one touchdown. He threw for 114 yards against the Miami Dolphins on December 20, 2001 and completed 12 passes against the St. Louis Rams on January 6, 2002.

Vick enjoyed a superb 2002 season, completing 231 of 421 passes (54.9 percent) for 2,936 yards and 16 touchdowns and throwing only eight interceptions. Vick led NFL quarterbacks in rushing with 113 carries for 777 yards (6.9-yard average) and eight touchdowns, compiling nearly as much rushing yardage as teammate Warrick Dunn in half as many carries. He guided the Falcons to second place in the National Conference South with a 9–5–1 regular season record, being named to the Pro Bowl team for the first time. From October 13 through December 2, Atlanta did not lose a game and averaged nearly 30 points.

The dangerous strong-armed playmaker provided the bulk of the Falcons' offense. With his double-threat potential, Vick changed the way quarterbacks and defenses played. Atlanta head coach Dan Reeves, observed, "I think every week you see something . . . that you go 'wow.' " Minnesota Vikings linebacker Henry Crockett added, "He's changed the game. There are going to be no more pocket passers anymore."

On December 2, 2002, Vick shattered the NFL record for the greatest rushing performance by an NFL quarterback, gaining a career-high and record-setting 173 yards against the Minnesota Vikings at the Metrodome. His 46-yard touchdown scamper in overtime gave the Falcons a 30–24 victory. Reeves boasted, "I've never seen anyone turn on the jets like that." Vick accounted for 346 of Atlanta's 379 yards, matching his rushing total with 173 yards and one touchdown in the air. He amassed the yardage in just 10 carries, shattering Bobby Douglass's quarterback record of 127 yards in 1972 and averaging 17.3 yards a carry to eclipse Marion Motley's (Cleveland Browns) 17.09 yards in 1950.

Vick led Atlanta to a 9–6–1 record and NFC Wild Card berth in 2002 and engineered a 27–7 victory over Green Bay, the first time the Packers ever lost a home playoff game. He connected on 22 of 38 aerials for 274 yards, was intercepted twice, and rushed six times for 30 yards, but the Philadelphia Eagles defeated the Falcons, 20–6, in the next round. He was selected to the NFC squad in the Pro Bowl for the first time following the 2002 season. Through 2002, Vick completed 281 of 534 passes (52.6 percent) for 3,721 yards and 18 touchdowns and rushed 144 times for 1,066 yards (7.4-yard average) and nine touchdowns. He won an ESPY award as NFL Player of the Year in 2002.

Vick suffered a broken right fibula in an NFL exhibition game against Baltimore in August 2003 and missed several regular season games. Vick, nicknamed "Ookie," combines a commendable sense of purpose and alluring verve and remains a warm, engaging personality wrapped with humility. "You have to be strong mentally to be successful," he asserts. For his part, coach Reeves explained, "he's very open-minded about things. He doesn't have a his-way or-no-way type of attitude. He's always looking to get better."

BIBLIOGRAPHY
Atlanta Falcons Media Guide, 2003; Jarrett Bell, "Vick Scrambles into NFL," *USA Today*, April 20, 2001, pp. 1C–2C; Dave Campbell, "Vick's Run Lifts Falcons 30–24 in OT," *USA Today*, December 2, 2002, p. 9C; Mike Lopresti, "Electrifying Vick Energizes Falcons," *Des Moines Register*, December 3, 2002, p. 2C; Joe Saraceno, "Vick a Runaway Top Value in NFL," *USA Today*, December 6, 2002, p. 3C; *The Sporting News Pro Football Register*, 2003; *Virginia Tech Football Media Guide*, 2000.

David L. Porter

JOSE VIDRO   Baseball
(August 27, 1974–)

Jose Vidro has batted over .300 for five consecutive seasons as a second baseman for the Montreal Expos (National League).

Jose Angel Cetty Vidro Jr. was born on August 27, 1974 in Mayaguez, Puerto Rico, the son of Jose Vidro Sr., a foreman in a Frito-Lay factory, and Daysi Vidro, an office worker for Sunkist Foods. Vidro graduated from Blanco Morales High School in Sabana Grande, Puerto Rico, in 1992 and married his hometown sweetheart, Annette, in January 1993. They have one son, Jose III.

Vidro grew up in Sabana Grande and began playing baseball daily as a 5-year-old. At age 17, the 5-foot 11-inch, 195-pound switch-hitter, who throws right-handed, was selected by the Montreal Expos (NL) in the sixth round of the June 1992 free-agent draft. Expos scout Fred Ferreira signed Vidro for a $30,000 bonus. For the next five years, Vidro improved his skills as a second baseman, third baseman, and shortstop in the Expos' minor league system. His first assignment in 1992 came with the Gulf Coast Expos (Gulf Coast League), where he batted .330 in 54 games.

Vidro spent 1993 with Burlington, Iowa (Midwest League) and 1994 with West Palm Beach, Florida (Florida State League). He split the 1995 season between West Palm Beach and Harrisburg, Pennsylvania (Eastern League). Vidro spent the 1996 season with Harrisburg and began 1997 with Ottawa, Ontario (International League). He joined the Montreal Expos in June, batting .249 in 67 games.

Vidro appeared in 83 games with the Expos and in 63 contests with Ottawa in 1998, batting .220 and .289, respectively. His first full season starting as second baseman with Montreal came in 1999. He worked hard to improve his defensive skills, and he ranks among the premier NL second basemen defensively. He finished 1999 second in the NL with 45 doubles, the third highest in Expo history, and second on the team with 38 multi-hit games. He connected for his first grand slam home run on August 6, 1999 against the San Diego Padres at Olympic Stadium. He fared among the NL's top 10 in several offensive categories batting .304 with 12 home runs, 45 doubles, and 59 runs batted in (RBI) in 140 games.

Vidro enjoyed a "career-season" in 2000. With his 200 base hits he trailed only Colorado's Todd Helton. Vidro finished seventh in the NL batting race with a .331 average. His 51 doubles ranked him third in the NL, while his 24 home runs, 97 RBIs, and 101 runs scored set club records for a second baseman. He was named as a reserve to the NL All-Star team for the first time in 2000 and finished third among NL second basemen with a .986 fielding percentage. Vidro tied the major league single-season record for fewest putouts by a second baseman (200) and most doubles by a switch-hitter (51). On July 3, 2000, he homered from each side of the plate against the Atlanta Braves.

Although missing 38 games in 2001 due to injuries, Vidro led the Expos with a .319 batting average, finishing second with 82 runs scored, and placed third with 155 base hits.

Vidro enjoyed another remarkable season in 2002 and was elected the starting NL second baseman in the All-Star game. He scored 103 runs, collected 190 base hits, including 43 doubles, 3 triples, and 19 home runs, and produced 96 RBIs in 152 games. His .315 batting average ranked sixth best in the NL, and second highest among the Expos. Vidro's 43 doubles tied him for third in the NL, and he shared the lead among his teammates. His 190 base hits and 103 runs scored placed him in third and eighth place, respectively, in the NL and second in both categories among all Expos teammates. He enjoyed another fine season in 2003, batting .310 with 36 doubles, 15 home runs, and 65 RBIs.

In seven seasons with Montreal between 1997 and 2003, Vidro has batted .306 with 473 runs scored, 940 hits, 233 doubles, nine triples, 87 home runs, 411 RBIs, 276 walks, and 342 strikeouts in 863 games.

BIBLIOGRAPHY:
Stephen Canvella, "Good Hit, Good Field," *Sports Illustrated* 23 (June 5, 2000), p. 88; "Jose Vidro," *Career Highlights*, www.mlb.com (2001); "Jose Vidro," *Career Stats*, www.mlb.com (2001); "Jose Vidro," *Career Stats*, www.tsn.ca.com (2002); "Jose Vidro," *Mystery Man*, www.puertoricoherald.com (June 24, 2002); "Jose Vidro," *Profile*, www.bigleaguers.com (2002); *The Sporting News Baseball Register*, 2003.

John L. Evers

OMAR VIZQUEL   Baseball
(April 24, 1967–)

Omar Vizquel, winner of nine consecutive Gold Gloves from 1993 to 2001, ranks among the most outstanding defensive players in major league baseball and has been a fixture at shortstop for the Cleveland Indians (American League) since 1993.

Omar Enrique Vizquel was born on April 24, 1967 in Caracas, Venezuela, the son of Omar Vizquel, an electrician and amateur baseball player. His family, middle class by Venezuelan standards, lived on the sixth floor of an apartment building, with he and his brother sharing a room. His childhood nickname was "earthquake" because he never stopped moving. Though mischievous, he rarely got into serious trouble with his parents or the authorities. Vizquel loved baseball and hung a poster of Venezuelan Cincinnati Reds shortstop Dave Concepcion over his bed. He and his childhood friends played baseball in the crowded streets of Caracas, using a broom handle for a bat and a wad of tape for a ball.

Vizquel played baseball in Francisco Espejo High School but also displayed many other typical adolescent interests. He grew his hair long and avidly followed the rock group Kiss. Though not a strong student, he graduated from Francisco Espejo in 1983 at just 16 years of age. In April 1984, he was signed as a nondrafted free agent by the Seattle Mariners (AL) and dispatched to Butte, Montana (Pioneer League).

Vizquel did not speak English and preferred to eat at the Denny's restaurant chain because their menu included pictures. Although two other Latinos played with Butte, Vizquel was homesick for his native land. But he was determined to have a baseball career and began to learn English by watching American television. Vizquel played in the Seattle minor league chain from 1984 through 1989. Although excelling defensively, he struggled with his hitting in the minor leagues.

Nevertheless, Vizquel's expertise with the glove earned his promotion to the major leagues. He became the shortstop for the Seattle Mariners in 1989, batting just .220 in 143 games. Injuries restricted him to 81 games in 1990, but he raised his batting average to .247. Vizquel enjoyed a breakout season offensively in 1992, hitting .294 and stealing 15 bases. The next year, the Venezuelan native earned his first Gold Glove award for defensive excellence. He enjoyed being in Seattle and married his wife, Nicole, in 1993.

In December 1993, while playing winter ball in Venezuela, Vizquel received a telephone call that he had been traded to the Cleveland Indians (AL) for shortstop Felix Fermin and designated hitter Reggie Jefferson. Initially, the trade devastated Vizquel and his wife. Besides being concerned about the climate and environment in Cleveland, Ohio, he knew the Indians had not finished higher than fourth for the previous quarter century.

But fortunes changed in Cleveland. Visquel and his wife found a home in suburban Westlake. Cleveland worked hard to attract tourism with fashionable restaurants and the Rock'n'Roll Hall of Fame and built a new home for the Indians at Jacobs Field.

The Indians also acquired Carlos Baerga, Sandy Alomar, and Roberto Alomar,* who reversed the club's fortunes. Cleveland dominated the Central Division, winning titles in 1995, 1996, 1997, 1998, 1999, and 2001. The Indians won AL pennants in 1995 and 1997 but lost the respective World Series to the Atlanta Braves and Florida Marlins.

For Vizquel losing the seventh game of the 1997 World Series to Florida marked the low point of his baseball career. Without his contributions, however, the Indians would not have emerged among the dominant AL teams. Besides garnering nine consecutive Gold Gloves between 1993 and 2001, Vizquel tied an AL record of 95 consecutive errorless games at shortstop from September 26, 1999 to July 1, 2000 and teamed with second baseman Roberto Alomar to form one of the most sensational double play combinations in baseball history. Vizquel developed into a fine hitter, batting a career-best .333 with 42 stolen bases in 1999. He continued his effective hitting, batting .287 in 2000 and .275 in 2002. His batting average slipped to .244 in 64 games in 2003.

Although Alomar was traded to the New York Mets following the 2001 season, the fan favorite remains a fixture at shortstop for the Indians. Vizquel has compiled a lifetime .273 batting average with 299 stolen bases, 59 home runs, and 656 RBIs in 1,990 major league games spanning 15 major league seasons.

The Vizquels have a son, Nico, and still reside in the Westlake section of Cleveland. Vizquel, active in many charitable enterprises, enjoys painting and is passionate about the arts. Nor has Vizquel forgotten about his native Venezuela, where he also has a home and plays winter ball. In December 1999, he worked with World Vision to raise over $500,000 in support of relief for flood victims in Venezuela.

BIBLIOGRAPHY:
Terry Pluto, "Omar Vizquel: Baseball's Best Defensive Shortstop," *Baseball Digest* 58 (February 1999), pp. 26–27; *The Sporting News Baseball Register*, 2003; Larry Stone, "Outstanding in His Field—With His Glove, Omar Vizquel Ranks Among the Best," *Baseball Digest* 60 (June 2001), pp. 62–65; Omar Vizquel with Bob Dyer, *My Life On and Off the Field* (Cleveland OH, 2002).

Ron Briley

HERSCHEL WALKER   Football, Track and Field, Bobsled
(March 3, 1962–   )

Herschel Walker ranks among the most versatile athletes in recent history, having participated in football, track and field, and the Olympic bobsled.

Herschel Junior Walker was born on March 3, 1962, in Wrightsville, Georgia, the fifth of seven children. His father, Willis Sr., farmed and worked in a clay products factory, while his mother, Christine (Taylor) Walker, worked in a clothing factory.

Walker's older brothers, Willis Jr. and Renneth, played football for the Johnson County High School team. Walker saw them as great role models and followed them into football. Willis Sr. considered running and racing important. "There was always an argument at night about who ran the fastest . . . there would be all this bragging, and the next day they would be all outside running." Walker attended the University of Georgia partly because his older sister, Veronica, accepted a track scholarship there.

At Johnson County High School, Walker showed extreme versatility as an athlete. Besides being a gifted sprinter, he also threw the shot and played basketball and football. In 1979 he won the Georgia State A Track and Field Championships in the 100-yard and 220-yard dashes and starred as a tailback. The Class A state football champions did not lose a single game. Walker's impressive performances included 3,167 rushing yards and 45 touchdowns. Not surprisingly, this prolific scorer attracted extraordinary attention from college recruiters. Over 100 institutions recruited the 6-foot 1-inch, 210-pound standout. Walker, much more than a muscular athlete gifted with amazing acceleration, was an excellent student, president of a scholarship honor society (Beta Club), and the valedictorian of his class.

Walker, a tough, brave, hard, menacing, and aggressive bulldog player, fearlessly used his missile-like body to gain yards as his team's premier ball carrier. Defense strategists devised whole new tackling strategies to stop the charging player, whose pace and power made him difficult to bring down.

At Georgia, Walker became only the seventh junior in National Collegiate Athletic Association (NCAA) history to win the Heisman Trophy. In three seasons as a "Bulldog," he amassed 5,259 rushing yards for the then third best in NCAA history. Many running backs simply get "worn down" and "run out of gas" if repeatedly given the ball and asked to bustle and bump and bruise their way for repeated yardage. Walker magically relished these challenges. In 1981 against the University of Florida, he carried the ball 47 times. As a "Bulldog," Walker averaged 159 rushing yards.

In February 1983, he signed with the New Jersey Generals (United States Football League). Many people believed that with Herschel aboard, the USFL would eventually rival the National Football League. Despite an optimistic start, the USFL struggled with many "growth" problems. The league survived only three seasons, but Walker continued his "Bulldog" road to success as its leading rusher in 1983 and 1985. In 1985, he gained 2,411 rushing yards for a then single-season professional football record.

In August 1986, following the collapse and disintegration of the USFL, he joined the Dallas Cowboys (NFL). Walker spent three years with the Cowboys and then in October 1989 was traded to the Minnesota Vikings (NFL). He played for the Vikings for two and one-half years and signed as a free agent with the Philadelphia Eagles (NFL) in June 1992. After being released by the Eagles in March 1995, he joined the New York Giants (NFL) a month later. He finished his NFL career in 1996 by completing a symbolic circle, returning home with the Dallas Cowboys. His NFL career record included 1,948 rushes for 8,205 yards and 61 touchdowns. He also made 498 pass receptions for 4,710 yards and 19 touchdowns.

In 1991 Walker took up a winter sport considerably different from football. He trained at Lake Placid, New York, with Winter Olympic hopefuls and made the bobsled team. His explosive strength and proven pickup speed made him ideally suited to a sport in which the start is all-important. Races are frequently won and lost by hundredths of a second. He was selected for the USA bobsled team at the 1992 Albertville, France, Winter Olympics.

Walker's professional football career record upon his 1997 retirement included rushing for 61 touchdowns and a 4.2-yard average; making 512 pass receptions for 4,859 yards, a 9.5-yard average, and 21 touchdowns; and making 215 kickoff returns for 5,084 yards, 23.6 yards per return, and two touchdowns.

Walker gave almost fanatical devotion to personal physical fitness. His high school coach initiated him into a spartan training regime of trunk curls (sit-ups), push-ups, and relay sprints. Despite his massive bulk and imposing physique, he built his body through physical "sculpting" and conditioning achieved outside of the weight room. He proudly spoke of exercise sessions in which he would complete hundreds of consecutive trunk curls, known as "crunches," and push-ups.

In 1983 Walker married Cynthia De Angelis, a former "Bulldog" track and field representative.

BIBLIOGRAPHY

George B. Kirsch et al., eds., *Encyclopedia of Ethnicity and Sports in the United States* (Westport, CT, 2000); David L. Porter ed., *African-American Sports Greats*

(Westport, CT, 1995); Chad Reese, Archives and Information Center, Pro Football Hall of Fame, Canton, OH, May 1, 2001; *The Sporting News Pro Football Register*, 1997.

Scott A.G.M. Crawford

CHRIS WEBBER Basketball
(March 1, 1973–)

Chris Webber starred as a forward-center in both college and professional basketball.

Mayce Edward Christopher Webber III, nicknamed "Chris" and "C-webb," was born on March 1, 1973 in Detroit, Michigan, the oldest of five children of Mayce Webber Jr., a General Motors assembly-line employee, and Doris Webber, a high school teacher. At his mother's insistence and over his father's objection, Webber attended Country Day High School, a predominantly white private school in exclusive Beverly Hills, Michigan. He excelled as a high school basketball player and in 1991 was selected as consensus High School Player of the Year.

A 6-foot 10-inch, 245-pound forward/center, Webber possessed strength, size, and quickness. He was rated the best player among the "Fab Five," the 1991 University of Michigan recruiting class that also included Juwan Howard, Jalen Rose, Jimmy King, and Ray Jackson. These five recruits started for the Wolverines as freshmen. In 1992 Webber led Michigan to a 25–9 won-lost record before losing, 71–51, to Duke University in the National Collegiate Athletic Association (NCAA) Division I Championship Game. The following year, the "Fab Five" established a school record of 31 regular season triumphs and advanced for the second straight year to the NCAA Tournament Championship Game. Webber was the leading rebounder and second leading scorer in the 1993 NCAA Tournament, but called an illegal timeout. At the close of the title game against the University of North Carolina, the Wolverines trailed by two points when Webber attempted to call a timeout. Michigan already had used their final timeout, was assessed a technical foul, and lost the game, 77–71.

A First Team All-America selection in 1993, Webber also was named a finalist for the Wooden and Naismith awards. He was selected to the NCAA All-Tournament team in 1992 and 1993 and led all NCAA Tournament players in rebounding and blocked shots both years. In two seasons at Michigan, he tallied 1,218 points and averaged 17.4 points in 70 games. Webber collected 702 rebounds and averaged 2.5 blocked shots. In 12 NCAA Tournament games, he averaged 17.8 points, 10.5 rebounds, and 2.7 blocked shots.

Webber entered the 1993 National Basketball Association (NBA) draft, becoming the first sophomore since "Magic" Johnson* in 1979 to be selected number one overall. The Orlando Magic (NBA) took Webber as the first pick and traded him to the Golden State Warriors (NBA) for Penny Hardaway* and three future first-round draft choices. Webber enjoyed an excellent first season, averaging 17 points, 9.1 rebounds, and 2.16 blocked shots and helping the Warriors to a 50–32 won-lost record and a playoff berth. Webber became the NBA's youngest player to win Rookie of the Year honors and made the NBA All-Rookie First Team. He and Golden State's coach Don Nelson often clashed. The Warriors traded Webber to the Washington Bullets (NBA) in November 1994 for Tom Gugliotta and three first-round draft choices.

Webber played four seasons in Washington, D.C., three with the Bullets and one when the franchise was renamed the Wizards. A shoulder separation and dislocation and resulting surgery limited his playing time in his first two seasons. In 1996–1997, he led the Bullets to their first playoff berth since 1988 and was selected for the NBA All-Star Game. After leading the Wizards in scoring, rebounding, and blocked shots the following season, in May 1998 Webber was traded to the Sacramento Kings (NBA) for Mitch Richmond and Otis Thorpe.

In four seasons with Sacramento, Webber has averaged 24.5 points and 11.0 rebounds. He led the Kings to four straight NBA playoff appearances, but Sacramento did not advance past the formidable Utah Jazz and the Los Angeles Lakers. He made the 1998–1999 All-NBA Second Team after leading the NBA in rebounds with a career-high 13 boards per game and ranking second in double-doubles with 36. The following season, Webber was selected to the All-NBA Third Team. He enjoyed his best season in 2000–2001, when he made his first start in the NBA All-Star Game, was twice named Player of the Week, and finished fourth in the Most Valuable Player (MVP) voting. He made the All-NBA First Team, averaging a career-high 27.1 points and 11.1 rebounds.

Webber ranked sixth in the NBA in scoring, eighth in rebounds, and fifth in double-doubles with 50 and, on January 5, 2001, recorded a career-high 52 points against the Indiana Pacers. He made the All-NBA Second Team in 2001–2002 scoring 1,322 points (24.5-point average) and 546 rebounds (10.1 average) in 54 games. He averaged 23.7 points, 10.1 rebounds, and 4.3 steals in the NBA playoffs before Los Angeles eliminated Sacramento in the Western Conference Finals. Webber again paced the Kings in 2002–2003 with 1,542 points (23.0 average) and 704 rebounds (10.5 average) in 67 games, making his fifth All-Star appearance and the All-NBA Second Team.

In 10 NBA seasons between 1993–1994 and 2002–2003, Webber compiled 13,209 career points and averaged 22.2 points. In 596 regular season games, he has collected 10.2 rebounds, 4.4 assists, 1.52 steals, and 1.71 blocked shots per game. In 47 NBA playoff games, he has posted 1,021 points, 468 rebounds, 209 assists, 55 steals, and 72 blocked shots.

Webber majored in psychology at the University of Michigan. He owns two Rottweilers, has his own record label and comic book (Webber's World), and enjoys water sports. He donated $100,000 to the Police Athletic League in Detroit, has been featured in numerous NBA television spots, owns a Gold's Gym fitness club, and has appeared in an episode of *New York Undercover*.

BIBLIOGRAPHY
"Chris Webber," *Players Background*, www.nba.com (2001); "Chris Webber," *Players Career Highlights*, www.nba.com (2001); "Chris Webber," *Player Career Statistics*, www.nba.com (2001); "Chris Webber," *Profile*, www.worldsportsmen.com (1998); *NCAA Men's Basketball's Finest* (Overland Park, KS, 1998); S. L. Price, "A Whole New Rap," *Sports Illustrated* 15 (April 12, 1999), pp. 42–46, 48; *The Sporting News Official NBA Register*, 2003–2004.

John L. Evers

REGGIE WHITE   **Football**
(December 19, 1961–)

Many football experts consider Reggie White the finest defensive lineman in gridiron history. In 15 National Football League (NFL) seasons with the Philadelphia Eagles (1985–1992), Green Bay Packers (1993–1998), and Carolina Panthers (2000), White set an NFL record with 198 sacks, was selected to play in 13 consecutive Pro Bowl games (1986–1998), and used his immense strength and explosive speed to excel even when double- or triple-teamed. The "Minister of Defense," as he was called, combined on-field excellence with active community involvement as an ordained Christian minister. "Playing football is helping me in my spiritual life because it's helping to build my character," he explained. "It's allowed me to see a lot of things . . . and it's also teaching me what the most important things are—like my family and, of course, God Himself."

Reginald Howard White was born on December 19, 1961 in Chattanooga, Tennessee, the son of Charles White and Thelma (Dodds) Collier. Although his parents never married and his grandparents were vitally involved in his upbringing, White continued to respect his father. He idolized Reverend Ferguson, an Anglo preacher of a largely African American Baptist Church who taught the Bible and preached racial reconciliation. "Reverend Ferguson was the greatest man of God I ever saw," White told *Sports Illustrated*. "He had a way with kids and teaching." White grew in physical strength and spiritual commitment, aspiring to become a football player and a minister. Both dreams later came true in remarkable ways.

At Howard High School, White gained All-America recognition in football, made All-State in basketball, and lettered in track and field. He also began guest preaching in churches at age 17. In a 1993 *Inside Sports* interview, he reflected, "I've always known that football was going to be a platform for me to help change peoples' lives for the sake of Jesus." On the field, he led postgame circle prayers, exhibited sportsmanship, and refused to use bad language.

Many National Collegiate Athletic Association (NCAA) football programs recruited White, but he signed with coach Johnny Majors's University of Tennessee team. With the Volunteers from 1980 through 1983, the 6-foot 5-inch,

285-pound defensive lineman made consensus All-America and Southeastern Conference Player of the Year his final season. Dean Steinkuhler of the University of Nebraska edged him for the Lombardi Award, given annually to the nation's outstanding collegiate lineman. White earned a Bachelor of Arts degree in Human Services in 1990.

White signed a five-year, $4 million contract with the Memphis Showboats of the short-lived United States Football League (USFL), making the All-Rookie team in 1984 and All-USFL in 1985. The USFL's instability and White's desire to play in the NFL led the Philadelphia Eagles (NFL) to buy out the remaining three years of his Memphis contract and sign him to a four-year, $1.85 million deal. The iron-man completed the 18-game USFL schedule and joined the Eagles for their final 13 games. He made 10 tackles and two-and-one-half sacks in his first start on his way to becoming National Football Conference (NFC) Defensive Rookie of the Year.

In 1986 the Philadelphia Eagles named Buddy Ryan, defensive coordinator for the Super Bowl champion Chicago Bears, as head coach. White became a game-changing force at the end of that year, making 18 sacks in 16 games and registering 4 more sacks in the Pro Bowl to become the game's Most Valuable Player (MVP). The following year, he set an NFC record with 21 sacks in a season shortened by the 1987 players' strike. In 1991 *Pro Football Weekly* voted him to the All-Decade team.

Although compiling a team-record 124 sacks in eight years with the Eagles, number 92 took the greatest pride in his all-around game. White told *Sports Illustrated*, "I get double-teamed on every play, so I expect it. Sacks are great, and they get you elected to the Pro Hall. But I've always felt that a great defensive lineman has to play the run and the pass equally well." White's straight talk, honesty, street-corner preaching, and antidrug and anti-abuse efforts, coupled with moral and financial support of Christian community outreach and development efforts in the Philadelphia area, won him widespread appreciation. His relationship with the Eagles grew strained, however, after he disagreed with management on the strike, personnel changes, and quality training facilities. He became one of the plaintiffs in a 1992 lawsuit against the NFL and won unrestricted free agency in 1993. *The Sporting News* commented, "Twenty years from now White . . . will be remembered not only for his Hall of Fame skills, but also for his role as a free agent pioneer who paved the way for non-quarterbacks to finally get their due."

The fierce competition among NFL teams for his services led to a much-publicized tour of major cities. White signed a $17 million, four-year contract with the Green Bay Packers (NFL), joining a great football tradition with renewed commitment to build a championship team. That dream was realized when the Packers defeated the New England Patriots in Super Bowl XXXI in 1997. Some questioned White's commitment to working for urban justice and social renewal when he signed with Green Bay, but the "Minister of Defense" broadened his humanitarian efforts. White helped establish programs in Tennessee (Hope Place for unwed mothers, Alpha and Omega Ministries, Knoxville Community Development Bank) and Wisconsin (Urban Hope for business entrepreneurs), and supported nationwide efforts through the Fellowship of Christian Athletes and local Christian churches. White made a one-season comeback with the Panthers after he, his wife, Sara, and children, Jeremy and Jecolia, moved to North Carolina. White told *Ebony*, "I'm trying to build up black people's morale, self-confidence and self-reliance to show that the Jesus I'm talking about is real."

White expresses outspoken personal views on biblical ethics and on multicultural issues. He has also made a sincere commitment to a healthy lifestyle stressing God and family. He related to *Sports Spectrum*, "Our kids are identifying themselves with what they want to do—not who they are. We need to begin to allow them to see that Jesus knew who he was. . . . Football is what I did, it's not who I am."

White retired from professional football in March 2001. Carolina coach George Seifert affirmed, "Reggie's records and accomplishments say it all. He is a Hall of Fame player and possibly the best defensive lineman ever to play the game."

BIBLIOGRAPHY
Barbara Carlisle Bigelow, ed., *Contemporary Black Biography*, vol. 7 (Detroit, MI, 1994); *Current Biography 1995* (New York, 1995), pp. 587–590; Tom Felton, "Catching Up with Reggie White," *Sports Spectrum* 14 (January–February 2000), p. 30; Peter King, "Trip to Bountiful," *Sports Illustrated* 78 (March 15, 1993), pp. 20–23; NFL Football Life Story: Reggie White, the Minister of Defense, VHS; "Reggie White," *Sports Spectrum* 9 (December 1995), p. 19; Reggie White, *Fighting the Good Fight* (Nashville, TN, 1999); Reggie White, *God's Playbook: The Bible's Game Plan for Life* (Nashville, TN, 1998); Reggie White, *Reggie White in the Trenches: The Autobiography* (Nashville, TN, 1996); Paul Zimmerman, "White Heat," *Sports Illustrated* 71 (November 27, 1989), pp. 65–69.

James D. Smith III

FRED WHITFIELD   Rodeo/Calf Roping
(August 5, 1967–)

Fred Whitfield popularized rodeo among African Americans, having won several world calf roping titles.

Fred Whitfield was born in Hockley, Texas, on August 5, 1967, the son of Willie Whitfield and Joyce Whitfield, and grew up in Cypress, Texas. As a youngster, he and his brother, Anthony, had lots of fun riding on a couple of Shetland ponies. They made lassos out of vacuum cleaner extension cords and lived five miles from a 7 Eleven store, making at least three trips per day for snacks and cool drinks. The Whitfield brothers and their sister, Tammy, were brought up by their mother, Joyce. The Whitfields divorced when Fred Whitfield was 9 years old. He very affectionately remembers his mother as a role model. "She worked hard and did it all."

Bill Pickett was the pioneering African American rodeo performer; African Americans made up less than 10 percent of all Professional Rodeo Cowboys Association (PRCA) cowboys. Whitfield and bull rider Charles Sampson remain the only African-Americans to win a World Championship.

Whitfield's career can be divided into two halves, with 1996 the dividing point. In 1996 the 6-foot 3-inch, 210-pound Whitfield competed at the top of his form. He had joined the PRCA in 1990 and won World Calf Roping Championships in 1991 and 1995. At the 1996 National Rodeo Finals, he competed at the Thomas and Mack Arena in Las Vegas, Nevada. Despite being the only points leader in the 1996 rodeo season in pursuit of the World Calf Roping Championship, Whitfield needed to perform well in the season finale. He commented, "I don't think it has bothered me the last couple of years, because I've gone in with the lead and I've managed to keep it. It could have been a lot better but then again it could have been a lot worse." Whitfield won the world calf roping contest and $58,336 at the National Finals, increasing his 1996 earnings to $155,336 and his career earnings to $799,229. Until the National Finals, his best 1996 winnings had been the $10,712 at the Reno, Nevada, meet.

As the National Finals competition moved into its frantic conclusion, Whitfield recalled: "The crowd was going crazy and I was pumped . . . I just got off my game plan." He performs with a simple personal philosophy, "Go for the jugular on the good calves, get by the bad ones."

After winning his third gold belt buckle, the special trophy awarded to the world champion calf roper, Whitfield described his high-pressure sport: "It's such a mental game out there. There's a sense of urgency in everybody. It's just great to be able to go out there and win."

Whitfield has continued to enjoy success since 1996, winning the world calf roping crown in 1999. In 2000, he captured his fifth world calf roping title, set a PRCA regular-season earnings record for calf roping with $129,516, married Cassie Loegel in April, and became a father for the first time in August when his daughter, Savannah, was born. His earnings of $194,936 in 2000 boosted his career earnings to $1,537,385.

Whitfield, an important inspirational, sociocultural sport icon, is the Tiger Woods* of rodeo. He observed in 1999, "I was the first African-American world champion calf roper . . . I have black people tell me all the time, 'You're the only reason I like to rodeo.' That makes me feel good inside, and it brings more people to the sport."

Whitfield, much more than an adept horseman, possesses extraordinary eye and hand coordination. He selects and trains a school of knowledgeable horses. In 1999 his favorite mounts were Reno (a sorrel), Moon (a bay), Rodeo, and Lightning P. He has survived several tumbles, including a July 1999 crash that sidelined him for three weeks.

Whitfield remains a fascinating symbol and link with an older America symbolized by the Wild West, the open range, the cowboy, Will Rogers, the lariat, and the vaudeville comedian. He embraces a modern athletic ethos in which breakneck speeds, thrills, and spills are the elixir of entertainment. For more than a decade, he has been a dominant performer in a fascinating sport with "the charm of big belt buckles, the insistent hiss of well-thrown hard-lay nylon rope, and the sweaty smell of an eager horse fidgeting in wait for competition."

Rodeo performers, such as Whitfield, may emerge as contemporary Western heroes. As with a Kit Carson, Billy the Kid, Wild Bill Hickok, and George Armstrong Custer, these horse and outdoors heroes personify traits that Americans have always admired. "Courage, self-reliance, and physical prowess have usually been rated high on the scale."

BIBLIOGRAPHY
Steve Fleming, Director of Communications, Professional Rodeo Cowboys Association, January 2, 1997; David Levinson and Karen Christensen, eds., *Encyclopedia of World Sport*, 2 (Santa Barbara, CA, 1996); Joe Naiman, "Whitfield Has Stay in East County," June 2002; Karl B. Raitz, ed., *The Theater of Sport* (Baltimore, MD, 1995); Kent Ladd Steckmesser, *The Western Hero—In History and Legend* (Norman, OK, 1997); Bob Welch and Ann Bleiker, Public Relations, Professional Rodeo Cowboys Association, May 2001.

Scott A.G.M. Crawford

BERNIE WILLIAMS   Baseball
(September 13, 1968–   )

The shy, soft-spoken Bernie Williams has accomplished what few athletes in New York City have been able to do. He has remained an underrated star, despite playing for a baseball dynasty and the most successful franchise in the history of the sport in the nation's largest media market.

Bernabe Figueroa Williams was born on September 13, 1968 in San Juan, Puerto Rico, the son of Bernabe Figueroa, who served in the Merchant Marine and worked as a night watchman with the Parks Department, and Rufina Williams, a public schoolteacher, principal, and college professor. Williams emerged as a talented athlete at a young age. He played Little League and Babe Ruth League baseball, competing against future major leaguers Juan Gonzalez* and Ivan "Pudge" Rodriguez.* The 15-year-old Williams, who attended Escuela Libre de Musica High School in San Juan, won four gold medals at an international track meet. One of the world's top 400-meter runners for his age group, he also excelled in the classroom and eventually studied at the University of Puerto Rico.

The 6-foot 2-inch, 225-pound Williams, who switch hits and throws right-handed, was signed by Fred Ferreira, the New York Yankees' (American League) top scout in Latin America. Williams made his professional debut in 1986, playing 61 games for Gulf Coast Yankees (Gulf Coast League). Within two years, he played for AAA Columbus, Ohio (International League) but was overmatched and sent to AA Albany, New York (Eastern League). There

Bernie Williams ©Photofest

Williams first showed the kind of power that he would display in the major leagues. After splitting the 1989 and 1990 seasons between AA and AAA ball, he made his major league debut with New York on July 7, 1991.

The job did not remain his without interruption. After playing only two games for the Yankees in 1992, Williams was returned to Columbus. He remained in the minor leagues until late August, when veteran outfielder Danny Tartabull went on the disabled list and created an opening for Williams on the

25-man roster. The 23-year-old outfielder played three games in left field and three games in right field before becoming the team's regular center fielder.

In 1996 Williams reached the 100-RBI mark for the first time in his career and emerged as the Most Valuable Player (MVP) of the AL Championship Series, spearheading the Yankees' first trip to the World Series since 1981. Williams struggled in the fall Classic but clouted a crucial home run in Game Three. The Yankees came back from a two-games-to-none deficit to pull off a stunning upset of the more talented Atlanta Braves.

Not satisfied with his first World Series ring, Williams advanced his level of play in 1997 when he batted .328 with 21 home runs. He also finally achieved some recognition for his standout defensive play, overcoming his below-average throwing arm to garner his first Gold Glove award. But the season would end in heartbreak for him. The Cleveland Indians defeated the New York Yankees in the AL Division Series.

The following three seasons, Williams's level of play peaked. In 1998 he completed an unprecedented trifecta by winning the AL's batting title with a .339 mark, capturing his second straight Gold Glove, and helping the Yankees thoroughly dominate the competition on their way to a four-game World Series sweep of the San Diego Padres. The following season, he posted some of the best offensive numbers of his career, including a personal best 202 hits and 116 runs, as the Yankees defended their World Series title against the Atlanta Braves. In 2000 he drove in a career-high 121 runs to help the Yankees win three straight World Series Championships.

Williams, sometimes criticized for his poor baserunning and lack of general baseball instincts, showed some slippage in 2001, making more frequent bad breaks on fly balls and watching the number of both his home runs and RBIs decline. Still, he maintained a .307 batting average and helped the Yankees return to the World Series for the fourth consecutive year. He and his teammates struggled against Arizona Diamondbacks' pitching during the World Series, as the Yankees' dynastic run was brought to a halt in Game Seven.

The 2001 season brought sadness and loss to Williams's personal life. He missed a 10-game stretch in April while visiting his father, Bernabe, who was seriously ill with pulmonary fibrosis. His father suffered a heart attack on May 13 and died later that day. Williams missed three more games while attending to his family's needs.

Williams experienced another successful season in 2002 but endured the disappointment of the Yankees' first-round playoff loss to the Anaheim Angels. For the first time since 1997, he did not appear in a World Series. Through 2003, he has batted .305 with 241 home runs and 1,062 RBIs. Williams batted .263 with 15 home runs and 64 RBIs in 2003, helping the Yankees win another AL East title. He hit .400 with 2 doubles and 3 RBIs in the AL Division Series against the Minnesota Twins, but Boston Red Sox pitchers limited him to a .192 batting average, one double, and 2 RBIs in the AL Championship Series. The Yankees lost the World Series to the Florida Marlins, but he batted .400 with 10 hits, 2 doubles, 2 home runs, and 5 RBIs.

Despite his success, Williams has remained humble and reserved. He has shown a level of well-roundedness seen in few professional athletes. A student of classical music in high school, he has become an accomplished guitar player and enjoys performing and listening to instrumental jazz. He married his wife, Waleska, on February 23, 1990, and they have three children, Bernie Alexander, Beatrice, and Bianca.

BIBLIOGRAPHY
Robert Dominguez, "Most Valuable (Guitar) Player," *New York Daily News*, October 3, 1999; Dan Graziano, "Williams Knows Throws Fall Far Short of Perfection," *Newark Star-Ledger*, March 11, 2003; Buster Olney, "Baseball's Shyest Superstar," *New York Times*, July 15, 1999; *New York Yankees Information and Record Guide*, New York Yankees Media Relations Department, 2003.

Bruce Markusen

RICKY WILLIAMS   Football
(May 21, 1977–)

Ricky Williams won the Heisman Trophy in 1998 as a tailback at the University of Texas at Austin and stars in the National Football League (NFL) as a running back with the Miami Dolphins (NFL).

Errick Lynne Williams Jr. was born on May 21, 1977 in San Diego, California, the son of Errick Williams Sr. and Sandy Williams, and was brought up mainly by his mother. He has a twin sister, Cassie. Williams excelled in football, baseball, track, and wrestling at Patrick Henry High School in San Diego. He played football for four years, rushing for 4,129 yards, scoring 55 touchdowns, and winning numerous All-State accolades. As a baseball player, he batted .333 with 31 stolen bases in his junior year and batted .340 with 26 stolen bases in his senior year.

The Philadelphia Phillies (National League) selected Williams in the eighth round of the 1995 amateur draft as an outfielder, but he was recruited by numerous colleges for his football skills. He decided to attend the University of Texas at Austin and then told school officials that he planned to sign with Philadelphia. Texas thereupon denied Williams a scholarship because of his professional baseball status. The Phillies then agreed to pay his college tuition and salary. He was taken in the 1998 Rule V Draft by the Montreal Expos (NL) and sold to the Texas Rangers (American League).

During his four-year football career at the University of Texas, Williams set 20 National Collegiate Athletic Association (NCAA) rushing records, including most rushing yards (6,279), eclipsing Tony Dorsett's 6,082 at the University of Pittsburgh 22 years earlier; all-purpose yards (7,206); highest average per carry (6.2 yards); rushing touchdowns (75); 200-yard rushing games (11) (tying Marcus Allen* of the University of Southern California, 1978–1981); points scored (452); games with touchdowns (33); and games with two or more scores (21). Williams also broke 44 school records and remains the only one of the top 13 all-purpose rushers to accomplish these feats without returning a kickoff.

After being switched from fullback to tailback in his junior year in 1997, Williams churned out more yardage. He gained 1,893 yards on 279 carries, winning the Doak Walker Award as the nation's top running back. He was named to the All-America team and finished fifth in the Heisman Trophy balloting. In his senior year in 1998, he rushed for 2,124 yards and 27 touchdowns on 361 carries to become only the eighth college football player to run for at least 2,000 yards in a season.

Williams took virtually every national award in 1998. He was chosen unanimously All-America and All–Big Twelve Conference and received the Heisman Trophy, Maxwell Award, Walter Camp Foundation Player of the Year Award, and Doak Walker Award, the first player to win the last named honor consecutively. He made two postseason appearances: a 38 to 15 loss to Penn State University in the 1997 Fiesta Bowl, and a 38 to 11 victory over the University of Mississippi in the 1999 Cotton Bowl.

After playing professional baseball for four summers, Williams concentrated on an NFL career. In the 1999 NFL draft, the 5-foot 10-inch, 236-pound Williams, who was blessed with size, power, and speed, was expected to be the first running back selected in the first round by the Indianapolis Colts. The Colts, however, chose Edgerrin James* from the University of Miami because of his ability to catch passes and run. James also provided one more dangerous receiver for quarterback Payton Manning.

The New Orleans Saints (NFL), desperate for a talented running back, held the fifth pick and selected Williams. Head coach Mike Ditka convinced the New Orleans management to trade away all their other choices in the 1999 NFL draft and their first- and third-round selections in 2000, to the Washington Redskins to obtain the rights to Williams. It was the first time in NFL history that one player became a team's total draft selection in a year. "It's a dream come true to have a chance to play in the NFL," Williams declared. "I was kind of upset that I was the second running back taken, but that's life. I'm going to go to New Orleans and make the best of things."

In his first NFL season, the dreadlocked back gained just 884 yards on 253 carries with two touchdowns in 1999. A nagging turf toe injury, however, forced him to miss four games. The Saints fired coach Ditka at the end of that season because Williams had not lived up to his college football accolades.

Williams criticized the Saints, their fans, and his contract in the March 20, 2000 issue of *Sports Illustrated*. Although he later issued an apology, the damage was already done. He limped to 1,000 yards in 2000 but missed the last six games with a broken ankle. He became only the fifth New Orleans running back to break the 1,000-yard barrier. The following season, he rushed for 1,245 yards on 313 carries with six touchdowns. In March 2002 the Saints traded Williams to the Miami Dolphins (NFL) for two future draft picks. That year Williams became the first Dolphin running back to lead the NFL in rushing, gaining 1,853 rushing yards (4.8-yard average) and 16 touchdowns. He became just the fourth NFL back to rush over 200 yards in five consecutive games and made the Pro Bowl.

Through the 2002 season, Williams has rushed 4,982 yards in 1,197 attempts (4.2-yard average) and 34 touchdowns and caught 179 passes for 1,455 yards (8.2-yard average) and three touchdowns.

Williams was an elementary education major. He has one daughter, Marley, and one son, Prince.

BIBLIOGRAPHY

New Orleans Saints Press Guide, 2001; *Pro Football Weekly*, May 1999, p. 4, April 2000; "Ricky Williams," *Current Biography Yearbook, 1999* (New York, 1999); *The Sporting News Pro Football Register*, 2003.

Richard Gonsalves

SERENA WILLIAMS   Tennis
(September 26, 1981–   )

Serena Williams, atop the Women's Tennis Association (WTA) world rankings until August 2003 won four consecutive Grand Slam finals from 2002 to 2003.

Serena Williams was born on September 26, 1981 in Saginaw, Michigan, the daughter of Richard Williams and Oracene Williams and the younger sister of fellow tennis professional, Venus Williams.* The sisters grew up in Compton, California. Serena, who is friendly and outgoing, attended a private school in Miami, Florida, and is a devout member of Jehovah's Witnesses. The youngest of five girls, she turned professional in 1995.

Although ranked only 304th in 1997, Williams defeated fourth-ranked Monica Seles and seventh-ranked Mary Pierce at a tournament in Chicago, Illinois, only her second Women's Tennis Association (WTA) Tour main draw event. She started 1998 ranked 96 but climbed to 40 after besting Lindsay Davenport to reach Australian Open semifinals in her first Grand Slam event. She lost in the finals to her older sister, Venus. She set the world record for defeating five top 10 players faster than any other player. Monica Seles had done it in 33 main-draw matches.

Williams enjoyed a 16-match winning streak in 1999, besting Steffi Graf's 1986 streak by three. She won her first singles title at the Paris Indoors tournament in Paris, France, in 1999, the same day Venus captured the Oklahoma City, Oklahoma, tournament. No sisters in professional tennis history had won titles in the same week. Williams won her first WTA title over Amelie Mauresmo, 6–2, 3–6, 7–6, in the Open Gaz de France in Paris, France. Her winning streak ended when she lost to her sister in the Lipton Championships title match, the first all-sister final in 115 years. Seeded seventh in the 1999 U.S.

Serena Williams ©Photofest

Open Tournament, Williams upset top-seeded Martina Hingis, second-seeded Davenport, and fourth-seeded Seles to win her first career Grand Slam singles title. She was the lowest seed to win the title since 1968 and only the second African American woman to take the singles crown. She also won the U.S. Open doubles title with Venus, becoming the fifth woman to win the singles and doubles crowns in the same year.

In 2000 Williams won singles titles in the Faber Grand Prix in Hannover, Germany, the Los Angeles Open, and Princess Cup, Tokyo, Japan, and reached the finals of the Open Gaz de France and du Maurier Open in Montreal, Quebec. She advanced to the semifinals of Wimbledon but lost to her sister, Venus. She and Venus teamed up to win the Wimbledon doubles title, triumphing over Julie Halard-Decugis and Ai Sugiyama, 6–3, 6–2, and the gold medal at the 2000 Olympic Games in Sydney, Australia.

Williams lost in the quarterfinals at the 2001 Australian Open to Hingis but teamed with Venus to win the Australian Open doubles. She was ousted by Jennifer Capriati in the quarterfinals of the French Open and Wimbledon.

Serena faced Venus in the 2001 U.S. Open finals, which drew the highest television tennis rating in 20 years. She lost to Venus, 2–6, 4–6, the first time since 1884 that two sisters met in a Grand Slam final and the first time that two African American sisters played in the final. Jeanne Moutoussamy-Ashe, widow of Arthur Ashe, remarked that "Arthur would have liked to have been here for them, because we're all beneficiaries. They've done a wonderful job." The two sisters have become very successful in a sport that has been traditionally dominated by white athletes. Serena was upset about losing to Venus, who did not enjoy triumphing over her sister. Their father had a difficult time watching the match and left before its conclusion. Serena told Venus, "You're the champion, you deserve it." Serena said later, "Enjoy it, because it might be my time next time."

The two tennis-playing sisters remain inseparable. They represent a new era in tennis and are the strongest players in the sport. Williams recognizes her role in the game and her relationship with her sister. "Tennis is just a game, and we're entertainers. People pay to see us play and perform. After that, we go home and we're always going to be family. We have to be able to separate tennis from family life." She attends classes at a Fort Lauderdale fashion college and earned a 3.4 grade point average in 2001. She receives endorsements from Avon, Nortel, and Sega and is represented by IMG, a sport marketing and management firm.

Williams fared 50–4 in 2002, losing only to Claudia Rubin after May. She won four consecutive Grand Slam events, defeating her sister, Venus; 7–5, 6–3 in the French Open finals; 7–6 (7–4), 6–3 in the Wimbledon finals; and 6–4, 6–3 in the U.S. Open finals. Serena, who has won 23 titles, has captured 7 of their 12 matches together. The Associated Press named her Athlete of the Year in 2002. Serena also won ESPY awards as Female Athlete of the Year and Top Female Tennis Player of 2002. She barely survived a second-set tiebreaker and finally prevailed, 3–6, 7–6 (5), 7–5 over fifty-sixth-ranked Emlie Loit in the first round of the 2003 Australian Open. She became the fifth woman to capture four consecutive Grand Slam titles, defeating Venus, 7–6 (7–4), 3–6, 6–4 in the Australian Open finals.

Williams faced a hostile crowd at the 2003 French Open and was upset by Justine Henin-Hardenne in the semifinals. She defeated Venus, 4–6, 6–4, 6–2, in the 2003 Wimbledon finals for her sixth Grand Slam and second consecutive Wimbledon crown, but did not defend her U.S. Open title because she underwent knee surgery. Her father, also her manager and coach, once predicted that Serena Williams would eventually become the better player of the two sisters. When Serena won the 1999 U.S. Open, she did what Venus had not been able to do, namely, win a Grand Slam. "That's something they've thought about all their lives: meeting in a final, two sisters. She feels she let everybody down." After Serena's upset victory, tennis star Andre Agassi remarked, "I like her game. She and Venus are incredible athletes, but it's my belief that Serena was more ready to win a big tournament. Her second serve is a lot better. Her forehand is better. And she's an efficient mover. They're both fast, and Venus can elevate into greatness as well. But she's going to end up taking a bit more work."

Pam Shriver, former player and commentator, called the two "best friends, doubles partners, practice partners. I don't think there have been players this close in the game, certainly not at the top." Mary Carillo, lead CBS analyst, said, "I think the sisters handle parental pressure beautifully. They understand what they have to do to defuse situations created by their father. Richard wants to be the story; he wants to be a big part of the Williams legend. He creates controversy and his kids have to react to it." Serena Williams stresses the importance of her sister and family to her life. "I don't see how tennis could separate us. Tennis only lasts a few years, and after that we have the rest of our lives."

BIBLIOGRAPHY

www.espn.go.com/tennis/s/wta/profiles/swilliams.html; Sally Jenkins and David Bailey, "Double Trouble," *Women's Sports and Fitness* (November/December 1998), pp. 102–106; Shirille Phelps, ed., *Contemporary Black Biography*, vol. 20 (1990), pp. 227–229; Peter Noel and Amanda Ward, "Fear of the Williams Sisters," *Village Voice* 45 (November 14, 2000), pp. 46–48; S.L. Price, "American Revolution," *Sports Illustrated* 95 (September 17, 2001), pp. 40–45; S.L. Price, "Father Knew Best," *Sports Illustrated* 91 (September 20, 2000), pp. 38–43; Michael Silver and Kevin Cook, "Serena's at Peace with Herself," *Sports Illustrated* 90 (March 22, 1999), pp. 38–39; Jon L. Wertheim, "We Told You So," *Sports Illustrated* 90 (April 5, 1999), pp. 68–71.

Maureen M. Smith

VENUS WILLIAMS
(June 17, 1980–)

Tennis

Venus Williams often ranked second in the Women's Tennis Association (WTA) world rankings behind her younger sister, Serena.*

Venus Ebone Starr Williams was born on June 17, 1980 in Lynwood, California, the fourth of five girls of Richard Williams, a former security agency owner, and Oracene Williams, a nurse. At age 10, Venus Williams won the under-12 division title in Southern California. She was on the front page of the *New York Times* and in *Sports Illustrated* as a fifth grader. In 1991 Richard moved the family from the tough Compton neighborhood so Williams could accept a scholarship at Rick Macci's tennis academy in Haines City, Florida.

Williams turned professional in October 1994 at the Bank of the West Classic in Oakland, California, and made limited appearances until the 1997 French Open and Wimbledon tournaments. In the Bank of the West Classic, she nearly upset second-ranked Arantxa Sanchez Vicario. In 1996 Williams possessed the ninth fastest serve on the tour, registering at 108 miles per hour at the Bausch & Lomb Championships in Amelia Island, Florida. She finished 7–5 in 1996. In 1997, she climbed from 211th to 64th in the world and reached the quarterfinals of two tournaments.

Williams ascended in the rankings during 1998, losing to eventual champion Lindsay Davenport in the semifinals of the U.S. Open. She advanced to the quarterfinals at the Australian Open, French Open, and Wimbledon tournaments. Her serve was clocked at 127 miles per hour at the Swisscom Challenge in Zurich, Switzerland. Her first career singles title came over South Africa's Joannette Kruger, 6–3, 6–2, in the IGA Tennis Classic in Oklahoma City, Oklahoma. She bested Anna Kournikova in the all-teen final at the Lipton Championships in Key Biscayne, Florida.

Venus defended her Lipton title in 1999 against her younger sister, Serena, in the first WTA Tour final match involving sisters. Williams won her first clay courts singles title in Hamburg, Germany, and her second two weeks later at the Italian Open. She reached the finals at Hannover, Germany, recording her first victory over tennis great Steffi Graf. In April 1999, Venus and Serena Williams became the first set of sisters to be ranked in the top 10 at the same time. They became the first sisters to win a Grand Slam doubles crown in the twentieth century at the French Open. Venus won her first Grand Slam singles title at Wimbledon in 2000, defeating Lindsay Davenport, 6–3, 7–6 (3) after besting Serena in the semifinals. Williams defeated Davenport again at the U.S. Open finals for her second Grand Slam singles title. At the 2000 Olympic Games in Sydney, Australia, she captured gold medals in the singles and in the doubles with Serena. The first tennis player to win both Olympic titles since 1924, Venus Williams enjoyed a 32-match winning streak in 2000.

Williams defended her Wimbledon title in 2001, over Justine Henin, 6–1, 3–6, 6–0, and won the Ericsson Open in Miami, Florida, over Jennifer Capriati, 4–6, 6–1, 7–6 (4). She lost to Martina Hingis, 6–1, 6–1, in the semifinals of the Australian Open, but she and Serena defeated Hingis and Monica Seles in the doubles competition.

At the 2001 U.S. Open, Williams faced her sister, Serena, in the finals. The big match drew high television ratings and celebrities. Venus triumphed

Venus Williams ©Photofest

over Serena, 6–2, 6–4, the first time since 1884 that two sisters met in a Grand Slam final and the first time that two African American sisters played in the final. Of their five meetings, Venus had won four. To cap off her banner year, she received the ESPY award for Outstanding Women's Tennis Performance.

The two African American sisters have become dominant players in a traditionally white upper class sport and have exposed urban youth to tennis. Williams explained, "We want to be just like Tiger Woods.* We want our success to extend to our communities, so others can enjoy the success that we're having."

As part of the sport's greatest sister act, the Williams sisters have dominated their opponents on the court. Venus, ranked second in the world, has lost 7 of 12 career matches with Serena through July 2003. Serena defeated Venus in four consecutive Grand Slam events: 7–5, 6–3 in the 2002 French Open finals; 7–6 (7–4), 6–3 in the 2002 Wimbledon finals, 6–4, 6–3 in the 2002 U.S. Open finals; and 7–6 (7–4), 3–6, 6–4 in the 2003 Australian Open finals. Venus, viewed as a more well-rounded and controlled strategist, observes, "I always want Serena to win. I'm the big sister. I take care of Serena. I make sure she has everything, even if I don't have anything." Off the court, they are best friends and live together. They also take courses together in fashion design.

Vera Zvonareva upset Williams in the fourth round of the 2003 French Open. She lost to Serena, 4–6, 6–4, 6–2 in the 2003 Wimbledon finals and withdrew from the U.S. Open because of an abdominal injury. Richard Williams has played a significant role in their careers and has written several books on his famous daughters, including *Venus Envy*. When his daughters sign endorsement deals, he requests that the companies donate goods to youth in the black community. His presence at tournaments often causes some tension, which he attributes to racism. "The WTA is a close-knit community that tends to embrace its own," he observed, "We've never been a part of it. But no one wants to see a tournament that Venus and Serena aren't in. We breathed life into this game, and people dislike us for it." He concluded, "The goals were for my girls to be good people and also the most powerful tennis players out there." Venus added, "If I'm not enhancing myself, I feel like I'm wasting my time." Her hard work paid off.

Venus Williams, 6 foot ½ inch tall and 168 pounds, recently signed a five-year, $40 million contract with Reebok International, the highest amount paid to a female athlete, and Serena has signed a deal with Avon. An Avon representative, states that "These were two very young women who were all about empowerment and caring and sharing. Their appeal goes very far and wide." Venus has also endorsed Wilson's The Leather Experts Inc. and Nortel Networks Corporation, and has appeared in a Sega video game. She will design a clothing line, which fits nicely into her plan to become a fashion designer. She studied fashion design at the Art Institute of Fort Lauderdale from October 1999 through December 2001.

Venus, managed and coached by her father, Richard, has won 28 career and four Grand Slam titles.

BIBLIOGRAPHY

www.espn.go.com/tennis/s/wta/profiles/vwilliams.html; Amanda Bower, "Williams Wins!" *Time* 158 (September 17, 2001), pp. 88–89; Shirille Phelps, ed., *Contemporary Black Biography*, vol. 7 (1990), pp. 207–210; Sally Jenkins and David Bailey, "Double Trouble," *Women's Sports and Fitness* (November/December 1998), pp. 102–106; Peter Noel and Amanda Ward, "Fear of the Williams Sisters," *Village Voice* 45 (November 14, 2000), pp. 46–48; S.L. Price, "American Revolution," *Sports Illustrated* 95 (September 17, 2001), pp. 40–45; Jon L. Wertheim, "We Told You So," *Sports Illustrated* 90 (April 5, 1999), pp. 68–71.

Maureen M. Smith

TIGER WOODS
(December 20, 1975–)

Golf

Tiger Woods has dominated golf since turning professional in 1996, winning eight majors. Eldrick Tiger Woods was born on December 20, 1975 in Cypress, California, the son of Earl Woods, a retired lieutenant colonel in the U.S. Army, and Kultida Woods, a native of Thailand. He has three half-brothers, Kevin, Earl Jr., and Royce, from his father's first marriage and was named after a Vietnamese soldier who saved his father from sniper fire.

Woods grew up in Cypress and began playing golf as a toddler. At 10 months old, he climbed out of his highchair, picked up his father's putter, and hit a ball right into the middle of a net in the family garage. His father recalled, "And then he hit another ball into the middle of the net." Earl screamed to Kultida, "We have a genius on our hands." Woods shot a 48 for nine holes at age 3, was featured at age 5 in *Golf Digest*, and scored a hole in one on an 85-yard hole at age 6. The 6-foot 2-inch, 180-pound smooth-swinging right-handed golfer graduated in 1994 from Western High School in Anaheim, California, where he won numerous golf tournaments and championships. His parents insisted that his schoolwork be completed before he played golf. He compiled an "A" average in high school and received an award for ranking among the top student-athletes in the United States.

When not in school, Woods either practiced or played golf in state or national tournaments. He won the Optimist International Junior tournament in 1983 at age 8 and repeated five more times by age 15. At age 14, he was the youngest golfer ever to prevail in the Insurance Youth Golf Classic. Woods triumphed in the U.S. Junior Amateur Championship from 1991 through 1993 and the U.S. Amateur Championship from 1994 through 1996. He also captured the Western Amateur Classic and represented the United States in the 1994 World Amateur Championships and the 1995 Walker Cup match. He compiled one of the most impressive amateur career records in United States Golf Association (USGA) history, being the only player to take both the Junior Amateur and Amateur titles. "I don't want to be known as the best black golfer," he said. "My goal has always been to be the best golfer, period."

Woods attended Stanford University between 1994 and 1996 before joining the Professional Golfers Association (PGA) tour in August 1996. He studied economics at Stanford University and was nicknamed "Urkel" by his teammates. He competed in 12 tournaments in 1994 and 1995, winning two and tying for fifth place in the National Collegiate Athletic Association (NCAA) Championship. The following season, he entered 14 tournaments and triumphed eight times. Woods won in his last five tournaments as a Stanford Cardinal. At the 1996 NCAA Championship, he shot a course-record 67 at the Honors Course in Chattanooga, Tennessee. He received the Fred Haskins and Jack Nicklaus College Player of the Year awards.

Tiger Woods ©Photofest

Although still an amateur, Woods participated in his first professional tournament, the 1992 Los Angeles Open, at age 16. He competed in three PGA events the following year and, in 1994, tied for thirty-fourth in the Johnnie Walker Asian Classic in Thailand and appeared in three other PGA events. He played in the 1995 Masters and British Open and finished the season by making the cut in the Motorola Western Open and Scottish Open. Before his first Masters, he said, "I've never been afraid of anything. I'm going down there to win." After playing in the Masters, U.S. Open, and British Open in 1996, he joined the PGA tour as a professional in late August.

Woods appeared in eight more events in 1996, earning $790,594 and finishing twenty fifth on the money list. He won the Las Vegas Invitational and the Disney Oldsmobile Classic and became the first player since Robert Gomez in 1990 to prevail in two tournaments in his first year as a professional. He also became the first golfer since Curtis Strange in 1982 to finish among the top 5 for five consecutive times.

In 1997 Woods won four PGA Tour events in 22 appearances. At age 21, he became the youngest player to win the Masters and the first person of African or Asian descent to triumph in a major golf championship. He triumphed by 12 strokes, a record victory margin for a Masters. "I never thought I would have the lead like I did," Woods recalled. He was also the youngest player to hold the top ranking in professional golf. "As soon as I saw Tiger Woods swing," golfer Gary Player observed, "I thought, Man, this young guy has got it." Besides receiving the Arnold Palmer Award, Woods led PGA golfers in money earned with a then-record $2,086,833. The following year, he took one event on the PGA Tour and three overall and finished fourth in earnings with $1,841,117.

In 1999 Woods became the first golfer in 25 years to capture eight PGA Tour events, including the season's last four tournaments. He took the PGA Championship in August by one stroke over Sergio Garcia. Golfer Colin Montgomerie remarked, "Tiger is so far ahead of everybody else. . . . He's going to be difficult to catch." Woods earned $6.6 million, breaking the single-season record by nearly $3 million.

Woods began the 2000 PGA Tour with two more triumphs, giving him six consecutive victories. He captured three major tournaments: the U.S. Open, the British Open, and the PGA Championship. The top-ranked player in the world won the U.S. Open by 15 strokes. His score broke the old record for a major tournament of 13, set by Tom Morris at the 1862 British Open. At age 24, Woods was the youngest player to prevail in all four majors—the Masters, the U.S. Open, the British Open, and the PGA Championship. He repeated as PGA champion in August in a sudden-death playoff victory over Bob May, becoming only the second player to garner three major titles in one year. (Ben Hogan took three majors in 1953.) Woods played in 20 PGA tour and World Wide events in 2000, winning nine times, finishing second four times, third once, and in the top ten 17 times, and amassing $9,188,321 in official money.

He compiled a scoring average of 68.17 strokes, breaking Byron Nelson's record of 68.33 strokes in 1945.

With his triumph at the Masters on April 8, 2001, Woods joined Bobby Jones as the only golfer to complete the Grand Slam by winning four major tournaments in a row. Woods captured four other tournaments in 2001, appearing in 19 events and finishing 18 times in the top 25.

In 2002 Woods prevailed in the Bay Hills Invitational, the Masters, and the U.S. Open, making him the first golfer since Jack Nicklaus to be victorious in the initial two major tournaments. At the British Open, he took 81 strokes to complete the third round. It was the worst round of golf in his professional career to that point and virtually eliminated any chances of winning his third major. Woods triumphed in the Buick Open and finished second to Rich Beem in the PGA Championship, just missing becoming the only player to win the three American majors in the same year. In a great come-from-behind effort, he fell one stroke short. He became the first golfer since Arnold Palmer to record at least five tour victories, capturing the American Express Championship in Kilkenny, Ireland, in September. He competed for the unsuccessful American team in the Ryder Cup play.

Woods underwent knee surgery in the fall of 2002 and failed to win a major tournament in 2003. He tied for fifteenth in the Masters, nine strokes behind Mike Weir. In the U.S. Open, Woods finished three over par and trailed winner Jim Furyk by 11 shots. He shared fourth in the British Open, two strokes behind Ben Curtis. Woods suffered his worst finish in a major at the PGA with a 12 over par and 16 strokes behind winner Shaun Micheel. Nevertheless, he won five of 18 PGA tour events and ranked first in the scoring. Woods's immeasurable impact on golf rivaled that of Jackie Robinson in baseball. In the last 25 years, only Michael Jordan* has possibly influenced the lives of more young people. Woods, who identifies with all age groups, has attracted people of all ages to golf, African American and white, not only because of his African-Asian descent, but also because of his talent, charisma, smile, cool, intelligence, and ability to come through under pressure.

Statistically, Woods's impact on golf will be difficult to equal. He has won 38 PGA tournaments, including three Masters, two PGAs, two U.S. Opens, and one British Open. He remains the only golfer to hold all four major titles simultaneously and leads active players in career victories and money earned. His adjusted 68.41 scoring average ranked as the second lowest ever and earned him the PGA of America Player of the Year Award. He ranked second behind Vijay Singh in earnings with $6,673,433 and compiled 12 Top-10 finishes.

Woods has achieved amazing success since 1996, being named the 1996 and 2000 *Sports Illustrated* Sportsman of the Year, the 2000 *L'Equipe* World Champion of Champions, the 1997, 1999, and 2000 Associated Press Male Athlete of the Year, and the 2000 Reuters Sportsman of the Year. He was chosen the 1997 ESPY Male Athlete of the Year and shared the award in 1999 and 2000 with Ken Griffey Jr. He was selected World Sportsman of the

Year in 1999 and 2000 by Laurens Sports Awards and received the Jack Nicklaus Award as PGA Player of the Year in 1997, 1999, 2000, 2001, and 2002. He won ESPY awards as Male Golfer of the Year from 1999 through 2002.

BIBLIOGRAPHY
Ross Atkin, "Tiger Woods Golf's Own Johnny Appleseed," *The Christian Science Monitor*, June 12, 1997, pp. 10–11; Harry Blauvelt, "Eye of Tiger Is Strictly on Winning," *USA Today*, November 8, 1999, pp. 1C–2C; Curry Kirkpatrick, "A Tiger in the Grass," *Newsweek* 133 (April 10, 1995), pp. 70–72; Rick Reilly, "Tiger Walks," *Sports Illustrated* 17 (April 27, 2002), pp. 40–45; John Strege, *Biography of Tiger Woods* (New York, 1997); "Tiger Woods," *Biography*, www.geocities.com (2000); "Tiger Woods," *Profile*, www.sportsline.com (2000); "Tiger Woods," *Related Information*, www.biography.com (2002); "Tiger Woods," *2001 Results*, www.pgatour.com (2001); "Tiger Woods," *2002 Results*, www.pgatour.com (2002).

John L. Evers and David L. Porter

CHARLES WOODSON   Football
(October 7, 1976–)

Charles Woodson won the Heisman Trophy in 1997 as a defensive back at the University of Michigan, helping the Wolverines win the 1997 National Collegiate Athletic Association (NCAA) Championship.

Charles Cameron Woodson was born in Fremont, Ohio, on October 7, 1976, the third child of Solomon Woodson, a forklift operator in a bottle factory and Georgia Woodson. Woodson grew up in Fremont, a blue-collar town in northern Ohio. He wore a metal brace on his feet from 20 months through age 4 to correct clubfeet. His parents divorced in 1982 when he was 5 years old. Woodson was brought up by his mother, Georgia, his older brother, Terry, and his sister, Shannon. He played "sock football" in the family's living room and flag football at the YMCA while in elementary school. He idolized Walter Payton and set his sights on winning the Heisman Trophy, But his mother would not let him play football his freshman year at Ross High School. As a sophomore, Woodson scored touchdowns receiving, rushing, and on punt returns, kickoff returns, an interception, and a fumble return. The brash, confident 6-foot, 200-pounder set Ross High School's all-time rushing record with 3,861 yards, earning Gatorade's Mr. Ohio Football honors and being in *Sports Illustrated* in 1994. His brother won football All-America accolades at Miami University of Ohio, while his sister attended the University of Arkansas on a track and field scholarship and qualified for the United States Olympic trials in 1992.

At the University of Michigan, Woodson started in football as a freshman. He won First Team Big Ten Conference (BTC) honors all three seasons for the Wolverines and started 42 of his 43 games at Michigan. He was selected

BTC Defensive Player of the Year and a First Team All-America cornerback in 1996 and 1997. He also starred as a punt returner and intermittent wide receiver. Coach Lloyd Carr declared, "He was a great football player from the very first day he arrived on campus." Carr added, "He has everything you want, physically and mentally. . . . Charles is big, strong. . . . He can make a mistake and recover." He was still one of the most popular players on our team. Noted for his quickness, tackling ability, and athleticism, Woodson ranked among the most versatile players in modern college football history. *College Football News* named him one of the 100 best college football players of all time.

In his last year at the University of Michigan in 1997, Woodson made seven interceptions, caught 11 passes for 231 yards and two touchdowns, and scored touchdowns on a 33-yard reverse and on a punt return. He also returned 33 punts for 282 yards. He led the BTC and finished second in the nation in interceptions. His heroics helped propel the University of Michigan to the BTC title, a Rose Bowl win over Washington State University, and a National Championship. Woodson won the *Chicago Tribune*'s Silver Football Award as the BTC's Most Valuable Player (MVP), the Bronko Nagurski Award, the Walter Camp Award as Player of the Year, the Jim Thorpe Award as Defensive Back of the Year, and the Bednarik Award as Defensive Player of the Year. He became the first defensive star in history to win the Heisman Trophy, college football's most prestigious award, ending 63 years of emphasizing offensive players. At Michigan, he stayed out of the public eye when not playing football and was not a materialistic person.

The Oakland Raiders (National Football League) selected Woodson as the fourth player in the first round of the 1998 NFL draft. In his first NFL season, he played all 16 games, a feat that no Raiders rookie had achieved in 27 years. During his first campaign with the Raiders, Woodson was credited with 63 tackles, five interceptions, and one touchdown. Woodson, whose peers voted him to the Pro Bowl, was named the NFL Defensive Rookie of the Year. Over the next four years, he averaged more than 60 tackles and made at least one interception per year. Woodson was selected a Pro-Bowler from 1998 through 2000. He helped the Raiders win the AFC West title and home field advantage in the playoffs with an 11–5 record in 2002. He averaged five tackles, as the Raiders eliminated the New York Jets, 30–10, in an AFC play-off Game, and walloped the Tennessee Titans, 41–24, in the AFC Championship game. Although still playing with a steel plate from a broken fibula, he recorded eight tackles and returned an intercepted pass 12 yards in the 48–20 loss to the Tampa Bay Buccaneers in Super Bowl XXXVII. He remained a defensive star at Oakland well into the twenty-first century.

Woodson, a trivia buff, loves to watch the television program *Jeopardy*. He excels in knowledge about biblical characters. He likes to watch movies and regularly attends church.

BIBLIOGRAPHY

Andrew Bagnato, "Heisman Stunner," *Chicago Tribune*, December 14, 1997, pp. 1, 5; "Charles Woodson's Career Accolades," 2001, University of Michigan Sports Information, Ann Arbor, Michigan; Jim Cnockaert, "Duel Personality: Woodson Fierce on Field, Remains Low-Key Off It," *Ann Arbor News*, December 12, 1997, p. 1B; Jay Mariotti, "Voters' Choice Easily Defended," *Chicago Sun-Times*, December 14, 1997, p. 3A; Charlie Vincent, "Woodson Makes Amends for Forgetting to Thank Teammates," *Detroit Free Press*, December 29, 1997, pp. 1D, 4D; Amy Whitesall, "Woodson's Mom Plays Major Role in Charles' Success," *Ann Arbor News*, December 12, 1997; Bob Wojonowski, "U-M's Woodson Makes Heisman History," *Detroit News*, December 14, 1997, pp. 1A, 6A.

Keith McClellan

ROD WOODSON   **Football**
(March 10, 1965–   )

When the Baltimore Ravens (National Football League) triumphed over the New York Giants in Super Bowl XXXV, one of the greatest defensive players in NFL history earned his first championship. After 15 years of outstanding play, future Hall of Famer Rod Woodson had won his first Super Bowl ring.

Roderick Kevin Woodson was born on March 10, 1965, in Fort Wayne, Indiana, the son of James Woodson, an African American laborer at International Harvester, and Linda Jo Doerflein, a white housewife. Of his mixed racial heritage, Woodson said, "I was taught to never back down." He attended Nelson Snider High School in Fort Wayne, where he played football and ran the hurdles in track and field. After being named to *Parade* magazine's High School Football All-America team, Woodson played football as a defensive back and kick returner at Purdue University. In 1986, he won First Team All-America honors. He also captured the Big Ten Conference Indoor Championship four times in the 55-meter hurdles.

The Pittsburgh Steelers (NFL) selected the 6-foot, 205-pound speedster in the first round of the 1987 NFL draft, the tenth player taken overall. In his first NFL season, Woodson played sparingly because legendary Steelers coach Chuck Noll continued his long-standing policy of not starting rookies. Woodson, however, became a mainstay of the Steelers defense the following year and remained there for the next eight seasons.

As cornerback and kick returner, in 1989 Woodson made the first of six consecutive appearances in the Pro Bowl. The Associated Press (AP) and the Pro Football Writers Association of America named him to their 1989 All-NFL teams as a kick returner. Several years of excellent play followed. In 1993 the AP and *College and Pro Football Newsweekly* selected him as the NFL Defensive Player of the Year. United Press International named him the American Football Conference Defensive Player of the Year, while his Steelers teammates voted him team Most Valuable Player (MVP) for an unprecedented third time.

After an outstanding 1994 season, the quiet, contemplative, passionately competitive Woodson tore his anterior cruciate ligament in the 1995 season opener. He returned to the Pro Bowl for the seventh time the following year,

Rod Woodson ©Courtesy of the Oakland Raiders

but he seemingly had lost a step. The New England Patriots exploited him in a 28–7 playoff victory over the Steelers.

After the 1996 season, Woodson's contract expired. The Steelers sought to re-sign Woodson at a lower salary and to switch him from cornerback to safety. The intensely proud Woodson balked at the change, maintaining that he was perfectly capable of playing cornerback. In July 1997 he joined the San Francisco 49ers (NFL).

After playing a year with the 49ers, in February 1998 Woodson signed with the Baltimore Ravens (NFL). Later that year, *Pro Football Weekly* named him to its NFL 75th Anniversary Team and tabbed him as the thirtieth-best player of all time. He considered this honor the highpoint of his career prior to winning the Super Bowl. After moving to safety in 1999, he intercepted seven passes to share the NFL lead. He returned those interceptions 195 yards, the second highest figure in the NFL and his single season best.

In 2000 Woodson played a key role on one of the greatest defenses in NFL history. The Ravens set an NFL record when its defense surrendered just 165 points during the regular 16 game season and won the Super Bowl. Woodson, who had returned to the Pro Bowl the previous season, made his ninth Pro Bowl appearance and garnered Second Team All-Pro honors. He remains the only player in NFL history to make the Pro Bowl at three different positions, including kick returner, cornerback, and safety.

In 2001 Woodson scored a touchdown off an interception for a NFL record-breaking tenth time. He recorded his sixty-first career regular-season interception, solidifying his position as the leader in interceptions among currently active players. His stellar performance earned him a tenth Pro Bowl appearance. In April 2002 he signed with the Oakland Raiders (NFL). That same year he equaled his career high with eight interceptions to move into third place on the all-time NFL list. Woodson made the Pro Bowl again, helping the Raiders win the AFC West title and home field advantage in the playoffs. He recorded five tackles, helping eliminate the New York Jets, 30–10, in the AFC playoffs. Woodson made six tackles in the 41–24 triumph over the Tennessee Titans in the AFC Championship Game, and seven tackles in the 48–20 loss to the Tampa Bay Buccaneers in Super Bowl XXXVII.

Woodson resides in Pittsburgh, Pennsylvania, where he is a popular figure. He owns a sports bar and an auto dealership and participates in charitable organizations, especially the fight against leukemia. He also sponsors several programs in Fort Wayne designed to reward academic excellence.

In 1989, Woodson married Nikki Theede. They have three daughters, Nemiah, Tia, and Marikah, and two sons, Demitrius, and Jarius.

BIBLIOGRAPHY

Baltimore Ravens Football Guide—2001; Jill Lieber, "Never Back Down," *Sports Illustrated* 77 (September 7, 1992), pp. 58–62; *Pittsburgh Steelers Media Guide*—1989; Michael Silver, "Gut Check," *Sports Illustrated* 86 (May 26, 1997), pp. 71–73; *The Sporting News Pro Football Register*, 2003.

Frank W. Thackeray

Index ───────────────────────────────────────

Note: The locations of main entries in the dictionary are indicated in the index by *italic* page numbers.

About the Editor and Contributors

Jack C. Braun, Associate Professor of History, Edinboro University of Pennsylvania, Edinboro, PA.

Ron Briley, Assistant Headmaster, Sandia Preparatory School, Albuquerque, NM.

Robert L. Cannon, lawyer and freelance writer, Santa Monica, CA.

Peter J. Cava, Press Information Director, USA Track & Field, Indianapolis, IN.

Dennis S. Clark, Instructor, Alternative Secondary Program, Lane Community College, Eugene, OR.

Scott A.G.M. Crawford, Associate Professor of Physical Education, Eastern Illinois University, Charleston, IL.

Robert A. Dunkelberger, University Archivist, Bloomsburg University of Pennsylvania, Bloomsburg, PA.

John L. Evers,* high school teacher and administrator, Carmi, IL.

Richard Gonsalves, head, conservation and watershed, City of Gloucester, Gloucester, MA and operator, Cape Ann Kicking Academy, Gloucester, MA.

Jorge Iber, Professor of History, Texas Tech University, Lubbock, TX.

Bruce Markusen, Manager of Program Presentation, National Baseball Hall of Fame and Museum, Cooperstown, NY, and freelance writer

Keith McClellan, editor, writer, Haworth Press, Oak Park, MI.

Richard D. Miller,* Air Force chaplain and freelance writer, Fort Thomas, KY.

William J. Miller,** Associate Professor Emeritus of History, St. Louis University, St. Louis, MO.

Scot E. Mondore, Manager of Museum Programs, National Baseball Hall of Fame and Museum, Cooperstown, NY.

John E. Mosher,* Guidance Counselor, Ferguson-Florissant School District, Florissant, MO.

Frank J. Olmsted, Pastoral Department, De Smet Jesuit High School, St. Louis, MO.

David L. Porter, Shangle Professor of History, William Penn University, Oskaloosa, IA, and freelance writer, Oskaloosa, IA.

James A. Riley, freelance writer, editor, and publisher, Canton, GA.

Victor Rosenberg, student, John Marshall Law School, Cleveland, OH, and freelance writer, Mayfield Heights, OH.

Terry W. Sloope, Assistant Director for Research, A. L. Burruss Institute of Public Service, Kennesaw State University, Kennesaw, GA.

James D. Smith III, Professor, Department of Theology and Religious Studies, University of San Diego, San Diego, CA, and Adjunct Professor, Bethel Seminary West, San Diego, CA.

Maureen M. Smith, Associate Professor of Kinesiology, California State University–Sacramento, Sacramento, CA.

Frank W. Thackeray, Professor of History, Indiana University Southeast, New Albany, IN.

John H. Ziegler, Professor, English, Film, and Humanities, Cochise College, Sierra Vista, AZ, and freelance writer, Tombstone, AZ.